THE ECONOMICS OF LEGAL RELATIONSHIPS

READINGS IN THE THEORY OF PROPERTY RIGHTS

THE ECONOMICS OF LEGAL RELATIONSHIPS

READINGS IN THE THEORY OF PROPERTY RIGHTS

Henry G. Manne
DISTINGUISHED PROFESSOR OF LAW
DIRECTOR, CENTER FOR STUDIES IN
LAW AND ECONOMICS
UNIVERSITY OF MIAMI LAW SCHOOL

WEST PUBLISHING COMPANY
St. Paul · New York · Los Angeles · San Francisco

Main entry under title:
The Economics of Legal Relationships: Readings in the Theory
    of Property Rights.
      Includes bibliographies and index.
        1. Law. 2. Economics. 3. Property. I. Manne, Henry G.
Law 343.04 75–4884

ISBN 0–8299–0048–9

3rd Reprint—1981

To Bobbie, Emily and Geoffrey

PREFACE

Law and economics as scholarly disciplines would seem to conflict
in more ways than they complement each other. They comprehend
distinctly different logical systems for looking at the world and solving
its problems. Economics is logically positivistic, scientifically rigorous,
and generally indifferent to normative issues. Its value lies mainly in
its ability to predict future outcomes and to explain the causes of past
events.

Law on the other hand has traditionally been a morally oriented, mechan-
istic system of dispute settlement which, by the standards of economics,
generates apparently random results. It gains its greatest majesty in
societies where the idea of a "rule of law, not men" is sacred, though
this phrase can be construed to exclude from the legal-decision process
the techniques of all men of science, including economists. See J.
Buchanan, Book Review, 60 *Va.L.Rev.* 483 (1974).

That ringing phrase, "the rule of law," implies that we should not try
to specify in advance the particular judicial result we want to reach in
resolving a certain kind of legal dispute, even if science offers us the
methods for reaching any stated goal. Rather the results should flow
automatically from precedent cases, from the interpretation of legislative
enactments, and from the words of a constitution, in accordance with a
traditional jurisprudential methodology. The emphasis in law is far
more strongly on process than on result. Not too many years ago,
even in respectable legal academic circles, to say that a decision was
"result-oriented" was a catchphrase method of criticizing an unpopular
judicial decision.

However, to the current generation of American legal scholars, strongly
influenced by a legal philosophy known as "Legal Realism," this all seems
nonsensical. Of course, the Realists hold, judges should (and in fact
always did) decide cases on the basis of their ideas about the desirability of particular results. The jurisprudential notion of a strict system
of legal precedent became for these scholars a kind of methodological
joke as they began their excursions into the world of the social and

natural sciences to get "better" results out of the legal system. A new debate on this point may be developing, and there are some recent signs of responsible disaffection with the value of the social sciences for law. For the moment, however, the integrationists have clearly carried the day.

It is not our purpose here to enter that debate. Rather our purpose is to advance economists' and lawyers' understanding of the range of possible interrelationships between law and economics. It is probably broader than casual observers have realized but not as helpful as the more ardent interdisciplinary advocates have hoped.

There are several good reasons for the widespread popularity of law and economics as complementary fields. One is the simple fact that economics is the most sophisticated and highly developed of the various social sciences; its analytical tools are simply more powerful and useful than those of the other social sciences. This is reflected today in the tremendous number of substantive areas of law that have received serious economic attention. That number is far too great for an all-inclusive collection of readings in one volume, and even texts purporting to be exhaustive must still be selective. Two recent efforts do show the breadth of concurrence between substantive law and economics, and the interested reader is strongly recommended to R. Posner's *Economic Analysis of Law* (1972) and G. Tullock's *The Logic of the Law* (1971).

But there may be an even more cogent explanation for the intensity of the romance between law and economics. In recent years economists, particularly some closely associated with law schools, have developed some extremely important new techniques and concepts that seem tailored to the needs and interests of legal scholars. Prior to these developments—which should probably be dated from Ronald Coase's now classic "The Problem of Social Cost" (1960, reprinted *supra*)—most academic economists were essentially preoccupied with aspects of macroeconomics that offered nothing of significant use to legal scholars. The major if not sole exception was the long-standing use of price and market theory in the field of antitrust law.

Unlike the way in which economics was normally used in antitrust law (in some ways not unlike the use of chemistry in a patent matter), the work pioneered by Coase and others took the legal system and various rules of liability as the critical data to be examined by the economists. Some legal scholars were probably attracted to economics by the flattery implicit in this attention and others by the necessity to comprehend the new language in which their own legal specialties were being discussed. At the same time it is important to note that certain individuals professionally identified as law professors were themselves making significant contributions to the economic analysis of their fields.

The economists' shift from their traditional focus on wealth maximization (with its connotation of a "dollar nexus" in all decision making), to the broader, more useful concept of utility maximization also had powerful ramifications for lawyers in diverse fields. So did the economists' increasingly refined analyses of public and private goods and of externalities. The new sophistication of these areas not only had obvious applications in areas of law dealing with economic planning and the like, but also opened to scientific study legal subjects long thought to be beyond economists' interests, such as criminal law, domestic relations, and litigation procedures.

Of late, developments growing out of this fertile joining have been accelerating at an almost dizzying pace. Law professors, at least those who have not already done graduate study in economics, are attending economics institutes in droves, and economists are slipping into law classes with increasing regularity. Economics students are making their interest in substantive legal policies felt by increasing their demand for applied economics courses, and law students increasingly demand law courses with a heavy economic content. And law firms are beginning to pay salary premiums for graduates with this dual training.

This interest has truly burst forth with startling speed, and teachers of economics and law are hard pressed to find appropriate textual materials to cope with it. Several new journals have made their appearance to service the market, and comprehensive texts, such as Posner's and Tullock's, *op. cit.*, have begun to appear; however, as indicated above, the interaction is probably already too great for any single text to cover every area of law in significant depth. We can expect, therefore, to see more economics texts specialized in individual legal fields and investigating them in greater depth.

This book of readings is itself specialized in one phase of the law-economics literature. Its main objective is to introduce both lawyers and economists to the fundamental economic literature in an expanding field most familiarly known to its initiates as "Property Rights." The term is highly misleading, especially to lawyers, and other phrases have gained some currency.

The term "property rights" is much broader than the word "rights" as used in the Hohfeldian jurisprudential system; it really refers to the whole system of substantive legal rules, whether the particular reference is to a legal right, privilege, duty or other such notion. (See Introduction, Part I.) Sufficient readings of these basic "property rights" materials are included in this book to serve the needs of either economists or law professors offering a course under this or similar titles.

In addition a few specific substantive legal areas have been covered in some depth in order to convey an idea of the extent to which the

newer economic analysis has made significant inroads into law.
In the interests of economy I have attempted to utilize as frequently
as possible articles that would both introduce new economic concepts
and build up a coherent pattern of the legal issues in a particular area.
Also to save space where appropriate, readings have been used which
summarize articles that might otherwise have been included.

That the selection process was difficult goes without saying, and that
some of the deletions were heart-rendering must also be acknowledged.
The deletion that hurt most was an entire section titled "Economics and
Jurisprudence" which would have contained several excellent reviews
of both Posner's book and of John Rawls' *Justice* (1971). The consensus one gathered from those materials was that we should develop
standards that will allow us carefully to delineate those areas of
law or decision-making in which economic science can be appropriately
applied and those in which the resulting loss of the law's moral force
may be too costly, or too risky.

I am in no way indebted for the production of this book to what Kenneth
Boulding has referred to as the "grants society." My financial arrangements were purely market, contractual ones. Still I am the grateful
beneficiary of the fantastic scholarship reflected in all the works
included here, and of others regrettably omitted. Regardless of the
form in which the authors might prefer their rewards in this life,
I should like to express my appreciation for their having made my own
intellectual life so much richer and more enjoyable.

There were some direct contributions of service in the form of suggestions
and criticisms. These came in varying amounts from Armen Alchian,
Harold Demsetz, William Riker, James Mofsky, Roger LeRoy Miller,
and Gordon Tullock. And generous gestures by Ronald Coase and
Richard Posner, editors respectively of the *Journal of Law and
Economics* and the *Journal of Legal Studies*, are also gratefully
acknowledged. And a special appreciation must be expressed to
Ms. Suzanne Sawada, my former student, secretary, research assistant,
and unflappable ally. Her performance in each of these capacities
made my effort far more pleasurable than it could otherwise have been.

Henry G. Manne
May 1975

CONTENTS

2

PROPERTY RIGHTS AND SOME
SUBSTANTIVE LEGAL RULES   121

3

PUBLIC GOODS, COLLECTIVE GOODS AND EXTERNALITIES

351

4

PROPERTY RIGHTS IN
ASSOCIATIONAL RELATIONSHIPS   481

This begins with some of the fundamental literature suggesting that there are problems in the operation of a private property, market exchange system causing divergences in individual instances between social (or aggregative) costs and private (or individual) costs. That is, the costs of certain activities may be imposed on others through private actions with no account of these costs being taken by the offender.

It has been popular for some time for economists to deride the private property system as being unable to cope with this kind of problem. The fascinating point now emerging, however, is that private exchange systems can and do for the most part satisfactorily deal with these problems through imaginative private contractual arrangements. Indeed, these parties have been far more imaginative than those economic critics who could only identify the problem but not see the likelihood of private solutions.

Part IV, entitled "Property Rights in Associational Relationships," applies the powerful concept of utility maximization as a substitute for the older and much more restrictive concept of wealth maximization. This concept, along with important recent advances in the theory of the firm, allows significant new insights into our understanding of modern corporations with their immense size and widely diffused ownership.

This same approach also opened up for rigorous analysis some areas that had never been readily available for study with earlier, cruder techniques. We now seem well along towards the development of predictive and satisfactory analytical theories about nonprofit organizations, labor unions and even government agencies. Unfortunately the fascinating literature in the last category has been omitted, even though it is already quite well developed. Suffice it to say that authors like William Niskanen, Roger Noll, Richard Posner, George Stigler, Gordon Tullock, Anthony Downs and others have us well on the way to a meaningful economic theory of bureaucrcy. Certainly no scholar interested in the field of administrative regulation, either from an economic or a legal point of view, can consider himself current in the field without a thorough knowledge of that impressive literature. Wherever feasible in other parts of this book, review articles with extensive bibliographies have been included, but unfortunately such a piece does not yet exist in the bureaucracy area.

We thus cover the gamut of the new economic techniques and concepts, while exposing the reader to a tremendous range of legal issues viewed in the new light. No one can fail to be impressed with the analytical powers offered by economic tools or by the genius of the writers who have been pioneering these areas. We are already beyond the threshold of a new field of scholarship, and dramatic advances can be anticipated almost daily.

INTRODUCTION

We are dealing in this set of readings with a number of tightly interdependent economic notions. There is no simple progression to the logic,
and articles in different sections overlap somewhat in subject matter.
However, it seemed more valuable to retain the integrity of the original
articles than to attempt to cut and paste small pieces of various articles
into a synthetic textbook.

Since this is a collection of readings on the economics of law, the
materials have been organized to present a somewhat systematic approach
to the law. Thus Part I deals with the formation and operation of legal
systems, sets of rules, and decision making institutions. Aside from the
fact that the language would sound strange to most legal philosophers,
these are fundamentally jurisprudential materials, since they examine
the origins of and justifications for legal systems relating to the ownership
and use of property, again using "property" in the broad sense of any
legal entitlement rather than in any legalistic or metaphysical sense.

Having examined theories regarding the formation and specification
of property rights, we turn in Part II to some detailed economic analyses
of the traditional legal rules that developed to regulate injuries to the
"property" of others, including negligence and products liability. These
areas, as it happens, have been the principal vehicles for the most important writings in the new field of property rights, including Coase's
classic "The Problem of Social Cost," the first article in Part II. This
organizational pattern allows us to introduce economics students to
these materials in terms of one of the most basic areas of common law,
liability for injuries to third parties.

Part III of the book extends this theme to an area of complex,
modern debate about property rights, cases in which numerous individuals
have rights in the same property or in which third persons are affected
by an individual's use of his property. Here we examine, first theoretically, and then as a more specific topical legal issue, that troublesome
but important problem of "externalities," though no single word can
connote all the nuances of this growing field of economics and law.

1

THE ECONOMICS OF LEGAL RELATIONSHIPS

READINGS IN THE THEORY OF PROPERTY RIGHTS

As a postscript to this introduction, I should mention that I intentionally make no effort to tell teachers how to use these materials. The readings are, I believe, quite sufficient for the purposes outlined in this Introduction, though some teachers may want to delete and others add materials. Nor do I advise professors at what level they should teach these materials or whether there should be prerequisite courses.

Since the book is not designed to serve any single academic constituency, these decisions are best left to those individuals who experience the tremendous excitement of new scholarly discoveries.

*

PART 1

The Economic Meaning and Development of Property Rights Systems

A Introduction

The first article in this section, W. Stubblebine's "On Property Rights and Institutions," is an elegant introduction to the whole subject matter of this book. While somewhat formalistic in its economics, it should be well within the capabilities of most law professors to understand and discuss. In addition to outlining a variety of classifications of legal systems that are possible, Stubblebine emphasizes the critical fact that we live in a world of constant, interacting change. "Laws modified in one period condition behavior in future periods . . . ; multi-period—uncertainty analysis seems unavoidable. . . . It may well be that men are destined to exist forever on the edge of the jungle." Or, we might add, *in* it. This theme of uncertainty, translated on occasion into "information costs," will play a large role in the analyses to follow.

Stubblebine's article is valuable in first position for still another reason. It is very important that economists and law professors alike understand at the outset that phrases such as "property rights," "legal structure," "economics of law," or "entitlements" all mean fundamentally the same thing, and while the term "property rights" seems to have the semantic lead at the moment, there is dissatisfaction with its apparent ambiguity, and another term may yet displace it. The important thing for lawyers to understand is that Hohfeldian concepts like rights, privileges, duties, etc., are all comprehended within any of the phrases mentioned above. A Hohfeldian "duty," for instance, would simply represent a disutility or cost attaching to some status or relationship, so that, in the case of goods, the value of ownership would be lessened. As useful as the Hohfeldian categories may have been for some legal analysis, they would present economists with the problem of adding apples and oranges. But by converting all of these varied utility pluses and minuses into one economic algebra, predictions and explanations of the motivation and behavior reponses of individuals living in society can be made with greater certainty.

Demsetz's "Toward a Theory of Property Rights (2)" serves two purposes. It clarifies, with specific illustrations, the concept of property rights, and it advances an extremely important hypothesis about how property rights in general emerge. His explanation of the differing property rights systems found among Indians in different parts of the North American Continent must surely rank among the classics of analytical reasoning about anthropology and law. The balance of Demsetz's article explains the special problem and significance of the enforcement of property rights, and touches briefly collective goods, externalities, and voluntary associations into firms, all points to be examined in more detail later.

In the next article (3), Pejovich shows us how the general theory already outlined in the previous articles aids substantially in the development of an economic theory of the state. Ironically Pejovich finds much that is similar in the writings of Marx and Engels on the one hand and modern property right theorists like Alchian and Demsetz on the other. While crediting the earlier writers with pioneering a sophisticated theory of property rights, Pejovich finds it to be marred ultimately by Marx's deterministic view of the history of mankind. Had Marx not been misled by this ideologically necessary view, that in turn colored his theory of the state and its relation to private property, he might well be hailed today as an originator of the modern theory of property rights.

The section concludes with a heavily edited review article on property rights literature by E. Furubotn and S. Pejovich (4). However, the article included the most complete bibliography on the subject available as of the end of 1972.

The second section of Part I addresses itself to issue of the formation of legal rights and governments on a somewhat less abstract level than found in the foregoing pieces, though we may still be dealing with positive laws at a fairly abstract level. In fact, the subject is really the economics of constitutional origins. James Buchanan, the undisputed doyen of this field, leads off with a game-theoretical analysis of the formation of constitutions and the inescapable complications resulting from changes in human preferences (5).

In this first work Buchanan alludes to the implications of a constitutional basis for property rights for such political issues as wealth redistribution. Then in his seminal paper, "The Political Economy of Franchise in the Welfare State" (6), he advances in some detail a theory of how much wealth redistribution we should anticipate under a constitution providing universal suffrage. Perhaps of even greater importance than this discussion is Buchanan's clear statement of the proposition that all constitutionally protected political rights, such as suffrage, or freedom of speech, or any others, must be viewed in any rigorous analysis as the analytical equivalent of property rights in goods. Furthermore, individuals may use these "rights" for the good or harm of others in society, just as they may utilize conventional material goods. And the value of any property right, be it material or political, is always discounted to the extent that enforceable rights of others may interfere with the full use or enjoyment of the right. Thus the constitutional right of a majority to tax away the wealth of a minority attenuates the value of the minorities' property.

Somewhat anticipating the Buchanan article was the 1964 contribution of Aaron Director, "The Parity of the Economic Market Place" (7), in which Director compares and contrasts the arguments for civil freedoms, including property ownership, with the arguments for democratic rule. He emphasizes the not untimely lesson that John Stuart Mill's *On Liberty* was *not* deploring encroachments on individual liberty through legislation but rather was condemning those resulting from "the tyranny of public opinion."

Director then turns a highly illuminating light on the paradoxical notion long popular in American political thought that a free market for ideas should be accorded a constitutional priority over a free market in so-called economic affairs. While Director has written little directly relevant to the subject at hand, an oral tradition has it that the more prolific writers in the field owe a considerable scholarly debt to this remarkable intellect. Some believe that he is more responsible than any other individual for the origins of the modern concept of property rights.

This section closes with a somewhat formal economic analysis of the concept of freedom by Moore (8). For those readers not attuned to Greek letters and mathematical symbols, the formal statement is summarized in quite clear prose later in the article. Moore's economic theory of civil liberties is a rather elaborate cost-benefit approach considering "only those externalities that physically affect some individual or affect the value of his wealth." Thus he rules out externalities such as the loss in welfare a member of the WCTU feels when someone else sips a martini.

Certainly this methodological rule makes life more convenient for economists, and it may even express an assumption that a great many civil libertarians would agree too. However, for a social scientist, it is difficult to see the objective basis on which Moore rests this assumption. If individualistic utilitarianism is the measure of all goods and bads, psychic harm cannot lightly be excluded. Still, if we do not make this assumption along with Moore, we are confronted with the terrible problem of how to justify the concept of social or

political freedoms in utilitarian terms.   While Linda Lovelace is not to
be sneezed at, by what logic do we absolutely disregard the interests
of those who gag on the very knowledge that *Deep Throat* is being
shown?   Moore's attempt to work his way out of this dilemma is
original and suggestive, but it is far from conclusive.   Perhaps the
problem is insoluble.   Still, as we shall see in the next section, externality problems are being dealt with every day without the use of police.

B The Development of Property Rights and Legal Institutions

1: ON PROPERTY RIGHTS AND INSTITUTIONS

WM. CRAIG STUBBLEBINE*

Some three or four years ago, I began an introductory principles course with Robinson Crusoe on his island, choosing between fish and coconuts subject to available technological-resource constraints. In this context, the students explored various hypotheses concerning Crusoe's production-consumption behavior. Once done, Friday was introduced to the island and several new scenarios were developed:

a) Friday retires to a part of the island far distant from Crusoe, and both continue thereafter to dwell in total isolation;

b) Crusoe enslaves Friday, turning him into an automaton such that Friday simply is another resource available to Crusoe;

c) Crusoe and Friday meet as equals, and agree to form a socialist democracy in which *all* decisions are made jointly and under a unanimity rule; and

d) Crusoe and Friday meet, and agree to a set of property rights which could be described as characteristic of a capitalist-free enterprise society.

Other than a) which is degenerative to Crusoe alone, the scenarios permit substantial exploration of concepts such as selfish versus benevolent dictatorships, two-person bargaining, comparative advantage, specialization of labor, and gains-from-trade—as well as *institutional* comparisons of the outcomes predicted under dictatorship, socialism, and capitalism.[1] At a later stage, Thursday, or Saturday, can be introduced to the island to per-

Explorations in the Theory of Anarchy. Gordon Tullock (ed.) (1972 Center for the Study of Public Choice, Blacksburg, Va.), p. 39.

mit exploration of several elementary propositions on majoritarian coalition formation.

Absent, conspicuously in the light of this seminar series, from that early course were the scenarios:

a) constructed by Professor Bush in which a Crusoe and a Friday "fight" their way to some initial equilibrium or *status quo* before undertaking to explore areas of potential agreement; and

b) implicit in Mr. Gunning's discussion in which a master exercises some control over a non-automaton slave.

That the scenarios can be multiplied more or less *ad infinitum* is not here of importance. What they do is to aid in the process of identifying, or delimiting, the set of attainable social relationships—that is, in delimiting the set from which will be selected the relationship prevailing at any given moment in time.

What is noteworthy about the scenarios is that Friday's arrival on the island fundamentally alters the environment in which *both* must operate. What neither Crusoe and Friday can escape is the fact that some social order must, and will, emerge. Some set of property rights must, and will, be created to condition the relationship between these two individuals—whether that set be characterized as capitalistic, socialistic, or something else. In a fundamental sense, any study of society must begin here, at the point where two or more individuals must accept the necessity of social relations, of creating property rights.

I. A Digression

I would digress briefly to reflect upon the activity in which the seminar participants find themselves engaged. One aspect is the formulation of an explanation of some (set of) observation(s) whether from the distant or near past, or from the near or distant future. By "explanation," I presume is meant the formulation of a theory which has among its hypotheses, or predictions, the outcomes observed.

Thus, for example, Bush has offered an explanation of why men initiate attempts to engage in trade. With but a slight modification of his model, one also may have an explanation of why men shun exchange: in Figure 1, point N—with its positive levels of E^A and E^B—is on the contract locus.[2] Similarly, Professor Buchanan has offered an explanation— an intriguing one—of why men resort to, as well as a theory of why men shun, anarchy or revolution.

I take as axiomatic that there are infinitely many alternative explanations for any given observation. I take also as axiomatic that: i) if two (or more) theories have exactly the same set of hypotheses, then the theories are mere transformations of each other; and ii) if there is at least one hypothesis not common to any two theories, then observation will reject at least one of the theories. Thus, if men are observed to shun exchange, it may be that there are no available gains-from-trade—because the rates of substitution are identical; or it may be that the observation comes from a part of the bargaining process prior to exchange; or it may be that the observation reflects the fact it takes time to learn of the availability of gains and how to exchange.

It also may be that a theory is compatible with some observations, but not with others. In this event, there is room to formulate a theory compatible with all observations. I accept however that this is not the occasion to debate the remark "a theory which explains everything explains nothing."

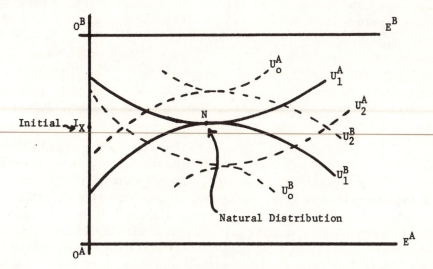

Figure 1

A second aspect has to do with the determination of "betterness." As a concept, it enters into the discussions of social scientists: (i) sometimes as an axiom in the statement of some theory of outcomes—usually as an axiom of choice from which follow, in conjunction with other axioms, hypotheses concerning observed behavior; and (ii) sometimes as a criterion outside of any theory of outcomes for ranking hypothetical or experienced outcomes.

There may be some who still are outraged morally by economists employing theories incorporating utility-income-profit maximization assumptions, as in i) above. In general, however, one trusts that most participating social scientists are prepared to judge such theories relative to other theories on the basis of their respective explanatory powers, on the extent to which each predicts the outcomes observed.

With respect to (ii), however, the situation is ambiguous. Economists, in particular, have formulated a number of non-theoretic criteria for ranking, or judging, outcomes—e. g., Pareto optimality, Kaldor-Hicks-Scitovsky (non-)compensation tests, Thompson-Tideman tests, etc.—and a number for ranking, or judging, decision-rules—e. g., equality of rates of substitution, distribution of income according to marginal product, equality of marginal social benefits and costs, preservation of competition, etc. From other disciplines, come other criteria: majority rule, abide by the Constitution, innocent men should not be punished for the crimes committed by others, etc. Each of these suffers from the same defect: the substitution of one criterion for another will enhance the interests of some individuals while damaging the interests of other individuals. From this dilemma there appears to be no escape. As a scientist, the social scientist has no basis on which to commend one criterion over another. Put another way, the social scientist is hopelessly lost as a *scientific* ranker of outcomes —whatever be his competence as a generator of theories of outcomes.

II. Property Rights

One of the most common activities engaging the energies and talents of men is discussion regarding the modification of existing property rights. Yet not too many years ago, use of the term "property rights," or "law structure," would have been a relatively rare event in the everyday conversation among economists. Today, some including myself would see in the notion a possible organizing principle for the study of society.

By way of definition: property rights, inextricable from technology-resources, serve to delimit the alternatives open to choice-making individuals in a society. The conjunction of individual choices yields an outcome dependent upon the tastes and technology-resources-property rights extant in that society.

Axiom of Existence: At any moment, property rights are specified fully to all choosing individuals.[3]

For example, the protagonists in the Bush model have the right to expend such levels of effort E as each sees fit; *and* to do whatever each wishes with his stock in the natural state; *and* to enter into whatever agreements they wish. By contrast, in a socialist democracy, either Crusoe or Friday may propose a course of action, but it may be undertaken if and only if both agree and if the action is feasible in the light of available resources. A's home ownership conveys on B the right to enter the property for the purpose of securing A's assistance in locating ambulance or police in an emergency, but not to sleep in A's doorway.

The notion that the oceans of the world are "not owned" must be interpreted as meaning that every individual possesses the (property) right to devote his energies to extracting from the waters the fish and other raw materials which abound there *without* any further agreement from any other individual or group of individuals. To now vest "ownership" must mean the deprivation of some individuals of the ocean rights which were theirs until now.

Axiom of Modification: Every individual seeks those property right modifications which he believes will improve his welfare. Since property rights condition behavior, he seeks those modifications which will induce others to make choices conveying on him an increased sense of satisfaction.

Unadorned, the axiom includes both barter and revolution.

Although it conjures up a picture in which a deer is moved physically from one man's shoulder to another's, "barter" may be viewed as a modification of existing property rights wherein A's rights to something (a deer) are conveyed to B in exchange for B's rights to some other thing (a beaver) being conveyed to A. It is the rights which are exchanged, not the goods. Similarly, revolution may be thought of, for example, as a mod-

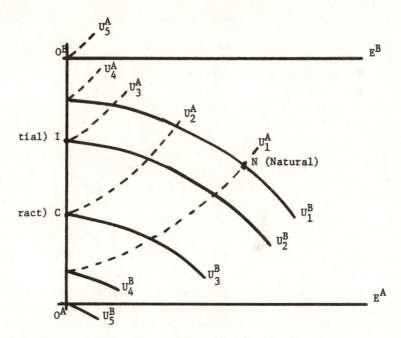

Figure 2

ification in which A conveys to B his (A's) right to engage in exchange with others in return for B's agreement not to put him (A) to death. Looked at in this way, every act is associated with the modification of some property right.

On the other hand, the barter of deer for beaver in no way has modified the more inclusive property right to engage in the exchange of rights with respect to deer and beaver. And the revolutionary merely has exerted his general property right to engage in revolution. Looked at in this way, no act modifies property rights.

One way out of this semantic thicket is to draw a (provisional) distinction between those rights exogenously or institutionally determined and those rights endogenous to a particular institution. Consider, for example, Figure 2 in which the three focal points of the Bush model are reproduced:[4] the initial distribution (I), the natural distribution (N), and the contract distribution (C).

Each of the focal points may be thought of as an outcome of some institution in which certain of the property rights are exogenous to each and every individual:

Institution *(Exogenous Property Rights)*	*Outcome* *(Distribution Point)*
I.1. One cannot expend effort (E) and cannot undertake exchange	Initial (I)
I.2. One cannot expend effort, but may undertake exchange	Initial (I)
I.3. One may expend effort, but cannot undertake exchange	Natural (N)
I.4. One may expend effort, and may undertake exchange	Contract (C)

Note that these instructions are mutually exclusive: being in one precludes being in any other institution at the same moment in time.

Properly understood, it is this relationship between institution and outcome which has been central to the scientific literature of economics—including the now burgeoning literature of property rights.[5] Indeed, perhaps the most central theorem of this literature is that, if they may, men will engage in the modification of existing property rights through exchange. And this is the major theorem of the Bush model.

By contrast, the dominant theme of welfare economics and of political economy, implicity or explicitly, has been evaluation of various institutional arrangements. For illustrative purposes, Figure 2 may be translated into a utility transformation function over outcomes such that every point in the area $OU_5^A U_5^B$ of Figure 3 is associated with some point in

Figure 2. For each institution, one and only one point in this space represents the outcome of that institution.

Given that more (utility) is preferred to less (utility), Figure 3 suggests the following theorem:

(i) institutions I.1, I.2, and I.4 will be preferred to institution I.3 by both individuals;

(ii) institutions I.1 and I.2 will be preferred to institution I.4 by individual A;

(iii) institution I.4 will be preferred to institutions I.1 and I.2 by individual B; and

(iv) institutions I.1 and I.2 will be equally preferred by both individuals.[6]

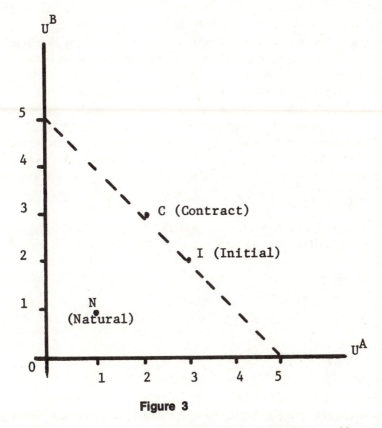

Figure 3

If the evaluation means comparison of the (relative) welfare accruing to each individual under various institutional arrangements, the task substantially is complete, given the limitations of the model under consideration. Specifically, comparison does not include any determination of "betterness"—however tempting is exclusion of I.3 by a Pareto criterion. Similarly, comparison does not admit conclusions concerning the predicted behavior of individuals in choosing among institutions. Why not? By definition, the institutional arrangements are determined exogenously; there is here no mechanism, no arrangement, through which individuals may effectuate their preferences among I.1 to I.4.[7]

In both the literature of welfare economics and of property rights, the notion that exchange enhances the welfare of a society has at least two interpretations:

(i) Some "god" of institutions may push out the welfare frontier by substituting a world of exchange (such as I.2), or a world of effort and exchange (such as I.4) for a world of effort alone (such as I.3); and

(ii) *Their* act of exchange in a world of effort and exchange (such as I.4) permits individuals to achieve the welfare frontier characteristic of that world, but does not alter the location of that frontier.

Although perhaps an oversight, economists normally do not admit to being predictors of godly behavior. However, failure to make clear, and to appreciate, the distinction between these two interpretations may explain the vacuousness of much of the welfare-policy literature.[8]

Alas, in a world the gods rarely visit, exogenous institutions are a fiction. What exists are laws having all the appearance of being man-made and man-enforced.[9] They distinguish between actions permitted and actions proscribed. Laws evolve through time. They and the property rights created thereby exist in any moment by virtue of choices and events in previous periods. The *status quo* is exogenous to the moment; modification of the *status quo* is endogenous to the moment.

This would suggest that a classification distinguishing among the means of permitted and proscribed property rights modification may be helpful:

1. Permitted
   a) Private exchange of rights.
   b) Collective or legislative action.
2. Proscribed
   a) Private crime.
   b) Social revolution.

Even here, care must be exercised. Labeling an act as permitted or proscribed in and of itself is of no consequence: the proscription of some action cannot preclude some individual from deciding to pursue that action. Nor can man possessed of incomplete information administer with certainty: some who violate the law will escape punishment, while some who do not violate the law will be punished as if they did. What law can do is to prescribe a structure of rewards and punishments to be associated with each action.[10]   This is its power.

   In that raw and uncivilized state characteristic of the Bush model, the application of energies to stealing, nowhere, is meaningfully proscribed. The exchange modification of property rights undertaken by the men therein always proceeds against the option to resort to theft.   Indeed, were theft meaningfully proscribed in this model, the operative institution would be I.2, not I.4; the outcome would be distribution I, not C.   Only at some later stage in man's development does a reward-punishment structure emerge which serves to distinguish between permitted and proscribed means of modifying property rights.

III.   Modification and Compensation

Changes in property rights inevitably lead to changes in some individual's perception of his wealth-utility position.   The approval of market exchange by classical and neo-classical economists is based in no small measure on the presumption that such transactions benefit all parties.   But what of the changes resulting from other means of modification?

   The question may be placed in perspective by considering a game of chance.[11]   Before deciding his course of action, the informed-rational individual would compute his expected wealth position were he to enter, and his position were he not to enter, into the play of the game.   If the opportunity offered to the individual be a fair game, his computed wealth position will be the same whether he chooses to accept or to reject an invitation to join the game.

   If, however, he decides to play, thereafter he will have an abiding interest in each roll of the die, or fall of the cards.   Before each new round, his expected wealth position may be recomputed—a computation which will reflect the outcomes experienced in past rounds, but remains unaffected by whether he now withdraws or continues on to future rounds.   Should his wealth position deteriorate in the course of the play, one might be properly sympathetic to his curses and lamentations without undertaking to compensate him for the change in his computed wealth.   Why not?   Because in a fundamental sense, he has suffered no damage: this is an outcome to which he exposed himself by entering into the game, a game which was then and is now fair.

   If, on the other hand, he concludes before the beginning of some round that the game can be modified to enhance his position in future rounds, he may propose such modification of the rules as seem appropriate to him. Should the modification be accepted by those who must agree, the game will continue in its new form.   If not, because one or more conclude that the modified game would be less attractive, either the proposal will be withdrawn and play continue under the old rules, or play will end.

So it is with the game of property rights. Each round modifies the existing set of rights without modifying the game itself. And, though losers may lament their losses during the rounds, none has suffered damages in the game. The lamentations mean only that their evokers would have fared better had they, and others, chosen to behave in some other way. If there is a difference between the game of chance and of property rights, it is that withdrawing from the latter means ending life. Only in the sense that life is preferred to death can property rights modification be said to be fair or positive-sum game for every player.

Perhaps it should be emphasized that the denial of damage to a player does not turn on any judgment—moral, ethical, or legal—concerning the manner in which modification takes place, applying equally to barter and to revolution. As among the *status quo*, a modification which incorporates compensation, and one which does not, the rational individual will choose that alternative best fulfilling the modification axiom. But this is a notion completely different from the criteria economists have sought to employ in judging betterness.

IV. Conclusion

Economic theory traditionally has dealt extensively with the modification of property rights through market exchange. The emergence of public choice in the 1950s provided substantive insights into political exchange. A small, but growing, literature has begun to examine private crime.[12] Of late, there has been a resurgence of interest in social evolution and revolution.

Ultimately, what seems destined to emerge is some general theory in which the modification of law structure plays a central role. If so, social scientists must learn to deal with models substantially more sophisticated than those currently at hand. Merely to consider the various means of modifying rights can be an exhausting task—to say nothing of specifying the structure of rights.[13] Laws modified in one period condition behavior in future periods; nature and men always in some measure are unpredictable; man's capacity to discover new modes of behavior and new technology seems unbounded. Multi-period—uncertainty analysis seems unavoidable.

Even if men in concert could discover a reward-punishment structure leading each individual to conclude that the expected pay-off to him of every proscribed act is negative, at this writing such a structure seems likely to gut the qualities which make life attractive.

It well may be that men are destined to exist forever on the edge of the jungle.

FOOTNOTES

* Virginia Polytechnic Institute and The Claremont Colleges. The paper draws substantially on my "Institutions and the Social Product Transformation Function" which has evolved over several seminar presentations beginning in 1968.

1 The complex of motivations which conditioned the evolving relationship between Crusoe and Friday in Defoe's 1719 classic is not of immediate interest here. One might note, however, that English involvement with North American slavery began some one hundred years prior to Defoe's publication.

2 Figure 1 is an alternative presentation of Bush's Figure 2. "1" represents the initial distribution between two individuals, A and B, of some fixed quantity $O_A O_B$ of an "all-purpose consumer good," $X.O^i E^i$ represents the effort expended by individual i "in taking income from individual j and protecting his own income from individual j." U^i represents individual i's indifference curve relating $O^i X^i$ and $O^i E^i$. "N" represents an equilibrium point in which neither A nor B finds it in his advantage further to adjust independently his own $O^i E^i$.

3 Although fully specified, there may be considerable uncertainty in the minds of some, or all, individuals as to just what the rights are.

4 Cf. Figure 1 and footnote 4.

5 Cf. E. G. Furabotn and S. Pejovich, *Property Rights and Economic Theory: A Survey of Recent Literature* supra p. —— (ed.).

6 In a world in which individuals receive initially two types of (consumer) goods, one predicts that I.2 would be preferred by both individuals to I.1 since the latter precludes the possibility of mutually advantageous trading leading to the elimination of differences in rates of substitution (in consumption).

7 If one did exist, it would constitute an exogenous institution from which would emerge some outcome, I or N or C. This suggests that students of social constitutions face a problem of infinite regression in which choice at any level is an outcome of a still more inclusive system of property rights.

8 To forestall misunderstanding on this point: shifts in the welfare frontier can and do occur—because new resources-technologies are discovered, not because men exploit the opportunities available under existing resource-technology conditions.

9 For present purposes, there is no need to distinguish among customary, statutory, and judicial law.

10 Structure is used here to cover two separate aspects: the likelihood of discovery-application (enforcement) and the money-utility value of the rewards-punishments to the actor prescribed by law. Among the laws in question are those calling for the allocation of resources to enforcement. There is no essential difference: the rewards accruing to the incompetent sheriff-enforcer are different from those accruing to the malfeasant sheriff-enforcer.

11 Although used here for a somewhat different purpose, the example will be recognized instantly by students of Rutledge Vining.

[12] Simon Rottenberg, ed., *Proceedings*, American Enterprise Institute Conference on Crime, 17–18 July 1972, Washington, D.C.

[13] Consider the property rights implicit in Bush's "contract distribution" (*cf.* Figure 2 above):

    i)   at the beginning of the period, B agrees to deliver to A an amount IC of X;

    ii)   both agree to expend zero E;

    iii) each may do whatever he wishes with his stock of $X(O^AC$ and $CO^B)$;

    iv) should B fail to deliver the required amount IC to A, each may expend such E as he sees fit;

    v)   should B deliver IC to A and then A(B) expend E_i^A (B), B(A) may expend such E_j^B (A) as he sees fit; and

    vi) A and B may enter into whatever additional agreements they wish.

B Continued

2: TOWARD A THEORY OF PROPERTY RIGHTS

HAROLD DEMSETZ
University of Chicago*

When a transaction is concluded in the marketplace, two bundles of property rights are exchanged. A bundle of rights often attaches to a physical commodity or service, but it is the value of the rights that determines the value of what is exchanged. Questions addressed to the emergence and mix of the components of the bundle of rights are prior to those commonly asked by economists. Economists usually take the bundle of property rights as a datum and ask for an explanation of the forces determining the price and the number of units of a good to which these rights attach.

In this paper, I seek to fashion some of the elements of an economic theory of property rights. The paper is organized into three parts. The first part discusses briefly the concept and role of property rights in social systems. The second part offers some guidance for investigating the emergence of property rights. The third part sets forth some principles relevant to the coalescing of property rights into particular bundles and to the determination of the ownership structure that will be associated with these bundles.

The Concept and Role of Property Rights

In the world of Robinson Crusoe property rights play no role. Property rights are an instrument of society and derive their significance from the fact that they help a man form those expectations which he can reasonably

57 Am.Ec.Rev. Proceedings Issue, May 1967, p. 347.

hold in his dealings with others.   These expectations find expression in the laws, customs, and mores of a society.   An owner of property rights possesses the consent of fellowmen to allow him to act in particular ways.   An owner expects the community to prevent others from interfering with his actions, provided that these actions are not prohibited in the specifications of his rights.

It is important to note that property rights convey the right to benefit or harm oneself or others.   Harming a competitor by producing superior products may be permitted, while shooting him may not.   A man may be permitted to benefit himself by shooting an intruder but be prohibited from selling below a price floor.   It is clear, then, that property rights specify how persons may be benefited and harmed, and, therefore, who must pay whom to modify the actions taken by persons.   The recognition of this leads easily to the close relationship between property rights and externalities.

Externality is an ambiguous concept.   For the purposes of this paper, the concept includes external costs, external benefits, and pecuniary as well as nonpecuniary externalities.   No harmful or beneficial effect is external to the world.   Some person or persons always suffer or enjoy these effects.   What converts a harmful or beneficial effect into an externality is that the cost of bringing the effect to bear on the decisions of one or more of the interacting persons is too high to make it worthwhile, and this is what the term shall mean here.   "Internalizing" such effects refers to a process, usually a change in property rights, that enables these effects to bear (in greater degree) on all interacting persons.

A primary function of property rights is that of guiding incentives to achieve a greater internalization of externalities.   Every cost and benefit associated with social interdependencies is a potential externality.   One condition is necessary to make costs and benefits externalities.   The cost of a transaction in the rights between the parties (internalization) must exceed the gains from internalization.   In general, transacting cost can be large relative to gains because of "natural" difficulties in trading or they can be large because of legal reasons.   In a lawful society the prohibition of voluntary negotiations makes the cost of transacting infinite.   Some costs and benefits are not taken into account by users of resources whenever externalities exist, but allowing transactions increases the degree to which internalization takes place.   For example, it might be thought that a firm which uses slave labor will not recognize all the costs of its activities, since it can have its slave labor by paying subsistence wages only.   This will not be true if negotiations are permitted, for the slaves can offer to the firm a payment for their freedom based on the expected return to them of being free men.   The cost of slavery can thus be internalized in the calculations of the firm.   The transition from serf to free man in feudal Europe is an example of this process.

Perhaps one of the most significant cases of externalities is the extensive use of the military draft.   The taxpayer benefits by not paying the full cost of staffing the armed services.   The costs which he escapes are the additional sums that would be needed to acquire men voluntarily for the services or those sums that would be offered as payment by draftees to taxpayers in order to be exempted.   With either voluntary recruitment, the "buy-him-in" system, or with a "let-him-buy-his-way-out" system, the full cost of recruitment would be brought to bear on taxpayers.   It has always seemed incredible to me that so many economists can recognize an externality when they see smoke but not when they see the draft.   The familiar smoke example is one in which negotiation costs may be too high (because of the large number of interacting parties) to make it worthwhile to internalize all the effects of smoke.   The draft is an externality caused by forbidding negotiation.

The role of property rights in the internalization of externalities can be made clear within the context of the above examples.   A law which establishes the right of a person to his freedom would necessitate a payment on the part of a firm or of the taxpayer sufficient to cover the cost of using that person's labor if his services are to be obtained.   The costs of labor thus become internalized in the firm's or taxpayer's decisions. Alternatively, a law which gives the firm or the taxpayer clear title to slave labor would necessitate that the slaveowners take into account the sums that slaves are willing to pay for their freedom.   These costs thus become internalized in decisions although wealth is distributed differently in the two cases.   All that is needed for internalization in either case is ownership which includes the right of sale.   It is the prohibition of a property right adjustment, the prohibition of the establishment of an ownership title that can thenceforth be exchanged, that precludes the internalization of external costs and benefits.

There are two striking implications of this process that are true in a world of zero transaction costs.   The output mix that results when the exchange of property rights is allowed is efficient and the mix is independent of who is assigned ownership (except that different wealth distributions may result in different demands).[1]   For example, the efficient mix of civilians and military will result from transferable ownership no matter whether taxpayers must hire military volunteers or whether draftees must pay taxpayers to be excused from service.   For taxpayers will hire only those military (under the "buy-him-in" property right system) who would not pay to be exempted (under the "let-him-buy-his-way-out" system).   The highest bidder under the "let-him-buy-his-way-out" property right system would be precisely the last to volunteer under a "buy-him-in" system.[2]

We will refer back to some of these points later. But for now, enough groundwork has been laid to facilitate the discussion of the next two parts of this paper.

The Emergence of Property Rights

If the main allocative function of property rights is the internalization of beneficial and harmful effects, then the emergence of property rights can be understood best by their association with the emergence of new or different beneficial and harmful effects.

Changes in knowledge result in changes in production functions, market values, and aspirations. New techniques, new ways of doing the same things, and doing new things—all invoke harmful and beneficial effects to which society has not been accustomed. It is my thesis in this part of the paper that the emergence of new property rights takes place in response to the desires of the interacting persons for adjustment to new benefit-cost possibilities.

The thesis can be restated in a slightly different fashion: property rights develop to internalize externalities when the gains of internalization become larger than the cost of internalization. Increased internalization, in the main, results from changes in economic values, changes which stem from the development of new technology and the opening of new markets, changes to which old property rights are poorly attuned. A proper interpretation of this assertion requires that account be taken of a community's preferences for private ownership. Some communities will have less well-developed private ownership systems and more highly developed state ownership systems. But, given a community's tastes in this regard, the emergence of new private or state-owned property rights will be in response to changes in technology and relative prices.

I do not mean to assert or to deny that the adjustments in property rights which take place need be the result of a conscious endeavor to cope with new externality problems. These adjustments have arisen in Western societies largely as a result of gradual changes in social mores and in common law precedents. At each step of this adjustment process, it is unlikely that externalities per se were consciously related to the issue being resolved. These legal and moral experiments may be hit-and-miss procedures to some extent but in a society that weights the achievement of efficiency heavily, their viability in the long run will depend on how well they modify behavior to accommodate to the externalities associated with important changes in technology or market values.

A rigorous test of this assertion will require extensive and detailed empirical work. A broad range of examples can be cited that are consistent with it: the development of air rights, renters' rights, rules for liability in automobile accidents, etc. In this part of the discussion, I shall present one group of such examples in some detail. They deal with the development of private property rights in land among American Indians. These examples are broad ranging and come fairly close to what can be called convincing evidence in the field of anthropology.

The question of private ownership of land among aboriginals has held a fascination for anthropologists. It has been one of the intellectual battlegrounds in the attempt to assess the "true nature" of man unconstrained by the "artificialities" of civilization. In the process of carrying on this debate, information has been uncovered that bears directly on the thesis with which we are now concerned. What appears to be accepted as a classic treatment and a high point of this debate is Eleanor Leacock's memoir on *The Montagnes "Hunting Territory" and the Fur Trade.*[3] Leacock's research followed that of Frank G. Speck [4] who had discovered that the Indians of the Labrador Peninsula had a long-established tradition of property in land. This finding was at odds with what was known about the Indians of the American Southwest and it prompted Leacock's study of the Montagnes who inhabited large regions around Quebec.

Leacock clearly established the fact that a close relationship existed, both historically and geographically, between the development of private rights in land and the development of the commercial fur trade. The factual basis of this correlation has gone unchallenged. However, to my knowledge, no theory relating privacy of land to the fur trade has yet been articulated. The factual material uncovered by Speck and Leacock fits the thesis of this paper well, and in doing so, it reveals clearly the role played by property right adjustments in taking account of what economists have often cited as an example of an externality—the overhunting of game.

Because of the lack of control over hunting by others, it is in no person's interest to invest in increasing or maintaining the stock of game. Overly intensive hunting takes place. Thus a successful hunt is viewed as imposing external costs on subsequent hunters—costs that are not taken into account fully in the determination of the extent of hunting and of animal husbandry.

Before the fur trade became established, hunting was carried on primarily for purposes of food and the relatively few furs that were required for the hunter's family. The externality was clearly present. Hunting could be practiced freely and was carried on without assessing its impact on other hunters. But these external effects were of such small significance that it did not pay for anyone to take them into account. There did not exist anything resembling private ownership in land. And in the *Jesuit Relations*, particularly Le Jeune's record of the winter he spent with the Montagnes in 1633–34 and in the brief account given by Father Druilletes in 1647–48, Leacock finds no evidence of private land holdings. Both accounts indicate a socioeconomic organization in which private rights to land are not well developed.

We may safely surmise that the advent of the fur trade had two immediate consequences. First, the value of furs to the Indians was increased considerably. Second, and as a result, the scale of hunting activity rose sharply. Both consequences must have increased considerably the importance of the externalities associated with free hunting. The property right system began to change, and it changed specifically in the direction required to take account of the economic effects made important by the fur trade. The geographical or distributional evidence collected by Leacock indicates an unmistakable correlation between early centers of fur trade and the oldest and most complete development of the private hunting territory.

> By the beginning of the eighteenth century, we begin to have clear evidence that territorial hunting and trapping arrangements by individual families were developing in the area around Quebec. . . . The earliest references to such arrangements in this region indicates a purely temporary allotment of hunting territories. They [Algonkians and Iroquois] divide themselves into several bands in order to hunt more efficiently. It was their custom . . . to appropriate pieces of land about two leagues square for each group to hunt exclusively. Ownership of beaver houses, however, had already become established, and when discovered, they were marked. A starving Indian could kill and eat another's beaver if he left the fur and the tail.[5]

The next step toward the hunting territory was probably a seasonal allotment system. An anonymous account written in 1723 states that the "principle of the Indians is to mark off the hunting ground selected by them by blazing the trees with their crests so that they may never encroach on each other. . . . By the middle of the century these allotted territories were relatively stabilized."[6]

The principle that associates property right changes with the emergence of new and reevaluation of old harmful and beneficial effects suggests in this instance that the fur trade made it economic to encourage the husbanding of fur-bearing animals. Husbanding requires the ability to prevent poaching and this, in turn, suggests that socioeconomic changes in property in hunting land will take place. The chain of reasoning is consistent with the evidence cited above. Is it inconsistent with the absence of similar rights in property among the southwestern Indians?

Two factors suggest that the thesis is consistent with the absence of similar rights among the Indians of the southwestern plains. The first of these is that there were no plains animals of commercial importance comparable to the fur-bearing animals of the forest, at least not until cattle arrived with Europeans. The second factor is that animals of the plains are primarily grazing species whose habit is to wander over wide tracts of land. The value of establishing boundaries to private hunting territories is thus reduced by the relatively high cost of preventing the animals from moving to adjacent parcels. Hence both the value and cost of establishing private hunting lands in the Southwest are such that we would expect little development along these lines. The externality was just not worth taking into account.

The lands of the Labrador Peninsula shelter forest animals whose habits are considerably different from those of the plains. Forest animals confine their territories to relatively small areas, so that the cost of internalizing the effects of husbanding these animals is considerably reduced. This reduced cost, together with the higher commercial value of fur-bearing forest animals, made it productive to establish private hunting lands. Frank G. Speck finds that family proprietorship among the Indians of the Peninsula included retaliation against trespass. Animal resources were husbanded. Sometimes conservation practices were carried on extensively. Family hunting territories were divided into quarters. Each year the family hunted in a different quarter in rotation, leaving a tract in the center as a sort of bank, not to be hunted over unless forced to do so by a shortage in the regular tract.

To conclude our excursion into the phenomenon of private rights in land among the American Indians, we note one further piece of corroborating evidence. Among the Indians of the Northwest, highly developed private family rights to hunting lands had also emerged—rights which went so far as to include inheritance. Here again we find that forest animals predominate and that the West Coast was frequently visited by sailing schooners whose primary purpose was trading in furs.[7]

The Coalescence and Ownership of Property Rights

I have argued that property rights arise when it becomes economic for those affected by externalities to internalize benefits and costs. But I have not yet examined the forces which will govern the particular form of right ownership. Several idealized forms of ownership must be distinguished at the outset. These are communal ownership, private ownership, and state ownership.

By communal ownership, I shall mean a right which can be exercised by all members of the community. Frequently the rights to till and to hunt the land have been communally owned. The right to walk a city sidewalk is communally owned. Communal ownership means that the community denies to the state or to individual citizens the right to interfere with any person's exercise of communally-owned rights. Private ownership implies that the community recognizes the right of the owner to exclude others from exercising the owner's private rights. State ownership implies that the state may exclude anyone from the use of a right as long as the state follows accepted political procedures for determining who may not use state-owned property. I shall not examine in detail the alternative of state ownership. The object of the analysis which follows is to discern some broad principles governing the development of property rights in communities oriented to private property.

It will be best to begin by considering a particularly useful example that focuses our attention on the problem of land ownership. Suppose that land is communally owned. Every person has the right to hunt, till, or mine the land. This form of ownership fails to concentrate the cost associated with any person's exercise of his communal right on that person. If a person seeks to maximize the value of his communal rights, he will tend to overhunt and overwork the land because some of the costs of his doing so are borne by others. The stock of game and the richness of the soil will be diminished too quickly. It is conceivable that those who own these rights, i. e., every member of the community, can agree to curtail the rate at which they work the lands if negotiating and policing costs are zero. Each can agree to abridge his rights. It is obvious that the costs of reaching such an agreement will not be zero. What is not obvious is just how large these costs may be.

Negotiating costs will be large because it is difficult for many persons to reach a mutually satisfactory agreement, especially when each hold-out has the right to work the land as fast as he pleases. But, even if an agreement among all can be reached, we must yet take account of the costs of policing the agreement, and these may be large, also. After such an agreement is reached, no one will privately own the right to work the land; all can work the land but at an agreed upon shorter workweek. Negotiating costs are increased even further because it is not possible under this system to bring the full expected benefits and expected costs of future generations to bear on current users.

If a single person owns land, he will attempt to maximize its present value by taking into account alternative future time streams of benefits and costs and selecting that one which he believes will maximize the present value of his privately-owned land rights. We all know that this means that he will attempt to take into account the supply and demand conditions that he thinks will exist after his death. It is very difficult to see how the existing communal owners can reach an agreement that takes account of these costs.

In effect, an owner of a private right to use land acts as a broker whose wealth depends on how well he takes into account the competing claims of the present and the future. But with communal rights there is no broker, and the claims of the present generation will be given an uneconomically large weight in determining the intensity with which the land is worked. Future generations might desire to pay present generations enough to change the present intensity of land usage. But they have no living agent to place their claims on the market. Under a communal property system, should a living person pay others to reduce the rate at which they work the land, he would not gain anything of value for his efforts. Communal property means that future generations must speak for themselves. No one has yet estimated the costs of carrying on such a conversation.

The land ownership example confronts us immediately with a great disadvantage of communal property. The effects of a person's activities on his neighbors and on subsequent generations will not be taken into account fully. Communal property results in great externalities. The full costs of the activities of an owner of a communal property right are not borne directly by him, nor can they be called to his attention easily by the willingness of others to pay him an appropriate sum. Communal property rules out a "pay-to-use-the-property" system and high negotiation and policing costs make ineffective a "pay-him-not-to-use-the-property" system.

The state, the courts, or the leaders of the community could attempt to internalize the external costs resulting from communal property by allowing private parcels owned by small groups of persons with similar interests. The logical groups in terms of similar interests, are, of course, the family and the individual. Continuing with our use of the land ownership example, let us initially distribute private titles to land randomly among existing individuals and, further, let the extent of land included in each title be randomly determined.

The resulting private ownership of land will internalize many of the external costs associated with communal ownership, for now an owner, by virtue of his power to exclude others, can generally count on realizing the rewards associated with husbanding the game and increasing the fertility of his land. This concentration of benefits and costs on owners creates incentives to utilize resources more efficiently.

But we have yet to contend with externalities. Under the communal property system the maximization of the value of communal property rights will take place without regard to many costs, because the owner of a communal right cannot exclude others from enjoying the fruits of his efforts and because negotiation costs are too high for all to agree jointly on optimal behavior. The development of private rights permits the owner to economize on the use of those resources from which he has the right to exclude others. Much internalization is accomplished in this way. But the owner of private rights to one parcel does not himself own the rights to the parcel of another private sector. Since he cannot exclude others from their private rights to land, he has no direct incentive (in the absence of negotiations) to economize in the use of his land in a way that takes into account the effects he produces on the land rights of others. If he constructs a dam on his land, he has no direct incentive to take into account the lower water levels produced on his neighbor's land.

This is exactly the same kind of externality that we encountered with communal property rights, but it is present to a lesser degree. Whereas no one had an incentive to store water on any land under the communal system, private owners now can take into account directly those benefits and costs to their land that accompany water storage. But the effects on the land of others will not be taken into account directly.

The partial concentration of benefits and costs that accompany private ownership is only part of the advantage this system offers. The other part, and perhaps the most important, has escaped our notice. The cost of negotiating over the remaining externalities will be reduced greatly. Communal property rights allow anyone to use the land. Under this system it becomes necessary for all to reach an agreement on land use. But the externalities that accompany private ownership of property do not affect all owners, and, generally speaking, it will be necessary for only a few to reach an agreement that takes these effects into account. The cost of negotiating an internalization of these effects is thereby reduced considerably. The point is important enough to elucidate.

Suppose an owner of a communal land right, in the process of plowing a parcel of land, observes a second communal owner constructing a dam on adjacent land. The farmer prefers to have the stream as it is, and so he asks the engineer to stop his construction. The engineer says, "Pay me to stop." The farmer replies, "I will be happy to pay you, but what can you guarantee in return?" The engineer answers, "I can guarantee you that I will not continue constructing the dam, but I cannot guarantee that another engineer will not take up the task because this is communal property; I have no right to exclude him." What would be a simple negotiation between two persons under a private property arrangement turns out to be a rather complex negotiation between the farmer and everyone else. This is the basic explanation, I believe, for the preponderance of single rather than multiple owners of property. Indeed, an increase in the number of owners is an increase in the communality of property and leads, generally, to an increase in the cost of internalizing.

The reduction in negotiating cost that accompanies the private right to exclude others allows most externalities to be internalized at rather low cost. Those that are not are associated with activities that generate external effects impinging upon many people. The soot from smoke affects many homeowners, none of whom is willing to pay enough to the factory to get its owner to reduce smoke output. All homeowners together might be willing to pay enough, but the cost of their getting together may be enough to discourage effective market bargaining. The negotiating problem is compounded even more if the smoke comes not from a single smoke stack but from an industrial district. In such cases, it may be too costly to internalize effects through the marketplace.

Returning to our land ownership paradigm, we recall that land was distributed in randomly sized parcels to randomly selected owners. These owners now negotiate among themselves to internalize any remaining externalities. Two market options are open to the negotiators. The first is simply to try to reach a contractual agreement among owners that directly deals with the external effects at issue. The second option is for some owners to buy out others, thus changing the parcel size owned. Which option is selected will depend on which is cheaper. We have here a standard economic problem of optimal scale. If there exist constant returns to scale in the ownership of different sized parcels, it will be largely a matter of indifference between outright purchase and contractual agreement if only a single, easy-to-police, contractual agreement will internalize the externality. But, if there are several externalities, so that several such contracts will need to be negotiated, or if the contractual agreements should be difficult to police, then outright purchase will be the preferred course of action.

The greater are diseconomies of scale to land ownership the more will contractual arrangement be used by the interacting neighbors to settle these differences. Negotiating and policing costs will be compared to costs that depend on the scale of ownership, and parcels of land will tend to be owned in sizes which minimize the sum of these costs.[8]

The interplay of scale economies, negotiating cost, externalities, and the modification of property rights can be seen in the most notable "exception" to the assertion that ownership tends to be an individual affair: the publicly-held corporation. I assume that significant economies of scale in the operation of large corporations is a fact and, also, that large requirements for equity capital can be satisfied more cheaply by acquiring the capital from many purchasers of equity shares. While economies of scale in operating these enterprises exist, economies of scale in the provision of capital do not. Hence, it becomes desirable for many "owners" to form a joint-stock company.

But if all owners participate in each decision that needs to be made by such a company, the scale economies of operating the company will be overcome quickly by high negotiating cost. Hence a delegation of authority for most decisions takes place and, for most of these, a small management group becomes the *de facto* owners. Effective ownership, i. e., effective control of property, is thus legally concentrated in management's hands. This is the first legal modification, and it takes place in recognition of the high negotiating costs that would otherwise obtain.

The structure of ownership, however, creates some externality difficulties under the law of partnership. If the corporation should fail, partnership law commits each shareholder to meet the debts of the corporation up to the limits of his financial ability. Thus, managerial *de facto* ownership can have considerable external effects on shareholders. Should property rights remain unmodified, this externality would make it exceedingly difficult for entrepreneurs to acquire equity capital from wealthy individuals. (Although these individuals have recourse to reimbursements from other shareholders, litigation costs will be high.) A second legal modification, limited liability, has taken place to reduce the effect of this externality.[9] *De facto* management ownership and limited liability combine to minimize the overall cost of operating large enterprises. Shareholders are essentially lenders of equity capital and not owners, although they do participate in such infrequent decisions as those involving mergers. What shareholders really own are their shares and not the corporation. Ownership in the sense of control again becomes a largely individual affair. The shareholders own their shares, and the president of the corporation and possibly a few other top executives control the corporation.

To further ease the impact of management decisions on shareholders, that is, to minimize the impact of externalities under this ownership form, a further legal modification of rights is required. Unlike partnership law, a shareholder may sell his interest without first obtaining the permission of fellow shareholders or without dissolving the corporation. It thus becomes easy for him to get out if his preferences and those of the management are no longer in harmony. This "escape hatch" is extremely important and has given rise to the organized trading of securities. The increase in harmony between managers and shareholders brought about by exchange and by competing managerial groups helps to minimize the external effects associated with the corporate ownership structure. Finally, limited liability considerably reduces the cost of exchanging shares by making it unnecessary for a purchaser of shares to examine in great detail the liabilities of the corporation and the assets of other shareholders; these liabilities can adversely affect a purchaser only up to the extent of the price per share.

The dual tendencies for ownership to rest with individuals and for the extent of an individual's ownership to accord with the minimization of all costs is clear in the land ownership paradigm. The applicability of this paradigm has been extended to the corporation. But it may not be clear yet how widely applicable this paradigm is. Consider the problems of copyright and patents. If a new idea is freely appropriable by all, if there exist communal rights to new ideas, incentives for developing such ideas will be lacking. The benefits derivable from these ideas will not be concentrated on their originators. If we extend some degree of private rights to the originators, these ideas will come forth at a more rapid pace. But

[handwritten margin note: This would tend to force up the interest rate on bonds.]

the existence of the private rights does not mean that their effects on the property of others will be directly taken into account. A new idea makes an old one obsolete and another old one more valuable. These effects will not be directly taken into account, but they can be called to the attention of the originator of the new idea through market negotiations. All problems of externalities are closely analogous to those which arise in the land ownership example. The relevant variables are identical.

What I have suggested in this paper is an approach to problems in property rights. But it is more than that. It is also a different way of viewing traditional problems. An elaboration of this approach will, I hope, illuminate a great number of social-economic problems.

FOOTNOTES

* Most of Professor Demsetz's writing was done while he was at the University of Chicago. He is presently Professor of the Department of Econmics at the University of California at Los Angeles.

1 These implications are derived by R. H. Coase, "The Problem of Social Cost," *J. of Law and Econ.*, Oct., 1960, pp. 1–44, supra, p. — [ed.].

2 If the demand for civilian life is unaffected by wealth redistribution, the assertion made is correct as it stands. However, when a change is made from a "buy-him-in" system to a "let-him-buy-his-way-out" system, the resulting redistribution of wealth away from draftees may significantly affect their demand for civilian life; the validity of the assertion then requires a compensating wealth change. A compensating wealth change will not be required in the ordinary case of profit maximizing firms. Consider the farmer-rancher example mentioned by Coase. Society may give the farmer the right to grow corn unmolested by cattle or it may give the rancher the right to allow his cattle to stray. Contrary to the Coase example, let us suppose that if the farmer is given the right, he just breaks even; i. e., with the right to be compensated for corn damage, the farmer's land is marginal. If the right is transferred to the rancher, the farmer, not enjoying any economic rent, will not have the wherewithal to pay the rancher to reduce the number of head of cattle raised. In this case, however, it will be profitable for the rancher to buy the farm, thus merging cattle raising with farming. His self-interest will then lead him to take account of the effect of cattle on corn.

3 Eleanor Leacock, *American Anthropologist* (American Anthropological Asso.), Vol. 56, No. 5, Part 2, Memoir No. 78.

4 Cf. Frank G. Speck, "The Basis of American Indian Ownership of Land," *Old Penn Weekly Rev.* (Univ. of Pennsylvania), Jan. 16, 1915, pp. 491–95.

5 Eleanor Leacock, op. cit., p. 15.

6 Eleanor Leacock, op. cit., p. 15.

7 The thesis is consistent with the development of other types of private rights. Among wandering primitive peoples the cost of policing property is relatively low for highly portable objects. The owning family can protect such objects while carrying on its daily activities. If these objects are also very useful, property rights should appear frequently, so as to internalize the benefits and costs of their use. It is generally true among most primitive communities that weapons and household utensils, such as pottery,

are regarded as private property. Both types of articles are portable and both require an investment of time to produce. Among agriculturally-oriented peoples, because of the relative fixity of their location, portability has a smaller role to play in the determination of property. The distinction is most clearly seen by comparing property in land among the most primitive of these societies, where crop rotation and simple fertilization techniques are unknown, or where land fertility is extremely poor, with property in land among primitive peoples who are more knowledgeable in these matters or who possess very superior land. Once a crop is grown by the more primitive agricultural societies, it is necessary for them to abandon the land for several years to restore productivity. Property rights in land among such people would require policing cost for several years during which no sizable output is obtained. Since to provide for sustenance these people must move to new land, a property right to be of value to them must be associated with a portable object. Among these people it is common to find property rights to the crops, which, after harvest, are portable, but not to the land. The more advanced agriculturally based primitive societies are able to remain with particular land for longer periods, and here we generally observe property rights to the land as well as to the crops.

8 Compare this with the similar rationale given by R. H. Coase to explain the firm in "The Nature of the Firm," *Economica*, New Series, 1937, pp. 386–405.

9 Henry G. Manne discusses this point in "Our Two Corporation Systems: Law and Economics," supra, p. —— (ed.).

B Continued

3: TOWARDS AN ECONOMIC THEORY OF THE CREATION AND SPECIFICATION OF PROPERTY RIGHTS *

SVETOZAR PEJOVICH
Ohio University

I

The alleged failure of the standard theory of production and exchange to explain a wide class of empirical observations has led to proliferation of *ad hoc* theorizing.[1] Without questioning the validity of some of those *ad hoc* theories, it is important to recognize that they are valid only for a small class of events. A generalization of the standard theory of production and exchange to obtain an expanded scope of its validity should, therefore, be regarded as a preferred alternative. The *property rights approach* represents such an attempt.

The line of reasoning that underlies the property rights approach to the explanation of economic events can be summarized as follows: the purpose of trade is to exchange bundles of property rights *to do things* with goods and services that are exchanged. The value of the goods that are traded and, consequently, the terms of trade depend on the content of property rights in those goods. For example, I will pay more for a house if the bundle of property rights I acquire permits me to exclude gasoline stations, chemical plants, etc. from the surrounding area. The possession of various property rights affects the allocation of resources, composition of output, income distribution, etc. To quote Professor

Reprinted from Review of Social Economy, Volume XXX, September 1972, Number 3.

Alchian: "In essence, economics is the study of property rights over re-sources . . . The allocation of scarce resources in a society is the assignment of rights to uses of resources . . . for the question of economics, or of how prices should be determined, is the question of how property rights should be defined and exchanged, and on what terms." [2] The cornerstones of a generalization of the standard theory via the property rights approach are then: (i) the concept of wealth maximization is replaced by that of utility maximization, and (ii) the effects of various property rights assignments over scarce resources on the penalty-reward system replace the classic constraint of private property rights with zero transaction costs.

That a relationship exists between property rights assignments and the allocation of resources might be intuitively obvious and readily observable. Yet, to convert, this relationship into an analytically useful and testable theory it is necessary to demonstrate that:

(i) Property rights assignments affect the allocation of resources in a *specific* and *predictable* way. This is an essential requirement that should help us to deduce some analytically important and empirically refutable propositions *re* the effects of changes in property rights assignments over scarce resources on formal equilibrium solutions. The on-going research on externalities, large corporations and regulated firms, and the economics of socialism has already provided strong evidence that the allocation and use of resources *is* constrained in a specific and predictable way by the prevailing property rights assignments.[3]

(ii) The creation and specification of property rights over scarce resources is endogenously determined; that is, it takes place in response to the desire of the interacting persons for more utility.

The purpose of this paper is to show that some strong support for the view that the creation and specification of property rights assignments over scarce resources are endogenously determined comes from three different sources. The sources of this support are: the logic of the standard economic theory of production and exchange, the writings of Marx and Engels, and empirical evidence.

II

A student of economics discovers early that the entire body of the standard theory of production and exchange is built upon the assumption of private property rights over resources with zero detection, police and enforcement costs, and the appreciation of the negatively sloped demand curve (which is independent of property rights assignments). He also learns that private property rights are a powerful and possibly necessary condition for the most efficient allocation of resources. The compulsive desire for more utility and the law of negatively sloped demand schedule combine with the right of private ownership to induce the utility maximizing individuals to increase the extent of exchange to the point where privately perceived marginal costs and benefits equal social costs and benefits.

An intelligent student will reject the idea that it is a mere accident when and where the importance of property rights assignments over resources is discovered. He will instead address himself to a fundamental economic question: is the standard theory of production and exchange capable of explaining the emergence of the institution of property rights over scarce resources. That is, can we deduce the development of property rights theoretically? The affirmative answer to this question has already been suggested by Cheung, Demsetz, North and others.[4]

Let us begin our discussion with the case where property rights in a resource are absent. A non-owned resource is a free good for individuals. However, it is a scarce good for society. The relevant questions are: what type of competition is used to allocate a non-owned good among the competing claimants, what is the cost of "purchasing" it, and what are the implications of the absence of property rights in a resource for its rate of exploitation and reproduction?

A person can derive utility (non-pecuniary as well as pecuniary) from a non-owned good only by taking it into his physical possession and for only as long as it remains in his possession. That is, the individual who postpones using that good *now* will find it taken by someone else. The rationing criterion is clearly: first come, first served. This type of competition suggests that the individual could hardly concern himself with either the cost of "planting" a non-owned good or its future value consequences (e. g., the value of lumber in the tree associated with aging). It follows that each person's "purchase" costs of a non-owned good equals his outlaid expenses (e. g., hunting rifle) and the highest-valued alternative. The latter can be taken to be of primary importance here.

The logic of economics then suggests that the rate of exploitation of a non-owned resource should be expected to exceed the rate that would prevail if some kind of transferable property rights in that good is established. Cheung and Gordon deduced the equilibrium solution of the industry as it occurs in the state of uncontrolled exploitation of a non-owned resource and demonstrated that the rent is completely eliminated and the *average* product of labor equals the *average* opportunity income.[5] That is, the marginal product of labor is below the social cost as represented by opportunity income. From the social point of view this situation implies economic waste. From the individual's point of view it implies a zero rent. Quite importantly this wasteful use of a resource should be attributed to the absence of property rights assignments in that good rather than the individual's greed or lack of social responsibility.

The rate of investment in a non-owned resource is also affected by the absence of property rights assignments. First, the investor must feel insufficiently confident that he will be able to capture the expected future value consequences of his investment decision. This would shorten his time horizon, raise the discount rate and, consequently, investment activity will stop short of what it would otherwise be. And this conclusion remains valid even if we assume that the investor is willing to incur the costs of policing his investment inputs. In that case the result will be a longer time horizon, lower discount rate, but also much higher costs associated with investment in a non-owned resource.

Second, the absence of property rights in a resource is also likely to affect the form of investment activity. For example, non-owned land in Tripolitania is used as a pasture by cattle owners rather than for planting more profitable almond trees. The reason for this wasteful behavior is that the costs of policing one's use of land for raising cattle that can be driven home at night is lower relative to the costs of policing investment in almond trees.[6]

The logic of economics is then capable of explaining that (i) from the social point of view the creation of property rights assignments is a powerful and possibly necessary condition for more efficient allocation and use of resources, and (ii) from the individual's point of view the specification of property rights is associated with his search for more utility. I conjecture that this latter point relates the standard theory of production and exchange to the creation of property rights over scarce resources.

The analysis of a non-owned resource indicates that the person would capture some rent for himself if he could exclude others from the free access to that good. The logic of economics then suggests that the individual or a group of individuals will try to exclude others from using a good whenever the expected benefits (rent) exceed the cost of policing and enforcing the "claim" to that resource. We note that to exclude others from the free access to a resource *means* to specify property rights over that good. For property rights are defined not as relations between men and things but, rather, as *the behavioral relations among men that arise from the existence of things and pertain to their use*. The prevailing system of property rights assignments in the community is, in effect, the set of economic and social relations defining the position of interacting individuals with respect to the utilization of scarce resources.

Probably the first step towards the creation of individual property rights was for a tribe to establish or to try to establish its exclusive right over a piece of land, fishing, or hunting grounds in order to consume some rent. Yet, privately perceived costs and benefits from the exploitation of a commonly held resource are different from total costs and benefits for at least two reasons: (i) not all costs of a person's activity are borne by himself (e. g., over-hunting, over-intensive use of land), and (ii) non-transferability of a commonly owned resource prevents a person from capturing for himself the full value of that good.[7] It follows that each member of the community could increase his benefits by either reducing the size of the group or capturing *more* property rights for himself. In other words, whenever contractual relationships result in the dissipation of a part of the rent to third parties there will be an incentive to alter the contractual relationship as long as the gains from so doing exceed the costs of specifying new property rights assignments. The marginal equivalences between the costs and benefits then become a major factor that governs the size of the group as well as changes in the content of property rights over a resource. As the size of the group is reduced and/or individuals acquire more property rights in a resource the difference between private and social costs as well as private and social benefits narrows down to be finally eliminated in a world of private property rights with zero transaction costs. This situation might easily amount to no more than a pious wish, but it is important to note that the man's compulsive desire for more utility combined with the cost-benefit calculus provides a rational explanation for both the creation as well as endogenously determined changes in the content of property rights assignments over scarce resources. Moreover, this explanation of the creation and specification of property rights is free from historical determinism. It does not proclaim a definite and pre-ordained sequence of changes in the specification of property rights. It merely suggests that the prevailing property rights assignments in the community reflect the costs and benefits of specifying property rights over scarce resources, and that changes in the property rights assignments are endogenously determined by changes in the cost-benefit ratio. Finally, the analysis does not preclude the possible influence of exogenous factors which could and indeed have affected the content of property rights over scarce resources (Communist revolution in Russia, governmental regulation of radio frequencies in the USA, etc.)

To incorporate our discussion into an expanded framework of the classical marginalism we have to specify all the important variables and parameters that affect, or might affect at various stages of the community's economic development, the determination of the costs and benefits of specifying property rights assignments over scarce resources. More importantly, we must also specify those factors that could bring about changes in the cost-benefit ratio and, thus, changes in the content of property rights. The result would be a formal and fully testable theory capable of explaining and possibly predicting the development of property rights assignments in response to changing economic conditions. Moreover, a generalization of the standard theory of production and exchange *via* the effects of property rights assignments on the penalty-reward system would substitute an integrated economic theory for *ad hoc* theorizing and hopefully improve our understanding of the economic processes, income distributions and resource allocations in various regions and at different times.

This is yet to be done. However, recent contributions have shown that the logic of economics and empirical evidence combine to suggest that the following three factors have frequently been responsible for changes in the cost-benefit ratio and, consequently, for changes in the content of property rights over resources.

(i) Technological Changes and Opening of New Markets. For example, the substitution of arabic numbers for Roman numerals and the invention of watches changed the extent of trade, the content of contractual stipulations, and provided incentives for the alteration of property rights; also, when people learned how to survey land, the cost of defining property rights in land fell relative to the gains from doing so. To quote Demsetz:

> New techniques, new ways of doing the same things, and doing new things—all invoke harmful and beneficial effects to which society has not been accustomed . . . It is my thesis . . . that property rights develop to internalize externalities when the gain from internalization becomes larger than the cost of internalization. Increased internalization, in the main, results from changes in economic values, changes which stem from the development of new technology and the opening of new markets, changes to which old property rights are poorly attuned.[8]

(ii) A Change in Relative Factor Scarcities and factor prices results in a change in the cost-benefit ratio and provides incentives for the modification of the existing or the creation of new property rights. North wrote:

> The revival of population growth as a result of the relative improvement in order led to local crowding and diminishing returns [in feudal Europe] . . . General diminishing returns appear to have set in the 12th century leading to changing relative factor scarcities. The rising value of land led to increasing efforts to provide for exclusive ownership and transferability. 13th century England witnessed the development of an extensive body of land law, the beginning of enclosure and finally the ability to alienate land.[9]

(iii) An Economic Theory of the State. Our comprehension of the development of property rights is obviously incomplete without an economic theory of the state. This is so because a political organization (tribe, princedom, kingdom, modern state, etc.) can be regarded as the firm that produces and sells protection and justice in exchange for revenue (taxes). The authority defines property rights over resources (including human resources, of course) *via* customs and/or laws and enforces those rights against both "insiders" (police, courts) and "outsiders" (military). The subjects pay for this service. The source of this payment is the rent which better specification of property rights makes possible. For example, Kings and Princes granted (and enforced) various property rights to merchants. This led to an expansion of trade, higher revenues, and the sharing of these gains by the authority and tradesmen. Similar events frequently occur in modern times. The states are known to close markets to all potential competitors by granting licenses to a selected few (a very valuable property right). This, in turn, is expected to raise the average return in the industry, a part of which then goes to the state treasury as licence fees.

A revenue seeking Prince is then moved by his own desire for more revenue to define and enforce property rights. It could be argued that changes in the content of property rights depend on the relationship between the benefits to the authority from granting new or modifying the existing property rights assignments and the costs of protecting them. If this line of reasoning is correct the "efficient" size of the political organization would be affected (and it is said affected and determined) by the size of markets and its military endowments. North argues in a recent paper that:

> An exchange economy and new weapons . . . made . . . a long struggle with numerous contenders . . . not only from within historically unified political units but also from without . . . The contenders were in competition with each other and the key to success was the fiscal revenues that the contenders could command. Each state therefore endeavored to price its services (i. e., taxes) in such a way as to maximize present value . . . The degree of monopoly power of the state in its contractual relationship with constituents reflected the degree to which other contenders appeared likely to be able to provide the same set of services. In short, the opportunity costs of the constituents lay behind the contractual relationships and changes in opportunity costs lead to efforts to alter the contract.[10]

One could venture to assert that our discussion throws some light on the purpose as well as the extent to which the ruling group can use its monopoly power to exogenously change property rights assignments over scarce resources and alter both the allocation of resources and income distribution.

Let us now summarize our discussion. The creation and specification of property rights over scarce resources is deduced from the standard theory of production and exchange. They both occur in response to the man's desire for more utility and, in turn, lead towards a more efficient allocation of resources. The term efficiency is defined here as the narrowing of the gap between privately perceived costs and benefits and social costs and benefits. As long as those are different, not all costs and benefits of a contract are borne by contractual parties and the inducements for better specification of property rights exist. Some important factors which govern changes in the content of property rights are asserted to be: technological innovations and opening of new markets, changes in relative factor scarcities, and the behavior of the state.

III

To the best of my knowledge Marx and Engels (hereafter: Marx) were the first economists (i) to raise the question of how and why property rights develop, (ii) to incorporate the institution of property rights into economic theory, and (iii) to assert that property rights assignments over scarce resources are endogenously determined. The purpose of this section is to present a brief discussion of the creation and specification of property rights, as understood by Marx.

In one of his major criticisms of classical political economy, Marx wrote:

> Political economy proceeds from the fact of private property, but it does not explain it to us. We have presupposed private property, the separation of labor, capital and land . . .   competition, the concept of exchange value, etc. Political economy expresses in general, abstract formulae the material process through which private property actually passes, and these formulae it then takes for granted what it is supposed to evolve. [Private property] is explained from external circumstances. As to how far these external . . .   circumstances are but the expression of a necessary course of [human] development, political economy teaches us nothing.[11]

I conjecture that the on-going research on a generalization of the standard theory *via* the property rights approach has been instigated by a similar set of objections.

A central theme in Marx's writings is the materialist or economic interpretation of history.

> Legal relations as well as forms of state could neither be understood by themselves nor explained by the so-called general progress of human mind but that they are rooted in the material conditions of life . . .   The mode of production in material life determines the general character of the social, political and spiritual processes of life.[12]

The objective of Marx's writings was to discover *causes* of social change, the dynamic laws of history. And he viewed the history of mankind as a continuous struggle of man against nature. The purpose of this struggle, which is but a reflection of man's survival instinct (that is, the compulsive desire for more), is to reverse the original relationship between man and nature, and to subordinate nature to man.

To reach the final historical stage of its development, where man becomes nature's master and where scarcity is eliminated, mankind must pass through definite types of *property relations*. Every set of property relation has its place in human progress toward ultimate affluence, and "new, higher relations of production . . . or—what is but a legal expression for the same thing—the property relations . . . never appear before the material conditions of their existence have matured in the womb of the old society." [13]   The term *relations of production* was habitually used by Marx in lieu of the term property relations and defined as relations among men in the process of production and exchange.[14]

The historical sequence begins with the primitive society where man is totally dependent for his subsistence on an alien and hostile environment. The entire life in a primitive society is geared towards the restricted objective of subsistence, the appropriation of the products in their natural state. The primitive community merely reproduces itself through time, and the spontaneous and unalterable division of labor explains its unchangeableness. The primitive society is a stagnant society, with no property, no state and thus no social and economic institutions to regulate the relations among men in the process of production and exchange.

Man's survival instinct, that is the instinct to labor, is arrested but not inoperative in a primitive society. And it is precisely on account of this instinct to labor, to produce subsistence more efficiently, that the circular flow of life in the primitive society breaks down and man makes the first step towards freeing himself from the dependence on nature. According to Marx, the institution of property rights is a *means* that makes the instinct to labor operative and breaks down the primitive society. The emergence of property rights is, therefore, the *historical necessity*. It is significant to note that Marx deduced the *historical necessity* of property rights theoretically from the initial alienation of man from nature and from his instinct to labor. Briefly, his argument is as follows:

Man's instinct to labor and his desire to produce subsistence more efficiently led to the progress in the production of food. For example, the discovery of fire made fish edible, while the bow and arrow rendered hunting a normal form of work. Eventually man learned how to increase the supply of subsistence by human activity. He produced a surplus above his own requirements and the existence of that surplus produced exchange and more efficient division of labor. The formation of the merchant class and the development of money followed the opening of new markets. Once man learned to apply human work to the products of nature it clearly became essential to regulate the relations among men with respect to the use of those products: the institution of property rights *had* to be born.

To the barbarian of the lower stage . . . human labor-power still does not produce any considerable surplus over its maintenance costs . . . The men were killed or adopted into the tribe . . . That was no longer the case after the introduction of cattle-breeding, metal working, weaving and lastly agriculture .   .   .   prisoners of war were turned into slaves .   .   .   and the first great division of labor arose.[15]

The creation of property rights in Marx's writings is then endogenously determined. The relevant questions are: what are the effects of property rights on the social structure, and what are some important factors that, according to Marx, govern changes in the content of property rights over scarce resources?

Engels related the origin of the family and variation in its size to changes in the content of property rights. He wrote:

> .   .   .   within this structure of society based on kinship groups the productivity of labor increasingly develops, and with it private property and exchange, differences of wealth, the possibility of utilizing the labor power of others .   .   .   .   the old society founded on kinship groups is broken up; in its place appears a new society, with its control centered in the state, the subordinate units of which are no longer kinship associations .   .   .   a system in which the system of family is completely dominated by the systems of property.[16]

Engels saw the origin of family as a consequence of a change in the content of property rights in land from communal to private ownership. He positively refused to identify the origin of marriage with love and passion. After all, he wrote, the "poets of love" romanticized adultery and not marriage.[17] Finally, Engels explored, in great detail, the relationship between the prevailing property rights structures in the community and the quality of family life. The following quote is but an example of his findings:

> In the countries where an obligatory share of the paternal inheritance is secured to the children by law and they cannot therefore be disinherited— in Germany, in the countries with French law and elsewhere—the children are obligated to obtain their parent's consent to their marriage. In the countries with English law, where parental consent to a marriage is not legally required the parents on their side have full freedom in the testamentary disposal of their property and can disinherit their childern at their pleasure.[18]

Creation of property rights reduced man's alienation from nature but, in turn, created a new type of alienation, that of man from man.

Marx's analysis of the concept of alienated labor consists of four successive steps: (1) Since it does not belong to him, the product of his labor appears to the workers as an alien object. (2) Consequently, the worker considers his work as imposed, forced labor. It is not the satisfaction of a need, but only a means for satisfying other needs. This is the relationship of the worker to his own activity as something alien and not belonging to him. (3) "Conscious labor reverses the relationship, in that man because he is a self-conscious being makes his life activity, his being, only a means for his existence . . .   Thus alienated labor turns the species life of man . . . into an alien being, and into a means for his individual existence. It alienates . . . his human life." [19] (4) "A direct consequence of the alienation of man from the product of his labor, from his life activity and from his species life is that man is alienated from other men." [20] From these considerations about the alienated labor stems the final conclusion concerning the nature of private property: "Private property is . . . the product . . . of alienated labor, of the external relations of the worker to nature and to himself." [21]

Thus, the emergence of property rights creates the possibility of progress, that is the subordination of nature to man, but it also creates hostile social classes. In this alienated environment the state emerges as a *means* of preserving the existing property relations and protecting the possessing class against the non-possessing class. Marx was very positive in his belief that the state does not create property relations; its function being to guarantee the existing ones. The existing property relations describe the prevailing social power and from them the passive role of the state is deduced analytically.

The final question concerns the factors which govern changes in the prevailing property relations. Those factors are the productive forces and the relationship between the productive forces and the prevailing property relations. Marx defined the concept of productive forces as the relation between man and nature in the production of the necessities of life. In the concept of productive forces Marx included technology, stock of capital on hand, labor force, working habits and education.

Given the prevailing property relations in the community, the productive forces develop. Each time a new development in the productive forces occurs man becomes a little less dependent on nature, and nature, in turn, becomes a little more subordinated to man. However, at some point the existing relations of production become fetters to further economic development. Then and only then, the old social structure breaks down and the new one, with a qualitatively new set of property relations emerges from within the old. This new set of property rights is then conducive for further development of the productive forces but only up to a point and the history continuously repeats itself until the final stage of affluence is reached. Thus, man pursues his objective of achieving a complete mastery over nature through historically pre-determined changes in the content of property rights which, in turn, are made necessary and, in fact, endogenously determined by changes in technology and the quantity and quality of inputs. A most significant statement by Marx reads as follows:

At a certain stage of their development the material forces of production in society come into conflict with the existing relations of production, or,

what is but a legal expression for the same thing, with the property relations within which they had been at work before. From forms of development of the forces of production these relations turn into their fetters.
Then comes the period of social revolution. With the change of the economic foundation the entire immense superstructure is more or less
rapidly transformed.[22]

It is clear that Marx and Engels viewed economics as the study of
property rights over scarce resources, and the emergence and specification
of property rights as being endogenously determined. According to them,
the man's compulsive desire for more (i. e., to subordinate nature to himself) on the one hand, and technology, relative factor endowments and the
quality of inputs on the other combine to explain historical changes in the
content of property rights. It is significant to note that the logic of the
standard theory of production and exchange suggested that the same set
of factors governs changes in the prevailing property rights assignments
over scarce resources. One notable exception is the role of state. Marx
argued that the state does not create property rights; its role being to
protect and enforce the existing property relations.

The importance of Marx's writings on property rights derives from
the fact that his point of departure, objectives and the method of analysis
are substantially different from the recent attempts by scholars like Alchian and Demsetz to incorporate the various types of property rights over
scarce resources into the standard theory of production and exchange.
Marx explained the development of property rights as occurring in a series
of historically pre-determined discontinuous sequences. If we make the
allowance for both the state of economic discipline some hundred years
ago as well as ideological underpinnings of Marx's works that imposed on
him a set of objectives that he had to arrive at, the fundamental difference
between Marx's analysis and that of modern theorists lies in Marx's deterministic view of the history of mankind. He clearly considered the sequence of events to be independent of the free action of man. While it is
true that Marx repeatedly said that men make their own history, he also
limited the ability of man to exercise his creative potentials. He subordinated his consciousness to class consciousness and then subordinated the
latter to the stage of development of the productive forces.

I conjecture that the modern economic analysis of the creation and
specification of property rights is superior to that of Marx because it has
more advanced tools of analysis at its disposal and is free from Marx's
deterministic approach to socio-economic changes. Given those fundamental differences between Marx and Engels on the one hand, and scholars
like Alchian and Demsetz on the other, the fact that Marx deduced property rights theoretically and suggested that changes in the content of property rights are governed by the same set of economic factors is, I conjec-

ture, an important source of indirect validation of the current research on the role of property relations in the community.

IV

A rigorous test of the set of conclusions suggested in Section I of this paper requires extensive and detailed empirical work. I hope that better experts in empirical work will eventually subject those conclusions to more detailed and extended tests. At this time I will limit myself to a few observations that appear consistent with the analysis suggested in this paper.

(i) In the early stages of the development of the Roman Empire, a form of communal ownership called *ager gentilicius* dominated the scene. *Agni gentilicii* were pastures and forests owned by Gens (a sort of clan of the same stock in the male line with the members having a common ancestor) which all members exploited in accordance with their needs. Then as agriculture developed the benefits from defining individual lots rose relative to the cost and the central authority sanctioned a change in the content of property rights. This change in property relations took the form of *consortium*—a sort of arrangement that permitted the family to exclusively enjoy but not to sell a well defined piece of land. An important consequence that followed the substitution of the *consortium* for the *ager gentilicius* was that the clan broke down into smaller family units.

(ii) The collapse of the Roman Empire and a complete disintegration of its legal structure resulted in the replacement of order by chaos. The concept of private property that was fully developed in the Roman Law and enforced by the state disintegrated. Violence became a predominant method of resolving conflict of interest among people in a world in which barbaric customs had replaced Roman Law. The cost of excluding outsiders from what one considered to be his property rose and the result, as our analysis would predict, was a return to a sort of property sharing by a larger group. The principal need in post-Roman Europe was for protection of family and security of its property (land). In order to survive, a weaker man turned to a stronger man and gave him the right of ownership in land he toiled in exchange for protection and a quasi right of tenancy; he *held the land of the lord*. The lord-vassal relationship then emerged as the basic social institution in medieval Europe, and the land which the vassal held was called *feud*. The new lord could and often did become the vassal of still another man; that is, he became both the lord of a weaker man and the vassal of a stronger man. In time, this chain between the lord at the top and the actual user of the land at the bottom lengthened and a socio-political system based on a method of holding property (feuds) developed. Only the lord (King) at the top was never a vassal. To reduce individual exploitation of *feud* a great many rules were developed regulating the use of land by vassals and serfs (peasants).

(iii) The revival of population growth as a result of the relative improvement in order led to local crowding and diminishing returns in local areas. The logical outcome . . . [was] the creation of new manors carved out of the wilderness—frequently, in order to provide incentive to peasants, conveying more liberal labor obligations and better specified property rights in land than the earlier manor. Settlement filled out northwest Europe and in consequence encouraged trade (1) by reducing the unsettled areas between manors that harbored brigands, (2) by encouraging the growth of towns in thickly settled areas where specialized skills were developed to produce manufactured goods, and in particular (3) by resulting in areas with very differentiated factor endowments which increased the gains from trade. The wine of Burgundy, Bordeaux, and the Mozella, the wool of England, the metal products of Germany, wool cloth from Flanders, fish and timber from the Baltic all betoken different factor endowments (both in terms of resources and human capital investment). In short, the frontier settlement movement was a sufficient reason to reduce the transaction costs of trade and increase the gains from trade.

The growth of trade and exchange economy basically altered feudal . . . [property] arrangements since the existence of an organized market negated the advantages of labor services as compared to a market system of landlord, tenant, and wage labor.[23]

(iv) Demsetz related the emergence of property rights among Indian tribes to the standard cost-benefit calculus.

Before the fur trade became established, hunting was carried on primarily for purposes of food and the relatively few furs that were required for the hunter's family. The externality was clearly present. Hunting could be practiced freely and was carried on without assessing its impact on other hunters. But these external effects were of such small significance that it did not pay for anyone to take them into account. There did not exist anything resembling private ownership in land. And in the Jesuit Relations, particularly Le Jeune's record of the winter he spent with the Montagnes in 1633–34 and in the brief account given by Father Druilletes in 1647–48, Leacock finds no evidence of private land holdings. Both accounts indicate a socioeconomic organization in which private rights to land are not well developed.

We may safely surmise that the advent of the fur trade had two immediate consequences. First, the value of furs to the Indians was increased considerably. Second, and as a result, the scale of hunting activity rose sharply. Both consequences must have increased considerably the importance of the externalities associated with free hunting. The property right system began to change, and it changed specifically in the direction required to take account of the economic effects made important by the fur trade. The geographical or distributional evidence collected by Leacock indicates an unmistakable correlation between early centers of fur trade and the oldest and most complete development of the private hunting territory.[24]

V

The analysis in this paper suggests the following conclusions:

(i) The creation and changes in property rights assignments can be deduced from the standard theory of production and exchange.

(ii) The creation and specification of property rights is endogenously determined; that is, it takes place in response to the desire of interacting persons for more utility.

(iii) The writings of Marx and Engels as well as some empirical evidence seem to be consistent with the logical deductions from the standard theory of production and exchange.

(iv) A generalization of the standard theory to obtain an expanded scope of its validity by incorporating into the analysis the effects of various property rights assignments seems possible.

FOOTNOTES

* The writing of this paper was facilitated by a grant from the National Science Foundation.

1 Endless division of externalities by types and the emergence of a number of theories of the modern firm are but a few examples.

2 A. Alchian, *Pricing and Society*, Westminster: The Institute of Economic Affairs, Occasional Paper No. 17, September 1967, pp. 2–3.

3 See for example, S. Cheung, "The Structure of a Contract and the Theory of a Non-Exclusive Resource," *Journal of Law and Economics*, Vol. 13, April 1971; A. Alchian, "Corporate Management and Property Rights" in *Economic Policy and the Regulation of Corporate Securities* (H. Manne, ed.), Washington, D. C.: American Enterprise Institute, 1969; and E. Furubotn and S. Pejovich, "The Soviet Manager and Innovation: A Behavioral Model of the Soviet Firm," *Revue de l'Est*, Vol. 3, January 1972.

4 See Cheung, ibid. S. Gordon, "The Economic Theory of a Common-Property Resource: the Fishery," *Journal of Political Economy*, Vol. 62, April 1954; H. Demsetz, "Toward a Theory of Property Rights," *American Economic Review*, Vol. 57, May 1967; D. North, "The Creation of Property Rights in Western Europe 900–1700 A.D.," unpublished manuscript.

5 Cheung, ibid. and Gordon, ibid. Gordon suggests an interesting example. An international agreement between the United States and Canada established a fixed-catch limit on halibut fishing in 1933. In 1933 the fishing season was six months long, while in 1952 it lasted only 26 days in the area from Willapa Harbor to Cape Spencer, and sixty days in the Alaska region. In other words, an increase in the average cost of fishing effort (long-

er and faster boat) allowed no gap between average productivity and average cost to appear, and hence no rent.

6 A. Bottomley, "The Effect of the Common Ownership of Land upon Resource Allocation in Tripolitania," *Land Economics*, Vol. 39, February 1963.

7 Demsetz wrote: "If a person seeks to maximize the value of his communal rights, he will tend to overhunt or overwork the land because some of the costs of his doing so are borne by others . . . . even if the agreement among all [members to curtail the rate at which they work the land] can be reached, we must yet take account of the costs of policing the agreement, and these may be large." op. cit., pp. 354–5.

8 Ibid., p. 350.

9 North, op. cit.

10 Ibid.

11 K. Marx, *Economic and Philosophical Manuscripts of 1844*, Moscow: Foreign Languages Publishing House, 1960, pp. 68–69.

12 K. Marx, "A Contribution to the Critique of Political Economy," in Marx-Engels, *Basic Writings on Politics and Philosophy* (L. Peuer, ed.), Garden City, New York: Doubleday, 1959, p. 43.

13 Ibid., p. 44.

14 For detailed analysis of the role of property relations in Marx's writings see E. Furubotn and S. Pejovich, *On Property Rights*, Washington DC American Enterprise Institute, forthcoming.

15 F. Engels, *The Origin of the Family, Private Property and the State*, New York: International Publishers, 1942, pp. 48 and 147.

16 Ibid., p. 6.

17 Ibid., p. 62.

18 Ibid., p. 65.

19 Marx, *Economic and Philosophical Manuscripts of 1844*, op. cit., pp. 101–103.

20 Ibid., p. 103.

21 Ibid., pp. 105 and 109.

22 Marx, "A Contribution to the Critique of Political Economy," op. cit., p. 43.

23 North, op. cit.

24 Demsetz, op. cit., pp. 351–2.

B Continued

4: PROPERTY RIGHTS AND ECONOMIC THEORY: A SURVEY OF RECENT LITERATURE *

EIRIK G. FURUBOTN
Texas A & M University

SVETOZAR PEJOVICH
Ohio University

As criticism of the traditional theory of production and exchange has mounted in the postwar period, increasing attention has been given to new analytical approaches that seek either to supplant classical marginalism or to extend its scope. In the latter category is the important body of literature that has grown up around the notion of property rights structures. The contributions here are quite diverse in style and content but are characterized by a common emphasis on certain basic ideas concerning the interconnectedness of ownership rights, incentives, and economic behavior. The purpose of the present paper is to summarize the essential features of this line of research, examine some of its important areas of application, and discuss the promise the approach holds for improved understanding of economic problems.

I. Extension of the Theory of Production and Exchange

The "property rights" literature begins with the presumption that modifications must be made in the conventional analytical framework if economic models having wider applicability are to be developed. Thus, several crucial changes are introduced into the theory of production and exchange. First, an entirely new interpretation is given to the role of in-

Journal of Economic Literature, Dec. 1972, Vol. X, No. 4, p. 1137.

dividual decision makers within the productive organization. The organization *per se* is no longer the central focus; rather, individuals are assumed to seek their own interests and to maximize utility subject to the limits established by the existing organizational structure. Second, account is taken of the fact that more than one pattern of property rights can exist and that profit (or wealth) maximization is not assured. By considering the effects of various possible property rights assignments on the penalty-reward system, detailed analysis of the interrelations between institutional arrangements and economic behavior becomes feasible. Third, transactions costs are recognized as being greater than zero in virtually all cases of practical importance. From a technical standpoint, these new ideas have straightforward application. The usual procedure is to formulate an optimization model that is analogous to, but in general distinct from, the traditional profit maximization case. In each instance, it is necessary to define the particular utility function that reflects the decision maker's preferences, and to determine the actual set of options (penalties—rewards) that is attainable by the decision maker. Then, the formal problem emerges as one of maximizing the utility function subject to the constraint imposed by the opportunity set. Of course, the usefulness of any such model depends on how skillfully the specification is made of the objective function and the opportunity set.

The rejection of profit maximization as the fundamental behavioral postulate explaining the actions of decision makers in the business sector represents a simple yet important step.[1] For, the shift to utility as the maximand opens up new possibilities for studying different patterns of managerial behavior, and permits greater insight into the operation of business firms in various socio-economic environments [1, Alchian and Kessel, 1962; 2, Alchian, 1965; 4, Alchian, 1969; 11, Averach and Johnson, 1962; 48, Furubotn, 1971; 49, Furubotn and Pejovich, 1970; 52, Furubotn and Pejovich, 1972; 83, Nichols, 1967; 90, Pejovich, 1969; 122, Williamson, 1964 and 123, Williamson, 1963]. This is so because regardless of the number, character, or diversity of the goals established by an individual decision maker, the goals can always be conceived as arguments in some type of utility function. And, as noted, the utility function can be maximized subject to appropriate constraints. Significantly, each decision maker is assumed to be motivated by self-interest and to move efficiently toward the most preferred operating position open.[2] It follows, therefore, that under the conditions envisioned, marginalism is not rejected; the standard techniques are merely extended to new applications [37, Crew, *et al*, 1971 and 60, Johnson, 1966].

To engage in something more than purely formal discussion the utility function must be given specific interpretation. Boulding's general comments on the "subjectivist" position make this clear.

If the firm will sacrifice "profits" (no matter how measured) for anything else, whether prestige, or good public or labor relations, or a quiet life, or liquidity, or security, or what have you, then it is clearly not maximizing profits. And if it is not maximizing profits it must be maximizing "utility," which is simply a more elaborate way of saying that it does what it thinks best. This can hardly be untrue, but it is also not very helpful unless some content can be poured into the empty utility functions [20, 1960, p. 4].

Relative to this argument, the property rights approach can be understood as an attempt to formulate empirically meaningful optimization problems by associating the utility function with the individual decision maker and then introducing specific content into the function. In this way, it becomes possible to consider the behavior of the decision maker within the firm, government bureau, or similar collective agency. The other key idea in the analysis is that different property rights assignments lead to different penalty-reward structures and, hence, decide the choices that are open to decision makers. An important shift of viewpoint is evident here. Instead of treating the *firm* as the unit of analysis and assuming that the owners' interests are given exclusive attention via the process of profit maximization, the utility maximizing model emphasizes *individual* adjustment to the economic environment and seeks to explain the behavior of the firm and other institutions by observing individual actions *within* the organization. In effect, an analytical basis is provided for examining the linkage between the objectives of decision makers and the particular strategies used to realize these objectives [123, Williamson, 1963, pp. 1033–40]. The presumption is, of course, that once human motivations are known, better understanding of the organization's allocation and use of resources becomes possible.

It is not difficult to accept the basic idea that "property rights" tend to influence incentives and behavior [35, Coleman, 1966]. The literature of the area, however, defines the concept of property rights with some precision and this special usage deserves comment. A central point noted is that property rights do not refer to relations between men and things but, rather, *to the sanctioned behavioral relations among men that arise from the existence of things and pertain to their use.* Property rights assignments specify the norms of behavior with respect to things that each and every person must observe in his interactions with other persons, or bear the cost for nonobservance. The prevailing system of property rights in the community can be described, then, as the set of economic and social relations defining the position of each individual with respect to the utilization of scarce resources.[3]

From a practical standpoint, the crucial task for the new property rights approach is to show that the content of property rights affects the allocation and use of resources *in specific and predictable ways.* For, without the latter assurance, there would be no possibility of developing analytically significant and empirically refutable propositions about the effects of various property rights assignments on the level and character of economic activity in the community. The essential assumption that systematic relations exist between property rights and economic choices lies in the background of discussion throughout the paper. At this stage, it is only necessary to emphasize one other point. Though sometimes forgotten, there should be no confusion about the fact that both trade and production involve *contractual arrangements*; these activities exist not so much to accomplish the exchange of goods and services but to permit the exchange of "bundles" of property rights.[4] Permission to do things with the goods and services is at issue.

The value of any good exchanged depends, *ceteris paribus*, on the bundle of property rights that is conveyed in the transaction. For example, the worth of a house to an individual will be relatively greater if the bundle of property rights acquired contains the right to exclude gasoline stations, chemical plants, etc. from the immediate vicinity of the house. It follows that the set of various property rights held over resources enters into the utility function of the decision maker. Consequently, a change in the general system of property relations must affect the way people behave and, through this effect on behavior, property rights assignments affect the allocation of resources, composition of output, distribution of income, etc. In the limit, one can say, as Alchian, that:

> . . . In essence, economics is the study of property rights over scarce resources. . . . The allocation of scarce resources in a society is the assignment of rights to uses of resources . . . the question of economics, or of how prices should be determined, is the question of how property rights should be defined and exchanged, and on what terms [3, Alchian, 1967, pp. 2–3].

This paper is concerned primarily with the effects of private property rights and state ownership on the allocation and use of resources. The right of ownership in an asset, whether by a private party or the state, is understood to consist of the right to use it, to change its form and substance, and to transfer *all rights* in the asset through, *e. g.*, sale, or *some rights* through, *e. g.*, rental. However, even though this definition suggests that the right of ownership is an exclusive right, ownership is not, and can hardly be expected to be, an unrestricted right. The right of ownership is an exclusive right in the sense that it is limited *only* by those restrictions that are explicitly stated in the law as it is interpreted from time to time. Such restrictions may range from the substantial to the minor. For example, on one hand, there is the serious case where an individual's right of ownership in an asset cannot be transferred for a price higher than the ceiling price stipulated by the government; on the other is the situation where a land owner is constrained from building a fence within two feet of the property line. In general, then, it is important to recognize that the attenuation of private (or state) property rights in an asset, through the imposition of restrictive measures, affects the owner's expectations about the uses to which he can put the asset, the value of the asset to the owner and to others, and consequently, the terms of trade. Because of these interrelations, the term attenuation represents a significant concept; when used in the paper, it will always signify the existence of some degree of restriction on the owner's rights to: (i) change the form, place, or substance of an asset, (ii) transfer all rights to an asset to others at a mutually agreed upon price.

Finally, the point must be stressed that most of the restrictions discussed here are those *imposed by the state*. To argue for a change in the content of the right of ownership, therefore, is to argue for a change in the allocation of resources to which legal support is given. In other words, as Samuels has noted:

> . . . opportunities for gain, whether pecuniary profit or other advantage, accrue to those who can use government. . . . If income distribution and risk allocation is a partial function of law (of property) then the law is an object of control for economic or other gain . . . whether the instances be tariff protection, oil subsidies, real estate agents' attempts to ban "for sale" signs on private homes or any other type of property rights [101, 1971, p. 444].

It follows, of course, that a theory of property rights cannot be truly complete without a theory of the state. And, unfortunately, no such theory exists at present. The ongoing research by J. Buchanan [24, 1962], R. McKean [75, 1971], W. Niskanen [84, 1968 and 85, 1971], D. North [86, 1972], G. Tullock [115, 1971] and other scholars gives promise of filling the gap, but this general line of investigation is still at a preliminary stage. Of special interest here is the fact that understanding of bureaucracy and the state can be developed from consideration of individual utility maximizing behavior. Professor North argues that the state has frequently traded inefficient property rights (e. g., licence to operate in a closed market) for revenue, and in doing so throttled economic growth. Indeed, it can be argued that changes in the content of property rights depend on the relationship between an *ex ante* estimate of benefits to the ruling elite from changing the existing property rights assignments and the *ex ante* or even *ex post* estimates of the costs to be incurred in policing and enforcing the changed structure of rights. If this reasoning is valid, the "efficient" size of the political organization should be affected by the size of markets and the state's military endowment, excluding considerations of *ex ante* errors or inoperable probabilities.

> An exchange economy and new weapons . . . made . . . a long struggle with numerous contenders . . . not only from within histori-

cally unified political units but also from without. . . . The contenders were in competition with each other and the key to success was the fiscal revenues that the contenders could command. Each state therefore endeavored to price its services (i. e., taxes) in such a way as to maximize present value. . . . The degree of monopoly power of the state in its contractual relationship with constituents reflected the degree to which other contenders appeared likely to be able to provide the same set of services. In short, the opportunity costs of the constituents lay behind the contractual relationships and changes in opportunity costs lead to efforts to alter the contract [86, North, 1972].

While systematic discussion of these themes cannot be attempted here, the basic hypothesis that changes in property rights are triggered by man's search for greater utility does seem worth exploring.

* * *

[Parts II and III omitted. (ed.).]

IV. Some General Observations

The preceding sections have attempted to give a systematic account of the major themes found in the property rights literature that has grown up in the last few decades. In a sense, it is somewhat artificial to think of the property rights contributions as falling into a distinct and separate area of specialization. For, as we have seen, a great variety of topics has been treated; and there is no absolute way to establish which works deserve inclusion in the property rights category and which do not. More important, the property rights analysis tends to build on and merge with the traditional theory so that, in the extreme, one might be tempted to say: microeconomic theory properly developed is the property rights approach. But, whatever the deeper questions of classification, there is some convenience in conceiving of a property rights literature and this body of writings does seem to possess certain characteristic features. The latter may be described as follows:

(1) Maximizing behavior is accepted as the norm; each decision maker is assumed to be motivated by self-interest and to move efficiently to the most preferred operating position open. Thus, the individual, whether he be a Soviet manager or a capitalist entrepreneur, is supposed to pursue his own goals within the limits allowed by the structure of the system in which he is operating and to reach an equilibrium position where utility is as great as it can be.

(2) The institutional environment in which economic activity takes place tends to be specified with precision. In particular, the existing property relations and the exchange, policing, and enforcement costs of contractual activities are spelled out in detail for each case studied. By making optimization models more general, the property rights literature per-

mits a greater range of institutional data to be considered and, thus, widens the applicability of the theory of production and exchange.

(3) There is confidence that the market logic can be applied fruitfully to a very great range of practical problems. Thus, the focus of discussion is on economic efficiency and the conditions under which markets should be, or should not be, extended into new areas.

(4) Strong concern is shown for the individualist basis of choice; the preferences or values of an individual are assumed to be revealed only through his market or political behavior. Social welfare functions are, therefore, either ignored or ruled out on grounds that such constructs have use only when choices are to be made by some agency or group external to the individuals directly affected.

(5) A central objective is to establish operationally meaningful propositions about the economy. Theory and empirical study tend to be blended so as to develop hypotheses that are subject to direct test and verification.

To say that the property rights literature has these distinguishing characteristics is, of course, not to suggest that other approaches share none of the qualities noted, or that other lines of investigation are without merit. Nevertheless, the property rights analysis does offer a fresh and useful way of looking at economic problems. Substantial advances have already been achieved and the literature gives evidence of continuing vitality and promise of future accomplishment.

FOOTNOTES

* The writing of this paper was facilitated by a grant from the National Science Foundation.

1 The analysis has also been extended to include the behavior of the state. See [22, Buchanan, 1968; 24, Buchanan and Tullock, 1962; 38, De Alessi, 1969; 75, McKean, 1971; 84, Niskanen, 1968 and 85, Niskanen, 1971].

2 The behavior of the firm (or other organization) is not interpreted in terms of the "satisficing" hypothesis that has been advanced by some authors who also reject profit maximization [109, Shubik, 1961; 110, Simon, 1959, pp. 265–66; 118, Vickers, 1968, Ch. 1].

3 Roman Law, Common Law, Marx and Engels, and current legal and economic studies basically agree on this definition of property rights.

4 Excellent discussion of the importance and content of contractual stipulations are found in S. Cheung [28, 1970] and S. MacCauley [66, 1963].

REFERENCES

Alchian, A. and Kessel, R. "Competition Monopoly and the Pursuit of Money" in National Bureau of Economic Research. *Aspects of labor economics*. Princeton: Princeton University Press, 1962, pp. 157–75.

Alchian, A. "The Basis of Some Recent Advances in the Theory of Management of the Firm," *J.Ind.Econ.*, Nov. 1965, *14*, pp. 30–41.

————, *Pricing and society.* Occasional Paper No. 17. Westminster: The Institute of Economic Affairs, 1967.

————, "Corporate Management and Property Rights" in H. Manne, ed. *Economic policy and the regulation of corporate securities.* Washington, D. C.: American Enterprise Institute for Public Policy Research, 1969, pp. 337–60.

————, "Information Cost, Pricing and Resource Unemployment," *Western Econ.J.*, June, 1969, *7*, pp. 109–28.

Alchian, A. and Allen, W. *University economics.* Belmont: Wadsworth, 1972.

Alchian, A. and Demsetz, H. "Production, Information Costs and Economic Organization," *Amer.Econ.Rev.* (forthcoming).

Arrow, K. "Economic Welfare and the Allocation of Resources for Invention" in National Bureau of Economic Research. *The rate and direction of inventive activity: Economic and social factors.* Princeton: Princeton University Press, 1962, pp. 609–25.

————, "An Extension of the Basic Theorems of Classical Welfare Economics" in J. Neyman, ed. *Proceedings of the Second Berkeley Symposium on Mathematical Statistics and Probability.* Berkeley, 1951, pp. 507–32.

Arrow, K. and Debreu, G. "Existence of an Equilibrium for a Competitive Economy," *Econometrica*, July 1954, *22*, pp. 265–90.

Averach, H. and Johnson, L. "Behavior of the Firm under Regulatory Constraint," *Amer.Econ.Rev.*, Dec. 1962, *52*, pp. 1052–69.

Bajt, A. "Property in Capital and in the Means of Production in Socialist Economies," *J.Law Econ.*, April, 1968, *11*, pp. 1–4.

Bator, F. "The Anatomy of Market Failure," *Quart.J.Econ.*, August 1958, *72*, pp. 351–79.

Baumol, W. *Business behavior, value and growth.* New York: Macmillan, 1959.

Becker, G. *Economics of discrimination.* Chicago: University of Chicago Press, 1957.

Berle, A. and Means, G. *The modern corporation and private property.* New York: Harcourt, Brace and World, 1968.

Berle, A. *Power without property.* New York: Harcourt, Brace and World, 1959.

Bornstein, M. and Fusfeld, D. *The Soviet economy: A book of readings.* Homewood, Illinois: Irwin, 1970.

Bottomley, A. "The Effect of the Common Ownership of Land upon Resource Allocation in Tripolitania," *Land Econ.*, Feb. 1963, *39*, pp. 91–95.

Boulding, K. "The Present Position of the Theory of the Firm" in K. E. Boulding and W. A. Spivy, eds., *Linear programming and the theory of the firm.* New York: Macmillan, 1960, pp. 1–17.

Bronfenbrenner, M. "A Reformulation of Naive Profit Theory," *Southern Econ.J.*, April 1960, *26*, pp. 300–09.

Buchanan, J., "Congestion on the Common: A Case for Government Intervention," *Il Politico*, 1968, *33*, pp. 776–86.

Buchanan, J. and Stubblebine, C. "Externality," *Economica*, Nov. 1962, *29* pp. 371–84.

Buchanan, J. and Tullock, G. *The calculus of consent*. Ann Arbor: University of Michigan Press, 1962.

Buchanan, J. and Devletoglou, N. *Academia in anarchy: An economic diagnosis*. New York: Basic Books, 1970.

Cheung, S. "Transaction Costs, Risk Aversion, and the Choice of Contractual Arrangements," *J.Law Econ.*, April 1969, *12*, pp. 23–42.

———, "Private Property Rights and Sharecropping," *J.Polit.Econ.*, Dec. 1968, *76*, pp. 1107–22.

———, "The Structure of a Contract and the Theory of a Non-Exclusive Resource," *J.Law Econ.*, April 1970, *13*, pp. 49–70.

Clarkson, K. "Property Rights, Institutional Constraints, and Individual Behavior: An Application to Short-term Hospitals," Ph.D. Dissertation, Department of Economics, University of California at Los Angeles, 1970.

Clayton, E. "Property Rights under Socialism," 1971 (unpublished manuscript).

———, "Price Appropriability and the Soviet Agricultural Incentives," paper presented at National Convention of the American Association for the Advancement of Slavic Studies, March 1972.

Coase, R. "The Federal Communications Commission," *J.Law Econ.*, Oct. 1959, *2*, pp. 1–40.

———, "The Problem of Social Cost," *J.Law Econ.* Oct. 1960, *3*, pp. 1–44.

———, "The Nature of the Firm," *Economica*, Nov. 1937, *4*, pp. 386–405.

Coleman, J. "Reward Structures and the Allocation of Effort" in P. F. Lazarsfeld and N. W. Henry, eds. *Readings in mathematical social science*. Cambridge: MIT Press, 1966, pp. 159–73.

Cooper, W. "Theory of the Firm: Some Suggestions for Revision," *Amer. Econ.Rev.*, Dec. 1949, *39*, pp. 1204–22.

Crew, M.; Jones-Lee, M. and Rawley, C. "X-Theory Versus Management Discretion Theory," *Southern Econ.J.*, Oct. 1971, *38*, pp. 173–84.

De Alessi, L. "Implications of Property Rights for Government Investment Choices," *Amer.Econ.Rev.*, March 1969, *59*, pp. 16–23.

Debreu, G. *Theory of value*. New York: Wiley, 1959.

Demsetz, H. "The Exchange and Enforcement of Property Rights," *J.Law Econ.*, Oct. 1964, *7*, pp. 11–26.

———, "Some Aspects of Property Rights," *J.Law Econ.*, Oct. 1966, *9*, pp. 61–70.

———, "Toward a Theory of Property Rights," *Amer.Econ.Rev.*, May 1967, *57*, pp. 347–73.

————, "Information and Efficiency: Another Viewpoint," *J.Law Econ.*, April 1969, *12*, pp. 1–22.

————, "When Does the Rule of Liability Matter," paper presented at the Southern Economic Association Meeting, November, 1971.

DeVany, A.; Eckert, R.; Meyers, C.; O'Hara, D. and Scott, R. "A Property System for Market Allocation of Electro-Magnetic Spectrum: A Legal-Economic-Engineering Study," *Stanford Law Rev.*, June 1969, *21*, pp. 1499–1561.

Domar, E. "The Soviet Collective Farm," *Amer.Econ.Rev.*, Sept. 1966, *56*, pp. 734–57.

Eckert, R. "Regulatory Commission Behavior: Taxi Franchising in Los Angeles and Other Cities," Ph.D. Dissertation, Department of Economics, University of California at Los Angeles, 1968.

Furubotn, E. "Toward a Dynamic Model of the Yugoslav Firm," *Can.J.Econ.*, May 1971, *4*, pp. 182–97.

Furubotn, E. and Pejovich, S. "Property Rights and the Behavior of the Firm in a Socialist State," *Z. für Nationalökon.*, Winter 1970, *30*, pp. 431–54.

————, "Tax Policy and Investment Decisions of the Yugoslav Firm," *Nat. Tax J.*, Sept. 1970, *23*, pp. 335–48.

————, "The Role of the Banking System in Yugoslav Economic Planning, 1946–1969" in D. Demarco, ed. *Revue Internationale D'Histoire de la Banque*, Vol. 4. Geneva, Librairie Droz, 1971.

————, "The Soviet Manager and Innovation: A Behavioral Model of the Soviet Firm," *Revue de L'Est*, Jan. 1972, *3*, pp. 29–45.

Furubotn, E. "Economic Organization and Welfare Distribution," *Swedish J.Econ.*, Dec. 1971, *73*, pp. 409–16.

Gordon, M. *The Investment, financing and valuation of the corporation.* Homewood, Illinois: Irwin, 1962.

Gordon, S. "The Economic Theory of a Common-Property Resource: The Fishery," *J.Polit.Econ.*, April 1954, *62*, pp. 124–42.

Graaff, J. *Theoretical welfare economics.* Cambridge: Cambridge University Press, 1957.

Hanvonen, J. "Postwar Developments in Money and Banking in Yugoslavia," *Int.Monet.Fund Staff Pap.*, Nov. 1970, *17*, pp. 563–601.

Heyne, P. "The Free Market System is the Best Guide for Corporate Decisions," *Financial Analysts J.*, Sept.-Oct. 1971.

Hindley, B. "Separation of Ownership and Control in the Modern Corporation," *J.Law Econ.*, April 1970, *13*, pp. 185–221.

Johnson, H. "Graphic Analysis of Multiple-Goal Firms: Development, Current Status and Critique," Pennsylvania State University, *Occasional Paper*, No. 5, 1966, pp. 1–36.

Kamerschen, D. "The Influence of Ownership and Control on Profit Rates," *Amer.Econ.Rev.*, June 1968, *58*, pp. 432–47.

Kaysen, C. "Another View of Corporate Capitalism," *Quart.J.Econ.*, Feb. 1965, *79*, pp. 41–51.

Larner, R. "The 200 Largest Nonfinanced Corporations," *Amer.Econ.Rev.*, Sept. 1966, *56*, pp. 777–87.

Levine, M. "Landing Fees and the Airport Congestion Problem," *J.Law Econ.*, April 1969, *12*, pp. 79–108.

Levy, F. "Economic Analysis of the Non-Profit Institution—The Case of the Private University," Thomas Jefferson Center for Political Economy, *Public Choice*, Spring 1968, *4*, pp. 3–17.

MacCaulay, S. "Non-Contractual Relations in Business: A Preliminary Study," *Amer.Sociological Rev.*, Feb. 1963, *28*, pp. 55–67.

Manne, H. "Good for General Motors," *Barron's*, May 18, 1970.

———, "The Parable of the Parking Lots," *Religion and Society*, Feb. 1972, *5*, pp. 22–27.

Marris, R. *The economic theory of managerial capitalism.* New York: Free Press of Glencoe, 1964.

Martin, D. "Claims to Work Opportunity: An Economic Analysis of Alternative Configurations of Hiring Rights," Ph.D. Dissertation, Department of Economics, University of California at Los Angeles, 1969.

———, "Job Property Rights and Job Defections," *J.Law Econ.*, Forthcoming.

Mayer, T. "The Distribution of Ability and Earnings," *Rev.Econ.Statist.*, May 1960, *42*, pp. 189–95.

McKean, R. "Products Liability: Implications of Some Changing Property Rights," *Quart.J.Econ.*, Nov. 1970, *84*, pp. 611–26.

———, "Divergences Between Individual and Total Cost Within Government," *Amer.Econ.Rev.*, May 1964, *54*, pp. 243–49.

———, "Property Rights Within Government and Devices to Increase Government's Efficiency," paper presented at the Southern Economic Association Meeting, November 1971.

Meade, J. "External Economies and Diseconomies in a Competitive Situation," *Econ.J.*, March 1952, *62*, pp. 54–67.

Meckling, W. "Management of the Frequency Spectrum," *Washington University Law Quart.*, Winter 1968, pp. 26–34.

Minasian, J. "Television Pricing and the Theory of Public Goods," *J.Law Econ.*, Oct. 1964, *7*, pp. 71–80.

Mishan, E. "The Postwar Literature on Externalities: An Interpretative Essay," *J.Econ.Lit.*, March 1971, *9*, pp. 1–26.

Moore, J. "Discretionary Behavior in a Worker-Managed Enterprise," paper presented at National Convention of the American Association for the Advancement of Slavic Studies, March 1972.

———, "On Incentives in Socialist Enterprises," paper presented at Southern Conference on Slavic Studies, October 1971.

Newhouse, J. "Toward a Theory of Nonprofit Institutions: An Economic Model of a Hospital," *Amer.Econ.Rev.*, March 1970, *60*, pp. 64–74.

Nicols, A. "Stock vs. Mutual Savings and Loan Associations: Some Evidence of Differences in Behavior," *Amer.Econ.Rev.*, May 1967, *57*, pp. 337–46.

Niskanan, W. "Nonmarket Decision Making: The Peculiar Economics of Bureaucracy," *Amer.Econ.Rev.*, May 1968, *58*, pp. 293–305.

———, *Bureaucracy and representative government*. Chicago: Aldine Publishing Company, 1971.

North, D. "The Creation of Property Rights in Western Europe 900–1700 A.D.," 1972 (unpublished manuscript).

Nove, A. *The Soviet economy*. New York: Frederick A. Praeger, 1969.

Nutter, W. "Markets Without Property: A Grand Illusion" in N. Beadles and A. Drewry, eds. *Money, the market, and the state*. Athens, Georgia: Georgia University Press, 1968, pp. 137–45.

Pejovich, S. "Liberman's Reforms and Property Rights in the Soviet Union," *J.Law Econ.*, April 1969, *12*, pp. 155–62.

———, "The Firm, Monetary Policy and Property Rights in a Planned Economy," *Western Econ.J.*, Sept. 1969, *7*, pp. 193–200.

———, "Fiscal Policy and Investment in Human Capital," *Rev.Soc.Econ.*, March 1970, *28*, pp. 53–59.

———, "Towards a General Theory of Property Rights," *Z. für Nationalökon.*, Spring 1971, *31*, pp. 141–55.

———, "Economic Reforms in the Soviet Union: Their Causes and Purpose," *Modern Age*, Jan. 1972, *16*, pp. 68–76.

———, "The Banking System and the Investment Behavior of the Yugoslav Firm" in M. Bornstein, ed. *Plan and market*. New Haven: Yale University Press, 1973.

Penrose, E. *The theory of the growth of the firm*. New York: J. Wiley and Sons, 1959.

Porter, A. *Job property rights*. New York: King Crown Press, 1954.

Prybyla, J. *Comparative economic systems*. New York: Appleton-Century-Crofts, 1969.

Quirk, J. and Saposnik, R. *Introduction to general equilibrium theory and welfare economics*. New York: McGraw-Hill, 1968.

Reder, M. "A Reconsideration of Marginal Productivity Theory," *J.Polit. Econ.*, Oct. 1947, *55*, pp. 450–58.

Rottenberg, S. "Property in Work," *Ind.Lab.Relat.Rev.*, April 1962, *15*, pp. 402–05.

Samuels, W. "Interrelations Between Legal and Economic Processes," *J.Law Econ.*, Oct. 1971, *14*, pp. 435–50.

Samuelson, P. *Economics*. 7th Edition. New York: McGraw-Hill, 1966.

Scitovsky, T. "To Concepts of External Economies," *J.Polit.Econ.*, April 1954, *62*, pp. 70–82.

Scott, A. "The Fishery: The Objectives of Sole Ownership," *J.Polit.Econ.*, April 1955, *63*, pp. 116–24.

Scott, M. "Relative Share Prices and Yields," *Oxford Econ.Pap.*, Oct. 1962, *14*, pp. 218–50.

Shalit, S. "Barriers to Entry in the American Hospital Industry," Ph.D. Dissertation, Chicago: University of Chicago, 1971.

Sherman, R. "The Design of Public Utility Institutions," *Land Econ.*, Feb. 1970, *46*, pp. 51–58.

Sherman, R. (with Thomas D. Willett), "Externality, Regional Development, and Tax-Subsidy Combinations," *Nat.Tax.J.*, June 1969, *22*, pp. 291–98.

Shubik, M. "Objective Functions and Models of Corporate Optimization," *Quart.J.Econ.*, August 1961, *75*, pp. 345–75.

Simon, H. "Theories of Decision-Making in Economics and Behavioral Science," *Amer.Econ.Rev.*, June 1959, *49*, pp. 253–88.

Smith, V. "On Models of Commercial Fishing," *J.Polit.Econ.*, March 1969, *77*, pp. 181–98.

Spulber, N. *The Soviet economy*. New York: Norton, 1962.

Steiner, P. "Monopoly and Competition in Television: Some Policy Issues," *Manchester School Econ.Soc.Stud.*, May 1961, *29*, pp. 107–31.

Stigler, G. "The Economics of Information," *J.Polit.Econ.*, June 1961, *69*, pp. 213–25.

Tullock, G. *The logic of the law*. New York: Basic Books, 1971.

Turvey, R. "Optimization and Suboptimization in Fishery Regulation," *Amer.Econ.Rev.*, March 1964, *54*, pp. 64–76.

Vanek, J. "Some Fundamental Considerations of Financing and the Right of Property Under Labor-Management," 1971 (unpublished manuscript).

Vickers, D. *The theory of the firm: Production, capital, and finance*. New York: McGraw-Hill, 1968.

Ward, B. "Workers Management in Yugoslavia," *J.Polit.Econ.*, Oct. 1957, *65*, pp. 373–86.

Weintraub, B. *Price theory*. New York: Pitman, 1949.

White, W. "Money, Information and Socialism," paper presented at the Western Economic Association Meetings, August 1971.

Williamson, O. *The economics of discretionary behavior: Managerial objectives in a theory of the firm*. Englewood Cliffs, New Jersey: Prentice-Hall, Inc., 1964.

———, "Managerial Discretion and Business Behavior," *Amer.Econ.Rev.*, Dec. 1963, *53*, pp. 1032–57.

Zaleski, E. *Planning reforms in the Soviet Union, 1962–1966*. Chapel Hill: The University of North Carolina Press, 1967.

*

**The Economics of
Constitutional Theory**

5: BEFORE PUBLIC CHOICE

JAMES M. BUCHANAN

A contract theory of the State is relatively easy to derive, and careful use of this theory can yield major explanatory results. To an extent at least, a "science" exists for the purpose of providing psychologically satisfying explanations of what men can commonly observe about them. Presumably, we "feel better" when we possess some explanatory framework or model that allows us to classify and interpret disparate sense perceptions. This imposition of order on the universe is a "good" in the strict economic sense of this term; men will invest money, time, and effort in acquiring it. The contract theory of the State, in all of its manifestations, can be defended on such grounds. It is important for sociopolitical order and tranquility that ordinary men explain to themselves the working of governmental process in models that conceptually take their bases in cooperative rather than in noncooperative behavior. Admittedly and unabashedly, the contract theory serves, in this sense, a rationalization purpose or objective. We need a "logic of law," a "calculus of consent," a "logic of collective action," to use the titles of three books that embody modern-day contract theory foundations.[1]

Can the contract theory of the State serve other objectives, whether these be normative or positive in character? Can institutions which find no conceivable logical derivation in contract among cooperating parties be condemned on other than strictly personal grounds? Can alleged improvements in social arrangements be evaluated on anything other than contractarian precepts, or, to lapse into economists' jargon, on anything other than Paretian criteria? But, even here, are these criteria any more legitimate than any other?

Explorations in the Theory of Anarchy, Gordon Tullock (ed.) (1972, Center for the Study of Public Choice, Blacksburg, Va.), p. 27.

In earlier works, I have tended to go past these fundamental questions. I have been content to work out, at varying levels of sophistication, the contractarian bases for governmental action, either that which we can commonly observe or that which might be suggested as reforms. To me, this effort seemed relevant and significant. "Political economy" or "public choice"—these seemed to be labels assignable to honorable work that required little or no methodological justification. It was only when I tried to outline a summary treatment of my whole approach to socio-political structure that I was stopped short. I came to realize that the very basis of the contractarian position must be examined more thoroughly.

We know that, factually and historically, the "social contract" is mythological, at least in many of its particulars. Individuals did not come together in some original position and mutually agree on the rules of social intercourse. And even had they done so at some time in history, their decisions could hardly be considered to be contractually binding on all of us who have come behind. We cannot start anew. We can either accept the political universe, or we can try to change it. The question reduces to one of determining the criteria for change.

When and if we fully recognize that the contract is a myth designed in part to rationalize existing institutional structures of society, can we simultaneously use the contractual derivations to develop criteria for evaluating changes or modifications in these structures? I have previously answered this question affirmatively, but without proper argument. The intellectual quality as well as the passionate conviction of those who answer the question negatively suggest that more careful consideration is required.

How can we derive a criterion for determining whether or not a change in law, or, if you will, a change in the assignment of rights, is or is not justified? To most social scientists, the only answer is solipsist. Change becomes desirable if "I like it," even though many prefer to dress this up in fanciful "social welfare function" or "public interest" semantics. To me, this seems to be pure escapism; it represents retreat into empty arguments about personal values which spells the end of rational discourse. Perhaps some of our colleagues do possess God-like qualities, or at least think that they do, but until and unless their godliness is accepted, we are left with no basis for discourse. My purpose is to see how far we can rationally discuss criteria for social change on the presumption that no man's values are better than any other man's.

Is *agreement* the only test? Is the Wicksellian-contractarian-Paretian answer the only legitimate one here? If so, are we willing to accept its corollaries? Its full implications? Are we willing to forestall all social change that does not command unanimous or quasi-unanimous consent?

Provisionally, let us say that we do so. We can move a step beyond, while at the same time rationalizing much of what we see, by resorting to "constitutionalism," the science of rules. We can say that particular proposals for social change need not command universal assent provided only that such assent holds for the legal structure within which particular proposals are enacted or chosen. This seems to advance the argument; we seem to be part of the way out of the dilemma. But note that this provides us with no means at all for evaluating particular proposals as "good" or "bad." We can generate many outcomes or results under non-unanimity rules. This explains my initial response to the Arrow impossibility theorem, and to the subsequent discussion. My response was, and is, one of nonsurprise at the alleged inconsistency in a social decision process that embodies in itself no criteria for consistency. This also explains my unwillingness to be trapped, save on rare and regretted occasions, into positions of commitment on particular measures of policy on the familiar efficiency grounds. We can offer no policy advice on particular legislative proposals. As political economists, we examine public choices; we can make institutional predictions. We can analyze alternative political-social-economic structures.

But what about constitutional change itself? Can we say nothing, or must we say that, at this level, the contractarian (Wicksellian, Paretian) norm must apply? Once again, observation hardly supports us here. Changes are made, changes that would be acknowledged to be genuinely "constitutional," without anything remotely approaching unanimous consent. Must we reject all such changes out of hand, or can we begin to adduce criteria on some other basis?

Resort to the choice of rules for ordinary parlor games may seem to offer assistance. Influenced greatly by the emphasis on such choices by Rutledge Vining, I once considered this to be the key to genuinely innovative application of the contractarian criteria. If we could, somehow, think of individual participants in a setting of complete uncertainty about their own positions over subsequent rounds of play, we might think of their reaching genuine agreement on a set of rules. The idea of a "fair game" does have real meaning, and this idea can be transferred to sociopolitical institutions. But how far can we go with this? We may, in this process, begin to rationalize certain institutions that cannot readily be brought within the standard Wicksellian framework. But can we do more? Can we, as John Rawls seems to want to do in his monumental, *Theory of Justice*,[2] think ourselves into a position of original contract and then idealize our thought processes into norms that "should" be imposed as criteria for institutional change? Note that this is, to me, quite different from saying that we derive a possible rationalization. To rationalize, to explain, is not to propose, and Rawls seems to miss this quite critical distinction. It is one thing to say that, conceptually, men in some genuinely constitutional stage of deliberation, operating behind the veil of ignorance, might have agreed to rules something akin to those that we actually observe, but it is quite another thing to say that men, in the here and now, should be forced to abide by specific rules that we imagine by transporting ourselves into some mental-moral equivalent of an original contract setting where men are genuine "moral equals."

Unless we do so, however, we must always accept whatever structure of rules that exists and seek constitutional changes only through agreement, through consensus. It is this inability to say anything about rules changes, this inability to play God, this inability to raise himself above the masses, that the social philosopher cannot abide. He has an ingrained prejudice against the status quo, however this may be defined, understandably so, since his very role, as he interprets it, is one that finds itself only in social reform. (Perhaps this role conception reflects the moral inversion that Michael Polanyi and Craig Roberts note; the shift of moral precepts away from personal behavior aimed at personal salvation and toward moral evaluation or social institutions.)

Just what are men saying when they propose nonagreed changes in the basic structure of rights? Are they saying anything more than "this is what I want and since I think the State has the power to impose it, I support the State as the agency to enforce the change"? We may be able to get some handles on this very messy subject by going back to Hobbes. We need to examine the initial leap out of the Hobbesian jungle. How can agreement emerge? And what are the problems of enforcement?

We may represent the reaction equilibrium in the Hobbesian jungle at the origin in the diagrammatics of Figure 1. If we measure "B's law abiding behavior" on the ordinate, and "A's law abiding behavior" on the abscissa, it is evident that neither man secures advantage from "lawful" behavior individually and independently of the other man's behavior. (Think of "law abiding" here as "not-stealing.") Note that the situation here is quite different from the usual public-goods model in which at least some of the "good" will tend to be produced by one or all of the common or joint consumers even under wholly independent adjustment. With law-abiding as the "good," however, the individual cannot, through his own behavior, produce so as to increase his own utility. He can do nothing other than provide a "pure" external economy; all benefits accrue to the other parties. Hence, the independent adjustment position involves a corner solution at the origin in our two-person diagram. But gains-from-trade clearly exist in this Hobbesian jungle, despite the absence of unilateral action.

It is easy enough to depict the Pareto region that bounds potential positions of mutual gains by drawing the appropriate indifference contours through the origin as is done in Figure 1. These contours indicate the internal or subjective rates of tradeoff as between *own* and *other* law-

abiding. It seems plausible to suggest that the standard convexity properties would apply. The analysis remains largely empty, however, until we
know something, or at least postulate something, about the descriptive
characteristics of the initial position itself. And the important and relevant point in this respect is that individuals *are not equal,* or at least need
not be equal, in such a setting, either in their relative abilities or in their
final command over consumables.[3] To assume symmetry among persons
here amounts to converting a desired normative state, that of equality
among men, into a fallacious positive proposition. (This is, of course, a
pervasive error, and one that is not only made by social philosophers. It
has had significant and pernicious effects on judicial thinking in the
twentieth century.) If we drop the equality or symmetry assumption,
however, we can say something about the relative values or tradeoffs as
between the relative "haves" and "have-nots" in the Hobbesian or natural
adjustment equilibrium. For illustrative purposes here, think of the
"natural distribution" in our two-person model as characterized by A's
enjoyment of 10 units of "good," and B's enjoyment of only 2 units. Both
persons expend effort, a "bad," in generating and in maintaining this
natural distribution. It is this effort that can be reduced or eliminated
through trade, through agreement on laws or rules of respect for property.
In this way, both parties can secure more "goods." The posttrade equilibrium must reflect improvement for both parties over the natural distribution or pretrade outcome. There are prospects for Pareto-efficient
or Pareto-superior moves from the initial no-rights position to any one of
many possible posttrade or positive-rights distributions.

Let us suppose that agreement is reached; each person agrees to an
assignment of property rights and, furthermore, each person agrees to
respect such rights as are assigned. Let us suppose, for illustration, that
the net distribution of "goods" under the assignment is 15 units for A and
7 units for B. Hence, there is a symmetrical sharing of the total gains-
from-trade secured from the assignment of rights. Even under such symmetrical sharing, however, note that the relative position of B has improved more than the relative position of A. In our example, A's income
increases by one-half; but B's income increases more than twofold. This
suggests that the person who fares relatively worse in the natural distribution may well stand to gain relatively more from an initial assignment of
rights than the person who fares relatively better in the pretrade state
of the world.

Agreement is attained; both parties enjoy more utility than before.
But again the prisoner's dilemma setting must be emphasized. Each of
the two persons can anticipate gains by successful unilateral default on the
agreement. In Figure 1, if E depicts the position of agreement, A can
always gain by a shift to N if this can be accomplished; similarly, B can
gain by a shift to M. There may, however, be an asymmetry present in

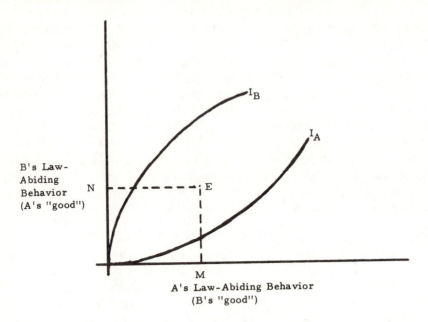

Figure 1

prospective gains from unilateral default on the rights agreement. The prospective gains may well be higher for the person who remains relatively less favored in the natural distribution. In one sense, the "vein of ore" that he can mine by departing from the rules through criminal activity is richer than the similar vein would be for the other party. The productivity of criminal effort is likely to be higher for the man who can steal from his rich neighbor than for the man who has only poor neighbors.

This may be illustrated in the matrix of Figure 2, where the initial pretrade or natural distribution is shown in Cell IV, and the posttrade or positive rights distribution is shown in Cell I. Note that, as depicted, the man who is relatively "poor" in the natural equilibrium, person B in the example, stands to gain relatively more by departing unilaterally from Cell I than person A. Person B could, by such a move, increase his quantity of "goods" from 7 to 12, whereas person A could only increase his from 15 to 17. This example suggests that the relatively "rich" person will necessarily be more interested in policing the activities of the "poor" man, as such, than vice versa. This is, of course, widely accepted. But the construction and analysis here can be employed for a more complex and difficult issue that has not been treated adequately.

Assume that agreement has been attained; both parties abide by the law; both enjoy the benefits. Time passes. The "rich" man becomes lazy and lethargic. The "poor" man increases his strength. This modifies the natural distribution. Let us say that the natural distribution changes to 6:6. The "rich" man now has an overwhelmingly more significant interest in the maintenance of the legal status quo than the "poor" man, who is no longer "poor" in natural ability terms. The initial symmetry in the sharing of gains as between the no-trade and the trade position no longer holds. With the new natural distribution, the "rich" man secures almost all of the net gains.

The example must be made more specific. Assume that the situation is analogous to the one examined by Winston Bush. The initial problem is how is manna which drops from Heaven to be divided among the two per-

	B Abides by "Law"	B Observes no "Law"
A Abides by "Law"	I 15, 7	II 6, 12
A Observes no "Law"	III 17, 3	IV 10, 2

Figure 2

sons. The initial natural distribution is in the ratio 10:2 as noted. Recognizing this, along with their own abilities, A and B agree that by assigning rights, they can attain a 15:7 ratio, as noted. Time passes, and B increases in relative strength, but the "goods" are still shared in the 15:7 ratio. The initial set of property rights agreed to on the foundations of the initial natural distribution no longer reflects or mirrors the existing natural distribution. Under these changed conditions, a lapse back into the natural equilibrium will harm B relatively little whereas A will be severely damaged. The "poor" man now has relatively little interest in adherence to law. If this trend continues, and the natural distribution changes further in the direction indicated, the "poor" man may find himself able to secure even net advantages from a lapse back into the Hobbesian jungle.

The model may be described in something like the terms of modern game theory. If the initial natural distribution remains unaltered, the agreed-on assignment of rights possesses qualities like the core in an n-person game. It is to the advantage of no coalition to depart from this assignment or imputation if the remaining members of the group are willing to enforce or to block the imputation. No coalition can do better on its own, or in this model, in the natural distribution, than it does in the assignment. These core-like properties of the assigned distribution under law may, however, begin to lose dominance features as the potential natural distribution shifts around "underneath" the existing structure of rights, so to speak. The foundations of the existing rights structure may be said to have shifted in the process.

This analysis opens up interesting new implications for net redistribution of wealth and for changes in property rights over time. Observed changes in claims to wealth take place without apparent consent. These may be interpreted simply as the use of the enforcement power of the State by certain coalitions of persons to break the contract. They are overtly shifting from a Cell I into a Cell II or Cell III outcome in the diagram of Figure 2. It is not, of course, difficult to explain why these coalitions arise. It will always be in the interest of a person, or a group of persons, to depart from the agreed-on assignment of claims or rights, provided that he or they can do so unilaterally and without offsetting reactive behavior on the part of the remaining members of the social group. The quasi-equilibrium in Cell I is inherently unstable. The equilibrium does qualify as a position in the core of the game, but we must keep in mind that the core analytics presumes the immediate formation of blocking coalitions. In order fully to explain observed departures from status quo we must also explain the behavior of the absence of the potential blocking coalitions. Why do the remaining members of the community fail to enforce the initial assignment of rights?

The analysis here suggests that if there has been a sufficiently large shift in the underlying natural distribution, the powers of enforcing adherence on the prospective violators of contract may not exist, or, if they exist, these powers may be demonstrably weakened. In our numerical example, B fares almost as well under the new natural distribution as he does in the continuing assignment of legal rights. Hence, A has lost almost all of his blocking power; he can scarcely influence B by threats to plunge the community into Hobbesian anarchy, even if A himself should be willing to do so. And it should also be recognized that "willingness" to enforce the contract (the structure of legal rules, the existing set of claims to property) is as important as the objective ability to do so. Even if A should be physically able to force B to return to the *status quo ante* after some attempted departure, he may be unwilling to suffer the personal loss that might be required to make his threat of enforcement credible.[4] The law-abiding members of the community may find themselves in a genuine dilemma. They may simply be unable to block the unilateral violation of the social contract.

In this perspective, normative arguments based on "justice" in distribution may signal acquiescence in modifications in the existing structure of claims. Just as the idea of contract, itself, has been used to rationalize existing structure, the idea of "justice" may be used to rationalize coerced departures from contract. In the process those who advance such arguments and those who are convinced may "feel better" while their claims are whittled away. This does, I think, explain much attitudinal behavior toward redistribution policy by specific social groups. Gordon Tullock has, in part, explained the prevailing attitudes of many academicians and intellectuals.[5] The explanation developed here applies more directly to the redistributionist attitudes of the scions of the rich, *e. g.*, the Rockefellers and Kennedys. Joseph Kennedy was less redistributive than his sons; John D. Rockefeller was less redistributive than his grandsons. We do not need to call on the psychologists since our model provides an explanation in the concept of a changing natural distribution. The scions of the wealthy are far less secure in their roles of custodians of wealth than were their forebears. They realize perhaps that their own natural talents simply do not match up, even remotely, to the share of national wealth that they now command. Their apparent passions for the poor may be nothing more than surface reflections of attempts to attain temporary security.

The analysis also suggests that there is a major behavioral difference fostered between the integenerational transmission of nonhuman and human capital. Within limits, there is an important linkage between human capital and capacity to survive in a natural or Hobbesian environment. There seems to be no such linkage between nonhuman capital and survival in the jungle. From this it follows that the man who possesses human capital is likely to be far less concerned about the "injustice" of his own position, less concerned about temporizing measures designed to shore up apparent leaks in the social system than his counterpart who possesses nonhuman capital. If we postulate that the actual income-asset distribution departs significantly from the proportionate distribution in the underlying and existing natural equilibrium, the system of claims must be acknowledged to be notoriously unstable. The idle rich, possessed of nonhuman capital, will tend to form coalitions with the poor that are designed primarily to ward off retreat toward the Hobbesian jungle. This coalition can take the form of the rich acquiescing in and providing defense for overt criminal activity on the part of the poor, or the more explicit form of political exploitation of the "silent majority," the Agnew constituency that possesses largely human rather than nonhuman capital.

This description has some empirical content in 1972. But what can the exploited groups do about it? Can the middle classes form a coalition with the rich, especially when the latter are themselves so insecure? Or can they form, instead, another coalition with the poor, accepting a promise of strict adherence to law in exchange for goodies provided by the explicit confiscation of the nonhuman capital of the rich? (Politically, this would take the form of confiscatory inheritance taxation.) The mythology of the American dream probably precludes this route from being taken. The self-made, the *nouveau riche*, seek to provide their children with fortunes that the latter will accept only with guilt.

All of this suggests that a law-abiding imputation becomes increasingly difficult to sustain as its structure departs from what participants conceive to be the natural or Bush-Hobbes imputation, defined in some proportionate sense. If the observed imputation, or set of bounded imputations that are possible under existing legal-constitutional rules, seems to bear no relationship at all to the natural imputation that men accept, breakdown in legal standards is predictable.

Where does this leave us in trying to discuss criteria for "improvement" in rules, in assignments of rights, the initial question that was posed in this paper? I have argued that the contractarian or Paretian norm is relevant on the simple principle that "we start from here." But "here," the status quo, is the existing set of legal institutions and rules. Hence, how can we possibly distinguish genuine contractual changes in "law" from those which take place under the motivations discussed above? Can we really say which changes are defensible "exchanges" from an existing status quo position? This is what I am trying to answer, without full success, in my paper in response to Warren J. Samuels discussion of the *Miller et al. v. Schoene* case.[6] There I tried to argue that, to the extent that property rights are specified in advance, genuine "trades" can emerge, with mutual gains to all parties. However, to the extent that existing rights are held to be subject to continuous redefinition by the State, no one has an incentive to organize and to initiate trades or agreements. This amounts to saying that once the body politic begins to get overly concerned about the distribution of the pie under existing property-rights assignments and legal rules, once we begin to think either about the personal gains from law-breaking, privately or publicly, or about the disparities between existing imputations and those estimated to be forthcoming under some idealized anarchy, we are necessarily precluding and forestalling the achievement of potential structural changes that might increase the size of the pie for *all*. Too much concern for "justice" acts to insure that "growth" will not take place, and for reasons much more basic than the familiar economic incentives arguments.

In this respect, 1972 seems a century, not a mere decade, away from 1962, when, if you recall, the rage was all for growth and the newfound concern about distribution had not yet been invented. At issue here, of course, is the whole conception of the State, or of collective action. I am far less sanguine than I was concerning the possible acceptance of the existing constitutional-legal framework. The basic structure of property rights is now threatened more seriously than at any period in the two-century history of the United States. In the paper, "The Samaritan's Dilemma," noted above, I advanced the hypothesis that we have witnessed a general loss of strategic courage, brought on in part by economic affluence. As I think more about all this, however, I realize that there is more to it. We may be witnessing the disintegration of our effective constitutional rights, regardless of the prattle about "the constitution" as seen by our judicial tyrants from their own visions of the entrails of their sacrificial beasts. I do not know what might be done about all this, even by those who recognize what is happening. We seem to be left with the question posed at the outset. How do rights re-emerge and come to command respect? How do "laws" emerge that carry with them general respect for their "legitimacy"?

FOOTNOTES

1 See Gordon Tullock, *The Logic of Law* (New York: Basic Books, 1970); James M. Buchanan and Gordon Tullock, *The Calculus of Consent* (Ann Arbor: University of Michigan Press, 1962); Mancur Olson, *The Logic of Collective Action* (Cambridge: Harvard University Press, 1965).

2 John Rawls, *Theory of Justice* (Cambridge: Harvard University Press, 1971).

3 The formal properties of the "natural distribution" that will emerge under anarchy have been described by Winston Bush in his paper, "Income Distribution in Anarchy."

4 For a more extensive discussion of these points, see my paper, "The Samaritan's Dilemma" (1971), to be published in *Economic Theory and Altruism*, edited by Edmund Phelps, Russell Sage Foundation (forthcoming).

5 See Gordon Tullock, "The Charity of the Uncharitable," *Western Economic Journal*, IX (December 1971), 379–91.

6 See Warren J. Samuels, "Interrelations Between Legal and Economic Processes," *Journal of Law and Economics*, XIV, 2 (October 1971), 435–50, and my, "Politics, Property and the Law," *Journal of Law and Economics* (forthcoming).

C Continued

6: THE POLITICAL ECONOMY OF FRANCHISE IN THE WELFARE STATE*

JAMES M. BUCHANAN
Virginia Polytechnic Institute
& State University

I. Pareto Optimal Redistribution

Introduction

In this paper I propose to examine carefully the implications concerning the voting franchise that are contained in the modern concept of Pareto-optimal income redistribution. This concept has been discussed at length in several papers in the late 1960's. I share some of the responsibility for generating this ·interest. In my early review of Musgrave's treatise,[1] I called explicitly for the derivation of a conceptual logic for redistribution that is on all fours with the logic for allocation in the public sector. It seemed inconsistent to me to adopt the stance of modern public finance theorists, exemplified by both Samuelson and Musgrave in somewhat different ways, who attempt to derive criteria for public-sector allocation from individualistic valuations but to reject these criteria for public-sector redistribution.[2] Hochman and Rodgers, in their much-cited paper, and Edgar Olsen, independently, responded, directly or indirectly to my suggestion. They attempted to construct a theory of income redistribution or a theory of transfers on the basis of individual utility interdependence.[3] This theory is open to either

Capitalism and Freedom: Problems and Prospects (R. Selden, ed.), Charlottesville, Va., Univ. Press of Virginia, 1975, pp. 52–77.

positive or normative interpretation, as "explaining" what is observed to take place through the fiscal process or as indicating what should take place under a regime characterized by utility interdependence of the sort postulated. Implicit in either interpretation, however, is the limitation of membership in the "fiscal club" of donors or potential donors. To the members of the donor group, whose utility functions contain arguments for the income or utility levels of other persons who are poor, the transfer of income to the latter group becomes a purely public good. And because of the jointness and non-exclusion attributes, a case is established, prima facie, for cooperative action, whether this is organized voluntaristically or politically.

If collective action takes its organizational form via political or governmental process, however, implications for the voting franchise are raised at the outset. If, in fact, the political decision mechanism is to serve, even to some remote approximation, as a surrogate for the idealized collective-cooperative fiscal club of potential donors, the voting franchise must be restricted to potential taxpayers, to those whose utility functions contain or might contain arguments for the income levels of poorer members of the larger community. Those persons to whom income transfers are to be made cannot be allowed to participate in the collective decision concerning the extent of this transfer itself since their own private interest will, of course, be unidirectional.

Elementary Analytics

Consider a community of $n + 1$ persons, composed of n i's and a single j. Each of the i's ($i = 1, 2, \cdots, n$) has the same utility function, which contains an argument for the income of j, designated in an all-purpose consumption good which also is the numeraire,

$$U^i = U^i (Y^i, Y^j), \tag{1}$$

where the Y's represent all-purpose consumption goods. Since the Y^j enters the utility functions of all i's, and since it is nonpartitionable among the i's, it qualifies as a purely public good in the Samuelsonian sense. The necessary condition for efficiency is familiar,

$$\sum_{i=1}^{n} \frac{u^i_{Y^j}}{u^i_{Y^i}} = 1, \tag{2}$$

where the small u's refer to the partial derivatives of the utility function. This condition states that the summed marginal evaluations over all i's, evaluated in the numeraire, equals marginal cost, which is simply one, owing to the monetary dimensionality of Y^j.

The satisfaction of (2) may be but need not be accompanied by the fulfillment of (3),

$$\frac{u^i_{Y^j}}{u^i_{Y^i}} = \frac{1}{n} \text{ for all } i. \tag{3}$$

If (2) is met, the Pareto frontier is attained since there exists no means of shifting from this position so as to improve the position of any person without harming another. All gains from trade in the most inclusive sense are exhausted, and, even allowing for full side payments at zero transactions costs, there is no proposal for change that could command unanimous agreement of all parties.

Note, however, that this seemingly straightforward application of the standard norm for public-goods efficiency does not contain the evaluation placed on the income transfer by the potential recipient, j.[4, 5] Since we are treating transfers of income or general purchasing power, it is clear that the marginal evaluation placed on a dollar's additional transfer by j will, at all levels, be a dollar, or,

$$\frac{u^j_{Y^j}}{u^j_{Y^j}} = 1. \tag{4}$$

If we now incorporate this evaluation of j into the summation over all members of the community, the necessary condition for efficiency seems to be,

$$\sum_{i,j=1}^{n+1} \frac{u^{i,j}_{Y^j}}{u^{i,j}_{Y^i}} = 1. \tag{5}$$

But (2) and (5) are not satisfied at equivalent levels of income transfer to j. In order to satisfy (5), the summed marginal evaluations over the i's, alone, must equal zero, or,

$$\sum_{i=1}^{n} \frac{u^i_{Y^j}}{u^i_{Y^i}} = 0. \tag{6}$$

When (6) is met, there is no utility interdependence at the margin. Note that *both* (2) and (5) describe positions on the Pareto welfare surface. These positions do not, of course, exhaust the Pareto set. *Any* level of income transfer at or beyond that which satisfies (2) will produce a result that qualifies as a Pareto-optimal position. Once attained, there will exist no means of changing or shifting from any such position under an idealized unanimity rule, when *both* the i's and the j's are franchised.

If the evaluation of recipients is included, note that (5) is *not* a necessary condition for Pareto-optimality. Summed marginal evaluations need not equal marginal cost. This apparent paradox arises from the particular nature of pure income transfers, and this nonuniqueness in outcomes makes the application of the standard tools difficult. For purposes of comparison, consider the collective or public provision of a lighthouse-type purely public good. In this latter instance, absent transactions costs and income-effect feedbacks, any departure from that allocation which satisfies the equivalent to (5) will set forces in motion that will return the system to the unique position where (5) is met.[6] No such equilibrating forces can emerge with pure income transfers because, despite a possible willingness of the donors, as a group, to offer amounts differing from a dollar for a dollar's change upward or downward in the amount of income transfer, such offer cannot be accepted by the recipient(s) since this total, also, must be computed as part of the transfer. In one sense, therefore, the condition defined by (5) alone is meaningless because, operationally, it is not different from any other among a subinfinity of positions.

By contrast, for the i's treated as a group, the members of which evaluate the transfer of income to j as a public or collective-consumption good, condition (2) is fully analogous to the orthodox efficiency norm in public-goods provision. Any change from that position defined or described by the satisfaction of (2) will set equilibrating tendencies in motion that will shift the outcome back to the equilibrium position, provided, of course, that the restricted assumptions about transactions costs and income-effect feedbacks are maintained.

Public Choice Implications

The formal analysis is simple enough, but its implications for the problems of collective decision-making must be examined. Three quarters of a century have passed since Knut Wicksell admonished his fellow economists for their failure to relate economic policy norms to the political setting within which policy takes place.[7] He accused economists of assuming that policy is made by an "enlightened and benevolent despot," whose criteria are those provided to him by pure-minded professors. Wicksell's strictures are almost wholly applicable in the current professional and quasi-professional discourse on income redistribution policy. The pros and cons of the various income maintenance plans, sometimes called negative income taxes, are discussed with little or no reference to the political-choice process.[8] In this context, the preliminary attempts to develop criteria for politically-implemented income redistribution from individual evaluations represent advance over the naivete inherent in the invocation of external value norms. These attempts have remained seriously incomplete, however, because of the failure to relate the analysis directly to the political decision mechanism, either that which is potential or in being.

In order to discuss this relationship systematically, it is useful to digress briefly and summarize the elementary methodology of the Pareto criterion itself. An initial or existing state of the economy is described by an imputation (assignment, allocation, distribution) of "goods" (positive and negative) among persons in the relevant community. In the normal case, individualized shares in total product are assumed to consist in full-fledged claims to the disposition of "goods" as their "owners" see fit, although behavioral limitations may be incorporated into the definitions without difficulty. Similarly, the "goods" are usually assumed to be fully partitionable among separate persons although, once again, the existence of joint and common ownership rights may be embodied in the appropriate definitions. In all cases, however, the imputation defines a structure of rights or claims that is presumed to be known with certainty. If individuals are informed about the qualities of the "goods" assigned to them, and if they are assumed to be rational utility maximizers, the private behavior of each person carries him to what we may call the nonexchange utility possibility frontier. That is to say, all gains from internal "trade" will be exhausted in the private or presocial behavioral calculus of individuals.

The Pareto criterion, whether applied to a classification of final positions, described by imputations of "goods" among persons, or to a distinction among changes from one position to another, is rooted in interpersonal or social *exchange*, the central institution that is analyzed variously in economic theory. Given any imputation, the Pareto criterion enables us to classify this into the nonoptimal or the optimal set.[9] If it is nonoptimal, it enables us also to calssify proposed moves or shifts as efficient or inefficient. The criterion can be applied positively to the observation of behavior as well as conceptually on the presumption that individual utility functions are known. Individuals, endowed with initial imputations, are presumed to engage in simple or ordinary trades that will shift the system in the direction of the Pareto frontier, exploiting the potentially available surplus obtainable. The Pareto norm can be utilized to assess the results of such trades, but its potential usefulness is found largely in the location and isolation of possible complex trading arrangements that may not emerge from the simpler trading processes. These complex trading prospects may, and normally will, involve simultaneous agreement on the part of more than two parties, and they may include trades in the form of "agreements" to change the rules or institutions within which orthodox trading can take place.

The Donor Cooperative or Club. If this summary description of the Pareto criterion is provisionally accepted, what can be said about "Pareto-optimal income redistribution"? Commencing from some initial imputation, unilateral transfers in some numeraire good (income) might be observed to take place voluntarily if utility functions exhibit interdependence.[10] Some such transfers would take place under wholly independent behavior but, as noted, there may exist both jointness and nonexclusion attributes that suggest superior results from joint or cooperative action. Potential donors would, in this setting, organize and join a voluntary cooperative for the purpose of making transfers to those persons designated as being eligible for "charity." The latter would, however, remain external to the acting donor group or club, and these recipients would treat the transfers as purely gratuitous. They could scarcely be expected to participate in decisions concerning the amount of transfer they receive and, of course, their evaluation of the transfer will not directly influence the decision of the donors.

Within the cooperative donor group or club, decisions must be made on the amount of transfer along with the distribution of the costs among individual members. In aggregate terms, the necessary condition for efficiency is that defined by (2) above. In a setting without decision-making costs, the group would operate under some effective rule of unanimity. Condition (2) would be satisfied, along with that defined in (3) for a set of equal i's. If members of the donor club should differ in preferences for income transfers, the equivalent of condition (3) would, of course, involve differing marginal costs among members. Decision-making costs exist, however, and these become significant where groups must reach agreement. Hence, even in purely voluntary donor clubs members might acquiesce in agreed-on, nonunanimity decision rules. Departure from unanimity removes any assurance that the aggregative marginal condition for efficiency, defined in (2), will be satisfied, or that the individualistic marginal conditions, defined in (3) or its equivalent, will be fulfilled. The voluntary nature of the arrangement embodied in the right of any member to withdraw unilaterally insures, however, that each person secure net gains from his participation. That is,

$$\int_0^T \frac{u^j_{Y^j}}{u^i_{Y^i}} \geq 1, \tag{7}$$

for all i's, where T measures the amount of income transfer to j by the fiscal club of the i's.[11]

In this more comprehensive setting that does allow for decision-making costs, the level of income transfer from donor groups to recipients under a regime of voluntary cooperative groups might appropriately be designated as "Pareto optimal." Conceptually, this seems to have been the organizational model assumed by several of those who have participated in the recent discussion.

Governmental Analogues to Voluntary Donor Cooperative. The observed institutional framework for much income redistribution is not voluntary; it is political or governmental. The analysis must somehow bridge the gap between voluntary and coercive organizational structure. How can analysis based on voluntary exchange, and utilizing the Pareto criterion, be extended to apply to political or governmental structure, since the latter must be, in its nature, coercive?

There are three institutions that would allow governmentally-determined income transfers to be brought under orthodox Pareto norms, and to be treated *as if* such transfers emerged from voluntary fiscal clubs with only minor variants. In each case, we make the preliminary and necessary assumption that decisions are made democratically through some voting process in which many persons participate, directly or indirectly. This rules out authoritarian decision-making on the part of governments.

Model I. In the first model, we can assume that a genuine rule of unanimity is operative, at least with respect to redistribution policy, and that all persons in the community have the voting franchise, both potential donors and potential recipients of transfers. The restrictiveness of unanimity may be relaxed sufficiently to allow for representative processes provided that the legislators selected represent all interests and that the unanimity requirement holds within the legislative assembly.

Commencing from an initial imputation of goods among persons, and with no voluntary redistribution, we may consider the results of an idealized decision process. It is clear that representatives of donors and recipients would agree on a level of income transfer that would satisfy condition (2) above. Proposals for additional income transfers beyond this level would be opposed by donor interests. Such extensions would, of course, be supported by representatives of recipient groups, as indeed would all proposals for additional transfers within meaningful limits. The political process would in this model accomplish essentially identical objectives as the cooperative or voluntary clubs organization discussed earlier. In practical fact, however, a political decision-structure organized in that fashion would probably generate a lower level of total income transfer than the alternative regime of wholly voluntary fiscal clubs. In the latter, the voluntary participation feature would make individual donors more acquiescent in departures from effective unanimity as a means of allowing some reduction in group decision costs. In political organization, departures from unanimity would be more strongly resisted.

Model II. Consider now a second model in which politically-determined income transfers might be discussed in an orthodox setting of Pareto optimality. If a regime of competitive governmental units exists, and if persons may shift membership among these at relatively little personal costs, each political unit may embody both an inclusive voting franchise and departures from an effective unanimity rule for collective choice while generating results that are akin to those broadly predictable under voluntary organization. This model is applicable, however, only in those situations where the utility interdependence, if such exists, involves members of the same "local" governmental jurisdiction. In this sort of setting, income redistribution takes on most of the properties of a "localized public good," and a Tiebout-like adjustment process places severe limits on the possible inefficiency that can emerge regardless of internal political decision rules.[12]

Model III. A third model is one in which the voting franchise is specifically limited to those who are actual or potential contributors or donors in the income-transfer system, that is, net taxpayers rather than net beneficiaries. In this model, those who receive income transfers are explicitly excluded from participation in the collective or governmental decisions that are concerned with either the level or the financing of the transfers. In this setting, income transfers to the "poor," treated here as an external group, can be analyzed as a purely public good whose benefits and costs are shared among members of the potential taxpayer and hence voting, group in the community. If, among this restricted set of persons, an effective rule of unanimity prevails for collective decisions, a regime closely analogous to that of voluntary clubs exists, with the differences previously noted. If the costs of decision-making suggest significant departures from unanimity, and if individual members of the group do not have available low-cost migrational alternatives, the moves or shifts in income distribution emerging from the political process may not be Pareto-superior. If, for example, a majority coalition, among the potential taxpayer group, desires to redistribute substantial income to the poor outside the voting group, at the expense of all potential taxpayers, the minority of the latter may suffer genuine fiscal exploitation. Nonetheless, the majority coalition need not act in such fashion, and the disenfranchisement of the transfer recipients removes the direct influence of those whose strictly private self-interest dictates extensions in transfers at all levels. Under such conditions, it seems plausible to treat observed political outcomes as indirect surrogates for something akin to genuinely voluntary transfers.

II. Property in Franchise

Observation tells us that none of the three models sketched briefly above describes the real world. What we do observe is politically-determined redistribution of income at jurisdictional levels that guarantee high-cost migrational alternatives and under the operation of decision rules that are basically majoritarian rather than unanimitarian. We observe, furthermore, that transfer recipients are not excluded from voting and otherwise participating in politics, including the politics of transfer policy itself. In this realistic setting, the Pareto criterion must either be judged of relatively little value in analyzing transfers or it must be modified substantially from its standard application.

Recall our summary of the methodology of the Pareto norm. Individuals in the social group are described in terms of an imputation or assignment of "goods," with well-defined limits as to rights of disposition. The orthodox Pareto criterion assists in evaluating or in proposing changes that involve simple and/or complex "trades" in these assigned "goods" among separate members of the community. I now think that this traditional approach that has been taken by many political economists, including me, has been seriously deficient. The deficiency may be identified and discussed in terms of the problems considered in this paper.

Nominal and Real Claims

In the distributional setting as observed in the real world, "goods" are *not* partitioned among separate persons (families) in the well-defined sense that is implicitly postulated in the standard analysis. To indicate this, I propose to distinguish "nominal" and "real" imputations or assignments over final "goods," over rights to the use of "goods." What we may actually observe, at any moment, is a set of nominal rights, which may be defined by an imputation, which may or may not accurately map the initial position or basis from which simple and complex trades among persons must commence. Alongside and accompanying the set of nominal claims over "goods," there exists a *membership* right in the social group or community, which may or may not be accompanied by a *voting* right in group or collective decisions. Both the membership right and the voting right have economic value to the holders, an economic value that takes its meaning in terms of some contingent claim on the "common fund" of "goods" available in the whole community.

Membership rights and voting rights are separate, and, in some cases, the distinction is important.[13]   But for purposes of this paper, these rights accompany each other; we simply assume that membership in the social group implies voting rights. What we observe, then, is a set of nominal claims, partitioned among persons and/or families in the group, along with universal and uniform voting rights (political equality) over all adults in the community. The latter rights take economic value in our model only through the indirect claims that they might represent over the total resource stock in the economy, all of which we assume is partitioned among persons in the nominal sense. For purposes of simplifying the analysis, we assume that there are no joint-consumption goods, no public goods of the standard variety.

Constitutional Restrictions

The value that a voting-membership right has for its holder depends on several things, including the allowable range for collective or political action. This will be defined by a political constitution, which may or may not be formally specified. We limit consideration in this paper to redistributional policy, and we specify the effective constitutional requirements to be as follows:

(1) Income redistribution shall be general rather than discriminatory, and redistribution, if it occurs, must take the form of transfers from higher to lower income categories, with equalization as the limit.

(2) No person in the recipient group who stands lower on the income scale before political redistribution shall secure less in total transfer than another who stands higher on the scale.

(3) No person in the taxpaying group who stands lower on the income scale before political redistribution shall be taxed by a higher amount than another who stands higher on the scale.

(4) Collective decisions are reached through simple majority voting.

These requirements seem plausible on their own account, as well as realistic if we confine attention to pure income transfer policy. Basically, these requirements state that arbitrarily composed political coalitions may not exploit minorities. "Regressive" and nondiscriminatory transfers as well as taxes are ruled out. Taken together, these requirements add stability to the expectations about redistribution policy, and they enable us to define more clearly the value of the membership-voting franchise.

No Production—No Utility Interdependence

I assume initially that there is no utility interdependence of the sort adduced to "explain" observed income transfers under the orthodox Pareto constructions discussed in Part One. In the absence of collective action, therefore, each person (family) retains all the "goods" under his assignment in the nominal sense. I assume, further, that agreed-on laws against theft are enforced perfectly. Finally, I assume in this model that the initial assignment of "goods" falls as manna with a distribution that is unchanging from one period to the next. "Goods" are not "produced" by human effort.[14]

Under the restricted conditions postulated, simple majority voting will generate an amount and type of income redistribution determined by the median income recipient acting to further his own position. His problem is one of simple maximization subject to the constitutional constraints imposed. In the no-production economy majority voting will tend to equalize all posttransfer incomes above and including the median and to equalize all positive transfers to persons below and including the median.

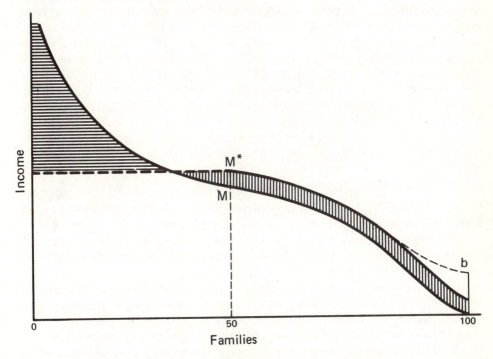

Figure 1
Constrained majority transfers in the no-production economy

Figure 1 depicts family distribution in a community in a shape that is similar to that which describes distribution in the United States. The median is located at M. If, in fact, this pattern should describe a distribution in a no-production setting, and if the constitutional limits were those indicated, the posttransfer income distribution would be shown by the dotted curve. The transfer to the median family, measured by MM* would be maximized subject to the constraints suggested, including the necessity that the two shaded areas be equal in size, that is to say, that the transfer budget be balanced.

We may now look at the value of the voting franchise to a person along the income scale in this model. It is clear that the franchise has value only through its indirect influence on the location of the median voter. Disenfranchisement of, say, persons at the lower levels of income would shift M leftwards on the diagram and the distance analogous to MM* would be smaller. This would impose monetary costs on all transfer recipients, not only those who might suffer disenfranchisement as such. Similarly, disenfranchisement of persons at the upper end of the scale would shift the median rightwards in the diagram. This would increase the amount of tax paid by each taxpayer, increase the number of taxpayers, increase the total amount of transfer, and increase the positive transfers received per recipient.

It may be noted from the construction of Figure 1 that, in the conditions of this model, the median voter will be harmed by the disenfranchisement of voters at either end of the scale; he will suffer from any shift of the median. A shift to the right will equalize incomes at and above the new median, but this must be at a lower level. A shift of the median to the left will reduce the total tax revenue collections while simultaneously increasing the number of recipients. This must involve a reduction in the amount of transfer per recipient, and hence the amount received by the initial median voter. It will not, therefore, be to the direct interest of the established median voter, presumed here to be the median pretransfer income recipient, to extend or to limit the franchise asymmetrically. He will, of course, be indifferent as to symmetrical changes.

No Production with Utility Interdependence

The introduction of utility interdependence into this model will have less effect on the results than might have been anticipated. The preference of certain upper income receivers for greater amounts of transfer than that emergent in the no interdependence framework will have an effect similar to their own disenfranchisement. The effective median position shifts to the right, with the results indicated above. Note particularly that this sort of utility interdependence will not allow for the inverse discrimination represented by larger transfers to the lowest pretransfer income recipients so long as the effective median voter's preference does not exhibit a concern for the utility of those standing lower along the pretransfer income scale. There will be no flaring of the dotted curve upwards as traced out by the extended segment shown by *b* in Figure 1. If such a flaring is to be produced, this must arise because of utility interdependence of voters in median income ranges, at least if we confine analysis to this very simple political choice model.

Production without Utility Interdependence

The introduction of production will drastically change the model. Instead of "goods" being initially distributed as manna, we now assume that "goods" are produced exclusively by human effort, and that the initially generated distribution is the same as before. In this model, the amount of redistribution that becomes rational for the median income recipient, and median voter, will be directly dependent on the incentive effects that taxation will exert on those from whom funds are to be exacted politically. It will clearly be inefficient to levy more than a revenue maximizing tax on any person. Hence, we should predict that the posttax distribution of income will reflect some inequality throughout the scale under the constitutional restrictions previously postulated. Figure 2 depicts the situation. The heavy curved line indicates the pretransfer distribution of initially received incomes *after* income earning adjustments to the transfers have been made. The dotted curve indicated the posttransfer distribution.

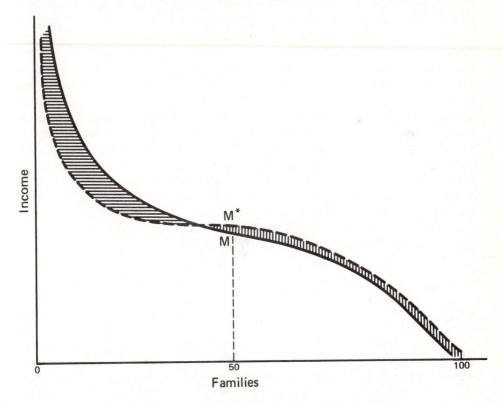

Figure 2
Constrained majority transfers in a production economy

As in the no production model, the median voter faces a constrained maximization problem. He will try to maximize the net transfer to him, shown by MM*. Let us assume that the dotted curve over the net taxpayer group represents the strict revenue maximizing locus. We want now to examine effects of a shift in the franchise as before. If persons at the lower extremities of the scale are disenfranchised, the median shifts to the left, as before, but note that this will have no effect on the total tax levied on those at the upper extremities of the scale. This is because these persons are, in all cases, being subjected to the revenue maximizing tax. Shifts in the median will not, therefore, modify their final positions. In such case, however, these highest income recipients will be totally indifferent as to whether or not they exercise their own franchise. The vote will have no value to them and they may be observed either to neglect the exercise of franchise or, more likely, to fulfill a presumed internal moral commitment by affecting to exhibit great concern for those at lower income levels.[15]

If this reaction on the part of the highest income recipients is fully recognized by the median voter, however, this, in itself, will cause the latter to refrain from imposing taxes at the strict revenue maximizing level. High income recipients will be taxed at a level sufficiently below such limits as to insure their attention to the voting process. The potential upward mobility in the income scale that enters into the expectations of the median voter will also modify or mitigate against impositions of taxes at the revenue maximizing limits.

In this model we should also note that changes in the location of the median voter along the income scale, brought about by voluntary voting abstention, utility interdependence, or explicit disenfranchisement, will not affect the net transfer to recipients at the lowest end of the scale nearly so much as in the no production setting. Because the highest income recipients are likely to be taxed at or near revenue maximizing limits regardless of the location of the median, over broad middle ranges, this source of funds remains invariant. Shifts in the median will affect the transfer per recipient slightly, but the primary effect will be that of shifting the break-even position, where a person is changed from a net taxpayer to a net beneficiary of the transfer scheme.

Democratic Income Transfers and Pareto Norms

It is tempting to extend the majoritarian transfer models, to introduce further qualifications, and to modify the assumptions. All of this offers challenging subject matter for the application of the tools of public choice theory. My purpose here, however, is neither such elaboration nor defense of the particular models chosen. Rather it is to relate the basic majoritarian transfer process to the Pareto criterion framework within which income transfers were discussed in Part I. As noted, I now recognize a serious deficiency in the standard application of the Pareto norms, and I want to discuss this deficiency explicitly with reference to the models introduced above.

Orthodox procedure would classify the income transfers generated by the working of pure majority voting rules, or by any political process that may reasonably be described by this model, as being coercive in nature, and, as such, clearly violative of the Pareto criterion as the latter is applied to changes or moves among positions. That is to say, a pure majoritarian transfer of income under the constitutional restrictions suggested would qualify as a "nonsuperior" move. I now think that this is an overly restricted usage of the Pareto norm, even as applied to changes. As I have noted at several places, the Pareto criterion, strictly speaking, is applicable only when the nominal imputation of "goods" among persons represents accurately the "real" set of claims or rights of persons over the final disposition of these "goods." It is erroneous, however, to acknowledge a nominal imputation as "real" in a setting that allows for income redistribution under collective or governmental auspices.

Consider, for example, the position of a single high income recipient. His nominal claim over the disposition of "goods" may be, relatively, very large indeed. But he secures (or earns) this nominal income in a polity (economy) that has extended universal and uniform suffrage to all its adult members. Furthermore, this recipient of the nominally high income cannot, by assumption, shift to alternative polities (economies) without undergoing major costs. In a very genuine sense, therefore, the high income recipient does not possess a full-fledged "property right" to the "goods" over which his nominal income apparently gives him claim. By the very nature of their simple voting or potential voting membership in a polity (economy) that constitutionally allows income transfers to take place under collective aegis, *all* other members in the community hold a contingent claim on the "goods" purchasable by the nominal income of the person in question. Hence, to say that the recipient of a nominally high income actively opposes a majoritarian transfer policy that makes him a net taxpayer and that this behavior, in itself, reveals that the policy does not reflect a Pareto-superior move or change, tends to obscure the underlying nature or basis of the complex interaction that is involved here. The majoritarian transfer can be viewed merely as the working out of the "real" set of claims to income in the community, the revision in the nominal set of claims predictable under the political structure in being, which includes "property rights" in franchise. The observed opposition of the rich man to transfer policy is akin to that of the person who has to pay an obligation previously made. Since the nominal income is not "his" by any "real" rights of ownership in the first place, his opposition can hardly be adduced in evidence that the transfer is violative of a meaningful welfare norm. To the extent that such a transfer appeared to violate clearly the Pareto criterion, as applied to the orthodox sense, many economists have rejected the Pareto framework in application to the whole set of issues involving income redistribution. Having no alternative, many of those who reject the Pareto criterion have sought to introduce external ethical norms to apply to all redistribution policy.

My own work, as well as those who have advanced the analysis of so-called "Pareto-optimal redistribution," has suffered in the opposite sense. Because political transfers seem to violate the standard Pareto norms, we have tended to opt out of any discussion and to say that nothing further can be constructed on the basis of individual evaluations. I now propose to modify this stance, and to do so in a substantial sense. Failure to carry out income transfer policy in a political setting such as that sketched out in the models above would represent a fundamental shift in the real assignment of rights, a shift in favor of those with the nominally higher incomes. Once the franchise has been extended to all adults, and once the constitution has allowed income transfers to take place collectively, the formal act of transfer becomes fully predictable from positive economic analysis. The basic property right inheres in the voting franchise, and the economic value of this franchise reflects the measure of the contingent claim to the incomes and wealth nominally imputed to individuals in the whole community.[16]

Pareto Optimality and the Status Quo

To this point, the income transfers from the nominally rich to the nominally poor that are predicted to occur under a democratic polity are derived from individual evaluations without normative content. The Pareto norms have not been utilized to evaluate these transfers, other than in the negative commentary suggesting their inapplicability. We may now, however, try to evaluate such redistribution in terms of the Paretian criteria. Is the institutional structure which embodies pure majoritarian transfers itself Pareto optimal? Does there exist a means of changing this structure that is Pareto superior; that is, does there exist any proposed change in constitutional-institutional rules that would, conceptually, command the assent of all members of the community?

At first glance, these questions may seem to reflect a return to the orthodox Pareto framework, which I have explicitly criticized. There is a major difference, however, which should be stressed. Paretian criteria have often been criticized because they lend support to the status quo. In a sense, this charge is correct, but my own response has always been that "we start from here," from the status quo, and, willy nilly, this constrains our analysis. The error in my own earlier methodological position has been my initial definition of the status quo, or starting point, in terms of a presumed imputation of "goods" among persons that ignores the political process in being and the genuine claims to "goods" inherent in this process.[17] This is properly to be regarded as much a part of the status quo as is any strictly defined nominal imputation. Having redefined the status quo, the Pareto criterion can be applied in the standard manner.[18]

It seems clear that any restriction on the voting franchise, once this has been universally extended, is nonoptimal; such a shift would harm some members of the community. Under universal franchise, we may then ask whether any of the constitutional constraints can be modified to the advantage of all parties. If we limit attention to income redistribution alone, and leave other collective activity out of account, there seems no apparent change that would qualify as Pareto superior. If this is the case, the total regime as described can be classified as Pareto optimal.

III. Impure Redistribution

The whole approach of Part II may be questioned, however, as regards its descriptive accuracy. Can the political process that we observe in the real world be approximated in such models, even if we accept the necessity of extreme simplicity and abstraction? Presumably, little distortion is created by the assumptions of universal suffrage. Effective majority voting rules, even when the complexities of actual political decision making are acknowledged, seem broadly acceptable in the context of the discussion here. The presence of high cost migrational alternatives can scarcely be challenged with reference to redistribution policy at the national government level.

More serious issues may be raised concerning the specific constitutional restrictions imposed on redistribution policy itself. We do not observe much "pure" income redistribution in the absence of collective provision of real goods and services. When the allocative role of the political sector is included in the analysis of distributional outcomes, quite different results may emerge. A more acceptable and alternative model would allow tax funds to be used (1) for financing publicly-supplied or publicly-subsidized real goods and services; or (2) for financing pure income transfers. In this setting, it may be to the advantage of the median voter-cum-income recipient to choose (1) rather than (2). This offers a means of escaping from constitutional restriction on regressively discriminatory transfers in the numeraire. While it may not be possible to discriminate in favor of the median voters by grants of larger absolute amounts of money than those offered to persons standing lower on the nominal income scale, the same purposes may be accomplished by choosing for public or governmental supply that set of real goods and services which is most highly valued by median voters. Once supplied, these goods and services may be available on equal terms to all members of the community, but the actual distribution of benefits, as valued, may be skewed dramatically toward middle income ranges.

This may be illustrated in Figure 3. The curve, Y_n, as before, depicts the nominal income distribution, after behavioral adjustments but before transfers. The curve, Y_d, represents the most preferred pure distributional scheme for the median voter under the constitutional restrictions imposed in

Part II. The curve, Y_p, depicts the alternative curve of effective final distribution under the regime that allows for collective provision of real goods and services. Note that Y_p falls *along* Y_d over high income ranges, and *below* Y_d over low income ranges.

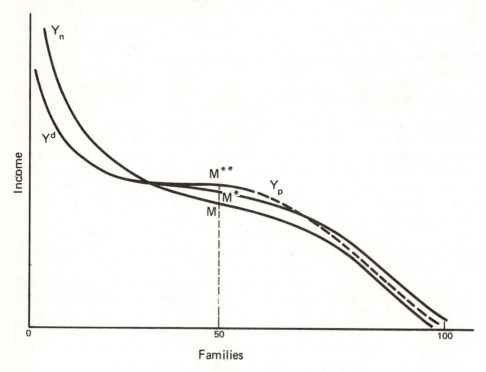

Figure 3
Unconstrained majority transfers

This alternative model of impure redistribution is in accord with the hypotheses advanced by Aaron Director, George Stigler, and Gordon Tullock, which suggest that the major beneficiaries of transfer policies are those in the median income ranges rather than the very poor. In neither of the basic models here do the "poor," as a group, possess decisive power via the voting process. Under a nondiscriminatory constitutional requirement, however, the very poor could do as well in terms of absolute pure transfers as median income recipients. This outcome is circumvented to the extent that in-kind goods and services are offered governmentally that are differentially valued by the median voters. Public education, at all levels, seems to provide the example here.

IV. Conclusions

Much of the confusion in the discussion of income redistribution stems from an inconsistency between our economic and our political attitudes. On the one hand, the ethics of capitalism suggest that the market earnings of resources become the property of the nominal owners, who may, presumably, dispose of these as they, personally, desire. They may, of course, select to worry about their fellows, but in such an attitudinal framework "charity" is merely another consumption "good." Any politically-determined transfer of income above minimal limits involves a coercive "taking." At the same time, however, the ethics of democracy suggest that restrictions on franchise are not to be tolerated. Few seem to have recognized the implications of the inconsistency between these value positions.

The inconsistency appears in its starkest form in redistribution policy, and it is the basis for the neoclassical dichotomy between allocation and distribution. Economists claim competence in defining and in identifying allocative efficiency, using as inputs the revealed (actually or conceptually) preferences (values) of individuals. They stop short when faced with distribution, and they often pull in external and nonindividualistic norms which they acknowledge to be less "scientific" than those introduced for the theory of allocation. Efficiency in allocation is defined to characterize a position where all of the potentially realizable surplus has been squeezed out of simple and complex trading arrangements. Essentially, this procedure is to describe the end point of a process, and economists have not carefully considered the starting point. Implicitly, they postulate an initial distribution of endowments and/or capacities among persons, and it is presumed that this imputation can be mapped directly into a set of final imputations of "goods" on the Pareto welfare surface. As noted, efforts have been made to bring this basic Pareto efficiency framework into the evaluation of distribution but without much success, largely because, here too, economists have not escaped from the inconsistency noted.

In this paper, I have tried to reconcile the inconsistency by going back to the starting point, and to call into question the orthodox definition of that imputation from which trade commences. If membership in a socio-political community carries with it a valued "right" of participation, this value must be somehow incorporated into any exhaustive partitioning of "potential goods" among persons, even if it is fully recognized that such value can, at best, be probabilistically estimated or determined. This procedure allows us, at least conceptually, to examine both allocation and distribution problems within a coherent analytical framework. The fact that the analysis, at all stages, becomes much more difficult, and perhaps less aesthetically satisfying, should not deter serious scholarship. Like it or not, we live in an environment where the workings and forms of capitalism are tempered by the workings and forms of majoritarian democracy.

FOOTNOTES

*I am indebted to both Winston Bush and Gordon Tullock for comments.
[1] "The Theory of Public Finance," *Southern Economic Journal*, 26 (January 1960), 234–238.

[2] In his now-classic formulation, Samuelson defined the necessary conditions for allocative efficiency with public-goods provision and then introduced a social welfare function to determine the final distribution. See Paul A. Samuelson, "The Pure Theory of Public Expenditures," *Review of Economics and Statistics*, XXXVI (November 1954), 387–389. Musgrave was less willing to introduce external welfare norms to determine distributional outcomes, but his conceptual separation of the allocation and distribution branches of the budget suggested different normative principles. See R. A. Musgrave, *The Theory of Public Finance* (New York: McGraw Hill, 1959).

[3] Harold M. Hochman and James D. Rodgers, "Pareto Optimal Redistribution," *American Economic Review*, LIX (September 1969), 542–557; Edgar O. Olsen, "A Normative Theory of Transfers," *Public Choice*, VI (Spring 1969), 39–58. The Hochman-Rodgers paper stimulated several comments, both in criticism and in extension. See Paul A. Meyer and J. J. Shipley, "Pareto Optimal Redistribution: Comment," *American Economic Review*, LX (December 1970), 988–990; R. A. Musgrave, "Comment," *American Economic Review* LX (December 1970), 991–993; R. "Comment," *American Economic Review*, LX (December 1970), 995–996; Harold M. Hochman and James D. Rodgers, "Reply," *American Economic Review*, LX (December 1970), 997–1002; E. J. Mishan, "Welfare Economics and Pareto Optimal Redistribution" (Typescript, June 1971).

[4] This has, of course, been recognized. Cf. W. C. Stubblebine, "Redistribution and Wicksellian Unanimity" (Unpublished Note, University of Virginia, 1962); George E. Peterson, "Welfare, Workfare, and Pareto Optimality," *Working Paper 1200-12*, Urban Institute, Washington, D.C. (December 1970).

[5] For simplicity, we assume that j is not concerned about the utility of the i's. That is, j's utility function is written $U^j = U^i (Y^j)$.

[6] This is the collective or public goods equivalent of the Coase theorem. Cf. R. H. Coase, "The Problem of Social Cost," *Journal of Law and Economics* III (1960), 1–44. In the transactions-costs rubric we must, of course, here include free-rider and preference revelation difficulties.

[7] Knut Wicksell, *Finanztheoretische Untersuchungen* (Jena: Gustav Fischer, 1896). Major portions of this work are published in translation as, "A New Principle of Just Taxation," in *Classics in the Theory of Public Finance*, edited by R. A. Musgrave and A. T. Peacock (London: Macmillan, 1958), pp. 72–118. The relevant passages are found on pages 82–87.

[8] There are notable exceptions of this generalization, among which are the contributions of both George Stigler and Gordon Tullock. See George J. Stigler, "Director's Law of Public Income Redistribution," *Journal of Law and Economics*, XIII (April 1970), 1–10; Gordon Tullock, "Welfare for Whom?," *Il Politico*, 33 (December 1968), 748–761, and "Charity of the Uncharitable," *Western Economic Journal*, IX (December 1971), 379–342.

[9] For background discussion, see Ragner Frisch, "On Welfare Theory and Pareto Regions," *International Economic Papers*, 9 (London: Macmillan, 1959), 39–92; and my "The Relevance of Pareto Optimality," *Journal of Conflict Resolution*, 6 (December 1962), 341–354.

[10] Transfers of specific goods, income-in-kind, might also occur. These are not discussed in order to keep the basic analysis simplified.

[11] In a regime of competing fiscal clubs each member must secure net benefits at least equal to that available to him from membership in any other club.

[12] For further discussion, see Mark Pauly, "Income Redistribution as a Local Public Good" (paper mimeographed for COUPE meeting, Fall 1971); and my "Who Should Distribute What in a Federal System" (paper mimeographed for Urban Institute Conference, March 1972).

[13] It is clear, for example, that open and free international migration would stimulate massive migration into nations even if migrants were wholly excluded from the voting franchise. It is precisely the claims that such migrants might make on the "common funds" of the community that provides one of the rational arguments against open migration. See Leland Yeager, "Immigration, Trade, and Factor Price Equilization," *Current Economic Comment*, 20 (August 1958), 3–8.

[14] The model here, and indeed much of the discussion in this Part, is influenced by my colleague, Winston Bush. See his, "Income Distribution in Anarchy" (Mimeographed, Virginia Polytechnic Institute and State University, January 1972).

[15] This explanation of the apparent charitable impulses of the very rich is akin to that offered for other groups by Gordon Tullock in his paper, "The Charity of the Uncharitable," op. cit.

[16] My own recognition of the basic point that the property-rights assignment takes place when the franchise is granted was, so far as I can tell, influenced by two sources. First, the discussion of my colleague, W. C. Stubblebine, in a seminar on property rights made clear that the presence of others in the social group must modify the environment for Crusoe and this must be taken into account in any analysis. See his, "On Property Rights and Institutions" infra (ed.).

Secondly, Nicolaus Tideman, of Harvard University, in a seminar discussion in Blacksburg, Virginia on 19 May 1972 advanced a proposal for using posterior probabilities as a means of getting around the revelation-of-preference problem in public goods settings. In this discussion, Tideman explicitly referred to the notion that, once choice alternatives are introduced for a vote, the property rights of those who hold differing positions on the alternatives have already been modified.

[17] This modification in my own position brings me close to that expressed by Musgrave in his "Comment," cited above, on the Hochman-Rodgers paper. Musgrave suggested that "primary" redistribution occurs as a result of the "social contract" within which political decision-making takes place. He did not, however, attempt to modify the applicability of the Pareto norms. Furthermore, Musgrave's position, as expressed in this "Comment" seems at variance with the explicitly normative stance taken in his presentation of the three-part budget. In that part of their "Reply" relating to Musgrave's criticism Hochman and Rodgers also take a position similar in many respects to that developed in this paper. However, they note, at one point, that "one cannot determine in welfare terms, whether the initial or market-determined distribution of income is satisfactory *until* Pareto optimal transfers have occurred." (P. 999.) This inference is directly contrary to that which emerges from the analysis of this paper. Taking the "property in franchise" approach, we can say that the initial positions from which Pareto-optimal redistribution (defined in the Hochman-Rodgers sense) may take place cannot be established until the political or majoritarian redistribution has occurred.

[18] In a discussion that is directly relevant to this paper, Alan T. Peacock and Charles K. Rowley criticize those who have developed models for Pareto-optimal redistribution on the grounds that the status quo starting point along with difficulties of securing unanimous agreement lend a conservative bias to the whole analysis; a bias that they consider contrary to liberal values. See, "Pareto Optimality and the Political Economy of Liberalism," *Journal of Political Economy*, 80 (May/June 1972), 476–490. Much of their criticism of the Pareto norms vanishes, however, under the reformulation suggested in this paper.

C Continued

7: THE PARITY OF THE ECONOMIC MARKET PLACE*

AARON DIRECTOR
University of Chicago Law School

I

Absolute doctrines are always easier to state and defend than doctrines which have to be limited. The claim which is made for complete laissez faire in the area of discussion is not part of the main tradition of liberalism in the area of economic life. While it is not possible to outline the proper division of labor between political and economic organization, a few preliminary observations on the appropriate scope of the free market seem necessary.

There is, first of all, the field of taxation, which is actually the field of public expenditures the basis of which is redistribution of income. How far this can be carried without ultimately undermining the competitive form of organization is indeed an open issue. But it can take a form which will minimize such undermining. Ideally it should take the form of transfers of money income between families. How far this ideal form can be pushed I do not know. It should further take a form which tends to remove the necessity for redistribution, that is, it should emphasize the goal of greater equality in earning capacity rather than greater equality in the distribution of results.

The main point I wish to make here is to call attention to the unnecessary increase of government activity which derives from the implicit assumption that, whenever there is a political decision to make certain expenditures by families compulsory, or to assure certain minimum stan-

The Journal of Law & Economics, Volume VII, October 1964, pp. 1–10.

dards of consumption, the organization of the resources involved must also be assigned to the state. Instead the test should always be whether the necessary organization is of a type which can be arranged on a competitive basis. A proper regard for this standard would, I believe, reduce significantly the area of political decisions without in any way impairing the equalitarian objectives. In fact, an incidental advantage of the separation would clarify the extent to which actual expenditures do in fact foster equalitarian objectives and the extent to which they reinforce the inequalities which already exist. The point can perhaps be best illustrated with Mill's observations on the organization of education, made, it is true, with the different objective of preventing the growth of uniformity of ideas:

> If the government would make up its mind to require for every child a good education, it might save itself the trouble of providing one. It might leave to parents to obtain the education where and how they pleased, and content itself with helping to pay the school fees of the poorer classes of children, and defraying the entire school expenses of those who have no one to pay them.[1]

Laissez faire has never been more than a slogan in defense of the proposition that every extension of state activity should be examined under a presumption of error. The main tradition of economic liberalism has always assumed a well-established system of law and order designed to harness self-interest to serve the welfare of all. The institution of private property—at least since Hume—has always been defended on this ground. And, wherever it seemed that this institution might be modified without subverting the general framework of a competitive society, the tradition has shown a readiness—perhaps exaggerated—to modify this basic institution. But the tradition goes much beyond this. It has always assumed that there were some economic results which cannot be attained at all or attained only in inappropriate amounts if left to the free market.

The tradition has always been hostile to private monopolies, whether contrived by enterprise or by labor. Inadequate attention to this problem in the earlier period is to be explained by the tacit assumption, which is not without merit, that under neutral rules the market would largely frustrate such contrivances. To the extent that this assumption was shown to be invalid, the tradition has displayed a readiness—although not matched by achievement—to formulate positive rules which will do so.

Where economic services can be provided only by monopoly form of organization because of underlying technical conditions, the liberal bias, in our own day at least, is against private exploitation of such monopolies. Fortunately, the area does not appear to be very extensive. If it were, the conflict between economic freedom and economic efficiency would become significant. Special reference should also be made to the recognition that a suitable monetary framework cannot be provided by competition and that it constitutes one of the requisite legal institutions.

Having noted these qualifications or "concessions," it is now in point to restate the "presumption-of-error doctrine." Every qualification is made because of some deficiency in the free-market type of organization. But every deficiency is met by an extension of state activity. It has been well said: "It is not possible to be continually taking steps toward socialism without one day arriving at the goal."

In this respect there is a remarkable similarity between the underlying basis for complete laissez faire in the market for ideas and the market for economic goods and services. The absolute doctrine of the first is defended even though it necessitates the protection of speech which no reasonable man wants or should want to see protected. But there is great wisdom in Justice Douglas' eloquent observation on the danger of encroaching interference:

> The Court in this and in other cases places speech under an expanding legislative control. Today a white man stands convicted for protesting in unseemly language against our decisions invalidating restrictive covenants. Tomorrow a Negro will be haled before a court for denouncing lynch law in heated terms. Farm laborers in the West who compete with field hands drifting up from Mexico; whites who feel the pressure of orientals; a minority which finds employment going to members of the dominant religious group—all of these are caught in the mesh of today's decision.[2]

II

The free market as a desirable method of organizing the intellectual life of the community was urged long before it was advocated as a desirable method of organizing its economic life. The advantage of free exchange of ideas was recognized before that of the voluntary exchange of goods and services in competitive markets. The explanation lies perhaps in the greater complexity of the theory of the market for goods and services, which came only with the actual emergence of a substantial amount of competition.

Moreover, freedom of speech and belief was advocated long before the growth of democracy. And Hume and Smith, the leading theorists of the competitive system, were not democrats. With Bentham and James Mill the argument for freedom merges with that for democracy. And this in a peculiar manner. Leslie Stephen tells us that liberty "means sometimes simply the diminution of the sphere of law and the power of legislators, or, again, the transference to subjects of the power of legislating, and therefore, not less control, but control by self-made laws alone."[3] Bentham and Mill argued for liberty in the second sense on the ground, as Bentham put it, of "responsibility to persons whose interest, whose obvious and recognisable interest, accords with the end in view—good government." [4]   And such identity of interest he found in nothing less than the numerical majority.   Bentham was not only a great reformer of the law but also a rigorous advocate of liberty in the sense of a diminution of the sphere of law and the power of legislators.   The argument for this was the same as that for democracy—interest.   "The interest which a man takes in the affairs of another, a member of the sovereignty for example in those of a subject, is not likely to be so great as the interest which either of them takes in his own: still less where that other is a perfect stranger to him." [5]   To this Bentham added the advantage of superior knowledge which is correlated with interest and the very shrewd remark that, if the "statesman were better acquainted with the interest of the trader than the trader himself, . . . simple information would be sufficient to produce the effect without any exercise of power." [6]

No conflict between the two types of freedom was at first expected. In point of fact democracy was expected to reinforce the other type of freedom.

Any Englishman at the end of the eighteenth century who, says Leslie Stephen, the historian of utilitarianism, demanded more power for the people "always took for granted their power would be used to diminish the activity of the sovereign power; that there would be less government and therefore less snobbery, less interference with free speech and free action, and smaller perquisites to be bestowed in return for the necessary services. The people would use their authority to tie the hands of the rulers, and limit them strictly to their proper and narrow functions." [7]

No conflict between the two types of freedom did in fact arise for a considerable period of time, and, when John Stuart Mill wrote the celebrated essay *On Liberty*, it was not to encroachment on individual liberty through legislation that he directed his eloquence but to the tyranny of public opinion.   This was also the main theme of Tocqueville's famous book which significantly strengthened Mill's own views on the dangers of democracy.

The subsequent decline of the attachment to individualism as dogma, and the gradual replacement of freedom in economic affairs by collectivist (*i. e.*, political) forms of organization, was admirably traced by Dicey first at the end of the century and again in 1914.   The further extension of collectivism in our time substantially enhances the reputation of Dicey as a prophet.   Putting to one side that part of intellectual opinion which has repudiated both the attachment to civil liberty and economic freedom, we note the marked divergence between the attachment to liberty as participation in government and the repudiation of liberty as restraint from government direction of economic life.   In the former I include the attachment to free speech, the only area where laissez faire is still respectable.

Bearing in mind the danger of generalization without empirical investigation, it may nevertheless be asserted with some confidence that among intellectuals there is an inverse correlation between the appreciation of the merits of civil liberty—including freedom of speech—and the merits of economic freedom. I believe this generalization will hold even after the exclusion from the evidence of that group whose attachment to civil liberty is limited to the transition from the capitalist hell to the authoritarian heaven. Lacking empirical data for this generalization, I must resort to intellectual pride as partial proof. Dissent from the generalization implies either that intellectual discussion is without influence in the formation of policy or that intellectual opinion is always two generations behind the times.

Some evidence is readily available. Justice Douglas has told us that "free speech, free press, free exercise of religion are placed separate and apart; they are above and beyond the police power; they are not subject to regulation in the manner of factories, slums, apartment houses, production of oil and the like." [8]   And Justice Black tells us with eloquent brevity that, when it comes to the fixation of prices of natural gas which goes into interstate commerce, "the alleged federal constitutional questions are frivolous." [9]

I am aware that the preferred position accorded to free trade in ideas is based on constitutional considerations, with which I am not concerned. But I believe that the preference goes beyond such considerations. Justice Black tells us: "My own belief is that no legislature is charged with the duty or vested with the power to decide what public issues Americans can discuss." He also tells us at the same time that "in a free country that is the individual's choice, not the state's." [10]

Dr. Meiklejohn not only tells us that the Constitution draws a distinction between the liberty of owning property and freedom of discussion; he also warns us that, by confusing the two, "we are in constant danger of giving to a man's possessions the same dignity, the same status, as we give to the man himself." [11]

III

I hold that this dichotomy is a mistaken one, and I turn to this aspect of the problem.

A superficial explanation for the preference for free speech among intellectuals runs in terms of vertical interests. Everyone tends to magnify the importance of his own occupation and to minimize that of his neighbor. Intellectuals are engaged in the pursuit of truth, while others are merely engaged in earning a livelihood. One follows a profession, usually a learned one, while the other follows a trade or a business. To cite a trifling example: For every opinion voiced in England against restriction of ordinary imports, there must be a hundred against restriction on foreign travel. Objective evaluation of the two restrictions would recognize that they differ only in that one involves bringing the goods to the consumer, while the other involves shipping the consumer to the goods. Intellectuals, on the other hand, see one restriction as interference with culture and the other as mere exclusion of cheap American movies.

Such an attitude does not accord with a proper respect for the ordinary activities of the bulk of mankind. Short of a revolution in tastes which would make people want much less than they now have of material well-being, or a revolution in technology while keeping present material wants constant, neither of which can be expected, the bulk of mankind will for the foreseeable future have to devote a considerable fraction of their active lives to economic activity. For these people freedom of choice as owners of resources in choosing within available and continually changing opportunities, areas of employment, investment, and consumption is fully as important as freedom of discussion and participation in government. The former freedom is at least important for those—even less than a majority—who wish to exercise such freedom.

It is perhaps of such people and of such activities that Tocqueville wrote:

> The principle of enlightened self-interest is not a lofty one, but it is clear and sure. It does not aim at mighty objects, but it attains without impracticable efforts, all those at which it aims. As it lies within the reach of all capacities, everyone can without difficulty apprehend and retain it . . . .
>
> The doctrine of enlightened self-interest produces no great acts of self-sacrifice, but it suggests daily small acts of self-denial. By itself it cannot suffice to make a virtuous man, but it disciplines a multitude of citizens in habits of regularity, temperance, moderation, foresight, self-command: and if it does not at once lead men to virtue by their will, it draws them gradually in that direction by their habits.[12]

The preference for the free market in ideas stems also from an undue emphasis on the definition of democracy as government by discussion or consensus and neglect of the older description of democracy as government by majority rule. We have no better alternative for making political decisions. But decisions are made by consensus in the sense that all participate in making them, and those who do not like the decisions are willing to accept them because of their initial preference for this method of making them. This does not alter the coercive character of government. "The minority gives way not because it is convinced that it is wrong, but because it is convinced that it is a minority." The consent is only moderately different from Hume's conception of consent which obtains under all forms of government.   And this suggests the wisdom of the older persuasion that coercion is increased as the area of political decision is enlarged.

It is only under a system of voluntary exchange that freedom is maximized.   It is there possible to choose between alternative voluntary association.   The choice which one has in moving from one coercive authority to another is very limited in any event and is further narrowed as economic affairs are increasingly converted into political discussion and decision.   It is surely no accident that mobility of people between states was greater when there was a more complete division of labor between political and economic institutions.   The choice for a minority which does not consent to socialist institutions, even assuming that other socialist societies will accept them, is that of departing with bare feet.   And such restriction is described as regulation of possessions or property rather than of men.

The priority accorded to the free market for ideas as against the free market for economic affairs is derived from an undue importance attached to discussion as a method of solving problems.   In consequence there is inadequate appreciation of the substantial merits of the impersonal character of the market when it is competitive.   The election is sufficiently recent to make superfluous an elaborate statement of the foolishness which passes for discussion when specific and important issues of policy such as trade between nations, fixing rents of houses, or subsidies to agriculture are made the subject of collective decision.   Perhaps the effectiveness of advertising and radio and television entertainment against the party which "talked sense to the American people" is a further illustration of the small part which discussion plays in collective decisions.   Professor Cooley, a not unsympathetic student of democratic institutions, has emphasized the great amount of "nonsense" which passed for discussion when such issues as the silver question were made the subject of political decision.   And he finds the saving feature of democracy in the skill of the ordinary man in choosing between persons.   This in turn brings to the fore the large element of discretionary authority inherent in increasing the scope of political authority over economic organization.

Finally, Professor Knight, who has explored the limitations of the impersonal voluntary exchange system of organization with greater subtlety than any critic of that system, has in turn warned us about the dangers of relying on collective rationality:

> Genuine, purely intellectual discussion is rare in modern society, even in intellectual and academic circles, and is approximated only in very small and essentially casual groups.   On the larger scale, what passes for discussion is mostly argumentation or debate.   The intellectual interest is largely subordinate to entertainment, i. e., entertaining and being entertained, or the immediate interest of the active parties centers chiefly in domi-

nance, victory, instructing others, or persuading rather than convincing, and not in the impartial quest of truth.[13]

The traditional defense of the free market as a method of organizing economic life has been utilitarian or instrumental. This emphasizes the consequent efficiency with which resources are used to achieve given ends. It derives its emphasis from the economist's desire to be scientific. The traditional defense of the free market in ideas has in the main also been utilitarian. Thus it plays an important role in Mill's defense of freedom of discussion. It has been challenged in both areas and more extensively in the sphere of economic matters. An empirical test of efficiency in the absence of experiment with alternative forms of organization is not readily available. The historical evidence is stronger—at any rate, less ambiguous —in the economic area. The short period of liberalism has been accompanied by as much material progress as took place in all prior times. But the evidence has not been persuasive. It is always easy to contrast the observed deficiencies with the unknown advantages. And cognizance of deficiencies tends—rightly—to grow with material progress. Very recent experience with alternative forms of organization has again strengthened the efficiency argument. This is all to the good: "The common man or average family has a far greater stake in the size of our aggregate income than in any possible redistribution of income." But I have tried to emphasize the importance of the free market as an end in itself, as an important aspect of freedom to choose between alternatives. While not always explicit, I believe it has always been implicit in the attachment of the great economists to the liberal tradition. In this context freedom means more than discussion and participation in government. It means responsibility, change, adventure, departure from accepted ways of doing things. It means freedom to choose one's ends as well as means for attaining them. In Leslie Stephen's phrase it means "energy, self-reliance, and independence, a strong conviction that a man's fate should depend upon his own character and conduct." [14] It is broader than Milton's dictum: "The whole freedom of man consists either in spiritual or civil liberty." [15]

More recently, with the spread of authoritarian regimes which have destroyed both economic and intellectual freedom, the instrumental character of the free economic market in an entirely new context has received substantial recognition. This is the argument that noneconomic freedom cannot flourish when the division of labor between voluntary organization and the coercive state is destroyed. Again the argument is not altogether new. Mill, whose defense of the free market was mainly in terms of efficiency, nevertheless added that if the "industries, the universities and the public charities, were all of them branches of the government; . . . if the employees of all these different enterprises were appointed and paid by the government, and looked to the government for every rise in life;

not all the freedom of the press and popular constitution of the legislature would make this or any other country free otherwise than in name." [16]

In this respect the political economists have shown better insight into the basis of all freedom than the proponents of the priority of the market place for ideas. The latter must of necessity rely on exhortation and on the fragile support of self-denying ordinances in constitutions. The former, on the other hand, have grasped the significance of institutional arrangements which foster centers of resistance against the encroaching power of coercive organization. Failure to appreciate this essential element of freedom protection among students of the law who minimize the importance of the free economic market is especially striking. In their own field they fully recognize the great significance of legal institutions—procedure—as against the substantive content of law in protecting the liberty of the subject.

The issue is no longer one of the general theory of the essential character of major economic decisions made by political organizations, which involves broad delegation of power to experts who cannot be disciplined by those for whom they act. "Such grants of power," as Knight tells us, "tend to become irrevocable and the power itself tends to grow beyond assignable limits." [17] As individual freedom is being challenged because we are no longer indifferent to diversity of views, we get an indication of what may happen when the state becomes the principal employer or determines the conditions of employment. The privilege against self-incrimination may not be an important protection of freedom. But any legal protection of this general type will become an empty piece of ceremonial apparatus when its exercise and protection are accompanied by the loss of one's livelihood. This may increase our esteem for martyrdom, but martyrs are not always rewarded in this world.

We can learn much from the acute observations of a recent comprehensive review of the privilege against self-incrimination. Without access to books and records we are told, "the enforcement of complicated regulation would break down or would involve additional cost not easily met in a period when the government is assuming staggering commitments. It is not surprising that a majority of the Supreme Court was convinced that the application of the privilege to require records is a luxury which a welfare-warfare state cannot afford." [18] Economists cannot distinguish between luxuries and necessities; other necessities may become mere luxuries which the welfare state cannot afford. Courts cannot provide satisfactory alternative areas of employment and promotion.

It is not essential to demonstrate that there is only one road to serfdom or that a particular road must inevitably lead to a specified destination. Some institutions are more flexible than others. We must choose those which minimize the risks of undesirable consequences.

FOOTNOTES

* This paper was first presented to the Conference on Freedom and the Law held at the University of Chicago Law School on May 7, 1953. It was printed in the University of Chicago Law School Conference Series, Number 13, pp. 16–25. The power and interest of Professor Aaron Director's treatment of a strangely neglected theme suggested that it should be made available to a wider audience.—*Editor*

1 Mill, On Liberty, in Utilitarianism, Liberty, and Representative Government 216–17 (1951).

2 Beauharnis v. Illinois, 343 U.S. 250, 286 (1952).

3 Stephen, 1 The English Utilitarians 132 (1900).

4 As expressed by John Stuart Mill. See his essay on Bentham in Mill, 1 Dissertations and Discussions 377 (1859).

5 Bentham, Manual of Political Economy, in 1 Jeremy Bentham's Economic Writings 229 (1953).

6 Id. at 231.

7 Stephen, op. cit. supra note 3, at 132.

8 Beauharnis v. Illinois, supra note 2, at 286.

9 Cities Service Co. v. Peerless Co., 340 U.S. 179, 189 (1950).

10 Beauharnis v. Illinois, supra note 2, at 270.

11 Meiklejohn, Free Speech and its Relation to Self-Government 2 (1948).

12 Tocqueville, 2 Democracy in America 149 (1864).

13 Knight, The Planful Act, in Freedom and Reform 349 (1947).

14 Stephen, op. cit. supra note 3, at 131.

15 Milton, The Ready and Easy Way to Establish a Free Commonwealth, in Prose Writings 239 (1958).

16 Mill, op. cit. supra note 1, at 223.

17 Knight, op. cit. supra note 13, at 369.

18 Meltzer, Required Records, The McCarran Act, and The Privilege against Self-Incrimination, 18 U.Chi.L.Rev. 687, 727–28 (1951).

C Continued

8: AN ECONOMIC ANALYSIS OF THE CONCEPT OF FREEDOM

THOMAS GALE MOORE
Michigan State University

Economists, especially of the libertarian variety, often discuss how the market increases personal freedom. Milton Friedman (1962) has ably described this relationship in his book *Capitalism and Freedom*. Paul Samuelson (1963) has recently taken Friedman and others to task for this. He has claimed that "complete freedom is not definable once two wills exist in the same interdependent universe. . . . What is actually called 'freedom' is really a vector of almost infinite components rather than a one-dimensional thing that can be given a simple ordering." While no one claims that complete freedom is possible, it is the intent of this paper to show that freedom can be measured in the same sense that welfare can be measured, and that a discussion of maximizing freedom can be made operational.

Before we do that let us consider why an individual in the United States is considered to be freer than one in Russia. There are many reasons, of course, but one element that I believe we would all agree on is that a citizen of the United States can criticize the government, the president, or his employer with *relative* impunity. In Russia (or any generally considered non-free society) such action will usually have severe repercussions—such as a few years' rest in Siberia. But even in the United States such action can have repercussions. If my employer is a Republican and a great supporter of the president, I may find myself looking for new work. If I work for the government, I may have to try to find employment in private industry. If I happen to be supporting communism I may actually find it difficult to secure a good job. In other words, the exercise of free speech, even in a

Journal of Political Economy, Vol. 77, No. 4, Pt. 1, 1969, p. 532.

*Capitalism and Freedom: Problems and Prospects (R. Selden, ed.), Charlottesville, Va., Univ. Press of Virginia (publication scheduled for Dec. 1974).

"free" society, may not be costless. In fact, the essential difference between a citizen here and a citizen in Russia is one of relative cost. In both places I can criticize the government and advocate a different economic system, but the relative costs of this behavior differ significantly.

The thesis, then, of this paper is that freedom can be defined in terms of welfare. A change in the cost of action (or non-action) can be considered to be a movement toward freedom if it increases welfare. We can consider that an individual has the desire to take all sorts of actions, each of which has a cost to himself and possibly to others. If the cost to the individual of performing some action is lowered without affecting the cost to others, then we will consider that a movement toward a freer society. For example, suppose there is a rule that says that speech against the state will be punished by five years in Siberia. Suppose this rule is changed so that such speech results simply in a lower-paying job. If this change in the rule does not lead to externalities such as higher costs for others in society, then it is a movement toward a free society. Much of the problem with the concept of freedom revolves around cases where externalities exist. For example, a person yelling "Fire!" in a crowded theater will levy serious externalities on others, and as a consequence, such action is not guaranteed by the concept of freedom of speech. But most forms of speech do not have these externalities. If one individual lectures another individual on the benefits of communism, LSD, or capitalism, and the other individual freely listens, then are there any externalities? The situation is analogous to a voluntary trade between two individuals. No such externality exists unless a third person is affected. There are two ways that such a speech could adversely affect a third person. First, if such a speech incited the listener or speaker to action and that action inflicted costs on others, it might be argued that the speech itself had external effects. It would also seem plausible to argue that it was solely the action that had the external effect. Alternatively, some people may not be indifferent to statements even if no one acts upon them. Thus I may object to statements in favor of capitalism even if no one is motivated to act in any way by the statements.

It might clarify matters if we consider a model. Assume there is only one action under consideration—for example, freedom of speech about communism. Let the utility function for one individual be given by the following relation:

$$U^1 = f^1(Y^1, Z^1, Z^2, \ldots, Z^m), \tag{1}$$

where Y^1 is the individual's income with given prices, Z^1 is the amount of discussion he carries on about communism, and $Z^2 \cdots Z^m$ is the amount carried on by each of the other $m-1$ persons. Then the relationship between changes in this individual's welfare and the other variables can be expressed:

$$dU^1 = \frac{\partial f^1}{\partial Y^1} dY^1 + \frac{\partial f^1}{\partial Z^1} dZ^1 + \cdots + \frac{\partial f^1}{\partial Z^m} dZ^m; \tag{2}$$

and for the individual to maximize his welfare with respect to the amount of Z he carries on, we get:

$$\frac{dU^1}{dU^1} = \frac{\partial f^1}{\partial Y^1} \frac{dY^1}{dZ^1} + \frac{\partial f^1}{\partial Z^1} = 0, \tag{3}$$

or in words, the marginal utility of income will be set equal to the ratio of the marginal utility of speaking to the marginal cost in terms of loss of income as a result of talking.

It might be objected that speaking on communism is not a single-dimensional variable; rather it is a vector of many dimensions relating to what is said, to whom, where, and so on. The analysis will still remain the same even if free speech is considered a vector of many dimensions. By letting Y be a function of all these dimensions, we can still differentiate (1) with respect to the vector Z^1 to get function (3), where dY^1/dZ^1 and $\partial f^1/\partial Z^1$ are vectors of dimension n and $\partial f^1/Y^1$ is a scalar. Basically, the problem is identical to the maximization problem facing a consumer of goods. Most goods are not homogeneous but have many dimensions; yet we treat them in analysis as a single good.[1] In this analysis, then, we will treat each separate aspect of freedom as a single good.

Now given this formulation, we can define maximization of freedom in terms of maximizing total welfare with respect to the cost imposed on doing the act. Let our welfare function be:

$$W = W(U^1, U^2, \ldots, U^m). \tag{4}$$

Then maximization of (4) requires that:

$$dW = \frac{\partial W}{\partial U^1} dU^1 + \frac{\partial W}{\partial U^2} dU^2 + \cdots + \frac{\partial W}{\partial U^m} dU^m = 0.$$

Now maximizing with respect to a change in costs requires:

$$\frac{dW}{dC} = \frac{\partial W}{\partial U^1} \frac{dU^1}{dC} + \cdots + \frac{\partial W}{\partial U^m} \frac{dU^m}{dC} = 0. \tag{5}$$

Let the effect of a change in C on any individual be expressed as follows. Call the income of an individual Y^0 if $Z^1 = 0$, and assume that the costs borne by the individual directly are reflected in lower income, so that his income $Y^1 = Y_0^1 + g^1(C, Z^1)$, where $\partial g^1/\partial Z^1 < 0$ and $\partial g^1/\partial C < 0$. Then for a single individual we have:

$$\frac{dU^1}{dC} = \frac{\partial f^1}{\partial Y^1} \frac{dY^1}{dC} + \frac{\partial f^1}{\partial Z^1} \frac{dZ^1}{dC} + \cdots + \frac{\partial f^1}{\partial Z^m} \frac{dZ^m}{dC} \tag{6}$$

and

$$dY^1 = \frac{\partial g^1}{\partial C} dC + \frac{\partial g^1}{\partial Z^1} dZ^1,$$

so (7)

$$\frac{dY^1}{dC} = \frac{\partial g^1}{\partial C} + \frac{\partial g^1}{\partial Z^1}\frac{dZ^1}{dC}.$$

Substituting (7) in (6) we find:

$$\frac{dU^1}{dC} = \frac{\partial f^1}{\partial Y^1}\frac{\partial g^1}{\partial C} + \left(\frac{\partial f^1}{\partial Y^1}\frac{\partial g^1}{\partial Z^1} + \frac{\partial f^1}{\partial Z^1}\right)\frac{dZ^1}{dC} + \cdots + \frac{\partial f^1}{\partial Z^m}\frac{dZ^m}{dC}. \tag{8}$$

Note that $dY^1/dZ^1 = \partial g^1/\partial Z^1$ for C held constant. Therefore, the term inside the parentheses in (8) equals zero since it is equal to (3). Now if external effects of Z on individuals are independent of who the other people are, we can write (8) as follows:

$$\frac{dU^1}{dC} = \frac{\partial f^1}{\partial Y^1}\frac{\partial g^1}{\partial C} + \frac{\partial f^1}{\partial Z}\sum_{i=2}^{m}\frac{dZ^i}{dC}, \tag{9}$$

where

$$\frac{\partial f^1}{\partial Z} = \frac{\partial f^1}{\partial Z^2} = \frac{\partial f^1}{\partial Z^3} = \cdots = \frac{\partial f^1}{\partial Z^m}.$$

Now assume that the individual can assign a dollar cost and that he would be indifferent between the options of paying and $\partial f^1/\partial Z$, the loss of utility per unit of Z. Thus we can write:

$$\frac{\partial f^1}{\partial Z} = \frac{\partial f^1}{\partial Y^1}\frac{\partial Y^1}{\partial Z},$$

where $\partial Y^1/\partial Z \lesseqgtr 0$ depending on whether $\partial f^1/\partial Z \lesseqgtr 0$. Now substituting in (9) we can write:

$$\frac{dU^1}{dC} = \frac{\partial f^1}{\partial Y^1}\left(\frac{\partial g^1}{\partial C} + \frac{\partial Y^1}{\partial Z}\sum_{i=2}^{m}\frac{dZ^i}{dC}\right). \tag{10}$$

Thus the net gain or loss from an infinitesimal change in C in terms of the individual's income can be expressed as

$$\frac{dY^1}{dC} = \frac{\partial g^1}{\partial C} + \frac{\partial Y^1}{\partial Z}\sum_{i=2}^{m}\frac{dZ^i}{dC}. \tag{11}$$

Thus, substituting (10) and (11) into (5) we find

$$\frac{dW}{dC} = \sum_{j=1}^{m}\frac{\partial W}{\partial U^i}\frac{\partial f^i}{\partial Y^i}\frac{dY^i}{dC} = 0. \tag{12}$$

Now $\partial W/\partial U^i \cdot \partial f^i/\partial Y^i$ can be considered weights to be attached to the net losses or gains experienced by individuals. Once the weights are assigned, the solution amounts to finding the weighted average gains and losses such that the weighted average gains equal the weighted average losses. Since it is impossible to compare $\partial f^i/\partial Y^i$ with $\partial f^j/\partial Y^j$, $i \neq j$, and since one reasonable, ethical approach is to assign the same weights to each individual, we will then extend the argument for the case when all the weights are made equal.[2] This assumption is not necessary but simplifies the exposition. Note that by this assumption we are implying that income is distributed optimally. If the reader feels that other weights are appropriate, then the analysis can be easily modified for any assigned weights. Thus we can now say that the sum of the marginal gains should equal the sum of the marginal losses from changing C. Therefore

$$\sum_{i=1}^{m} \frac{\partial g^i}{\partial C} = - \sum_{i=1}^{m} \frac{\partial Y^i}{\partial Z} \sum_{\substack{j=1 \\ j \neq 1}}^{m} \frac{dZ^j}{dC} ,$$

where $\partial g^i/\partial C < 0$, $\partial Z^j/dC < 0$, and $\partial Y^i/\partial Z \gtrless 0$. Now if $\partial Y^i/\partial Z > 0$, then C should be reduced.

It is clear from the above analysis that if $\partial Y^i/\partial Z = 0$, then $C = 0$ would maximize welfare. The whole problem then revolves around the size of $\partial Y^i/\partial Z$ and its sign. In general, $\partial Y^i/\partial Z$ reflects the external gain or loss from the action Z. Part of the problem with the concept of freedom is over the admissible set of externalities. It could be that we include everything that anyone considers relevant. Then if I object to your way of worshipping God, it becomes relevant. It is useful at this point to accept an individualistic ethic (value judgment) that the only relevant externalities will be those which affect an individual's senses or the value of his wealth. Thus most normal forms of religious worship would not affect the value of my wealth nor would they affect my hearing, sight, taste, or touch. Thus by ruling out such externalities, we find that the optimum cost for any normal type of religious practice is zero (above the opportunity costs of the resources involved).

Let us be more specific about the admissible set of externalities. In a sense, everything that an individual is aware of must have come through his senses. Then to say that the externality must affect his senses could be interpreted to include everything. We will restrict it to those externalities which directly impinge on his senses. If he hears about someone doing something he objects to, this will not count. On the other hand, if he is forced to watch what he objects to, that is an admissible externality. Thus, for example, a fervent member of the WCTU would suffer a relevant externality from being forced to witness a drunk on her front step, but would not if she hears about a man drinking in a bar.

It should be emphasized that this is a value judgment that not all readers will wish to accept. If any externality is permitted, then we can put no restrictions on the types of activities which could be taxed. Free speech, freedom of religion, and so on, can only be justified if some restrictions are placed on the admissible set of externalities.

Let us consider the relevance of this value judgment for the subject of speech. If I advocate to another individual LSD, a particular product, or free love, and the individual willingly listens, the net externalities can be considered zero unless the individual is stimulated to action *and* the action has externalities.

Let us work through a simple model. Let $C_i = f^i(n)$ be the cost in money terms to the ith individual from n people doing an activity y. Let n be a function of the number of speeches z made in favor of activity y, so we can write: $n = y(z)$.

Let B_j be the income equivalent gain to the jth speechmaker from speaking in favor of y. Let G_k equal the gain to the kth individual from actually doing action y. Thus if we allow additions of monetary welfare, we get total welfare W as a function of z and the cost of z, C_z:

$$W = \sum_{j=1}^{m} C_i + \sum_{k=1}^{z} B_j + \sum_{i=1}^{n} G_k, \tag{13}$$

where m is the size of the population. So we want to maximize W with respect to z, the cost of speaking in favor of y, and C_y, *the cost of actually doing* y. Now let Δz be the change in number of speeches made due to a change in the cost of making speeches, ΔC_z; let r be the change in number of people acting due to Δz. Now consider a reduction in cost of speaking, ΔC_z. If $\Delta W > 0$, then cost of speaking should be reduced:

$$\Delta W = \sum_{i=1}^{m} \frac{\Delta C_i}{\Delta n} r + \sum_{j=0}^{\Delta z} B_{z-j} + \sum_{k=0}^{r} G_{k+n}. \tag{14}$$

Note that $\Delta C_i / \Delta n$ can be positive if some people gain from the action as well as lose. Now if ΔW is positive, the reduction in C_z should be carried out. Eventually, however, further reductions in C_z would lead to a loss in welfare and hence should not be made. Why should ΔW ever become negative? Well, the first term must be negative; if not, then C_z should be lowered toward zero until it is negative, since there are no net externalities from speech. Assume the first term is negative. As C_z is lowered, B_j will fall, since each individual maximizing his well-being will speak until $B_j \geq C_z$ and on the margin $B_z = C_z$. So when $C_z = 0$, $B_z = 0$. The last term is positive and decreasing as n increases, since it seems likely that $G_j > G_{j+1}$ for all j, because those who gain the most are likely to be the first to act. Thus B_j can be made negative if need be by paying for speech, and G_j is declining, so eventually the sum of the last two terms will be negative. Even if the first term rises toward zero, the sum of all the terms should eventually be negative, since eventually r will equal zero, that is, further speeches will not increase the number of doers. That will make the first term and the last term zero, and hence with a negative or zero C_z, implying a negative or zero B_z, ΔW will be negative or zero.

Note that if our activity is voting between two candidates and we presume that a vote transferred from one candidate to another has equal and opposite welfare effects on the two candidates and their supporters, then $C_z \leq 0$. That is, we should impose no costs on speeches and maybe subsidize campaign information if at $C_z = 0$,

$$\sum_{k=0}^{r} G_{n+k} > 0,$$

that is, if there are further benefits to voters from provision of more information. The assumption made above that benefits and losses from voting are exactly offsetting may appear to be extreme. But by our individualistic value judgment of welfare benefits and costs, only those actions count which affect a person physically or affect his wealth. Thus only votes which shift the outcome count. Since a vote that shifts the outcome must reflect a situation where about half the voters are on one side and half on the other, the assumption of offsetting benefits and losses does not appear to be so extreme.

Now if

$$\sum_{i=1}^{m} \frac{\Delta C_i}{\Delta n} < 0,$$

then costs should be imposed on the activity and on speech advocating it. Consider the costs imposed on the activity itself. Let p be the change in number of persons acting due to a change in the cost of the activity. These costs should be reduced as long as the resultant $\Delta W > 0$:

$$\Delta W = \sum_{i=1}^{m} \frac{\Delta C_i}{\Delta n} p + \sum_{k=0}^{p} G_{k+n}. \tag{15}$$

It can be seen that expression (15) requires a $C_y > 0$, since at $C_y = 0$, $G_n = 0$, and as long as

$$\sum_{i=1}^{m} \frac{\Delta C_i}{\Delta n} < 0,$$

then the cost of doing the activity has been lowered too far. Now if we measure ΔC_y so that $p = 1$ we can write

$$\Delta W = \sum_{i=1}^{m} \frac{\Delta C_i}{\Delta n} + G_{n+1} \geq 0. \tag{16}$$

Now if we can approximate function (16), by a continuous function we can say that at the maximum:

$$\Delta W = \sum_{i=1}^{m} \frac{\Delta C_i}{\Delta n} + G_{n+1} = 0, \tag{17}$$

or

$$\sum_{i=1}^{m} \frac{\Delta C_i}{\Delta n} = - G_{n+1}. \tag{18}$$

Assuming therefore C_y is set so that (17) is satisfied, we can substitute (18) in (14) and get:

$$\Delta W = \sum_{j=1}^{r} (G_{n+j} - G_{n+1}) + \sum_{j=1}^{\Delta z} B_{z-j}. \tag{19}$$

Now, since the first term is negative the second term must be positive for $\Delta W \geq 0$. If we accept the convention of measuring ΔC_z so that $\Delta z = 1$, we can write (19) as follows:

$$\Delta W = \sum_{j=1}^{r} (G_{n+j} - G_{n+1}) + B_z \geq 0, \tag{20}$$

and since the marginal individual will speak up to the point that $B_z = C_z$, we can conclude that C_z must be positive. Moreover, an individual or individuals will do z up until, for the marginal individual n or for the marginal act, $G_n = C_y$. Substituting in (20) and rearranging, we get

$$\sum_{j=1}^{r} G_{n+j} + C_z \geq rC_y. \tag{21}$$

We can conclude from (21) that minimization of costs of actions in society may involve imposing costs on speech and that such costs may be greater than the cost of doing if one speech leads to more than one person acting.

Let us summarize the previous section so that the implications of this approach to the concept of freedom are clear. First, by our individualistic value judgment we will count only those externalities that physically affect some individual or affect the value of his wealth. Thus we rule out all externalities such as the loss in welfare that a member of the WCTU feels when I sip a martini. As a general rule we can conclude that if there are external costs, then some sort of cost should be imposed on the activity. If we treat each individual identically and assign equal weights to dollar losses by different individuals, the marginal cost of performing the activity should equal the sum of the marginal externalities for all other people. Thus if we consider that the action is speech, then such speech should only be completely free if it imposes no externalities or offsetting externalities. For most public policy issues and for most voting situations, offsetting externalities can reasonably be inferred. Even if such externalities are not offsetting in some cases, it may not be feasible to tax only those speeches, and so an assumption can be made that in the long run such discussion will have offsetting externalities. On the other hand, there is some speech where it is clear that the externalities are not offsetting, for example, if a man urges others to burn down a school. This type of speech imposes costs on all or most others but does not confer benefits to anyone except the person doing the burning and the person urging the burning.[3] For a maximization of welfare, costs should be imposed both on the doer and on the speaker provided that the speech does lead to some action.

Those familiar with welfare economics will notice that this model is, similar to those used to derive the standard welfare theorems. Many of the qualifications of that analysis also extend to the area of freedom. In particular we might note that the theory of the second best (Lipsey and

Lancaster, 1956) may be important in this context. If, for example, the cost of doing something is higher than justified, then actions taken to convince others of this situation should not necessarily be taxed at the level suggested by the above analysis.

Let us extend our model and use it to analyze some currently pressing issues which are related to the concept of freedom. There has been considerable agitation for open housing legislation in many communities. Proponents of the legislation have supported it on the grounds that the freedom of Negroes and other minority groups would be increased if the legislation were enacted so they could buy houses wherever they wished. On the other hand, opponents of the legislation have argued that such legislation would infringe upon the freedom of property owners to sell to whomever they wished. Now first, it is clear that such legislation if enforced will reduce the cost of buying a house in a particular area by a member of a minority group. It is not true to say that he could not have bought a house; there always exists some price at which he could have bought a house in that area, but it was presumably above that at which a white person could have bought it. Now the difference between the price to a white person and the price to a Negro reflects the costs, as seen by the seller, of selling to the Negro. Since Negroes did not buy into the neighborhood at that price, the marginal valuation of a house in that neighborhood must have been smaller than the marginal cost to the seller of having a Negro in his area. Therefore, if we assume that we should count a white dollar as much as a black dollar, such legislation is unwise and would not in general increase welfare. There are two qualifications to this statement that should be considered.

First, the passage of the law might itself lower the costs. The costs before the passage of open housing legislation might cause the seller to be ostracized by his friends and relations. But after the passage of a statute making it illegal to discriminate, he could plead that, while he did not want to make the sale, the law compelled him to. Note that the trouble with this rationale is that it ignores why his friends would have ostracized him if he had made the sale before the passage of open housing. Presumably they would have acted that way only because such a sale was expected to inflict costs on them. These costs will not be reduced by the open housing legislation, and if the original owner had correctly estimated these costs to his friends and neighbors, the open housing legislation can be considered to have shifted the costs to the neighbors directly and in about the same magnitude that was reflected in the original price to a Negro. But note that our value judgment ruled out counting any costs resulting from simply knowing that a black lives down the block. Therefore, the original price to the Negro may reflect costs not permitted by our individualistic ethic, and open housing legislation may be a movement toward a freer society.

Moreover, individuals who face discrimination might be willing to pay something for the right not to be discriminated against. That is, a Negro might be willing to pay more than the reservation price of the white seller provided whites were being asked to pay a similar sum, but a black might be unwilling to pay much more than whites for the same property. Thus the true value to the black might exceed the original price to him provided discrimination was not involved.

Given our definition of freedom, we might apply it to the Bill of Rights to show that we can interpret each provision which has to do with freedom or justice in terms of costs and benefits. Freedom of speech has already been discussed above. Freedom of the press can be defended analogously. People can read what they want to read and ignore what they wish. The only externality arises if such reading leads to some change in behavior of the reader. It is alleged that pornography has such an effect on unstable personalities and therefore is not covered by the provisions of the Constitution. Of course, banning pornography adversely affects those who would like to buy it. It is an empirical question whether pornography has external effects and whether such costs exceed those borne by individuals who wish to read it and are barred. If it does impose externalities, the appropriate response is to tax pornography but not to ban it. All political literature is aimed at leading the reader to take action which will affect other individuals, specifically those in power and those who wish to get into power. If we consider that the benefits to someone of achieving power equal the benefits to the person in power of staying there, then bans on literature advocating one candidate over another have equal and offsetting effects. Since the provision of the information is desired by both the provider and the reader, on balance it is clearly less costly to allow freedom of the press than to deny it.

Freedom of religion can also be explained in economic terms. For most religions there are few discernible externalities. The only issues in freedom of religion arise when there are externalities—usually connected with children. Christian Science offers an excellent example. Since advocates do not believe in the practice of professional medicine, problems arise concerning vaccinations, inoculations, and blood transfusions. Vaccinations and inoculations clearly have externalities for non-Christian Scientists. But most of the controversy has swirled around blood transfusions, especially for children. There seems to be the general feeling that if an adult wishes not to be given a blood transfusion even if it results in his death, that this is his prerogative. But for the parents of a child to refuse permission may mean the child's death. Whether this is an externality or not depends on the relevant unit, the family or the individual. To the extent that we make the decision-making unit the family there is no externality, but if it is considered to be the individual then plainly there exists a real externality.

Freedom of peaceable assembly and petition also exert few externalities on others, and therefore their guarantee in the constitution lowers the cost of some actions to the public while inflicting negligible costs on others. Basically, these provisions increase the flow of information in society by allowing individuals with grievances to express them to the authorities.

The rest of the articles in the Bill of Rights can also be construed in terms of costs and benefits. Article II, for example, deals with the right to keep and bear arms. This amendment has been limited in many jurisdictions by licensing laws and limits on the types of arms allowed. There is an increasingly strong movement to limit the flow of all arms to the public. The reason for the less liberal interpretation of this article than for other articles is that the externalities of guns are more obvious.

Articles III and IV and the last provision of Article V in essence deal with the rights of private property and essentially provide that those rights cannot be arbitrarily taken away without specifically considering each case. In other words, costs cannot be inflicted on individuals by reducing their property rights without specifically weighing the costs and benefits and in general compensating the loser.

Articles V through VIII deal with the administration of the law and justice. They each contribute to making individuals feel more secure in their daily life and therefore can be considered to lower the cost of justice in general. There is, of course, some probability that any single individual will be accused falsely of some crime and convicted. These amendments are designed to either reduce the probability of such an occurrence or the cost of such an occurrence when it arises. Thus it lowers the expected cost of justice to innocent individuals. Here again the problem of externalities arises. The cost of justice to innocent individuals could be reduced to zero if and only if no one was prosecuted for any crime. But this would increase the cost of crime and hence lead to higher costs for innocent individuals. The appropriate objective, if costs are to be minimized, is to find that set of rules where, on the margin, the increased cost to innocent individuals of increasing the probability of catching and convicting a malefactor is equal to the increased cost of the crime he would commit if the probability of being convicted is lowered. Thus the varying court interpretations of these amendments have presumably been intended to find this balance. Some argue that the costs to the public of increasing the difficulty in achieving convictions have far exceeded the gains; others argue for the opposite point of view. But in any case, it seems appropriate to consider this in terms of probabilities of certain costs being inflicted on innocent individuals in our society.

In conclusion, we might note that this interpretation of the concept of freedom removes the distinction between property rights and personal rights. If we are interested in the cost of doing certain actions, it makes little sense to consider a tax on travel abroad as somehow different from legal prohibition from traveling. Whether the cost is higher in one instance or the other depends on the amount of tax and the punishment that is levied for illegal travel. It could easily be that the cost would be higher in the case of the tax than in the case of the legal prohibition.

It is clear that costs should be levied on the activities that impose external costs on others. In actual practice these are usually enforced by a trial and by a judge. But this procedure leads to considerable uncertainty in what the cost will be, since judges and juries will impose different costs in each case. Moreover, the cost of a jail sentence will differ considerably depending on whether it is imposed on a professional man or on an unskilled worker. From the point of view of efficiency, then, it would be preferable to convert, wherever possible, unlawful activity to activity which is taxed. From this viewpoint a tax on foreign travel is clearly preferable to a legal prohibition.

There is one other welfare implication that should be brought out of this analysis. If the objective is to maximize a Bergson welfare function, which is a function not only of the quantities of marketplace goods and services but also a function of the costs of other activities such as free speech, it does not follow that it is always desirable to maximize the economic component of the welfare function. That is, total welfare might be higher when some of the usual marginal conditions are violated in the market sector, if freedom has not been maximized. In other words, we must generalize the theory of the second best to include both market variables and freedom variables. To see this, assume that the social cost of writing about a particular topic is below the optimum as defined above. Then it may improve matters if the cost of printing were raised above marginal cost. In general, since marketplace variables and other variables in the welfare function interact, the subject of maximization is dependent on the variation of all factors in the welfare function simultaneously.

This analysis has shown that it is possible to define freedom meaningfully. The analysis also is fruitful because it has implications for public policy. As a minimum, it suggests the right questions to ask when one is dealing with public policy issues. In addition, since a free competitive market tends to internalize externalities, it suggests that such a market will result in a free society.

REFERENCES

Baumol, William J. "Calculation of Optima; Product and Retailer Characteristics: The Abstract Product Approach," *J.P.E.*, LXXV, No. 5 (October, 1967), 674-85.

Friedman, Milton. *Capitalism and Freedom*. Chicago: Univ. Chicago Press, 1962.

Lancaster, K. J. "A New Approach to Consumer Theory," *J.P.E.*, LXXIV, No. 2 (April, 1966), 132-57.

Lipsey, R. G., and Lancaster, K. "The General Theory of Second Best," *Rev. Econ. Studies* (October, 1956), 11-32.

Little, I. M. D. *A Critique of Welfare Economics*. 2nd ed. New York: Oxford Univ. Press, 1957.

Meade, J. E. *Trade and Welfare*. New York: Oxford Univ. Press, 1955.

Samuelson, Paul. "Modern Economic Realities and Individualism," *The Collected Scientific Papers of Paul A. Samuelson*, edited by J. E. Stiglitz. Vol. 2. Cambridge, Mass.: M.I.T. Press, 1966.

FOOTNOTES

[1] See Lancaster (1966) and Baumol (1967) for a discussion of methods of handling the multidimensional problem.

[2] See Little (1957) for a discussion of the necessity to assign weights.

[3] This is true because of our individualistic welfare assumption.

Property Rights and Some Substantive Legal Rules

*

A Introduction

When Ronald Coase wrote "The Problem of Social Cost" (9), he was addressing himself to a rather basic error in the conventionally accepted tenets of Pigovian welfare economics. There is no internal evidence in Coase's article that he thought he was developing anything that would become universally known as the "Coase theorem," but it is the measure of the importance of this work that while it corrected a significant error in the modern economic literature, it also developed a generalized hypothesis with application to a vast number of legal and social issues.

The modern treatment of the subject, though recognized before Alfred Marshall's time, dates mainly to Pigou's *The Economics of Welfare* (4th ed., 1946). The problem begins when individuals or firms, through their own maximizing behavior, impose costs on others without the consent of the other parties. Pigou and most welfare-economists who followed concluded that in order to correct for the ensuing inefficiency in the allocation of resources, it would be appropriate to impose legal liability on the acting party, impose a tax, or forbid the offending behavior. In the course of demonstrating the weaknesses in each of these positions, Coase pointed out that in the absence of negotiation or other transactions costs, and assuming private property and competitive markets, the rule of liability had absolutely no effect on the allocation of resources, though any change in law would have a one-time wealth transfer effect.

It remained for H. Demsetz fully to elaborate the broad implications of the Coase theorem, while at the same time successfully staving off a variety of criticisms made of it. Demsetz's brilliant commentary on the Coase theorem, "When Does the Rule of Liability Matter?" (10), demonstrated that the Coase theorem is independent of long run versus short run considerations; that the "extortion criticism" is really nothing more than the classical monopoly problem stated in new terminology; and that the value of the Coase theorem is not lost because in the real world transactions costs are never zero.

Another elaboration of some of the specific qualifications to the Coase theorem appears in Demsetz's "Some Aspects of Property Rights" (11). Here the discussion focuses on necessary and sufficient preconditions for individuals or firms to efficiently internalize social costs.

This issue more than any other has occupied the attention of applied economists and lawyers interested in policy problems. The issue, as Demsetz sees it, is that costs and benefits of any particular prospective change in property rights cannot always be accurately predicted. When they can be estimated accurately (i. e. information costs are not too high to warrant the expense), and especially if this can be done before the costs in question have been incurred, voluntary market exchanges will generally create the most appropriate allocations. In other situations, which are not really too common, less satisfactory measuring techniques, such as cost-benefit analysis or political voting must be used.

Coase had explicitly recognized that there would generally be wealth transfer effects to any particular rule of liability, and again Demsetz's elaboration of this point (12) generates important new insights for the legal scholar. What he shows is that the amount of wealth effect or wealth transfer implicit in any change in the rule of liability is an inverse function of the costs of negotiating new private arrangements among the parties directly interested in the rule change. This in turn may be a function of the duration of the pertinent contractual or "title" arrangements.

Thus, a labor contract which can be renegotiated between employers and employees relatively frequently will cause them to negate most wealth-transfer effects implicit in any change in the liability rules for employee injuries. On the other hand, where relatively permanent expectations have been created, especially as with ownership rights in specialized goods such as land, the wealth effects of legal rule changes will be greater. Thus, Demsetz rationalizes a point lawyers have long seemed to understand by intuition, namely, that stability of legal arrangements and rules is more important in a field like real property law than it is, say, in connection with the sale of goods or services. The implications of this finding are of special significance to those who advocate sudden changes in settled land uses and rights.

In the article following, by G. Calabresi (13), a law professor with considerable economic sophistication addresses himself to the fundamental question of how legal scholars can best use the Coase theorem. He correctly cautions us about the tremendous difficulties in gathering the data necessary to take full and correct advantage of the implications

of the Coase theorem for policy-making. When this empirical evidence
becomes very costly, Calabresi—with undertones running quite
contrary to those found in Demsetz's treatment of this subject—
concludes that all manner of government interventions based on our intuition and upon our informed guesses about transactions costs (amounts
and least-cost bearers) can be rationalized in light of the Coase
theorem. The issue is, to put it simply, not yet settled.

The readings in Section C examine one kind of legal problem in
considerable detail. The authors begin with both legal and economic
theory and then try to reach specific policy proposals based on
either casual or sophisticated data (14 through 17). But these materials on negligence law and products liability should make clear that
we are still at a fairly primitive stage in developing reliable empirical
techniques for resolving these legal issues. Scholars interested in the
Coase theorem have worked this subject area in more depth than
any other topic. Yet, as the materials make clear, there is still no
complete agreement on even one subcategory of the subject, as the
battle rages between advocates of "liability for fault" and advocates of
the "no-fault" approach.

Readers are strongly recommended to an article by Professor Walter
Y. Oi, "The Economics of Product Safety," in the *Bell Journal of Economics and Management Science,* Volume IV, No. 1, Spring 1973, pp.
3–28. Professor Oi develops the theory that a system of absolute
liability constitutes a required tied sale of the product and an insurance
policy for any consumer of risky goods. He develops a conclusion,
based on consumer minimization of full price paid for this package,
that more rather than less of the high-risk goods will be produced
under this rule than under a rule of *"caveat emptor."* Professor Oi's
article is highly formalistic and mathematical, so that its inclusion in
this collection did not seem warranted. Nonetheless, it is an important
analysis of this field and will serve economics scholars well.

It is interesting that economists, such as Professor Oi, are often
at the mercy of legal writers for the materials they discuss.
In this regard it is highly instructive to note that at the same time that
Professor Oi was preparing his fine work, the rules of the game were
being changed by a highly influential and imaginative law professor,
J. O'Connell. As co-author with R. Keeton of *Basic Protection for the
Traffic Victim* (1965), O'Connell has succeeded in making most
states in the United States consider, and many adopt, some form of no-
fault insurance for compensating automobile accident victims. Now
he has proposed a totally different approach for all other kinds of accidents (18). He terms this "elective no-fault liability insurance," and
it must surely be reckoned with as one of the more significant proposals
to be advanced in this area. An elaboration will appear soon in book form.

Basically, Professor O'Connell is proposing that we remove government (in the form of courts) as much as possible from the provision of dispute resolution services, although the issue is not stated in quite these terms. Nonetheless, O'Connell recognizes that the "moral hazard" costs of repealing all doctrines of liability would be too great, and he explains why the cost of general government accident insurance would also be prohibitive. But he proposes an ingenious solution whereby firms or individuals can offer their goods and services either under the existing legal arrangement or under a system of no fault liability for out-of-pocket expenses. His proposal seems to provide an effective, market oriented device for minimizing transactions costs in a wide range of accident situations. It will undoubtedly be widely discussed in the future.

The final article in this section, by Professor Komesar (19), makes a singularly important point about the relationship of law and economics in personal injury fields. He suggests that, on balance, the rules of liability discussed in the prior articles in this section are quite apt to be less important than the rules for computing the *amount* of recoveries. Professor Komesar reminds us that until quite recently legal scholars were almost exclusively concerned with the rules of liability, largely perhaps because damage issues were difficult for lawyers to conceptualize and because the economics literature provided little assistance or direction.

However, all of that has begun to change, Professor Komesar suggests, under the influence of imaginative new economic theories associated mainly with the name of Gary Becker. Sophisticated consideration of measurement issues by law-economic scholars still lags behind that addressing itself to the abstract liability rules. But it is a safe prediction that attention in the future will focus more and more on this aspect of the total picture.

It would not have been remiss to have included in this same Part II a section dealing with the economics of crime and criminal laws. However space considerations dictated the deletion of even the two works with which any interested reader is recommended to begin that subject. The first is G. Stigler, "The Optimum Enforcement of Laws," 78 *J.Pol.Econ.* 526 (1970); and the second is G. Becker and G. Stigler, "Law Enforcement, Malfeasance, and Compensation of Enforcers," 3 *J.Legal Studies* 1 (1974). The latter piece especially is full of the kind of intellectual surprises that are creating such excitement and interest for interdisciplinary legal and economics scholars today.

B Non-Contractual Liability Rules— The Theory

9: THE PROBLEM OF SOCIAL COST

R. H. COASE

I. The Problem to Be Examined [1]

This paper is concerned with those actions of business firms which have harmful effects on others. The standard example is that of a factory the smoke from which has harmful effects on those occupying neighbouring properties. The economic analysis of such a situation has usually proceeded in terms of a divergence between the private and social product of the factory, in which economists have largely followed the treatment of Pigou in *The Economics of Welfare*. The conclusions to which this kind of analysis seems to have led most economists is that it would be desirable to make the owner of the factory liable for the damage caused to those injured by the smoke, or alternatively, to place a tax on the factory owner varying with the amount of smoke produced and equivalent in money terms to the damage it would cause, or finally, to exclude the factory from residential districts (and presumably from other areas in which the emission of smoke would have harmful effects on others). It is my contention that the suggested courses of action are inappropriate, in that they lead to results which are not necessarily, or even usually, desirable.

II. The Reciprocal Nature of the Problem

The traditional approach has tended to obscure the nature of the choice that has to be made. The question is commonly thought of as one in which A inflicts harm on B and what has to be decided is: how should we re-

The Journal of Law & Economics, Volume III, October 1960, pp. 1–44.

strain A? But this is wrong. We are dealing with a problem of a reciprocal nature. To avoid the harm to B would inflict harm on A. The real
question that has to be decided is: should A be allowed to harm B or should
B be allowed to harm A? The problem is to avoid the more serious harm.
I instanced in my previous article [2] the case of a confectioner the noise and
vibrations from whose machinery disturbed a doctor in his work. To
avoid harming the doctor would inflict harm on the confectioner. The
problem posed by this case was essentially whether it was worth while, as
a result of restricting the methods of production which could be used by
the confectioner, to secure more doctoring at the cost of a reduced supply
of confectionery products. Another example is afforded by the problem
of straying cattle which destroy crops on neighbouring land. If it is inevitable that some cattle will stray, an increase in the supply of meat can
only be obtained at the expense of a decrease in the supply of crops. The
nature of the choice is clear: meat or crops. What answer should be given
is, of course, not clear unless we know the value of what is obtained as well
as the value of what is sacrificed to obtain it. To give another example,
Professor George J. Stigler instances the contamination of a stream.[3] If
we assume that the harmful effect of the pollution is that it kills the fish,
the question to be decided is: is the value of the fish lost greater or less
than the value of the product which the contamination of the stream makes
possible. It goes almost without saying that this problem has to be looked
at in total *and* at the margin.

III.   The Pricing System with Liability for Damage

I propose to start my analysis by examining a case in which most economists would presumably agree that the problem would be solved in a completely satisfactory manner: when the damaging business has to pay for
all damage caused *and* the pricing system works smoothly (strictly this
means that the operation of a pricing system is without cost).

A good example of the problem under discussion is afforded by the
case of straying cattle which destroy crops growing on neighbouring land.
Let us suppose that a farmer and a cattle-raiser are operating on neighbouring properties. Let us further suppose that, without any fencing between the properties, an increase in the size of the cattle-raiser's herd increases the total damage to the farmer's crops. What happens to the marginal damage as the size of the herd increases is another matter. This depends on whether the cattle tend to follow one another or to roam side by
side, on whether they tend to be more or less restless as the size of the herd
increases and on other similar factors. For my immediate purpose, it is
immaterial what assumption is made about marginal damage as the size
of the herd increases.

To simplify the argument, I propose to use an arithmetical example. I shall assume that the annual cost of fencing the farmer's property is $9 and that the price of the crop is $1 per ton. Also, I assume that the relation between the number of cattle in the herd and the annual crop loss is as follows:

Number in Herd (Steers)	Annual Crop Loss (Tons)	Crop Loss per Additional Steer (Tons)
1	1	1
2	3	2
3	6	3
4	10	4

Given that the cattle-raiser is liable for the damage caused, the additional annual cost imposed on the cattle-raiser if he increased his herd from, say, 2 to 3 steers is $3 and in deciding on the size of the herd, he will take this into account along with his other costs. That is, he will not increase the size of the herd unless the value of the additional meat produced (assuming that the cattle-raiser slaughters the cattle), is greater than the additional costs that this will entail, including the value of the additional crops destroyed. Of course, if, by the employment of dogs, herdsmen, aeroplanes, mobile radio and other means, the amount of damage can be reduced, these means will be adopted when their cost is less than the value of the crop which they prevent being lost. Given that the annual cost of fencing is $9, the cattle-raiser who wished to have a herd with 4 steers or more would pay for fencing to be erected and maintained, assuming that other means of attaining the same end would not do so more cheaply. When the fence is erected, the marginal cost due to the liability for damage becomes zero, except to the extent that an increase in the size of the herd necessitates a stronger and therefore more expensive fence because more steers are liable to lean against it at the same time. But, of course, it may be cheaper for the cattle-raiser not to fence and to pay for the damaged crops, as in my arithmetical example, with 3 or fewer steers.

It might be thought that the fact that the cattle-raiser would pay for all crops damaged would lead the farmer to increase his planting if a cattle-raiser came to occupy the neighbouring property. But this is not so. If the crop was previously sold in conditions of perfect competition, marginal cost was equal to price for the amount of planting undertaken and any expansion would have reduced the profits of the farmer. In the new situation, the existence of crop damage would mean that the farmer would sell less on the open market but his receipts for a given production would remain the same, since the cattle-raiser would pay the market price for any crop damaged. Of course, if cattle-raising commonly involved the destruction of crops, the coming into existence of a cattle-raising industry might raise the price of the crops involved and farmers would then extend their planting. But I wish to confine my attention to the individual farmer.

I have said that the occupation of a neighbouring property by a cattle-raiser would not cause the amount of production, or perhaps more exactly the amount of planting, by the farmer to increase. In fact, if the cattle-raising has any effect, it will be to decrease the amount of planting. The reason for this is that, for any given tract of land, if the value of the crop damaged is so great that the receipts from the sale of the undamaged crop are less than the total costs of cultivating that tract of land, it will be profitable for the farmer and the cattle-raiser to make a bargain whereby that tract of land is left uncultivated. This can be made clear by means of an arithmetical example. Assume initially that the value of the crop obtained from cultivating a given tract of land is $12 and that the cost incurred in cultivating this tract of land is $10, the net gain from cultivating the land being $2. I assume for purposes of simplicity that the farmer owns the land. Now assume that the cattle-raiser starts operations on the neighbouring property and that the value of the crops damaged is $1. In this case $11 is obtained by the farmer from sale on the market and $1 is obtained from the cattle-raiser for damage suffered and the net gain remains $2. Now suppose that the cattle-raiser finds it profitable to increase the size of his herd, even though the amount of damage rises to $3; which means that the value of the additional meat production is greater than the additional costs, including the additional $2 payment for damage. But the total payment for damage is now $3. The net gain to the farmer from cultivating the land is still $2. The cattle-raiser would be better off if the farmer would agree not to cultivate his land for any payment less than $3. The farmer would be agreeable to not cultivating the land for any payment greater than $2. There is clearly room for a mutually satisfactory bargain which would lead to the abandonment of cultivation.[4] But the same argument applies not only to the whole tract cultivated by the farmer but also to any subdivision of it. Suppose, for example, that the cattle have a well-defined route, say, to a brook or to a shady area. In these circumstances, the amount of damage to the crop along the route may well be great and if so, it could be that the farmer and the cattle-raiser would find it profitable to make a bargain whereby the farmer would agree not to cultivate this strip of land.

But this raises a further possibility. Suppose that there is such a well-defined route. Suppose further that the value of the crop that would be obtained by cultivating this strip of land is $10 but that the cost of cultivation is $11. In the absence of the cattle-raiser, the land would not be cultivated. However, given the presence of the cattle-raiser, it could well be that if the strip was cultivated, the whole crop would be destroyed by the cattle. In which case, the cattle-raiser would be forced to pay $10 to the farmer. It is true that the farmer would lose $1. But the cattle-raiser would lose $10. Clearly this is a situation which is not likely to last indefinitely since neither party would want this to happen. The aim of the farmer would be to induce the cattle-raiser to make a payment in return for an agreement to leave this land uncultivated. The farmer would not be able to obtain a payment greater than the cost of fencing off this piece of land nor so high as to lead the cattle-raiser to abandon the use of the neighbouring property. What payment would in fact be made would depend on the shrewdness of the farmer and the cattle-raiser as bargainers. But as the payment would not be so high as to cause the cattle-raiser to abandon this location and as it would not vary with the size of the herd, such an agreement would not affect the allocation of resources but would merely alter the distribution of income and wealth as between the cattle-raiser and the farmer.

I think it is clear that if the cattle-raiser is liable for damage caused and the pricing system works smoothly, the reduction in the value of production elsewhere will be taken into account in computing the additional cost involved in increasing the size of the herd. This cost will be weighed against the value of the additional meat production and, given perfect competition in the cattle industry, the allocation of resources in cattle-raising will be optimal. What needs to be emphasized is that the fall in the value of production elsewhere which would be taken into account in the costs of the cattle-raiser may well be less than the damage which the cattle would cause to the crops in the ordinary course of events. This is because it is possible, as a result of market transactions, to discontinue cultivation of the land. This is desirable in all cases in which the damage that the cattle would cause, and for which the cattle-raiser would be willing to pay, exceeds the amount which the farmer would pay for use of the land. In conditions of perfect competition, the amount which the farmer would pay for the use of the land is equal to the difference between the value of the total production when the factors are employed on this land and the value of the additional product yielded in their next best use (which would be what the farmer would have to pay for the factors). If damage exceeds the amount the farmer would pay for the use of the land, the value of the additional product of the factors employed elsewhere would exceed the value of the total product in this use after damage is taken into account. It follows that it would be desirable to abandon cultivation of the land and to release the factors employed for production elsewhere. A procedure which merely provided for payment for damage to the crop caused by the cattle but which did not allow for the possibility of cultivation being discontinued would result in too small an employment of factors of production in cattle-raising and too large an employment of factors in cultivation of the crop. But given the possibility of market transactions, a situation in which damage to crops exceeded the rent of the land would not endure. Whether the cattle-raiser pays the farmer to leave the land uncultivated or himself rents the land by paying the land-owner an amount slightly greater than the farmer would pay (if the farmer was himself renting the land), the final result would be the same and would maximise the value of production. Even when the farmer is induced to plant crops which it would not be profitable to cultivate for sale on the market, this will be a purely short-term phenomenon and may be expected to lead to an agreement under which the planting will cease. The cattle-raiser will remain in that location and the marginal cost of meat production will be the same as before, thus having no long-run effect on the allocation of resources.

IV.   The Pricing System with No Liability for Damage

I now turn to the case in which, although the pricing system is assumed to work smoothly (that is, costlessly), the damaging business is not liable for any of the damage which it causes. This business does not have to make a payment to those damaged by its actions. I propose to show that the allocation of resources will be the same in this case as it was when the damaging business was liable for damage caused. As I showed in the previous case that the allocation of resources was optimal, it will not be necessary to repeat this part of the argument.

I return to the case of the farmer and the cattle-raiser. The farmer would suffer increased damage to his crop as the size of the herd increased. Suppose that the size of the cattle-raiser's herd is 3 steers (and that this is the size of the herd that would be maintained if crop damage was not taken into account). Then the farmer would be willing to pay up to $3 if the cattle-raiser would reduce his herd to 2 steers, up to $5 if the herd were reduced to 1 steer and would pay up to $6 if cattle-raising was abandoned. The cattle-raiser would therefore receive $3 from the farmer if he kept 2 steers instead of 3. This $3 foregone is therefore part of the cost incurred in keeping the third steer. Whether the $3 is a payment which the cattle-raiser has to make if he adds the third steer to his herd (which it would be if the cattle-raiser was liable to the farmer for damage caused to the crop) or whether it is a sum of money which he would have received if he did not keep a third steer (which it would be if the cattle-raiser was not liable to the farmer for damage caused to the crop) does not affect the final result. In both cases $3 is part of the cost of adding a third steer, to be included along with the other costs. If the increase in the value of production in cattle-raising through increasing the size of the herd from 2 to 3 is greater than the additional costs that have to be incurred (including the $3 damage to crops), the size of the herd will be increased. Otherwise, it will not. The size of the herd will be the same whether the cattle-raiser is liable for damage caused to the crop or not.

It may be argued that the assumed starting point—a herd of 3 steers —was arbitrary. And this is true. But the farmer would not wish to pay to avoid crop damage which the cattle-raiser would not be able to cause. For example, the maximum annual payment which the farmer could be induced to pay could not exceed $9, the annual cost of fencing. And the farmer would only be willing to pay this sum if it did not reduce his earnings to a level that would cause him to abandon cultivation of this particular tract of land. Furthermore, the farmer would only be willing to pay this amount if he believed that, in the absence of any payment by him, the size of the herd maintained by the cattle-raiser would be 4 or more steers. Let us assume that this is the case. Then the farmer would be willing to pay up to $3 if the cattle-raiser would reduce his herd to 3 steers, up to $6 if the herd were reduced to 2 steers, up to $8 if one steer only were kept and up to $9 if cattle-raising were abandoned. It will be noticed that the change in the starting point has not altered the amount which would accrue to the cattle-raiser if he reduced the size of his herd by any given amount. It is still true that the cattle-raiser could receive an additional $3 from the farmer if he agreed to reduce his herd from 3 steers to 2 and that the $3 represents the value of the crop that would be destroyed by adding the third steer to the herd. Although a different belief on the part of the farmer (whether justified or not) about the size of the herd that the cattle-raiser would maintain in the absence of payments from him may affect the total payment he can be induced to pay, it is not true that this different belief would have any effect on the size of the herd that the cattle-raiser will actually keep. This will be the same as it would be if the cattle-raiser had to pay for damage caused by his cattle, since a receipt foregone of a given amount is the equivalent of a payment of the same amount.

It might be thought that it would pay the cattle-raiser to increase his herd above the size that he would wish to maintain once a bargain had been made, in order to induce the farmer to make a larger total payment. And this may be true. It is similar in nature to the action of the farmer (when the cattle-raiser was liable for damage) in cultivating land on which, as a result of an agreement with the cattle-raiser, planting would subsequently be abandoned (including land which would not be cultivated at all in the absence of cattle-raising). But such manoeuvres are preliminaries to an agreement and do not affect the long-run equilibrium position, which is the same whether or not the cattle-raiser is held responsible for the crop damage brought about by his cattle.

It is necessary to know whether the damaging business is liable or not for damage caused since without the establishment of this initial delimitation of rights there can be no market transactions to transfer and recombine them. But the ultimate result (which maximises the value of production) is independent of the legal position if the pricing system is assumed to work without cost.

V.   The Problem Illustrated Anew

The harmful effects of the activities of a business can assume a wide variety of forms. An early English case concerned a building which, by obstructing currents of air, hindered the operation of a windmill.[5] A recent case in Florida concerned a building which cast a shadow on the cabana, swimming pool and sunbathing areas of a neighbouring hotel.[6] The problem of straying cattle and the damaging of crops which was the subject of detailed examination in the two preceding sections, although it may have appeared to be rather a special case, is in fact but one example of a problem which arises in many different guises. To clarify the nature of my argument and to demonstrate its general applicability, I propose to illustrate it anew by reference to four actual cases.

Let us first reconsider the case of *Sturges v. Bridgman*[7] which I used as an illustration of the general problem in my article on "The Federal Communications Commission." In this case, a confectioner (in Wigmore Street) used two mortars and pestles in connection with his business (one had been in operation in the same position for more than 60 years and the other for more than 26 years). A doctor then came to occupy neighbouring premises (in Wimpole Street). The confectioner's machinery caused the doctor no harm until, eight years after he had first occupied the premises, he built a consulting room at the end of his garden right against the confectioner's kitchen. It was then found that the noise and vibration caused by the confectioner's machinery made it difficult for the doctor to use his new consulting room. "In particular . . . the noise prevented him from examining his patients by auscultation[8] for diseases of the chest. He also found it impossible to engage with effect in any occupation which required thought and attention." The doctor therefore brought a legal action to force the confectioner to stop using his machinery. The courts had little difficulty in granting the doctor the injunction he sought. "Individual cases of hardship may occur in the strict carrying out of the principle upon which we found our judgment, but the negation of the principle would lead even more to individual hardship, and would at the same time produce a prejudicial effect upon the development of land for residential purposes."

The court's decision established that the doctor had the right to prevent the confectioner from using his machinery. But, of course, it would have been possible to modify the arrangements envisaged in the legal ruling by means of a bargain between the parties. The doctor would have been willing to waive his right and allow the machinery to continue in operation if the confectioner would have paid him a sum of money which was greater than the loss of income which he would suffer from having to move to a more costly or less convenient location or from having to curtail his activities at this location or, as was suggested as a possibility, from having to build a separate wall which would deaden the noise and vibration. The confectioner would have been willing to do this if the amount he would have to pay the doctor was less than the fall in income he would suffer if he had to change his mode of operation at this location, abandon his operation or move his confectionery business to some other location. The solution of the problem depends essentially on whether the continued use of the machinery adds more to the confectioner's income than it subtracts from the doctor's.[9] But now consider the situation if the confectioner had won the case. The confectioner would then have had the right to continue operating his noise and vibration-generating machinery without having to pay anything to the doctor. The boot would have been on the other foot: the doctor would have had to pay the confectioner to induce him to stop using the machinery. If the doctor's income would have fallen more through continuance of the use of this machinery than it added to the income of the confectioner, there would clearly be room for a bargain whereby the doctor paid the confectioner to stop using the machinery. That is to say, the circumstances in which it would not pay the confectioner to continue to use the machinery and to compensate the doctor for the losses that this would bring (if the doctor had the right to prevent the confectioner's using his machinery) would be those in which it would be in the interest of the doctor to make a payment to the confectioner which would induce him to discontinue the use of the machinery (if the confectioner had the right to operate the machinery). The basic conditions are exactly the same in this case as they were in the example of the cattle which destroyed crops. With costless market transactions, the decision of the courts concerning liability for damage would be without effect on the allocation of resources. It was of course the view of the judges that they were affecting the working of the economic system—and in a desirable direction. Any other decision would have had "a prejudicial effect upon the development of land for residential purposes," an argument which was elaborated by examining the example of a forge operating on a barren moor, which was later developed for residual purposes. The judges' view that they were settling how the land was to be used would be true only in the case in which the costs of carrying out the necessary market transactions exceeded the gain which might be achieved by any rearrangement of rights. And it would be desirable to preserve the areas (Wimpole Street or the moor) for residential or professional use (by giving non-industrial users the right to stop the noise, vibration, smoke, etc., by injunction) only if the value of the additional residential facilities obtained was greater than the value of cakes or iron lost. But of this the judges seem to have been unaware.

Another example of the same problem is furnished by the case of *Cooke v. Forbes*.[10] One process in the weaving of cocoa-nut fibre matting was to immerse it in bleaching liquids after which it was hung out to dry. Fumes from a manufacturer of sulphate of ammonia had the effect of turning the matting from a bright to a dull and blackish colour. The reason for this was that the bleaching liquid contained chloride of tin, which, when affected by sulphuretted hydrogen, is turned to a darker colour. An injunction was sought to stop the manufacturer from emitting the fumes. The lawyers for the defendant argued that if the plaintiff "were not to use . . . a particular bleaching liquid, their fibre would not be affected; that their process is unusual, not according to the custom of the trade, and even damaging to their own fabrics." The judge commented: " . . . it appears to me quite plain that a person has a right to carry on upon his own property a manufacturing process in which he uses chloride of tin, or any sort of metallic dye, and that his neighbour is not at liberty to pour in gas which will interfere with his manufacture. If it can be traced to the neighbour, then, I apprehend, clearly he will have a right to come here and ask for relief." But in view of the fact that the damage was accidental and occasional, that careful precautions were taken and that there was no exceptional risk, an injunction was refused, leaving the plaintiff to bring an action for damages if he wished. What the subsequent developments were I do not know. But it is clear that the situation is essentially the same as that found in *Sturges v. Bridgman*, except that the cocoa-nut fibre matting manufacturer could not secure an injunction but would have to seek damages from the sulphate of ammonia manufacturer. The economic analysis of the situation is exactly the same as with the cattle which destroyed crops. To avoid the damage, the sulphate of ammonia manufacturer could increase his precautions or move to another location. Either course would presumably increase his costs. Alternatively he could pay for the damage. This he would do if the payments for damage were less than the additional costs that would have to be incurred to avoid the damage. The payments for damage would then become part of the cost of production of sulphate of ammonia. Of course, if, as was suggested in the legal proceedings, the amount of damage could be eliminated by changing the bleaching agent (which would presumably increase the costs of the matting manufacturer) and if the additional cost was less than the damage that would otherwise occur, it should be possible for the two manufacturers to make a mutually satisfactory bargain whereby the new bleaching agent was used. Had the court decided against the matting manufacturer, as a consequence of which he would have had to suffer the damage without compensation, the allocation of resources would not have been affected.

It would pay the matting manufacturer to change his bleaching agent if the additional cost involved was less than the reduction in damage. And since the matting manufacturer would be willing to pay the sulphate of ammonia manufacturer an amount up to his loss of income (the increase in costs or the damage suffered) if he would cease his activities, this loss of income would remain a cost of production for the manufacturer of sulphate of ammonia. This case is indeed analytically exactly the same as the cattle example.

Bryant v. Lefever [11] raised the problem of the smoke nuisance in a novel form. The plaintiff and the defendants were occupiers of adjoining houses, which were of about the same height.

> Before 1876 the plaintiff was able to light a fire in any room of his house without the chimneys smoking; the two houses had remained in the same condition some thirty or forty years. In 1876 the defendants took down their house, and began to rebuild it. They carried up a wall by the side of the plaintiff's chimneys much beyond its original height, and stacked timber on the roof of their house, and thereby caused the plaintiff's chimneys to smoke whenever he lighted fires.

The reason, of course, why the chimneys smoked was that the erection of the wall and the stacking of the timber prevented the free circulation of air. In a trial before a jury, the plaintiff was awarded damages of £40. The case then went to the Court of Appeals where the judgment was reversed. Bramwell, L. J., argued:

> .   .   .   it is said, and the jury have found, that the defendants have done that which caused a nuisance to the plaintiff's house. We think there is no evidence of this. No doubt there is a nuisance, but it is not of the defendant's causing. They have done nothing in causing the nuisance. Their house and their timber are harmless enough. It is the plaintiff who causes the nuisance by lighting a coal fire in a place the chimney of which is placed so near the defendants' wall, that the smoke does not escape, but comes into the house. Let the plaintiff cease to light his fire, let him move his chimney, let him carry it higher, and there would be no nuisance. Who then, causes it? It would be very clear that the plaintiff did, if he had built his house or chimney after the defendants had put up the timber on theirs, and it is really the same though he did so before the timber was there. But (what is in truth the same answer), if the defendants cause the nuisance, they have a right to do so. If the plaintiff has not the right to the passage of air, except subject to the defendants' right to build or put timber on their house, then his right is subject to their right, and though a nuisance follows from the exercise of their right, they are not liable.

And Cotton, L. J., said:

> Here it is found that the erection of the defendants' wall has sensibly and materially interfered with the comfort of human existence in the

plaintiff's house, and it is said this is a nuisance for which the defendants are liable. Ordinarily this is so, but the defendants have done so, not by sending on to the plaintiff's property any smoke or noxious vapour, but by interrupting the egress of smoke from the plaintiff's house in a way to which . . . the plaintiff has no legal right. The plaintiff creates the smoke, which interferes with his comfort. Unless he has . . . a right to get rid of this in a particular way which has been interfered with by the defendants, he cannot sue the defendants, because the smoke made by himself, for which he has not provided any effectual means of escape, causes him annoyance. It is as if a man tried to get rid of liquid filth arising on his own land by a drain into his neighbour's land. Until a right had been acquired by user, the neighbour might stop the drain without incurring liability by so doing. No doubt great inconvenience would be caused to the owner of the property on which the liquid filth arises. But the act of his neighbour would be a lawful act, and he would not be liable for the consequences attributable to the fact that the man had accumulated filth without providing any effectual means of getting rid of it.

I do not propose to show that any subsequent modification of the situation, as a result of bargains between the parties (conditioned by the cost of stacking the timber elsewhere, the cost of extending the chimney higher, etc.), would have exactly the same result whatever decision the courts had come to since this point has already been adequately dealt with in the discussion of the cattle example and the two previous cases. What I shall discuss is the argument of the judges in the Court of Appeals that the smoke nuisance was not caused by the man who erected the wall but by the man who lit the fires. The novelty of the situation is that the smoke nuisance was suffered by the man who lit the fires and not by some third person. The question is not a trivial one since it lies at the heart of the problem under discussion. Who caused the smoke nuisance? The answer seems fairly clear. The smoke nuisance was caused both by the man who built the wall *and* by the man who lit the fires. Given the fires, there would have been no smoke nuisance without the wall; given the wall, there would have been no smoke nuisance without the fires. Eliminate the wall *or* the fires and the smoke nuisance would disappear. On the marginal principle it is clear that *both* were responsible and *both* should be forced to include the loss of amenity due to the smoke as a cost in deciding whether to continue the activity which gives rise to the smoke. And given the possibility of market transactions, this is what would in fact happen. Although the wall-builder was not liable legally for the nuisance, as the man with the smoking chimneys would presumably be willing to pay a sum equal to the monetary worth to him of eliminating the smoke, this sum would therefore become for the wall-builder, a cost of continuing to have the high wall with the timber stacked on the roof.

The judges' contention that it was the man who lit the fires who alone caused the smoke nuisance is true only if we assume that the wall is the given factor. This is what the judges did by deciding that the man who erected the higher wall had a legal right to do so. The case would have been even more interesting if the smoke from the chimneys had injured the timber. Then it would have been the wall-builder who suffered the damage. The case would then have closely paralleled *Sturges v. Bridgman* and there can be little doubt that the man who lit the fires would have been liable for the ensuing damage to the timber, in spite of the fact that no damage had occurred until the high wall was built by the man who owned the timber.

Judges have to decide on legal liability but this should not confuse economists about the nature of the economic problem involved. In the case of the cattle and the crops, it is true that there would be no crop damage without the cattle. It is equally true that there would be no crop damage without the crops. The doctor's work would not have been disturbed if the confectioner had not worked his machinery; but the machinery would have disturbed no one if the doctor had not set up his consulting room in that particular place. The matting was blackened by the fumes from the sulphate of ammonia manufacturer; but no damage would have occurred if the matting manufacturer had not chosen to hang out his matting in a particular place and to use a particular bleaching agent. If we are to discuss the problem in terms of causation, both parties cause the damage. If we are to attain an optimum allocation of resources, it is therefore desirable that both parties should take the harmful effect (the nuisance) into account in deciding on their course of action. It is one of the beauties of a smoothly operating pricing system that, as has already been explained, the fall in the value of production due to the harmful effect would be a cost for both parties.

Bass v. Gregory [12] will serve as an excellent final illustration of the problem. The plaintiffs were the owners and tenant of a public house called the Jolly Anglers. The defendant was the owner of some cottages and a yard adjoining the Jolly Anglers. Under the public house was a cellar excavated in the rock. From the cellar, a hole or shaft had been cut into an old well situated in the defendant's yard. The well therefore became the ventilating shaft for the cellar. The cellar "had been used for a particular purpose in the process of brewing, which, without ventilation, could not be carried on." The cause of the action was that the defendant removed a grating from the mouth of the well, "so as to stop or prevent the free passage of air from [the] cellar upwards through the well. . . ." What caused the defendant to take this step is not clear from the report of the case. Perhaps "the air . . . impregnated by the brewing operations" which "passed up the well and out into the open air" was offensive to him. At any rate, he preferred to have the well in his yard stopped up. The court had first to determine whether the owners of the public house could have a legal right to a current of air. If they were to have such a right, this case would have to be distinguished from *Bryant v. Lefever* (already considered). This, however, presented no difficulty. In this case, the current of air was confined to "a strictly defined channel." In the case of *Bryant v. Lefever*, what was involved was "the general current of air common to all mankind." The judge therefore held that the owners of the public house could have the right to a current of air whereas the owner of the private house in *Bryant v. Lefever* could not. An economist might be tempted to add "but the air moved all the same." However, all that had been decided at this stage of the argument was that there could be a legal right, not that the owners of the public house possessed it. But evidence showed that the shaft from the cellar to the well had existed for over forty years and that the use of the well as a ventilating shaft must have been known to the owners of the yard since the air, when it emerged, smelt of the brewing operations. The judge therefore held that the public house had such a right by the "doctrine of lost grant." This doctrine states "that if a legal right is proved to have existed and been exercised for a number of years the law ought to presume that it had a legal origin." [13] So the owner of the cottages and yard had to unstop the well and endure the smell.

The reasoning employed by the courts in determining legal rights will often seem strange to an economist because many of the factors on which the decision turns are, to an economist, irrelevant. Because of this, situations which are, from an economic point of view, identical will be treated quite differently by the courts. The economic problem in all cases of harmful effects is how to maximise the value of production. In the case of *Bass v. Gregory* fresh air was drawn in through the well which facilitated the production of beer but foul air was expelled through the well which made life in the adjoining houses less pleasant. The economic problem was to decide which to choose: a lower cost of beer and worsened amenities in adjoining houses or a higher cost of beer and improved amenities. In deciding this question, the "doctrine of lost grant" is about as relevant as the colour of the judge's eyes. But it has to be remembered that the immediate question faced by the courts is *not* what shall be done by whom *but* who has the legal right to do what. It is always possible to modify by transactions on the market the initial legal delimitation of rights. And, of course, if such market transactions are costless, such a rearrangement of rights will always take place if it would lead to an increase in the value of production.

VI. The Cost of Market Transactions Taken into Account

The argument has proceeded up to this point on the assumption (explicit in Sections III and IV and tacit in Section V) that there were no costs involved in carrying out market transactions. This is, of course, a very unrealistic assumption. In order to carry out a market transaction it is necessary to discover who it is that one wishes to deal with, to inform people that one wishes to deal and on what terms, to conduct negotiations leading up to a bargain, to draw up the contract, to undertake the inspection needed to make sure that the terms of the contract are being observed, and so on. These operations are often extremely costly, sufficiently costly at any rate to prevent many transactions that would be carried out in a world in which the pricing system worked without cost.

In earlier sections, when dealing with the problem of the rearrangement of legal rights through the market, it was argued that such a rearrangement would be made through the market whenever this would lead to an increase in the value of production. But this assumed costless market transactions. Once the costs of carrying out market transactions are taken into account it is clear that such a rearrangement of rights will only be undertaken when the increase in the value of production consequent upon the rearrangement is greater than the costs which would be involved in bringing it about. When it is less, the granting of an injunction (or the knowledge that it would be granted) or the liability to pay damages may result in an activity being discontinued (or may prevent its being started) which would be undertaken if market transactions were costless. In these conditions the initial delimitation of legal rights does have an effect on the efficiency with which the economic system operates. One arrangement of rights may bring about a greater value of production than any other. But unless this is the arrangement of rights established by the legal system, the costs of reaching the same result by altering and combining rights through the market may be so great that this optimal arrangement of rights, and the greater value of production which it would bring, may never be achieved. The part played by economic considerations in the process of delimiting legal rights will be discussed in the next section. In this section, I will take the initial delimitation of rights and the costs of carrying out market transactions as given.

It is clear that an alternative form of economic organisation which could achieve the same result at less cost than would be incurred by using the market would enable the value of production to be raised. As I explained many years ago, the firm represents such an alternative to organising production through market transactions.[14] Within the firm individual bargains between the various cooperating factors of production are eliminated and for a market transaction is substituted an administrative decision. The rearrangement of production then takes place without the need for bargains between the owners of the factors of production. A landowner who has control of a large tract of land may devote his land to various uses taking into account the effect that the interrelations of the various activities will have on the net return of the land, thus rendering unnecessary bargains between those undertaking the various activities. Owners of a large building or of several adjoining properties in a given area may act in much the same way. In effect, using our earlier terminology, the firm would acquire the legal rights of all the parties and the rearrangement of activities would not follow on a rearrangement of rights by contract, but as a result of an administrative decision as to how the rights should be used.

It does not, of course, follow that the administrative costs of organising a transaction through a firm are inevitably less than the costs of the market transactions which are superseded. But where contracts are peculiarly difficult to draw up and an attempt to describe what the parties have agreed to do or not to do (e. g. the amount and kind of a smell or noise that they may make or will not make) would necessitate a lengthy and highly involved document, and, where, as is probable, a long-term contract would be desirable; [15] it would be hardly surprising if the emergence of a firm or the extension of the activities of an existing firm was not the solution adopted on many occasions to deal with the problem of harmful effects. This solution would be adopted whenever the administrative costs of the firm were less than the costs of the market transactions that it supersedes and the gains which would result from the rearrangement of activities greater than the firm's costs of organising them. I do not need to examine in great detail the character of this solution since I have explained what is involved in my earlier article.

But the firm is not the only possible answer to this problem. The administrative costs of organising transactions within the firm may also be high, and particularly so when many diverse activities are brought within the control of a single organisation. In the standard case of a smoke nuisance, which may affect a vast number of people engaged in a wide variety of activities, the administrative costs might well be so high as to make any attempt to deal with the problem within the confines of a single firm impossible. An alternative solution is direct Government regulation. Instead of instituting a legal system of rights which can be modified by transactions on the market, the government may impose regulations which state what people must or must not do and which have to be obeyed. Thus, the government (by statute or perhaps more likely through an administrative agency) may, to deal with the problem of smoke nuisance, decree that certain methods of production should or should not be used (e. g. that smoke preventing devices should be installed or that coal or oil should not be burned) or may confine certain types of business to certain districts (zoning regulations).

The government is, in a sense, a super-firm (but of a very special kind) since it is able to influence the use of factors of production by administrative decision. But the ordinary firm is subject to checks in its operations because of the competition of other firms, which might administer, the same activities at lower cost and also because there is always the alternative of market transactions as against organisation within the firm if the administrative costs become too great. The government is able, if it wishes, to avoid the market altogether, which a firm can never do. The firm has to make market agreements with the owners of the factors of production that it uses. Just as the government can conscript or seize property, so it can decree that factors of production should only be used in such-and-such a way. Such authoritarian methods save a lot of trouble (for those doing the organising). Furthermore, the government has at its disposal the police and the other law enforcement agencies to make sure that its regulations are carried out.

It is clear that the government has powers which might enable it to get some things done at a lower cost than could a private organisation (or at any rate one without special governmental powers). But the governmental administrative machine is not itself costless. It can, in fact, on occasion be extremely costly. Furthermore, there is no reason to suppose that the restrictive and zoning regulations, made by a fallible administration subject to political pressures and operating without any competitive check, will necessarily always be those which increase the efficiency with which the economic system operates. Furthermore, such general regulations which must apply to a wide variety of cases will be enforced in some cases in which they are clearly inappropriate. From these considerations it follows that direct governmental regulation will not necessarily give better results than leaving the problem to be solved by the market or the firm. But equally there is no reason why, on occasion, such governmental administrative regulation should not lead to an improvement in economic efficiency. This would seem particularly likely when, as is normally the case with the smoke nuisance, a large number of people are involved and in which therefore the costs of handling the problem through the market or the firm may be high.

There is, of course, a further alternative, which is to do nothing about the problem at all. And given that the costs involved in solving the problem by regulations issued by the governmental administrative machine will often be heavy (particularly if the costs are interpreted to include all the consequences which follow from the Government engaging in this kind of activity), it will no doubt be commonly the case that the gain which would come from regulating the actions which give rise to the harmful effects will be less than the costs involved in Government regulation.

The discussion of the problem of harmful effects in this section (when the costs of market transactions are taken into account) is extremely inadequate. But at least it has made clear that the problem is one of choosing the appropriate social arrangement for dealing with the harmful effects. All solutions have costs and there is no reason to suppose that government regulation is called for simply because the problem is not well handled by the market or the firm. Satisfactory views on policy can only come from a patient study of how, in practice, the market, firms and governments handle the problem of harmful effects. Economists need to study the work of the broker in bringing parties together, the effectiveness of restrictive covenants, the problems of the large-scale real-estate development company, the operation of Government zoning and other regulating activities. It is my belief that economists, and policy-makers generally, have tended to over-estimate the advantages which come from governmental regulation. But this belief, even if justified, does not do more than suggest that government regulation should be curtailed. It does not tell us where the boundary line should be drawn. This, it seems to me, has to come from a detailed investigation of the actual results of handling the problem in different ways. But it would be unfortunate if this investigation were undertaken with the aid of a faulty economic analysis. The aim of this article is to indicate what the economic approach to the problem should be.

VII.   The Legal Delimitation of Rights and the Economic Problem

The discussion in Section V not only served to illustrate the argument but also afforded a glimpse at the legal approach to the problem of harmful effects. The cases considered were all English but a similar selection of American cases could easily be made and the character of the reasoning would have been the same. Of course, if market transactions were costless, all that matters (questions of equity apart) is that the rights of the various parties should be well-defined and the results of legal actions easy to forecast. But as we have seen, the situation is quite different when market transactions are so costly as to make it difficult to change the arrangement of rights established by the law. In such cases, the courts directly influence economic activity. It would therefore seem desirable that the courts should understand the economic consequences of their decisions and should, insofar as this is possible without creating too much uncertainty about the legal position itself, take these consequences into account when making their decisions. Even when it is possible to change the legal delimitation of rights through market transactions, it is obviously desirable to reduce the need for such transactions and thus reduce the employment of resources in carrying them out.

A thorough examination of the presuppositions of the courts in trying such cases would be of great interest but I have not been able to attempt it. Nevertheless it is clear from a cursory study that the courts have often recognized the economic implications of their decisions and are aware (as many economists are not) of the reciprocal nature of the problem. Furthermore, from time to time, they take these economic implications into account, along with other factors, in arriving at their decisions. The American writers on this subject refer to the question in a more explicit fashion than do the British. Thus, to quote Prosser on Torts, a person may

> make use of his own property or . . . conduct his own affairs at the expense of some harm to his neighbors. He may operate a factory whose noise and smoke cause some discomfort to others, so long as he keeps within reasonable bounds. It is only when his conduct is unreasonable, *in the light of its utility and the harm which results* [italics added], that it becomes a nuisance. . . . As it was said in an ancient case in regard to candle-making in a town, "Le utility del chose excusera le noisomeness del stink."

> The world must have factories, smelters, oil refineries, noisy machinery and blasting, even at the expense of some inconvenience to those in the vicinity and the plaintiff may be required to accept some not unreasonable discomfort for the general good.[16]

*   *   *

[Discussion of English cases omitted (ed.).]

The legal position in the United States would seem to be essentially the same as in England, except that the power of the legislatures to authorize what would otherwise be nuisances under the common law, at least without giving compensation to the person harmed, is somewhat more limited, as it is subject to constitutional restrictions.[28] Nonetheless, the power is there and cases more or less identical with the English cases can be found. The question has arisen in an acute form in connection with airports and the operation of aeroplanes. The case of *Delta Air Corporation v. Kersey, Kersey v. City of Atlanta*[29] is a good example. Mr. Kersey bought land and built a house on it. Some years later the City of Atlanta constructed an airport on land immediately adjoining that of Mr. Kersey. It was explained that his property was "a quiet, peaceful and proper location for a home before the airport was built, but dust, noises and low flying of airplanes caused by the operation of the airport have rendered his property unsuitable as a home," a state of affairs which was described in the report of the case with a wealth of distressing detail. The judge first referred to an earlier case, *Thrasher v. City of Atlanta*[30] in which it was noted that the City of Atlanta had been expressly authorized to operate an airport.

> By this franchise aviation was recognised as a lawful business and also as an enterprise affected with a public interest . . . all persons using [the airport] in the manner contemplated by law are within the protection and immunity of the franchise granted by the municipality. An airport is not a nuisance per se, although it might become such from the manner of its construction or operation.

Since aviation was a lawful business affected with a public interest and the construction of the airport was authorized by statute, the judge next referred to *Georgia Railroad and Banking Co. v. Maddox* [31] in which it was said:

> Where a railroad terminal yard is located and its construction authorized, under statutory powers, if it be constructed and operated in a proper manner, it cannot be adjudged a nuisance. Accordingly, injuries and inconveniences to persons residing near such a yard, from noises of locomotives, rumbling of cars, vibrations produced thereby, and smoke, cinders, soot and the like, which result from the ordinary and necessary, therefore proper, use and operation of such a yard, are not nuisances, but are the necessary concomitants of the franchise granted.

In view of this, the judge decided that the noise and dust complained of by Mr. Kersey "may be deemed to be incidental to the proper operation of an airport, and as such they cannot be said to constitute a nuisance." But the complaint against low flying was different:

> . . . can it be said that flights . . . at such a low height [25 to 50 feet above Mr. Kersey's house] as to be imminently dangerous to . . . life and health . . . are a necessary concomitant of an airport? We do not think this question can be answered in the affirmative. No reason appears why the city could not obtain lands of an area [sufficiently large] . . . as not to require such low flights. . . . For the sake of public convenience adjoining-property owners must suffer such inconvenience from noise and dust as result from the usual and proper operation of an airport, but their private rights are entitled to preference in the eyes of the law where the inconvenience is not one demanded by a properly constructed and operated airport.

Of course this assumed that the City of Atlanta could prevent the low flying and continue to operate the airport. The judge therefore added:

> From all that appears, the conditions causing the low flying may be remedied; but if on the trial it should appear that it is indispensable to the public interest that the airport should continue to be operated in its present condition, it may be said that the petitioner should be denied injunctive relief.

In the course of another aviation case, *Smith v. New England Aircraft Co.*,[32] the court surveyed the law in the United States regarding the legalizing of nuisances and it is apparent that, in the broad, it is very similar to that found in England:

> It is the proper function of the legislative department of government in the exercise of the police power to consider the problems and risks that arise from the use of new inventions and endeavor to adjust private rights and harmonize conflicting interests by comprehensive statutes for the public welfare. . . . There are . . . analogies where the invasion of the airspace over underlying land by noise, smoke, vibration, dust and disagreeable odors, having been authorized by the legislative department of government and not being in effect a condemnation of the property although in some measure depreciating its market value, must be borne by the landowner without compensation or remedy. Legislative sanction makes that lawful which otherwise might be a nuisance. Examples of this are damages to adjacent land arising from smoke, vibration and noise in the operation of a railroad . . . ; the noise of ringing factory bells . . . ; the abatement of nuisances . . . ; the erection of steam engines and furnaces . . . ; unpleasant odors connected with sewers, oil refining and storage of naphtha. . . .

Most economists seem to be unaware of all this. When they are prevented from sleeping at night by the roar of jet planes overhead (publicly authorized and perhaps publicly operated), are unable to think (or rest) in the day because of the noise and vibration from passing trains (publicly authorized and perhaps publicly operated), find it difficult to breathe because of the odour from a local sewage farm (publicly authorized and perhaps publicly operated) and are unable to escape because their driveways are blocked by a road obstruction (without any doubt, publicly devised), their nerves frayed and mental balance disturbed, they proceed to declaim about the disadvantages of private enterprise and the need for Government regulation.

While most economists seem to be under a misapprehension concerning the character of the situation with which they are dealing, it is also the case that the activities which they would like to see stopped or curtailed may well be socially justified. It is all a question of weighing up the gains that would accrue from eliminating these harmful effects against the gains that accrue from allowing them to continue. Of course, it is likely that an extension of Government economic activity will often lead to this protection against action for nuisance being pushed further than is desirable. For one thing, the Government is likely to look with a benevolent eye on enterprises which it is itself promoting. For another, it is possible to describe the committing of a nuisance by public enterprise in a much more pleasant way than when the same thing is done by private enterprise. In the words of Lord Justice Sir Alfred Denning:

> . . . the significance of the social revolution of today is that, whereas in the past the balance was much too heavily in favor of the

rights of property and freedom of contract, Parliament has repeatedly intervened so as to give the public good its proper place.[33]

There can be little doubt that the Welfare State is likely to bring an extension of that immunity from liability for damage, which economists have been in the habit of condemning (although they have tended to assume that this immunity was a sign of too little Government intervention in the economic system). For example, in Britain, the powers of local authorities are regarded as being either absolute or conditional. In the first category, the local authority has no discretion in exercising the power conferred on it. "The absolute power may be said to cover all the necessary consequences of its direct operation even if such consequences amount to nuisance." On the other hand, a conditional power may only be exercised in such a way that the consequences do not constitute a nuisance.

> It is the intention of the legislature which determines whether a power is absolute or conditional. . . . [As] there is the possibility that the social policy of the legislature may change from time to time, a power which in one era would be construed as being conditional, might in another era be interpreted as being absolute in order to further the policy of the Welfare State. This point is one which should be borne in mind when considering some of the older cases upon this aspect of the law of nuisance.[34]

It would seem desirable to summarize the burden of this long section. The problem which we face in dealing with actions which have harmful effects is not simply one of restraining those responsible for them. What has to be decided is whether the gain from preventing the harm is greater than the loss which would be suffered elsewhere as a result of stopping the action which produces the harm. In a world in which there are costs of rearranging the rights established by the legal system, the courts, in cases relating to nuisance, are, in effect, making a decision on the economic problem and determining how resources are to be employed. It was argued that the courts are conscious of this and that they often make, although not always in a very explicit fashion, a comparison between what would be gained and what lost by preventing actions which have harmful effects. But the delimitation of rights is also the result of statutory enactments. Here we also find evidence of an appreciation of the reciprocal nature of the problem. While statutory enactments add to the list of nuisances, action is also taken to legalize what would otherwise be nuisances under the common law. The kind of situation which economists are prone to consider as requiring corrective Government action is, in fact, often the result of Government action. Such action is not necessarily unwise. But there is a real danger that extensive Government intervention in the economic system may lead to the protection of those responsible for harmful effects being carried too far.

VIII.   Pigou's Treatment in "The Economics of Welfare"

The fountainhead for the modern economic analysis of the problem discussed in this article is Pigou's *Economics of Welfare* and, in particular, that section of Part II which deals with divergences between social and private net products which come about because

> one person A, in the course of rendering some service, for which payment is made, to a second person B, incidentally also renders services or disservices to other persons (not producers of like services), of such a sort that payment cannot be exacted from the benefited parties or compensation enforced on behalf of the injured parties.[35]

Pigou tells us that his aim in Part II of *The Economics of Welfare* is

> to ascertain how far the free play of self-interest, acting under the existing legal system, tends to distribute the country's resources in the way most favorable to the production of a large national dividend, and how far it is feasible for State action to improve upon 'natural' tendencies.[36]

To judge from the first part of this statement, Pigou's purpose is to discover whether any improvements could be made in the existing arrangements which determine the use of resources. Since Pigou's conclusion is that improvements could be made, one might have expected him to continue by saying that he proposed to set out the changes required to bring them about. Instead, Pigou adds a phrase which contrasts "natural" tendencies with State action, which seems in some sense to equate the present arrangements with "natural" tendencies and to imply that what is required to bring about these improvements is State action (if feasible). That this is more or less Pigou's position is evident from Chapter I of Part II.[37] Pigou starts by referring to "optimistic followers of the classical economists"[38] who have argued that the value of production would be maximised if the Government refrained from any interference in the economic system and the economic arrangements were those which came about "naturally." Pigou goes on to say that if self-interest does promote economic welfare, it is because human institutions have been devised to make it so. (This part of Pigou's argument, which he develops with the aid of a quotation from Cannan, seems to me to be essentially correct.) Pigou concludes:

> But even in the most advanced States there are failures and imperfections. . . . there are many obstacles that prevent a community's resources from being distributed . . . in the most efficient way. The study of these constitutes our present problem. . . . its purposes is essentially practical. It seeks to bring into clearer light some of the ways in which it now is, or eventually may become, feasible for governments to control the play of economic forces in such wise as to promote

the economic welfare, and through that, the total welfare, of their citizens as a whole.[39]

Pigou's underlying thought would appear to be: Some have argued that no State action is needed. But the system has performed as well as it has because of State action. Nonetheless, there are still imperfections. What additional State action is required?

If this is a correct summary of Pigou's position, its inadequacy can be demonstrated by examining the first example he gives of a divergence between private and social products.

> It might happen . . . that costs are thrown upon people not directly concerned, through, say, uncompensated damage done to surrounding woods by sparks from railway engines. All such effects must be included—some of them will be positive, others negative elements—in reckoning up the social net product of the marginal increment of any volume of resources turned into any use or place.[40]

The example used by Pigou refers to a real situation. In Britain, a railway does not normally have to compensate those who suffer damage by fire caused by sparks from an engine. Taken in conjunction with what he says in Chapter 9 of Part II, I take Pigou's policy recommendations to be, first, that there should be State action to correct this "natural" situation and, second, that the railways should be forced to compensate those whose woods are burnt. If this is a correct interpretation of Pigou's position, I would argue that the first recommendation is based on a misapprehension of the facts and that the second is not necessarily desirable.

Let us consider the legal position. Under the heading "Sparks from engines," we find the following in Halsbury's Laws of England:

> If railway undertakers use steam engines on their railway without express statutory authority to do so, they are liable, irrespective of any negligence on their part, for fires caused by sparks from engines. Railway undertakers are, however, generally given statutory authority to use steam engines on their railway; accordingly, if an engine is constructed with the precautions which science suggests against fire and is used without negligence, they are not responsible at common law for any damage which may be done by sparks. . . . In the construction of an engine the undertaker is bound to use all the discoveries which science has put within its reach in order to avoid doing harm, provided they are such as it is reasonable to require the company to adopt, having proper regard to the likelihood of the damage and to the cost and convenience of the remedy; but it is not negligence on the part of an undertaker if it refuses to use an apparatus the efficiency of which is open to bona fide doubt.

To this general rule, there is a statutory exception arising from the Railway (Fires) Act, 1905, as amended in 1923. This concerns agricultural land or agricultural crops.

In such a case the fact that the engine was used under statutory powers does not affect the liability of the company in an action for the damage. . . . These provisions, however, only apply where the claim for damage . . . does not exceed £ 200, [£ 100 in the 1905 Act] and where written notice of the occurrence of the fire and the intention to claim has been sent to the company within seven days of the occurrence of the damage and particulars of the damage in writing showing the amount of the claim in money not exceeding £ 200 have been sent to the company within twenty-one days.

Agricultural land does not include moorland or buildings and agricultural crops do not include those led away or stacked.[41]   I have not made a close study of the parliamentary history of this statutory exception, but to judge from debates in the House of Commons in 1922 and 1923, this exception was probably designed to help the smallholder.[42]

Let us return to Pigou's example of uncompensated damage to surrounding woods caused by sparks from railway engines. This is presumably intended to show how it is possible "for State action to improve on 'natural' tendencies." If we treat Pigou's example as referring to the position before 1905, or as being an arbitrary example (in that he might just as well have written "surrounding buildings" instead of "surrounding woods"), then it is clear that the reason why compensation was not paid must have been that the railway had statutory authority to run steam engines (which relieved it of liability for fires caused by sparks). That this was the legal position was established in 1860, in a case, oddly enough, which concerned the burning of surrounding woods by a railway,[43] and the law on this point has not been changed (apart from the one exception) by a century of railway legislation, including nationalisation. If we treat Pigou's example of "uncompensated damage done to surrounding woods by sparks from railway engines" literally, and assume that it refers to the period after 1905, then it is clear that the reason why compensation was not paid must have been that the damage was more than £ 100 (in the first edition of *The Economics of Welfare*) or more than £ 200 (in later editions) or that the owner of the wood failed to notify the railway in writing within seven days of the fire or did not send particulars of the damage, in writing, within twenty-one days. In the real world, Pigou's example could only exist as a result of a deliberate choice of the legislature. It is not, of course, easy to imagine the construction of a railway in a state of nature. The nearest one can get to this is presumably a railway which uses steam engines "without express statutory authority." However, in this case the railway would be obliged to compensate those whose woods it burnt down. That is to say, compensation would be paid in the absence of Government action. The only circumstances in which compensation would not be paid would be those in which there had been Government action. It is strange that Pigou, who clearly thought it desirable that compensation should be paid, should have chosen this particular example to demonstrate how it is possible "for State action to improve on 'natural' tendencies."

Pigou seems to have had a faulty view of the facts of the situation. But it also seems likely that he was mistaken in his economic analysis. It is not necessarily desirable that the railway should be required to compensate those who suffer damage by fires caused by railway engines. I need not show here that, if the railway could make a bargain with everyone having property adjoining the railway line and there were no costs involved in making such bargains, it would not matter whether the railway was liable for damage caused by fires or not. This question has been treated at length in earlier sections. The problem is whether it would be desirable to make the railway liable in conditions in which it is too expensive for such bargains to be made. Pigou clearly thought it was desirable to force the railway to pay compensation and it is easy to see the kind of argument that would have led him to this conclusion. Suppose a railway is considering whether to run an additional train or to increase the speed of an existing train or to install spark-preventing devices on its engines. If the railway were not liable for fire damage, then, when making these decisions, it would not take into account as a cost the increase in damage resulting from the addtional train or the faster train or the failure to install spark-preventing devices. This is the source of the divergence between private and social net products. It results in the railway performing acts which will lower the value of total production—and which it would not do if it were liable for the damage. This can be shown by means of an arithmetical example.

Consider a railway, which is *not* liable for damage by fires caused by sparks from its engines, which runs two trains per day on a certain line. Suppose that running one train per day would enable the railway to perform services worth $150 per annum and running two trains a day would enable the railway to perform services worth $250 per annum. Suppose further that the cost of running one train is $50 per annum and two trains $100 per annum. Assuming perfect competition, the cost equals the fall in the value of production elsewhere due to the employment of additional factors of production by the railway. Clearly the railway would find it profitable to run two trains per day. But suppose that running one train per day would destroy by fire crops worth (on an average over the year) $60 and two trains a day would result in the destruction of crops worth $120. In these circumstances running one train per day would raise the value of total production but the running of a second train would reduce the value of total production. The second train would enable additional railway services worth $100 per annum to be performed. But the fall in the value of production elsewhere would be $110 per annum; $50 as a result of the employment of additional factors of production and $60 as a result of the destruction of crops. Since it would be better if the second train were not run and since it would not run if the railway were liable for damage caused to crops, the conclusion that the railway should be made liable for the damage seems irresistable. Undoubtedly it is this kind of reasoning which underlies the Pigovian position.

The conclusion that it would be better if the second train did not run is correct. The conclusion that it is desirable that the railway should be made liable for the damage it causes is wrong. Let us change our assumption concerning the rule of liability. Suppose that the railway is liable for damage from fires caused by sparks from the engine. A farmer on lands adjoining the railway is then in the position that, if his crop is destroyed by fires caused by the railway, he will receive the market price from the railway; but if his crop is not damaged, he will receive the market price by sale. It therefore becomes a matter of indifference to him whether his crop is damaged by fire or not. The position is very different when the railway is *not* liable. Any crop destruction through railway-caused fires would then reduce the receipts of the farmer. He would therefore take out of cultivation any land for which the damage is likely to be greater than the net return of the land (for reasons explained at length in Section III). A change from a regime in which the railway is *not* liable for damage to one in which it *is* liable is likely therefore to lead to an increase in the amount of cultivation on lands adjoining the railway. It will also, of course, lead to an increase in the amount of crop destruction due to rail-way-caused fires.

Let us return to our arithmetical example. Assume that, with the changed rule of liability, there is a doubling in the amount of crop de-struction due to railway-caused fires. With one train per day, crops worth $120 would be destroyed each year and two trains per day would lead to the destruction of crops worth $240. We saw previously that it would not be profitable to run the second train if the railway had to pay $60 per an-num as compensation for damage. With damage at $120 per annum the loss from running the second train would be $60 greater. But now let us consider the first train. The value of the transport services furnished by the first train is $150. The cost of running the train is $50. The amount that the railway would have to pay out as compensation for damage is $120. It follows that it would not be profitable to run any trains. With the figures in our example we reach the following result: if the railway is not liable for fire-damage, two trains per day would be run; if the railway is liable for fire-damage, it would cease operations altogether. Does this mean that it is better that there should be no railway? This question can be resolved by considering what would happen to the value of total produc-tion if it were decided to exempt the railway from liability for fire-damage, thus bringing it into operation (with two trains per day).

The operation of the railway would enable transport services worth $250 to be performed. It would also mean the employment of factors of production which would reduce the value of production elsewhere by $100. Furthermore it would mean the destruction of crops worth $120. The coming of the railway will also have led to the abandonment of cultivation of some land. Since we know that, had this land been cultivated, the value of the crops destroyed by fire would have been $120, and since it is unlikely that the total crop on this land would have been destroyed, it seems reasonable to suppose that the value of the crop yield on this land would have been higher than this. Assume it would have been $160. But the abandonment of cultivation would have released factors of production for employment elsewhere. All we know is that the amount by which the value of production elsewhere will increase will be less than $160. Suppose that it is $150. Then the gain from operating the railway would be $250 (the value of the transport services) minus $100 (the cost of the factors of production) minus $120 (the value of crops destroyed by fire) minus $160 (the fall in the value of crop production due to the abandonment of cultivation) plus $150 (the value of production elsewhere of the released factors of production). Overall, operating the railway will increase the value of total production by $20. With these figures it is clear that it is better that the railway should not be liable for the damage it causes, thus enabling it to operate profitably. Of course, by altering the figures, it could be shown that there are other cases in which it would be desirable that the railway should be liable for the damage it causes. It is enough for my purpose to show that, from an economic point of view, a situation in which there is "uncompensated damage done to surrounding woods by sparks from railway engines" is not necessarily undesirable. Whether it is desirable or not depends on the particular circumstances.

How is it that the Pigovian analysis seems to give the wrong answer? The reason is that Pigou does not seem to have noticed that his analysis is dealing with an entirely different question. The analysis as such is correct. But it is quite illegitimate for Pigou to draw the particular conclusion he does. The question at issue is not whether it is desirable to run an additional train or a faster train or to install smoke-preventing devices; the question at issue is whether it is desirable to have a system in which the railway has to compensate those who suffer damage from the fires which it causes or one in which the railway does not have to compensate them. When an economist is comparing alternative social arrangements, the proper procedure is to compare the total social product yielded by these different arrangements. The comparison of private and social products is neither here nor there. A simple example will demonstrate this. Imagine a town in which there are traffic lights. A motorist approaches an intersection and stops because the light is red. There are no cars approaching the intersection on the other street. If the motorist ignored the red signal, no accident would occur and the total product would increase because the motorist would arrive earlier at his destination. Why does he not do this? The reason is that if he ignored the light he would be fined. The private product from crossing the street is less than the social product. Should we conclude from this that the total product would be greater if there were no fines for failing to obey traffic signals? The Pigovian analysis shows us that it is possible to conceive of better worlds than the one in which we live. But the problem is to devise practical arrangements which will correct defects in one part of the system without causing more serious harm in other parts.

I have examined in considerable detail one example of a divergence between private and social products and I do not propose to make any further examination of Pigou's analytical system. But the main discussion of the problem considered in this article is to be found in that part of Chapter 9 in Part II which deals with Pigou's second class of divergence and it is of interest to see how Pigou develops his argument. Pigou's own description of this second class of divergence was quoted at the beginning of this section. Pigou distinguishes between the case in which a person renders services for which he receives no payment and the case in which a person renders disservices and compensation is not given to the injured parties. Our main attention has, of course, centred on this second case. It is therefore rather astonishing to find, as was pointed out to me by Professor Francesco Forte, that the problem of the smoking chimney—the "stock instance" [44] or "classroom example" [45] of the second case—is used by Pigou as an example of the first case (services rendered without payment) and is never mentioned, at any rate explicitly, in connection with the second case.[46] Pigou points out that factory owners who devote resources to preventing their chimneys from smoking render services for which they receive no payment. The implication, in the light of Pigou's discussion later in the chapter, is that a factory owner with a smokey chimney should be given a bounty to induce him to install smoke-preventing devices. Most modern economists would suggest that the owner of the factory with the smokey chimney should be taxed. It seems a pity that economists (apart from Professor Forte) do not seem to have noticed this feature of Pigou's treatment since a realisation that the problem could be tackled in either of these two ways would probably have led to an explicit recognition of its reciprocal nature.

In discussing the second case (disservices without compensation to those damaged), Pigou says that they are rendered "when the owner of a site in a residential quarter of a city builds a factory there and so destroys a great part of the amenities of neighbouring sites; or, in a less degree, when he uses his site in such a way as to spoil the lighting of the house

opposite; or when he invests resources in erecting buildings in a crowded
centre, which by contracting the air-space and the playing room of the
neighbourhood, tend to injure the health and efficiency of the families living there." [47] Pigou is, of course, quite right to describe such actions as
"uncharged disservices." But he is wrong when he describes these actions
as "anti-social." [48] They may or may not be. It is necessary to weigh the
harm against the good that will result. Nothing could be more "anti-
social" than to oppose any action which causes any harm to anyone.

The example with which Pigou opens his discussion of "uncharged disservices" is not, as I have indicated, the case of the smokey chimney but
the case of the overrunning rabbits: " . . . incidental uncharged disservices are rendered to third parties when the game-preserving activities
of one occupier involve the overrunning of a neighbouring occupier's land
by rabbits. . . . " This example is of extraordinary interest, not so
much because the economic analysis of the case is essentially any different
from that of the other examples, but because of the peculiarities of the
legal position and the light it throws on the part which economics can play
in what is apparently the purely legal question of the delimitation of rights.

The problem of legal liability for the actions of rabbits is part of the
general subject of liability for animals.[49] I will, although with reluctance,
confine my discussion to rabbits. The early cases relating to rabbits concerned the relations between the lord of the manor and commoners, since,
from the thirteenth century on, it became usual for the lord of the manor
to stock the commons with conies (rabbits), both for the sake of the meat
and the fur. But in 1597, in *Boulston*'s case, an action was brought by one
landowner against a neighbouring landowner, alleging that the defendant
had made coney-burrows and that the conies had increased and had destroyed the plaintiff's corn. The action failed for the reason that

> . . . so soon as the coneys come on his neighbor's land he may kill
> them, for they are ferae naturae, and he who makes the coney-boroughs
> has no property in them, and he shall not be punished for the damage
> which the coneys do in which he has no property, and which the other
> may lawfully kill.[50]

As *Boulston*'s case has been treated as binding—Bray, J., in 1919, said
that he was not aware that *Boulston*'s case has ever been overruled or
questioned [51]—Pigou's rabbit example undoubtedly represented the legal
position at the time *The Economics of Welfare* was written.[52] And in this
case, it is not far from the truth to say that the state of affairs which
Pigou describes came about because of an absence of Government action
(at any rate in the form of statutory enactments) and was the result of
"natural" tendencies.

Nonetheless, *Boulston's* case is something of a legal curiosity and Professor Williams makes no secret of his distaste for this decision:

> The conception of liability in nuisance as being based upon ownership is the result, apparently, of a confusion with the action of cattle-trespass, and runs counter both to principle and to the medieval authorities on the escape of water, smoke and filth. . . . The prerequisite of any satisfactory treatment of the subject is the final abandonment of the pernicious doctrine in *Boulston's* case. . . . Once *Boulston's* case disappears, the way will be clear for a rational restatement of the whole subject, on lines that will harmonize with the principles prevailing in the rest of the law of nuisance.[53]

The judges in *Boulston's* case were, of course, aware that their view of the matter depended on distinguishing this case from one involving nuisance:

> This cause is not like to the cases put, on the other side, of erecting a lime-kiln, dye-house, or the like; for there the anoyance is by the act of the parties who make them; but it is not so here, for the conies of themselves went into the plaintiff's land, and he might take them when they came upon his land, and make profit of them.[54]

Professor Williams comments:

> Once more the atavistic idea is emerging that the animals are guilty and not the landowner. It is not, of course, a satisfactory principle to introduce into a modern law of nuisance. If A. erects a house or plants a tree so that the rain runs or drips from it onto B.'s land, this is A.'s act for which he is liable; but if A. introduces rabbits into his land so that they escape from it into B.'s, this is the act of the rabbits for which A. is not liable—such is the specious distinction resulting from *Boulston's* case.[55]

It has to be admitted that the decision in *Boulston's* case seems a little odd. A man may be liable for damage caused by smoke or unpleasant smells, without it being necessary to determine whether he owns the smoke or the smell. And the rule in *Boulston's* case has not always been followed in cases dealing with other animals. For example, in *Bland v. Yates,*[56] it was decided that an injunction could be granted to prevent someone from keeping an *unusual and excessive* collection of manure in which flies bred and which infested a neighbour's house. The question of who owned the flies was not raised. An economist would not wish to object because legal reasoning sometimes appears a little odd. But there is a sound economic reason for supporting Professor Williams' view that the problem of liability for animals (and particularly rabbits) should be brought within the ordinary law of nuisance. The reason is not that the man who harbours rabbits is solely responsible for the damage; the man whose crops are eaten is equally responsible. And given that the costs of market transactions make a rearrangement of rights impossible, unless we know the particular circumstances, we cannot say whether it is desirable or not to make the man who harbours rabbits responsible for the damage committed by the rabbits on neighbouring properties. The objection to the rule in *Boulston*'s case is that, under it, the harbourer of rabbits can *never* be liable. It fixes the rule of liability at one pole: and this is as undesirable, from an economic point of view, as fixing the rule at the other pole and making the harbourer of rabbits always liable. But, as we saw in Section VII, the law of nuisance, as it is in fact handled by the courts, is flexible and allows for a comparison of the utility of an act with the harm it produces. As Professor Williams says: "The whole law of nuisance is an attempt to reconcile and compromise between conflicting interests. . . ." [57] To bring the problem of rabbits within the ordinary law of nuisance would not mean *inevitably* making the harbourer of rabbits liable for damage committed by the rabbits. This is not to say that the sole task of the courts in such cases is to make a comparison between the harm and the utility of an act. Nor is it to be expected that the courts will always decide correctly after making such a comparison. But unless the courts act very foolishly, the ordinary law of nuisance would seem likely to give economically more satisfactory results than adopting a rigid rule. Pigou's case of the overrunning rabbits affords an excellent example of how problems of law and economics are interrelated, even though the correct policy to follow would seem to be different from that envisioned by Pigou.

Pigou allows one exception to his conclusion that there is a divergence between private and social products in the rabbit example. He adds: " . . . unless . . . the two occupiers stand in the relation of landlord and tenant, so that compensation is given in an adjustment of the rent." [58] This qualification is rather surprising since Pigou's first class of divergence is largely concerned with the difficulties of drawing up satisfactory contracts between landlords and tenants. In fact, all the recent cases on the problem of rabbits cited by Professor Williams involved disputes between landlords and tenants concerning sporting rights.[59] Pigou seems to make a distinction between the case in which no contract is possible (the second class) and that in which the contract is unsatisfactory (the first class). Thus he says that the second class of divergencies between private and social net product

cannot, like divergences due to tenancy laws, be mitigated by a modification of the contractual relation between any two contracting parties, because the divergence arises out of a service or disservice rendered to persons other than the contracting parties.[60]

But the reason why some activities are not the subject of contracts is exactly the same as the reason why some contracts are commonly unsatisfactory—it would cost too much to put the matter right. Indeed, the two cases are really the same since the contracts are unsatisfactory because they do not cover certain activities. The exact bearing of the discussion of the first class of divergence on Pigou's main argument is difficult to discover. He shows that in some circumstances contractual relations between landlord and tenant may result in a divergence between private and social products.[61] But he also goes on to show that Government-enforced compensation schemes and rent-controls will also produce divergences.[62] Furthermore, he shows that, when the Government is in a similar position to a private landlord, e. g. when granting a franchise to a public utility, exactly the same difficulties arise as when private individuals are involved.[63] The discussion is interesting but I have been unable to discover what general conclusions about economic policy, if any, Pigou expects us to draw from it.

Indeed, Pigou's treatment of the problems considered in this article is extremely elusive and the discussion of his views raises almost insuperable difficulties of interpretation. Consequently it is impossible to be sure that one has understood what Pigou really meant. Nevertheless, it is difficult to resist the conclusion, extraordinary though this may be in an economist of Pigou's stature, that the main source of this obscurity is that Pigou had not thought his position through.

IX.   The Pigovian Tradition

It is strange that a doctrine as faulty as that developed by Pigou should have been so influential, although part of its success has probably been due to the lack of clarity in the exposition. Not being clear, it was never clearly wrong. Curiously enough, this obscurity in the source has not prevented the emergence of a fairly well-defined oral tradition. What economists think they learn from Pigou, and what they tell their students, which I term the Pigovian tradition, is reasonably clear. I propose to show the inadequacy of this Pigovian tradition by demonstrating that both the analysis and the policy conclusions which it supports are incorrect.

I do not propose to justify my view as to the prevailing opinion by copious references to the literature. I do this partly because the treatment in the literature is usually so fragmentary, often involving little more than a reference to Pigou plus some explanatory comment, that detailed examination would be inappropriate. But the main reason for this lack of reference is that the doctrine, although based on Pigou, must have been largely the product of an oral tradition. Certainly economists with whom I have discussed these problems have shown a unanimity of opinion which is quite remarkable considering the meagre treatment accorded this subject in the literature. No doubt there are some economists who do not share the usual view but they must represent a small minority of the profession.

The approach to the problems under discussion is through an examination of the value of physical production. The private product is the value of the additional product resulting from a particular activity of a business. The social product equals the private product minus the fall in the value of production elsewhere for which no compensation is paid by the business. Thus, if 10 units of a factor (and no other factors) are used by a business to make a certain product with a value of $105; and the owner of this factor is not compensated for their use, which he is unable to prevent; and these 10 units of the factor would yield products in their best alternative use worth $100; then, the social product is $105 minus $100 or $5. If the business now pays for one unit of the factor and its price equals the value of its marginal product, then the social product rises to $15. If two units are paid for, the social product rises to $25 and so on until it reaches $105 when all units of the factor are paid for. It is not difficult to see why economists have so readily accepted this rather odd procedure. The analysis focusses on the individual business decision and since the use of certain resources is not allowed for in costs, receipts are reduced by the same amount. But, of course, this means that the value of the social product has no social significance whatsoever. It seems to me preferable to use the opportunity cost concept and to approach these problems by comparing the value of the product yielded by factors in alternative uses or by alternative arrangements. The main advantage of a pricing system is that it leads to the employment of factors in places where the value of the product yielded is greatest and does so at less cost than alternative systems (I leave aside that a pricing system also eases the problem of the redistribution of income). But if through some God-given natural harmony factors flowed to the places where the value of the product yielded was greatest without any use of the pricing system and consequently there was no compensation, I would find it a source of surprise rather than a cause for dismay.

The definition of the social product is queer but this does not mean that the conclusions for policy drawn from the analysis are necessarily wrong. However, there are bound to be dangers in an approach which diverts attention from the basic issues and there can be little doubt that it has been responsible for some of the errors in current doctrine. The belief that it is desirable that the business which causes harmful effects should be forced to compensate those who suffer damage (which was exhaustively discussed in section VIII in connection with Pigou's railway sparks example) is undoubtedly the result of not comparing the total product obtainable with alternative social arrangements.

The same fault is to be found in proposals for solving the problem of harmful effects by the use of taxes or bounties. Pigou lays considerable stress on this solution although he is, as usual, lacking in detail and qualified in his support.⁶⁴ Modern economists tend to think exclusively in terms of taxes and in a very precise way. The tax should be equal to the damage done and should therefore vary with the amount of the harmful effect. As it is not proposed that the proceeds of the tax should be paid to those suffering the damage, this solution is not the same as that which would force a business to pay compensation to those damaged by its actions, although economists generally do not seem to have noticed this and tend to treat the two solutions as being identical.

Assume that a factory which emits smoke is set up in a district previously free from smoke pollution, causing damage valued at $100 per annum. Assume that the taxation solution is adopted and that the factory owner is taxed $100 per annum as long as the factory emits the smoke. Assume further that a smoke-preventing device costing $90 per annum to run is available. In these circumstances, the smoke-preventing device would be installed. Damage of $100 would have been avoided at an expenditure of $90 and the factory-owner would be better off by $10 per annum. Yet the position achieved may not be optimal. Suppose that those who suffer the damage could avoid it by moving to other locations or by taking various precautions which would cost them, or be equivalent to a loss in income of, $40 per annum. Then there would be a gain in the value of production of $50 if the factory continued to emit its smoke and those now in the district moved elsewhere or made other adjustments to avoid the damage. If the factory owner is to be made to pay a tax equal to the damage caused, it would clearly be desirable to institute a double tax system and to make residents of the district pay an amount equal to the additional cost incurred by the factory owner (or the consumers of his products) in order to avoid the damage. In these conditions, people would not stay in the district or would take other measures to prevent the damage from occurring, when the costs of doing so were less than the costs that would be incurred by the producer to reduce the damage (the producer's object, of course, being not so much to reduce the damage as to reduce the tax payments). A tax system which was confined to a tax on the producer for damage caused would tend to lead to unduly high costs being incurred for the prevention of damage. Of course this could be avoided if it were possible to base the tax, not on the damage caused, but on the fall in the value of production (in its widest sense) resulting from the emission of smoke. But to do so would require a detailed knowledge of individual preferences and I am unable to imagine how the data needed for such a taxation system could be assembled. Indeed, the proposal to solve the smoke-pollution and similar problems by the use of taxes bristles with difficulties: the problem of calculation, the difference between average and marginal damage, the interrelations between the damage suffered on different properties, etc. But it is unnecessary to examine these problems here. It is enough for my purpose to show that, even if the tax is exactly adjusted to equal the damage that would be done to neighboring properties as a result of the emission of each additional puff of smoke, the tax would not necessarily bring about optimal conditions. An increase in the number of people living or of business operating in the vicinity of the smoke-emitting factory will increase the amount of harm produced by a given emission of smoke. The tax that would be imposed would therefore increase with an increase in the number of those in the vicinity. This will tend to lead to a decrease in the value of production of the factors employed by the factory, either because a reduction in production due to the tax will result in factors being used elsewhere in ways which are less valuable, or because factors will be diverted to produce means for reducing the amount of smoke emitted. But people deciding to establish themselves in the vicinity of the factory will not take into account this fall in the value of production which results from their presence. This failure to take into account costs imposed on others is comparable to the action of a factory-owner in not taking into account the harm resulting from his emission of smoke. Without the tax, there may be too much smoke and too few people in the vicinity of the factory; but with the tax there may be too little smoke and too many people in the vicinity of the factory. There is no reason to suppose that one of these results is necessarily preferable.

I need not devote much space to discussing the similar error involved in the suggestion that smoke producing factories should, by means of zoning regulations, be removed from the districts in which the smoke causes harmful effects. When the change in the location of the factory results in a reduction in production, this obviously needs to be taken into account and weighed against the harm which would result from the factory remaining in that location. The aim of such regulation should not be to eliminate smoke pollution but rather to secure the optimum amount of smoke pollution, this being the amount which will maximise the value of production.

X.   A Change of Approach

It is my belief that the failure of economists to reach correct conclusions about the treatment of harmful effects cannot be ascribed simply to a few slips in analysis. It stems from basic defects in the current approach to problems of welfare economics. What is needed is a change of approach.

Analysis in terms of divergencies between private and social products concentrates attention on particular deficiencies in the system and tends to nourish the belief that any measure which will remove the deficiency is necessarily desirable. It diverts attention from those other changes in the system which are inevitably associated with the corrective measure, changes which may well produce more harm than the original deficiency. In the preceding sections of this article, we have seen many examples of this. But it is not necessary to approach the problem in this way. Economists who study problems of the firm habitually use an opportunity cost approach and compare the receipts obtained from a given combination of factors with alternative business arrangements. It would seem desirable to use a similar approach when dealing with questions of economic policy and to compare the total product yielded by alternative social arrangements. In this article, the analysis has been confined, as is usual in this part of economics, to comparisons of the value of production, as measured by the market. But it is, of course, desirable that the choice between different social arrangements for the solution of economic problems should be carried out in broader terms than this and that the total effect of these arrangements in all spheres of life should be taken into account. As Frank H. Knight has so often emphasized, problems of welfare economics must ultimately dissolve into a study of aesthetics and morals.

A second feature of the usual treatment of the problems discussed in this article is that the analysis proceeds in terms of a comparison between a state of laissez faire and some kind of ideal world. This approach inevitably leads to a looseness of thought since the nature of the alternatives being compared is never clear. In a state of laissez faire, is there a monetary, a legal or a political system and if so, what are they? In an ideal world, would there be a monetary, a legal or a political system and if so, what would they be? The answers to all these questions are shrouded in mystery and every man is free to draw whatever conclusions he likes. Actually very little analysis is required to show that an ideal world is better than a state of laissez faire, unless the definitions of a state of laissez faire and an ideal world happen to be the same. But the whole discussion is largely irrelevant for questions of economic policy since whatever we may have in mind as our ideal world, it is clear that we have not yet discovered how to get to it from where we are. A better approach would seem to be to start our analysis with a situation approximating that which actually exists, to examine the effects of a proposed policy change and to attempt to decide whether the new situation would be, in total, better or worse than the original one. In his way, conclusions for policy would have some relevance to the actual situation.

A final reason for the failure to develop a theory adequate to handle the problem of harmful effects stems from a faulty concept of a factor of production. This is usually thought of as a physical entity which the businessman acquires and uses (an acre of land, a ton of fertiliser) instead of as a right to perform certain (physical) actions. We may speak of a person owning land and using it as a factor of production but what the landowner in fact possesses is the right to carry out a circumscribed list of actions. The rights of a land-owner are not unlimited. It is not even always possible for him to remove the land to another place, for instance, by quarrying it.   And although it may be possible for him to exclude some people from using "his" land, this may not be true of others.   For example, some people may have the right to cross the land.   Furthermore, it may or may not be possible to erect certain types of buildings or to grow certain crops or to use particular drainage systems on the land.   This does not come about simply because of Government regulation.   It would be equally true under the common law.   In fact it would be true under any system of law.   A system in which the rights of individuals were unlimited would be one in which there were no rights to acquire.

If factors of production are thought of as rights, it becomes easier to understand that the right to do something which has a harmful effect (such as the creation of smoke, noise, smells, etc.) is also a factor of production. Just as we may use a piece of land in such a way as to prevent someone else from crossing it, or parking his car, or building his house upon it, so we may use it in such a way as to deny him a view or quiet or unpolluted air.   The cost of exercising a right (of using a factor of production) is always the loss which is suffered elsewhere in consequence of the exercise of that right—the inability to cross land, to park a car, to build a house, to enjoy a view, to have peace and quiet or to breathe clean air.

It would clearly be desirable if the only actions performed were those in which what was gained was worth more than what was lost.   But in choosing between social arrangements within the context of which individual decisions are made, we have to bear in mind that a change in the existing system which will lead to an improvement in some decisions may well lead to a worsening of others.   Furthermore we have to take into account the costs involved in operating the various social arrangements (whether it be the working of a market or of a government department), as well as the costs involved in moving to a new system.   In devising and choosing between social arrangements we should have regard for the total effect.   This, above all, is the change in approach which I am advocating.

FOOTNOTES

1 This article, although concerned with a technical problem of economic analysis, arose out of the study of the Political Economy of Broadcasting which I am now conducting. The argument of the present article was implicit in a previous article dealing with the problem of allocating radio and television frequencies (The Federal Communications Commission, 2 J.Law & Econ. [1959]) but comments which I have received seemed to suggest that it would be desirable to deal with the question in a more explicit way and without reference to the original problem for the solution of which the analysis was developed.

2 Coase, The Federal Communications Commission, 2 J.Law & Econ. 26–27 (1959).

3 G. J. Stigler, The Theory of Price 105 (1952).

4 The argument in the text has proceeded on the assumption that the alternative to cultivation of the crop is abandonment of cultivation alogether. But this need not be so. There may be crops which are less liable to damage by cattle but which would not be as profitable as the crop grown in the absence of damage. Thus, if the cultivation of a new crop would yield a return to the farmer of $1 instead of $2, and the size of the herd which would cause $3 damage with the old crop would cause $1 damage with the new crop, it would be profitable to the cattle-raiser to pay any sum less than $2 to induce the farmer to change his crop (since this would reduce damage liability from $3 to $1) and it would be profitable for the farmer to do so if the amount received was more than $1 (the reduction in his return caused by switching crops). In fact, there would be room for a mutually satisfactory bargain in all cases in which a change of crop would reduce the amount of damage by more than it reduces the value of the crop (excluding damage)—in all cases, that is, in which a change in the crop cultivated would lead to an increase in the value of production.

5 See Gale on Easements 237–39 (13th ed. M. Bowles 1959).

6 See Fontainebleu Hotel Corp. v. Forty-Five Twenty-Five, Inc., 114 So.2d 357 (1959).

7 11 Ch.D. 852 (1879).

8 Auscultation is the act of listening by ear or stethoscope in order to judge by sound the condition of the body.

9 Note that what is taken into account is the change in income after allowing for alterations in methods of production, location, character of product, etc.

10 L.R. 5 Eq. 166 (1867–1868).

11 4 C.P.D. 172 (1878–1879).

12 25 Q.B.D. 481 (1890).

13 It may be asked why a lost grant could not also be presumed in the case of the confectioner who had operated one mortar for more than 60 years. The answer is that until the doctor built the consulting room at the end of his garden there was no nuisance. So the nuisance had not continued for many years. It is true that the confectioner in his affidavit referred to "an invalid lady who occupied the house upon one occasion, about thirty years before" who "requested him if possible to discontinue the use of the mortars before eight o'clock in the morning" and that there was some evidence that the garden wall had been subjected to vibration. But the court had little difficulty in disposing of this line of argument: ". . . this vibration, even if it existed at all, was so slight, and the complaint, if it can be called a complaint, of the invalid lady . . . was of so trifling a character, that . . . the Defendant's acts would not have given rise to any proceeding either at law or in equity" (11 Ch.D. 863). That is, the confectioner had not committed a nuisance until the doctor built his consulting room.

14 See Coase, The Nature of the Firm, 4 Economica, New Series, 386 (1937). Reprinted in Readings in Price Theory, 331 (1952).

15 For reasons explained in my earlier article, see Readings in Price Theory, n. 14 at 337.

16 See W. L. Prosser, The Law of Torts 398–99, 412 (2d ed. 1955). The quotation about the ancient case concerning candle-making is taken from Sir James Fitzjames Stephen, A General View of the Criminal Law of England 106 (1890). Sir James Stephen gives no reference. He perhaps had in mind *Rex. v. Ronkett*, included in Seavey, Keeton and Thurston, Cases on Torts 604 (1950). A similar view to that expressed by Prosser is to be found in F. V. Harper and F. James, The Law of Torts 67–74 (1956); Restatement, Torts §§ 826, 827 and 828.

* * *

28 See Prosser, op. cit. supra n. 16 at 421; Harper and James, op. cit. supra n. 16 at 86–87.

29 Supreme Court of Georgia, 193 Ga. 862, 20 S.E.2d 245 (1942).

30 178 Ga. 514, 173 S.E. 817 (1934).

31 116 Ga. 64, 42 S.E. 315 (1902).

32 270 Mass. 511, 523, 170 N.E. 385, 390 (1930).

33 See Sir Alfred Denning, Freedom Under the Law 71 (1949).

34 M. B. Cairns, The Law of Tort in Local Government 28–32 (1954).

35 A. C. Pigou, The Economics of Welfare 183 (4th ed. 1932). My references will all be to the fourth edition but the argument and examples examined in this article remained substantially unchanged from the first edition in 1920 to the fourth in 1932. A large part (but not all) of this analysis had appeared previously in Wealth and Welfare (1912).

36 Id. at xii.

37 Id. at 127–30.

38 In Wealth and Welfare, Pigou attributes the "optimism" to Adam Smith himself and not to his followers. He there refers to the "highly optimistic theory of Adam Smith that the national dividend, in given circumstances of demand and supply, tends 'naturally' to a maximum" (p. 104).

39 Pigou, op. cit. supra n. 35 at 129–30.

40 Id. at 134.

41 See 31 Halsbury, Laws of England 474–75 (3d ed. 1960), Article on Railways and Canals, from which this summary of the legal position, and all quotations, are taken.

42 See 152 H.C.Deb. 2622–63 (1922); 161 H.C.Deb. 2935–55 (1923).

43 Vaughan v. Taff Vale Railway Co., 3 H. and N. 743 (Ex.1858) and 5 H. and N. 679 (Ex.1860).

44 Sir Dennis Robertson, I Lectures on Economic Principles 162 (1957).

45 E. J. Mishan, The Meaning of Efficiency in Economics, 189 The Bankers' Magazine 482 (June 1960).

46 Pigou, op. cit. supra n. 35 at 184.

47 Id. at 185–86.

48 Id. at 186 n. 1. For similar unqualified statements see Pigou's lecture "Some Aspects of the Housing Problem" in B. S. Rowntree and A. C. Pigou, Lectures on Housing, in 18 Manchester Univ. Lectures (1914).

49 See G. L. Williams, Liability for Animals—An Account of the Development and Present Law of Tortious Liability for Animals, Distress Damage Feasant and the Duty to Fence, in Great Britain, Northern Ireland and the Common Law Dominions (1939). Part Four, "The Action of Nuisance, in Relation to Liability for Animals," 236–62, is especially relevant to our discussion. The problem of liability for rabbits is discussed in this part, 238–47. I do not know how far the common law in the United States regarding liability for animals has diverged from that in Britain. In some Western States of the United States, the English common law regarding the duty to fence has not been followed, in part because 'the considerable amount of open, uncleared land made it a matter of public policy to allow cattle to run at large" (Williams, op. cit. supra 227). This affords a good example of how a different set of circumstances may make it economically desirable to change the legal rule regarding the delimitation of rights.

50 5 Coke (Vol. 3) 104 b. 77 Eng.Rep., 216, 217.

[51] See Stearn v. Prentice Bros. Ltd., (1919) 1 K.B., 395, 397.

[52] I have not looked into recent cases. The legal position has also been modified by statutory enactments.

[53] Williams, op. cit. supra n. 49 at 242, 258.

[54] Boulston v. Hardy, Cro.Eliz., 547, 548, 77 Eng.Rep. 216.

[55] Williams, op. cit. supra n. 49 at 243.

[56] 58 Sol.J. 612 (1913–1914).

[57] Williams, op. cit. supra n. 49 at 259.

[58] Pigou, op. cit. supra n. 35 at 185.

[59] Williams, op. cit. supra n. 49 at 244–47.

[60] Pigou, op. cit. supra n. 35 at 192.

[61] Id. 174–75.

[62] Id. 177–83.

[63] Id. 175–77.

[64] Id. 192–4, 381 and Public Finance 94–100 (3d ed. 1947).

10: WHEN DOES THE RULE OF LIABILITY MATTER?

HAROLD DEMSETZ*

The active interface between law and economics has been limited largely to antitrust and regulation, but recent work, primarily in economics, has revealed a much wider area of common interest. The new development, which deals with the definition and structure of property rights, has implications for central areas of the law, such as real property, torts, and contracts, although it originated in an economic analysis of the divergence between private and social cost. While still in its embryonic stage, the analysis has proceeded far enough for it to be called to the attention of a wider audience.

The questions with which we shall be concerned are whether and under what conditions a legal decision about liability affects the uses to which resources will be put and the distribution of wealth between owners of resources. If ranchers are held liable for the damage done by their cattle to corn fields, how will the outputs of meat and corn be affected? If drivers or pedestrians, alternatively, are held liable for automobile-pedestrian accidents, how will the accident rate be affected? What implications for extortion (an extreme form of wealth redistribution) are found in the decision about who is liable for damages?

I

Recent developments in this area began with an article by Professor R. H. Coase.[1] Coase's work presented a penetrating criticism of the conventional

Journal of Legal Studies, Vol. 1, No. 1, 1972, p. 13.

treatment by economists of divergences between private and social cost. The social cost of furthering an economic activity is the resulting reduction in the value of production that is obtainable from other activities. Such reductions occur because the resources required to further an activity are scarce and must be diverted from other possible uses. According to the view that Coase challenged, social cost, being the sum total of the costs incurred to carry on any activity, might very well differ from private cost. For example, the social cost of running steam locomotives properly includes the fire damage done to surrounding farm crops by sparks from the locomotive. If the railroad is not required to pay for these damages, perhaps through a tax per train, then, according to the conventional analysis, the railroad would not take account of crop damage costs in deciding how many trains to run. In the absence of a specific public policy to intervene, the rate at which an activity is carried forth, which is determined solely by private cost, would diverge from the optimum rate, which is determined by social cost. In the present example, the private cost of running additional trains, being less than the social cost because crop damage is not taken into account, would encourage the railroad to run too many trains per day. The conventional economic analysis called for the levy of a tax per train, equivalent to the damages, in order to bring social cost and private cost into equality.

Coase demonstrated that the imposition of such a tax could, in some circumstances, aggravate the difficulty, but two other aspects of his work are of more concern to us. Coase (1) showed that powerful market forces exist that tend to bring private and social cost into equality without the use of a tax, and (2) discussed the conditions under which the legal position toward liability for damages would and would not alter the allocation of resources. Coase discusses an interaction between two productive activities, ranching and farming, in the context of a competitive regime in which the cost of transacting (or negotiating) is assumed to be zero.[2] His analysis concludes that social cost and private cost will be brought into equality through market negotiations—and this regardless of which party is assigned the responsibility for bearing the cost that results from the proximity of ranching and farming.

The law, reasoning that crops *stand in the way* of a neighbor's cattle, can leave the farmer to bear the cost of crop damage; alternatively, reasoning that cattle *stray errantly* across farm fields, the law can assign liability for crop damages to ranchers. Coase's work demonstrates that either legal position will result in the same resource allocation—i. e., in the same quantities of corn and meat—and, also, that negotiations between the parties to the damage will, with either legal position, eliminate any divergence between private and social cost. If the law favors ranchers by leaving farmers to bear the cost of crop damage, then there exist incentives for farmers to pay ranchers to reduce the sizes of the herds, or to take other measures that will reduce the amount of damage. A summary arithmetic example reveals how such market transactions lead to Coase's results.

Suppose that the net return to an owner of ranchland would be increased by $50 if herd size were increased by one head of cattle but that the additional head of cattle would impose corn damage on the owner of neighboring farmland that reduced his net return by $60. If the law did *not* require the rancher to compensate the farmer, the farmer would offer to pay the rancher a sum up to $60, the damage he would suffer if the rancher increased his herd by one head. The rancher would accept the offer since any amount above $50 would be more than ample compensation for the reduction in net returns associated with the smaller herd size.

Farmer liable : Negotiations would continue until the net return to the rancher of a head of cattle exceeded the reduction in net return to the farmer associated with the damage done by that head of cattle. Such negotiations would bring the total value of corn and beef produced to a maximum since herd size would be reduced only when the consequent increase in the net value of corn output ($60 in the above example) exceeded the decrease in the net value of beef output ($50 in the example) required to reduce crop damage.

Rancher liable : If the rule of liability were the reverse, requiring the owner of ranchland to compensate the farmer for the crop damage, the same equilibrium would be reached. Since the rancher earns a net return of only $50 and must pay damages of $60 if he raises an additional head of cattle, he would find it in his interest not to increase the size of his herd. Moreover, he would reduce the size of his herd as long as the net return forgone was smaller than the resulting increase in the net return to farming since this would be the liability to him if he did not reduce herd size by another unit. He would be led to settle upon the same herd size, with the same consequence for crop size, as he would have chosen in the absence of liability. The mix of output is not changed [3] because negotiations between the parties eliminate all divergence between private and social cost.

The resulting equality between social and private cost is important enough to warrant a few more words. The conventional analysis of the farmer-rancher interaction would have concluded that in the absence of liability for damage (or of an appropriate tax per head of cattle) the social cost of increasing herd size would have exceeded the rancher's private cost by the $60 damage done to the neighboring farmer's crops. The rancher, if he were neither held liable nor taxed, would have no reason to take account of this damage and would therefore be led to raise too many cattle and impose too much damage on farm crops. It is the supposed existence of this gap between private and social cost that seems to call for a tax per head of cattle or for an assignment of liability to the rancher. Coase's reasoning shows this logic to be in error. Even in the absence of a tax or liability for damage, the harmful effects of his activities on surrounding crops would be brought to bear on the private calculations of the owner of ranchland, for he must reckon as a true (but implicit) cost of increasing herd size the payment from the farmer that he must forgo if he refuses to agree to the farmer's request for a reduction in herd size. Market negotiations bring the full cost of his decision to bear on him through the offers made by the farmer and thereby eliminate any difference between private and social cost. This, as Coase recognized, would not be true if the cost of negotiating could not be assumed to be negligible. We shall return to this problem later.

It is not generally appreciated that Coase's reasoning has legal applications that extend beyond problems of the divergence between social and private cost as these typically are conceived. What is at issue in the farmer-rancher case is which party has a particular property right. In the one case the farmer has the right to allow or prohibit cattle grazing on certain specified lands, while in the other case it is the rancher who has the right. Private property takes the form of a bundle of rights, of which different components may be held by different persons. In the absence of significant negotiating cost, the use to which these property rights is put is independent of the identities of the owners since each owner will be given market incentives to use his property right in the most valuable way. Just what is the most valuable way depends on market conditions and not owner identities.

The analysis can be extended to many types of property right problems. One that is of current interest to lawyers is the continuing litigation about the legal status of the reserve clause in organized baseball. An important defense of the reserve clause has been the assertion that it prevents wealthy baseball clubs from acquiring too large a share of the good players. By applying the above analysis to this problem it is possible to refute the assertion, especially since the cost of negotiations would seem to be negligible in this case. For what is at issue is whether the identity of the owner of a player's baseball services will alter the location of his playing activities. An application of Coase's analysis to this problem suggests that the reserve clause should have no effect on the identity of the team for which a player plays.

When signing initially with a major league organization, a player owns his baseball talent in the sense that he has the right to offer his services for sale to any ball club. But once he signs with a major league club, he can no longer negotiate with other clubs for the sale of his services, although he retains the right to refuse to play. The reserve clause, which is written into every major league contract, requires major league clubs who wish to acquire the services of a player who is already under contract to purchase his contract from the club currently owning it.

Thus, once a player signs with a major league organization, part of the bundle of property rights to his services are transferred from the player to the club with which he signs. The right to play on various teams passes via the reserve clause from the player to the club owning his contract, and this club can reserve the player for its own use even though other teams might be willing to pay the player more than he is receiving.

The question considered here is *not* whether there exists a correlation between the wealth of a club and the quality of its players. The relevant question is whether the distribution of players among teams would change were the reserve clause to be declared illegal. Would wealthier clubs acquire more good players if the right to negotiate with other teams always resided with the player? [4]

In the absence of the reserve clause, a player would change clubs only if he found it in his interest to do so. With the reserve clause, a player will change clubs only if the club that owns his contract finds it in its interest. It appears that a different pattern of player migration between clubs might exist with the reserve clause than without it. But the appearance is deceptive. No matter who owns the right to sell the contract for the services of a baseball player, the distribution of players among teams will remain the same.

To see why this is so, assume that a player *not* subject to the reserve clause receives a $15,000 per annum wage from club A for which he currently plays. Club B offers him $16,000 to play for them. If this amount exceeds the value of the player to club A, the club will not find it in its interest to make a counteroffer large enough to retain the player's services and he will join club B. However, if his services are worth more than $16,000 to club A, the club will find it in its interest to make a counteroffer large enough to retain his services. With no reserve clause the player plays for the club that most highly values [5] his services.

Let us now suppose that the reserve clause is effective and, as before, that the player is currently paid $15,000 by club A. Club B now offers club A $1,000 per annum (or its present value equivalent) for the player's contract, so that if the negotiations succeed club B will pay $16,000 for the player's services of which $15,000 is paid to the player under the terms of the purchased contract and $1,000 is paid to club A. If $1,000 per annum exceeds the player's net value to club A after it pays his $15,000 annual salary, then it will be in club A's interest to sell his contract to club B, but if the player is worth more to club A than $16,000 (equal to the $1,000 offer from club B plus the player's $15,000 salary), it will refuse to sell his contract.

The condition under which the player is transferred to club B when he is subject to the reserve clause is precisely the condition under which he will elect to transfer to club B when he is not subject to the reserve clause. He transfers to club B if club B finds his services more valuable than does club A whether or not the reserve clause is in effect. The reserve clause, therefore, cannot be expected to result in a different distribution of players among teams than would prevail in its absence.

The reader may object, suggesting that nonpecuniary considerations might make the distribution of players different depending on the legal status of the reserve clause. But this objection also would be in error. Suppose that the player, presently owned by a California club, has developed a preference for working in California. If there were no reserve clause, his preference would lead him to ask at least $1,000 more to play ball with a Chicago club than he earns playing for a California club; and, in the absence of a reserve clause, a Chicago club would need to bid $1,000 more than a California club to obtain his services. But this is also true with the reserve clause. Under reserve clause arrangements, suppose that the Chicago club offers the California club only $500 more than the player's net value to the California club. The California club, indeed, will be tempted to sell the player's contract to Chicago. It appears that the $500 increment, which would be too small to move the player were there no reserve clause, is large enough to move him if there is a reserve clause. This is incorrect because the player, when working under the reserve clause arrangement, would be willing to offer a sum of up to $1,000 (the value of the nonpecuniary amenities to him of California) to the California club to induce it to refuse to sell his contract to Chicago. Any amount above $500 would be sufficient to make the California club reject Chicago's offer since Chicago is offering only $500 more than the player is worth to the California club. (The player can "offer" such an amount by accepting a pay reduction.) With or without the reserve clause, then, the player will locate where the value he places on amenities plus the value of his baseball talent is greatest.

II

The significance of Coase's work quickly led to critical responses by Wellisz,[6] Calabresi,[7] and others, although Calabresi withdrew his criticism in a later paper.[8] The criticism centered around two allegations— that the Coase theorem neglects long-run considerations that negate it and that the spirit of the work endorses the use of resources for the undesirable purpose of "extortion." The long-run issue is discussed here and the "extortion" problem in Part III. In Part IV, I discuss the problems introduced when the assumption of negligible transaction cost is dropped.

The question of long-run considerations has been raised because it would seem that different liability rules would alter the profitability of remaining inside or outside each industry. It is alleged that if farmers are left to bear the cost that arises from proximity to cattle, the rate of return to farming will fall and resources will therefore leave the farming industry. Alternatively, if ranchers are left to bear the cost, the resulting reduction in rate of return to ranching will lead to the exit of resources from that industry. Hence, even if transaction cost is zero, the market will allocate resources differently in the long run depending upon which rule of liability is chosen.

But short-run versus long-run considerations should have no bearing on the Coase theorem, which is based on the proposition that an implicit cost (the forgone payment from the farmer) is just as much a cost as is an explicit cost (the liability damage), and this proposition surely must hold in the long run as well as in the short run. One way of demonstrating this is by allowing the two activities to be merged under a common owner. A detailed example of this is given by G. Warren Nutter.[9] If there is no special cost to operating a multiproduct firm, the costly interaction between farming and ranching will be fully brought to the owner's attention in his operation of a farming-ranching enterprise. The mix of output that he produces will be that which maximizes his earnings. The rule of liability that is chosen can have no effect on his decisions because the owner of such a firm must bear the interaction cost whichever legal rule is adopted. The cost interdependence is a technical-economic interdependence, not a legal one. Since such merged operations are possible, the rule of liability is rendered irrelevant to the choice of output mix. But a refutation of the criticism that is based on the use of the joint product enterprise gives rise to the (incorrect) suspicion that the basic problem has been begged, since the rule of liability that is chosen cannot in this case alter the wealth of the owner of a farming-ranching enterprise. The spirit of the argument can be preserved, while the suspicion is allayed, by assuming that the advantages offered by specialization of ownership are so great that it is uneconomic to merge the two activities into a single ranching-farming firm.

If owners of farmland bear the cost of crop damage, what must be the cost conditions that are associated with an equilibrium allocation of land to farming, ranching, and other uses? For such damage to arise there must be a sufficient scarcity of land to force farms and ranches into proximity. Marginal farm acreage (acreage that just "breaks even") must earn revenue sufficient to cover all cost, including the cost of crop damage done by straying cattle. Suppose the proximity of ranching and farming reduces the net return to the owner of farmland by $100 as compared with what could be earned were there no neighboring ranch. If ranching continues on the neighboring acres, it must be true that the net return to the owner of the ranchland exceeds $100, for otherwise the farmer would have been able to purchase the removal of cattle from neighboring land by offering $100 to the neighboring ranchers. The reduction in net return to farming brought about because of crop damage is thus implicitly taken into account by the owner of the ranchland when he refuses the offer of the owner of the neighboring farmland. The money offered by the farmer is refused by the rancher precisely because the continued use of the land for grazing brings in additional net revenue in excess of $100.

Land that is submarginal as farm or ranchland (land that cannot be profitably farmed or ranched) is unable to earn revenue sufficient to cover the explicit $100 damage cost if it is put to the plough or the $100 implicit cost if it is employed in ranching. Were this land to be employed in farming, its owner would suffer losses attributable in part to the damage done to his crops by straying cattle, whereas if it were employed in ranching its owner would suffer the implicit loss of foregoing a $100 payment from the neighboring farmer (the owners of farmland bearing the cost of crop damage). Submarginal land by definition can be neither farmed nor ranched profitably.

Now let the rule of liability be changed so that ranchers become liable for crop damage. If there is to be a long-run effect, it must be true that the cost interrelationships change in a manner that causes either the conversion of ranchland to farmland or submarginal land to farmland. But neither conversion can be made profitable by the change in liability.

Acreage that was marginally profitable in ranching must remain ranchland because it had been earning net revenues in excess of the $100 damages done by cattle to surrounding farmland. If a producing ranch were to be switched from ranching to farming to avoid the new liability its owner would forgo revenues (in excess of $100) that exceeded the resulting reduction in liability ($100). The owner of what was marginal ranchland, therefore, will continue to employ his land in ranching under the new liability rule.

The land that previously was submarginal must remain submarginal. The changed liability rule will not attract this land into farming. Submarginal lands under the original rule of liability earned insufficient revenues in farming to cover the $100 cost of crop damage. Under the new rule of liability, neighboring ranchers will succeed in negotiating with the owners of this land to keep it out of farming. Operating ranches, under the old rule of liability, had been yielding net revenues in excess of $100; therefore it will be possible and profitable for ranchers, in order to avoid the $100 crop damage that otherwise would result, to offer an amount to the owners of submarginal land that is sufficient to keep the land out of farming.

There is a temptation at this point in the argument to believe that an error has been made. Suppose that the farmer suffers damages equal to

$100 and the rancher enjoys a net return equal to $110. If the rancher is not liable he will choose to continue ranching and to refuse a payment from a neighboring farmer of $100 to stop ranching. But if the rule of liability is reversed, he will continue ranching only if his $110 net return is sufficient to cover the cost imposed on the farmer ($100) *plus* the payment required to keep submarginal land (which can be assumed to border on another boundary of the ranch) out of farming. There has been no error in the argument, but there is an error in introducing the second neighbor halfway through the analysis. With the rancher not liable, he would have elected to remain in ranching only if the net return to ranching exceeded the payments to leave ranching offered to him by *both* his neighbors. If the rancher finds it remunerative to remain in ranching in the face of both these offers he must earn a sufficient net return from ranching, after the rule of liability is changed and he is held liable, to be able to pay damages to his neighboring farmer *and* to pay the owner of neighboring submarginal land to keep that land out of production.

The change in the rule of liability does not lead to a conversion of ranchland or submarginal land to farming. The use of land that maximized returns before the change in liability rule continues to maximize returns after the new rule is adopted, and the mix of output is unaffected by the choice of liability rule even when long-run considerations are analyzed. To understand the effect of altering the rule of liability it is important to recognize that the owner of a resource who finds it in his interest to employ that resource in a particular way when he bears the cost of an interaction will be paid to employ that resource *in the same way* when the rule of liability is reversed. What can happen, and in this case does happen, when the rule of liability is changed is that present owners of land having a comparative advantage in ranching suffer a *windfall* loss in the value of their land while owners of farmland enjoy a *windfall* gain. But this redistribution of wealth cannot alter the uses of these lands.

III

The problem of "extortion" is part of the larger problem of wealth redistribution that may accompany a change in the rule of liability. Our concern here is with situations in which such a redistribution takes place. However, it should be noted that, when there is no restriction on contracting, a change in the rule of liability need not be accompanied by wealth redistribution. If owners of firms are made liable for industrial accidents, for example, then the equilibrium wage will move downward to reflect the shifting of this explicit cost from workers to employers. Employers no longer will need to cover the cost of industrial accidents in the wages they pay since this cost will be paid by them in the form of industrial accident insurance or self-insurance required by the new rule of liability.   The general effect of shifting accident liability directly to firms will be merely to change the classification, not the amount, of remuneration.   What under no employer liability were simply wages become under employer liability wages plus accident benefits.   No redistribution of wealth accompanies the change in liability.   Workers who, when they had to bear the cost of accidents directly, received $X in wages will, under the new rule of liability, receive part of the $X in the form of accident compensation and the remainder in wages, but there will be no change in their total income after taking account of expected accident costs under the two systems.

This holds strictly only if workers and employers are allowed to enter into voluntary contractual arrangements for reshifting the explicit cost back to workers, a matter that need not be discussed in detail here.   If such agreements are disallowed by the law—i. e., if the costs of making such agreements is prohibitively high because of their illegality—then some wealth may be redistributed from those workers who would have found it advantageous to self-insure to workers who find it advantageous to buy insurance; such a law would force workers, in the wage reductions they must accept, to purchase insurance for industrial accidents from their employers.

The problem of "extortion" arises when a change in liability gives rise to a redistribution in wealth.   In the farmer-rancher case, the relative values of nearby farm and ranchlands will be changed when the rule of liability is altered.   Under one rule of liability, with farmers required to bear the cost of crop damage, farmers will need to pay ranchers to reduce herd size; under the other rule ranchers will have to pay farmers for damages or for any alteration in the quantity of corn grown nearby. The change in the direction of payments must affect the rents that can be collected by owners of these lands and thus the market values of these lands.

In these cases the owner of the specialized resource, ranchland or farmland, that is not required to bear the cost of the interaction may threaten to increase the intensity of the interaction in an attempt to get his neighbor to pay him a larger sum than would ordinarily be required to obtain his cooperation in adjusting the intensity of the interaction downward.   The owner of ranchland, if he is not liable for crop damage done by straying cattle, might, in the absence of a neighboring farmer, raise only 1,000 head of cattle.   With proximity between farming and ranching, a neighboring owner of farmland might be willing to pay the rancher the sum required to finance a 200-head reduction in herd size.

However, if the owner of ranchland *threatens* to raise 1,500 head, he may be able to secure more than this sum from the farmer because of the additional crop damage that would be caused by the larger herd size. With or without this "extortion" threat, the size of the herd will be reduced to 800 because that is the size, by assumption, that maximizes the total value of both activities. Given the interrelationship between the two activities, that is the herd size that will maximize the return to the farmer and, indirectly, the sum available for possible transfer to the rancher. What is at issue is the sharing of this maximum return.

To the extent that there exist alternative farm sites, the ability of the owner of ranchland to make such a threat credible is compromised. Competition among such owners will reduce the payment that farmers make to ranchers to that sum which is just sufficient to offset the revenue forgone by ranchers when herd size is reduced. No rancher could succeed in a threat to increase herd size above normal numbers because other ranchers would be willing to compete to zero the price that farmers are asked to pay to avoid abnormally large herd sizes. Abnormally large herd size, in itself, will generate losses to owners of ranchland and, for this reason, competition among such owners will reduce the price that owners of farmland must pay to avoid such excessive herd sizes to zero.

But if a ranchland owner has a locational monopoly, in the sense that there are no alternative sites available to farmers, then the rancher may succeed in acquiring a larger sum from his neighboring farmer in order to avoid abnormally large herd sizes. The acquisition of a larger sum by the owner of ranchland generally will require him to incur some cost to make his threat credible, perhaps by actually beginning to increase herd size beyond normal levels. If the cost of making this threat credible is low relative to the sum available for transfer from the owner of farmland, the rancher will be in a good position to accomplish the transfer. The sum available for transfer will be the amount by which the value of the neighboring land when used as farmland exceeds its value in the next best use. If the rancher were to demand a larger payment from his neighbor, the neighboring land would be switched to some other use.

The temptation to label such threats extortion or blackmail must be resisted by economists for these are legal and not economic distinctions. The rancher merely attempts to maximize profits. If his agreements with neighboring farmers are marketed in competition with other ranchers, profit maximization constrained by competition implies that an agreement to reduce herd size can be purchased for a smaller payment than if effective competition in such agreements is absent. The appropriate economic label for this problem is nothing more nor less than monopoly. It takes on the cast of such legal classifications as extortion only because the context seems to be one where the monopoly return is received by threatening to produce something that is not wanted—excessively large herds.   The conventional monopoly problem involves a reduction or a threat to reduce the output of a desired good.   In the unconventional monopoly problem presented here, there is a threat to increase herd size beyond desirable levels.   But this difference is superficial.   The conventional monopoly problem can be viewed as one in which the monopolist produces more scarcity than is desired, and the unconventional monopoly problem discussed here can be considered one in which the monopolist threatens to produce too small a reduction in crop damage.   Any additional sum that the rancher succeeds in transferring to himself from the farmer is correctly identified as a monopoly return.

The temptation to resolve this monopoly problem merely by reversing the rule of liability must be resisted.   Should the liability rule be reversed and the owner of ranchland now be held liable for damage done by his cattle to surrounding crops, the specific monopoly problem that we have been discussing would be resolved.   But if the farmer enjoys a locational monopoly such that the rancher has nowhere else to locate, the shoe will now be on the other foot.   The farmer can threaten to increase the number of bushels of corn planted, and hence the damage for which the rancher will be liable, unless the rancher pays the farmer a sum greater than would be required under competitive conditions.   The potential for monopoly and the wealth redistribution implied by monopoly is present in principle whether or not the owner of ranchland is held liable for damages.   Both the symmetry of the problem and its disappearance under competitive conditions refute the allegation that Coase's analysis implicitly endorses the use of resources in undesirable activities.

Should the law treat such classes of monopoly problem as "extortion" or "blackmail"?   It may not be useful for the law to take this step because the threat is made credible by increasing the output of an economic good— cattle if the rancher is not liable, corn if he is.   Because it is difficult to sort desirable from undesirable increases in herd or crop size, there is a real danger of penalizing desirable increases in herd or crop size by mistake if such wealth transfers are treated as extortion.   Activities to which anti-extortion laws normally apply typically involve the use of violence or the threat to take some action that falls within a general class of actions considered socially undesirable.   The application of anti-extortion legal measures in such cases is less likely to penalize socially desirable actions by mistake.   In other cases, it may be possible for the courts to limit the amount of payments to levels that are reasonable compensations for costs incurred (or profits forgone), although it is not clear how easily such determinations can be made by courts.   Alternatively, it is possible to attempt to eliminate the source of the problem—monopoly—but the wisdom of relying on antitrust in this context is a matter on which the author is unprepared to speak.

IV

The costly interaction between farming and ranching is not properly attributed to the actions of either party individually, being ("caused," instead, by resource scarcity, the scarcity of land and fencing materials. If transaction cost is negligible, it would seem that the choice of liability rule cannot depend on who "causes" the damage since both jointly do, or on how resource allocation will be altered, since no such alteration will take place, but largely on judicial or legislative preferences with regard to wealth distribution.

Once significant transacting or negotiating cost is admitted into the analysis, the choice of liability rule will have effects on resource allocation, and it no longer follows that wealth distribution is the main or even an important consideration in choosing the liability rule. The assumption of negligible transacting cost can be only a beginning to understanding the economic consequences of the legal arrangements that underlie the operations of the economy, but little more can be done here than to illustrate the nature of the considerations.[10]

The most obvious effect of introducing significant transacting cost is that negotiations will not be consummated in those situations where the expected benefits from exchange are less than the expected cost of exchanging. Exchange opportunities will be exploited only up to the point where the marginal gain from trade equals the marginal cost of trade. Of course, there is nothing necessarily inefficient in halting exchange at this point. If this were all that could be said on the subject, there would be little more to do than call the reader's attention to the similar analytical roles of transport cost in international trade and transacting cost in exchange generally. But there is more to say.

Significant transacting cost implies that the rule of liability generally will have allocative effects (as Coase recognizes). Consider the problem of liability for automobile-pedestrian accidents. To the extent that "accident" has any economic meaning it must mean that circumstances are such that voluntary negotiations between the driver and the pedestrian are prohibitively costly in many driving situations. The parties to an accident, either because of the speed with which the accident occurs or because of a failure to notice the presence of a competing claimant for the right-of-way, cannot conclude an agreement over the use of the right-of-way at costs that are low enough, *ex ante*, to make the effort worthwhile.

Partly as a consequence of the costliness of such negotiations, rules of the road are developed. Speed limits, traffic signals, and legal constraints on passing are substituted for the development of saleable private rights. In a specific case it may be possible to assign private rights to use the road in a way that makes the exchange of these rights feasible, but, in general, if these rules make economic sense it is precisely because the cost of transacting is expected to be too high in most cases to warrant the development of saleable private rights to the use of roads.

The practicality of such rules is not an argument for or against government action, but a rationale for the substitution of rules for negotiation. The use of rules to eliminate costly negotiations can be found in the management of privately owned parking lots and toll roads as well as in those that are publicly owned.

Such rules notwithstanding, accidents do take place. Assuming that the cost of transacting is too high to make negotiated agreements practical in such cases, we can compare the effect on resource allocation of the rule of liability that is chosen. If drivers are held liable in automobile-pedestrian accidents, the incentives for pedestrians to be careful about how and where they cross streets will be reduced. The incentives for drivers to be careful will be increased. Indeed, if each pedestrian could be guaranteed *full* compensation for all financial, physical, and psychological costs suffered in an accident, then pedestrians would become indifferent between being struck by an auto and not being struck. Drivers, however, would actively seek to avoid accidents since they would always be liable, whereas if it were possible to have a system of complete and full pedestrian liability it would be the drivers who became indifferent between accidents and no accidents and it would be the pedestrians who actively sought to avoid accidents.

In a regime in which transacting cost was zero, either system of liability would generate the same accident-avoiding behavior, as the Coase analysis suggests. With driver liability, drivers would themselves avoid accidents or, if such avoidance could be purchased at lower cost from pedestrians, drivers would pay pedestrians to avoid accidents. Under a scheme of pedestrian liability it would be the pedestrians who took direct action to avoid accidents or indirect action by paying drivers to avoid accidents. Under either rule of liability those accidents are avoided for which the accident cost exceeds the least cost method of avoiding accidents, where the least cost is the lesser of either the driver or pedestrian cost of avoiding accidents. Both rules of liability, assuming zero transacting cost, yield the same accident rate and the same accident-avoiding behavior. The effect of switching from one rule of liability to another is limited to wealth redistribution.

In a situation in which transacting cost is prohibitively high, driver liability leads to the avoidance only of those accidents for which the cost of avoidance to the *driver* is less than the expected accident cost, and pedestrian liability leads to the avoidance of only those accidents for which the cost of avoidance to the *pedestrian* is less than the expected accident cost. In general, the accident rate that results will differ under these two systems since the cost of avoiding accidents will not be the same for drivers and pedestrians. Both systems will lead to higher accident rates than would be true if transacting costs were zero. The effect of positive transacting cost is to raise the cost of avoiding accidents through the foreclosure of the use of possibly cheaper cost-avoidance techniques when these can be employed only by the other party to the accident. A similar conclusion can be reached for all liability problems when transacting cost is prohibitive and when the law cannot particularize the rule of liability to take account of who is the least-cost damage avoider in every instance.

One liability rule may be superior to another if transacting costs are more than negligible precisely because the difficulty of avoiding costly interactions is not generally the same for the interacting parties. It may be less costly for pedestrians to avoid accidents or for farmers to relocate their crops than it is for drivers to avoid accidents or ranchers to reduce the number of cattle they raise. If information about this were known, it would be possible for the legal system to improve the allocation of resources by placing liability on that party who in the usual situation could be expected to avoid the costly interaction most cheaply.

The use of words such as "blame," "responsible," and "fault" must be treated with care by the economist because they have no useful meanings in an economic analysis of these problems other than as synonyms for the party who could have most easily avoided the costly interaction. Whether the interaction problem involves crop damage, accidents, soot, or water pollution, the qualitative relationship between the interacting parties is symmetrical. It is the *joint* use of a resource, be it geographic location, air, or water that leads to these interactions. It is the demand for scarce resources that leads to conflicting interests.

The legal system does produce rules for determining *prima facie* "fault," but in this context "fault" means only according to some acceptable and applicable legal precedent. In an accident involving a rear-end collision, the court generally will place the burden for proving the absence of negligence on the party driving the following car. If a car strikes a person running across a fenced expressway at night the burden of proving the absence of negligence is likely to be placed on the pedestrian. In treating such cases differently, the law bases its decisions on acceptable and appropriate precedents, but the acceptability of these precedents should not be confused with the morality of the interacting parties. A deeper analysis of these precedents may reveal that they generally make sense from the economic viewpoint of placing the liability on that party who can, at least cost, reduce the probability of a costly interaction happening. Less care need be taken by the driver of the following car in a rear-end collision than would need to be taken by the lead driver to avoid the accident, and less care is needed by a pedestrian to refrain from running across an expressway than is needed by a driver to avoid striking the pedestrian.   Nor need the acceptability of such precedents be based on restitution since, as these precedents become known, their long-run effect is to deter accidents at least cost.   If courts are to ignore wealth, religion, or family in deciding such conflicts, if persons before the courts are to be treated with regard only to the cause of action and available proof, then, as a normative proposition, it is difficult to suggest any criterion for deciding liability other than placing it on the party able to avoid the costly interaction most easily.

FOOTNOTES

* Professor of Business Economics, Law School and Graduate School of Business, University of Chicago.   The author wishes to thank the Charles R. Walgreen Foundation for financial aid through its grant to the University of Chicago, and, also, the Lilly Endowment through its grant to the University of California.

1 R. H. Coase, The Problem of Social Cost, 3 J.Law & Econ. 1 (1960).

2 Id. at 2–8.

3 I ignore other possibilities such as building a fence.   These are discussed by Coase (id. at 3).   Consideration of them changes the exposition but not the results.

One further assumption is required for the mix of output to remain unchanged.   Any redistribution of wealth resulting from a change in the rule of liability is assumed to have no consequences for the demands for the products produced.   Owners of farmland and ranchland should be vegetarians in equal proportions, for otherwise a redistribution of wealth between these two groups would alter the market demands for corn and beef and thereby indirectly alter the mix of output produced.   The wealth redistribution problem will be discussed later when we turn to the subject of extortion.

4 The reserve clause and other aspects of organized baseball are discussed in Simon Rottenberg, The Baseball Players' Labor Market, 64 J.Pol.Econ. 242 (1956).   The reasoning employed by Rottenberg is similar but not identical to the above argument.   Rottenberg's argument is based partly on the premise, not used here, that it takes two fairly well matched teams to produce a good game.

5 Nonpecuniary aspects of his employment are discussed later, but it should be noted that the argument for retention of the reserve clause is not based on nonpecuniary job amenities.

6 Stanislaw Wellisz, On External Diseconomies and the Government Assisted Invisible Hand, 31 Economica (N.S.) 345 (1964).

7 Guido Calabresi, The Decision for Accidents: An Approach to Nonfault Allocation of Costs, 78 Harv.L.Rev. 713 (1965).

8 Guido Calabresi, Transaction Costs, Resource Allocation and Liability Rules—A Comment, 11 J.Law & Econ. 67 (1968).

9 G. Warren Nutter, The Coase Theorem on Social Cost: A Footnote, 11 J.Law & Econ. 503 (1968).

10 Other considerations that arise when the cost of transacting is positive are discussed in Harold Demsetz, Some Aspects of Property Rights, 9 J.Law & Econ. 61 (1966).

11: SOME ASPECTS OF PROPERTY RIGHTS *

HAROLD DEMSETZ
University of Chicago

The tradition in microeconomic theory is to take wants and technology as givens and to proceed from these to deduce from the assumption of scarcity testable implications and normative propositions. These assumptions, together with variety in tastes and abilities and differences in the number of rivals, give rise to most economic laws. In this way, laws such as those that relate to demand, comparative advantage, equalization of factor returns, and the relationship of price to cost are deduced. The role of property rights is not explicitly dealt with in this approach. But imbedded in the whole process is a third class of given datum. There must be assumed a set of social arrangements which define ownership. In this paper, I will examine some aspects of property rights that bear both on issues to which we have been led by the traditional approach and to some which we have ignored because property rights have not been treated explicitly.

An example will make clear the necessity of assumptions about social arrangements. Consider the two economic laws which state that (1) demand curves are negatively sloped and that (2) queues will tend to be eliminated by a price that is free to fluctuate. The first law is true even if ownership does not include the right to buy or sell; it does not even depend on the existence of exchange. Thus, from the first law it follows that an increase in the unpleasantness of my neighbor (an increase in the

Journal of Law and Economics, Vol. 9 (1966), p. 61.

price of association) will diminish the frequency of my visits. Nothing is bought or sold but the law holds true.

The second law holds true generally only when the right to sell is included in ownership. And this is so for nontautological reasons. Queues usually do exist for the use of public parking at zoos, beaches, etc., on popular holidays when no freely fluctuating price is charged for the use of facilities. Of course, the trouble and delay associated with waiting for parking will limit the length of queue and the hotter the day the shorter the queue will tend to be; this is a reflection of the law of negatively sloped demand. But the queue, which can be either of demanders or suppliers, is not generally reduced to insignificance by the heat of the day. And therein lies a difference between the economic laws that prevail when ownership includes right of sale and when it does not. When sale is included, the price will *tend* to rise and the length of queue will *tend* to be reduced. Self-interest and the relatively small cost of most price adjustments assure this.

Methods other than relying on the heat of the day or on the height of price can be used to reduce queues. Entry into public parking places can be made more or less difficult; directions on how to get there can be hidden from sight or placed in prominent positions, etc. These methods are generally more costly to employ and no one has a clear self-interest in employing them. Consequently, according to the first law, they are employed to a lesser degree than flexible pricing. Therefore, queues can be expected to be more significant where the right of sale is not included in ownership.

A private property system is difficult to define in a few words, and I shall not attempt a complete definition here. Crucially involved is the notion that individuals have control over the use to which scarce resources (including ideas) can be put, and that this right of control is saleable or transferable. A private property right system requires the prior consent of "owners" before their property can be affected by others. The role of the body politic in this system is twofold. Firstly, the government or courts must help decide which individuals possess what property rights and, therefore, who has the power to claim that his rights are affected by others. Secondly, property rights so assigned must be protected by the police power of the state or the owners must be allowed to protect property rights themselves. Presumably the best mix of public and private protection will depend on ethical and other considerations.

There are three important implications of a private property system that are valid in a world in which all property rights are assigned and in which the cost of exchanging and of policing property rights are zero. A private property system under such conditions, implies that (1) the value of all harmful and beneficial effects of alternative uses of property rights will be brought to bear on their owners, (2) to the extent that owners of property rights are utility maximizers, property rights will be used efficiently, and (3) the mix of output that is produced will be independent of the distribution of property rights among persons except insofar as changes in the distribution of wealth affect demand patterns.

These implications follow directly from the recent work of R. H. Coase.[1] We will not derive them in detail here, but the nature of the forces which produce them can be grasped easily by way of example. Whether or not a new product will be profitable is, in the absence of exchange and police costs, independent of which of the following property right assignments is chosen:

(A) Producers of new products are assigned the right to sell new products without compensating competitors who are injured.

(B) Producers of old products are assigned the right to retain their customers.

Under right assignment (A), injured producers of old products will need to bear the cost imposed upon them by the introduction of new products, but they will be able to bring this cost to the attention of new product producers by offering to pay them to withdraw the new products. Competitors will be willing to pay a sum up to the amount which measures the harmful effects visited upon them. They can do this by offering such a sum to the new product producer to withdraw his product or, what is more likely, they can offer such a sum to buyers in the form of price cuts in order to retain their patronage. If the cost imposed on injured producers of old products is greater than the gain conferred on buyers by the new product, the injured competitors will be able to retain their customers and the new product will fail. If the gain conferred on buyers by the new product exceeds the cost imposed on producers of old products, the new product will succeed.

Under right assignment (B), the new product producers will need to pay an acceptable sum to producers of old products before buyers can shift to the new product. The amount which old product producers will find acceptable will be a sum no smaller than the value of the harmful effects of losing customers. The sum that producers of old products will accept under right assignment (B) is precisely the same as the sum they pay under right assignment (A). If this sum exceeds the gains that buyers would enjoy from the new product, the new product will be withdrawn. Given the gains and the costs generated by the new product, the profitability of producing it will be the same under either and any system of completely specified property rights.

Since all costs and gains of exercising property rights are brought to bear on property owners no matter what right assignment is adopted, the output mix will remain invariant with respect to the property right system used, provided only that all rights are assigned. This result should not be too surprising; it states that in the absence of exchange and police costs property rights will always be used where they assume their maximum value. This is a standard proposition of economics with regard to any economic resource. The property right in our example is the right to produce a new product. Whether this right is initially owned by new product producers or by their competitors, it will end up being owned by that party which will find it more valuable. Who this party is will be independent of the initial right assignment.

Although the proposition that property rights will find their most valuable use turns out to be a standard deduction from economic theory, it is a very important variant. It calls to our attention the possibility that the solution of many problems may be arrived at by a more complete specification of property rights.

Our conclusions do *not* depend on the degree of competitiveness. In the absence of exchange and policing costs all monopolists could discriminate freely or could be paid by purchasers of their products to act competitively. Exchange surplus would, of course, accrue to the monopolists.

A world without exchange or police costs can only be a starting point for analyzing the implications of alternative property right systems. Where such costs are positive, alternative assignments of property rights will generally imply different mixes of output. I am unable at present to specify the procedure that should be followed for the assignment of property rights, but I wish to call attention to some characteristics that will have an important bearing on the choice of such a procedure. I shall call these characteristics *valuation costs* and *realignment costs*.

Valuation Costs. The efficiency with which property rights are used depends on whether their value in the use to which they are put is sufficient to cover the cost of foregoing alternative uses. However, for most uses of property rights only some beneficial and harmful effects are easily known. Other effects can be discovered only with great cost. Most of the harmful effects imposed on workers and on the suppliers of many inputs can be known beforehand with little cost. A property right system which requires the *prior* agreement of these input owners before they can be put to a particular task insures that these costs will be taken into account. But the inputs upon which smoke from the factory will eventually descend, such as distant farmland (and these are inputs in every sense of the word), can be known only with great cost.

While it is difficult to draw a neat line, it is clear that as the uncertainty increases about whose rights will be affected and by how much, a point will be reached beyond which the expected cost of a prior determining of effects exceeds the expected gain. The greater the uncertainty of effect, the less inclined we should be to require that prior compensation be paid to those harmed or prior fees be charged of those benefited. The cost of sorting out and measuring legitimate claims in cases of great uncertainty would be so high as to undermine efficient resource use. Property right uses which, with omniscience, would be known to be profitable, would be discouraged by the imposition of such costs in the presence of uncertainty. Innovation and change would be uneconomically hampared by a commitment to a policy of prior compensation.

Denial of prior compensation when those who will be affected are known with a fair degree of accuracy, however, would also be inefficient. For in these instances, the most economical way to measure accurately the costs and benefits of a given use of property rights is to insist on the right to prior compensation for accepting a harmful effect or on prior payment for delivering a beneficial effect. The right to prior compensation implies the right to insist on *voluntary* consent, and insisting on voluntary consent tends to produce information accuracy when many costs and benefits are known only by the individuals affected.

The requirement of prior compensation if those affected can be ascertained easily and the denial of prior compensation when those affected can be identified only with great difficulty does not deny the efficiency of requiring compensation in many of the uncertain cases *after the fact*. The cost of acquiring information will be lowered after property rights have been put to a particular use, so that assessment of effects may become sufficiently easier in some instances to make the payment of compensation economic.

It is difficult to define boundary lines for prior as compared with after-the-fact compensation, but sometimes it is possible to assign rights in a way that reduces valuation costs. A clear prescription seems to stand in one important case—pecuniary effects. We have discussed above two alternative assignments of rights and argued that they would have the same effect on resource allocation if exchange and police costs were zero. The example involved compensation for pecuniary effects and whether a new product producer should compensate competitors for taking away customers. Once we recognize the cost of discovering and accrediting claims, a difference between the two right assignments emerges.

Damaged competitors know they are losing customers and they can reflect the cost imposed on them by offering customers lower prices. They do not need to know who is taking customers from them and the costs of establishing such knowledge is rendered unnecessary. If, alternatively, we should give competitors the right to their customers, prior compensation would need to be paid by a new entrant before he could engage in business. The cost of establishing which firms are damaged and by how much would be so great as to discourage entry even though entry would have been profitable had there been no problem of resolving uncertainty. It follows from efficiency requirements that persons and firms be given the right to compete without compensating those who are financially damaged. Those who are harmed by competition can voluntarily bid to retain customers. In some cases the harmful effects may be so obvious that prior compensation to a competitor would not affect resource allocation. Such cases are very unlikely where the effects stem from the loss or gain of buyers but are more likely where they result from physical damage.

Realignment Costs. Alternative assignments of property rights will affect the resources devoted to exchanging for reasons other than valuation costs. Even if uncertainty in the valuation of resource in alternative employments is taken as given, it will be efficient to assign *new* property rights in a way that is expected to minimize the cost of transacting that will be required subsequently. Given variety in demands and abilities, it is unlikely that a correct initial assignment of rights will eliminate all recontracting, but it may be possible to reduce recontracting costs significantly.

For example, let us consider the property right problems associated with the introduction of home air conditioners. The question arises as to whether homeowners should have the right to prevent noise levels from rising above a given intensity or whether air conditioner owners should have the right to run their sets even though noise levels on surrounding land will be raised. If it is generally true that owners of air conditioners will so strongly desire to operate their sets that they will purchase most of the noise control rights from their neighbors, then exchange costs could be reduced by giving the initial assignment of rights to set owners. If set owners are given these rights, some homeowners will contract to buy them from set owners, but, by assumption, the number and presumably the cost of such exchanges would be less than under the alternative assignment of rights. A number of sets that approximates the efficient number would be arrived at with the use of less resources for conducting exchange if set owners are given the right rather than homeowners.

This prescription for the assignment of property rights is most clearly applicable when these rights are new. The age of air transportation suddenly made the right to traverse upper airspace a valuable right, whereas the airplane merely provided a competing claimant for the already valuable right to use lower airspace. The right to use upper airspace was not clearly defined because a definition was rarely demanded; it could be argued that there was no involuntary taking of property when the right to use upper airspace was assigned to airplane owners and to the government. Since a decision was needed and since it appeared that airplane owners would eventually acquire the right to use upper airspace, an efficient allocation seemed to demand that exchange costs be reduced by initially assigning the new right where it was finally expected to reside. (The assigned right is greatly limited. The right of sale is not generally included with the right of use, so that if other competing claims for the use of upper airspace arise, a reallocation through the courts will be required.)

The right to use (and to sell the use of) lower airspace has been defined rather clearly to reside with landowners. The existence of this definition attests to the fact that landowners do find the right to use lower airspace a valuable right for such purposes as insuring quiet and building high structures. In the case of lower airspace, we are dealing with the problem of whether or not the right to use or own lower airspace should be involuntarily *reassigned*. The existence of serious competing claims to the use of lower airspace should create doubt about our ability to judge which use is most valuable and, hence, should lead us to rely to a larger extent on voluntary negotiations between competing claimants and landowners.

Should the practice of involuntary reassignment become common, all confidence in the longevity of property rights will be reduced and all long-run consequences of using property rights in various ways will tend to be neglected. Nonetheless, it must be realized that some degree of involuntary reassignment of property rights is desirable if most persons agree to a reassignment that, because of high police or exchange costs, cannot easily take place in the market. Taxing for the provision of national defense is the classic example. The great cost that would be required to confine the benefits of national defense only to those who pay for them (that is, the great cost of preventing nonpayers from "stealing" benefits), is what makes the voluntary exchange of property rights in the production of national defense rather impractical.

However, it is sometimes the case that a public taking of property will benefit one fairly well defined group of persons at the expense of another. Indeed, the compensation principle of welfare economics presumes that it is possible to determine who will be harmed or benefited and by how much. But, in the absence of voluntary exchange of already existing property rights, it is difficult to see how this valuation information is obtained.

Valuation in the Absence of Voluntarism. Once the property right system has been changed to allow the nonvoluntary taking of property from and for identifiable groups of persons, we can no longer rely on market negotiations to produce valuation information. In some cases, it may be thought that market transactions are too costly to bring about a proper resource allocation and that substituting political machinery for the market will reduce this cost. In such cases the rule now incorporated into much of welfare economics is that, if a change in resource allocation will produce enough benefit so that those who are harmed by the change *could* be compensated adequately, then the change should be made.

Some economists have argued that the compensation need not be paid to those harmed, that such a payment should be viewed as a problem of wealth distribution and not one of efficiency. Others have argued that compensation must be paid so that we can be assured that no one is made worse off by the change. There is, however, a separate reason for the payment of compensation. This reason, which is explained below, is based on strictly interpreted efficiency requirements that arise from the need for accurate information; it does not rely on the ethical postulate that no person should be left worse off because of a government sponsored change in the *status quo*.

The costs and benefits of a prospective change in resource allocation cannot be treated as given datum. The marginal cost and benefit curves associated with a prospective realignment of resources are not known by the government. Each affected individual knows his benefit or cost, and, in the absence of high exchange cost, this information would be transmitted to others in the form of market negotiations. The primary problem of the government *is* the estimation problem. The compensation principle by its assumption that costs and benefits are known begs the most difficult question posed by a prospective change.

Our argument can be made without loss of generality by considering a particular activity that harmfully affects some persons while benefiting others. We assume that exchange or police costs are too high for the harmful and beneficial effects of the activity to be brought to bear adequately on participants by private property adjustments. Our problem is illustrated in Figure I where mc_1 and mb_2 measure, respectively, the marginal costs which accrue to group 1 and the marginal benefits which accrue to group 2 for various levels of the prospective action. The ethical symmetry of the problem should be underscored. To allow the action will benefit group 2 and harm group 1. To disallow the action will benefit group 1 and harm group 2. A neutral ethical position would allow us to portray the situation equally well by reversing the identification of costs and benefits. The marginal cost of curtailing the activity would be the mb_2 curve, and the marginal benefit of curtailing the activity would be the mc_1 curve.

Whichever way one views the problem, the efficient level of the activity in the absence of market or political adjustment costs is q_1. Given that exchange or police costs are prohibitively high, the marginal cost (marginal benefit) to group 1 cannot be brought to bear on group 2 and the marginal benefit (marginal cost) to group 2 cannot be brought to bear on group 1. Let us suppose that the political costs of adjusting the ac-

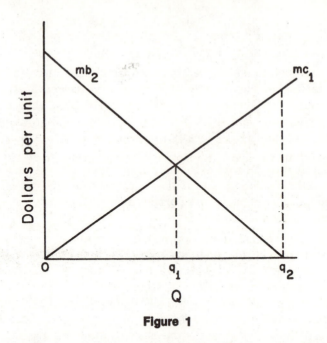

Figure 1

tivity level are low enough to make such an adjustment desirable and, further, so that q_1 remains efficient, let us assume that these political costs are independent of the degree to which the adjustment is made.

If the government should merely question those who alleged that they will be harmed by the activity, it will be in their interest to exaggerate the harmful effects so that they can increase the probability that the activity will be prohibited. Those who allege that they will be harmed if the activity is prohibited have an incentive to exaggerate the benefits they will derive from the activity. Assessing these benefits and costs by simple-minded questionnaires or by relying on the publicity of complaints will lead to the decision being based on inaccurate information, although this is a fair description of the way in which the political calculus sometimes operates. However, it is conceptually possible for the government to acquire information of greater accuracy.

But there will be a hold-out problem.

Let the government attempt to buy the permission of those who feel that they will be harmed by allowing the activity and also let the government attempt to buy the permission to restrict the activity from those who feel that they will benefit from the activity. That action should be taken for which permission can be purchased at lower cost. By assuming the role of middleman, the government through the payment of compensation can increase the accuracy of the information upon which it acts.

The difficulty is that it is not easy to see why the government can play the middleman role more cheaply than can private middlemen. But if the government can be a better innovator in this marketing function it is clear that compensation may be desirable to improve the accuracy of information, that is, for efficiency reasons.

A tool of analysis frequently used by economists to uncover such information when market negotiations are prohibitively costly is modern cost-benefit analysis. I suppose that systems analysis is the best we can do in some circumstances, but some of the practitioners of systems analysis fail to realize how imperfect is the information that is produced.

Suppose that we are interested in determining how much the state should spend on automobile safety devices. To answer this question we can calculate the cost of an additional safety device and compare it to the value of the lives we expect it to save. If we are sophisticated, we can calculate this latter value by multiplying the expected decrease in deaths by the value of a typical live person. The value of a typical live person is frequently taken to depend on the discounted value of that portion of his earnings that an accidental death will eliminate.

The difficulty with this analysis is that the correct solution will be to equate the marginal cost of safety devices to the *price* that persons are willing to pay for expected reductions in their accident rate. This price will be an individual matter. It will depend on a person's demand to live longer, on his income, on the prices of other things, and on his *taste for life*. The latter fact is knowable only to himself in principle, and, although it will be revealed through negotiation in the market place over the exchange of private property, it is only poorly approximated by a sophisticated cost-benefit analysis. A poor man may be willing to pay a higher price than a rich man for additional expected years of life, especially if he has a greater fear of hell.

FOOTNOTES

* The author wishes to thank the Lilly Endowment for financing his work for several weeks at the University of California at Los Angeles through a grant to that institution for the study of property rights.

1 See Coase, The Problem of Social Cost, 3 J.Law & Econ. 1 (1960).

B Continued

12: WEALTH DISTRIBUTION AND THE OWNERSHIP OF RIGHTS

HAROLD DEMSETZ*

Introduction

In the first issue of the *Journal* I discussed the allocative effects of right ownership,[1] expanding on Professor R. H. Coase's important contribution to this subject,[2] but I referred to the problem of wealth distribution only when comparing the legal concept of extortion with the economic concept of monopoly. The present paper explores more deeply the relationship between the structure of ownership and the distribution of wealth. But before proceeding to this task, it will be useful to repeat one point covered in my earlier paper.

When a new cost arises, resources will tend to be reallocated in a manner that minimizes the fall in the value of output that results from this cost. For example, the innovative application of agricultural herbicides may kill neighboring grapevines as a result of wind-carried spillovers. In such situations, some (marginal) vineyards may be sufficiently unproductive that the cheapest way of accommodating to the new cost is for these lands to be converted to other uses. Or it may be that land owners will respond to the new cost by tending to locate vineyards upwind from other crops.

Such new costs generate allocation effects, not only within the directly interacting activities, but also in related industries that supply inputs and complementary or substitute products. These allocative effects will be the same whether or not the farmer must compensate the vineyard owner for damages done—a conclusion that follows from and is subject to the

Journal of Legal Studies, Vol. 1, No. 2, 1972, p. 223.

conditions underlying Coase's analysis, the main condition being the assumption that the cost of transacting is negligible. A reduction in wine output will have effects on the glass container industry, the beer industry, and the demand for farm workers. The changes in price and output in these related industries generally will redistribute wealth, but such redistributions are *not* of concern in this paper because they are unrelated to the legal decision about the ownership of airspace rights above the vineyards. Whether the courts decide that neighboring farmers have certain rights in that airspace, and hence are under no obligation to compensate vineyard owners for damage done to grapevines, or decide the opposite, the same vineyards and the same farms will be retired from production. The distributive effect for resources employed in *related* industries is invariant with respect to this legal decision. The effect on the wealth of those who own the resources used in related industries depends on the particular mix of grape and corn output that results from the use of herbicides. This mix generally will be independent of the legal decision as to who owns what rights (assuming zero transacting cost). What is relevant to the present paper is how the legal assignment of rights affects the distribution of wealth between the directly interacting parties, between the owners of vineyards and the owners of farm land.

Our first objective is to ascertain just what it is that allows legal decisions about right ownership to alter the distribution of wealth. We can proceed toward this objective by considering two cases that appear to yield different distributive effects, but, upon closer examination, can be shown to be qualitatively the same. The first case involves the assignment of rights when the interaction cost arises as a result of a market exchange between the parties affected. It would *appear* in this case that no wealth redistribution follows from the manner in which rights are assigned. The second case reconsiders the problem when the interaction cost does not arise as a result of a market exchange between the parties. In this case, it *appears* that the distribution of wealth is altered by the particular assignments of rights.

Exchange Situations. The exchange of commodities and services in the market place often gives rise to costs (and, in a more general analysis, to benefits) that were not taken into account explicitly in the transaction. The outward manifestation of this can be found in the record of litigation and legislation. For example, consumers of birth control pills had up to 1970 filed more than 300 lawsuits against manufacturers, primarily alleging harmful side effects. A history of such legal actions is characteristic of many commodities and services, and in some cases, for example liability for on-the-job accidents, the problem has been resolved in the legislature. A question that arises in such cases is to what extent the welfare of the parties is altered by the legal position taken in the legislature or the court.

There can be little doubt that a specific court decision will alter the distribution of wealth between the contending parties; that, after all, is the main motivation for litigation. A more difficult question is the extent to which the wealth of buyers as a *group*, and sellers as a *group*, will be altered by the legal position.

Consider the problem of liability for on-the-job accidents. The legal question of concern here is the effect of requiring employers to compensate workers for costs arising from industrial accidents. Should employers be liable for such costs, then firms will count the expected compensation for accidents as part of the explicit cost of employing labor. Because expected compensation is an explicit cost to the employer under this arrangement, he will offer to employ a given quantity and quality of labor only at a wage rate sufficiently low that, after adding expected compensation, the sum is just equal to the higher wage that he would have been willing to pay in the absence of employer liability. What the worker would have received simply as a wage if the employer were not liable for injury costs he now receives as the sum of a lower wage and an implicit accident insurance premium purchased for him by his employer, competition among workers leading him to accept lower wages when accompanied by such a premium. It would seem that the distribution of wealth between workers and shareholders is unaffected by the legal position because of the offsetting alteration in explicit wages.

This conclusion, which is subject to some qualifications to be discussed below, can be illustrated with the aid of figure 1. Supply and demand curves for labor are shown in this figure. The S and D curves are drawn on the assumption that employers are not liable for industrial accidents, and the primed curves are based on the opposite assumption. Let $\overline{FR}$ represent the expected accident cost per man-year of labor and let the vertical axis measure the annual wage per laborer. If employers are not liable for the cost of industrial accidents, the equilibrium wage rate is given by F, where S and D intersect. Employees bear accident costs equivalent to $\overline{FR}$ per year against which they can purchase accident insurance or self-insure, as each sees fit. With employer liability, the demand for labor is reduced and the supply of labor increased until the new wage, indicated by R, is just sufficient to allow employers to purchase accident insurance from the proceeds earned by the firm through its employment of labor.

The distribution of wealth appears to be unaffected by the legislation because workers and employers capture the same amounts of producer and consumer surplus with either legal position. With employees explicitly bearing accident costs, the producer surplus will be the triangle GHF and the employee surplus will be the triangle GYF, and with employer liability these surpluses will be given, respectively, by triangles TXR and STR. Since TXR and GHF are identical, as are STR and GYF, the distribution of wealth between the two groups seems to be invariant with respect to the legal position that is taken.

Implicit in the above analysis is the assumption that the cost of transacting can be neglected safely for the purpose at hand. But the role of transaction cost should be understood. If employees are left to bear accident costs, and are compensated through their wages for these costs, they can either purchase accident insurance or self-insure. Those employees who believe that they are less accident prone, or who are less averse to risk, would tend to self-insure: others would tend to purchase accident insur-

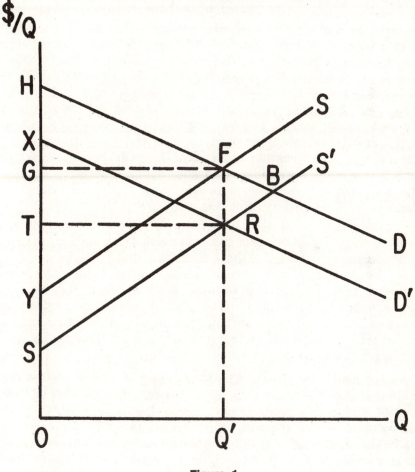

Figure 1

ance. But if the law assigns the liability for accidents to employers and prohibits employees and employers from contracting out of employer liability, then those workers who would have self-insured will be deprived of the opportunity to do so, for they will be compelled to accept lower wages in return for insurance provided them by the employer.

When transaction cost becomes significant, the legal position is more likely to have consequences for the distribution of wealth. In the present case, those workers who would wish to but who are prevented from securing higher wages by voluntarily bearing accident costs would seem to be harmed as compared to what their situation would be under a system of worker liability for accidents. In effect, the prohibition of such contractual arrangements denies them the opportunity to take advantage of their willingness to assume risk or their belief that they are more careful than others. Of course, to the extent that the employer's insurance company can recognize careful workers, it will be possible for the worker to receive higher wages than others because the insurance premium paid on his behalf by the employer will reflect the care taken by the worker. But, for this to be the case, the cost to the insurance company of transacting such special arrangements must be low.

In all of these matters, it is important to separate financial liability from actual performance. The fact that employees may explicitly bear the cost of industrial accidents in no way implies that they will be the ones to undertake accident prevention or even that they will negotiate directly with insurance companies for accident insurance. If management, or some third party, can perform these tasks more effectively, then the services of these parties can be purchased by employees or by groups of employees.

It should be noted that we have not dealt here with the resource allocation question of what accident rate will result from the legal position regarding financial liability. I have discussed that issue in my previous article. Nonetheless, it is worth calling attention to the incentive to reduce the accident rate that is offered to employers even though they are not held liable for industrial accidents. Offering employees a safer environment in which to work should allow an employer to secure his labor supply for lower wages than he would be required to pay if his firm did not have an excellent reputation for giving attention to safety.

Non-exchange Situations. The development of a herbicide, we assume, has brought about a costly interaction between the growing of corn, to which the herbicide is applied, and the growing of grapevines, which are killed by wind-carried deposits of the herbicide. This problem actually arose in Monee, Illinois in 1969. The Ramey and Allen Winery planted its first grapevines in 1963 in an ambitious undertaking to produce a Midwestern champagne. In 1967 a promising champagne successfully met its first market test. But the bubbling hopes of the small company were spiked by a grape-killing agricultural herbicide carried by the wind from surrounding cornfields, and in 1969 the 35 acres of the winery were put up for sale.

In situations such as these, the costly interaction is not associated with an exchange transaction. There is no market price, such as the wage rate in our previous example, that can vary to offset the wealth redistributions that might accompany a particular legal decision on the ownership of rights to use airspace.

If the owners of cornland are given the right to airspace, then the damage done to vineyards becomes an *implicit* cost of growing corn. It is implicit because neighboring vineyard owners would be willing to pay this sum to next-door farmers to induce the latter to abandon corn growing. For the land to remain in corn, the price of corn must be sufficiently high to yield a land rent greater than this implicit cost.

If the legal position now is reversed, owners of vineyards being given the right to control airspace, then what was an implicit cost—an economic rent—to growing corn is converted to an explicit cost borne by owners of cornfields when compensating vineyard owners for damages done by the herbicide. Wealth is thereby redistributed from those owning resources specialized to corn production to those owning resources specialized to grape growing.

Unlike industrial accidents, where the cost is associated with a market transaction, the legal position will alter neither the price of corn nor the price of grapes. The decision merely reclassifies costs from explicit to implicit for the parties to the interaction. But such a reclassification is merely a way of describing the resulting redistribution of wealth. The consequence of such a reclassification of cost can be observed in the prices of land specialized to the production of grapes or corn. A legal position that confers the right to control airspace on owners of land specialized to corn production should result in a higher price for such land and a lower price for vineyards compared to the prices that would prevail if vineyard owners were able to control the use of airspace. The land price changes that would follow upon a legal decision on the ownership of airspace rights are in the nature of windfall gains or losses to the parties.

The Common Element in the Two Cases. It is possible now to join the two situations that we have been discussing. In the cornfield-vineyard example, a wealth redistribution is produced by a change in the definition of property rights because the interacting parties are contractually committed to the ownership of land that has comparative advantages, respectively, in growing corn and growing grapes. By owning the titles to their land, they are assured of bearing all the windfall losses or gains that occur because of an unforeseeable new cost and an unpredictable legal reaction to that cost. After these developments take place, prices to these land titles adjust appropriately to reflect which land will enjoy windfall gains and which windfall losses, and subsequent purchasers avoid all windfall effects.

The *apparent* absence of any wealth redistribution in the industrial accident case is attributable to the implicit (and generally incorrect) assumption that similar contractual commitments are absent. Employer and employee are assumed to stand in the relationship of *prospective* purchaser and supplier of labor services. But if we suppose that an effective labor contract had been negotiated in a situation in which employees bear all industrial accident costs and in which the wages for which they contract are high enough to offset the actuarial value of expected accident costs, and the courts then unexpectedly shift the liability to employers, a redistribution of wealth from employers to those employees already under contract will take place. Thus, the essential condition for a reassignment of rights to alter the distribution of wealth is that the persons whose activities interact must have engaged in these activities through contractual obligations whose terms are incongruous in light of the new rule of liability. And the difference between the cases we have been examining is simply the length of time such incongruous contractual arrangements persist after the structure of rights has been altered. The purchase of land titles usually is not subject to renegotiation, but rather is binding over an indefinite period. A wage contract, however, usually binds the parties over a relatively short time period. For land, then, a restructuring of rights of action implies that the wealth effects that will be capitalized into the price of land titles should reflect a long-term alteration in the revenues and costs of owners, whereas the alteration in liability for industrial accidents contemplates only a short-run alteration in revenues and costs.

This suggests that the duration of the contracts that are entered into will be directly related to the stability of legal arrangements. Risk-averse buyers and sellers will prefer shorter-term contracts in situations where established property arrangements are more likely to be overturned, and, where possible, such persons also would prefer to acquire title to less durable assets.

The Problem of Exclusivity. The above discussion of the relationship between the definition of rights of action and the redistribution of wealth assumes the existence of *exclusive* rights. Whether the owner of cornland or of vineyards is given the right to use and control airspace, it is possible for the parties involved to control the level of interaction costs because the right to airspace is exclusive. The owner of vineyards may pay for a reduction in crop size if the law absolves the corn grower of liability for damage done to grapes by the herbicide that he uses, but once such an agreement is reached, it is assumed that a reduction in the use of herbicide can be brought about through agreement by the parties. The geographical features of this particular problem suggests that such control can be approximated closely, since herbicide from a more distant farm cannot be carried as easily by the wind to a given vineyard. Hence, effective exclusion of the herbicide can be purchased by an owner of vineyards merely by obtaining agreements with nearby owners of cornland and attaching this agreement, as a covenant, to the land title.

But there may exist situations that, because of their very nature, or neglect by the law, deny exclusive rights to affect the level of the costly interaction. If anyone and everyone have the right to put chemicals into a stream (or to prevent chemicals from being put into the stream) without compensating those who are thereby harmed, then it is impossible for a party to enter into a contractual agreement that effectively controls the level of the activity. The most he can guarantee is his own action. He cannot effectively guarantee how others will act. A person wishing to reduce the chemical content of the river would need to pay all those who were willing to use the stream for waste disposal. But if exclusive rights of access to the stream were owned by only one party, then only he would need to be paid to obtain a specific reduction in chemical content. The problems that arise when the power to exclude is absent are difficult to analyze because they often reduce to processes involving strategic considerations. Nonetheless, it is possible to discern in broad outline the wealth distribution consequences of the absence of exclusive rights of action.

Consider the problem of highway congestion that arises when one and all have the right to enter an expressway and no one has the right to exclude such entry. An individual who values his time highly might wish to reduce traffic congestion during peak hours. Since anyone has the right of entry, he must pay others to adopt alternative routes or times of travel. If he pays a user to adopt such alternatives he can reduce congestion, except that another person who already uses one of these alternatives would be attracted to the expressway by the absence of the first person. One who desires to buy less congestion must be prepared to pay all those not now using the expressway who would be willing to use it if congestion levels were reduced moderately. This includes not only those who find the expressway of potential use in the resolution of their transport problems but also those whose time and alternatives are so unimportant that they would be willing to enter the freeway merely to exact a payment not to do so. If the supply of those who have low-value alternatives is highly elastic, those persons who desire reduced congestion will have to offer the full monetary value of the benefit they derive from quicker transit to those who agree to stay off the road. The communal right to enter the expressway exacts as much wealth from those who wish to reduce congestion as would be taken from them by a perfectly discriminating monopolistic supplier of reduced congestion.

Strategic bargaining problems are enmeshed in such transactions. Who will offer a payment to reduce congestion when all who do not offer such payments may benefit at no expense to themselves? How is the value of the benefit of reduced congestion to be divided among the many who agree to remain off the expressway? These questions are beyond the scope of the present paper, but it is worth noting that they become unimportant if there is an owner of the road who has the right to collect tolls and can exclude from the use of the road those who do not pay. He would not have to negotiate with those who in the previous instance were attracted to the road merely to receive payments for not using it.

Another view of the wealth redistribution process that is implied by the nonexclusivity of rights is offered by the subject of "extortion." Assume that the public police department is unable to hamper persons who seek "protection" money from shopkeepers, or, what comes to the same thing, assume that society has given to everyone the right to break windows. Unless strategic bargaining problems can be resolved and complex transactions effected at low cost, no shopkeeper would pay to prevent window breakage if a succession of other persons threatening to break his window can be anticipated. And even then the shopkeeper would be pushed to the point of indifference, with the sum exacted in total by all prospective window breakers just equal to the benefit of retaining the window.

However, if the payment to one prospective window breaker helps to ensure that others will not be in line for a payoff, that is, if the one who is paid can effectively deliver an exclusive right by taking over the policing function neglected by the community police—if, in this way, the market can create exclusive rights—then a mutually satisfactory arrangement that saves the window by transferring wealth can be made. If there is competition among "extortionists," each of whom can police the territory if he is awarded the contract, the amount of wealth transferred to obtain unbroken glass may be little more than the cost of policing.

More on Extortion. Many activities that seem outwardly identical to those that we identify as extortionate are perfectly legal. Thus, if A threatens to open a business identical and next door to B's business, it is not generally unlawful for B to pay A to refrain from doing so, whereas if A were to ask payment for not delivering to B's wife a photograph embarrassing to B then A's activity would generally be held to be illegal. How do the two cases differ? It cannot be said that A's threat, if carried out, has social utility in the first case but not the second. If society frowns upon promiscuous activity, the possibility that such a photograph might be shown to B's wife may deter B from his transgressions, just as, if B should build a railroad next to A's additional transportation services would be made available to society. Yet in the one case society does not object to the wealth transfer and in the other it does.

The explanation may lie in the fact that there are cases in which it is plausible to suppose that the activity clearly yields social cost in excess

of social benefit.   An example would be the threat to break windows unless paid not to do so.   Since the social purposes to be served by window
breaking are weak at best, it seems sensible to make wealth transfers
brought about through this activity illegal, although some government
policies, such as payments for not growing crops and for burying pigs to
raise pork prices, are highly similar activities.

As we proceed through the spectrum of such activities toward those in
which it is more difficult to determine whether the social cost exceeds the
benefit, we run greater risks of deterring desirable activities by making
them illegal.   Thus, in general we would not want to prohibit the attempt to
open a new firm even if its business was identical to that of an older
firm in the same neighborhood and even though, on occasion, the threat
of opening the new firm in the same neighborhood might be intended to
induce the older firm to pay the new firm not to open.   The more likely
it is that the benefits of an activity exceed its cost, the more reluctant we
should be to deter redistributions of wealth associated with the activity.

The general method adopted by the legal system in these situations
is essentially to alter the definition of property rights.   Thus, firms generally do not own the right to control the kind of business that opens
down the street (unless they also own the location down the street).   But a
person does own the right to some aspects of his privacy, and this is interpreted to mean that he has some control over the photographs taken
of him.   The legal situation is complex, for the same photograph taken
without his permission may be legally taken if it serves the purpose of establishing grounds for divorce.   Such a photograph might very well be
the evidence used to secure alimony, which, of course, is not extortion because it is legal!

FOOTNOTES

* Professor of Business Economics, Law School and Graduate School of Business,
University of Chicago.

[1] Harold Demsetz, When Does the Rule of Liability Matter?, 1 J.Leg.Studies 13
(1972).

[2] R. H. Coase, The Problem of Social Cost, 3 J.Law & Econ. 1 (1960).

13: TRANSACTION COSTS, RESOURCE ALLOCATION AND LIABILITY RULES— A COMMENT *

GUIDO CALABRESI
Yale Law School

In his article on "The Problem of Social Cost" Professor Coase argued that (assuming no transaction costs) the same allocation of resources will come about regardless of which of two joint cost causers is initially charged with the cost, in other words regardless of liability rules.[1] Various writers —including me—accepted that conclusion for the short run, but had doubts about its validity in the long run situation. The argument was that even if transactions brought about the same short run allocation, liability rules would affect the relative wealth of the two joint cost causing activities, and in the long run this would affect the relative number of firms and hence the relative output of the activities.[2]

Further thought has convinced me that if one assumes no transaction costs—including no costs of excluding from the benefits the free loaders, that is, those who would gain from a bargain but who are unwilling to pay to bring it about—and if one assumes, as one must, rationality and no legal impediments to bargaining, Coase's analysis must hold for the long run as well as the short run. The reason is simply that (on the given assumptions) the same type of transactions which cured the short run misallocation would also occur to cure the long run ones. For example, if we assume that the cost of factory smoke which destroys neighboring farmers' wheat

Calabresi, "Transaction Costs, Resource Allocation and Liability Rules—A Comment," 11 J.Law & Econ. (1968), from pages 67 to page 73.

can be avoided more cheaply by a smoke control device than by growing a smoke resistant wheat, then, even if the loss is left on the farmers they will, under the assumptions made, pay the factory to install the smoke control device. This would, in the short run, result in more factories relative to farmers and lower relative farm output than if the liability rule had been reversed. But if, as a result of this liability rule, farm output is too low relative to factory output those who lose from this "misallocation" would have every reason to bribe farmers to produce more and factories to produce less. This process would continue until no bargain could improve the allocation of resources.

The interesting thing about this analysis, however, is that there is no reason whatsoever to limit it to joint cost causers. Thus, if one assumes rationality, no transaction costs, and no legal impediments to bargaining, *all* misallocations of resources would be fully cured in the market by bargains.[3] Far from being surprising, this statement is tautological, at least if one accepts any of the various classic definitions of misallocation. These ultimately come down to a statement akin to the following: A misallocation exists when there is available a possible reallocation in which all those who would lose from the reallocation could be fully compensated by those who would gain, and, at the end of this compensation process, there would still be some who would be better off than before.

This and other similar definitions of resource misallocation merely mean that there is a misallocation when a situation can be improved by bargains. If people are rational, bargains are costless, and there are no legal impediments to bargains, transactions will *ex hypothesis* occur to the point where bargains can no longer improve the situation; to the point, in short, of optimal resource allocation.[4] We can, therefore, state as an axiom the proposition that all externalities can be internalized and all misallocations, even those created by legal structures, can be remedied by the market, except to the extent that transactions cost money or the structure itself creates some impediments to bargaining.[5]

It may be that this welfare economics analogue to Say's law has always been quite obvious to economists, although if it has its relevance has too frequently been ignored. In any event, lawyers who use economics have in virtually every case been hopelessly confused on the subject.[6] For this reason, if no other, it is worthwhile elaborating on the practical implications of the proposition.

The primary implication is that problems of misallocation of resources and externalities are not theoretical but empirical ones. The resource allocation aim is to approximate, both closely and cheaply, the result the market would bring about if bargaining actually were costless.[7] The question then becomes: Is this accomplished most accurately and most cheaply by structural rules (like anti-trust laws), by liability rules, by taxation and governmental spending, by letting the market have free play or by some combination of these? This question depends in large part on the relative *cost* of reaching the correct result by each of these means (an empirical problem which probably could be resolved, at least approximately, in most instances), and the relative *chances* of reaching a widely *wrong* result depending on the method used (also an empirical problem but one as to which it is hard to get other than "guess" type data). The resolution of these two problems and their interplay is *the* problem of accomplishing optimal resource allocations.

Two points are implied in the foregoing discussion. The first is that since transactions do cost money, and since substitutes for transactions, be they taxation, liability rules, or structural rules, are also not costless, the "optimal" result is not necessarily the same as if transactions were costless. Whatever device is used, the question must be asked: Are its costs worth the benefits in better resource allocations it brings about or have we instead approached a false optimum by a series of games which are not worth the candles used? This does not mean, though, that the actual optimum is necessarily the one an unaided market would reach. Further market improvements may well be prohibitive at a stage where laws and their enforcement are still a relatively cheap way of getting nearer the goal.[8]

The second point is that both the unreachable goal of "that point which would be reached if transactions were costless," and the gains which reaching nearer the goal would bring are not usually subject to precise definition or quantification. They are, in fact, largely defined by guesses. As a result, the question of whether a given law is worth its costs (in terms of better resource allocation) is rarely susceptible to empirical proof. This does not mean, of course, that the best we can do is adopt a laissez faire policy and let the market do the best it can. It is precisely the province of good government to make guesses at to what laws are likely to be worth their costs. Hopefully it will use what empirical information is available and seek to develop empirical information which is not currently available (how much information is worth *its* costs is also a question, however). But there is no reason to assume that in the absence of conclusive information no government action is better than some action. This is especially so if the guesses made take into account two factors. The first is: Action in an uncertain case is more likely to be justified if the market can correct an error resulting from the proposed action more cheaply than it could an error resulting from inaction. The second is: Action in an uncertain case is more likely to be justified if goals *other* than resource allocation (like proper income distribution) are served by the action. In effect the first factor says, in uncertainty increase the chances of correcting an error, while the second says, the achievement of other goals is accomplished very cheaply where the most that can be said about the resource allocation effect of a move is that we cannot be *sure* that it will be favorable.[9]

The relevance of the foregoing analysis may be seen in various areas of government intervention. I shall briefly mention three because they have brought forth different governmental responses: (1) the monopoly area, (2) highways or parks, (3) automobile accidents.

(1) Why should be have laws which attempt to control monopolies? Assuming no transaction costs, those who lose from the relative under-production of monopolies could bribe monopolists to produce more. We know, however, that such market action is usually unrealistic—that is, it would be too expensive relative to the benefits it would bring. The problem of excluding free loaders, would—absent any other problems—suffice to make it so. We believe that a series of structural rules, a series of laws in this case, are cheaper than market correction would be, and more important, we believe they are cheap enough to be worth having. This last belief involves certain guesses about what a "costless" market would do, and what the gains of approaching that goal by legislation are. Even if we assume that these guesses are in large terms fairly supported by empirical information, we certainly reach a point where the putative gains of further more stringent legislation or of more stringent enforcement are hard to justify in terms of the costs of such programs. In such a situation how far we go cannot help but be affected, and properly so, by what other goals—like dilution of power, or income redistribution—we think a further step will accomplish. Far from being irrelevant, these factors may be made an integral part of the law, if not the economics, of antitrust.[10]

(2) The question of why we have public highways is not totally dissimilar. One can view the decision to have public highways as the product of certain assumptions about what people would do if there were no transaction costs. These assumptions are largely guess work—perhaps even more guess work than in the monopoly case. As in the monopoly situation, government intervention is believed to bring us nearer, and more cheaply, to what a costless market would establish than would the real market. The reason may be that exclusion of free loaders seems substantially more expensive than compulsion of payment by all putative gainers, including would-be free loaders. The result is taxation, in part, of those who supposedly gain from the presence of a better highway system. I say in part, because here again the guesses made are inevitably affected by other goals. "Free" parks can be analyzed in the same way. The validity of the assumptions, the availability of empirical information and the effect of other goals may be quite different. But the basic analysis remains the same.

(3) The case of automobile accidents is somewhat more complex. It presents in fairly typical fashion the problem of multiple cost causers. As such it raises quite clearly the issue of short and long run misallocations, and the issue of which governmental interventions are, if incorrect, more subject to market corrections.

Assume that the cheapest short run way of minimizing the sum of accident costs and of the costs of avoiding accidents involving pedestrians and cars is to have rubber bumpers rather than to have pedestrians wear fluorescent clothes. In a world of costless transactions rubber bumpers would become established in the market regardless of liability rules, regardless of whether cars or pedestrians bore the loss initially. Since transactions cost money, the short run effect would in fact be quite different, depending on who was held liable. Making the car owner liable would establish the proper number of rubber bumpers. This would be the desired short run resource allocation, unless, of course, the cost of establishing car owner liability were too great relative to the gains it brought about.[11] But making the car owner liable also has long run effects affecting the relative number of cars and pedestrians. Our assumption as to the best short run liability bearer does not carry with it any guarantee that the car owners are the best long run bearers. It might be that in a world of no transaction costs rubber bumpers would be established, but more cars relative to pedestrians would be desired than would come about if liability were placed on car owners.

Depending on how sure we are of our long and short run guesses, this problem can be handled by using different devices. For example, the short run allocation could be accomplished by a car-owner liability rule, while the long run hypothetical misallocation could be corrected by a subsidy to car makers raised from taxes on pedestrians. But the sureness necessary to justify this subsidy, in the absence of nonresource allocation goals which might support it, seems very hard to come by.

The automobile accident situation also raises the point that different devices for accomplishing seemingly "optimal" resource allocation vary in desirability depending on their relative costs and on the relative likelihood of error in our guess work. Returning to the rubber bumper example, if we are perfectly sure that rubber bumpers are always the cheapest way of minimizing the sum of car-pedestrian accident costs and the costs of avoiding such accidents, it seems likely that the cheapest way of getting rubber bumpers is by a law that requires them, rather than by liability rules. It is quite a different thing if the "cheapest way" is more complex and involves some rubber bumpers, and some more careful driving by owners without rubber bumpers.

This in turn suggests another factor in the decision. Suppose we are not sure whether rubber bumpers or wearing fluorescent clothing is the "cheapest way" of handling the car-pedestrian accident problem. In this case it may become necessary to consider the following question: Is an erroneous placing of liability on car owners or an erroneous placing of liability on pedestrians more likely to be corrected in the market? Whether car owners (or car makers) can bribe pedestrians more cheaply than pedestrians can bribe car owners or makers, becomes the relevant issue. Similarly, it becomes crucial to decide whether an error brought about by a "liability rule" is more subject to market correction than an error resulting from a law requiring a particular type of rubber bumper.

Clearly this sketchy description of the automobile accident problem (like those of monopoly and highways) can only indicate the range and complexity of the issues involved in deciding whom to hold liable, and what safety devices to require. A full analysis of the resource allocation issue in auto accidents has, to my knowledge, not yet been attempted. A fully adequate decision would clearly require immense amounts of empirical data. But here (as in the monopoly and highway cases) the lawyer cannot wait for near certainty. He must propose solutions which seem to be the best on the basis of data and impressions currently available. And here too he will be aided in making practical proposals by the fact that goals other than optimal resource allocations may give clear indications of the desirable course in situations where resource allocations policy gives only a hint. One such goal may well be the often mentioned goal of "adequate" loss spreading (which is, in fact, closely analogous to the income distribution policy).

The conclusion is that Coase's analysis, read as a kind of Say's law of welfare economics, gives us an admirable tool for suggesting what kind of empirical data would be useful in making resource allocation decisions, and for indicating what kinds of guesses are likely to be justifiably made in the absence of convincing data. Some may take Coase's analysis to suggest that little or no government intervention is usually the best rule. My own conclusions are quite different. His analysis, combined with common intuitions or guesses as to the relative costs of transactions, taxation, structural rules and liability rules, can go far to explain various types of heretofore inadequately justified governmental actions. This is especially so if one considers the relevance of goals other than resource allocations to those situations where inadequate data makes resource allocations an unsatisfactory guide. Perhaps more precise data will some day prove some of these interventions to be improper from the standpoint of resource allocation. Then we shall have to choose, as we often do, between the bigger pie and other aims. Coase's analysis certainly suggests situations where this has been done. Its principal importance lies, however, in helping to delineate those areas of uncertainty where more facts would help us make better resource allocation judgments, and where, at least in the absence of more facts, the lawyer must be guided by guess work as to what the facts are and by goals other than resource allocations in suggesting workable solutions for problems which cannot wait till all the facts are in.

FOOTNOTES

*I am particularly indebted to Professor R. H. Coase of Chicago, and Professor Ward Bowman, of Yale, with each of whom I have discussed parts of this comment.

1 Coase, The Problem of Social Cost, 3 J.Law & Econ. 1 (1960).

2 See, for example, Calabresi, The Decision for Accidents: An Approach to Nonfault Allocation of Costs, 78 Harv.L.Rev. 713, 730 n. 28, 731 n. 30 (1965) and Calabresi, Fault, Accidents and the Wonderful World of Blum and Kalven, 75 Yale L.J. 216, 231–232 and accompanying footnotes (1965).

3 See note 5 infra.

4 Any given individual qua individual might well be richer or poorer as a result of the liability rules in force at the beginning of the bargaining process. But this difference in distribution of wealth would *ex hypothesis* not be one which would affect total social product.

5 By transaction costs, I have in mind costs like those of getting large numbers of people together to bargain, and costs of excluding free loaders. But one may properly ask the question: in what way are these qualitatively different from the cost of establishing a bargain between two parties, i. e., the cost of walking over and dickering? And if they are not, then how are they different from common selling costs, which we all assume the market normally handles optimally? Perhaps the difference is a qualitative one which escapes me. If it is not, it may be that as to normal selling costs, or costs of one-for-one dickering we readily accept the probably justifiable empirical conclusion that no substitute for the market can achieve a similar result as cheaply. But see e. g., Calabresi, The Decision for Accidents, 78 Harv.L.Rev. 713, 725–729 (1965), and Calabresi, Fault, Accidents and the Wonderful World of Blum and Kalven, 75 Yale L.J. 216, 223–231 (1965) (suggesting that liability rules may occasionally be crucial even in these cases). With the kinds of costs which Coase seems to call transaction costs, that conclusion, though possibly often still valid, cannot be accepted without more data. See Coase, supra note 1.

6 One notable recent exception is Professor Frank I. Michaelman. See Michaelman, Property, Utility and Fairness: Comments on the Ethical Foundations of "Just Compensation" Law, 80 Harv.L.Rev. 1165, 1172–1176 (1967).

7 Professor Harold Demsetz in a very provocative article has recently suggested that the institution of private property and its protection by the law can be explained in these terms, Demsetz, Toward a Theory of Property Rights, 57 Am.Econ.Ass'n.Pap. & Proc. 347 (1967). Surprisingly, he does not suggest that one of the examples which he gives of externalities not internalized by private property, that of factory smoke pollution, might also be handled by a change in property rights, that is, by making the factory owner liable for the smoke, id. at 357. This might resolve the problem if transaction costs were significantly lower if the factory owner were initially liable than if home-owners bore the loss, a not unlikely hypothesis.

8 See Demsetz, supra note 7.

9 Some may argue that other goals, like income redistribution, are best achieved not through *ad hoc* decisions but rather as part of a general policy implemented through devices (like some forms of progressive taxation) chosen with the goal specifically in mind. Even if this position is accepted, it is possible that a general policy in favor of a particular distribution of income could be arrived at and its implementation be intentionally left to particular cases where no provably adverse resource allocation effects would come about. This would be especially attractive to those who accept the view that most forms of progressive taxation misallocate resources.

The mention of other goals may suggest that their benefits can be established with substantial certainty. That obviously is not so, but the process of deciding whether to accomplish these goals does not, in our society, seem to depend on the ability of social scientists to prove their desirability with substantial certainty.

10 Obviously there are also many cases where these other goals are pursued without regard to possible adverse resource allocation effects. My object in this comment is not to criticize or even to discuss such situations. Mine is a minimalist position and suggests only that taking such other goals into account is justified where doing so gives rise to no provable adverse resource allocation effects.

11 This caveat has a long history in torts law and is in large part the basis of Holmes' famous justification of the fault system. See Holmes, The Common Law, 94–96 (1881). Needless to say, the caveat is perfectly valid even if it fails, as I believe it does, to justify the fault-liability system today.

*

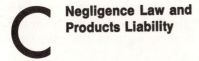

Negligence Law and Products Liability

14: A THEORY OF NEGLIGENCE

RICHARD A. POSNER*

Negligence—the failure to exercise the care of an ordinarily prudent and careful man—has been the dominant standard of civil liability for accidents for the last 150 years or so, in this as in most countries of the world; and accident cases, mainly negligence cases, constitute the largest item of business on the civil side of the nation's trial courts. Yet we lack a theory to explain the social function of the negligence concept and of the fault system of accident liability that is built upon it. This article attempts to formulate and test such a theory, primarily through a sample of 1528 American appellate court decisions from the period 1875–1905.

I

There is an orthodox view of the negligence concept to which I believe most legal scholars and historians would subscribe that runs as follows: Until the nineteenth century a man was liable for harm caused by his accidents whether or not he was at fault; he acted at his peril. The no-fault standard of liability was relaxed in the nineteenth century under the pressure of industrial expansion and an individualistic philosophy that could conceive of no justification for shifting losses from the victim of an accident unless the injurer was blameworthy (negligent) and the victim blameless (not contributorily negligent). The result, however, was that accident costs were "externalized" from the enterprises that caused them to workers and other individuals injured as a byproduct of their activities.

Journal of Legal Studies, Vol. 1, No. 1, 1972, p. 29.

Justification for the shift, in the orthodox view, can perhaps be found in a desire to subsidize the infant industries of the period but any occasion for subsidization has long passed, laying bare the inadequacy of the negligence standard as a system for compensating accident victims. The need for compensation is unaffected by whether the participants in the accident were careless or careful and we have outgrown a morality that would condition the right to compensation upon a showing that the plaintiff was blameless and the defendant blameworthy.[1]

There are three essential points here. The first, that the adoption of the negligence standard was a subsidy to the expanding industries of the nineteenth century, is highly ambiguous. It is true that if you move from a regime where (say) railroads are strictly liable for injuries inflicted in crossing accidents to one where they are liable only if negligent, the costs to the railroads of crossing accidents will be lower, and the output of railroad services probably greater as a consequence. But it does not follow that any subsidy is involved—unless it is proper usage to say that an industry is being subsidized whenever a tax levied upon it is reduced or removed. As we shall see, a negligence standard of liability, properly administered, is broadly consistent with an optimum investment in accident prevention by the enterprises subject to the standard. Since it does not connote, as the orthodox view implies,[2] an underinvestment in safety, its adoption cannot be equated with subsidization in any useful sense of that term. We shall also see that many accident cases do not involve strangers to the enterprise (such as a traveler at a crossing), but rather customers, employees, or other contracting parties, and that a change in the formal law governing accidents is unlikely to have more than a transient effect on the number of their accidents. Finally, whether the period before the advent of the negligence standard is properly characterized as one of liability without fault remains, so far as I am aware, an unresolved historical puzzle.[3]

The second major point implicit in the orthodox view is that the dominant purpose of civil liability for accidents is to compensate the victim for the medical expenses, loss of earnings, suffering, and other costs of the accident. Hence, if it is a bad compensation system, it is a bad system. Yet Holmes, in his authoritative essay on the fault system, had rejected a compensation rationale as alien to the system.[4] People, he reasoned, could insure themselves against uncompensated accidents,[5] and there was accordingly no occasion for a state accident-compensation scheme. Holmes left unclear what he conceived the dominant purpose of the fault system to be, if it was not to compensate. The successful plaintiff does recover damages from the defendant. Why? Suppose a major function of the negligence system is to regulate safety. We are apt to think of regulation as the action of executive and administrative agencies. But the creation of private rights of action can also be a means of regulation.[6] The rules are made by the judges aided by the parties. The burdens of investigation and of presenting evidence are also shouldered by the parties. The direct governmental role is thus minimized—a result highly congenial to the thinking of the nineteenth century. Such a system cannot function unless the damages assessed against the defendant are paid over to the plaintiff. That is the necessary inducement for the plaintiff to play his regulatory role of identifying violations of the applicable judge-made rule, proving them, and when appropriate pressing for changes in the rule.

The third essential point in the orthodox view is that negligence is a moral concept—and, in the setting of today, a moralistic one. The orthodox view does not explore the moral roots of fault, but contents itself with asserting that such moral judgments as can be made in the usual accident case are an anachronistic, even frivolous, basis for determining whether to grant or withhold redress. The rejection of moral criteria as a basis for liability follows easily from the conception of the fault system as a compensation scheme and nothing more: it would be odd to deny welfare benefits on the ground that the recipient's misfortune was not the product of someone's wrongful conduct.

Characterization of the negligence standard as moral or moralistic does not advance analysis. The morality of the fault system is very different from that of everyday life. Negligence is an objective standard. A man may be adjudged negligent though he did his best to avoid an accident and just happens to be clumsier than average.[7] In addition, a number of the established rules of negligence liability are hard to square with a moral approach. Insane people are liable for negligent conduct though incapable of behaving carefully. Employers are broadly responsible for the negligence of their employees. The latter example illustrates an immensely important principle. In less than four per cent of the cases in our sample was the defendant accused of actually being negligent. In all other cases the defendant was sued on the basis of the alleged negligence of employees or (in a few cases) children. The moral element in such cases is attenuated.

Moreover, to characterize the negligence concept as a moral one is only to push inquiry back a step. It is true that injury inflicted by carelessness arouses a different reaction from injury inflicted as the result of an unavoidable accident. We are indignant in the first case but not the second. The interesting question is why. What causes us to give the opprobrious label of careless to some human conduct but not other and to be indignant when we are hurt by it? The orthodox view gives no answer.

II

It is time to take a fresh look at the social function of liability for negligent acts. The essential clue, I believe, is provided by Judge Learned Hand's famous formulation of the negligence standard—one of the few attempts to give content to the deceptively simple concept of ordinary care. Although the formulation postdates the period of our primary interest, it never purported to be original but was an attempt to make explicit the standard that the courts had long applied. In a negligence case, Hand said, the judge (or jury) should attempt to measure three things: the magnitude of the loss if an accident occurs; the probability of the accident's occurring; and the burden of taking precautions that would avert it.[8] If the product of the first two terms exceeds the burden of precautions, the failure to take those precautions is negligence. Hand was adumbrating, perhaps unwittingly,[9] an economic meaning of negligence. Discounting (multiplying) the cost of an accident if it occurs by the probability of occurrence yields a measure of the economic benefit to be anticipated from incurring the costs necessary to prevent the accident. The cost of prevention is what Hand meant by the burden of taking precautions against the accident. It may be the cost of installing safety equipment or otherwise making the activity safer, or the benefit forgone by curtailing or eliminating the activity. If the cost of safety measures or of curtailment—whichever cost is lower—exceeds the benefit in accident avoidance to be gained by incurring that cost, society would be better off, in economic terms, to forgo accident prevention. A rule making the enterprise liable for the accidents that occur in such cases cannot be justified on the ground that it will induce the enterprise to increase the safety of its operations. When the cost of accidents is less than the cost of prevention, a rational profit-maximizing enterprise will pay tort judgments to the accident victims rather than incur the larger cost of avoiding liability. Furthermore, overall economic value or welfare would be diminished rather than increased by incurring a higher accident-prevention cost in order to avoid a lower accident cost. If, on the other hand, the benefits in accident avoidance exceed the costs of prevention, society is better off if those costs are incurred and the accident averted, and so in this case the enterprise is made liable, in the expectation that self-interest will lead it to adopt the precautions in order to avoid a greater cost in tort judgments.

One misses any reference to accident avoidance by the victim. If the accident could be prevented by the installation of safety equipment or the curtailment or discontinuance of the underlying activity by the victim at lower cost than any measure taken by the injurer would involve, it would be uneconomical to adopt a rule of liability that placed the burden of accident prevention on the injurer. Although not an explicit part of the Hand formula this qualification, as we shall see, is implicit in the administration of the negligence standard.

Perhaps, then, the dominant function of the fault system is to generate rules of liability that if followed will bring about, at least approximately, the efficient—the cost-justified—level of accidents and safety.[10] Under this view, damages are assessed against the defendant as a way of measuring the costs of accidents, and the damages so assessed are paid over to the plaintiff (to be divided with his lawyer) as the price of enlisting their participation in the operation of the system.   Because we do not like to see resources squandered, a judgment of negligence has inescapable overtones of moral disapproval, for it implies that there was a cheaper alternative to the accident.   Conversely, there is no moral indignation in the case in which the cost of prevention would have exceeded the cost of the accident.   Where the measures necessary to avert the accident would have consumed excessive resources, there is no occasion to condemn the defendant for not having taken them.

If indignation has its roots in inefficiency, we do not have to decide whether regulation, or compensation, or retribution, or some mixture of these best describes the dominant purpose of negligence law.   In any case, the judgment of liability depends ultimately on a weighing of costs and benefits.

In order to explore the hypothesis that liability for negligence is designed to bring about an efficient level of accidents and safety, I sampled American appellate decisions in accident cases from the period 1875–1905. That was the classical flowering of the negligence concept.   Before 1875 the standard was rather new (although most of its major doctrines had been announced) and the reported decisions few.   After 1905 the tort system entered a new phase.   The first Federal Employers' Liability Act was passed in 1906 and the first workmen's compensation statute a few years later.   These enactments cut deeply into the domain of the traditional negligence doctrines and, after initial constitutional difficulties, brought the classical period of the negligence standard to an end.[11]   The disadvantage of choosing such a period is that it obscures the dynamics of legal change.   The negligence system may have reached maturity in 1875, but it did not begin then.   The process of selection and rejection by which earlier doctrines and procedures were woven into the coherent system that we will be examining in the following pages is of the highest interest, but it is a study in itself.

The sample was constructed in the following manner.   I read every published accident opinion of an American appellate court (state or federal, final or intermediate) issued in the first quarter of 1875, 1885, 1895, and 1905.[12]   A few categories of borderline cases were excluded, primarily those involving lost freight, nondelivery of telegrams, nuisances, and sales of liquor to drunkards.   I abstracted the information in the opinions and then tabulated that information.   The opinions in the sample constitute about one thirtieth of all the appellate accident opinions issued during the period.[13]   By taking such a sample, rather than following the conventional approach in legal scholarship of analyzing "leading" cases, I hoped to obtain a representative view of the actual functioning of the negligence system.   The reader may wonder at the use of appellate cases rather than trial-court cases for this purpose.   Since most cases are never appealed a sample of appellate cases gives only a partial, and perhaps distorted, glimpse of the operation of the negligence system.   It would have been impractical, however, to base this study on trial-court records.   At least in the period with which we are concerned, such records as are available typically contain less information about a case, especially with regard to its facts, than the typical appellate opinion.   Furthermore, trial-court records are neither published nor indexed, and are dispersed among thousands of county and municipal court houses—circumstances that interpose formidable obstacles to obtaining a proper sample.   Finally, even a good sample of trial-court cases would not solve the tip-of-the-iceberg problem.   Nowadays at most 2 per cent of accident claims are actually tried; [14] in a somewhat higher but still small percentage a lawsuit is begun but settled in advance of trial.[15]   The vast majority of claims leave no trace in judicial records.   Comparable statistics for the period 1875–1905 are unavailable, but it would seem that then, too, the majority of claims were settled without any litigation although the ratio of litigated claims to all claims may have been higher than today.[16]   Unfortunately, so far as I have been able to ascertain, the claims records of railroads and other companies frequently involved in accidents and of liability insurers no longer exist for the period.

A sample limited to appellate cases turns out to be more varied and apparently representative than one might have expected.   Negligence cases appealed during our period were not limited to cases involving very large sums of money or novel issues of law.   Most of the cases in the sample involve neither.   Of the 64 cases involving damage to property in which the amount of the judgment is reported, more than 25 per cent involve judgments of less than $100 and more than 75 per cent judgments of less than $1000.[17]   And only about 20 per cent of the cases in the sample involve pure questions of law.   The issues on appeal typically involve the sufficiency of the evidence, the trial judge's rulings on admissibility, and the clarity and accuracy of his instructions to the jury.   Yet there must be some biases in a sample limited to appellate cases.   In an effort to identify and correct these a sample of 111 railroad and street-railway accident cases for the relevant period was drawn from the records of Cook County, Illinois (the county in which Chicago is located) and rural Du Page County to the west.   I shall indicate at the appropriate places where these cases require modification of conclusions drawn from the appellate cases.   The trial-court sample confirms that only a small percentage of cases are appealed: of the 47 cases in the sample that went to trial, only 6 were decided on appeal.

III

We begin by looking at the broad institutional and doctrinal framework of the negligence system as revealed by the appellate cases. Both in this and the next part (specific rules of liability) I have tried to report the information revealed by the sample as fully as possible rather than simply mine it for examples, although I have excluded a certain amount of redundant or peripheral material.

It will be helpful to make an initial distinction between two broad categories of accident: accidents to strangers (for example, a streetcar running down a pedestrian), and accidents to parties in a contractual or other bargaining relationship (customers, employees, tenants, and the like). Of the 1494 cases in the sample for which the requisite information is available, 54 per cent involve accidents between strangers, 30 per cent involve accidents to employees, 12 per cent involve accidents to passengers (mostly railroad and streetcar passengers), and 4 per cent involve accidents to other customers and other contracting parties, mostly tenants. The regulatory function of negligence liability is evident in cases involving accidents to strangers. Where the costs of transacting are high, an unregulated market will not bring about an optimum level of accidents and safety. More than 90 per cent of the cases in this group involve types of accidents in which the costs of transacting are probably very high—mainly cases involving railroad and steetcar crossing accidents, railroad collisions with trespassing people and cattle, accidents to pedestrians and other travelers involving defects in the sidewalk or street, other road accidents, ship collisions, and dog bites.[18] In such chance-encounter accidents it is unrealistic to expect much bargaining between the parties in advance over the level of safety and the economic function of liability is evident: it is to bring about the level of accidents and safety that the market would bring about if transactions were feasible —the efficient level. In the second group of cases, the parties already have a contractual relationship and the impact of liability rules on accidents and safety is more problematic. The parties are normally free to rearrange by contract whatever liabilities are imposed by the law: the stagecoach company can contract with its passengers for a lower or higher standard of care.

Even here, the costs of explicit agreement on safety may not be negligible. Many transactions take place without a formal written contract. The costs associated with specifying in detail the performance contracted for are too high. When buying a train ticket, one doesn't receive a contract spelling out the railroad's undertaking with respect to safety appliances and to the careful selection and supervision of engineers, firemen, conductors, and dispatchers. It is left to the courts to decide, should the need arise, what safety precautions the parties would have agreed upon if negotiations had taken place, and this is doubtless on the whole a cheaper way of proceeding. The level of safety that the parties would have negotiated would presumably have been the efficient level, in the sense that the passenger would have demanded and the company supplied that quantum of safety precautions at which the cost of preventing an additional accident (in a higher price for the ticket, in less comfort, more delay, etc.) would have just exceeded the cost of the accident, if it occurred, discounted by the probability of its occurrence. In the event of an accident and a consequent suit by the injured passenger, it is the court's job to determine whether the company lived up to its bargain—whether, that is, it supplied the optimum amount of safety. The inquiry is thus the same as in the case of an accident to a stranger and this, together with the similarity in the type of injury that results, may explain why the courts treat both stranger and contracting-party cases mostly without distinction under the negligence standard. They make some distinctions, however, with respect to cases involving accidents to employees, and in discussing the elements of the doctrinal framework of the negligence system we will therefore treat those cases separately.

Breach of the Defendant's Duty. The general rule is that the defendant owes to those whom he might chance upon and injure a duty to exercise due care—the care of an ordinarily prudent and careful man. The breach of that duty is actionable negligence. However, a higher duty—the duty of the highest practicable care, the duty to avoid the slightest negligence—is owed by a common carrier (usually, in our period, a railroad) to its passengers while they are on board. As an approximation to the likely understanding of the parties to the contract of carriage, the exception seems a reasonable one. Strictly speaking, it is nonsense to speak of a standard of care higher than that of due care. An enterprise will not spend $100 in safety appliances to avert a $90 accident when it can satisfy its legal obligations by paying a $90 judgment. The rule that common carriers owe a higher duty to their passengers signifies that passengers expect (and are willing to pay for) a high level of safety—because the railroad has a comparative advantage in accident prevention (indeed, passengers are normally helpless to avert an accident) and because a collision or derailment (like a plane crash today) is likely to kill or seriously injure them. These factors are absent or attenuated in the case of a passenger injured on the station grounds—say by a loose board in the platform—or a passenger injured in a private vehicle, and, as we would predict, the standard of highest practicable care is not applied in those cases.

The second major exception to the ordinary-care standard concerns the liability of land occupiers, in our period usually railroads, to uninvited entrants, usually trespassers using the track as a path. Here the duty (with some exceptions discussed later) is a lesser one: not to use due care, but only to avoid a knowing injury. The rule is a corollary of a system of property law that is designed to protect rights of exclusive possession. Since it is often difficult to exclude trespassers, the imposition of a duty to look out for their safety would interfere with the landowner's use of his property. The rule of no liability may also rest on a judgment that the utility of trespassing, in general, is less than the cost that would have to be incurred to prevent injury to trespassers along railroad rights of way and in other areas that the general public is not invited to enter.

It is difficult to particularize the standard of ordinary care without discussing particular types of accident, a later inquiry, but there are two general principles relating to its implementation that are significant. The first is that the violation of a statute prescribing a duty of care is negligence per se as to a member of the class intended to be protected by the statute who is injured as a result of the violation. The theoretical interest of this principle is that it potentially displaces a good deal of the judicial function in negligence cases, including the Hand formula. If the legislature fixes a speed limit of 10 miles per hour for trains at crossings, it is no longer open to the court to decide, by a balancing of costs and benefits, what speed under what conditions will optimize railroad crossing accidents. It would be comforting for the economic theory of negligence liability to think that legislatures, too, used a Hand-type formula in fixing statutory duties of care but as we shall see the theoretical basis for expecting them to do so is much weaker than in the case of courts.

Another critical element in applying the standard of due care is the weight assigned customary practices. Can a plaintiff argue that the failure to have air brakes is negligence, at a time when no railroad has them? Or is it a defense that the railroad has the same safety appliances as every other railroad or as the average railroad of its class? If compliance with the average or customary practice in the trade automatically discharged the defendant's duty of due care, there would be cases where the negligence system failed to optimize safety. Suppose the only benefit of a safety appliance is to a stranger to the industry in our earlier sense—someone with whom the enterprise has no contractual relationship and will not enter into one because of transaction costs. No firm in the industry will have an incentive to install the appliance, for it will not be able to recover its cost by charging a higher price to customers or setting a lower wage to employees (notice, however, that air brakes are not that kind of appliance). Thus, the market will not induce the adoption of such an appliance even if its benefits in accident prevention exceed its costs —and neither would the negligence system if compliance with industry custom were a defense. It is therefore interesting, in terms of principle, to observe that the courts in our period held that custom was not a defense, although, as we shall see, in practice a plaintiff faced an uphill struggle to convince a court that failure to adopt an appliance nowhere in use in an industry exhibited a want of ordinary care.

Contributory Negligence. Another fundamental principle of the common law of negligence is that if the victim of the accident failed to exercise due care, and his breach contributed to the accident, he is barred from recovery even though the defendant was negligent. That the plaintiff has a duty of care flows directly from our exegesis of the Hand formula. There are cases where the cheapist accident preventer is the prospective victim himself and so should be liable. But the principle of contributory negligence, as the name implies, is commonly applied in cases where the defendant is also negligent and the question arises, why bar recovery in those cases too? The answer, I suggest, is that it is impossible, in general, to show that permitting recovery in cases where either party could have avoided the accident (if the plaintiff was negligent but the accident would have happened anyway the defense of contributory negligence fails) would bring the level of safety and accidents closer to the optimum point. If we make the defendant always liable in such a case, defendants as a class will have more incentive to take safety precautions than if they are never liable, since in the latter instance the cost of accidents to them would be lower. But correspondingly plaintiffs as a class would have less incentive to take safety precautions in the first case than in the second, because the accident cost to them would be higher in the second—more of their accidents would be uncompensated. If the effects are thus symmetrical, there is no economic basis for attempting to shift the loss from injured to injurer.

This analysis ignores, however, the case where, although either party, victim or injurer, could have prevented the accident at a lower cost than the accident cost discounted by the probability of its occurrence, the cost of prevention to the injurer would have been lower than the cost of prevention to the victim. The correct economizing rule here is to make the injurer liable, even though the victim may be said to have been contributorily negligent. This refinement is nowhere explicit in the cases, but it may have been implicit. Glancing ahead for a moment at the specific rules of contributory negligence discussed in the next part, one finds only rare instances where the sacrifice required of the victim by the law to avert an accident is disproportionate to that required of the injurer.

Causation. The courts require proof of a causal connection between the breach of duty, either defendant's or plaintiff's, and the injury. Dispense with such proof, and you are no longer talking about the costs of accidents. If the defendant was negligent but the accident would have occurred anyway, it would be incorrect to view the costs of the accident as the consequence of his negligence since they would not have been avoided by the exercise of due care. Yet the defendant was negligent: would not an award of damages serve a useful purpose, therefore, by punishing him for his breach of duty, thereby encouraging him to comply in the future with the requirements of efficiency? This I question. Where the standard of care applied to a particular activity is economically correct there will be incentive enough for firms to comply. If they do not they face a judgment bill (for accidents occasioned by their failure to comply with the standard) larger than the cost of taking the precautions required by the standard. Punishment—an exaction that exceeds the costs to society (here, accident costs) imposed by the particular violation being punished—is necessary where the violator is frequently not apprehended, because a rational lawbreaker will discount the gravity of any legal sanction by the probability that it will be imposed.[19] There are hit-and-run accidents, and if they are a more serious problem in the age of the automobile, there must have been cases in the period covered by this study in which the injurer was not apprehended, especially when trains killed livestock or lone walkers on the track or engine sparks ignited crops or buildings. But such cases must have been exceptional and it is unlikely that most victims of negligence injuries failed to assert their claims because they couldn't identify the injurer. It is, in contrast, quite likely that most price-fixing conspiracies (for example) are never brought to bar, due to their covert character.[20] One is therefore not surprised to find that punitive damages are normally disallowed in negligence cases and allowed in price-fixing cases. Moreover, an appropriate punishment component is built into the negligence system. If an injurer attempts to conceal his identity and is sued, his efforts at concealment may be considered evidence of willfulness justifying the imposition of punitive damages (however, the sample contains no such cases).

Punishment for negligence would close an important safety valve in the negligence system. A standard of care is necessarily a crude approximation to optimality. Allowing enterprises a choice whether to comply or pay the social costs of violation may permit a closer approximation. Suppose there is a rule that a dam owner is responsible for flood damage unless his dam is at least 16 feet high. Presumably the rule reflects a judgment that the cost of raising the dam is less than the cost of the floods that a lower dam would fail to contain. One owner thinks the rule is incorrect. He estimates that the only flood likely to occur is one that would swamp a 16-foot dam and therefore that he can save money by violating the rule. Courts are not infallible and we give maximum play to individual judgment if we let the dam owner act on his estimate. If he is wrong, he will have to pay a judgment, but if he is correct an unnecessary expenditure on dam building will have been saved.[21]   One can reply that it is just as likely that a standard of care will be too lax as too strict; and if the former a punitive sanction will tend to compensate for the laxity.   But this leads to the same stand-off as in our earlier discussion of contributory negligence, and with the same implications.   If the only recognized basis for invoking legal processes to shift an accident loss from the victim to another party is the expectation of improving the efficiency of resource use, then before we can recognize a right of action (in this case a right to sue for injuries that would have occurred anyway) we must be able to say that the shift will improve efficiency; and we cannot.

Foreseeability. Courts invoke the doctrine of "proximate cause" to excuse defendants from liability for unforeseeable consequences of negligence.   A train stops at a crossing and a group of rowdy passengers debark.   A lady driving a carriage waiting at the crossing for the train to move on is frightened.   After a delay the passengers reembark and the train moves on but the lady is now late, it is growing dark, her driving is erratic because of fright and anxiety, she drives into a ditch and is injured.   The railroad may have been negligent in permitting the train to be delayed at the crossing and the rowdy passengers to debark but the courts do not view its negligence as the "proximate cause" of her accident.   Such a result follows from the economic standard of negligence.   If negligence is a failure to take precautions against a type of accident whose cost, discounted by the frequency of its occurence, exceeds the cost of the precautions, it makes sense to require no precautions against accidents that occur so rarely that the benefit of accident prevention approaches zero. The truly freak accident isn't worth spending money to prevent.   Moreover, estimation of the benefits of accident prevention implies foreseeability.

Respondeat Superior. As mentioned earlier, in few cases in the period covered by the sample was the defendant accused of being personally negligent.   Most suits are based on the doctrine of respondeat superior, which makes an employer liable to third parties for the torts of his employees committed in furtherance of their employment.   The doctrine at first glance seems inconsistent with the economic theory of negligence.   A careless workman is like a defective machine.   A company should devote resources to screening out careless workmen just as it should devote resources to inspecting its machinery for defects but there comes a point where a further expenditure on supervision of employees or on inspection of machinery would exceed the accident costs that the expenditure would save.   The law recognizes this quite clearly with respect to machinery.   A firm was liable (in the period covered by the sample at any rate) only for those defects that a reasonable inspection would have discovered. But the law seemingly takes an inconsistent position with respect to the careless workman. The employer is liable regardless of his care in attempting to prevent carelessness.

The inconsistency is more apparent than real. A machine is inanimate and undeterrable. A workman is not. But liability for negligence will not deter a workman who has no money to pay for the accidents he causes. This greatly complicates the formulation of an appropriate standard of care for the employer. Suppose that a railroad in hiring locomotive engineers makes a reasonable effort to screen out clumsy, irresponsible, accident-prone individuals. A serious problem would remain. An engineer—let him be as prudent and skillful as you want—is running behind schedule, so he opens the throttle. The resulting speed is dangerous to pedestrians at crossings but if the engineer is a coldly rational man the danger will not inhibit him. Being judgment-proof, he is not answerable for the consequences to pedestrians. Thus, a railroad not only must exercise care in hiring workers; it must impose sanctions on them for carelessness, because tort law cannot deter the judgment-proof. By making the railroad strictly liable for the torts of its employees in the scope of their employment, which is the effect of respondeat superior, the law creates a mechanism by which the railroad can decide for itself how much to invest in preventing its workers from being careless. It will invest until the last cent of its investment in worker safety saves one cent in accident costs. There will be cases where no reasonable expenditure would have averted the accident and where, therefore, the effect of respondeat superior is to shift losses without affecting the level of safety. But the only alternative would have been for the courts to regulate in great detail the company's methods of selecting, supervising, and disciplining employees.

Our interpretation of respondeat superior derives additional support from the distinction that the courts of the period made between employees and independent contractors. If you hired a contractor to do a job and left the manner of work entirely up to him, you were not liable for injuries caused by his negligence or the negligence of his employees. But if you supervised the details of his work you were liable. These distinctions are economically defensible. If there is no supervision of the work in which the accident occurs, there is no basis for anticipating that the work will be done more safely if the principal is liable. Nor is there a presumption that an independent contractor is insolvent and therefore undeterrable by the threat of tort liability from behaving, or permitting his employees to behave, carelessly. But the principal has a duty to select a competent contractor and if the work involves large risks to safety, such as bridge construction, this duty cannot be discharged, the courts held, by perfunctory inquiry.

The principle of respondeat superior was not applied to the family. Parents were liable for the torts of their children only if negligent in supervising them.   Perhaps the reason for treating employers and parents differently is that employers in fact have greater control over the behavior of their employees on the job than do parents over their children.   The employer can select his employees, discharge them, and prescribe rewards and punishments to which rational beings will respond. Children tend to be ungovernable; natural parents do not choose their children; children cannot be fired for having been careless.   A rule of strict parental liability would have little regulatory effect—and would thus violate what we have tentatively identified as the basic character of the negligence system—because in most cases parents would be incapable at reasonable cost of preventing careless behavior of their children.

Industrial-Accident Doctrine.   In cases where the accident victim is a worker suing his employer, the courts in our period applied a number of special doctrines.   The most fundamental was that respondeat superior was inapplicable: with important exceptions to be noted, an employer was not liable to his employees for injuries inflicted by their fellow employees. A comparison between this principle and the contrary principle in the case of accidents to strangers brings out clearly the essential economic logic of the negligence system.   A pedestrian at a crossing doesn't know the engineer or fireman of any of the trains that pass and is in no position to play a role in preventing accidents by identifying careless workers. In contrast, a fellow employee is in the best position to identify a careless worker, at least if they work in reasonable proximity.   The fellow-servant rule as the exception to respondeat superior is known, provides, in principle at least, a powerful instrument for industrial safety when combined with the rule making the employer liable for injuries inflicted on an employee through the negligence of a fellow employee if the employer was on notice of the fellow employee's habitual neglect or incompetence.   The effect of the two rules is to give employees a strong incentive to report careless fellow workers to their supervisors.   Some incentive would exist anyway because people generally don't like to be injured, but it is reinforced when an employee knows that if he does not report his fellow's negligence and is injured he will have no right to compensation from his employer.   Any rational human being, but perhaps especially a worker lacking assets or adequate insurance, private or social, fears an uncompensated accident even more than a compensated accident.   The fellow-servant rule was evidently designed to direct that fear into constructive channels.

The major question in implementing the rule is what criteria to use in deciding whether one employee of a company is a fellow of another. To deem all the workers of a company fellow servants would carry well beyond the rationale of the rule, because an employee doesn't have the opportunity to observe and evaluate the work habits of all the other employees of a large firm. Several tests competed for judicial favor in our period. We shall examine them later. For now it is enough to note the major limitation on the scope of the rule: it did not immunize the employer from liability for the negligence of those employees responsible for the conditions in which the injured employees worked. The brakeman may be barred from recovery if injured through the negligence of a locomotive engineer, but not if the negligence is an employee's whose duty was to inspect the car for defective hand holds or clear the roadbed or repair the automatic couplers or install a block system. Such work is not done in proximity to the operating employees and the latter will neither know who the responsible workers are or have any basis for evaluating the care with which they have worked until an accident occurs.

The rule of contributory negligence applied in cases where an employee was suing his employer. A distinct although related doctrine, assumption of risk, also applied and figures in many of the cases. Under this doctrine an employee was barred from recovering damages where the accident was the result of hazards known by or obvious to him. If a brakeman is employed on a train that is not equipped with the standard safety appliances, he knows this, and he is injured in an accident that would not have occurred had it been so equipped, the employer is not liable, even if the cost of the appliances is less than the discounted accident cost. This result is supported by economic logic. Attitudes toward risk are not distributed uniformly among the population. Some people will pay a good deal more than $1 for a lottery ticket that gives the holder a chance of 1 in 1000 to win $1000; others won't pay anything. The former have a preference for risk, the latter an aversion to it. Suppose in our train example that the cost of the standard appliances would be $10 per worker per year and they would produce a $15 saving in accident costs by reducing the likelihood that the worker would sustain a $1000 injury from $\frac{1}{50}$ to $\frac{1}{200}$. Since the brakeman knew that the train was not equipped with the standard appliances, and therefore that his chances of injury were higher than normal, why was he willing to continue working? Presumably he was paid to take the risk. We can draw the further inference that he was a risk preferrer. Had he been risk neutral, and the going wage for brakemen on trains equipped with the standard appliances was (say) $500 a year, the railroad would have had to pay him $515 to compensate him for the increased risk; but it would not have done so since it could have employed him at a lower net cost ($510) by installing the devices. If a brakeman is willing to work for less than $510, as our example assumes, the efficient (cost-minimizing) solution is for the railroad to hire him and not install the safety appliances. This solution would be frustrated if assumption of risk were not a defense, because then the railroad would have to install the safety appliances in order to avoid a judgment bill larger than their cost.

The assumption of risk doctrine enables the risk preferrer to market his taste for risk, but it also allows the risk averse to exploit their aversion. Let the going wage for a locomotive engineer be $750 a year with a 1/1000 chance of sustaining a $3000 injury in the course of the year, and let the cost of reducing that chance to 1/2000 be $2 per engineer per year in additional safety appliances. Since the cost of the additional appliances exceeds the benefits, the railroad would not be guilty of negligence if it failed to install them. But suppose that enough locomotive engineers to staff the company's trains are highly risk averse. They are so eager to minimize the likelihood of an accident that if the company will install the appliances they will accept a wage reduction from $750 to $745 a year. The company will install the appliances and save $3 a year per engineer. If the company later removes the appliances without informing the engineers and one of them is injured in an accident that would have been prevented by the appliances, the company will be liable to him for the costs of the accident under the rule that a company is liable to an employee for breach of its customary safety standards.

Damages. For the Hand formula to optimize safety, the rules for determining damages once the defendant's liability has been established must measure with reasonable accuracy the social costs of accidents. In cases involving bodily injury short of death, an accident victim's economic loss has the following components: (1) any damage to property; (2) any medical and hospital expenses and other outlays necessitated by the accident; (3) the present value of all earnings lost or likely in the future to be lost as a result of any temporary or permanent disability caused by the accident; and (4) any suffering to the victim, his family, and in some cases perhaps others, resulting from pain, disfigurement and impairment of ability to enjoy life. In general the rules of damages during the period embraced by the sample track the elements of economic loss. Damage to property is fully recoverable, as are any outlays for medical or other expenses incurred in consequence of the accident. Lost earnings, past and future, are compensable. Damages for "pain and suffering," a category nearly coterminous with item (4) above, are also allowable although the only one whose suffering may be considered is the victim himself. In two respects the courts evidenced some economic sophistication. They allowed compensation for loss of nonpecuniary but real earnings, such as a housewife's; and by providing for compensation in a lump sum paid at the time of judgment rather than in periodic payments during the period of disability they avoided the disincentive effects of tying continued compensation to continued inability to work and economized on administrative and policing costs.

The measurement of damages in death cases presents special problems. It is difficult to discover the value that an individual places on his life. If you ask someone how much money he would demand in exchange for giving up his life on the spot, he is likely to reply that no price would be high enough—his price is infinite. But that is because he would have only an infinitesimal amount of time in which to enjoy the proceeds of his sale. Judging from how people risk their lives constantly for small gains in convenience, the average individual will, and in effect does, sell years of his life quite cheaply so long as he expects to have some time in which to enjoy the gains from the sales. The solution of the courts of our period was to allow no damages to the victim's estate for the death itself (there might, of course, be pain or suffering before death and they would be compensable), but to compensate the pecuniary loss suffered by the victim's family. They measured this loss not by the amount of earnings that the victim lost by his death but by the amount of contribution from his earnings to the family's support that the family lost by his death, which is the correct economic measure.

No damages were allowed for the survivors' grief. Since this is a real cost, its exclusion seems economically unsound, even if we assume that the family in working-class homes of the nineteenth century was a less romantic institution than the family of today (we shall see that the working class were the main victims of accidents). Cases involving the death or disability of children may seem especially anomalous in their exclusion of sentimental factors. The basic measure of damages was the child's contribution to his parents' income, which had two components: the child's earnings until he reached his majority, which by law belonged to the parents, minus the expenses of his upkeep; and the likely support that the child would contribute in the parents' old age. This is correct so far as it goes, and perhaps in an era of large families, high infant mortality, little knowledge of contraception, and no social security, a child of working-class parents was sometimes viewed by them as an income-producing asset whose destruction could be compensated for in much the same way as the destruction of property. That would be consistent with a notable study of working-class families of the period.[22] The modern view of children is different and the basis on which damages are computed in children's death cases has changed greatly since the period with which we are concerned.[23]

A seemingly peculiar feature of the law of damages is that the defendant is liable to the full extent of the victim's injuries, even if the extent could not have been foreseen. A team accidentally runs down a man with a preternaturally thin skull and kills him. A normal man would not have been injured seriously. The driver is nonetheless fully liable for the death if the accident resulted from his negligence. The result seems at first glance inconsistent with the principle discussed earlier that one is not liable for the unforeseeable consequences of negligence. However, there is a good reason for distinguishing in this regard between the fact of injury and its extent. We want the total liability of negligent injurers to equal the total cost of their accidents. If instead of attempting to determine damages in each case on an individual basis, we used an average figure (the injury a man of average strength and health would have sustained in an accident of the same type), then we would be overcompensating some (those who are stronger or healthier than average) as well as undercompensating the weaker. But overcompensating for injuries may cause the accident rate to rise. Insurance companies will not insure a building against fire for more than it is worth lest arson be encouraged. Nor should the law of negligence encourage the strong to court injury by overcompensating them when an injury occurs. But then the weak must not be undercompensated, lest the total liability of negligent injurers fall short of the total cost of their accidents.

We have considered the major substantive doctrines of the negligence system as revealed by the sample. It remains to consider the institutional framework of the system. The essence of the system in its institutional or procedural aspect is that it is adversary, decentralized, and nonpolitical in a sense that I shall explain. The motive force of the system is supplied by the economic self-interest of the participants in accidents. If the victim of an accident has a colorable legal claim to damages, it pays him to take steps to investigate the circumstances surrounding the accident; if the investigation suggests liability, to submit a claim to the party who injured him or the party's insurance company; if an amicable settlement cannot be reached, to press his claim in a lawsuit, if necessary to the highest appellate level. The other party has a similar incentive to discover the circumstances of the accident, to attempt a reasonable settlement, and, failing that, to defend the action in court. By creating economic incentives for private individuals and firms to investigate accidents and bring them to the attention of the courts, the system enables society to dispense with the elaborate governmental apparatus that would be necessary for gathering information about the extent and causes of accidents had the parties no incentive to report and investigate them exhaustively. The parties, of course, are not disinterested, but competition between them to persuade a judge can be expected to produce a reasonable approximation to the underlying reality. And while most cases will be settled, enough will not be settled to assure the courts a continuous and voluminous stream of data. As mentioned earlier, the 1528 cases in our sample probably represent about one thirtieth of the appellate negligence cases decided between 1875 and 1905, from which we can infer that some 45,000 such cases were decided during the period. By 1905 the cases are apparently running at a rate of almost 3000 a year. And these are only the appellate cases.

I have stressed the informational role of the adversary system as a counterweight to the frequently expressed view that common law adjudication, with its focus upon the individual case, is an implausible method of obtaining efficient general standards of safety. The common law method may be compared with the economic market—also a highly decentralized, competitive and largely private system that generates strong pressures for efficient performance. The parties to a lawsuit are in competition for the favor of the tribunal in much the same way that sellers compete for the patronage of customers. Both systems create powerful incentives to furnish information. The analogy must not be pressed too far; we shall consider some important differences later. However a rule based on an adversary presentation of information may be expected to correspond to reality at least as well as one based on the self-serving declarations of one of the accident participants, and a hundred lawsuits based on rigorous adversary scrutiny of the parties' allegations may be a firmer base for a rule of safe conduct than unverified contentions by injured and injuring parties in legislative and administrative rule-making hearings. The point is illustrated by a case in the sample that the plaintiff lost because, while alleging that he had been made a cripple for life as the result of injuries to many vital organs, he proved only a minor injury to his toe—a member omitted from his enumeration.

A common criticism of the negligence system as a method of regulation is that standards of conduct are established after the accident has occurred. However, the same is true, in practice, of legislative and administrative regulation as well: it is the shocking accident, rather than the expectation of an accident, that evokes regulation. Whether the lags involved in negligence adjudication are markedly greater than those associated with legislative and administrative processes is an empirical question. As shown in Table 1, the mean duration from the accident to the appellate opinion for all cases in our sample is 40 months; declines during the period; and in 1905 is only 37 months. The criticism of adjudicative regulation as *post hoc* also ignores anticipation. Prediction of how courts will decide is of the essence of legal training and expertise. A rule announced by an appellate court will often have been anticipated long in advance—possibly since before the accident. And courts may in general be more predictable than legislative or administrative bodies.

Another important characteristic of the adversary system of negligence adjudication is that it is calculated to encourage the formulation and application of safety principles that will be grounded in considerations of efficiency. Because punitive damages, as mentioned, are not allowed in negligence cases, evidence concerning the poverty, wealth, or other attractive or repulsive characteristics of the parties unrelated to whether the accident was brought about by a failure to take cost-justified precau-

Table 1
Duration of Cases (months)

Region	Date	Mean	0–12 months	13–24	25–36	37–48	49–60	61–72	73–84	Above 84	Number of Observations	Mean—Intermediate Appellate Decisions Only	Number of Observations	Second or Other Subsequent Trial or Appeal
New England	1875	28		2	5	2					9			
	85	50			3	2				1	6			1
	95	31			4						4			
	1905	33		5	6	5	2				18			
Total a		34		7	18	9	2			1	37			1
Mid-Atlantic	1875	60		1	1		1	3	1	1	8	48	5	
	85	39		2	11	4	2	3			22	38	9	
	95	45	1	7	12	7	6	4	2	3	42	40	24	4
	1905	36	1	19	17	10	8	4	1	2	62	34	38	6
Total a		41	2	29	41	21	17	14	4	6	134	37	76	10
South	1875	78		1				1		1	3			
	85	39									2			
	95	38		3	6	1	2	2			14			
	1905	28		18	11	4	2				35			2
Total a		34		22	18	6	4	3		1	54			2
North Central	1875	77			1					2	3			
	85	42		3	9	3	1	1		2	19	37	5	3
	95	40		6	21	16	7	11	2	1	55	38	24	3
	1905	44		13	25	27	11	2	2	3	92	46	52	7
Total a		43		22	56	46	19	14	4	8	169	43	81	13
Border	1875													
	85	107							1	1	2			
	95	41		1	3	3	2	1			10			
	1905	32	1	3	6					1	11			3
Total a		42	1	4	9	3	2	1	2	1	23			3
West	1875	39		1	4	1	1	1			8	43	1	1
	85	47		2		5	1	3	1		12	50	4	1
	95	44	1	8	19	12	12	7	1	5	65	37	33	1
	1905	36	1	34	20	17	10	4	2	3	91	31	51	10
Total a		40	2	45	43	35	24	15	4	8	176	34	89	13
Federal Courts	1895	38	1	8	3	6	1		2	1	22	30	19	
	1905	41		3	10	6	2		2	1	24	38	23	1
Total a		40	1	11	13	12	3		4	2	46	34	42	1
Grand total a		40	6	140	198	132	71	47	18	27	639	37	288	43
Total b—1875		49		5	11	3	2	5	1	4	31	47	6	1
Total b—1885		45		7	24	24	4	7	2	4	63	40	18	5
Total b—1895		42	2	25	65	39	29	16	5	9	190	38	81	8
Total b—1905		37	3	92	85	63	33	19	6	8	309	37	141	28

Source: Judicial reports.
a Or average.
b Or average. Federal cases excluded.

tions is excluded at trial, although such characteristics can often be inferred.

The division of functions between judge and jury is consistent with emphasis on efficiency. The heavy use of juries is a striking feature of the negligence system during the period covered by the sample. Plaintiffs recovered judgments in jury trials in 945 of the cases in the sample, but recovered judgments in nonjury trials in only 59; defendants recovered judgments in jury trials in 98 cases, but recovered judgments in nonjury trials in only 23.[24] In one sense the use of the jury assures, insofar as possible, that the trial of the case will not be tainted by evidence or argument involving the income or wealth of the parties or other inadmissible grounds: such grounds are literally excluded from the jury's consideration.   On the other hand, formally excluded considerations are often obvious and a jury is a less disciplined adjudicator than a judge. The use of the jury does bring to bear on safety problems the judgment and experience of a broader segment of the community than if judgments of negligence were made by judges alone.   Judges may not know a great deal about driving a farm wagon, boarding a streetcar, operating a rip-saw, or the other activities in which accidents were common during our period.   They were drawn from the professional class and most accidents did not involve members of that class.   As mentioned earlier, 30 per cent of the cases in the sample involve accidents to employees, with only one exception that I recall workers rather than executives.   Although the occupation or income group of the remaining plaintiffs usually cannot be determined from the cases, of 145 cases in which the information is available 106—73 per cent—are cases where the plaintiff is a worker or a member of a worker's family.[25]   If this proportion holds for the remaining non-employee cases in the sample, then 81 per cent of all the cases in the sample involve injury to members of an economic class to which judges do not belong.   Although we know little about the composition of the juries of this period, they were probably more representative of the population of accident victims (and injurers) than the judges, and may therefore have had a better feel for the facts in many accident situations.

The jury's function was not limited to finding the facts; it was also resposible for deciding whether the facts found constituted negligence. It was the jurors who applied, within certain broad limits set by the judge, the Hand formula.   It may seem paradoxical to entrust to laymen selected largely by chance so much of the lawmaking function, but the paradox disappears when we recall that the formula requires a common sense lay judgment rather than a technical lawyer's judgment.   If due care is taking cost-justified precautions, panels of randomly selected laymen, operating with such guidance as is afforded by the testimony of witnesses, the argument of counsel and the instructions of the judge, should be able to make roughly adequate judgments, at least much of the time.   The nature of the required judgment, after all, should be familiar to anyone with experience of everyday life.   We are constantly reckoning in our minds, in most instances unconsciously to be sure, the probability of an accident, the magnitude of the loss if it occurs, and the cost of taking precautions to prevent it from occurring.   These judgments are implicit in the decision to climb a ladder, cross a street, step into the shower, or fly in an airplane, and similar judgments were no less inescapable in the period covered by the sample.   Doubtless the cost judgments of juries are very crude in comparison to those that would be made by a market were a market in accidents feasible.   But such a market does not appear to be feasible.   The meaningful comparison is therefore to decisions by judges or administrators or legislators.   And in that frame of reference juries may do quite well.

The evidence thus far examined indicates that the basic formal structure of the negligence system broadly supports an economic theory of negligence. However, there is a danger of being fooled when all one is looking at is the formal level of an institution, so the remaining portion of the article attempts a closer examination of the specific rules and results of the negligence system.

* * *

[Section IV omitted (ed.).]

Particularization of the Standard of Care.   In conclusion of our discussion of the rules of liability, it is interesting to observe the *number* of particular rules of liability that may be found during our period. The reader should bear in mind that the rules we have discussed are based on only a small fraction of the total number of accident cases decided by appellate courts between 1875 and 1905. The frequent criticism of the fault system as the unpredictable product of the caprices of individual juries ignores the continuous and pervasive rulemaking, some statutory and some common law, that went on. The set of negligence rules constituted not an ambiguous moral imperative but a comprehensive code of safety regulation, lending point to Holmes' comment, made with specific reference to accident liability, that the tendency of the common law is to become more certain and to precipitate specific rules of conduct from general principles.[38]

V

To summarize the evidence thus far discussed, I discern no systematic bias in the law of negligence as it was applied between 1875 and 1905 in favor of industrial growth and expansion, except insofar as the efficient use of resources may be thought to foster, or perhaps to be the equivalent of, economic development. The common law seems to have been fairly evenhanded in its treatment of the claims of victims and injurers. The rules of liability seem to have been broadly designed to bring about the efficient (cost-justified) level of accidents and safety, or, more likely, an approximation thereto. The tendency of legislatures in safety matters, in contrast, was to retard industrial expansion by enacting statutes protecting farmers and workers. The rhetoric of the protectionist movement portrayed the common law courts as indifferent to safety. But this characterization is imprecise. One can think of many rules, common law and legislative, that would have reduced the accident bills of railroads and other industries below an efficient level (and thereby have stimulated more rapid industrial growth), but we do not find such rules.

Our examination of the evidence, however, is not complete. Rules of liability and general organizing principles are not the only components of a legal system. Even if we were confident that the thrust of the system was toward achieving an efficient level of accidents and safety, we would want to explore how far it had carried. We need to look more closely at the practical operating level of the system. Unfortunately the data are fragmentary and only the most tentative conclusions possible.

The Economic Adequacy of the Common Law Negligence Rules. In principle, we have said, the negligence system should bring about the cost-justified level of investment in safety, but what about in practice? We lack sufficient information about the actual costs of alternative safety methods and appliances in the period between 1875 and 1905 to go much beyond the general appraisal of liability rules attempted in the preceding part of the paper. But there is important indirect evidence. Almost half the cases in the sample involve accidents arising in the course of a contractual relationship between the participants. The costs of contracting specifically with reference to safety need not be negligible merely because the parties have contracted with reference to some other term of their relationship, but neither should they be completely prohibitive. If, therefore, the common law rules were markedly inefficient we would expect to find numerous cases in which the participants in the accident had specified in advance their respective liabilities yet we find almost none. Nor do we find much statutory activity that can plausibly be interpreted as having been evoked by the inability of the common law to bring about efficient levels of safety.

But in one respect there are both analytical and empirical grounds for thinking the common law probably did not do a very good job. We referred earlier to the relevance of customary practices in defining the standard of care and to the significance, for an economic analysis of the negligence concept, of the courts' rejection of compliance with custom as a defense to a negligence action. The sample contains no case in which an enterprise was held to have been negligent for having failed to introduce a safety method or appliance not generally in use in the industry. All kinds of safety appliances were introduced during the period embraced by the sample: in railroading alone, there were the automatic coupler, the air brake, the steel car, steel rails, the electric block system for preventing collisions, and many others.[39] The safety standard is higher at the end of the period than at the beginning but there is no evidence that the law of negligence had anything to do with raising it. On reflection this is not surprising. A plaintiff who before the first railroad had installed the Westinghouse air brake tried to prove that the cost of the appliance was less than its benefits in accident prevention faced a terribly uphill struggle. There was a natural reluctance to permit a jury or even a series of juries to decide that the railroad industry, not just one backward line, should be investing very substantial sums in an unproven and inevitably controversial new appliance: the air brake was much derided in railroading circles when it was first invented.[40]

If the law is not responsible for major innovations in safety methods, what is? Although the question lies somewhat outside of the scope of this paper, I shall venture an answer. There are few areas, certainly in railroading, where the introduction of a safety appliance would benefit only third parties, whose injuries an enterprise will take account of only if forced to do so by the state. Spark-arresting equipment is one, and it is perhaps significant that the courts required railroads to install the "best and latest," not merely the customary, such equipment. But the air brake, for example, protected not only, or even primarily, trespassers on the track and travelers at crossings. It protected passengers, thereby increasing the demand for railroad travel; the railroad's equipment, thereby reducing its repair and replacement bill; and the railroad's employees, thereby reducing the risk premium that it had to pay its workers and the loss of human capital invested in injured workers. Industry had strong incentives, wholly apart from liability, for introducing air brakes and this is true of most other safety appliances.

I remarked earlier the affinity between the economic market and common law adjudication as methods of allocating resources. Our discussion of the difficulties faced by courts in compelling adoption of major safety innovations points to a fundamental difference between the methods. A market is strongly conducive to an honest valuation of goods. If you say that something is worth a dollar, and then actually buy it, I will be inclined to believe what you said; you put your money where your mouth was. The credibility conferred by a demonstrated willingness to pay is wanting in negligence suits. The plaintiff may argue that the expenditure by the railroad industry of $X million on safety appliances will prevent $2X million in accident losses, properly discounted, but since he is not about to make any such investment himself, his statement will be greeted with a measure of skepticism. The cost of overcoming that skepticism is likely to exceed his stake in the outcome of the case.

For the same reason we should not expect the courts to attempt interindustry safety comparisons, although the Hand formula, followed literally, would require them to do so. Suppose the cost of installing air brakes would exceed the cost of the accidents that they would prevent; that does not conclude the analysis. If a system of canals and roads provides nearly as fast and cheap a method of transportation as the railroads, and one that is a good deal safer, the economically optimizing solution may be neither to require the installation of air brakes nor to countenance the accidents resulting from their absence, but, rather, by making the railroads liable, to induce the substitution of canals for railroads.

The displacement of one industry by another is a common result of the operation of the market, but one can understand why courts would be unwilling to attempt to determine analytically whether such a displace-ment was justified. This is a serious limitation of the negligence system as a method of optimizing the allocation of resources to safety. Yet the courts did not brush the problem under the rug entirely. They carved an important exception to the standard of negligence for ultrahazardous ac-tivities, such as blasting. Those are by definition activities where un-avoidable accident costs are great, and therefore where one is most likely to find that an alternative method of achieving the same result (digging instead of blasting) is cheaper when unavoidable accident costs are taken into account. A rule of strict liability—the rule applied to activities classified as ultrahazardous—compels them to be taken into account.

Railroads are dangerous, but the danger is mostly to passengers and employees,[41] who are presumably compensated by the railroads for any danger. The social benefits of railroad transportation in the late nine-teenth century greatly exceeded any reasonable estimate of the costs of unavoidable railroad accidents to strangers and enable us to conclude that railroads would not have been displaced by canals and roads if railroads had been made liable for those costs.[42]

The problem of the honest valuation also plagues the negligence sys-tem in computing damages. If I testify in a negligence suit that the loss of my little finger was a source of unbearable psychological agony, for which $100,000 would barely compensate me, I am likely to be disbelieved; not so if I refuse a bona fide offer of $100,000 for my little finger. Yet the variance in the values that people attach to avoiding pain and dis-figurement is doubtless great. A market in accidents would recognize and reflect this diversity of tastes; the judicial surrogate for the mar-ket tends to suppress it.

* * *

[Balance of article omitted (ed.).]

FOOTNOTES

* Professor of Law, University of Chicago, Gary S. Becker, Owen M. Fiss, Morton J. Horwitz, Stanley N. Katz, John H. Langbein, George J. Stigler, and Hans Zeisel made helpful comments on an earlier draft of this article. Wendy Binder and Robert Schuwerk rendered valuable research assistance. Financial support was provided by the National Bureau of Economic Research under a grant from the National Science Foundation for research in law and economics; however, my findings and conclusions have not been re-viewed or approved by the National Bureau.

1 The various strands of the orthodox view are exemplified by P. S. Atiyah, Accidents, Compensation and the Law ch. 19 (1970); Guido Calabresi, The Costs of Accidents, A Le-gal and Economic Analysis pts. 4–5 (1970); Grant Gilmore, Products Liability: A Com-mentary, 38 U.Chi.L.Rev. 103 (1970); Cornelius J. Peck, Negligence and Liability Without

Fault in Tort Law, 46 Wash.L.Rev. 225 (1971); Herman Miles Somers and Anne Ramsay Somers, Workmen's Compensation—Prevention, Insurance, and Rehabilitation of Occupational Disability ch. 2 (1954).

[2] And as is made explicit in Guido Calabresi, Some Thoughts on Risk Distribution and the Law of Torts, 70 Yale L.J. 499, 515–17 (1961).

[3] Holmes argued brilliantly that it was not. See Oliver Wendell Holmes, Jr., The Common Law 100–05 (1881), and for the same argument in slightly different form, his article Trespass and Negligence, 1 Am.L.Rev. (N.S.) 1, 15–20 (1880). Other historical discussions are cited in Cornelius J. Peck, supra note 1, at 225–27.

[4] See Oliver Wendell Holmes, Jr., The Common Law, supra note 3, at 96, 110.

[5] Life and accident insurance was apparently fairly common during our period, at least among workers. See Gilbert Lewis Campbell, Industrial Accidents and Their Compensation ch. III (1911). In 1907–1908, some 49 per cent of workers in New York State involved in accidents carried some type of insurance. 1910 Rep't New York State Employers' Liability Commission 101.

[6] A book published by the Association of Railway Claim Agents exhorting railroad personnel to observe safety rules laid down in the book illustrates the regulatory function of private law. R. C. Richards, Raiload Accidents, Their Cause and Prevention (1906).

[7] See Oliver Wendell Holmes, Jr., The Common Law, supra note 3, at 108.

[8] United States v. Carroll Towing Co., 159 F.2d 169 (2d Cir. 1947); Conway v. O'Brien, 111 F.2d 611 (2d Cir. 1940).

[9] But it should be noted that Hand was no stranger to economic analysis. See especially United States v. Corn Products Co., 234 Fed. 964 (S.D.N.Y.1916).

[10] The first systematic attempt to explain a portion of tort law by economic theory was R. H. Coase, The Problem of Social Cost, 3 J.Law & Econ. 1 (1960) (English nuisance law). The extension of the approach to negligence is suggested, but not developed, in Harold Demsetz, Issues in Automobile Accidents and Reparations from the Viewpoint of Economics (June 1968), in Charles O. Gregory and Harry Kalven, Jr., Cases and Materials on Torts 870 (2d ed. 1969); and Guido Calabresi, in The Cost of Accidents, A Legal and Economic Analysis (1970), and in his earlier articles, cited id. at 321, has used economic theory to mount an attack on the negligence system. The utility of economic theory in explaining the law of intentional torts is explored in Richard A. Posner, Killing or Wounding To Protect a Property Interest, 14 J.Law & Econ. 201 (1971).

[11] These developments are traced in Herman Miles Somers and Anne Ramsay Somers, supra note 1, ch. 2. The texts of the early federal employers' liability acts are set forth in W. W. Thornton, A Treatise on the Federal Employers' Liability and Safety Appliance Acts 545–48 (3d ed. 1916).

[12] Federal cases prior to 1895 are excluded because in the earlier periods there were no federal appeals courts other than the Supreme Court, and the Court decided few negligence cases (only one in the first quarter of 1885, for example). A problem with the 1875 and 1885 cases in the sample is that decisions in these early periods were not always dated, and some guesses had to be made. As a result, some of the cases included in the sample for 1875 were probably decided in 1874 and 1876; and in order to circumvent the dating problem I went to the first quarter of 1887, by which time dates can be found for all cases, for cases in a few of the jurisdictions in place of the first quarter of 1885. A spot check indicated that these modifications of the sampling method made no significant difference in the number and type of cases collected.

[13] This is a rough estimate. The flow of appellate decisions is not even throughout the year; in particular it tends to be thinner in the summer. In this respect, the sample may represent more than ¼ of the year's cases. But in two other respects the sample is in-

complete: (1) not all appellate decisions were reported or reported sufficiently completely to identify the nature of the case, although I believe that most were; (2) decisions were sometimes reported long after they were rendered and some of these I must have missed in my search of the reports.

14 See, e. g., H. Laurence Ross, Settled Out of Court—The Social Process of Insurance Claims Adjustments 179, 216 (1970); Alfred F. Conard, et al., Automobile Accident Costs and Payments, Studies in the Economics of Injury Reparation 237, 241 (1964); Hans Zeisel, Harry Kalven, Jr., and Bernard Buchholz, Delay in the Court 40 (Table 14) (1959); Marc A. Franklin, Robert H. Chanin, and Irving Mark, Accidents, Money and the Law: A Study of the Economics of Personal Injury Litigation, in Dollars, Delay and the Automobile Victim, Studies in Reparation for Highway Injuries and Related Court Problems 39 (Walter E. Meyer Research Institute ed. 1968); Vernon K. Dibble, What Is, and What Ought To Be: A Comparison of Certain Formal Characteristics of the Ideological and of the Legal Styles of Thought 70 (Table 4) (Third Draft, July 1971, unpublished).

15 See, e. g., H. Laurence Ross, supra note 14, at 216–17.

16 In one sample of 614 fatal accidents in Illinois, 281 families settled without court proceedings, and there were 135 lawsuits. Report of the Ohio Employers' Liability Commission, pt. 1, xxxi (1911). In a sample of 370 Ohio death cases in which compensation was paid 285 were settled without litigation. Id. at xl; id. at xxxvii indicates a lower ratio of litigated to all claims. In a sample of 125 New York death cases in which some compensation was paid, 104 cases were settled without the filing of a suit. Computed from New York State Employers' Liability Commission, supra note 5, at 30–31, note 1. Another sample of New York death cases contains 111 cases in which compensation was paid without any litigation and 73 lawsuits. Id. at 97. All of these statistics involve industrial accidents only (i. e., accidents arising in the course of the employment relationship), and relate to the period 1905–1910 (they were compiled as part of the movement for workmen's compensation), which is somewhat later than the period of the present study. The higher ratio of litigated to all claims than today is intelligible when one reflects that the contemporary statistics relate primarily to automobile accidents. The fact that a few liability insurance companies handle virtually all claims and that most automobile accidents involve simple and highly recurrent factual situations facilitate massive disposition outside of the judicial system. The accident picture in the period covered by this study was more heterogeneous and therefore less susceptible of routinized settlement.

17 See Table 9, infra.

18 See Tables 2 and 3, infra.

19 See Gary S. Becker, Crime and Punishment: An Economic Approach, 76 J.Pol.Econ. 169 (1968).

20 See Richard A. Posner, A Statistical Study of Antitrust Enforcement, 13 J.Law & Econ. 365, 401–11 (1970).

21 Cf. Gary S. Becker, supra note 19, at 199.

22 See Stephan Thernstrom, Poverty and Progress—Social Mobility in a Nineteenth Century City 155 (1964).

23 See, e. g., Wycko v. Gnodtke, 361 Mich. 331, 105 N.W.2d 118 (1960).

24 In our trial sample, however, the jury was waived about 25% of the time.

25 I exclude ship-collision cases tried in federal courts under the admiralty jurisdiction. These are cases where the plaintiff is invariably an enterprise, and where, it is interesting to note, there is no right to trial by jury.

38 Oliver Wendell Holmes, Jr., The Common Law, supra note 3, at 111–129. A number of treatises were written during our period on or relating to specific areas of negligence, and setting forth specific duties of care in great profusion, such as Wharton on Negligence,

Campbell on Negligence, Bishop on Noncontract Law, Addison on Torts, Cooley on Torts, Keasberg on Electric Wires, Baldwin on Railroad Law, Elliott on Railroads and Street Railroads, Beach on Law of Railways, Dillon on Municipal Corporations, Labatt on Master and Servant, Nellis on Street Surface Railroads, Beach on Contributory Negligence, Bailey on Master's Liability for Injuries to Servants. These works are much cited by the courts in the cases in our sample.

[39] See Charles Francis Adams, Jr., supra note 29; Carl S. Vrooman, American Railway Problems in the Light of European Experience 182–204 (1910).

[40] Charles Francis Adams, Jr., supra note 29, at 204.

[41] In 1891, for example, of 40,910 people reported to have been killed or injured by railroads, 32,065 were passengers or employees (and some of the others also had a contractual relationship with the railroad). United States Department of Commerce, Bureau of the Census, Historical Statistics of the United States—Colonial Times to 1957, 437 (1960).

[42] The social saving resulting from the existence of railroads has been estimated, for the year 1890, as somewhat more than $400 million. See Introduction to Part III, in The Reinterpretation of American History 98, 101–02 & n. 4 (Robert William Fogel and Stanley L. Engerman eds. 1971). If we assume that under the negligence standard railroads would not have been liable to one half of the 8,845 killed or injured in railroad accidents to strangers in 1891 (see note 41 supra; statistics for 1890 not available), and we assume an average cost of $3944 per fatal and $4227 per nonfatal accident (see Table 7 infra), then strict liability would have increased the costs of railroading by a little more than $18 million that year. And this ignores the fact that the substitute modes of transportation, especially roads, were not accident-free. To be sure, railroads probably could not capture in their rates the full social saving from railroading. But if we compare our estimate of unavoidable accident costs to strangers with total railroad operating revenues in 1890, we find that the former is only 1.7% of the latter. See Historical Statistics of the United States, supra note 41, at 434.

Continued

15: STRICT LIABILITY: A COMMENT

RICHARD A. POSNER*

Within the last year there have appeared several major articles [1] that, while otherwise extremely diverse, share a strong preference (in one case implicit) for using the principle of "strict liability" to resolve legal conflicts over resource use.[2] I shall argue in this comment that the authors of these articles fail to make a convincing case for strict liability, primarily because they do not analyze the economic consequences of the principle correctly.

I

To explicate these consequences I shall use the now familiar example of the railroad engine that emits sparks which damage crops along the railroad's right of way. I shall assume that the costs of transactions between the railroad and the farmers are so high that the liability imposed by the law will not be shifted by negotiations between the parties.

The economic goal of liability rules in such a case is to maximize the joint value of the interfering activities, railroading and farming.[3] To identify the value-maximizing solution requires a comparison of the costs to the railroad of taking steps to reduce spark emissions to various levels, including zero, and the costs to farmers of either tolerating or themselves taking steps to reduce the damage to their property from the sparks. The value-maximizing solution may turn out to involve changes by both parties in their present behavior; for example, the railroad may have to install

Journal of Legal Studies, Vol. 2, No. 1, 1973, p. 205.

a good but not perfect spark arrester and the farmer may have to leave an unplanted buffer space between the railroad right of way and his tilled fields.   Or, the value-maximizing solution may involve changes by the railroad only, by the farmer only, or by neither party.

Let us consider what, if any, different effects negligence and strict liability—competing approaches to the design of liability rules—might have in nudging railroad and farmer toward the value-maximizing (efficient) solution, under various assumptions as to what that solution is.

The railroad will be adjudged negligent if the crop damage exceeds the cost to the railroad of avoiding that damage.[4] But the farmer will still not prevail if the cost of the measures *he* might have taken to avoid the damage to his crops is less than the crop damage; this is the rule of contributory negligence.

If the efficient solution requires only that the railroad take some measure to reduce the farmer's crop damage, then the negligence approach leads us toward the efficient solution.   Since the railroad is liable for the damage and the damage is greater than the cost to the railroad of preventing it,[5] the railroad will adopt the preventive measure in order to avoid a larger damage judgment.   If the efficient solution is either that the railroad do nothing or that both parties do nothing, the negligence standard will again lead to the efficient solution.   Not being liable, the railroad will have no incentive to adopt preventive measures; the farmer will have no incentive to take precautions either, since by hypothesis the cost of doing so would exceed the crop damage that he suffers.   If the efficient solution requires only the farmer to take precautions, the negligence approach again points in the right direction.   The railroad is not liable and does not take precautions.   The farmer takes precautions, as we want him to do, because they cost less than the crop damage they prevent.

That leaves only the case where the efficient solution involves avoidance by both parties.   Again the negligence standard should lead toward an efficient solution.   The farmer will adopt his cost-justified avoidance measure so as not to be barred by the contributory negligence rule and once he has done so the railroad will adopt its cost-justified avoidance measure to avoid liability for the accidents that the farmer's measure does not prevent.

The foregoing discussion must be qualified in one important respect. If the efficient solution requires only the railroad to take precautions but the farmer could take a precaution that, although more costly than the railroad's (otherwise *it* would be the optimum solution), would be less costly than the crop damage, the farmer's failure to adopt the measure will, nonetheless, be deemed contributory negligence.   He will therefore adopt it and the railroad will have no incentive to adopt what is in fact the cheaper method of damage prevention.

A principle of strict liability, with no defense of contributory negligence, would produce an efficient solution where that solution was either for the railroad alone to take precautions or for neither party to do so,[6] but not in the other two cases. In the case where the efficient solution is for the farmer alone to take avoidance measures, strict liability would not encourage efficiency, for with the railroad liable for all crop damage the farmer would have no incentive to avoid such damage even if it was cheaper for him to do so; he would be indifferent between the crops and compensation for their destruction. Similarly, in the case where the efficient solution consists of precautions by both railroad and farmer, strict liability would give the farmer no incentive to shoulder his share of the responsibility. But we need only add a defense of contributory negligence in strict liability cases in order to give the farmer an incentive to take precautions where appropriate. There would still be the problem of inefficient solutions where the farmer's precaution, although less costly than his crop damage, was more costly than the railroad's precaution; but this could be remedied by redefining the contributory negligence defense—a step that should be taken in any event.

At least as a first approximation, then, a strict liability standard with a defense of contributory negligence is as efficient as the conventional negligence standard, but not more efficient. This conclusion would appear to hold with even greater force where, as in a products liability case, there is (or can readily be created) a seller-buyer relationship between injurer and victim. Indeed, it can be shown that in that situation an efficient solution is likely to be reached not only under either strict liability (plus contributory negligence) or negligence, but equally with no tort liability at all.

The cost of a possibly dangerous product to the consumer has two elements: the price of the product and an expected accident cost (for a risk-neutral purchaser, the cost of an accident if it occurs multiplied by the probability of occurrence). Regardless of liability, the seller will have an incentive to adopt any cost-justified precaution, because, by lowering the total cost of the product to the buyer, it will enable the seller to increase his profit.[7] Where, however, the buyer can prevent the accident at lower cost than the seller, the buyer can be counted on to take the precaution rather than the seller, for by doing so the buyer will minimize the sum of the price of the product (which will include the cost of any precautions taken by the seller) and the expected accident cost.[8]

Although both strict liability and negligence appear to provide efficient solutions to problems of conflicting resource uses, they do not have identical economic effects. The difference comes in cases where the efficient solution is for neither party to the interference to do anything. This is the category of interferences known in negligence law as "unavoidable accidents." They are rarely unavoidable in the literal sense. But frequently the cost either to injurer or to victim of taking measures to prevent an accident exceeds the expected accident cost and in such a case efficiency requires that the accident be permitted to occur.   Under a negligence standard, the injurer is not liable; under strict liability, he is.   What if any economic difference does this make?

It can be argued that unless an industry is liable for its unavoidable accidents, consumers may be led to substitute the product of the industry for the safer product of another industry. Suppose the only difference between railroads and canals as methods of transportation were that railroads had more unavoidable accidents. If the railroad industry were not liable for those accidents, the price of railroad transportation would be the same as the price of transportation by canal, yet we would want people to use canals rather than railroads because the former were superior in the one respect—safety—in which the two methods differed. In principle, a negligence standard would require the railroad to bear the cost of those accidents. They are not unavoidable. In fact, they could be avoided at zero cost by the substitution of canal for railroad transportation. But perhaps courts are incapable of making inter-industry comparisons in applying the negligence standard. Nonetheless the argument affords no basis for preferring strict liability to negligence, since an identical but opposite distortion is created by strict liability. Compare two dfferent tracts of land that are identical in every respect except that one is immediately adjacent to a railroad line and one is well back from any railroad line. If the railroad is strictly liable for crop damage inflicted by engine sparks there will be no incentive to use the tract near the railroad line for fire-insensitive uses and to shift the growing of flammable crops to the tract that is remote from a railroad line, even though such a rearrangement may eliminate all crop damage at zero cost.

A related misconception involves the question of the comparative safety level in the long run under strict liability versus negligence liability. The level of safety is unaffected in the short run by which liability rule is chosen. Even if the injurer is strictly liable, he will not try to prevent an accident where the cost of prevention exceeds the accident cost; he will prefer to pay the victim's smaller damages. However, he will have an incentive to invest in research and development efforts designed to develop a cost-justified method of accident prevention, for such a method would lower the cost of complying with a rule of strict liability. It is tempting to conclude that strict liability encourages higher, and in the long run more efficient, levels of safety, but this is incorrect. Rather than creating an incentive to engage in research on safety, a rule of strict liability merely shifts that incentive. Under the negligence standard the cost of unavoidable accidents is borne by the victims of accidents. They can reduce this cost in the long run by financing research into and development of cost-justified measures by which to protect themselves. The victims will not themselves organize for research, but they will provide the market for firms specializing in the development of new safety appliances.[9]

Let us consider some other possible differences, in economic effect, between strict liability and negligence. It might appear that strict liability would reduce the costs of tort litigation, both by simplifying the issues in a trial and thereby reducing its costs and by removing an element of uncertainty and thereby facilitating settlements, which are cheaper than trials. But the matter is more complex than this. By increasing the scope of liability, strict liability enlarges the universe of claims, so even if the fraction of cases that go to trial is smaller the absolute number may be larger. And, by increasing the certainty that the plaintiff will prevail, strict liability encourages him to spend more money on the litigation; conceivably, therefore, the costs of trials might actually increase.[10]

Under strict liability, in effect the railroad (in our example) insures the farmer against the loss of his crops; under negligence liability, the farmer must obtain and pay for insurance himself (or self-insure). Thus, although strict liability, under the name "enterprise liability," has long been defended on the ground [11] that it permits accident losses to be spread more widely, there is little to this argument: the farmer can avoid a concentrated loss by insuring. However, if we were confident that the cost of insuring was lower for the railroad than for the farmer, we might on this ground prefer strict liability.[12]

Strict liability increases the costs of railroading, in our example, and negligence the costs of farming. But the implications for the overall distribution of income and wealth are uncertain, at least in the example, so intertwined were the economic interests of railroads and farmers during the period when the modern system of negligence liability was taking shape. Any increase in the cost of railroading would be borne in significant part by farmers since they were the railroads' principal customers. The intertwining of economic interests is characteristic of many modern tort contexts as well, such as automobile and product accidents. Most victims of automobile accidents are owners of automobiles; victims of defective products are also consumers.

Additional considerations come into play where there is a buyer-seller relationship between victim and injurer; but they relate primarily to the question whether sellers' liability (either strict liability or negligence) has different consequences from no liability (i. e., buyers' liability). There are two reasons for believing that there might be different safety consequences. First, if the buyers of a product are risk preferring, they may be unwilling to pay for a safety improvement even if the cost is less than the expected accident cost that the improvement would eliminate. Under a rule of no liability, the improvement will not be made;

under a rule either of strict liability or of negligence liability, the improvement will be made.[13]   But the higher level of safety is not optimum in the economic sense, since it is higher than consumers want.

Second, consumers may lack knowledge of product safety.   Criticisms of market processes based on the consumer's lack of information are often superficial, because they ignore the fact that competition among sellers generates information about the products sold.   There is however a special consideration in the case of safety information: the firm that advertises that its product is safer than a competitor's may plant fears in the minds of potential consumers where none existed before.   If a product hazard is small, or perhaps great but for some reason not widely known (*e. g.*, cigarettes, for a long time), consumers may not be aware of it.   In these circumstances a seller may be reluctant to advertise a safety improvement, because the advertisement will contain an implicit representation that the product is hazardous (otherwise, the improvement would be without value).   He must balance the additional sales that he may gain from his rivals by convincing consumers that his product is safer than theirs against the sales that he may lose by disclosing to consumers that the product contains hazards of which they may not have been aware, or may have been only dimly aware.   If advertising and marketing a safety improvement are thus discouraged, the incentive to adopt such improvements is reduced.   But make the producer liable for the consequences of a hazardous product, and no question of advertising safety improvements to consumers will arise.   He will adopt cost-justified precautions not to divert sales from competitors but to minimize liability to injured consumers.

In principle, we need not assume that the only possible sources of information about product safety are the manufacturers of the product. Producers in other industries would stand to gain from exposing an unsafe product, but if their products are not close substitutes for the unsafe product, as is implicit in our designation of them as members of other industries, the gain will be small and the incentive to invest money in investigating the safety of the product and disseminating the results of the investigation slight.   Firms could of course try to sell product information directly to consumers;   the problem is that because property rights in information are relatively undeveloped, the supplier of information is frequently unable to recover his investment in obtaining and communicating it.

The information problem just discussed provides an arguable basis for rejecting *caveat emptor* in hazardous-products cases, but not for replacing negligence with strict liability in such cases, which is the trend of the law.   The traditional pockets of strict liability, such as respondeat superior and the liability of blasters and of keepers of vicious animals, can be viewed as special applications of negligence theory.[14]   The question whether a general substitution of strict for negligence liability would improve efficiency seems at this stage hopelessly conjectural; the question is at bottom empirical and the empirical work has not been done. Finally, it is interesting to note that in the area of tort law that is in greatest ferment, liability for automobile accidents, the movement appears to be from negligence to no liability![15]

II

A

Now to our authors. I begin with Professor Baxter. His discussion of strict liability is brief and largely implicit, and in focusing upon one small aspect of a long and excellent study I hope I will not be understood as intending a general criticism of his article.

Baxter is concerned with the problem of airport noise. The airlines correspond to the railroad in our example. The owners of residences in the vicinity of the airport who are disturbed or annoyed by airplane noise correspond to the farmer. Baxter seeks a rule of liability that will lead to an efficient level of noise damage. One approach that he considers is the noise easement. Under existing law an airline that flies low enough to create a high noise level is required to obtain from the owner of the subjacent property (by condemnation, if the airline cannot come to terms with him) an easement for the airline to maintain that noise level. The price of the easement in a condemnation proceeding will be equal to the reduction in the market value of the property caused by the noise.

Baxter is troubled by the fact that the easement is perpetual. He points out that should an airplane noise-suppression device one day be developed that enabled a reduction in the noise level at a cost lower than the increase in property values brought about by the device, the airline would have no incentive to install the device[16] and the result would be to perpetuate a solution to the conflicting uses that was no longer optimum. To remedy this he proposes that easements be limited to ten years. If at the end of that period a method for reducing noise at a cost lower than the increase in property value had been developed the airline would install it in order to minimize the cost of acquiring easements for the next period.[17]

This solution solves the problem identified by Professor Baxter but in so doing unsolves another, and for all one knows as serious, a problem that perpetual easements avoid. Just as one method of maximizing the joint value of railroading and farming may be for the farmer to take certain precautions, so one method of maximizing the joint value of air travel and of land use may be for the landowners in the vicinity of airports to reduce the damage from noise by soundproofing or by shifting to a land use that is relatively insensitive to noise. Assume that sometime after the airline obtains perpetual easements, an improved method of sound-proofing residences is developed; its adoption would reduce noise damage by more than it costs. Under existing law the homeowners would have an adequate incentive to adopt the method, because the entire resulting increase in the value of their homes would inure to them. Under Baxter's proposed system of time-limited easements the homeowners' incentive to install such devices would be much smaller. A part of the improvement would inure to the benefit not of the homeowner but of the airline, in the form of a reduced easement price in the next period. The method of time-limited easements, therefore, will discourage efficient cost-reduction measures by noise victims.

To demonstrate the fundamental difficulty with Baxter's proposal, let us imagine that the periods are made shorter and shorter (a process Baxter would object to, I take it, only on the basis of administrative costs, which let us assume are zero). In the limit, the system of time-limited easements becomes a system of strict liability: the airline pays for noise damage as it occurs. But we saw earlier that a rule of strict liability, unless modified by a defense of contributory negligence, will not produce an efficient solution (assuming, as Baxter does, heavy transaction costs) if the solution requires a change in the victims' behavior.[18]

B

Professor Calabresi proposes that liability be placed on the party to an interaction who is in the better position to "make the cost-benefit analysis between accident costs and accident avoidance costs and to act on that decision once it is made."[19] The application of this rule would lead in many, although not in all, cases to strict liability without any defense of contributory negligence. For example, suppose that people are frequently injured because the blade of their rotary mower strikes a stone and that these accidents could be prevented at least cost by the operator of the mower, who need only remove the stones in his path. Calabresi suggests that the manufacturer of the mower might nonetheless be liable under his approach. The injury is an expectable one and the manufacturer is in a better position than the user to figure out how to minimize the relevant costs.

To impose liability on the manufacturer in this case, however, is inefficient: it eliminates the incentive of the operator to adopt a more economical method of preventing the injury. One could argue, perhaps, that the incentive created by fear of physical injury is already so great that adding or subtracting a pecuniary cost will not affect behavior. But Calabresi does not take this position.

He allows himself an escape hatch. The mower case might be one where, in his terminology, although the producer is in the better position to determine the efficient solution he is not in the better position to implement it, since implementation requires a change in behavior by the user. But this circumstance, while relevant, is not, for Calabresi, decisive: where the party in the better position to determine the efficient solution is not the one in the better position to implement it, "the decision requires weighing comparative advantages." [20]

I am mystified by this approach. The only reason that Calabresi offers for not placing liability in every case on the party whose behavior we want to influence in order to produce the efficient solution is that identification of that party is often very difficult; but his approach requires such identification in every case, since it is always relevant, although never decisive, to inquire whether the party best able to judge the costs and benefits of alternative courses of action is also the party whom we want to act upon that judgment.

I can only speculate on the reasons that have led Calabresi into such an odd corner. He is, of course, strongly committed to the proposition that the negligence system is incapable of producing efficient solutions to problems of conflicting resource use.[21] And he must now believe, perhaps for reasons similar to those presented in part I of this comment, that strict liability is not sharply distinguishable from negligence so far as the production of efficient solutions to problems of conflicting resource use is concerned. He has therefore shifted discussion to a new level, where the inability of either principle to optimize accident costs is admitted and strict liability defended on another ground altogether: that it is the appropriate method of compelling the party better able to determine the efficient solution to make that determination. Where, however, that party is incapable of acting on the determination—because the solution turns out to require a change in behavior by the other party and transaction costs preclude him from paying that party to make the change—it is very difficult to see what has been accomplished. That is presumably why Calabresi added a second prong to his test, requiring that the party best able to make the cost-benefit analysis also be able to act upon it. But to use the second prong the court (or legislature) must make precisely the determination about which Calabresi is so skeptical when it is made in a negligence case: the determination of which party is in the better position to optimize the costly interaction.

C

Let us turn now to the moralists, Professors Fletcher and Epstein. Fletcher discusses two competing paradigms, or theories, of tort liability. One is the entirely novel "paradigm of reciprocity," under which the injurer is strictly liable if he created a risk to the victim that was disproportionate to the risk the victim created to him. He sets out "to demonstrate the pervasive reliance of the common law on the paradigm of reciprocity," [22] but many of the examples he uses in the demonstration are odd.[23] His reasons for promoting the paradigm of reciprocity emerge from his criticism of the competing theory, which he terms the "paradigm of reasonableness" and which corresponds roughly to the negligence standard interpreted in economic terms. Fletcher dislikes this paradigm because it is instrumentalist: that is, it involves a comparison of the utility of the victim's conduct with the utility of the injurer's. In cases where the negligence principle results in the denial of compensation to someone injured by one of Fletcher's nonreciprocal (disproportionate) risks, an innocent victim is sacrificed on the altar of community needs.[24] He believes that the refusal to compensate in these circumstances is the moral equivalent of punishing for bigamy a woman who honestly believed that her first husband was dead.

The relationship of the paradigm of reciprocity to strict liability is not one to one. But railroads vis-à-vis farmers, drivers vis-à-vis pedestrians, and many other interactions traditionally governed by the negligence principle would become, under his approach, areas of strict liability. Fletcher's analysis, however, is unsound. Reciprocity in his sense is a function purely of the rule of liability that happens to be adopted, and not of any underlying physical or economic relationships. Were the railroad strictly liable for crop damage caused by engine sparks it could not injure the farmer; he would be indifferent as between having crops and being fully compensated for their destruction. But he could injure the railroad —by planting additional crops (perhaps closer to the railroad right of way), by planting more flammable or more valuable crops, by stacking hay ricks near the tracks, by erecting wooden buildings near the tracks, and so on. Any of these actions would increase the railroad's damage bill and might ultimately force the railroad to discontinue its line, with resulting losses to the railroad's shareholders, employees, and customers (perhaps most of whom are farmers). One can make the element of victimization even clearer by assuming that the railroad line was built before the adjacent lands were used for farming. This is plausible since the construction of a railroad line typically increased the agricultural value of land proximate to it. In such a case are the farmers so morally innocent as to be entitled to compensation regardless of the costs to the railroad? Would denying them compensation really be just like imposing a criminal penalty on a woman who honestly and reasonably believed her husband was dead?

Most torts arise out of a conflict between two morally innocent activities, such as railroad transportation and farming. What ethical principle compels society to put a crimp in the former because of the proximity of the latter, rather than a crimp in the latter because of the proximity of the former? The farmer crowds the railroad, and the railroad the farmer. A rule of strict liability taxes the railroad for the benefit of the farmer; a rule of no liability would tax the farmer for the benefit of the railroad. Under a rule of strict liability, the railroad pays for the crop damage even if the cheapest way of minimizing that damage is for the farmer to modify his behavior; the result is a reduction in the value of the railroad that is greater than the farmer's gain. Under a rule of no liability the farmer pays for all crop damage even when the cheapest way of minimizing the damage is for the railroad to modify its behavior; the result is a reduction in the value of farmland greater than the railroad's gain. Why is not the railroad morally innocent when it must pay for damage that the farmer could have avoided at lower cost and the farmer morally innocent when he is forced to absorb damage costs that the railroad could have avoided at lower cost?

The situation is not clarified by restating the issue in terms of individual interests versus community needs.[25] The rule of strict liability, imposed in the case where the farmer is the cheaper cost avoider, harms both individual interests—those of the customers (many of them farmers), employees, suppliers, and shareholders of the railroad—and the community interest in efficiency. It benefits other individuals—farmers, consumers of food products (except their gains may be offset by higher railroad costs), etc.

Fletcher would in effect apply a rule of strict liability, without a defense of contributory negligence,[26] to a number of areas now governed by the negligence standard. Such an approach, as explained in part I of this comment, is inefficient. Apparently he considers this irrelevant.[27] Yet it cannot be an ethical imperative that society dissipate an indefinite amount of its members' resources in order to operate a scheme for the compensation of accident victims, who, after all, can insure against the consequences of an accident. Fletcher seems at least troubled by the point. He says, for example, that he desires only to tax and not to prohibit socially useful activity. But this is not responsive to the problem. A tax, if high enough, becomes prohibitory. Even a moderate tax will have some resource effects. A compensation system that fails to give farmers an incentive to economize on their activities will result in the waste of valuable resources. In another place he states: "If imposing a private duty of compensation for injuries resulting from nonreciprocal risk-taking has an undesirable economic impact on the defendant, the just solution would not be to deny compensation, but either to subsidize the defendant or institute a public compensation scheme."[28] But this is not responsive to the problem either. Subsidizing the railroad, in our example, will not give the farmer an incentive to take cost-justified methods of damage avoidance, and it is the failure to create such incentives that is the source of in-efficiency under Fletcher's approach.

D

Professor Epstein adopts still a different approach. His position is that a person should be prima facie liable for any injury that he causes, "cause" to be defined with reference to the structure of ordinary language rather than in the strained ways in which it has frequently been used by judges and legal commentators. This view naturally leads him to prefer strict liability to negligence as the standard of tort liability, although by em-phasizing that people should only be prima facie liable for the injuries they cause he leaves open the possibility of various defenses.

It might appear that Epstein has committed the same error as Fletch-er, that of failing to understand the reciprocal nature of an accident or other tort injury. He reinforces the impression of error by quoting and then criticizing the passage from Professor Coase's article on social cost in which Coase, in explaining the reciprocal relationship, says that the crop is as much the cause of the spark damage as the engine.[29] But Epstein has not in fact committed this error. He is prepared to concede that from an economic standpoint an inquiry into causation is vacuous; but he insists that in an ordinary-language sense it is proper to view the engine as the cause of the crop damage and improper to view the crop as a cause.

Epstein's achievement is in demonstrating, contrary to the dominant view of several generations of tort scholars, that a principle of liability based on causation is not incapable of being reduced to a set of operational rules that conform to an acceptable notion of cause. But this reader is perplexed *why* a society should decide to allocate accident costs in ac-cordance with Epstein's admittedly plausible notions of causation. What social or ethical end is advanced?

Part of Epstein's answer emerges from his discussion of negligence as an alternative to strict liability. He makes two major criticisms of negligence. The first, expressed in various ways, is that we rarely have enough information to know what the optimum solution to a problem of conflicting resource uses is. This is true, and it follows that the negli-gence system produces, at best, crude approximations of the result one could expect if market rather than legal processes were operative. But why despise crude approximations? In any event, Epstein cannot, mere-ly by embracing strict liability, escape the necessity of making such approximations unless he is prepared not to recognize any defenses that require a comparison of the costs of alternative methods of resolving the conflict. Whether he is prepared to do so is uncertain; he has adopted the risky tactic of postponing consideration of the issue to a subsequent article. We shall return to this point.

His second major criticism of the negligence system brings us to the heart of his reasons for preferring to base liability on causation: it is that the negligence system, if administered in accordance with its basic logic, would give too much power to judges to impose restrictions on human liberty. He illustrates this point with the "good Samaritan" rule of tort law. If I see another person in danger and at trivial cost to myself could save him but fail to do so, I am not liable to him; the law does not require me to be a good Samaritan. But this result, Epstein (who approves of it) argues, is inconsistent with the basic logic of the negligence system and shows that logic to be wrong. If the cost to me of taking a measure that will avert an accident to another is lower than the expected accident cost, the law should shift the accident cost from the victim to me if I fail to take the measure, for this will give me an incentive to incur the lesser cost to avoid the greater, and thereby increase efficiency. No less an authority on utility maximizing than Jeremy Bentham would agree with Epstein's point.[30]

Nor, says Epstein, can the economic optimizer limit liability to the case where the cost to the rescuer is trivial. Even where there is a substantial risk of bodily harm to the rescuer he should be liable for failure to rescue, so long as the cost to the victim of not being rescued is greater than the expected harm to him. From here it is but a step to situations in which judges might conscript people for all sorts of activity upon a finding that the benefit of the activity exceeded the cost to them.

But Epstein is incorrect that there is no logical stopping point under an economic analysis in imposing liability on people in order to induce them to perform socially productive activity. The rescue case is a plausible one for liability because transaction costs are so high: when I see a flower pot about to fall on someone's head I cannot pause to negotiate with him over an appropriate fee for warning him of the impending danger. There is no occasion for compelling transactions where negotiations are feasible. Indeed, because market transactions are preferable to legal transactions except where market transaction costs are prohibitive,[31] a system of liability that coerced people into performing services in circumstances where negotiations between them and the beneficiaries of the services were possible would be economically unsound.

Nor is the law's handling of the good Samaritan case quite so inconsistent with the basic logic of economic analysis as Epstein implies. Affirmative duties to avert harm to strangers are frequently imposed, the doctrines of attractive nuisance and of last clear chance being examples. The principal exception is the pure bystander case. Even here, the law will sometimes create an incentive to help a stranger by recognizing a good Samaritan's legal right to be compensated for the assistance rendered; indeed, Fletcher and Epstein's favorite case, *Vincent v. Lake Erie Transp. Co.*,[32] may be viewed as a case in which a suit for such compensation was vindicated.[33]

But I am quite prepared to assume that the law is out of phase with economic analysis in the matter of warnings and rescues; it is hardly a point in favor of Epstein's argument. His theory of strict liability is normative rather than positive. His own proposal for dealing with the good Samaritan problem is contrary, he admits, to the common law solution.

The final question that must be asked of Professor Epstein is how high a price he is willing to pay to vindicate the interest in preventing judges from imposing affirmative duties. It may be quite high. He hedges, as I have remarked, on defenses, but there is a strong implication that no version of contributory negligence will be permitted.[34] Moreover, the logic of his argument would appear to compel him to tolerate—paradoxically in view of his sensitivity to judicial overreaching—a substantial and potentially quite costly expansion in the degree to which people's freedom of action may be limited by common law liabilities. Suppose I make a completely innocent gesture, such as removing my hand from my pocket, and a highly nervous bystander, mistaking the purpose of the gesture, faints with fright. Under Epstein's theory of liability I may well be liable to the bystander because my gesture caused him to faint.[35] Now the fact that I am liable in such situations does not mean that I will never take my hand out of my pocket. But I may hesitate before making any gestures and the aggregate costs of such hesitations will be substantial. The cheaper way of avoiding the accident would have been for the victim to obtain treatment for his nervous ailment or to avoid situations in which an innocent gesture would be likely to frighten him. But this efficient solution is not possible under Epstein's approach. He would say that the driver who without fault injures a blind pedestrian is liable, while the present law would inquire whether the pedestrian was carrying a blind man's stick (to alert drivers) and otherwise taking inexpensive but effective measures to protect himself from injury.

III

The analysis of the comparative economic properties of strict liability and negligence, in part I of this paper, yielded conclusions that may be summarized as follows:

  1. Economic theory provides no basis, in general, for preferring strict liability to negligence, or negligence to strict liability, provided that some version of a contributory negligence defense is recognized. Empirical data might enable us to move beyond agnosticism but we do not have any.

2. A strict liability standard without a contributory negligence defense is, in principle, less efficient than the negligence-contributory negligence standard. Empirical data could of course rebut the presumption derived from theory.

The relevance of these findings to the articles discussed in part II is that each author argues for strict liability without any version of a contributory negligence defense. Each thus prefers a standard that, on the basis of existing (and inadequate) knowledge, must be regarded as presumptively less efficient than alternative standards. Since the efficient use of resources is an important although not always paramount social value, the burden, I suggest, is on the authors to present reasons why a standard that appears to impose avoidable costs on society should nonetheless be adopted. They have not carried this burden.

FOOTNOTES

* Professor of Law, University of Chicago, Harold Demsetz and Hein D. Kötz commented helpfully on an earlier draft. This paper is part of a study of liability rules being conducted under a grant from the National Science Foundation to the National Bureau of Economic Research for research in law and economics. The paper is not an official National Bureau publication since it has not undergone the full critical review accorded National Bureau studies, including approval by the Bureau's board of directors.

1 William F. Baxter & Lillian R. Altree, Legal Aspects of Airport Noise, 15 J.Law & Econ. 1 (1972); Guido Calabresi & Jon T. Hirschoff, Toward a Test for Strict Liability in Torts, 81 Yale L.J. 1055 (1972); George P. Fletcher, Fairness and Utility in Tort Theory, 85 Harv.L.Rev. 537 (1972); Richard A. Epstein, A Theory of Strict Liability, 2 J.Leg.Studies 151 (1973). My analysis is also an implicit criticism of Marc A. Franklin, Tort Liability for Hepatitis: An Analysis and Appraisal, 24 Stan.L.Rev. 439 (1972), especially id. at 462–64, and of much judicial writing on the subject; see, e. g., Escola v. Coca-Cola Bottling Co., 24 Cal.2d 453, 462, 150 P.2d 436, 440–41 (1944) (Traynor, J., concurring).

2 The concept of strict liability is a various one, but at its core is the notion that one who injures another should be held liable whether or not the injurer was negligent or otherwise at fault.

3 Or, stated otherwise, to maximize the joint value of the railroad's right of way and the farmer's land.

4 The meaning of negligence is explored in Richard A. Posner, A Theory of Negligence, 1 J.Leg.Studies 29 (1972). The example in text assumes that the probability of the damage occurring is one; the assumption is not essential to the analysis. It also assumes that the only possibilities are no crops, or no sparks; this assumption, which is again not essential to the analysis, will be relaxed.

5 If the cost of prevention exceeded the damage cost, prevention would not be the efficient solution. The efficient solution would be to permit the damage to take place.

6 In the first case, the railroad would be liable and would have an incentive to adopt the precaution. In the second case, the railroad would still be liable but it would have no incentive to adopt precautions; it would prefer to pay a judgment cost that by hypothesis would be lower than the cost of the precautions.

7 Suppose the price of a product is $10 and the expected accident cost 10¢; then the total cost to the (risk-neutral) consumer is $10.10. If the producer can reduce the expected accident cost to 5¢—say at a cost of 3¢ to himself—then he can increase the price of the product to $10.05, since the cost to the (risk-neutral) consumer remains the same. Thus his profit per unit is increased by 2¢. (In fact, he will be able to increase his total profits even more by raising price less.) The extra profit will eventually be bid away by competition from producers but that is in the nature of competitive advantages.

8 This is actually a more efficient solution than either negligence or strict liability, since it avoids the problem we noted earlier of the law's economically incorrect definition of contributory negligence.

The economics of products liability is debated at length in Symposium, Products Liability: Economic Analysis and the Law, 38 U.Chi.L.Rev. 1 (1970). See in particular Roland N. McKean, Products Liability: Trends and Implications, id. at 3.

9 In principle, the costs of research should be included in the basic negligence calculus; in practice, we may assume they are not.

10 On the determinants of the choice to litigate rather than to settle and of expenditures on litigation see Richard A. Posner, The Behavior of Administrative Agencies, 1 J. Leg.Studies 305–23 (1972); see also William M. Landes, An Economic Analysis of the Courts, 14 J.Law & Econ. 61 (1971).

11 Not an economic ground. See Richard A. Posner, Book Review, 37 U.Chi.L.Rev. 643 (1970).

12 The farmer may not want to insure; he may be a risk preferrer. A risk preferrer is someone who likes to take chances. He will pay $1 for a lottery ticket although the prize is $1000 and his chances of winning only one in 2000. And he may prefer to accept a one one-thousandth chance of a $1000 loss rather than pay $1 to insure against the loss. He will be especially hostile to the idea of paying $1.10 for that insurance, a more realistic example since insurance involves administrative expenses that consume a part of the premium. Hence, if many farmers are risk preferring and do not want insurance, the benefits of strict liability, as perceived by them, may be slight.

13 This assumes that the producer cannot disclaim liability; the effect of a disclaimer is to shift liability to the consumer.

14 See note 23, infra; Richard A. Posner, supra note 4, at 42–44, 76.

15 Most no-fault auto compensation plans involve (1) compulsory accident insurance and (2) exemption from tort liability.

16 Since it had already paid for the right to maintain the noise level that the device, not without cost to the airline, would enable it to reduce. It might attempt to sell back a portion of the easement to the property owners, but each owner would have an incentive to decline to enter into the transaction in the hope that others would do so; for once the airline purchased the device all the subjacent property owners, those who had not paid the airline along with those who had, would benefit from the reduced level of noise.

17 See William F. Baxter & Lillian R. Altree, supra note 1, at 17–21, 92–113.

18 It is noteworthy that in an earlier article, Professor Baxter recognized the importance of a defense of contributory negligence to strict liability. See William F. Baxter, The SST: From Watts to Harlem in Two Hours, 21 Stan.L.Rev. 1, 53 (1968).

19 Guido Calabresi & Jon T. Hirschoff, supra note 1, at 1060.

20 Id. at 1060, n. 19.

21 See Guido Calabresi, The Costs of Accidents, A Legal and Economic Analysis, pt. IV (1970); Guido Calabresi & Jon T. Hirschoff, supra note 1, at 1075 and n. 74.

22 George P. Fletcher, supra note 1, at 543.

23 For example, assault and battery. How would Professor Fletcher deal with the rule that permits both parties to an illegal combat to obtain damages from the other if he is injured (see Clarence Morris, Morris on Torts 30–31 (1953))? It is a rule of strict liability, but under his view should not be; so far as the reciprocity of the risk (in his terms) is concerned, an illegal combat is just like a mid-air collision. Another of his odd examples is the strict liability of owners of vicious dogs. The common law rule (see id. at 239) is that the dog's owner must have reason to believe that the dog is vicious (the "one-bit" rule), and so understood represents an application of the negligence principle rather than of strict liability.

24 See, e. g., George P. Fletcher, supra note 1, at 564.

25 See id. at 573.

26 See id. at 549, n. 44. The article is not entirely clear on this point. Fletcher points out that sometimes contributory negligence results in the imposition of excessive risks on the defendant (see id. at 549), and therefore creates a situation of reciprocity in his sense of that term. Where, as in many cases, the plaintiff's contributory negligence does not create any risk to the defendant's safety or property, presumably it would not be a defense under his view (see id. at 549, n. 44).

27 See id. at 540–41, 573. His position on this point is not entirely clear due to the obscurity of his discussion of excuses. See, e. g., id. at 553.

28 Id. at 551, n. 51.

29 Richard A. Epstein, supra note 1, at 164–65, quoting Ronald H. Coase, The Problem of Social Cost, 3 J.Law & Econ. 1, 2 (1962).

30 Jeremy Bentham, Theory of Legislation 189–90 (R. Hildreth ed. 1864).

31 See Richard A. Posner, supra note 4, at 74–77. The point is further developed in Richard A. Posner, Economic Analysis of Law, chs. 6, 27 (forthcoming).

32 109 Minn. 456, 124 N.W. 221 (1910).

33 The common law and especially Continental rules governing the legal rights and liabilities of rescuers are discussed in John P. Dawson, *Negotiorum Gestio*: The Altruistic Intermeddler, 74 Harv.L.Rev. 1073 (1961). As he points out, the principal examples in common law of the rescuer's being entitled to compensation from the rescued (in the absence of any contractual or other preexisting relationship between the two) are maritime salvage and the right of physicians to recover fees from people whom they treat under emergency conditions. See id. at 1096–98, 1119 and n. 107; Cotnam v. Wisdom, 83 Ark. 601, 104 S.W. 164 (1907). Both liability for failure to rescue and the right to compensation for rescuing are much greater in Continental jurisprudence. See, e. g., section 330c of the German Penal Code, which makes it a crime to fail to render aid to someone in danger, even at risk of bodily harm to the rescuer.

34 See, e. g., Richard A. Epstein, supra note 1, at 181, 197 and n. 108.

35 Professor Epstein remarks that so vulnerable an individual would in all probability not survive long enough to be done in by the defendant's gesture. But this is not a convincing point. He must be done in by someone or something, even if it is only a nurse in the hospital where he is born, who would presumably be liable under Epstein's view. Moreover, susceptibility to injury from fright might be the result of an illness or accident at any age. I am also unpersuaded by his suggestion that there might be a defense, consistent with his general approach, in such a case. Id. at 172–73, n. 65. The general impression that Epstein creates in the mind of this reader is that, while he will not admit explicit considerations of cost in his analysis, he is hopeful that his noneconomic approach will not do serious economic damage.

16: PRODUCTS LIABILITY: IMPLICATIONS OF SOME CHANGING PROPERTY RIGHTS *

ROLAND N. McKEAN

The use of products, from tractors to glass shower doors, often results in accidents and damages, sometimes to the purchaser and sometimes to bystanders. Who should be liable for these costs has for many years been a subject of much concern. Politicians and officials have become increasingly aroused about the safety of items ranging from Corvairs to "shamburgers," leading in part to complaints about liability assignment (though mainly to advocacy of product specifications). In the legal profession, this subject of who is or should be liable has been labeled "products liability" and has caused concern, particularly because of its connection to individuals' notions of equity or fairness. In economics, since accidental damages are a special case of externalities, the subject is also of great concern, especially because of the connection between externalities—those interdependencies that are not mutually, voluntarily accepted—and economic efficiency.

The existence of any externality is related to the rules for and costs of assigning and exchanging property rights. The basic things that we exchange are not products' physical features as such but rather packages of rights to do things with those features. *If* all rights were clearly defined and assigned, *if* there were zero transaction costs, and *if* people agreed to abide by the results of voluntary exchange, there would be no

84 Quarterly Journal of Economics (1970), p. 611.

externalities.   Accidental damage is no exception.   Wherever it results
in an externality, this is related to the rules for and costs of assigning
and exchanging rights.   In this instance, one of the principal rights involved [1] is the right not to be liable for damages or, to look at the other
side of the coin, the obligation to pay for damages.   As is the case with
other rights, this one exists as some sort of expectation, not as a certainty.

The right to avoid liability, like the right to resell one's land, is a
feature of an asset that has value.   Alternative right assignments may
have different impacts on equity (as conceived of by each individual) and,
since there are transaction costs, different impacts on production processes and costs, insurance carried, the allocation of resources among uses,
and the options open to consumers.   In this article I shall discuss some of
those impacts of different right assignments pertaining to liability for
damage.   The coverage will not include "safety legislation," e. g., requiring that all cars be equipped with safety belts.   Such legislation is a big
topic in itself, and while requiring certain behavior affects right-assign-
ment, the discussion here will be confined to requiring right-reassign-
ments that affect behavior.   First, however, I shall sketch out some of
the background concerning products liability.

I.   Developments Concerning Products Liability

After the development of industrial societies, one of the most important
conditions for the existence of products liability was that privity, or a direct
contractual relationship, had to exist.[2]   In other words, a manufacturer
might be liable to the wholesaler, the wholesaler to the retailer, and the
retailer to his customer, but the manufacturer was not liable to remote
customers or to third parties because he had no contractual relationship
with them.   For the most part this requirement of privity was upheld
in England and the United States throughout the nineteenth century.
In one famous case, *Winterbottom v. Wright* (1842), in which a coach
with a defective wheel had overturned, Lord Abinger said: "There is no
privity of contract between these parties; and if the plaintiff can sue,
every passenger, or even any person passing along the road, who was
injured by the upsetting of the coach, might bring a similar action.   Unless we confine the operation of such contracts as this to the parties who
entered into them, the most absurd and outrageous consequences, to which
I can see no limit, would ensue." [3]

A.   Evolution of Sales Law

In connection with certain products and activities, quite a few exceptions
to the privity rule developed, especially late in the nineteenth and early

in the twentieth centuries.[4]   There is a long history of special concern about foods and about "inherently or imminently dangerous" or "ultra-hazardous" products, e. g., explosives.   In developing special rules for these categories, the courts may have been groping for changes in rights that would yield more gain than cost, as gauged by the judges.[5]   Concern about liability for injuries from these products rose whenever people became more impressed with the hazards.   For instance, concern about foods soared after the publication of Upton Sinclair's work.[6]

The big breakthrough, however, was the decision in the famous case of the collapsing automobile, *MacPherson v. Buick Motor Company*.[7] This 1916 decision held the manufacturer liable, in the absence of privity, for injuries resulting from the use of a product, whether or not inherently dangerous, if there is evidence of "negligence" in the manufacture or assembly of the product.   Afterward, this position was adopted in case after case and state after state.   The ruling was applied, not just to special categories, such as food, beverages, firearms, and explosives, but to such varied items as a sanitary napkin,[8] an inflammable celluloid comb,[9] and a defective bar stool.[10]   The product usually had to pose significant danger to life and limb, and the courts sometimes refused to make awards for minor hazards, such as a defective high heel or coffee-can key.[11]   Nonetheless, there was unquestionably a shift toward making producers liable in a wider range of circumstances.

Other extensions of producers' liability were brought about by means of special ad hoc devices.   It is often difficult to prove negligence on the part of a manufacturer, but in some instances the courts applied the doctrine of "res ipsa loquitur": let the matter speak for itself.   If a sealed bottle of soft drink was found to contain a cockroach, it seemed highly unlikely that anyone, after the bottling was done, had opened the container and inserted the insect.   The courts were prepared to assume that the production process did involve negligence.   Similarly, if a sealed unit in a machine caused damage, the courts often concluded that the matter spoke for itself.   Another device for getting around the privity requirement was to regard the wife as an agent for her husband so that, even if he has no direct contractual relationship with the seller, the latter may be liable if the husband suffers injuries while using the product.

These devices are often criticized as being tortured or "artificial" attempts to move toward strict producer liability, but with uncertainty one might without being illogical judge these rules to be better than the alternatives.   The courts were uneasy about proceeding to strict liability lest it yield more harm than good, yet they felt that these small steps with comparatively unambiguous cut-off points would yield more good than harm.   Similarly one might be uneasy about permitting automobiles to proceed in the face of a red traffic light whenever drivers deem it safe, yet feel confident that allowing *right* turns on a red light would yield more good than harm.

Express warranty and especially implied warranty have been extended by recent interpretations of the law, further reflecting the shift toward "let the seller beware."   There may now be an implied warranty of fitness for a particular purpose as distinct from the item's ordinary purpose. For this warranty to hold, the seller must have reason to know that purpose, but it is not necessary for the buyer to have informed the seller; the buyer must be relying on the seller's judgment in selecting *or furnishing* the goods (formerly the seller was liable only if he selected the goods); and purchase by trade name no longer means that the seller's judgment is not being relied upon. The course of dealing and trade usage may generate implied warranties, e. g., may give the seller "reason to know" the particular purpose to which goods are put in a particular locality.[12] Advertising directly to consumers can generate warranties to them. In *Baxter v. Ford Motor Co.*, the manufacturer was held to be liable because a windshield advertised as shatterproof did in fact shatter when struck by a stone.[13]

B.   Shifts toward Strict Liability under Tort

Strict liability under tort can be roughly defined as liability simply because a wrong was done, not because a contract was unfulfilled. No attribution of negligence is necessary (though the presence of a "defect," which may simply substitute another word for negligence, is necessary), and no contract need be involved. To many observers it seems that products liability has been evolving rapidly toward strict liability under tort. The following are typical comments: "With privity on the wane, *caveat venditor* will be the rule, not *caveat emptor*; the time has come to hold a requiem for this . . . anachronism."[14] "It seems safe to predict that strict liability for products will soon be the established law in this country." [15]

A crucial case was that of *Henningsen v. Bloomfield Motors, Inc.* in 1960.[16] Mrs. Henningsen suffered injuries when the car suddenly turned right and ran into a wall, presumably due to a defective steering gear. Without any evidence of negligence, the court held Chrysler as well as the dealer liable, saying: "an implied warranty that it [the product] is reasonably suitable for use as such accompanies it into the hands of the ultimate purchaser. Absence of agency . . . is immaterial." [17] There had been earlier and unsuccessful attempts to put automobiles under the heading of "deadly and dangerous instrumentalities" or to apply the rules for "ferocious animals" to the "devil wagon," [18] but the Henningsen case appeared to eliminate the requirements for privity or negligence with respect to *all* products, and to cast doubt on the effectiveness of disclaimers. Within a few years the Henningsen precedent was applied to a wide variety of products, including a glass door, shotgun, dental chair, and hula skirt. Liability to bystanders, and other extensions of manufacturer liability, have been established more recently.[19]

Even strict tort liability, however, would still require that there be a defect in the product. The issues about proof of injury and defect, abnormal use (a manufacturer will not be held liable simply because he produces a hammer with which someone manages to hit his head), intervening conduct, and knowledge of the defect will still exist and relieve the producer of liability in many circumstances.[20] Thus the full development of strict liability under tort would simply go further to raise the probability that the producer would be held liable. It would reassign certain property rights in a probabilistic sense.

C.   Moves toward Other Liability Assignments

Some writers appear to have in mind more than strict tort liability, however, for they urge or foresee more comprehensive compensation of victims than would occur under strict liability. One writer explicitly supports eliminating the requirement of a defect.[21] For some situations, compulsory accident insurance has been urged, assigning the liability to a large group of potential victims without regard to fault. Automobile accidents especially—with the high court costs and long delays, the difficulties of determining fault, and the large financial consequences—have given rise to proposals such as the Keeton-O'Connell plan.[22] Debate about these liability assignments may lead in turn to serious consideration of social accident insurance under which the taxpayers would be liable.

II.   Implications of Alternative Assignments of Liability

I shall attempt, not to identify optimal policies, but simply to discuss some of the consequences of alternative products-liability arrangements.[23] (Indeed, while each individual can identify the policies *he* prefers, there is no criterion of optimality that *all* members of a group are compelled by logic to accept.) These consequences will be mainly certain costs generated by the alternative arrangements—costs in terms of the price tags that are implicit in a predominantly voluntary exchange system and that would help direct one toward Pareto-optimal policies. Such costs may not be relevant from the standpoint of every individual, but I believe that the value judgments of many persons would cause these costs to be pertinent to their choosing among products-liability arrangements.

Let us examine a spectrum of possibilities from customer liability without fault to taxpayer liability without fault.

A. Caveat Emptor

As a starter, what would be the consequences of complete *caveat emptor*—of having customers watch out for themselves and bear the losses that occur during the use of a product? As Coase has shown,[24] that arrangement would lead to economic efficiency—to the production of safety features, caution in using products, and so on, by those parties having a comparative advantage in accident prevention—*if* there were zero transaction costs, and *if* people agreed to accept the results of voluntary exchanges. Purchasers of products would hire producers to include safety features and hire themselves to be careful as long as these actions paid. What about third parties who were injured? If owners of products were liable, they would modify their choices of products and hire bystanders to be careful as long as the gains outweighed the costs. Bargaining would lead to economic efficiency in producing safety features, warnings, instructions to users, instructions to bystanders, caution in using products, caution in standing or walking nearby, and so on. (Or, another possible arrangement would be to make the third parties liable for injuries to themselves. In this case, the third parties could costlessly get together and pay as much as it would be worth to them to have safer products or more cautious use of them.)

Transaction costs, it might be noted, include the costs of negotiation, contracting, and enforcement, which therefore include the costs of acquiring information about the features of products and about contract violations. If we are to consider products-liability issues in a world of zero transaction costs, however (and in my view it is useful to *start out* that way), that world cannot mean zero information costs in the sense of complete certainty about everything; for in those circumstances there would be no defects, carelessness, chance, accidents, or questions of liability.[25]

In actuality, of course, there are heavy transaction costs. Sometimes one may judge that alternative assignments of rights would bring roughly equivalent results, but often transaction costs vary markedly with different right assignments.[26] With customer liability, however, note that *certain* transaction costs are in fact *comparatively* low. The costs of hiring producers to make safer products and issue warnings and instructions are relatively low, for the market is a mechanism through which customers are able to bid for safer products, instructions, and so on. If one is injured, financially or physically, by defective merchandise, he feels after the event that he has been at the mercy of producers and completely without influence on the design of products. (Moreover, *caveat emptor* may strike one as being inequitable—but for the present let us confine our attention to costs and economic efficiency.)   Nonetheless, as disappointments occur to thousands of customers, they turn to rival products or producers—unless upon reflection they prefer the lower price plus that risk to higher prices with reduced risks; and producers find it profitable to make a larger percentage of their products relatively safe, to issue instructions and warnings, to carry liability insurance, and to have broader warranties or more generous returned-goods policies.   Hence, while disappointments and injuries never cease, users are able in the aggregate to register their preferences by turning to competitors and bidding more for the goods that they prefer.

Transaction costs become higher if they deal with producers whose profits are regulated or who are sheltered from entry (even through the purchase of existing enterprises), since such producers will be less responsive to consumers' willingness to pay.   Such costs will be still higher if one buys from a government agency and tries to hire this producer to offer a safer or otherwise modified product.   If a publicly owned highway or reservoir strikes you as being dangerous, the threat of your turning to competitors will not influence the design of the output.   Hiring these producers to alter their products takes the comparatively expensive form of organizing pressure groups.

Customer liability would hold another kind of transaction cost in check: the cost of information about what degree of product safety in particular uses is economical.   The buyer is in a better position than anyone else to know the exact use to which he plans to put a product and what alternative qualities, or degrees of safety, in the product would mean to his costs and gains.   The customer, if he is liable, has an extra incentive to acquire and make appropriate use of information.   To get the information, he must deal, not with thousands of individuals, but with the seller and a few other identifiable persons.   Now the result will *not* be zero information cost or complete information or zero mistakes.   All that is being asserted is that customer liability tends to keep *part* of the information costs relatively low.

On the other hand, *caveat emptor* may keep other types of information cost comparatively high.   The manufacturers do know more than anyone else about the nature of their products, and unless they probe and offer consumers numerous alternative amounts of information, customers may never know how much information they would be willing to pay for.   This could be especially serious with enterprises that do not count heavily on repeat business and customer goodwill.   With any arrangement, many resources will go into acquiring and providing information about products.   At present, buyers utilize consumer reports, producer brochures, telephone enquiries, conversations with friends and salesmen, advertisements that convey information, engineers' and other experts' services, and directories and the Yellow Pages to help them find out where to make enquiries. But useful information about products is very costly. How difficult it is to inspect many modern products; how little one discovers about color TV sets or psychiatric treatment or new plumbing fixtures even after investigation. With high costs, potential buyers settle for relatively little information and either forego exchanges that might be mutually advantageous or accept risks that would be rejected—*if* information costs were lower. One may judge that overall costs—information, transaction, foregone-exchange, and accident costs—could be reduced by directing government,[27] or inducing producers, to provide additional information.

The amount of information that it is economical to generate and the costs of generating information will be different for different products. For example, producers surely provide all the information that customers are willing to pay for in the case of simple familiar products like ordinary tools and supplies. When one considers new, changing, or complex products like new drugs or power tools, however, it may take years of transactions before customers can determine what kind of extra information can be offered and how much various amounts will cost. For complex secondhand items, great effort to gather information will still leave enormous uncertainty. Information about items that one does not buy frequently— e. g., swimming pools, gas furnaces, specialized medical-care equipment, food at unknown restaurants, a house in an unfamiliar city—is also comparatively expensive per unit of the product purchased. (In addition, the consequences of a bad outcome or of nonoptimal calculations by consumers may be particularly serious for certain products, which may bring forth value judgments that consumers should be protected against themselves.) Thus different treatment, e. g., liability assignments, for different product categories (such as "ultrahazardous" or "highly complex" products) may make sense even though it might be foolish in some ideal world with zero transaction costs.

Caveat emptor would also keep another transaction cost relatively low—that of hiring the users to be careful in employing the product. For the user is most frequently the buyer of the product or an acquaintance or a member of his family. Thus if he is liable for losses, he has to obtain the cooperation, not of thousands of strangers, but of himself and a few individuals with whom he has direct personal contact, in seeing that an appropriate degree of care is exercised. This does not mean that he will be as careful as it is humanly possible to be; it merely means that he will choose by weighing the costs of extra care, such as loss of time, against the gains, such as the reduced risk of suffering uncompensated losses or injuries.

With customer liability it is costly—as it would also be with either victim or producer liability—for bystanders to register their bids. It would be very expensive for potential third-party victims to acquire information about the myriad contingencies, and then to get together and bid for safer products, better instructions, more warnings, greater care by the user, and so on. Again, one may judge that total costs could be reduced by reassigning rights so as to elicit safer products, more warnings, and more careful use from the standpoint of bystanders. (And, with regard to fairness, rather than efficiency, *most* people would probably say that product users or producers, or perhaps taxpayers, should compensate injured bystanders.)

Incidentally, when third-party effects or any externalities are large and one sees no way of reducing the costs of voluntary negotiations, one may judge that the use of compulsion would cut total costs. When people are denied options, e. g., when producers are forbidden to produce items that do not have specified safety features, there is no objective evidence about the magnitude of certain costs and gains, since there is no way to see how much people would be willing to pay for options denied or items they are forced to take. Nonetheless, one must sometimes make judgments about these costs and gains. For instance, I understand that in the early days of television, each receiving set emitted signals that interfered with the reception of other sets in the vicinity. Bargaining among set owners to hire each other to install shielding or to watch television only at designated times would have been extremely expensive. The government ordered producers to install shielding on all future sets, thus compelling even isolated set owners to buy this extra feature. Most of us would probably agree in this instance that this action was preferable to doing nothing, i. e., we would judge that the gains exceeded the costs.

On balance, customer liability probably does bring relatively low transaction costs for many product categories. Wherever this is so, bargaining under customer liability would effect additional Pareto-optimal exchanges in comparison with other liability assignments. There are nonetheless several major reasons that might make one oppose *caveat emptor*. (1) One might believe that he could negotiate through the political process for liability assignments that would yield more equitable [28] outcomes, yet that high negotiation costs preclude making tax-subsidy arrangements that would yield an equally desirable wealth distribution *and* economic efficiency. (2) One might attach value to certain political procedures or arrangements per se (e. g., for ideological reasons) and simply not care much about costs that are relevant to Pareto-optimal steps. (3) One might attach value to preventing people from taking the risks they would voluntarily choose to take. (4) One might still believe that customer liability leads to less economic efficiency than other arrangements, since the issue is in doubt once transaction costs are recognized. It is in doubt because we do not know exactly what information, negotiation, and enforcement costs would be with some other assignment of rights (or compulsory product specifications). Since some of these costs will be in doubt, one must in the end make personal judgments in deciding what arrangement he believes would be efficient. One individual, or a majority of individuals, may judge that total costs could be reduced by departing from customer liability.

B.   Producer Liability with Defect

What are the consequences of moving further toward producer liability— of reducing the chances that the purchaser will be held liable and increasing the chances that the producer will face liability? (And this, to repeat, is what seems to have happened.) In my judgment the effects would not have great quantitative significance but would be along the following lines. I would expect more court cases and court costs, since under complete customer liability, the product owner is not compensated, and there is no court determination of the extent of injury, the presence of defects, or the existence of negligence. There would now be higher costs of hiring purchasers to exercise care, for this would now require myriad special contracts with prohibitive enforcement costs, and those higher transaction costs would result in the existence of more externalities; i. e., accident rates would rise.[29] Producers would turn increasingly to liability insurance, and since it would not be economical to adjust the premiums continuously or precisely, producers might, up to certain thresholds, find it efficient to neglect safety features,[30] diluting the shift toward safer products that is noted below.

With the customer facing a lower probability of being liable, relatively hazardous designs would be less unattractive to him, and the demand curve for such products would rise relative to the demand curve for comparatively safe products. With the producer facing a higher probability of being liable and with his either carrying liability insurance or paying damages, relatively hazardous designs would be more costly, and the supply curve for such products would decrease. On the basis of this shift in liability assignment by itself, there is no presumption that the quantity of hazardous products sold would change, and while the consumer would pay a higher price to the producer, he would simply be forced to buy insurance from the producer instead of having the option of insuring himself. The only thing that would happen to the consumer's position is that he would be denied the opportunity of taking the risk. Since that option would be preferred by some consumers, especially by the poor, this would mean in effect a rise in the price of hazardous products relative to the price of "safe" products, resulting in the end in some shift toward safer products and working to the detriment of the poor.

The shift in liability assignment would decrease efficiency, however, if there was a net increase in transaction costs. (As noted above, producer liability would surely raise the costs of hiring users to be careful and raise some, though not all, information costs.)   If this happened, the supply curve would decrease still further, resulting in higher prices for hazardous relative to safer products and in a net shift from hazardous to safer products.

C.   Producer Liability without Defect

Let us turn now to a rather extreme arrangement that has been mentioned in recent years—producer liability *without fault or defect*. The manufacturer would simply be held liable for all injuries occurring with the use of his product, regardless of circumstances. As in the other cases, if there were zero transaction costs, producers could hire purchasers to be careful, third parties could hire users to be careful and producers to issue safer products, and purchasers could hire manufacturers to provide various safety features. Each would take these actions as long as the extra gain exceeded the extra cost, and resource use would end up at an efficient point. With transaction costs, however, manufacturer liability without fault or defect would alter resource allocation, and, unless the transactions costs could be measured, it would be uncertain which liability assignment would lead to an efficient point.

I conjecture that costs would be affected in the following ways and that the changes would be important quantitatively. The cost of hiring thousands of purchasers or third parties to exercise care would be enormous, and therefore these persons would now find it relatively inexpensive to be careless. Accident rates would rise. Insurance premiums would become high except on relatively safe products, increasing the net price of hazardous products relative to the price of safe products. As in the preceding case, there would be a shift away from the comparatively hazardous product lines toward the safer products. The net impact on accident costs is not clear, but total costs would rise, because accident prevention would not be produced by those having a comparative advantage in doing so. Court costs per case would decline in comparison with the fault system, but the number of claims would rise; and, unlike the case of *caveat emptor*, disputes and court costs would not be nil, because even if fault did not have to be established, the fact and extent of injury would have to be determined. (Otherwise, claims would be infinitely large.) Consumers would face a narrower range of choice—a significant sacrifice, but one that is impossible to quantify in any generally valid fashion. As far as this particular sacrifice is concerned, poor people would be hardest hit, because their options would now be to buy relatively expensive safe products, or hazardous products plus high producer-insurance costs, or nothing at all.

The higher accident prevention costs would be borne largely by the customers and potential customers in each industry in the form of higher prices and restricted choice (though I would predict legislative intervention in an effort to check the rising costs). Some of the burden might be passed on to customers in other industries, as people shifted their purchases, and input rents might be reshuffled somewhat. Whether or not one regarded these changes in wealth distribution as being equitable would depend upon the precise impacts and upon one's value judgments.

D. Taxpayer Liability

Many persons believe that it would be more equitable to spread the burdens more widely, e. g., to spread the burden of aircraft accidents over input owners in, and customers of, airlines or aircraft manufacturers or both. As far as equity is concerned, however, such redistributions still seem rather arbitrary. Why not put the burden on taxpayers in general?

One way to do this would be to have government compensate people for all injuries without regard to fault. Of course a claim that an injury had occurred would have to be checked; so there would still be this sort of administrative cost. Note, however, that neither purchasers nor producers (nor third parties) would now have to worry about being liable, so that carelessness in design and use of products would become relatively inexpensive to these persons. With the customer not liable, hazardous products would be less unattractive. As the cost of selling unsafe or defective products went down from producers' standpoints, they would expand supplies. Thus both the demand curve and the supply curve of relatively hazardous products would increase, and, without government regulation, there would be a shift toward the use of dangerous products. As the cost of failing to inspect products or of employing products carelessly went down from purchasers' standpoints, they would take more of these actions. If officials or taxpayers thought of hiring these persons to behave differently, ordinary bargaining would be prohibitively expensive.

It is virtually certain that voters and their representatives would find this situation unsatisfactory. Costs would soar too high. Liability insurance, warnings, and disclaimers—in this extreme arrangement and without governmental regulation—would practically disappear. To make taxpayer liability workable, government would have to draw up a network of specifications for products, regulations of their use, and required instructions and warnings. Some "unavoidably unsafe products" might be banned altogether. Producers would inevitably face penalties (a kind of liability) for violating the requirements. Again, consumers would find their choice restricted, this time by law; they would be unable to buy relatively cheap, albeit relatively unsafe, products if they preferred them. Some new kind of penalties for negligence in using products, and perhaps for carelessness by bystanders, would be devised. Administrative and enforcement costs would be high. In the end there would be increased sacrifices in general, and these burdens would be shifted around according to the complex factors that determine tax incidence. One cannot say that social accident insurance would be a "bad" policy, but he can say with confidence that it would not amount to a "free lunch."

In short, as with property right assignments in general, different liability assignments would often bring about significant differences in resource use because of differential transaction costs. It is important to know more about the variation of transaction costs under alternative institutions and about the implications for wealth distribution and resource allocation of different right or liability assignments.

FOOTNOTES

* The author is primarily indebted to the Joint AEA–AALS Committee (American Economic Association and Association of American Law Schools) and through the committee to the Walter E. Meyer Research Institute for financing the study on which the article is based. The author also wishes to thank the Center for Advanced Studies at the University of Virginia, and the Lilly Endowment grant to the University of California at Los Angeles for the purpose of studying property rights, for support of work that contributed to the study. Thanks are due to numerous lawyers and economists who talked to me about the study or took part in a critique of the study, and especially to James M. Buchanan, Guido Calabresi, Harold Demsetz, Robert Dorfman, Grant Gilmore, and Donald L. Martin for their criticisms.

1 Others would include rights to use items for various purposes and with varying degrees of care.

2 Only the high spots will be reviewed here. For more detail see such articles as Dix W. Noel, "Manufacturers of Products—The Drift Toward Strict Liability," *Tennessee Law Review*, 24 (Spring 1957), 963–1018 or William L. Prosser, "The Assault Upon the Citadel (Strict Liability to the Consumer)," *Yale Law Journal*, 69 (June 1960), 1099–1148.

This section will be nonanalytical, but I hope that the background will be of interest to economists. The AEA–AALS Committee arranged for the study in the hope of stimulating interest among economists in the evolving legal framework and its analysis (and to stimulate lawyers to be more concerned with the *economic* implications of that framework).

3 10 M & W 109, 152 Eng.Rep. 402 (Exch.1842).

4 Lester W. Feezer, "Tort Liability of Manufacturers and Vendors," *Minnesota Law Review*, 10 (Dec. 1925), 1–27.

5 Ronald H. Coase, "The Problem of Social Cost," *Journal of Law and Economics*, 3 (Oct. 1960), 19–20.

[6] Upton Sinclair "said later that he had aimed at the public's heart, and by accident hit it in the stomach" (C. C. Regier, "The Struggle for Federal Food and Drugs Legislation." *Law and Contemporary Problems*, 3 (1933), 9, cited by Prosser, op. cit. 1106).

[7] 217 N.Y. 382, 111 N.E. 1050 (1916).

[8] *La Frumento v. Kotex Co.*, 131 Misc. 314, 226 N.Y.Supp. 750 (N.Y.C.City Ct.1928).

[9] *Farley v. Edward E. Tower Co.*, 271 Mass. 230, 171 N.E. 639 (1930).

[10] *Okker v. Chrome Furniture Mfg. Co.*, 26 N.J.Super. 295, 97 A.2d 699 (1953).

[11] *Timpson v. Marshall, Meadows and Stewart, Inc.*, 198 Misc. 1034, 101 N.Y.S.2d 583 (Sup.Ct.1950); *Boyd v. American Can Co.*, 249 App.Div. 644, 291 N.Y.S. 205 (2d Dep't 1936). For a discussion and other citations see Noel. op. cit.

[12] K. Sidney Neuman, "The Uniform Commercial Code and Greater Consumer Protection Under Warranty Law," *Kentucky Law Journal*, 49 (Winter 1960–61), 240–69.

[13] 168 Wash. 456, 12 P.2d 409.

[14] Walter H. E. Jaeger, "Privity of Warranty: Has the Tocsin Sounded?" *Duquesne University Law Review* (1963), 1.

[15] John W. Wade, "Strict Tort Liability of Manufacturers," *Southwestern Law Journal*, 19 (1965), 5–25.

[16] 32 N.J. 358, 161 A.2d 69 (1960). See William L. Prosser, "The Fall of the Citadel (Strict Liability to the Consumer)," *Minnesota Law Review*, 50 (1966), 791–848.

[17] 32 N.J. 384, 161 A.2d 84.

[18] *Lewis v. Amorous*, 3 Ga.App. 50, 55; 59 S.E. 338, 340 (1907).

[19] *Time Magazine*, May 23, 1969, p. 66.

[20] Prosser, "The Fall of the Citadel," *loc. cit.*, 824–48.

[21] Thomas A. Cowan, "Some Policy Bases of Products Liability," *Stanford Law Review*, 17 (July 1965), 1094.

[22] Robert E. Keeton and Jeffrey O'Connell, *Basic Protection for the Traffic Victim* (Boston: Little, Brown, 1965).

[23] See also Walter J. Blum and Harry Kalven, Jr., *Public Law Perspective on a Private Law Problem: Auto Compensation Plans* (Boston: Little, Brown, 1965); Guido Calabresi, "Does the Fault System Optimally Control Primary Accident Costs?" *Law and Contemporary Problems*, 33 (Summer 1968), 429–63; and Oliver E. Williamson, Douglas G. Olson, and August Ralston, "Externalities, Insurance, and Disability Analysis," *Economica*, 34 (Aug. 1967), 235–53 for other pertinent analyses.

[24] Coase, op. cit.

[25] Another condition for applying the Coase theorem, according to some, is that there be perfect competition, which may seem inconsistent with the existence of products-liability issues (since they often involve brand names, differentiated products, and warranties on such products). In the zero-transaction-cost case, however, monopolists would be hired by consumers to act like competitors. Also, homogeneity of products *to customers* does not necessarily imply that retailers, wholesalers, and manufacturers of particular items cannot be identified. In any event, one can discuss the implications of right assignments for costs and Pareto-optimal *changes* without assuming conditions that would lead to overall Pareto-optimality; "second-best" complications raise doubts, but they raise the same doubts about *any* partial equilibrium analysis.

[26] For example, if one knew that group A would nearly always buy certain rights from group B, he could reduce transaction costs by assigning these rights to group A in the first place (see Harold Demsetz, "Some Aspects of Property Rights," *Journal of Law and Economics*, 9 (Oct. 1966), 66).

27 It should be remembered, however, that governments are often inefficient providers of useful information: the incentives of those who write government pamphlets will not reflect a premium placed on gaining customers' goodwill.

28 I. e., distributional impacts that one prefers.

29 Some people argue that removing liability from users, thus reducing the monetary cost of their having accidents, would not induce those persons to have additional painful and perhaps fatal accidents. To be sure, if more carelessness meant a 100 per cent probability of having a serious accident, prospective pain would be deterrent enough, but what more carelessness really means is ordinarily a *modest* increase in the probability of having *some* sort of accident. We trade such increased chances of having an accident for a saving of money or time every day. If carelessness is made to cost less, more will be taken. (Admittedly, the costs that people associate with extremely low risks are unclear. For instance, they may treat a trivial chance, and a still lower chance, of a large loss as being equivalent. There is all the more reason, it seems to me, to expect people to respond to clearly perceived costs in money or time.)

30 Williamson, Olson, and Ralston, op. cit.

17: EDITED TRANSCRIPT OF AALS-AEA CONFERENCE ON PRODUCTS LIABILITY

HENRY G. MANNE, editor*

Roland McKean.[1] Professor Buchanan's comments on the defense of *caveat emptor* posed few issues with which I would disagree. Using different terminology, I did make the central point that *caveat emptor* as the basis for products liability does at least lower certain costs in connection with certain product categories. That does not mean that there is a clear-cut case that any logical man must accept for approving *caveat emptor*. It just means that there are certain consequences of having that arrangement that can logically be agreed upon.

Professor Calabresi perceptively emphasized categories of products as the correct approach to a fuller discussion of products liability. I did say that for some products one might prefer *caveat emptor* while for other products one might prefer government intervention or producer liability. But I did neglect the analysis of particular product categories, aside from choosing specific examples from different product categories to illustrate different points. This is a direction in which one could profitably move. For particular kinds of product categories what would the costs be of having different liability assignments, different arrangements? Calabresi has made some progress in that direction, and my hunch is that we can profitably go still further and look at the categories in greater detail.

A minor matter of disagreement between Calabresi and myself might occur in connection with this idea of trading fairness for efficiency. I think of myself as occasionally making a trade-off of what I consider a fair

University of Chicago Law Review, Vol. 38, no. 1, 1970, p. 117.

or equitable arrangement for a bit of something else—greater efficiency or some other objective. If there were really and truly zero transaction costs, we would not have to make that trade-off. But since there are not zero costs, I think sometimes one is forced to ask himself would he prefer an arrangement which corresponds more closely to what he would regard as equitable, or would he prefer another arrangement which gives up a little equity for some other objective. Now Professor Calabresi prefers to look at this in a different way, but it seemed to me that we were not really in substantial disagreement about this. The disagreement was a minor one about the terminology or a particular way of looking at the matter and not about the substance.

One of the critics apparently concluded that I felt that *caveat emptor* was always the best arrangement. I do not really believe that, at least with respect to all product categories. I expect the idea emerged because the bulk of my analysis was devoted to "let-the-buyer-beware," and I may have sounded as though I really thought that was the best arrangement. I meant, however, to convey that one can prefer any one of these arrangements without being illogical. We just do not have any criterion dictating what is the best arrangement from some group standpoint.

There seemed to be some doubt whether, if we do not have any criterion for what is good, the matter need be discussed at all. Actually, however, all any science can do is to throw a little more information in the pot to help each of us determine his preference. I do not believe that is useless even though one cannot say precisely what is the optimal policy from everyone's standpoint.

I was a bit shaken to realize that Professor Dorfman thought I was applying the Coase theorem and leaving it at that. He seemed to be regarding me as saying, in accord with the Coase theorem, that the liability assignment really does not make any difference in the real world. This may have resulted because the bulk of the discussion was devoted to an elaboration of notions of comparative advantage in the zero transaction costs case. I regard the Coase theorem as an important point of departure from which to go forward into the real world and ask which arrangement most reduces total costs in comparison with other arrangements for a particular product category. I did not devote as much space as I might have to the analysis of these pertinent issues.

Professor Gilmore felt that I was remiss in saying there had not already been an important revolution in products liability developments. Certainly there has been a revolution in a legal sense, and most people would say that the changes within the last fifty years have been great compared to the changes in the previous century or so. But from the standpoint of the economic implications of the alternative arrangements, changes so far strike me as having been fairly modest, particularly in comparison with some of the proposals that are being discussed, such as really strict liability, perhaps with no requirement of a defect, or a more extreme arrangement, social insurance for all accident victims. These, I think, would have quite important economic implications, while the changes so far in the direction of producer liability do not strike me as having had crucial economic implications.

I think it may have been Professor Gilmore too who felt that since the Coase theorem was only taken as a point of departure which did not necessarily give real world implications, that maybe it was of little relevance. I do not agree. I think that this theorem, even though it is far from having assumptions that correspond to the real world, is terribly important in thinking about liability or property rights assignments and things of that sort. But, I emphasize again, it is only a point of departure.

The real disagreements will regard the criterion. Some people will say economic efficiency is the most important. Others would rather put more emphasis on equity, even if they have to sacrifice a good deal of efficiency. Some will simply have a wish to interfere with other people's choices, while others find it intolerable to tell somebody else what is good for him.

James Buchanan.[2] In one sense I am in a fair degree of agreement not only with McKean but with Dorfman and Calabresi, if you properly delineate the issues. My paper really takes off from one aspect of the general problem that McKean mentioned in his basic monograph but did not develop fully. And, I think, Professor Dorfman largely assumes away the issues that I discuss. He in a sense assumes away the possibility of putting liability on the producers, if in fact the producer had no fault, whereas I emphasize the inherent possibility of the pure accident as an aspect of the product. And, I am not in disagreement essentially with Professor Calabresi either, since he too assumes away the problem I was discussing. He discusses the most effective cost-reducing assignment of liability on the presumption that the technology of the product, or, I should say, the quality of the product, is fixed. Only if you define a fixed product quality, in a world where transaction costs exist, does it seem to me that Calabresi's problem arises. Then I think I would agree that we should search for the cost-minimizing way of assigning the liability. I was emphasizing that the assignment of liability may in fact itself affect the quality of the product. So in a sense I do not disagree with him, but the problem that I discussed was somewhat different from his.

I think I do disagree fundamentally with Professor Gilmore. He suggests that law is like language, and therefore we cannot do anything about it. I simply would refuse, in part on faith, to accept this world. I don't like to think the world is hopeless. Now I am going to be very interested to see what the lawyers around here today have to say about this approach. I would not be happy if I thought we were all wasting our time.

There are two aspects of this problem that have not been fully distinguished. One is the degree of riskiness—or flip it over and call it safety—the consumer is to be allowed to bear. And, second, once you agree on that, is the question of how to assign liability. These are two separate problems.

I was trying to examine the effects in these terms of the shift toward more and more liability being placed on the producers, which McKean instanced as being part of our experience. This implies that consumers or buyers are being constrained to purchase products which have inherently less riskiness than would have been true under *caveat emptor*. I tried to argue that if you ignore third party effects and, temporarily, information problems, this result can be condemned on both equity and efficiency grounds. There would be no conflict between equity and efficiency because the people who suffer in this case are the poor. We condemn this on both equity and efficiency grounds, so the only justification for departure from *caveat emptor* then is that there may be third party effects.

You can argue a general shift in this direction if you argue that products are more and more exerting third party effects. But if we focus on third party effects and examine each product as a separate category, what does this do to the law? Law by its nature has some generality in it, and if you start talking about particular products and product subcategories, maybe you get into Professor Gilmore's world after all. That does worry me.

Products by and large are getting more complicated. The problem confronting the buyer in choosing amongst competing products is getting more difficult. But this does not in itself justify a departure from *caveat emptor*. Because of this information problem you can perhaps justify a larger public role in information supply. I have not really developed this fully, but it does seem to me that there is what some economists call a public good aspect to information. It seems to me this might be discharged directly through information supply rather than by trying to accomplish the same thing very crudely and indirectly by a shift toward producer liability.

Guido Calabresi.[3] I think that Professor Buchanan's formulation has a basic error in it. He talks about how much risk consumers should be allowed to bear. And, he says, if we have *caveat venditor*, producer liability, then consumers cannot choose to pay less and take risks. My problem is one of symmetry. If we have *caveat emptor*, consumer liability, then the poor producer who wishes to take a risk of a product which causes injury, because he likes to take risks, is deprived of that opportunity. In the theoretical model that Professor Buchanan poses of a large number of consumers, there may also be a large number of producers, and there is no particular reason to assume that one of these risk-taking groups is more important than the other. None of this would matter, of course, if we had no transaction costs. We need not keep repeating that; in addition, it would not matter too much if we had some transaction costs if we allowed what are called exculpatory or indemnificatory agreements. That is, it is not the decision about whom we put the liability on in the first place that diminishes choice in Buchanan's model. The problem of diminution of choice arises only if we forbid transactions to shift the initial burden. But in the first instance, one is as good as the other for this purpose.

The difficulties arise since transaction costs may make exculpatory clauses too difficult to establish. The moment we come to this point we have to decide who is going to be liable. Whose risk-taking do we want to maximize? Do we want to give more chance to risky producers or more chance to risky consumers? That is the kind of empirical question about which I think Professor McKean quite properly says there would be disagreement. It all depends on how you look at it, on what you think is important.

Beyond this, often the law not only places initial liability on the producer but also bars exculpatory clauses. Then we have in effect decided that we do not want consumers to take risks. When we do this, we usually do it because we think that we have problems of information costs. I think we might profitably spend some time on why it is that as we have moved from the world of one man trading face to face with another man, where we certainly did not want to bar any exculpatory clauses, to the world of today, we tend to bar more of these. That is, I think, the crucial issue. There is nothing in theory about either consumer liability or producer liability which increases economic efficiency. The two are as a theoretical matter completely equivalent.

As you start bringing in practical matters, differences begin to appear. It is there that the nuances of Professor McKean's and my paper may be different. I tend to emphasize more those factors which suggest the importance of the choices on the part of producers. None of this can be proven in any economic sense. I suppose we could get more empirical data than we have, but I suggest that as lawyers we do not have to wait for proof because we have to make a decision between the two. Professor Gilmore's paper suggests that the choices are being made politically, and the choice is being made precisely in the direction Gilmore suggests.

In addition, Professor McKean suggests that every case of collective decision-making is one of wanting to tell someone else how to behave because we know better. I would suggest that there are times when we make collective decisions on grounds that are really akin to the economic efficiency argument. That is the situation where, because of transaction costs, it is cheaper to do something by a collective decision. We know that this will destroy some choice, but we make the empirical judgment that more important choices are maintained. In effect that is analogous to what we do, given transaction costs, when we decide on either producer or consumer liability.

A more direct case occurs when we bar people from going through a red light. It is very hard to put the cost of running through red lights to them at that point. We cannot do it. So what we do is to recognize that some people might prefer to run the red light if given that choice. But they are so few that by forbidding it we come nearer to what we think would happen if we were able without cost to give everybody his choice. I think there is a whole series of collective decisions whose justification is not that "I know better than you" but that we come closer to what would happen in the world of no transaction costs by making this collective decision than by not making the collective decision.

Robert Dorfman.[4] The central issue of the whole discussion goes in part to the way that economists on the one hand and lawyers on the other hand seem to look at the problem. We are faced with the difficulty that economics is like the law of gravity in this sense—it works best in a vacuum. The law of gravity works just fine in dealing with objects in orbit way out there. It is not helpful at all in predicting more terrestrial projectories. The problem both for ballistics experts and for economists is that we really are not concerned with problems in a vacuum.

A great deal of economic policy in law and elsewhere is designed for no other purpose than to correct the various imperfections that are experienced in actual markets—transaction costs, information costs, and various other kinds of frictions—many of them quite technical. If you take one of these policies and examine it in the light of a perfect economy, in a vacuum, with no information costs or transaction costs, it will usually turn out that that policy will do no good and very likely some harm. Then no one, not even a non-economist, would recommend those policies. But the policies are actually designed to overcome the windage and the frictions and complications that make our world different from the abstract world in which economic theory works most effectively. So the split in our camp is a difference in judgment as to how far we think the inspection of perfect markets can take you in dealing with our specific issue.

Grant Gilmore.[5] I find the economic analysis in the papers not only fascinating but extremely valuable. However, as a lawyer, I would inject a precautionary note against any belief that theoretical understanding of so complex a phenomenon can be a guide for action. We may feel that if we can develop a theory which everybody believes to be correct and if the theory tests out empirically, then we lawyers should draft a statute reflecting the conclusions arrived at or at least formulate a statement to guide judges so that they could arrive at better decisions. But I doubt strongly and instinctively—and that is the part of my paper which so saddens Professor Buchanan—that there really is any carryover, even from the most correct understanding of what transpires in the real world, to what ought to be done about it as a matter of law reform. As Professor Calabresi remarked, the process of law reform or law change is essentially political not technological.

The principal point I tried to suggest in my comments on Professor McKean's paper was that the developments that appear to have been going on in this isolated field of products liability have been part of a much larger phenomenon with the same reversal of risks between active and passive parties. It has occurred across the whole spectrum of our law of civil obligations. It has been going on over a long period of time and is essentially a political process.

I assume that the economists are on the whole opposed to this development. Let us further assume that they can be proved to be correct, not only in the other world of the Coase theorem but in the real world. What follows? Suppose it was a statute implementing the correct conclusions which the economists have drawn with respect to products liability. That would move developments in this area in the opposite direction from the course which instinctively has been followed in all other areas of obligation over the last fifty to seventy-five years. This would, I think, set up intolerable strains within the legal system. One cannot isolate for action—although one can profitably isolate for analysis and description—a field as narrowly circumscribed as this.

George Stigler.[6] I should like to start by complaining against the anti-theoretical attitude of all of the speakers. They are playing a game, popular in fields like labor-economics, but which I hope would not get a foothold here, of erecting a very formal theoretical model and then saying once you depart from it a couple of inches nothing is left. The theory has enormous real vitality, as I shall try to illustrate. You could take a surface, a uniform space, and distribute resources and preferences over it, and assume (1) zero transportation costs and (2) any assignment of the costs of adjustment of space, that is, of locating yourself as either a buyer or a seller. You quickly get to the result that it does not matter where you assign the latter responsibility in this regime of zero transportation costs. If now you introduce transportation costs it still makes no difference where you assign the responsibility for the movement. Furthermore, the movement will be optimal, no matter what the transportation cost, up to and including complete immobility. There is no sense in which the theory loses its validity as you move away from that extreme.

It is similar in the case of products liability, although everybody says that once we put transaction costs in, we are playing in a different ballpark. But that is not so. There are very strong incentives in the economic system to minimize transaction costs, to make the appropriate amount of transactions and not to embark upon unnecessary ones. I find a failure to recognize this, for example, when Calabresi says, "The existence of large transaction costs are obvious in products liability situations where third parties are injured. The cost of gathering all pedestrians who might be injured by an unsafe car or an unsafe driver and getting together to bribe the car makers is obviously enormous." But one of the clever things the economic system does is not engage in those transactions which are never going to occur. It is not expensive to have one unsafe car identified by having it hit somebody and then have the appropriate redress by legal action. So an immense number of transactions never have to be engaged in. When people say that the theory no longer holds once we have departed from the zero transaction case, they are making what I think is an unfounded conjecture.

Calabresi. Of course, the tendency for the market to minimize transaction costs exists and will minimize the error which our interference, our placing of liability, will make. It will minimize it up to the point where the size of the transaction cost makes further changes not worthwhile. And, in this sense, once we have allocated liability, the market will always work best to minimize our mistake. But, if you have transaction costs, where you put the liability in the first place makes a difference.

Stigler. Why does it make a difference to us? You have not proved that. I take it that the assignment of liability is in itself a transaction-cost-economizing device, and that you could have no rules of liability and let all people who engage in trades establish them.

Calabresi. One could. We evidently choose to have liability rules because we think that this collective decision is cheaper than these transaction costs. That is another example of the red light situation. We do this throughout society. That is what all legal rules in effect are; that is what I think Professor Demsetz's article on property [7] made quite clear. Now, the problem, I suppose, is to decide which assignment of liability, between the two, is going to get us nearer to what would happen if we did not have transaction costs. That does not mean that once we have done this, but imperfectly, we would not have new, advantageous transactions. But it is as wrong to say that it does not matter where we put liability initially.

Harold Demsetz. [8] I would like to join Professor Stigler in defending the Coase theorem, but defending it in a different fashion. I think that the theorem is extremely useful for the purpose for which it was set out and also for this conference. The purpose for which it was originally developed was to dispel some nonsense in economics which had nothing at all to do with transaction costs. It had to do with clearly wrong positions about where you assign liability or whether tax methods were appropriate measures of adjustment. In that context it was an extremely powerful theorem.

But, even if we do remove it from that context and place it in the context of this conference, it seems to me that the Coase theorem serves a very useful purpose. There is a lot of naivete about what happens when the courts decide that one person or another is liable. The Coase theorem makes you reconsider simplistic notions about what the effect of the law is going to be. I think that it is a tribute to the Coase theorem that everybody here is now aware of the fact that, until you start playing this game of transaction costs, the law may not have any effect at all. I do not think that people realized that until the Coase proposition was launched.

W. Page Keeton.[9] We have talked here about costs as if we knew what they were. You have somebody whose eye is put out by an exploding Coca-Cola bottle; that is the typical products liability case. Now assume with me that that represents a thousand dollar liability. But the system that we are talking about here involves probably a charge of two thousand dollars on the manufacturer. In addition to what it repays under the legal standard which sets the thousand dollar figure, it has to clear its own investigation expense, its own counsel fees, and its own system of prevention and all the rest. Meanwhile, the person whose eye was put out receives only $500, since typically in these small claims the contingent fee for the lawyer will run something in the order of 50% or maybe a little less. But the great bulk of this legal business is done not through courts but through the threat of using the courts and through negotiation between the lawyers. I think it is fair to say that long before the courts changed the law the settlement practices had abandoned the search for fault pretty largely and really just looked to see if the man's eye was really out. I think this is what you mean by transaction costs, but I am never sure because this is an information cost. I do not know if you count that as part of the transaction costs or not. I also do not know whether you are calling the cost of keeping the jury away from other useful work a transaction cost or not. To me the label "transaction cost" does not fit that too well. Part of what is troubling me is that I do not have a clear picture of just what these costs are.

Melvin Reder.[10] I think it is fruitful to consider that each producer of a product is producing a joint product. One would be the product itself; the other would be a liability contract. As a concrete example, when

Sears Roebuck sells many of its appliances, it also offers the option of a service contract. In principle one could have a variety of alternative service contracts each of which would, in principle, specify the location and extent of the liability. So Sears or any seller could, in principle, offer a variety of joint products. A customer then selects which among the possible products and combinations he wants. Indeed, legally to assert where the liability must lie is really to limit the possibility of choice among these alternative products. This has disadvantages from the economist's point of view. Once we look at the matter in this way, the information cost really becomes a species of policing costs and the cost of the uncertainty of how the courts are going to interpret the contract, since you cannot specify exactly what a liability contract will mean in every little case.

One could urge the development of consumer advisory services to tell non-specialized buyers what the contract might mean; conceivably the state might even subsidize legal counseling about the contracts. Perhaps the market for information itself would generate it. I have something of Professor Buchanan's feeling, however, that this may be a place where market failure has a greater than usual chance of appearing. Looked at in this way, it seems to me that one could come much closer than otherwise to *caveat emptor*. Give the buyer a variety of options from which he may pick and give him free or cheap technical advice, and let him go to it. Occasionally, where there are externalities, the state may decide that as a condition of having the product put on the market at all, a certain minimum type of guarantee ought to be required.

Robert Braucher.[11] As I think of myself drawing up a contract for Sears Roebuck for warranty liability, the difference between that and taking that same provision and putting it in a state statute seems much smaller than economists seem to think it is.

Reder. What you forget is that there is Montgomery Ward, and if Sears puts in a provision that a substantial set of customers do not want, those customers will shift to the outlet that gives them the kind of quality they do want. Your legislature is not that indulgent of minority tastes.

Keeton. On the contrary, quite often in the process of drafting this type of plan Sears Roebuck puts in a provision and Montgomery Ward is likely to follow suit. When they go to the state legislature they are likely to be there together.

Reder. But somebody may not. Somebody may say, "Look, there is still this minority group over here and it would pay us to cater to them."

Gilmore. The statutes in any case would start off: "Unless otherwise agreed . . . ."

Calabresi. I do not understand why Professor Reder reaches the conclusion that one should start with the rule of *caveat emptor* with warranties sold to the appliance buyer. One could, I take it, just as well start with the rule of *caveat venditor* and have exculpatory clauses. If you accept what Professor Reder says or what follows from Coase, it does not matter where you start, just as long as you allow this free contract. Then the question focuses on this free contract. Professor Reder suggests that there is a substantial role for the government in policing this free contract and in seeing that this free contract actually is based on adequate information for all the parties. But if you once say that the government ought to step in and make this information available or ought to help people, it is at least conceivable that people's wants are more nearly catered to more cheaply if you come in with a government rule that says you shall not do that.

Now this certainly destroys the desires of some people. But what we have to do as lawyers is compare the loss of these people's choice with the costs of setting up the kind of policing device necessary to make Professor Reder's suggestion work.

Richard Musgrave.[12] I would distinguish between two entirely different aspects to note about transaction costs. One is the opportunity cost of putting resources into the negotiation or decision process. I do not think this is terribly interesting. The real problem arises because you have small numbers involved in the bargaining process and this may lead to solutions which are quite different from the competitive ones. In other words, the imperfections result from the bargaining process. You have a kind of bilateral situation, and don't know how it is going to come out. It seems to me that the term "negotiation cost" should be used for the differences between the actual outcome and that which would arise if we had a perfectly competitive market process.

Stigler. Transactions do not have a natural definition. We used to have big fights twenty or thirty years ago over whether you could draw an absolutely sharp line between production costs and selling costs. That literature petered out with the conclusion that you could not make such a distinction except in polar cases. The simplest kind of transaction would be an exchange of one clearly valid currency for another clearly valid currency at a currency exchange. There are almost pure transaction costs in this exchange of titles. There are almost no costs of research for the validity of the product and so forth, and it is all very clean.

But in ordinary consumer product transactions there are services performed, and the transaction does not end the day that the title transfer takes place. There may be continuing latent responsibilities, and there may be continuing contractual relationships influenced by this initial contract. Thus, the contrast between a transaction cost and a non-transaction cost is an impirical rather than a purely formal classification.

Demsetz. If by great good luck you are put into an optimal position, then it would not matter if it cost a great deal to move or not because you do not have any desire to move. By transaction costs here we are talking about those costs of being in a non-optimal position that it does pay to bear. I agree with Stigler that we attempt to minimize them, but I do not agree that where we start from does not matter. The legal system that starts you in a very bad position costs more than a legal system which starts you close to the optimal position. It seems to me that the notion of transaction costs refers to the lesser of these two costs, one of which is not merely a cost of movement or transaction but a cost of the non-optimality which may be less than the movement cost, a kind of opportunity cost.

Calabresi. Is not the crucial question whether this movement is accomplished best by leaving it up to the market or to some kind of collective rule? Demsetz says it is a matter of good luck to be there in the first instance, but it might be a matter of having more intelligence. Suppose bad luck puts us in a particular position but the market would not get us to a better position because it is too expensive. We then make a judgment, which involves comparisons of utility, that we can by coercion, by a legal rule, move from that position to another one. And we may decide to do that because we think that is more efficient than staying where we are, though there is then the problem that once some collective decisions are accepted, other collective decisions, not based on efficiency notions, become more likely.

Braucher. One of the great cases in the products liability field is the *Henningsen* case. And, one of the things that motivated the court was precisely that General Motors, Ford, and Chrysler used the same products liability system which put all the costs on the ordinary consumer who buys a car, and they had done it by what was called a "free contract." It was no more a free contract than a statute is a free contract, but there it was. Now, as I understand the Coase theorem, it says that if General Motors, Ford, and Chrysler get together to put the entire load of products liability on the consumer, then as long as there are no transaction costs, that would not affect resource allocation. Well, if that is true, then I submit further that if all of the people who drive cars and own cars get together and get the legislature to put the burden back on General Motors and Ford and Chrysler, there is also no effect on resource allocation and that we should go to some other question.

William Klein.[13] I would like to bring up a point which might give some sort of framework for all of this, the distinction in products liability between a sale by the manufacturer of an automobile and a sale by an individual. Suppose that I sell my car to somebody else, that it is eight years old, and that I know from experience that cars that are eight years old have brake failure, among other things; but I do not know specifically that anything is wrong with this car. If the brake linings fail a month later and the buyer is injured, I take it that the rule is quite clear that that buyer does not have a cause of action against me. On the other hand, if General Motors sells cars knowing that in the course of manufacture there will be a number of cases in which brake linings fail, General Motors is liable.

Dean Keeton says that the explanation that fits this situation is that General Motors is in a better position to spread the risk—to take out insurance—than is the individual. I do not agree. I would say that the individual is in a better position to spread the risk because he can decide for himself what his own life is worth, whether or not he wants protection against accidents, and so forth. But, it seems fair to me to say that if companies like General Motors tell people that here is a marvelous, hotsy-totsy car and do not give them an option to buy insurance policies or a better car that has been inspected more, I think it very reasonable to say, "O.K., we are going to take you at your word as it appears in all your advertising rather than in this little contract that you have given us."

Braucher. In McKean's paper there is a reference to the automobile liability schemes, and I think also to the workmen's compensation scheme, but we have not seen how the apparatus we have been discussing would work in a non-traditional legal arrangement.

Calabresi. Well, the workmen's compensation scheme would look the following way: Assume a world in which there is employee liability for work-associated accidents. In order to maintain a given quality of labor, as a first approximation, employers have to pay wages that are high enough to reimburse the employees for the costs of accidents that they are likely to incur. So the employer has an incentive to economize on accidents. If he economizes on accidents, he reduces his wage bill, since the actuarial wage equivalent he would have to pay would be reduced if he economized on accidents. Now take the liability scheme and switch it over, making the employer liable for accidents—work-associated accidents —or making him buy insurance to cover work-associated accidents. He pays an actuarial premium to the insurance company to cover the work-associated accidents and, at a first-level approximation, in order to get the same given quality of labor, he now has to pay a correspondingly lower wage rate. So that in either situation, at the first-level approximation, there is no difference as regards the accident rate; in both cases you have the same financial incentive to economize on accidents.

Braucher. As Gilmore said, if you have a general trend in your society to make the big industrial corporations liable for everything in sight, it is simply not possible to carve out a little thing called "products liability" and say that it is going to be different. There is a certain tendency for everything to work together in this same general way, and if that is what happened with workmen's compensation first, and we are now getting to where automobile accidents are going to be on the no-fault scheme or social insurance scheme or something, it sticks in my mind that products liability is going to go along with that trend too.

Walter Blum.[14] I wonder whether anybody thinks that in any major industry the differential transaction costs from going one way or another on products liability make any significant difference. Are we not talking about something that in the overall picture of cost allocation is relatively trivial? It really does not matter much which way it comes out. Is it likely that there are a significant number of circumstances in which putting the liability originally on the manufacturer or seller as against putting it on the user is likely to make a significant difference, assuming that the law does not prohibit contracting out of it?

Calabresi. I am puzzled by one thing, because you telescoped again the question of initial liability and the question of contracting out of it, and I think we cannot attack the problem you pose unless you pull these two things apart. The question of initial liability would have to be whether this is the kind of defect which, either because of risk-awareness or because of the existence of transaction costs, is one which the manufacturer can more cheaply avoid. If, instead, you move to the question of whether a liability-shifting contract is to be allowed or not, then you are immediately faced with the question of whether the consumer has made a conscious or adequate choice that he wishes to bear this particular type of risk. And this leads you right back to the difference between the situations where the defect is known and where the defect is knowable and the degree of risk-awareness of the parties. Where the consumer has made a conscious choice, consumer liability would seem to offer an attractive scheme. But because of the tendency of people to insure, we must also consider the expense of making insurance categories which are sufficiently differentiated and personal. Because of that expense we find that very often a collective method of control—a non-insurable fine, jail, the whip, hanging, any nice thing, or driver's license removal—is a more effective way of controlling consumer behavior.

When we move to the manufacturer's side, we may find that there the market works surprisingly effectively because there each company is its own insurance population. It can respond to the risk. If true, this would be a good reason for choosing producer liability. We must also consider Professor McKean's point that, on what might be called "fairness grounds," society may require consumer recoveries or social insurance of some sort, so that no one is rendered destitute or his income level changed dramatically as a result of accidents. Then the choice realistically may be between a system like social insurance, paid out of taxes, which has a totally different economic effect, and a system of manufacturer liability, which there are some of us who would say might even improve matters economically. There are some who might say it may make matters worse, but certainly it is clear that it would not be as undesirable in efficiency terms as social insurance. I think that is the battle that is going to be fought.

McKean. I would like to give a brief reaction to Professor Blum's question. It does seem to me that there are instances in which it might make considerable difference which way you assign the liability, even allowing for contracting out or internalizing some of the burdens. I think drugs may be a case of a product where it makes a difference which way you assign liability. This may well be a case in which, if you change the liability drastically from consumer to manufacturer's liability without fault (even though he can then contract out by insurance and so on), there would be a considerable difference in the total costs of accidents, the accident rates and total costs.

Marshall Shapo.[15] Recently I was in the back yard on a Sunday afternoon with my little boy who just turned five. He cut his finger, ran into the house and came out a couple of minutes later wearing a bandaid. When I went back in the house, I found an open medicine cabinet that I had not considered he could reach. So I would like to pose a specific question: I am a judge with a case of a five-year-old child who has killed himself by taking too many aspirin from an aspirin bottle that does not have the safety-lock cap. I want to know what the economic consequences are of holding the aspirin manufacturer for not having this kind of cap.

Musgrave. It seems to me that where no variation in the product's safety is possible, one can better afford to be indifferent about where the burden should lie. But where greater safety can be provided at relatively little cost by the manufacturer, as in this aspirin bottle case, one would prefer manufacturer's liability. The manufacturer is more likely to know the possibilities of technical change in the product which will affect safety than is the consumer. There are really two things: one is the insurance problem given the risk characteristics; and the other is the effect of changes in the product on the level of accidents. Placing the liability on the manufacturer will make him respond more effectively by introducing safety features because he knows the technology which is involved in doing this.

Demsetz. There is a simple way to handle it: give the choice to the consumer. You can have cheaper aspirin bottles which thoughtful and intelligent parents will put where no child can reach them, and you can have those for the careless and superficial and label them accordingly, and let people buy the kind they want.

Shapo. That assumes one can distinguish between a class of intelligent people and a class of careless people. There is really only one class of people and they are occasionally intelligent and careful and occasionally negligent, but they are the same people all the time.

Calabresi. If I were presenting that case [assuming that the object were only economic efficiency], I would say, first: "Your Honor, if you do not become convinced that it makes any difference which way, in terms of economics, we put this liability, let me suggest that there is a great deal of pressure on equity, justice, and whatever grounds, to move towards social insurance which covers all these accidents. Such a move clearly would make a very substantial efficiency difference, because it would remove this cost both from the careless parent and from the careless manufacturer. Because this pressure will increase if we have consumer liability, you should put the burden of proof on the economist to convince you that consumer liability is more efficient than producer liability." Then I would ask whether it is cheaper to have an arrangement which lets a parent choose a cheaper bottle which he can put in a higher place, or the opposite. If there is sufficient information, we feel confident that the choice will be made intelligently. If the cost of giving this information is too great, we may choose not to allow this kind of transaction. You would first have to decide how much information and what kind of information would be required in order to be confident that we were really dealing with people rationally choosing to buy a cheaper product because as to *them* it was sufficiently safe. Then the inconvenience cost for people to find out which aspirin bottle was safest as against the cost of making a safer bottle would become the principal question.

In order to make the case more interesting, we might allow contracting out of liability only if the contract met certain requirements of information. Then the cost of meeting such requirements might be so great that whichever way we put the initial liability, it would actually stay, because no one could meet the requirements for a contract.

Stigler. You play a one-sided game. We talked about how the market acquires information and how people react to it, but on the other hand you seem to presume that the legislature gets free, accurate, and immediate information on new developments and that it has an efficient bureaucracy to enforce its policies.

Demsetz. It seems to me that in this kind of example there is inevitably a disagreement among people about whether or not they should be protected from themselves, in other words whether or not you want to interfere with their choices, and I think that is probably present here. The people that Mr. Shapo has in mind are probably the kind that Professor Gilmore mentioned, and it includes a lot of us who are intelligent part of the time and have some lapses. The question is, are we smart enough to hedge against the contingencies by buying the more careful product, or do we deliberately take the other, or do we take it without thinking? On this sort of thing I do not see any way to resolve a disagreement. "There are two types of people," as the old saying goes, "those who agree that there are two types of people and those who don't." And some people believe in interfering with other people's choices and some people do not.

Walter Oi.[16] Suppose simply that the government faces the decision of whether or not to insist on safety caps. The government really does not know what the reduction is in the probability of an accidental death, and that might be very slight. It is misleading then to talk about an individual instance where some child actually commits the fatal act. What you must ask is how much safety caps reduce the probability or the expected loss for a typical customer as against the cost we impose on buyers of aspirin by insisting on the caps. When you put it in this kind of probabilistic terms, I do not see any clear direction in which you ought to move.

Calabresi. You have made a jump, because by putting liability on the manufacturer we do not quite insist on safety caps. Let us assume we do put liability on the manufacturer and that an adequate exculpatory contract is too expensive. At that point we have not compelled the cap. We have compelled the manufacturer to choose between paying the damages, plus the administrative costs entailed in the damages, and putting on the cap. The government may be capable of forcing this choice when it is not capable of making the collective decision: "You must use the cap."

Buchanan. May I make a comment on this, not so much as an economist, but maybe a little in support of Professor Gilmore? It seems to me that we slipped too quickly into talking about the government making this decision. We were talking about the case as posed. We are talking about the single judge faced with this problem, and, obviously, from this discussion, no matter what kind of evidence the judge is going to get, it is going to be conflicting. So the judge makes a decision, and he makes a decision somehow on the basis of these costs and benefits, and on the basis of his own judgment. This seems to me to be a pretty good way of solving this, provided we do not have a centralized court that uniquely decides this for everyone for all time. This is a strong argument for allowing a judicial system which has decentralized decision centers in which one judge is free to decide one way, and another in a different way. The emergence of law out of this kind of context might well be justified in the sense of a provisional way of arriving at an answer about which nobody is certain.

Shapo. A year or so ago a study was made of Chicago's schoolchildren —I think the sample was about thirty thousand—and it was found that 757 had toxic levels of lead in their bodies, presumably from housepaint. There is a strong feeling that we should find ways of preventing such occurrences, of protecting children against these hazards, which, after all, result from products with which they had no contractual connection in any sense. What does the economist have to contribute to the judgment that has to be made about an issue like this?

Calabresi. I am not an economist, but I want to put one thing which you said in context. You suggested that we want to protect people in some way. I would put that same notion in a slightly different way. People in some ways like to protect themselves against themselves. We may not like this, but it is a recurring phenomenon. We pass a Bill of Rights in our Constitution so that when we are tempted at a particular moment to enact some laws which violate something which in a calmer moment we felt was important, we protect ourselves from the temptation. There is at least one sense in which a system of liability rules may be this kind of thing, a protection designed at a calm moment. When I go into a polling booth I may not want all people to have to do certain things. But I may want them to force me, perhaps, to buy medical insurance, even though as a result I force other people who may not want it. The majority of us require this because we find it necessary to protect ourselves against a later moment when the trip to Florida looks like an awfully good idea.

I am not quite sure how you handle this; I do not think that the discussion has addressed this question at all, and I think it is in large part behind Shapo's query. It is not that these people are incompetent; it is that they themselves will vote to protect themselves against a subsequent incompetence.

Demsetz. I would accept Professor Calabresi's point—you can derive a certain logic for some legislation or liability rules as people somehow protecting themselves. But I think Shapo meant something quite different. He seemed concerned with the widely held view that some people are simply incompetent to judge their own well-being and incompetent to choose as consumers. Therefore, it is incumbent on us, as on the rest of the community, to impose standards which will in fact prevent them from doing themselves damage. It may well be that we are forced to that sort of position, but I think we ought to be clear that it is completely contradictory to accept that view. If we start worrying about our liability laws on the presumption that some people are incompetent, how can we then go along and say that those same people should be allowed to vote for liability rules or a government, which is a far more complicated problem than purchasing food. If we start talking about our liability laws in that context, we must examine the whole logic of political democracy. Now, if you are willing to go that far—and I am not—I have to fall back and say that I assume that people are intelligent enough to make their own decisions.

Keeton. I think it is not a question of intelligence or competence on the part of the people. But it is certainly true that each of us is limited in what he can learn about. Now in most instances it seems to me perfectly clear that the manufacturer who makes his product has to know more about the risk and the incidence of harm that is likely to result from his product than anybody else. If you assume that he is going to pass all this on and that the consumers can drink in all the information that comes from a thousand different sources, well, then you assume something that is completely irrational. They cannot know about it; it is impossible for them to learn about it; I do not care how smart they are. But the manufacturer knows about his product.

Armen Alchian.[17] I have heard the statement made often that consumers just do not appreciate the risks they are faced with. But consider the fact that 500 people get killed every year flying in airplanes. Does that mean that people undervalue the risk of flying an airplane? Not at all. People are ignorant and realize that information is expensive. Just because one man knows something someone else does not know does not mean that he is going to use the information to someone else's benefit. The economic problem is to produce the amount of information people want.

The automobile warranty provides a beautiful illustration, and it would affect everybody in this room. We are all intelligent, over-educated people, literate and logical, and none of us, I will bet, has read with understanding the warranty on his automobile. This contract is freely made, with no coercion, and everybody in the United States buys a car this way. The contract says that if the steering wheel should come loose in your hands and you should run off a cliff and if you should take the defective part, if there is one, and send it back to Detroit, freight prepaid, and if this happens before you have had the car ninety days or three thousand miles, whichever happens first, and if in the sole judgment of General Motors, Ford, or Chrysler, it agrees that the part was defective, it will supply you a new part and charge you only for labor.

Stigler. The warranty does not consist of that piece of paper; it consists of a set of practices of the manufacturer, his agents and dealers when product defects are displayed to them. Let us not let the difficulty of wording a contract so that it does not crucify one party disguise the fact that economic reality consists of a set of practices that are actually engaged in.

Gilmore. Which are quite contrary, of course, to what they have said earlier. Of course, the practice of the manufacturer after the steering wheel broke in poor Mrs. Henningsen's hands was to say "sure, we will take care of this."

Keeton. This information gap reminds me of some of the cases in medical malpractice holding that a doctor does not have to explain all of the details involved in surgical procedures. I do not want my doctor trying to explain all of that to me. I would not understand him—and I would rather just have him go ahead and do what he thinks he ought to do and get it over with.

Henry G. Manne.[18] There is some confusion here because one group is, I think, assuming that the pieces of paper you have with writing on them are part of the information; the economists, I think, are talking about information which is an operative factor in everyone's decision-making, viewed in the aggregate. If pieces of paper do not affect anyone's action or anyone's wealth decision, they are not a relevant part of the information process for the economist.

Reder. Part of what the economists have been saying is in fact what the students have been saying. No *"in loco parentis."* What we are saying is that, given the way that people get information, they are going to do as good a job, as far as they are concerned, as some other person or agency can do for them. However poor this may be, the alternative to having individuals make their own individual decisions is to have them made by some other mechanism, and in general what we are saying is that in practice most people will indicate that they think this is inferior. The cigarette-smoking case is, I think, the classic example.

Shapo. I want to come back to the paint case, which is a third party case in which the injured party is not one of the contracting parties. It seems to me that the no-*in-loco-parentis* argument does not apply there and I want to know what help an economist can give me in making a normative judgment on that problem.

Demsetz. Let us approach the problem generally rather than specifically. We would like to go on the premise that freedom of action is something that is good. We would like to have it produced, but it is not producible without costs. One of the costs of producing freedom is that people are going to make mistakes in using their freedom. Even from their own viewpoint they are going to make mistakes.

If we approach the system from that viewpoint, we next ask who is going to make decisions for children. As a general rule we feel that children's self-interest will on the average be best taken care of if we allow the decisions to rest in the hands of their parents, knowing at the same time that some parents are going to make mistakes. We feel that if we tried to bring up the children in government camps, we would make worse mistakes of a different kind.

It is not a question of no mistakes versus some mistakes, it is a question of having mistakes of one kind versus mistakes of another kind. Obviously no one has perfect knowledge. Somehow you must decide when you are going to stop trying to rectify the mistakes that arise from people's exercise of freedom. And maybe the line is not drawn in the right place, maybe you want to shove it one way or another, but merely citing the fact that some people have made mistakes that have hurt third parties is not in itself a convincing argument to me that we ought to draw the line someplace else.

Alchian. Economic theory does not tell what you ought or ought not to do; it merely points out the consequences of actions that you choose for reasons based on other criteria. But do not ask the economists or economic theory what you ought to do; they will never tell you. All they can do is to avoid common fallacies as well as give you other implications that you had not foreseen.

Musgrave. It seems to me that economists can say a little more than that. Suppose these children who had this toxic poisoning did not have it from the painting of their own house, but, let us say, from paint in the neighborhood, so that we do not make the children the third party with their parents the first party. It is a real third party case. Then, it seems to me, the situation is one where the use of this paint has a certain externality which is overlooked by the market because the people who buy this paint do so at the cost of producing this paint. The cost of the damage to children is overlooked. I think the economist in this case can say that this is a market failure, that the cost of this externality should be allowed for and that there should be, say, a cost in the form of an excise tax on the production of that paint. Now, whether the proceeds of that excise tax should be used to make restitution payments to the children is what I call the problem of fairness. The economist can certainly say that the consumers of the paint ought to pay the external cost of their using it.

Peter Steiner.[19] I would even say a little more than Mr. Musgrave. The economists know two things: They know that sometimes markets work, and they know that sometimes markets fail. I think they know some of the circumstances under which the probability of failure is likely and when there may be some case for interference. It seems to me in general that we economists are not in the position to say simply that freedom is in general always preferred to any alternative when in fact we know that in some cases interfering is more likely to result in a more desirable result. Though we cannot solve the normative question, we can define the conditions under which a market failure is likely to occur. I do not know where that line would be drawn, but I would urge that we get some work done on this.

Calabresi. Let us take the paint case in the third party situation. I suppose if all the people who are likely to be injured by this paint were aware of their risk and could get together and bribe the manufacturer, they would pay the manufacturer not to make this kind of paint. Obviously that is absurd. The costs of that are too great and that is what we mean by saying that that is an externality. Even so we have a choice to make, because the moment we decide that this is one of those situations where we put the liability on the manufacturer, no paint will any longer have lead in it. We will have deprived some people, who would have been able to use leaded paint in situations where it might harm no one, of that opportunity. That is some deprivation. On the other hand, if we fail to put liability on the manufacturer, we are inducing all manufacturers to produce leaded paint because it is cheaper and because they do not have to bear the real cost because the transaction cost of putting that full cost on them is too great. So this poses, in a somewhat more dramatic way, precisely the question we all have been talking about. With third parties the question as to who has the lowest costs of cost avoidance must be faced. I think most people judge the cheapest cost avoider in that situation to be the paint manufacturer. If economists could come up with a good deal of information we might convince the public of the opposite. At the moment, however, whether economists like it or not, that is where the burden of proof rests, because uninformed people, who are not going to spend money to inform themselves, guess on this empirical question that way.

Musgrave. There are all types of legislation which have been passed to protect children. A classic case is, of course, forced education. All children must go through this process because we do not trust the parents to invest in the children. Our society has been quite prepared to go into the family and attempt to control the relationship between parents and children in a very extensive fashion, as illustrated in education or in child labor legislation. Certainly we have made this judgment without the fear that thereby we have tremendously constrained freedom.

The historical change in the law which we have talked about may be a function of the economic progress that we have. As we move into an increasingly affluent society, there is a tremendous growth in the amount of goods and purchases of commodities. Time is the scarce factor. Yet, with the growth in wealth one must make a great many more decisions, and the time available for decisions is becoming more and more valuable. We may be prepared to pay more for information, but with the increase in the number of goods, the cost of information will mount considerably, while the payoff for any given improvement, any given commodity, is relatively small. In other words, the increased value to you of being able to choose more intelligently between A and B is relatively small, while the costs of making informed decisions are increasing.   We may therefore be increasingly prepared to accept the judgment of the government or some other group who will do the screening, provide us with information, guarantee the safety of the products, etc., even though this involves some cost in terms of reducing the range of available commodities.

FOOTNOTES

* Kenan Professor of Law, Department of Political Science, University of Rochester.

1 Professor of Economics, University of Virginia.

2 Professor of Economics, Virginia Polytechnic Institute.

3 Professor of Law, Yale University.

4 Professor of Economics, Harvard University.

5 Professor of Law, The University of Chicago.

6 Professor, Graduate School of Business, The University of Chicago.

7 Demsetz, *Some Aspects of Property Rights*, 9 J.Law & Econ. 61 (1966) [ed.].

8 Professor, Graduate School of Business and Law School, The University of Chicago.

9 Dean and Professor of Law, The University of Texas.

10 Professor of Economics, Stanford University.

11 Professor of Law, Harvard University.

12 Professor, Department of Economics and Law School, Harvard University.

13 Professor of Law, University of Wisconsin.

14 Professor of Law, The University of Chicago.

15 Professor of Law, The University of Texas.

16 Professor, Graduate School of Management, University of Rochester.

17 Professor of Economics, University of California at Los Angeles.

18 Professor of Law, Department of Political Science, University of Rochester.

19 Professor, Department of Economics and Law School, University of Michigan.

C Continued

18: ELECTIVE NO-FAULT LIABILITY INSURANCE FOR ALL KINDS OF ACCIDENTS: A PROPOSAL*

JEFFREY O'CONNELL

It seems likely that the outstanding success of even limited no-fault auto insurance laws (witness the successful experience in both Massachusetts and Florida, the first states to enact them) [1] will eventually result in the spread of better and better no-fault auto laws.

But what about other accident victims—those injured by power tools, or falls in stores, or in the course of medical treatment?

Difficulties Confronting Plaintiffs in Products Liability Actions

The plight under traditional tort law of those who suffer losses from such accidents is much worse than that of auto accident victims. At least for auto accidents, a large total number of people are paid a large total sum of money under tort law. The situation in other areas of accident law is much grimmer. In contrast to most auto claims which most lawyers feel competent to handle, "[i]n the best of circumstances," according to the Final Report of the National Commission on Product Safety, "a products [liability] case is still a bruising, frequently heartbreaking, always onerous undertaking for client and lawyer." [2] In order to impose liability on a manufacturer for injury caused by his product, the product must be proven in some way defective. But proving a product

September, 1973 Issue of The Insurance Law Journal, pp. 495–515.

defective most often involves engineering evidence and testimony of the most technical and arcane kind. And all the while these expensive personnel—lawyers and engineers—are huddling and conferring and appearing in court, a *very* expensive meter is ticking.

The decision to invest all the time and money required in a products liability suit is not lightly undertaken. Manufacturers defend products liability cases with a passion—and often win. The plaintiff's lawyer, on the other hand, is paid on a contingent fee basis: if the case is lost, the lawyer is out of pocket a large investment in time and money. Nor are the problems of legal doctrine and factual proof by any means limited to proving a defect. The manufacturer will most often defend with an almost endless variety of technical and legal hurdles that can often only be resolved after exhaustive trials and then appeals. Keep in mind that these snags can each lead to expensive, prolonged disputes, with that horrendously expensive meter again ticking away for both sides as highly paid experts examine all aspects of the accident. As far as the defense is concerned, according to the Final Report of the National Commission on Product Safety:

> The manufacturer employs a battery of attorneys and technical experts with ample resources at their disposal. The consumer must prove that it was the manufacturer's product, that it did cause the injury, that the defect existed at the factory, that the suit lies within the statute of limitations, that the infrequency of the injury does not absolve the manufacturer from liability, and so on.

> Meanwhile the defense can muster volumes of evidence against each statement by the consumer. The defense can also stall: it can appeal to the next highest court. While the consumer waits and pays, the defense, if it expects to lose, can offer a modest settlement.[3]

The obstacles facing a victim injured by a manufactured product, in contrast to those faced by a traffic victim (bad as are the latter obstacles) are exacerbated by the deep umbrage the typical manufacturer takes at facing or paying a products liability claim. After all, his product is accused of being "defective." Quite apart from the adverse publicity involved, it deeply offends the pride of most manufacturers to be challenged in this way. It denigrates the great effort they believe they expend on such things as careful design and quality control.

The consequence of these factors, according to the Final Report of the National Commission on Product Safety, is that "[t]he most serious limitation on recovery of damages for [product] injuries to consumers is the cost of trial: witnesses testified that it hardly pays to press a defective product claim for less than $5,000 to $10,000."[4]

Most Injuries Are Not Compensated

As a result of all this, says the Final Report, "most injuries to consumers [from manufactured products] go uncompensated." [5]   Indeed, in light of how difficult it is to to prosecute a products liability claim, the Report comments that "[t]o advise a battered consumer to sue may simply add insult to injury." [6]

This situation would be tragic enough even without the huge losses due to personal injury inflicted by manufactured products in this country.   The National Commission on Product Safety found that 20 million Americans are injured annually by consumer products alone, with "a number of makes, models, or types" of the following categories of products harboring especially "unreasonable hazards to the American consumer: architectural glass, color television sets, fireworks, floor furnaces, glass bottles, high-rise bicycles, hot-water vaporizers, household chemicals, infant furniture, ladders, power tools, protective headgear, rotary lawnmowers, toys, unvented gas heaters, and wringer washers." [7]

Of the 20 million injured, 110,000 are permanently disabled and 30,000 killed.[8]   The annual costs to society from such injuries may well exceed $5.5 billion, acording to the Commission, with a calculation of over $4 billion in "costs to the injured persons, their families, and close friends or relatives, whether or not the monies are reimbursed." [9]

As to examples of particular products, architectural glass or ordinary window glass injures 150,000 annually, with 100,000 of these injuries alone caused by people walking through glass doors; [10]   injuries as a result of using ladders amount to 125,0000 to 200,000 per year, with 400 to 600 of these resulting in death; [11]   rotary lawnmowers caused an estimated 140,000 injuries in 1969; [12]   children's toys and play equipment cause around 1,400,000 injuries per year.[13]

Despite such harrowing but actuarially predictable carnage, the total amount of compensation available to victims from products liability insurance is negligible, even when compared with the scanty benefits flowing to traffic victims from automobile liability insurance.   For auto accidents, a United States Department of Transportation study found that, with compensable losses totalling $5.1 billion [14] in serious injuries and death cases, auto liability insurance paid out only $800 million, or 15 per cent of compensable losses.[14a]   For consumer products, the percentage is apparently *much* less.   According to the National Commission on Product Safety's Report, products liability insurance covers "only a few per cent of the medical cost of injuries." [15]

In another way, too, the products liability insurance system nonetheless makes the frightful auto liability insurance system look good by comparison.   Much more than half—56 cents—of every auto insurance premium dollar is chewed up in administrative and legal costs.[16] This is in contrast to administrative and legal expenses of 3 cents for Social Security, 7 cents for Blue Cross, and 17 cents for health and accident plans.[17] Although precise figures for products liability insurance are not available, given what we know about the greater need for expensive experts and the greater likelihood of recalcitrant resistance to claims, along with the lack of payment of smaller nuisance claims, the percentage of the premium dollar spent on administrative and legal expenses for products liability insurance is *much* greater even than for auto insurance.[18]

That may explain why the public derives so little from the much vaunted explosion of products liability suits. Less than 10 years ago, there were approximately 50,000 products liability claims in the United States courts; today there are about 500,000. Similarly the gross amount of products liability premiums has skyrocketed: in 1950 it is estimated it amounted to $25 million; in 1970, $125 million.[19]

But, except for a few victims "lucky" enough (1) to be seriously injured by a product with a demonstrably provable defect, (2) to hire a very expensive plaintiff's lawyer, and (3) to possess a case which—miracle of miracles—can run the gauntlet of countless legal and practical pitfalls, the many millions of dollars in products liability insurance largely accrue to a few highly skilled lawyers on both sides, a number of highly skilled engineers and technical experts, and some casualty insurance companies (with the latter, of course, loudly complaining about how much money they are losing on the whole operation).[20]

Difficulties Confronting Plaintiffs in Medical Malpractice Actions

The scenario for medical malpractice cases follows that for products liability as in a litmus test, as demonstrated by the recent voluminous report of the National Commission on Medical Malpractice to HEW Secretary Caspar Weinberger.[21]

As to complex issues, one lawyer who has intensively studied medical malpractice has recently spoken of "the almost Byzantine nature of trying to find fault in malpractice litigation . . . ."[22] This stems from the fact that surgical procedures, for example, along with the range of their possible consequences, are so very complicated that trying to determine whether they were properly executed makes even many difficult products liability cases look easy.

The problem of complexity of issues and the need for expert witnesses is greatly exacerbated in medical malpractice cases by the so-called "conspiracy of silence" among doctors.

Many grim examples can be cited of such reluctance to speak out. As just one, doctors were asked by the Boston University Law Medicine Institute whether they would testify in behalf of a claimant in a malpractice case where the surgeon had made a mistake by removing a wrong kidney: 70 per cent of the doctors stated they would refuse to testify despite the clear merit of the claim.[23]

Such a feeling of closed ranks shows that the doctor—even more than the manufacturer—resents and resists a lawsuit deeply and bitterly. The widely held view of the medical profession is that responsibility for medical malpractice suits can be laid at the feet of greedy, grasping, unethical shysters, stirred by their unconscionable contingent fees, to in turn stir up—or at least join with—ungrateful, unrealistic and ignorant patients. According to a recent Congressional study entitled "Medical Malpractice: The Patient versus the Physician":

> "Physicians contend that a large number of claims and suits filed against them have no basis—that no negligence is involved. The physician believe their patients regard them as 'easy targets' for litigation and sizable judgments and claims." [24]

As the result of such intransigence, only a few of the biggest claims for medical malpractice are worth pursuing. According to Dr. David Rubsaman, who holds both medical and law degrees and is an expert on medical malpractice:

> "A considerable number of patients who have a medical injury, even though probably negligently caused, and who go to see a first-class malpractice attorney, will not be accepted by him. A patient may have lost a month's work and be out of pocket a thousand dollars for medical expenses because of the doctor's negligence. Assume he is now completely recovered and feels fine. That month of work and the $1,000 for medical expenses is a heavy burden for a man making $500 a month. But no first-class attorney in California will take that case because the malpractice insurance carriers will not settle, and it just costs too much money for the plaintiff's attorney to try them." [25]

All this means too that very little of the total loss suffered as a result of medical treatment is compensated. According to a recent publication on medical malpractice by the Center for the Study of Democratic Institutions:

> "Mr. [Eli P.] Bernzweig [an attorney and executive director of the Secretary's Commission on Medical Malpractice of the Department of Health, Education and Welfare] cited an American Medical Association professional liability survey which indicated that for every patient who files a malpractice suit 'there are probably ten times as many who never become aware of the fact that they have legitimate fault claims under our system.' " [26]

But medical malpractice claims and premiums, like those for products liability, are skyrocketing. Medical malpractice claims are being filed at the rate of about 18,000 a year,[27] with a total cost of malpractice claims in court judgments and out-of-court settlements equalling at least $80.3 million annually;[27a] it is not unusual for a doctor to pay from $5,000 to $12,000 *annually* in medical malpractice insurance premiums.[28]

But, according to a Congressional study of medical malpractice: "The lion's share of the total cost to the insurance companies of malpractice suits and claims goes to the legal community."[29] According to Rick Carlson, an attorney engaged in a study of medical malpractice, "[only] between sixteen and seventeen cents of the premium dollar ends up as benefits to victims of medical injuries,"[30] in contrast to 97 cents for Social Security, 93 cents for Blue Cross, 83 cents for much health insurance, and 44 cents for tort liability auto insurance.[31]

Cases of auto accidents, products liability, and professional malpractice constitute the most significant categories of personal injury litigation in our society. (Industrial accidents, the other great category of accidents, were largely removed from courtroom litigation by no-fault workmen's compensation statutes passed by the various states, for the most part early in this century.) Other categories remain, however, such as falls in stores, hunting accidents, and other almost countless ways accidents can happen. For these cases, too, the cumbersomeness of the fault system operates with its heavy hand. Nor are the problems by any means limited to the difficulties of establishing the fault of the defendant. Myriad other legal barriers remain to an intelligent—not to say, humane—way of compensating victims of accidents.

They include the following:

(1) Rules of so-called "contributory fault" barring an accident victim guilty of fault from any—or at least full—compensation.[32]

(2) A requirement of one final lump-sum payment of losses, as opposed to periodic payment as losses accrue, with resultant hardship or perhaps malingering in the meantime.[33]

(3) The so-called "collateral source" rule calling for double or triple—or more—payment for the same loss by various insurance coverages, thereby making running up medical bills or lost work often very profitable.[34]

(4) Payment for so-called pain and suffering often measured as a multiple of medical bills, thereby leading to even more padding of medical bills, especially in trivial cases, with the further result that those suffering the pain the least are often paid for it the most and those suffering pain the most are often paid for it the least.[35]

Inadequacies of the Present Tort Insurance System

This, then, is the present tort insurance system: not a system for paying accident victims from accident insurance (as sensible as that simple idea would seem to be), but a system for *fighting* accident victims about paying them from accident insurance; a system so cumbersome that the typical accident victim, after consulting a lawyer (indeed, even a highly paid specialist), cannot know *when* he will be paid, *what* he will be paid, or *if* he will be paid;[36] a system so hugely wasteful of insurance dollars in sending so much into the pockets of lawyers and insurance companies and so little to victims themselves; a system so highly dilatory that, when it finally gets around to disposing of cases, is usually cruelly vindictive to most and occasionally relatively generous to others, with the outcome more dependent on luck and emotion than need and reason.

Solving the problem of compensating on a no-fault basis very large losses from auto accidents, and more generally for other accidents not covered by auto reform, is much more difficult than compensating on a no-fault basis smaller auto accident losses. No-fault auto insurance has been relatively easy to effectuate because of two interrelated factors:

(1) A system of widespread fault liability insurance, readily and simply transferable into no-fault loss insurance, without much fear that the transformation would impose new and formidable burdens on anyone.

(2) A sufficiently dangerous—or otherwise distinctive [36a]—activity, that is, driving a motor car, such that the statute can readily identify who is to be required to pay for what loss.

But with many other accidents—those from medical malpractice or manufactured products, for example—no-fault insurance poses much greater problems because neither factor is generally applicable. For example, as to the first factor, if ladder manufacturers were to be made liable for falls from ladders, regardless of any fault or defect, wouldn't this very likely expand their liability exponentially? As to the second factor, is building a cement patio a sufficiently dangerous activity that, say, the subcontractor laying the concrete should be automatically and indefinitely liable to anyone falling on the concrete and injuring himself?[37]

Indeed even for auto accidents, the fear of the high costs in providing unlimited no-fault benefits has similarly meant reluctance to provide such benefits on the grounds it might cost substantially more than present required liability insurance.

Limited no-fault auto insurance has left us, then, with a lack of coverage for the more seriously injured traffic victim and, of course, even much less coverage for other accident victims.

Application of No-Fault Concept to Other Accident Victims

And so, the question is how to apply the no-fault concept to this crucial remainder?

One apparent solution to compensating accident victims is simply to abandon tort liability of any kind and pay everyone injured by accidents for his wage loss and medical expenses under Social Security.[38]   Indeed, won't impending national health insurance largely meet the needs of those suffering serious personal injury?

Unfortunately, the costs in the United States would be imposing indeed if we were to cover, under Social Security or some other forms of social insurance, wage loss and medical expenses stemming from all accidental injuries.   In the United States, the costs of impending national health insurance are already causing great unease.   Estimates vary widely, but even under President Nixon's more modest national health insurance proposal (the status of which at this point is highly questionable), the Social Security Administration has estimated that federal expenditures would amount to $34 billion of a total 1974 national health expenditure of about $107 billion (up from a total expenditure of $67 billion in 1970); under Senator Edward Kennedy's more ambitious bill, the Social Security Administration estimated federal expenditures of $114 billion.[39]   It is precisely the spectre of such costs—along with the resistance of the medical profession—that makes passage of national health insurance so remote at this time.

Certainly, the spiralling and originally grossly underestimated costs of Medicare and Medicaid give pause when contemplating the costs of vast extensions of medical insurance.   Annual Medicaid costs in New York State, amounting to $1.99 billion, now exceed amounts spent there for welfare.[40]

And all this in the face of a landslide victory to a President determined to curb rising public expenditures.

But even if national health insurance were to be passed in the immediate future on a comprehensive scale, it would still meet only a relatively small portion of the total personal injury losses of accident victims, since it almost certainly would not cover wage loss.   In the case of auto accidents, for example, estimates are that 74 per cent of injury losses is for wage losses, and only 22 per cent for medical losses (with 4 per cent for "other expenses").[41]   Given the high costs that any national health insurance will be likely to impose, it will be a long time indeed before any national health insurance or Social Security is extended to cover wage loss as well.   And one doubts that such protection will ever cover more than very modest levels of subsistence income.

The point is that covering wage losses, as well as medical expenses, of *all* injury victims under social insurance, as is being tested in New

Zealand,[42] is going to have to face cruel competition for public spending in coming years. One doubts very much that dismantling the tort liability system, and replacing it with a vast scheme of social insurance to cover middle class accidental wage loss, will soon rank high in social priority. All the more reason, then, to think in terms of reforming tort law itself, as was done with no-fault auto insurance.

Think for a moment on the European experience. Compared to the United States, all European countries have traditionally had much higher levels of social insurance and much lower levels of affluence, with many fewer people in the prosperous middle or upper middle classes. Thus, social insurance covers much more accident loss than in the United States, but the tort claim for losses above social insurance remains intact.[43] Both at the bottom and the top, there is much less need for tort law in Europe than in the United States but it remains. *A fortiori*, it will remain in the United States.

Even if we could cover all losses from all injuries under Social Security, or general health insurance, economists specializing in loss allocation, such as Professor Guido Calabresi [44] of the Yale Law School, tell us it would be unwise to have all injuries from whatever cause paid for out of a big, undifferentiated pool of "insurance" such as Social Security. Rather, they argue, a given activity or industry should be made to pay for the particular losses it causes. Otherwise, the argument goes, there is less incentive to keep that activity or industry safe. Isn't your incentive to produce a safe product greatly lessened, it is asked, if persons injured by your product are paid exclusively from general tax revenues or the like? [45] Professor Leonard Ross of the Columbia Law School has spoken of so-called "market deterrence" of accidents, achieved by charging given enterprises for the special losses each engenders.

> [Market] . . . deterrence operates by placing the costs of accidents on the activities which cause them; for example, by making power lawn mower manufacturers liable for all [personal injury] damage[s] caused by . . . their mowers [regardless of anyone's fault]. In theory, mower prices would then rise and sales fall; some families would be induced to shift to manual mowers, the total amount of power mowing would be reduced, and the level of accidents would abate. Moreover, manufacturers might become choosy about customers, raising prices to noninstitutional buyers or perhaps simply to obvious schlemiels. Finally, they would have an incentive to redesign mowers to improve safety features. A variety of market forces would be set in motion to lower the total loss through accidents.[46]

For a variety of reasons, then, we shouldn't soon expect a solution from Social Security or general health insurance to the problem of accident compensation.[47] How then to make more sense of accident compensation short of a Social Security solution?

A New No-Fault Law of "Enterprise Liability"?

Could one lump all injuries together from other than auto or work accidents under one general statute, creating a new no-fault law of "enterprise liability?" Such a law might provide that every enterprise entailing distinctive risks of personal injury (such as the production of ladders or power tools) must pay for the injuries it typically generates, without regard to anyone's fault. That way when someone loses his eye from a flying rock from a power mower, he would be automatically recompensed without endless litigation over whether the mower was defectively constructed or whether he was careless in using it, just as he would be compensated under no-fault auto insurance without regard to anyone's fault for the loss of an eye from an auto accident. Under such a law—as under no-fault auto insurance—hugely expensive investigations and litigation over defects and fault would be eliminated. Also, as under no-fault auto insurance, in order to help finance paying the more vital and measurable losses of medical expenses and lost wages, no payment would be made for so-called pain and suffering.[48]

Would this trade-off work? That is, assuring payment for out-of-pocket loss, regardless of anyone's fault, merely on the happening of an accident, to replace the gamble of greater compensation dependent on trying to prove who was at fault in the accident? Or put it this way: Would it work for non-auto accidents, as it is obviously working in the case of auto and employment accidents?

There is good reason to think that it would. In addition to not paying for pain and suffering, such a law should provide—as many no-fault auto proposals have—that no payment would be made for amounts already covered by other sources such as Blue Cross or sick leave—or even life insurance. By such a provision, personal injury law would be made to serve a most worthwhile function for it: payments tailored to large, individual losses not met by other forms of payment such as Social Security or health insurance, which, although growing, are always going to remain inadequate to cover all losses. And enterprise liability would accomplish this in a way that would eliminate most of the expensive and often fruitless arguments over fault and the value of pain which dominate personal injury law today.

The crucial question in deciding whether to adopt a system of no-fault enterprise liability is this: Will the claims over which enterprise's risk created the loss end up equally—or more—cumbersome and technical compared to those over who was at fault?

One can't be sure. One can argue that, statistically, serious accidents probably don't happen in that many different ways. There seems to be, in other words, a pattern to accidents, so deciding what risks operated in most accidents won't be that difficult.   Think again of the list of products classified by the National Commission on Product Safety as especially dangerous.   Enterprise liability might obviously apply, for example, against:

(1) Those who manufacture and sell architectural glass, when people are cut by it;

(2) Those who manufacture and sell fireworks, when the fireworks explode and injure;

(3) Those who manufacture and sell floor furnaces, when the furnaces cause burns;

(4) Those who manufacture and sell high-rise bicycles, when people fall off the bicycles;

(5) Those who manufacture and sell hot-water vaporizers, when the vaporizers cause burns;

(6) Those who manufacture or sell power tools, when the tools mutilate.

In other words, arguably, we know right away what risk of what enterprise is involved concerning most serious accidental injuries.

It must be admitted though, as indicated earlier, that it is easy to pose difficult questions about the applicability of such "enterprise liability." Take that guest who falls on the cement patio at a neighbor's house and cracks his skull.   Who pays if there are still losses once all the victim's own insurance has run out?   Not the householder: he is in no better position to bear—or pass on—the loss than his neighbor.   How about the contractor who built the house?   Or the subcontractor who built the patio? Or the seller of the cement?   If all of them, in what proportion?

Obviously, then, as these questions suggest, such a proposal of enterprise liability, while more modest than trying to cover all losses from all injury under Social Security, is still relatively revolutionary.   No firm cost data as to what it would cost in the aggregate or to individual enterprise is available to legislatures, and even if available, the data would be subject to dispute and uncertainty, in light of the scope of the proposed change. Manufacturers and professional men, already plagued by myriad legal and other economic uncertainties in a swiftly changing society, would probably robustly—and successfully—resist passage of such legislation on either a federal or state level.

Without doubt, then, a proposal for such no-fault enterprise liability poses daunting questions.

There is, therefore, the question whether legislation of this scope ought to be enacted at one stroke if there are other alternatives.   Even the stoutest-hearted liberals have been perhaps more than a little shaken by the unpredictable results often stemming in the 1960's from implementing untried proposals for ambitious social reform as formulated by academics and civil servants. (It is not without significance, though, that no-fault auto insurance is one such proposal that seems to be working as well as the professors said it would.) D. P. Moynihan has pointed out that in the light of this experience, "The nation can ill afford full scale social programs of unknown value that cost large amounts but have no [experimental] . . . features—no way of genuinely assessing their contributions so that policy can be improved." [49] Feminist Ingrid Bengis has put it more pungently: "I am very wary," she says, "of conclusions that precede experience." [50]

How to go about experimenting with no-fault insurance for various kinds of accidents beyond auto and workmen's compensation insurance?

Proposed Solution: Elective No-Fault Liability

I suggest a solution whereby any enterprise would be allowed to elect, if it choose, to pay from then on for the injuries it causes on a no-fault basis, thereby foreclosing claims based on fault. The enterprise would be allowed to select all, or if it chose, just certain risks of personal injury it typically creates and agree to pay for out-of-pocket losses when injury results from those risks. To the extent—and only to the extent—a guarantee of no-fault payment exists at the time of the accident, as under no-fault auto or workmen's compensation insurance, no claim based on fault (or a defect) would be allowed against the party electing to be covered under no-fault liability insurance.[50a]

The incentives to elect no-fault liability in place of traditional liability based on fault would be that, although the enterprise may have to pay more people for injury, it would pay them much less: it would not have to pay anything already covered by other insurance, nor anything for pain and suffering. This would eliminate paying *anything* in most cases of smaller injuries: it would also cut down substantially on what is to be paid in cases of larger injuries. Also, the enterprise would save on the huge amounts now spent on legal fees and expert witnesses to determine that intractable question of whether there was fault or a defect in causing the accident. Of great importance, too, for manufacturers and doctors, the *stigma* of liability would be substantially—and often totally—removed. No longer would the enterpriser be paying because his product is defective or because he malpracticed but rather on the morally neutral ground that the accident was just that—an "accident."

Certainly, an astute enterpriser, concerned about skyrocketing products liability premiums under present law, would be inclined to check on what paying under elective no-fault liability would cost him in comparison to regular tort liability. At least for some categories of injuries, the enterpriser might find it advantageous to pay only for out-of-pocket loss, albeit on a no-fault basis. The availability of such an option would certainly encourage many enterprises at least to develop data and focus on the question of which system of compensation would be to their advantage. Some enterprises might find the cost much less, so wasteful is the regular tort system. This would be especially true for enterprises facing myriad regular tort claims of a nuisance nature, such as falls in stores, irritatingly deleterious matter in food, and so forth, where relatively trivial claims dwarf those for very serious injury. Others might find the costs closer, but it's not inconceivable that humanitarian instincts would then operate to tip the scale in favor of electing enterprise liability.

When the no-fault auto insurance controversy was reaching an early peak, a chief executive of a major car rental company read of the fantastic waste of the auto liability insurance system, resulting in so little of the premiums being paid to traffic victims. Shocked and concerned by this waste—and by how little traffic victims were being paid from auto liability insurance, despite its cost—he called in his general counsel to investigate the matter further, with the eventual result that his company, along with other car rental companies, became advocates of no-fault auto insurance, even to the point of testifying and lobbying in various legislative forums, including the Congress. It is true that in this instance, projected cost savings under no-fault served as an additional spur, but the businessman's outrage at the waste and cruelty of the tort liability system was a real catalyst. It may be too much to hope that many businessmen would see a competitive advantage in being able to advertise their willingness to pay for injuries caused by their products, in that businessmen, understandably perhaps, are reluctant to raise in their advertising the spectre of injury by their products. But a concern for the inevitable actuarial toll imposed by their products is not unimaginable on the part of many businessmen, and no-fault liability will give a beneficial outlet for that concern.

Elective no-fault liability may make especially good sense for the medical profession, as well as pharmaceutical houses. Unquestionably, there are medical procedures giving rise to adverse but expectable results regardless of fault, but which often lead to medical malpractice claims. For many such procedures, it would make sense to allow health care providers to elect to pay out-of-pocket loss simply on the happening of those adverse results. Areas of anesthesia, for instance, and neurosurgery and orthopedics, and certain side effects from drugs immediately come to mind.[51] It is not without significance that doctors—abhorring the stigma of malpractice suits—have already been advocating no-fault insurance payments covering medical injuries. Keep in mind, too, that the stunning success of no-fault auto insurance in allowing more people to be eligible for payment, while at the same time stabilizing and even reducing insurance premiums, is going to greatly increase the receptivity of all kinds of enterprises—medical and otherwise—to experimenting with no-fault insurance.[52]

Actually, there is already strong precedence for such an elective approach to no-fault accident law in the provisions of many workmen's compensation laws in many states which allow employers to elect to be covered under no-fault workmen's compensation, thereby avoiding liability based on fault.[53] These laws were passed in light of early 20th Century court decisions outlawing compulsory workmen's compensation as unconstitutional.[54] Although compulsory workmen's compensation has long been upheld [55] as to accidents from other than employment or autos, the political unfeasibility of compulsory no-fault enterprise liability immediately applicable to all businesses has already been suggested.[56] The *relative* unfeasibility of even a law imposing no-fault liability on comparatively hazardous businesses can be readily imagined in light of lobbying disputes over just which enterprises are to be singled out.[57] And so, to repeat the workmen's compensation experience, once again experimental no-fault liability would seem to make sense as a compromise, albeit this time not for constitutional reasons. Indeed, even as to employment injuries, about one-third of the states still have elective workmen's compensation laws.[58] In those states, most eligible employers choose to be covered,[59] which would seem to augur well for businesses and professional men electing to be covered under no-fault liability.

In effect, elective no-fault liability makes both factors which facilitate no-fault auto insurance applicable to many other kinds of accidents:

(1) Those electing no-fault can decide for themselves if their fault liability insurance is readily and simply transferable into no-fault loss insurance, without therefore fearing that the transformation will impose new and formidable burdens on them.

(2) Similarly the decision as to who is to be required to pay for what is not left open-ended, but defined by the one electing in his own elective no-fault liability policy.

Of course, the question will be raised as to why anyone should be allowed to elect to pay under no-fault liability a possibly lesser total amount for injuries associated with his product or activity than he might pay under tort liability based on fault. The answer is this: the premise of no-fault liability is that the regular tort liability is often absurdly and unnecessarily wasteful, dilatory, and cruel. Far better, if necessary, to spend less and spend it wisely. Paying injured parties when their needs outstrip their resources—without the expense and delay of establishing fault or a defect in a product—is much wiser than funnelling money through the regular tort liability system where available funds so largely end up in the pockets of lawyers, expert witnesses, and insurance companies.

In addition, as elective no-fault liability proves feasible, on the basis of its success in given instances, compulsory no-fault liability could be *imposed* on more and more enterprises for more and more injuries, if society wished to do so.

But the great virtue of allowing injurers to elect no-fault liability is in flexibility through encouraging experimentation. Given the undeniable evils of the present system, who will be hurt by such experimentation? There are some victims who, viewed *ex post facto,* will receive less under no-fault liability than they would have under the regular tort system. But looking at the matter from the vantage of *before* an accident—that being the fairest way to measure various options as to insurance—it seems that the public favors relative certainty of payment of out-of-pockets loss, as compared to a gamble for payment of out-of-pocket loss plus pain and suffering.[60] Several reliable surveys have indicated that preference. Indeed, according to one survey conducted in Illinois, few of those who were successful in claiming for compensation based on who was at fault in the accident knew about—or learned about—or cared about being paid for pain and suffering by the so-called "wrongdoer."[61] Accident victims perceive what lawyers do not: "Accidents" are just that, and what accident victims want is prompt payment for their real out-of-pocket losses with a minimum of fuss and argument.

Note, too, the layers of flexibility possible under elective no-fault liability. The enterpriser could be allowed to experiment with no-fault liability for, say, products produced during a given period. He might also be allowed to limit the age of the product for which he assumes no-fault liability. The enterpriser might, in addition, be allowed to limit the amount of no-fault benefits for which he is liable to, say, multiples of $10,000, with the enabling legislation requiring a corresponding tort exemption for claims above the no-fault benefits of, say, one-half of the $10,000 multiple measured in pain and suffering (for example, if no-fault benefits of $20,-000 are provided, no tort suit could be maintained unless the value of pain and suffering exceeded $10,000, and so forth). Alternatively the enabling legislation could measure the tort exemption as, say, one-third of the amount of no-fault benefits, measured in medical bills (for example, if no-fault benefits of $30,000 are provided, no tort suit could be maintained unless medical bills exceeded $10,000). The problem with any formula tied to medical bills is that it can encourage the padding of medical bills to exceed the tort exemption.[62]

Another problem of allowing a cut-off point for no-fault benefits and preserving the tort action above it is that the elector—which would be paying both fault and no-fault claims for some serious injuries—might well be tempted to use the availability of no-fault benefits in bargaining perhaps unfairly over the disposition of the tort claim.[63] But that disadvantage must be weighed against the flexibility of experimentation imparted by allowing an elector to cut off the amount of no-fault benefits for which it assumes liability.

In point of fact, there is no reason the law should limit elective no-fault liability to enterprises. Normally, it is true, individuals probably will not find it as advantageous as enterprises to shift to no-fault liability in that premium savings will be less likely. No savings would likely accrue from a switch in homeowners' coverage, for example. But motorists might well find it better and/or cheaper to elect no-fault liability to cover losses in a state without any no-fault law or to cover their liability above the "threshold" for tort suits under limited no-fault laws. Any motorist could thus insure to pay anyone injured in or by his car on a no-fault basis, just as an enterprise elects no-fault liability in return for the abolition of tort claims against the insured.[63a] Allowing any and all to thus replace the cumbersome fault liability with no-fault liability will encourage further experimentation with no-fault coverage, with all the advantages all round flowing therefrom.

Indeed, elective no-fault auto insurance could do much to alleviate the problems posed by inadequate no-fault auto insurance laws already enacted and even worse ones being urged by trial lawyers and some in the insurance industry.[64] If, for example, the tort exemption threshold under a no-fault law is very low (as in Massachusetts) or even nonexistent (as in Delaware and Oregon), motorists could be expected to choose to initiate or greatly increase the exemption as it applies to them, in return for agreeing to pay their victims' losses on a no-fault basis when all other sources of the accident victims are exhausted.

Another leaf from the experience under early legislation dealing with industrial accidents might be applied to nonemployment injuries. Prior to enactment of workmen's compensation statutes, some early employers' liability statutes, while retaining a requirement of proof of negligence against an employer, nonetheless abrogated the defenses of contributory negligence and assumption of risk for industrial accidents.[65] With such common law defenses abolished in a state allowing elective workmen's compensation, an employer is under that much greater incentive to opt to be covered under elective workmen's compensation. Similarly, in order to encourage any and all to opt to be covered under elective no-fault liability insurance, the defenses of assumption of risk and contributory negligence could be abolished against any and all defendants in personal injury actions. Such a move would have the additional advantage of eliminating, at least in part, the cumbersome arguments over fault—that is, the plaintiffs' fault—even when no-fault coverage is not elected.

Of course, the question might be asked as to why the victim's conduct should *never* be a factor in influencing payment after an accident. Professor Calabresi tells us that our primary goal in imposing accidental losses (whether by transferring or leaving them) is to influence conduct in such a way as to lessen the number and severity of accidents.[66] But speaking only of personal injuries, imposing losses on individual victims can never have a significant deterrent effect, since the desire to avoid being hurt is invariably much more compelling than the desire to avoid financial loss. As a practical matter, individuals driving cars or using power tools—or deciding to do such things—will never be significantly influenced by fear of the effect of their conduct on their being paid by insurance once an accident occurs, even in the unlikely event they understand the laws of contributory negligence and assumption of risk.[67] Moreover, only payment from liability insurance is sacrificed by careless conduct; accident and health insurance, sick leave, fire insurance—even life insurance to survivors—are paid regardless of fault. As a result, imposing economic loss on the victim of an accident by denying him liability insurance payment because he was at fault will virtually never contribute to reducing the number or severity of accidents by making potential victims more careful.

And even to the extent one can imagine that rules of law and insurance can induce more careful behavior on the part of a potential accident victim, a rule of law such as that under elective no-fault liability denying payment for the victim's pain and suffering imposes a substantial portion of the loss on him. (But the reason for not paying for the victim's pain and suffering is not so much to influence his behavior; rather, it is because insurance dollars are so precious; there are probably never going to be enough to go around; better, then, to use those dollars to replace dollars lost than to use them to replace something essentially irreplaceable by dollars, namely pain and suffering.[68])

By way of contrast, when one turns to the person conducting an enterprise—say, a manufacturer or doctor—one sees that financial considerations are bound to predominate over fear of personal injury as a deterrent against unsafe conduct. The impersonal institutional enterprise, by definition, cannot suffer personal injury. Of course, its officers—or the practitioner providing, say, medical services—will most likely not want patrons to get hurt for humanitarian reasons. But economic motives are always going to be operating and probably often predominate. Another way to think about this is to recognize that the potential individual injury victim has only one personal injury to think about—his own. And it would be so awful to his person that he doesn't get around to thinking about its financial or insurance consequences. But for the entrepreneur, personal injury losses mean losses to *others*, and as to them, he is inevitably going to be thinking about them in the aggregate, and therefore, about their financial repercussions on him. This explains why fear of paying damages may well influence a potential defendant to be more careful, whereas fear of not being paid damages will not influence a potential plaintiff to be more careful.[69]

* * *

[Pages omitted (ed.).]

Conclusion

Turning back in closing to elective no-fault liability, D. P. Moynihan, in discussing the advantages of no-fault auto insurance, stated that the proponents of no-fault insurance are "right in the all important perception as to what it is Americans are good at. We are good at maintaining business relationships once a basis for mutual self interest is established. [No-fault insurance] . . . would establish one." [81]

Elective no-fault liability, by allowing the businessman and his customer, or a doctor and his patient, to bypass the lawyers, with all their acrimonious, inappropriate and self-serving cumbersomeness, in the event of accidental injury in the course of using a product or service, is also surely an excellent example of establishing a relationship based on mutual self interest.

The United States applied no-fault insurance to work accidents at the turn of the *last* century. One would hope we would not wait to attempt to apply it to all kinds of accidents until the turn of the *next* century. But time is running out.

FOOTNOTES

* This article is a revised, shortened version of an article entitled "Expanding No-Fault Beyond Auto Insurance," 59 *Virginia Law Review* 749 (May 1973). Both articles are adapted from portions of a forthcoming book dealing with extending the no-fault concept beyond auto insurance. All these writings are part of a study by the author financed by the John Simon Guggenheim Memorial Foundation, Consumers Union, the Foundation for Insurance Research Study and Training (FIRST) of the League Insurance Group, Detroit, Michigan, and the Center for Advanced Study, University of Illinois. The author is also grateful to the Centre for Socio-Legal Studies, Wolfson College, Oxford University, England, where he was a Visiting Fellow for six months in 1973.

1 ". . . [T]he Massachusetts law has resulted in substantial savings in bodily injury premiums, as well as an unexpected decline in claims for damages. Favorable reports on the state's experience were largely responsible for the enactment of a no-fault law by its neighbor Connecticut." *New York Times*, Oct. 3, 1972, at p. 23, col. 5. For a favorable report on the similar Florida no-fault law, see *New York Times*, Nov. 24, 1972, at p. 59, cols. 2–3. But for a discussion of spurious no-fault laws which fail to limit the right to sue based on fault, see *New York Times*, Nov. 27, 1972, at p. 55, cols. 1–2, and April 8, 1973, at p. 32, col. 1; and J. O'Connell, *The Injury Industry*, Commerce Clearing House, Chicago, Ill. (1971), at pp. 111–114 (1971). See also footnote 64 below and accompanying text.

2 National Commission on Product Safety, Final Report, p. 73 (1970), CCH Consumer Product Safety Guide ¶ 400.

3 Id.

4 Id., at p. 74.

5 Id.

6 Id.

7 Id., at p. 1.

8 Id.

9 Id., at p. 68.

10 Id., at p. 12.

11 Id., at p. 25.

12 Id., at p. 29.

13 Id., at p. 30.

14 United States Department of Transportation, *Economic Consequences of Automobile Accident Injuries, Report of the Westat Research Corp.*, Vol. I, pp. 40, 118 (Table 11 FS) (1970).

14a Id., at pp. 146–147 (Table 15 FS).

15 National Commission on Product Safety, cited at footnote 2, at p. 70.

16 R. Keeton, *Compensation Systems: The Search for a Viable Alternative to Negligence Law*, p. 33 (1969).

17 Warne "Let's Hear from the Insurance Consumer," 36 *Insurance Counsel Journal* 494, 496 (1969). See also United States Department of Transportation, *Economic Consequences of Automobile Accident Injuries, Report of the Westat Research Corp.*, Vol. I, pp. 37–38 (1970); A. Conard, J. Morgan, M. R. Pratt, C. Voltz & R. Bombaugh, *Automobile Accident Costs and Payments: Studies in the Economics of Injury Reparation*, pp. 172, 186 (1964).

18 For medical malpractice insurance—where the insured event is similarly tangled—it has been estimated that only between 16 and 17 cents (!) ends up in victims' pockets. Footnote 30 below and accompanying text.

19 *Business Insurance*, Nov. 6, 1972, p. 55, col. 2.

20 Cf. *National Underwriter* (Prop. & Cas.Ed.), Jan. 12, 1973, at p. 2, col. 4.

21 *Report*, Secretary's Commission on Medical Malpractice (HEW) (1973).

22 *Medical Malpractice: A Discussion of Alternative Compensation and Quality Control Systems*, a Center Occasional Paper, p. 17 (Center for the Study of Democratic Institutions, D. McDonald, Ed., 1971).

23 M. Gross, *The Doctors* 520 (1966).

24 Subcommittee on Executive Reorganization, 91st Cong., 1st Sess., "Medical Malpractice: The Patient versus the Physician," p. 5 (Comm.Print 1969). But see *Report*, cited at footnote 21, at p. 10.

25 Center Occasional Paper, cited at footnote 22, at p. 4.

26 Id.

27 *Report*, cited at footnote 21, at p. 6.

27a *Report*, Secretary's Commission on Medical Malpractice (HEW) 8 (App.1973).

28 R. E. Keeton, "Compensation for Medical Accidents," 121 *University of Pennsylvania Law Review* 590, 595, n. 16 (1973).

29 "Medical Malpractice," cited at footnote 24, at p. 2.

30 Center Occasional Paper, cited at footnote 22, at p. 5.

31 Footnote 17 above and accompanying text.

32 J. O'Connell, cited at footnote 1, at pp. 13–14.

33 Id., at p. 16.

34 Id., at pp. 29–30.

35 Id., at pp. 30–36.

36 Id., at p. 4. That the system also does little, if anything, to serve a deterrent purpose against unsafe products, see Whitford, "Products Liability," in Supplemental Studies, National Commission on Product Safety, pp. 221, 228–230 (1970); Denenberg, Statement, 9a Hearings, National Commission on Product Safety, IX–311, IX–312 to IX–317 (1970). For an indication that the present tort liability system does little, if anything, to encourage better medical care, but on the contrary, has deleterious effects on health care, see *Report*, cited at footnote 21 above, at pp. 14–17.

36a See footnote 37 below.

37 For an excellent discussion of the problems of applying the no-fault concept to medical accidents, see R. E. Keeton, cited at footnote 28. See also J. O'Connell, "Expanding No-Fault Beyond Auto Insurance," 59 *Virginia Law Review* 749, 790–795 (1973).

The reader will note I referred to "a sufficiently dangerous—or otherwise distinctive—activity, such that the statute can readily identify who is to be required to pay for what loss." Driving a car is sufficiently a dangerous activity that we know without much confusion the parameters of liability involved in paying for all the injuries caused by driving. In the case of any very dangerous activity—such as blasting—arguably the same is true. That is one reason it has been so feasible to impose liability without reference to any fault or defect on extra-hazardous enterprises under the common law. Employment, it will be noted, is often not dangerous, but it is sufficiently severable in time and space that no-fault workmen's compensation statutes have been able to define in a manageable way who is to be required to pay for what loss (granted the vexing—but not insurmountable—problems in defining the phrase "arising out of and in the course of employment").

38 For a New Zealand statute in substantial measure doing just that, see Accident Compensation Act, 1972, No. 43 (N. Z.). For a discussion of the Act, see Palmer, "Compensation for Personal Injury: A Requiem for the Common Law in New Zealand," 21 *American Journal of Comparative Law* 1 (1973); Palmer & Lemons, "Toward the Disappearance of Tort Law—New Zealand's New Compensation Plan," 1972 *University of Illinois Law Forum* 693; and Palmer, "Abolishing the Personal Injury Tort System: The New Zealand Experience," 9 *Alberta Law Review* 169 (1971). See also Franklin, "Replacing the Negligence Lottery: Compensation and Selective Reimbursement," 53 *Virginia Law Review* 774 (1967); and T. Ison, *The Forensic Lottery: A Critique on Tort Liability as a System of Personal Injury Compensation* (1967).

39 *New York Times*, Aug. 6, 1971, at p. 13, col. 1.

40 *New York Times*, Nov. 30, 1972, at p. 1, col. 1.

41 United States Department of Transportation, *Motor Vehicle Crash Losses and Their Compensation in the United States: A Report to the Congress and the President*, March 1971, p. 6. These figures were computed using the losses listed in Table 2 for Medical Expense, Wage Loss, and Other Expenses.

42 Footnote 38 above.

43 For a discussion of the interaction of tort law and social insurance in Europe, see R. Keeton & J. O'Connell, *Basic Protection for the Traffic Victim*, pp. 189–218 (1965); United States Department of Transportation, *Comparative Studies in Automobile Accident Compensation* (1970).

44 G. Calabresi, *The Costs of Accidents* (1970).

45 See generally, J. O'Connell, cited at footnote 1, at pp. 143–146.

46 Ross, book review of *The Costs of Accidents*, 84 *Harvard Law Review* 1322, 1323 (1971).

47 For a much more extensive discussion—along with supporting statistics—which rejects, at least for the immediate future, a Social Security solution to accident compensation, see J. O'Connell, cited at footnote 37, at pp. 805–812.

[48] For a much more extensive discussion of this proposal, including an appraisal of incorporating Professor Calabresi's "economic" criteria to replace "fault" as the basis of tort liability, see J. O'Connell, cited at footnote 37.

[49] F. Mosteller & D. P. Moynihan, *On Equality of Educational Opportunity*, pp. 51–52 (1972).

[50] As quoted in *Newsweek*, Jan. 22, 1973, at p. 89.

[50a] For further discussion of elective no-fault liability, see J. O'Connell, cited at footnote 37, at pp. 796–801.

[51] Under elective medical no-fault liability, some problems such as "informed consent" remain. A doctor at least arguably should remain liable in regular tort for an adverse result he elected to cover under no-fault liability where he failed to properly warn the patient of the risk. But by delineating the risks covered—and for whom—elective no-fault liability will encourage, I expect, better focusing on these areas. If, for example, a doctor knows his insurance is payable for an adverse result from a given procedure regardless of how it happens, he's more likely to make sure the patient is in an appropriate condition for the procedure, is he not? And to discuss those risks with the patient? (Actually, though, the extent to which doctors do in fact—and ideally should—discuss adverse possibilities with patients is a racking problem indeed, the subtleties of which often seem to escape us lawyers. See M. Halberstam, "The Doctor's New Dilemma—'Will I Be Sued?,' " *New York Times*, Feb. 14, 1971, Sec. 6 (magazine), at pp. 8, 34–35. At any rate, it would seem that a precise focusing encouraged by elective no-fault liability on the risks involved in a given procedure would have a salutary effect here, as well as solving many other problems.)

If, however, litigation over informed consent mushrooms and proves to be cumbersome and wasteful on the scale of other medical malpractice litigation, a case might be made for abolishing the tort action based on lack of informed consent once the doctor agrees to cover the adverse result on a no-fault basis. Better to rely on medical peer group review (which might well be more aggressive with the spectre of much resented malpractice litigation removed) and even criminal sanctions to encourage medical propriety than to rely on civil litigation insulated by impersonal insurance payment, especially where relying on civil litigation diverts funds from other—and arguably better—uses, namely, payment for out-of-pocket losses.

[52] The argument may be raised in opposition to elective no-fault liability for medical cases that freeing doctors from medical malpractice tort liability will lessen deterrence of medical malpractice. But in the case of medical malpractice, the deterrence seems particularly slight under regular tort liability in light of the "conspiracy of silence" enveloping so much malpractice. At any rate, with an insurance system returning 17 cents out of a dollar premium in benefits to victims (see footnote 30 above and accompanying text), shouldn't we be ready to at least experiment with something new?

But what *is* the effect on deterrence if doctors opt for no-fault liability because it removes all stigma and is economically preferable? In other words, given the absence of stigma and reduced insurance premiums, where would the deterrent come from? And if stigma is so much more important than money that doctors will elect, even though they pay more, won't the greatest incentive for the exercise of care be eliminated?

The answer is that the episodic and irrational nature of present malpractice claims and litigation simply does not provide much incentive to due care. Even if elective no-fault liability costs less than present fault liability insurance, the premiums will still be substantial, and they should vary with a doctor's record. The only way he can control costs is to be careful. So incentives from insurance costs will still operate, and arguably more rationally than before.

The wisdom of experimenting with no-fault insurance for injuries incurred in the course of medical treatment is echoed by the Final Report of the Secretary's Commission on Medical Malpractice, sponsored by the Department of Health, Education and Welfare. See footnote 21 above. The Report, a result of a year-long study, states "The principle of compensating for injury without the necessity of proving fault is an old one and growing ever more popular," but then cautions that there are "difficult problems we face in seeking to develop any effective medical injury compensation system which is not fault-based . . . [and] the Commission . . . does not believe that we should leap headlong from a system that works (with however many faults) into an untested one that may cause even more severe problems." *Report*, cited at footnote 21, at pp. 100–101. In addition, the Report states, that various proposals "[should] be developed, tested and demonstrated through both public and private initiatives . . . ." Also, "the Federal Government [should] fund one or more demonstration projects at the state or local level in order to test and evaluate the feasibility of possible alternative medical injury compensation systems." *Report*, cited at footnote 21, at p. 107. See also *Report Appendix*, cited at footnote 27a, at p. 450.

53 2 A. Larson, *Workmen's Compensation Law*, Sec. 67, at pp. 152.8–152.28 (1970). Of course, it is true that under elective workmen's compensation, employees as well as employers are given an election to be covered under workmen's compensation. (West Virginia, though, does allow the employer to elect, but not the employee. W.Va.Code Ann. Secs. 2516, 2517 (1943)). But that is feasible under workmen's compensation because one has a feasible fixed point in time prior to an accident when the employee must make his election, namely, at the time of employment. One could not allow election *after* injury without imposing on the employer the problem of adverse selection. But actually the right of an employee to elect not to be covered is highly theoretic. In Massachusetts, for example, where the employee retains the right not to be covered (although the Act is compulsory as to an employer), no employees ever elect not to be covered, and, as a practical matter, wouldn't be hired if they did. Horowitz & Bear, "Would a Compulsory Workmen's Compensation Act Without Trial by Jury Be Constitutional in Massachusetts?" 18 *Boston University Law Review* 35–36 (1938).

54 For example, *Ives v. South Buffalo R.R.*, 201 N.Y. 271, 94 N.E. 431 (1911).

55 *New York Cent. R.R. v. White*, 243 U.S. 188 (1917); *Hawkins v. Bleakly*, 243 U.S. 210 (1917); *Mountain Timber Co. v. Washington*, 243 U.S. 219 (1917).

56 Footnotes 48–50 above and accompanying text.

57 For a proposal of such no-fault extra-hazardous enterprise liability, see footnotes 74–80 below and accompanying text.

58 *Report of the National Commission on State Workmen's Compensation Laws*, p. 44 (1972). See id., at p. 45, Table 2.3.

59 Id., at pp. 44–45.

60 For a comprehensive review of the public opinion surveys on this topic, see O'Connell & Wilson, "Public Opinion on No-Fault Auto Insurance: A Survey of the Surveys," 1970 *University of Illinois Law Forum* 307; also appearing in O'Connell & Wilson, "Public Opinion Polls on the Fault System: State Farm versus Other Surveys." 568 Insurance Law Journal 261 (May 1970), and O'Connell & Wilson, "The Department of Transportation and Market Facts Public Opinion Polls on No-Fault Auto Insurance," 580 Insurance Law Journal 239 (May 1971). But for a report on a statewide vote in Colorado rejecting a no-fault law under an initiative procedure, see *National Underwriter* (Prop. & Cas.Ed.), Nov. 10, 1972, p. 1, col. 4. In that instance, the complications of trying to enact a complex statute by an initiative process render the vote doubtful as a reflection of public opinion on no-fault. Id.

61 J. O'Connell & R. Simon, *Payment for Pain and Suffering: Who Wants What, When & Why?* 29–34 (1972); also printed in 1972 *University of Illinois Law Forum* 1, 29–34.

[62] But see J. O'Connell, cited at footnote 1, at p. 118, indicating that fear of padded medical bills decreases with the seriousness of the injury. Increasingly, a tort exemption tied to a medical expenditure "threshold" is gaining acceptance in no-fault auto legislation enacted by the states.

[63] See R. Keeton & J. O'Connell, cited at footnote 43, at p. 350.

[63a] The mechanics of such elective no-fault auto liability might be structured to preserve an insured, his family, and the occupants of his car being paid by his own insurance company. Thus, in a typical two-car collision between driver A and driver B, if both had elected no-fault liability, A's insurer would pay the occupants of A's car (including A) on a no-fault basis and B's insurer would pay the occupants of B's car (including B) on the same basis, with concomitant tort exemptions. If only A had elected no-fault liability, A's insurer would be required to pay the occupants of A's car on a no-fault basis, as well as the occupants of B's car (including B). But A, as well as the occupants of both A's car and B's car, would then retain their tort actions against B, and out of any proceeds of any recovery from B, they would be required to reimburse A's insurer for any amounts previously paid to them. As to accidents involving only one car insured for no-fault liability (whether the accident involved two cars or only one), any motorist could be offered optional no-fault coverage for himself. Perhaps indeed such coverage should be compulsory for anyone choosing no-fault liability coverage, just as I would be inclined to make no-fault coverage of one's own family compulsory, even where the jurisdiction has intrafamily immunity from regular tort liability.

[64] See footnote 2 above.

[65] H. Somers & A. Somers, *Workmen's Compensation*, p. 21 (1954).

[66] G. Calabresi, cited at footnote 44, at pp. 25–26.

[67] For an indication that somewhere between 40 to 50 per cent of the public does not understand that contributory negligence bars recovery in tort claims, see United States Department of Transportation, *Public Attitudes Toward Auto Insurance: A Report of the Survey Research Center, Institute for Social Research. The University of Michigan*, p. 71 (Automobile Insurance and Compensation Study 1970); J. O'Connell & W. Wilson, *Car Insurance and Consumer Desires*, pp. 12–13 (1969).

[68] R. Keeton & J. O'Connell, cited at footnote 43, at pp. 361–362.

[69] When, as in the case of auto accidents, one is dealing with two individual drivers, fear of higher insurance premiums *may* influence each of them to be more careful. But to the extent they are thinking that way, they are not really thinking about getting seriously hurt. The minute that possibility enters their heads, it isn't a financial consideration—such as, a denial of payment for personal injury—that exerts any influence, but rather the horror of the spectre of personal injury itself. So although an increase or decrease of insurance premiums *may* influence an individual's behavior to the extent one is concerned with being seriously injured, it is only the fear of personal injury that influences behavior, not fear of being denied payment for it.

[81] D. P. Moynihan, "Next: A New Auto Insurance Policy," *New York Times*, Aug. 27, 1967, Sec. 6 (Magazine) at pp. 26, 82.

C Continued

19: TOWARD A GENERAL THEORY OF PERSONAL INJURY LOSS

NEIL K. KOMESAR*

This article employs a recent change in the economic analysis of the household to reexamine the legal framework for assessing the loss resulting from physical injury.

It is important at the outset to distinguish between loss from personal injury and the amount of the loss that is or should be compensable by legal action. Thus, despite oft-repeated assertions that "full compensation" is the objective of the personal-injury damage machinery,[1] it would be ingenuous to claim that every element of loss should be compensated. There are strong policy grounds for setting damages below losses. The two most basic of these are the social costs of measurement or assessment and the implicit adjustment in the amount of damages made in recognition of different degrees of liability or fault. The marginal social costs of measuring or assessing less tangible forms of loss may be greater per dollar of loss than with more tangible forms. As such, society may wisely choose to limit not only the amount but also the type of loss compensated. The liability considerations are more subtle but also important. It is already thought that juries which hear both liability and damage questions employ information about the former in considering the latter.[2] Such an approach seems sensible since it is doubtful that liability is really a binary phenomenon, "liable" or "not liable." The limitation on compensable loss which is implicitly part of the present damage rules may be an institutionalization of a view that a tortfeasor cannot be totally responsible.

Journal of Legal Studies, Vol. III, No. 2, June 1974, p. 457.

While either "measurement" or "liability" considerations may explain the observed divergence between loss and compensable damages, the present structure has failed to consider systematically such policy grounds. While such a failure makes proof of their existence difficult to establish, this article will remain sensitive to the potential role of these factors as determinants of the observed legal rules.

Cognizant of these other policy grounds and of the many other complexities in the damage area, including the mysterious processes of the jury,[3] this article makes no direct proposals for reform of the damage rules. Its object is a clarification of the meaning of personal injury loss. In that light it will examine the general structure of personal injury damages. To the extent that existing damage rules are the product of a mistaken perception of actual loss, the rules may need reform.

The recent surge of conceptual economic analyses of the liability side of the personal injury question [4] provides two reasons for a similar examination of the damage side. First, the discrepancy in analytical effort afforded these two closely related areas creates an incentive to examine the slighted area.[5] Second, although the liability discussion has not given much attention to damages, the proposed reforms eliminating liability considerations create the possibility that the damage structure itself will be changed, perhaps in the direction of schedule damages.[6] While the nuances of liability may provide valid grounds for a limitation of damages, the specifics of that limitation need careful consideration. To the extent that present legal perceptions of loss from personal injury place the wrong weight on certain forms of loss due to a misunderstanding of the economic nature of those forms, a limitation of liability based on present perceptions would choose the wrong forms of loss for extinction.

Another reason for examining damage concepts lies in the growing concern of the law with assessing nonconventional sources of loss. There have been recent changes in the articulation and measurement of such categories as wrongful death of children or of wives and mothers, loss of wife's services, and loss of husband's consortium. Although these changes have been sporadic and piecemeal, they do signify pressures on the personal injury damage rules toward recognition of real, but unconventional, forms of loss.

I. Conceptual Framework

Aside from certain out-of-pocket costs such as "medical expenses," [7] the crux of personal injury is the value of time. Time is perhaps the most important basic resource possessed by individuals and households. An individual's market income is usually at least a partial product of the sale of his time on the market, and his pleasures are at least partially the product of the use of his time in pleasurable activity. The victim of personal injury suffers loss through the reallocation or extinction of time: extinction to the extent that death ensues immediately or through shortened life expectancy; reallocation to the extent that the incident forces the injured party to employ his time in a manner he would not have chosen in the absence of the injury.

The present personal injury damage structure explicitly considers the value of time in the context of lost earnings or lost earning capacity. There the plaintiff is compensated because his time has been or will be employed in a less remunerative manner. The crux of the analysis which follows is that *all* personal injury damages can be analyzed profitably in the same terms as those accepted for earning capacity and that the present damage structure may have disregarded or at least misperceived a large part of the value of the time loss.

Recently a change in economic analysis has focused more attention on household resources, and in particular time resources.[8] Previously the attention of economists had been centered almost exclusively on the workings of the national economy and the market firm. The household received only passing attention as the provider of labor inputs for the market and the final depository for the goods and services produced on the market. Traditional economics viewed the household's decisions in terms of its reaction to the market. The household's utility function (its basic decision-making structure) was expressed exclusively in terms of the amount of market goods and services which the household "consumed."[9] The household's ability to acquire these goods and services was constrained by the amount of market income that it received (wages, dividends, interest).[10] In general the most important component of this income is wage income obtained by time spent in the labor market. Thus the older theory conceived household happiness in terms of goods and services purchased from the market with income received primarily in the form of wages. The manner in which these purchases were used within the household remained shrouded in mystery so far as economic theory was concerned.

So long as this conceptual framework was not pushed too hard it worked passably well in the general analysis of the demand for market goods and services. However, when economists began to search more deeply into the determinants of the supply of labor, such as investment in human capital (education), labor force participation (labor-leisure choice), birth rates, morbidity, and mortality, this featureless, passive conception of the household proved to be inadequate.

The newer conceptual framework provides more substance to the household, examining how the household employs market goods and services and allocates its time resources, part of which it sends out into the labor force. The analysis of market production had never been limited simply to counting the amount of raw material or the number of machines and laborers used by the factory; the process of combining these factors of production into the final output had received equal if not greater attention. The new analysis of the household, called "household production theory," takes the same conceptual path and examines the process by which the household combines its factors into its final outputs. Household utility and therefore decisions are no longer conceived of as primarily dependent on market goods and services. Instead the ultimate sources of utility, termed commodities, are produced by the household by combining market goods and services with time of the household members just as the market firm combines material and labor inputs into production of its final output.[11]

The commodities produced can include procreation, meals, recreation, childrearing, protection, health, etc. These categories can be broken down further or defined at points closer to the ultimate utility object. However, the important aspect of the theory is not the final product, but the productive process. When economic analysis is focused more closely on the workings of the household, it does more than provide a more realistic view of final consumption.[12] It allows for a more complete integration of household time inputs into an analysis of the household. Health, meals, childrearing, etc. are produced by inputs of household members' time as well as inputs of market goods and services. The opportunity costs of the time of household members and the substitution between household time and market-produced goods and services can now be considered in the context of elements that have traditionally entered into the analysis of production by market firms: changes in factor prices, technological capacity, externalities, etc.

Even more importantly for the present context, as the general framework changed so did the basic measure of the household's resources, the "budget constraint." In the traditional theory, since utility was derived from market goods and services, the household's ability to gain utility was measured by its *market income,* consisting primarily of wages received for time employed in the labor force. However, the new theory bases utility on commodities which in turn are produced by market goods and services *and* direct time inputs by household members. Thus, the new budget must include the time available for direct household production as well as the market income available for the purchase of market-produced inputs.

Nor is it necessary to measure household resources strictly in terms of two separate entities, market goods and services and time in household production. Since the major component of the household's access to market goods and services, its market income, is primarily wage income, the household's *total* income can now be measured primarily in terms of its *total* time resources, some of which are sold on the market as a means of obtaining the market inputs employed in household production and some of which are employed directly in household production. This new budget constraint is called "full income." [13]

As noted previously, the crux of personal injury loss lies in the reallocation or extinction of the time resources of the household. The budget constraints of both the traditional and household production approaches to consumer behavior stress time. But while the traditional theory explicitly recognized the time of a household member only when it was spent in the labor force, the new theory recognizes the time of the household member in both his market (labor) and nonmarket activities. More importantly, it recognizes them on an equal footing. A particular commodity might be produced with more home time and fewer market goods and services or vice versa. There are no a priori grounds to assume that one set of factors is more important to the household.

Like the traditional economic conception of the household, personal injury damage law stresses market time. While earnings or earning capacity are not the only allowable categories of damages, they are the most commonly accepted and the only ones figured on an incremental hourly basis. Although it is not possible to determine the extent to which the emphasis on market activity that characterized the older economic perception of the household affected the law's perception of personal injury damage, the similarity in emphasis in the two areas does raise the possibility of cross-fertilization or perhaps theories independently evolved given the same intellectual climate. As Professor McCormick has noted, economic theory plays a role in the determination of damage rules.[14] Thus, there may be reason to believe the older economic conceptions of the household influenced the emphasis on market time which characterizes the present law of personal injury damages.[15]

II. Applications

A. Nonmarket Time

1. Integration of the Concept. Given the conceptual framework, it is next relevant to inquire how the damage structure might integrate these notions. It was previously noted that the only existing rubric of personal injury damages which explicitly recognizes the value of time is "earning capacity." The treatment of earning capacity will continue to be an important source of comparison with the treatment of nonmarket time. In addition to this comparison, reconsideration of the treatment of nonmarket time can also profit from a comparison with the damage rules applicable to the loss of inputs into market-firm production and the destruction of personal property.

Since the new economic analysis of the household employs the same analysis generally applied to the market firm, the damage rules applicable to losses incurred by such firms through tortious acts are relevant.   In this connection the following two simple hypotheticals yield some useful insights.   First, consider the X Corporation, famous for the laundry detergent, Sudso, which it produces by combining a number of ingredients including a scouring powder.   It produces this scouring powder itself. Approximately one-third of the powder is used as an ingredient in Sudso, one-third is sold to the Y Corporation, a processor of industrial solvents, and one-third is used by the X Corporation to keep its own plant clean. The corporation separately stockpiles the scouring powder for each of the various uses.   Due to the negligence of a neighbor, all three of the stockpiles are destroyed.   Second, consider a dairy farmer who raises corn to feed his cows and sells the surplus corn on the market using the funds received from the sale to purchase inputs for his milk production: machines, veterinary services, milk pails, paint for his barn, etc.   Due to the negligence of a neighbor, his corn is destroyed.

These hypotheticals reveal the obvious fact that a market firm can recover for loss of its inputs due to the tortious act of another without regard to the manner in which those inputs would have entered the productive process.   The soap corporation can recover for the loss of all three stockpiles despite the fact that one was to be directly sold on the market, another was to be a physical input into the firm's major product, Sudso, and another was never to reach the marketplace at all.   The farmer can recover for the value of the corn he would have input directly into the productive process as well as the corn he would have sold on the market in order to obtain funds used to purchase other direct inputs for his milk production.

There are no conceptual grounds for treating the household firm differently.   The loss of household time that would have been employed directly in household production deserves the same recognition accorded the loss of time which would have been sold on the market in order to obtain the funds used to purchase the other direct inputs employed in household production.

There is another important insight provided by the market-firm analogy.   The amount that the farmer could have received for his corn on the market or the soap corporation could have received for the scouring powder provides a useful lower-bound estimate of the value of those inputs in internal production.   One use of the hypothetical factors of production (corn and scouring powder) was direct sale of the market. The benefit or product from the sale of a unit of the scouring powder or corn is the market price of that unit.   This figure can be employed to value the use of the factor in internal production.   Given diminishing returns to internal use, the value of the marginal unit in internal use would be equal to the market price while the value of nonmarginal units would be greater than the market price. Thus, it is accurate to say that the value of a factor of production in internal production is worth *at least* the amount that would have been received from its direct sale on the market. Similarly, the value of a unit of time in internal household production is worth *at least* the amount that would have been received from its direct sale on the market (the applicable wage rate).

The approach taken by the law of damages to the tortious damage or destruction of personal property provides another useful source of comparison with the approach to the tortious injury of the person. As previously noted, the household produces its ultimate commodities by combining the time of its members with goods and services purchased on the market. While household-production theory treats these two forms of inputs similarly, the law of damages does not. If an automobile, television set, pleasure boat, polo pony, stove, refrigerator, or any other chattel is damaged or destroyed because of the tortious act of a third party, the loss would clearly be compensable under present damage rules.[16] There would be no necessity to show that the chattel was employed to produce market income for the household. Thus, in an automobile collision, the destruction of the automobile or the loss of its services would be compensable (given liability) without any distinction between those services associated with earning market income and those associated with household activities. Should the destruction of the driver and loss of his or her services be treated differently?

These chattels are inputs into the household processes which produce the ultimate pleasure and well-being of the household.[17] The loss to the household is the decrease in its ability to produce the same state of welfare associated with the original state of these chattels. These chattel inputs are conceptually identical to the time that is used with them in order to produce the desired state of welfare. Damage or destruction of the time input occasions the same sort of loss as damage or destruction of the material input.

While the law of damages recognizes the inputs into market production despite the manner in which they enter the productive process,[18] and the material inputs into household production without the necessity of showing any direct pecuniary return from the input, the emphasis of the personal-injury damages rules on market activities ignores all but a small segment of the time inputs of the household. The law's conception of personal injury loss seems to treat each week as though it contained 40 hours (eight hours per day, five days per week) rather than 168 hours (24 hours per day, seven days per week).[19]

Here it becomes relevant to note the secular decline in the number of hours worked per capita despite the secular increase in the real wage.

There are several interpretations of this somewhat remarkable phenomenon.[20] However, all of the interpretations emphasize the apparently increased value of nonmarket time. The substitution of nonmarket for market time despite the increase in real wages indicates that at the margin the value of nonmarket time increased even more rapidly than that of market time.

This secular substitution of nonmarket for market time has some important implications in the present context. First, although the previous discussion has indicated that nonmarket time is conceptually similar to market time, it might still be argued that nonmarket time had in fact little actual value relative to market time. One measure of the value of nonmarket time—or more accurately of the lower-bound on the value of nonmarket time—is its alternative earnings in the market (*i. e.*, its "opportunity costs").[21] In some instances the market value of time now spent in nonmarket activities is arguably quite low and perhaps negative.[22] However, the substitution of nonmarket for market time in the face of increased real wages indicates that at least some nonmarket time has a market alternative approximately equal to the wage rate observed for the market hours.

Second, the secular decline in hours allocated to the market provides the paradoxical possibility that the present personal injury damage structure may be the process of further narrowing its conception of loss. Thus, most of the recent articles extolling the benefits of the economist-statistician as an expert witness on personal injury damage issues have concentrated on the importance of the secular upward trend in real wages in the determination of lost earning capacity.[23] Failure to consider this increase in real wages would produce an underestimation of the potential hourly earnings lost by the injured plaintiff. But, as indicated, the increased real wages have been associated with a decrease in hours allocated to the labor force. This decrease is a source of reduction in the estimate of lost earning capacity which will partially offset the increase associated with the increased real wage. Thus, paradoxically, as time becomes more valuable, less of it will be considered by the earning-capacity component of the personal-injury damage structure. As noted previously that damage structure has already narrowed its perceived week from 168 to 40 hours. The thrust of the secular trends in real wages and hours worked means that the perceived hours per week will be diminished further.[24]

   2. **Legal Approaches to Nonmarket Time.** While the personal injury damage rules do not recognize nonmarket time as such, they have recognized losses beyond those of earnings and earning capacity. Some of this residual constitutes, albeit indirectly, a reaction to loss of nonmarket time. This section will consider that patchwork body of law. The discussion will focus on the conception of loss embodied in each of these categories

and the loss still uncompensated by them.   The discussion will be organized by household role: child, wife, husband.

Thus far, the personal injury damage rules have been treated as a whole.   It is necessary now to distinguish between at least three different approaches.   If the victim lives, the personal injury damage rules are applied.   If the victim dies there are two different general approaches to "wrongful death" damages: loss to estate and loss to survivor.   Since the wrongful-death concept is the product of statutory rather than common law, the applicable standard is dependent on the statutes of the particular jurisdiction.   The "loss to estate" approach is an extension of personal-injury law that allows the representative of the estate to collect for damage suffered by the victim.   The "loss to survivors" approach creates a new cause of action based on the damage suffered by the survivors due to the death of the victim.[25]   It is important to distinguish between these three general approaches because they vary in their treatment of nonmarket time.[26]

a. *Child and Housewife.*   Not surprisingly, most of the legal recognition of nonmarket time loss is to be found in situations where the directly injured party devoted little, if any, time to market activities. Where substantial market earnings are in evidence, it is possible to ignore other aspects of loss under cover of the seemingly sizable recoveries.   However, where severe physical incapacity is present but the injured party can show no market activity, the legal system is faced with the quandary of either providing negligible recovery or searching beyond the safe confines of market activity.   Two groups that have traditionally had minor roles in the market are children and married women.[27]

(1) *Injury to a Housewife.*   Where the tortious act leaves the housewife alive but injured, the damage law provides a mechanism for recognition of the value of her nonmarket time.   It provides recovery for loss of her household services and loss of "consortium."   The latter category covers the less tangible aspects of the wife's nonmarket time—companionship, society, and conjugal relations.

The loss occasioned by injury to the housewife could have been valued in terms of the opportunity costs of the housewife's time rather than in terms of the value of her services.   The two methods have different relative merits from the standpoint of measurement; these will be discussed subsequently.[28]   However, in its recognition of housewife's services, the law of personal injury damage comes closer to a conceptually valid perception of nonmarket time than it does in any other area.

The problem that arises in connection with the injured housewife is not the perception of the loss but the peculiarly limited standing to recover it.   The right of recovery does not belong to the injured victim or even to the household per se.[29]   It belongs to the husband.   The right evolved from the common law perception of the wife as an extension of her husband. In return for the obligation to provide support, the husband received the right to the proceeds of the wife's time. Initially this right involved all of the wife's time. The wife's own right of recovery was limited to her pain and suffering. By statute the wife now has the right to recover for the loss to her market time (lost earnings or earning capacity). But the nonmarket time still belongs to the husband.[30]

Several insights can be drawn from this process. First, it is not surprising that the wife's services should be an area of nonmarket time recognized by the law while other nonmarket time was not. The treatment of a wife's services is not an outgrowth of an advanced and sophisticated perception of the value of nonmarket time, but is, rather, an unsophisticated application of the traditional perception of chattels. The wife was a chattel of her hubsand and the loss of her services was no more than the loss of the services of other chattels. Second, it is interesting that nonmarket time is perceived as separate from pain and suffering. The husband collects for the former while the wife collects for the latter. It appears that the damage law conceives of pain and suffering as a category distinct from the loss of value of time, either market or nonmarket time.

If the wife dies as a result of the tortious act, the wrongful-death approaches come into play and they may have substantially different outcomes. Under the survivorship approach, the household (i. e., its remaining members) is eligible to recover for the loss caused it by the death of the wife (mother). This situation is different if the woman lives, since then only the husband, if there is one, can recover. But under the wrongful-death approach the husband or children can recover for the loss of the woman's household services as it affects them.

While the loss-to-survivors approach to the wrongful death of a housewife or mother combines the sensible perception of nonmarket time characteristic of the approach to the personal injury of the housewife with a broader standing to recover, the loss-to-estate approach presents substantial problems. From a strict application of the rules, it would appear that the instantaneous death of a housewife who had no history of labor force participation and no evidence of any future participation would go uncompensated. Aside from some recovery for pain and suffering prior to death (a factor eliminated here by the assumption of instantaneous death), damages based on lost earning capacity are figured according to one of three methods: net earnings, accumulation (savings), and gross earnings. Whatever the method chosen, a victim who was specializing and would have continued to specialize in nonmarket activity would receive no recovery.

Faced with this stark example of failure of the personal injury damage structure to perceive the value of time, some courts and legislatures have altered the law by simply borrowing the loss-of-services category from the loss-to-survivors jurisdictions. Faced with the choice between economic reality and doctrinal consistency, these courts and legislatures opted for the former. A solution consistent with both would lie in the recognition of the loss of nonmarket and market time on the same basis.

Even in those jurisdictions where the rationale of the loss-to-estate doctrine is strictly followed, one suspects that courts and juries may avoid the outcome by basing awards on some hypothesized future labor force participation notwithstanding that the real probability of any such participation is virtually zero.[31] Anything but a nominal award in such a case reveals the tension between reality on the one hand and a formal legal perception that sees only market time on the other.

Thus, where a housewife is the victim of tortious acts, recovery for damages can range from payment for her household services as wife and mother (wrongful death, loss-to-survivors theory) to virtually nothing (wrongful death, loss-to-estate theory). Any recovery for her nonmarket time belongs neither to her nor to her administrator, but to her statutory survivors, usually her husband or children. The problems with so limited a concept of standing to recover are most apparent in the case of an unmarried woman, discussed later.

(2) *Injury to a Child.* If the child is injured but not killed, the father has a right of recovery for the loss of earnings or services during the child's minority. The child can recover for the present value of any lost income after majority plus any pain and suffering. If the child is killed, the two wrongful-death approaches apply: loss to survivors and loss to estate. The former involves loss of services to the surviving parents or other family; the latter involves an estimate based on future market earnings.

While the formal structure applicable to a child is similar to that applicable to a housewife, implementation has created different sorts of difficulties. The greatest difficulties in the case of the housewife arose as we saw in the loss-to-estate wrongful death context. The child cases encounter the greatest difficulty in connection with the services-to-the-household construct which is present in both personal-injury and loss-to-survivor wrongful death actions. While the services of the housewife have received much attention and methods of approximating the loss via market replacement have been devised, no such success has attended consideration of the child's services.

There are two sources of conventional pecuniary returns that a household might receive from a child: the child's prospective market activities while a minor (*e. g.*, delivering newspaper, farm work, summer or part-time jobs);[32] and the prospective "pension" provided by the child's support of the parents after the child's majority. While in individual cases it is possible that any of these items might represent a sizable portion of the real loss to the household,[33] it is likely that in most cases such recovery would be minimal. These items hardly capture the essence of a child's role in the household. The percentage of children who are labor force participants in any meaningful sense is small. The essence of the average child's role is in the *direct production* of household commodities. It is the value of his *nonmarket* time that provides the real source of loss given injury or death.

Nor is the essence of the child's role in the production of household commodities the performance of household chores. While he may perform conventional household services (*e. g.*, mowing the lawn, setting the table, washing the dishes, walking the dog), it is likely that a greater percentage of his time inputs are reflected in less tangible commodities such as familial affection or parental pride. The major source of benefits reflected in the choice to have children is to be found in the value of these commodities rather than in the value of the market income or close equivalents within the household that the child might provide the household.[34]

Thus, unlike the case of the wife, there is usually no easy recourse to either market opportunity costs or market replacement services as sources of estimation of the loss. Does this mean that the value of the child is zero? The answer to this question is yes only to the extent that the value of the *use* of a T.V., automobile, stove, pet dog, etc. is determined solely by the value of its *market*-income-producing ability. This value is different from its price or market value and is so precisely because its price or market value reflects the value of its nonmarket use. Because of legal restraints, there is no open market in children. But one need only observe the long waiting lines and black markets for adoption to infer a substantial market price. In addition, adopted and natural children are probably not perfect substitutes—the price of a natural child, if such a price existed, would most probably exceed that for an adopted child.

If talk of markets in children disturbs the reader, consider the expenditures made by parents on young children. They involve not only substantial out-of-pocket costs (*e. g.*, medical services, education, clothing, etc.), but probably an even more costly allocation of parental time.[35] Assuming some level of rationality on the part of prospective parents, the benefits of children would appear substantial and, in most cases, greatly in excess of the addition to the household's pecuniary income provided by the child.

I am aware of the fact that measurement of the value of a child is difficult. However, it seems a poor solution to this difficult problem to use criteria for damage recovery that are unrelated to the real value and therefore the real loss. Even if no better criteria can be found,[36] it would seem more appropriate to describe the general role of the child in the household in meaningful terms and allow the jury to assess the loss based on its view of the role of this particular child than to inform the jury that it is to search for loss in terms of pecuniary sources of income that are inapplicable. One expects that this is an area where the jury already disregards the artificial criteria supplied to it by the court and applies its own sense of the loss.[37] It would seem rational to recognize the process explicitly. The advantage of such recognition would lie in the possibility of jury decisions based on direct evidence on the pertinent matters rather than simply jury impressions gathered indirectly. It would also provide a basis for the evolution of a better articulated standard and more sensitive measures of the value of the child.

In the loss-to-estate jurisdictions, the wrongful death of a child has been evaluated in terms of the market earnings of the child for his expected life. Such an approach creates two problems. First, to the extent that the real purpose of the statute is to compensate survivors, the problems raised in the discussion of the pecuniary-approach measures used in survivor jurisdictions apply here. But while the problems are the same the end result is probably not. It would appear less likely that the amount of recovery would underestimate the actual loss.[38] Indeed the recovery could be in excess of the actual loss suffered by the family.

If, on the other hand, the loss-to-estate statutes really are aimed at providing the correct recovery for the actual loss to the deceased child, then the emphasis on market earnings ignores a substantial amount of loss. Death extinguishes more than 40 hours per week. There is no conceptual reason to single out the eight-hour segment of a 24-hour day for which the person would have received wages. In this context, the problems of recovery for the loss to a child are the same as the problems for all victims.

b. *The Other 128 Hours: Husbands and Unmarried Adults.* While the loss of nonmarket time has received some recognition in the case of housewives and children, it has received little recognition in the case of husbands and none in the case of single people. Persons in these categories are likely to be employed in market activities on a "full-time" basis, but "full-time" means 40 hours per week, not 168. Even in the case of the housewife or the child, one suspects that the law's attempt to compensate nonmarket time are based on approximations of a 40-hour "nonwork" week rather than of a 168-hour week.

If a husband is injured but not killed, he may recover for his lost earnings and earning capacity and his pain and suffering. At common law, his wife could not recover for any lost services or for consortium. Even today only a minority of American jurisdictions recognize the wife's right to recover for loss of husband's consortium.[39] If the husband is killed, then nonmarket services are recognized in loss-to-survivors jurisdiction, but these are usually provided in connection with those services associated with the raising of children—educational and moral upbringing [40]—and then only when there is evidence that these services have "practical and financial value." [41] In loss-to-estate jurisdictions, the nonmarket time of a deceased husband is ignored, especially if he followed normal patterns of employment. Such a result follows again from the application of the rules associated with loss to estate. In these cases, where there is evidence of lost earnings or lost earning capacity, there is little incentive for *sub rosa* accommodation of nonmarket time.

Where the victim injured but not killed is unmarried, there is no source of recovery for nonmarket time or even nonmarket services except to the extent that he or she collects for the pain component of this time under the aegis of pain and suffering.[42]

The disregard of nonmarket time is hardly more sensible in the case of a single-person household than in the case of a larger household. Consider the following hypothetical. A young law professor is injured through the fault of a third party and the injury takes the form of some impairment in the movement of her left arm. Assume that she is single, lives alone and the injury causes her little or no pain or humiliation. She is hurt during a school recess and is able to return quickly to work. There is no evidence that her ability to teach or research law is impaired. However, she cannot perform basic household functions such as cooking and cleaning, and she cannot take part in certain athletic activities such as golf or swimming in which she had spent a substantial part of her time.[43]

Is her loss, aside from medical expenses, zero? Do these losses of productivity in household activities constitute "pain and suffering"? Suppose, by way of comparison, that a different injury impairs only her ability to function on the job. She can no longer talk or read for long periods, the basic skills of a law professor. She must take a lower-paying job. Is her loss, aside from medical expenses, zero? Do these losses of productivity in market activities constitute "pain and suffering"?

In both instances, the injury impaired the value of the time of the victim. There are no a priori grounds for assuming that the loss is greater in one situation than the other. If the loss does not constitute pain and suffering in the second instance, it is difficult to understand why it should in the first instance. We return to this point later.[44]

    c. *Medical Expenses: A Brief Note on Household Production of Health.* Throughout the preceding discussion, the recovery of out-of-pocket costs such as medical expenses has been assumed or ignored. The actual loss to a household includes the costs to that household of convalescence but these costs include more than medical expenses, which represent only the expense of the material inputs in the household production of restored health. The standard "medical expense" item of damages does not include the value of household time inputs involved in this productive process.   The value of the victim's time inputs are reflected in the damage award to the extent that he missed time at work and the failure to count the value of his nonmarket time has already been discussed.   But there are other household time inputs beyond those of the victim.   Given any serious injury, adjustments are made within a household.   The time of the spouse spent tending to the victim may be substantial.   To the extent that the household produced this tending with market inputs (nurses, housekeepers, hospital room, hospital meals, physicians, etc.), the loss could be recovered.   But the value of any household time expended cannot.

The failure to consider a real loss here involves more than issues of fairness and adequate compensation.   There is also the possibility that the rules of damage recovery generate artificial incentives to employ market inputs.   While it is unlikely that households would allocate appreciably more time to the labor force because the personal injury damage structure failed to recognize nonmarket time adequately, it is not unlikely that they would choose an appreciably more market-input-intensive production of convalescence because of the damage structure's disregard of nonmarket time there.   In the general case, the effect of the differential treatment of market and nonmarket time is substantially reduced because it is discounted by the low probability of tortious injury.   In the case of convalescence, the injury has already occurred and the probability of damage recovery is high.[45]

Considering the apparently short supply (high social cost) of hospital and physician services, the household choice that employs these services as though they were free (because the decision-making household will not pay) may be highly inefficient.   Providing compensation for household time inputs as well as market inputs would eliminate this source of inefficiency.

B.   Pain and Suffering

It is difficult to generate a definition of "pain and suffering" which captures its intuitive meaning, and still can be consistently applied to actual fact situations.   If pain and suffering is defined as a measure of the decrease in life's enjoyment or loss of utility, then it is the total and sole measure of loss from personal injury.   Under either the old or new economic perception of the household, the ultimate goal is utility and either market income or full income is merely a means to that goal.   Thus, if a category of damages is meant to measure all decrease in utility, it measures all loss and it would be double counting to allow recovery for lost earning capacity or lost household services.

The present legal structure does not reflect such a broad definition of pain and suffering. On the market side, the law allows recovery for earning capacity and lost earnings as well as pain and suffering. On the non-market side, the law allows separate treatment of housewife's services and pain and suffering.

The less encompassing definition forces a distinction to be made between pain and loss of pleasure—not an easy distinction to make. One approach is to distinguish between physical discomfort and "loss of productivity," as the present system does. To understand the tentative distinction between these two things, consider the following somewhat fanciful hypothetical. A man enters the emergency room of a hospital with a cut on his arm. He receives immediate attention from Dr. X who stitches up the wound and gives the patient some mild sedative. While he is dozing, he is spotted by Dr. Y who mistakes him for one of his patients and has him deeply sedated. Through a series of further bungles he is kept sedated for over a week. He awakes to find himself in good physical shape, thoroughly rested, but missing a week. Did the patient-victim suffer loss? He felt no pain. In fact, he avoided some of the pain that would have otherwise been associated with his lacerated arm. But he did lose the use of one week of time, both market and nonmarket, and so a substantial real loss is likely.

The separation of physical discomfort and lost productive capacity is a separation of each unit of time into two potential components. These components are potentially present for *all* time units, both nonmarket and market. To suggest that pain and suffering is the law's measure of loss of nonmarket time while earning capacity is its measure of the loss of market time is to make a strange perception stranger: an individual is productive only eight hours a day, five days a week and suffers physical discomfort only during the remaining 16 hours per day and on weekends. The correct definition of pain and suffering is that it is a component of loss potentially associated with all 168 hours of the week.[46]

The separation of each hour into several components, which characterizes this analysis of pain and suffering, opens up consideration of other possible subdivisions of each hour. In particular, it is possible that hours seemingly spent in nonmarket activities contain market components and that hours seemingly spent in market activities contain nonmarket components. The first group would include that amount of sleeping, eating, exercise, etc. which increases the market productivity of the person. This increased productivity should be reflected in the wage received by the person for his market time and therefore covered by the present lost earning capacity and lost earnings categories.[47]

The second group is more interesting. It deals with that part of the value of market time captured directly by the household or individual in nonmarket amenities rather than in his observed wage.   Individuals in choosing market occupations have varying sensitivities to nonmarket amenities.   Location of the employment, characteristics of fellow employees, prestige, respect, social goals, etc. are common examples of nonmarket amenities that may provide trade-offs for money wages.   To the extent that such elements are present, existing legal approaches may not sufficiently compensate for lost market time.

This area has more than academic interest.   The present measures of lost earning capacity reveal an ambivalence about the applicable wage rate that reflects the tension between the observed wage rate and the full value of the hour.   This ambivalence is illustrated by the "earning potential" measures employed in cases where the victim has not yet had any market experience.[48]   For example, where the victim is still in school, his observed wage rate is often zero.   The law does not award zero recovery, but instead examines the earning capacity of individuals who have characteristics similar to the victims except that they are older and already labor-force participants.   To the extent that the legal system concentrates on those "similar" individuals who choose occupations with the highest observed real wage, it is applying a different standard to the victim without market experience than it applies to a victim who has a history of labor-force participation.   A victim of the latter type would present evidence of his actual real wage.   He might be able to adjust this wage rate by showing that his employment at the time of the incident was different than his normal employment.   But he could not point to individuals who had similar characteristics, but higher observed wage rates, and insist that the higher wage rates be used in the valuation of his lost market time.

The law's failure to consider the potential rather than the observed wage rate may, by ignoring the value of lost amenities, underestimate the real loss caused by the tortious injury.   Consider the earlier example of the young law professor who lost her job because she could no longer display the necessary speaking and reading stamina.   Many law professors could receive higher money wages in the practice of law.   They choose legal teaching for its nonpecuniary benefits.   Thus, if our hypothetical law professor had chosen to practice law, she might receive a more substantial recovery for her lost market time than she will receive given her professional choice.

There remains the question whether, in the case of an injury, a loss of the total value of the hours affected has occurred.   The time has not been extinguished; it has been reallocated.   The loss is the difference between the hour's value in its present and previous use.   This is a pervasive problem—it is present in recovery for lost earning capacity or lost earnings as well as in the case of nonmarket time units.   The present system awards the full observed wage to the plaintiff who cannot work despite the fact that the nonmarket use in which the plaintiff now employs his time may have substantial value in direct household production.

III. Measurement

The measurement of unconventional forms of loss is often difficult. However, there are at least two potential sources of improvement in measurement capability. One is the work of economists who are employing the household-production theory in analyses of the household's allocation of its time resources, market and nonmarket, and their productivity. The second is the strong incentive that personal-injury victims and the plaintiff's bar have to establish these additional real losses as bases of recovery. The bar has made use of economists to refine and expand existing loss concepts. A significant number of economists have gained some expertise in providing such information.[49] It is likely that, given a broader legal framework, the bar, and these economists, can find better measures of the unconventional forms of losses.

A.   Housewife's Time

Several recent articles discuss techniques for evaluating the loss of a housewife's or mother's services. Some suggest that the services be enumerated and their value measured in terms of the pecuniary costs of replicating each of these services on the market.[50] In theory, such a system would provide an accurate measure of the loss to the extent that (1) all services were enumerated, (2) each was adjusted for the quality of performance, and (3) a substitute market service could be identified. In fact, each of these conditions for accuracy presents substantial problems, especially the last two. It appears that, in practice, the valuation is limited to a few basic domestic services that have easily identifiable market substitutes. While such a system is superior to no evaluation, it is likely to underestimate seriously many losses.

Another approach would be the valuation of the time of the wife or mother in terms of her market wage rate. To the extent that a wife or mother could earn $5 per hour on the market but devotes her time to nonmarket activity, the value of that time is *at least* $5 per hour.[51] However, this approach to measuring the lost value of a wife's or mother's time also involves practical problems. First, it is necessary to generate information about the market alternative, a task that may be difficult for married women even for the standard eight-hour day. Second, the opportunity cost represents only the lowest estimate of the actual value of the time. Where a woman has been recently employed or has a long history of full-time employment, her hourly wage rate adjusted for normal advancement or secular wage changes would provide a basic source of information on opportunity costs. However, if the woman was never employed, or never employed to the reasonable extent of capabilities, the data on her opportunity costs will be more difficult to generate.

In this connection, the recent work of several household-production economists, principally Reuben Gronau, provides some useful insights.[52] Gronau estimated the household value of the time of nonworking women from information about the working experience of women with similar characteristics. The use of information about a class of persons of similar characteristics to approximate the potential earnings of an individual victim is, as we saw earlier, not unknown in personal-injury damages law. Gronau's approach could be used to generate information on the range of opportunity costs for working women with similar characteristics to an injured wife or mother, and the jury could choose the applicable wage rate from that range.

There is reason to believe, however, that the opportunity-costs approach, even if accurately applied, would underestimate the real value of the lost nonmarket time. Opportunity costs represent the value in the next best alternative use. Economics generally begins with the assumption that the market will operate to equalize returns in alternative uses so that opportunity costs provides a close measure of the actual value of a resource. However, this assumption is not always realistic. The resource may have attributes for one use which are relatively unique. This uniqueness may generate above-normal returns—economic rents—for the resource in the particular use. For example, Bill Walton, the celebrated center for the UCLA basketball team, may have unique skills at the sport which will command a large return when he turns professional. If the value of Walton's basketball time were computed by using the market wage in his next best (next-highest-paying) occupation, it would be significantly lower than the actual value of that time in basketball.

The role of a given wife or mother in a given household would seem to have sufficient uniqueness to raise a strong possibility of the presence of economic rents, and therefore of a substantial difference between the market wage rate and her household value of time. These economic rents might be estimated by combining the opportunity-costs and catalogue-of-services methods—a recent article attempted a combined approach that was apparently accepted as evidence in a personal-injury case.[53]

B. Beyond the 40-Hour Week

As noted previously, the law of damages virtually ignores the nonmarket time of the market-employed victim. The other 128 hours per week are not easy to value. Economists have produced no actual estimates of its value despite the importance of such estimates in such areas as transportation and the environment.

However, there does exist a method of estimation, and a readily available source of data, which could be used to generate estimates for at least a part of the remaining 128 hours. In the context of unemployed wives and mothers, it was suggested that an opportunity-cost method be employed which took as a base figure the available wage rate for those in the labor force with similar characteristics. A similar approach could be employed for at least a part of the nonmarket time for employed adults.

As of May 1971, approximately five per cent of those males employed in full-time jobs had second jobs and these second jobs sometimes involved 30 or more hours per week. The percentage of employed females with second jobs is lower, but even here the absolute number was approximately 300,000. These figures come from the report of a Labor Department study on multiple job holding which contains information on the sexual, racial, occupational, and age characteristics of these job holders, and on the median earnings from both the first and second jobs and the median hours employed in the second job.[54]

The average marginal wage rate for the second job appears to be approximately $2.50 and may not decrease appreciably even beyond the thirtieth extra hour.[55] Data such as these provide the basis for estimating the opportunity costs of time beyond the normal work week from the market wage rate earned by multiple job holders with *characteristics similar to the victims'*. Such estimates are not different in type from, nor less trustworthy than, the estimates of lost earning capacity for a victim who has not yet entered the labor force—estimates routinely used as evidence in personal-injury cases.

C. Children's Time

Neither the catalogue-of-services approach employed in the context of housewife's time nor the opportunity-cost approach will be of much assistance in estimating the nonmarket time loss caused by the personal injury of a child. Most of the services performed by children do not have readily identifiable market substitutes and there does not exist a sample of market-employed children of sufficient size and generality to generate acceptable opportunity-cost estimates.

Aside from reliance on the gestalt impression of the jury, I can imagine only one method that might generate sensible estimates, and it is limited to the case of the death of a child. That method would employ an investment approach in which the child was valued as one might value the loss from the destruction of a home-built stereo or TV or a unique machine or structure built by a market firm for its own internal use. The value of the child would be a function of the amount of household resources expended on the creation and rearing of the child. This resource expenditure would include out-of-pocket expenses (*e. g.*, hospital and doctors' fees, education, clothing) plus the value of the parental time inputs employed in creating and rearing the child estimated in the manner suggested in the previous two sections.

There would be problems in determining the value of the adult time inputs and the child's share of general household expenditure, but they are soluble. A more difficult problem is that if the family were to receive damages equal to its entire investment (out-of-pocket and time), it might be overcompensated to the extent that it had already received some benefits from the investment. In the extreme, if the child's benefit to the household was fully realized at the moment of the outlay of resources (costs), there would be no loss (except a possible loss of economic rent).[56]

At least one court has articulated an "investment" rationale to uphold a sizable recovery for the wrongful death of a child. In *Wycho v. Gnotke*, the Michigan Supreme Court provided the following sensible analysis:

> The pecuniary value of a human life is a compound of many elements. The use of material analogies may be helpful and inoffensive. Just as with respect to a manufacturing plant, or industrial machine, value involves the costs of acquisition, emplacement, upkeep, maintenance service, repair, and renovation, so in our context, we must consider the expenses of birth, of food, of clothing, of medicines, of instruction, of nurture and shelter. Moreover, just as an item of machinery forming part of a functioning industrial plant has a value over and above that of a similar item in a showroom, awaiting purchase, so an individual member of a family has a value to others as part of a functioning social and economic unit. This value is the value of mutual society and protection, in a word, companionship. The human companionship thus afforded has a definite, substantial, and ascertainable pecuniary value and its loss forms a part of the "value" of the life we seek to ascertain.[57]

The addition of companionship may be an attempt to capture the loss of economic rent as well as the outlays on the child. While it may be accurate to include part of the output as well as the inputs, it would be double counting to include the full measure of both.

Estimates of the investment in a child have been available for some time.[58] In addition to the older efforts, the present work on the economics of fertility contains interesting data and the potential for additional insights in the future.[59]

D.   Concluding Comments on Measurement

The methods that have been or can be devised to measure the value of the loss of nonmarket time are not inherently more costly to apply, or less reliable, than the measures employed for some elements of market time and some forms of material goods.   The evaluation of earning capacity for those not yet at full capacity at the time of the incident involves the same difficulties as the estimation of the opportunity costs of a housewife's time and of at least part of the time beyond the standard work week.   The evaluation of a unique machine, consumer durable, or structure involves the same problems as are involved in evaluating the investment value of a child.

Several of the measures suggested deal with nonmarket time on an incremental, or hour-by-hour, basis, much the way market time is viewed. There has apparently been some controversy over the attempt to interject such an incremental approach (e. g., $10 per minute of pain) into personal-injury damage considerations other than earning capacity.   Melvin Belli long ago proposed an incremental approach, no doubt with an eye to larger recoveries.[60]   The courts appear to have come to differing conclusions on the validity of this "per diem" approach.[61]   Given the conceptual framework and measurement guidelines offered here, the extension of the incremental approach to the valuation of nonmarket time seems appropriate. Market time and nonmarket time are conceptual equivalents.   They play perfectly analogous roles in the well being of a household.   In many instances, they can be measured in quite analogous ways.

Without joining in the sometimes strained philosophical debate over the meaning of compensation,[62] it is important to discuss one implication of the failure to compensate the real loss represented by the loss of nonmarket time.   Even if the average nonmarket hour were only one third as valuable as the average market hour, the value of nonmarket time per week would exceed the value of market time (based on a 40-hour work week).   To the extent that the law allows only the loss of market time to be compensated, more than half of the actual loss is unrecoverable. Such a system implies a de facto comparative negligence standard that finds the plaintiff *at least* as liable as the defendant in each case.   In such circumstances, what is the exact meaning of "liability"?   While as mentioned at the outset of this article there are policy grounds for setting damages at less than actual losses, one wonders whether those grounds justify such a large threshold loss by the plaintiff.

Conclusion

A recent change in economics sharpens perception of the role of time in the household.   It shows that time spent in the market in exchange for market income is only one means to the end of greater household satisfaction and that the same end is also attained by inputs of time directly into "household production."   These insights raise questions about the present legal approaches to the assessment of damages for tortious injury to the person—approaches that seem to concentrate on the value of market time and to give little recognition to the value of nonmarket time.

The present article offered a conceptual framework based on this change in economics. It employed this framework to examine the present personal injury damage rules, particularly those that attempt to deal with nonmarket activity. It attempted to generate more realistic and better integrated perceptions of these losses. It closed with a discussion of measurement techniques employed or employable in estimating the new forms of loss suggested.

While there are possibly valid reasons for greater consideration and compensation of market than of nonmarket time, it is not obvious that these are the bases for the observed difference in the law's treatment. To the extent that the difference stems from misperception of the role or value of nonmarket time, and to the extent that the misperception can be corrected within the framework of present or future liability and compensation systems, the change in economic perception discussed here should lead to a change in law.

FOOTNOTES

* Associate Professor of Law, University of Wisconsin Law School, and Associate, Institute for Research on Poverty.

1 See Cornelius J. Peck & William S. Hopkins, Economics and Impaired Earning Capacity in Personal Injury Cases, 44 Wash.L.Rev. 351 (1969); Harry Kalven, Jr., The Jury, the Law and the Personal Injury Damage Award, 19 Ohio St.L.J. 158, 160 (1958); A. I. Ogus, Damages for Lost Amenities: For a Foot, a Feeling, or a Function?, 35 Modern L.Rev. 1 (1972); Fleming James, Jr., Damages in Accident Cases, 41 Cornell L.Q. 582, 583 (1956); Charles T. McCormick, Damages, §§ 20, 137 (1935) [hereinafter cited as McCormick]; 1 Theodore Sedgewick, A Treatise on the Measure of Damages, § 29 (1912); Restatement of Torts, § 903, comment a (1939).

2 Harry Kalven, Jr., supra note 1, at 165. Where the jury is no longer employed, courts have had to give much more consideration to unconventional forms of loss. Apparently this effort has not been rewarded with unqualified success. See A. I. Ogus, supra note 1.

3 Consider the findings of the University of Chicago Jury Project in connection with the "gestalt" verdict. See Harry Kalven, Jr., supra note 1, at 161–62.

4 Among the recent examples are Guido Calabresi & A. Douglas Melamed, Property Rules, Liability Rules, and Inalienability: One View of the Cathedral, 85 Harv.L.Rev. 1089 (1972), Richard A. Posner, A Theory of Negligence, 1 J.Leg.Studies 29 (1972); Richard A. Epstein, A Theory of Strict Liability, 2 J.Leg.Studies 151 (1973); and Richard A. Posner, Strict Liability: A Comment, 2 J.Leg.Studies 205 (1973).

[5] The failure to consider the damage side with even approximately the same care as that given the liability side has been decried several times. Twenty years ago, Professor Jaffe explained the different treatment in the following terms:

I suggest that the crucial controversy in personal injury torts today is not in the area of liability but of damages. Questions of liability have great doctrinal fascination. Questions of damage—and particularly their magnitude—do not lend themselves so easily to discourse. Professors dismiss them airily as matters of trial administration. Judges consign them uneasily to juries with a minimum of guidance, occasionally observing loosely that there are no rules for assessing damages in personal injury cases. There is analogy for this situation in Jerome Frank's complaint that fact finding, though of paramount importance, is neglected by teachers who devote themselves too exclusively to appellate law. This may reflect not so much their judgment of relative importance (as Judge Frank supposes) as the relative adaptability of the subjects to conceptualization. And so it probably is with the subject of damages.

Louis L. Jaffe, Damages for Personal Injury: The Impact of Insurance, 18 Law & Contemp.Prob. 219, 221–22 (1953). See also Robert J. Nordstrom, Damages as Compensation for Loss, 2 N.C.Central L.J. 1, 20 (1970).

[6] The following observations of Professor James made before the recent explosion of consideration of the liability question are indicative of the kind of adjustments in damage rules which may be expected:

The principle of compensation is a natural enough corollary of the fault principle. If defendant is a wrongdoer and he is to pay damages to an innocent plaintiff, it seems eminently fair that these damages should (at least) put the plaintiff, as nearly as may be, in the same position he would have been in if the defendant's wrong had not injured him. . . . Today, however, the trend in accident law is running heavily towards diluting the requirement of fault for liability and the defense of the victim's fault. Increasingly the personal participants in the accident—even where their fault is clear—do not pay the judgments awarded. These are paid by absentee employers or by insurance companies and through them distributed widely over a large segment of society. Accident law is approaching—perhaps by faltering steps—an enterprise liability without fault. If such a system is to be justified, it cannot be in terms of the personal ethical evaluation which gave rise to the compensatory theory of damages. Justification must come, rather, from the kind of considerations of social morality which led to workmen's compensation. . . . The reason for strict liability here is to provide assurance that accident victims will be rehabilitated, and that they and their dependents will be cared for during the period of disability without imposing on the victims or their families a crushing burden. The amount of damages measured by this functional standard may be less than the compensatory damages provided by the common law, especially since compensation is presently attempted for many speculative nonpecuniary items. Even when we consider the victim's pecuniary loss, we must remember that accidents bring a net pecuniary loss to society as a whole—the social wealth and income is thereby diminished—so that if the victim is made entirely whole, he will fare better than society and will not himself share the economic burden he is asking society to distribute. If social need is invoked to justify strict liability without regard to moral fault, then the demands of that need should measure the extent of the liability. In that context, what is fair is only what is needed, though here as elsewhere in life too stingy a view of the need might frustrate the meeting of it.

Fleming James, Jr., supra note 1, at 583–85.

[7] Even these costs are "time-related" and fit within the proposed framework. Medical expenses are given explicit consideration at pp. 476–77, infra.

[8] The basic reference here is Gary S. Becker, A Theory of the Allocation of Time, 75 Econ.J. 493 (1965) [hereinafter cited as Becker]. However, the conception of the im-

portance of household time pre-dates Becker. See Wesley C. Mitchell, The Backward Art of Spending Money and Other Essays (1937); Margaret G. Reid, Economics of Household Production (1934). Recently it has been expanded and applied broadly, beginning with Becker, and Kevin J. Lancaster, A New Approach to Consumer Theory, 74 J.Pol.Econ. 132 (1966). The recent surge of interest in this approach can be dated from these works.

Some of the formal structure and assumptions of the new theory have been criticized within the economics profession. See Marc Nerlove, The "New Home Economics" : A Theory of Household Choice and Decision-Making? (paper presented to the 1973 Annual Meeting of the Population Ass'n. of America, April 22, 1973); Robert A. Pollack & Michael L. Wachter, the Relevance of the Household Production Function and its Implications for the Allocation of Time (Wharton Sch. of Finance, Dep't. of Econ. Discussion Paper No. 262, 1973). Both of these critiques discuss the manner in which the new theory is employed (i. e., the range of questions about which it can yield unambiguous answers, and the validity of technical assumptions made in various mathematical developments of the theory). They do not argue with the basic necessity for an expanded conception of household economies, especially one which examines the role of household time in household production. It is these generally accepted aspects of the new theory that are employed here.

9 The conventional functional form was usually written:

$$U = U(x_i, \ldots, x_n)$$

where U is utility and x_i, the ith good or service purchased on the market.

10 The conventional budget restraint was written:

$$Y = \sum_{i=1}^{m} w_i t_i + V,$$

where Y is market income, t_p the ith hour, w_p the wage rate applicable to the ith hour, and V, non-wage market income.

11 The new utility function is written as follows:

$$U = U(Z_i, \ldots, Z_8) = U(x_i, \ldots, x_n ;\ t_i, \ldots, t_m),$$

where Z_i is the ith "commodity," x_i the ith market purchased good or service, and t_i the ith time input.

12 "Doctors' services, for example, instead of being treated as a final good that directly increases household utility, are considered an input into household commodities such as health. Few receive direct pleasure from the ministrations of doctors; few would expend resources just to be stuck with needles, poked with tongue depressers, and subjected to the tensions and delay of the waiting room. These unpleasantries are inputs rather than outputs." Neil K. Komesar, A Theoretical and Empirical Study of Victims of Crime, 2 J.Leg.Studies 301, 302 (1973).

13 The new budget constraint is written as follows:

$$S = \sum_{i=1}^{168} \sum_{j=1}^{P} w_{ij} t_{ij} + V,$$

where w_{ij} is the wage rate applicable to the ith hour of the jth member of the household, t_{ij} is the associated hour, S is the "full income" and V is non-wage income. The "168" limit on the summation represents the physical upper bound on hours per week (24 hours per day, seven days per week). Thus the budget constraint as shown represents one week's full income. For a discussion of the subtleties of this concept and method of actual approximation of the applicable wage, see Becker at 497–500.

14 McCormick at 160.

15 In this connection, it is interesting to note Professor Jaffe's criticism of "pain and suffering," the category of damages which has traditionally provided most of the recovery available beyond lost earning capacity:

But why we may ask *should* the plaintiff be compensated in money for an experience which involves no financial loss? It cannot be on the principle of returning what is his own. Essentially that principle rests on an economic foundation: on maintaining the integrity of the economic arrangements which provide the normally expectable basis for livelihood in our society. Pain is a harm, and "injury," but neither past pain nor its compensation has any consistent economic significance. The past experience is not a loss except insofar as it produced deterioration. It will be said, however, that these arguments betray a limited, a Philistine view of the law's concern, one that the law has happily transcended. This objection mistakes the argument. Of course, the law is concerned, and properly so, with other than economic interest. The criminal law and the tort law insofar as punitive (that is to say insofar as the conduct of the plaintiff warrants punishment) is much concerned with the protection of non-economic interest

. . . .

Louis L. Jaffe, supra note 5, at 461–62. This statement can be read in two ways. Either "pain and suffering" was intended to compensate for something beyond the loss of household nonmarket time resources, an idea which will be explored subsequently, or "economic significance" is to be attached solely to resources which produce financial loss in the form of reduced market income. The latter view may be consistent with the older economic analysis of the household, but it is not consistent with the newer conception.

A similar perception is exemplified in a recent case note where the author asserts that in modern society children are no longer "economic assets." Note, 22 Drake L.Rev. 200, 202 (1972). The point the author seeks to make is generally valid, but his usage reveals the association of economic asset and market-income-producing asset. The latter is an example of the former, but not the sole example.

16 See generally McCormick, ch. 19, at 467.

17 More accurately, it is the flow of services from these chattels which is input into household production. The loss of the chattel is really the loss of a stock: the present value of a flow of services.

18 Time inputs into market production are usually recovered by households. The assessment of impaired earning capacity for a self-employed person does need to consider the particular market context of the victim. It is interesting to note that the legal system is willing to assess damages here despite the substantial measurement difficulties inherent in disassociating the value of the victim's time from the value of other inputs in the final product. See McCormick at 309–14.

19 Such a statement may be subject to some qualification given the *ad hoc* personal injury categories to be discussed subsequently, although as will be seen the short week is probably an accurate characterization in general.

20 The traditional interpretation and an alternative are provided in the following interesting passage from Becker at 505–06:

Most of the large secular increase in earnings, which stimulated the development of the labour-leisure analysis, resulted from an increase in the productivity of working time due to the growth in human and physical capital, technological progress and other factors. Since a rise in earnings resulting from an increase in productivity has both income and substitution effects, the secular decline in hours worked appeared to be evidence that the income effect was sufficiently strong to swamp the substitution effect.

The secular growth in capital and technology also improved the productivity of consumption time: supermarkets, automobiles, sleeping pills, safety and electric razors, and telephones are a few familiar and important examples of such developments. An improvement in the productivity of consumption time would change relative commodity prices and increase full income, which in turn would produce substitution and income effects. The interesting point is that a very different interpretation of the observed decline in hours of work is suggested because these effects are precisely the opposite of those produced by improvements in the productivity of working time.

. . . Instead of claiming that a powerful income effect swamped a weaker substitution effect, the claim would have to be that a powerful substitution effect swamped a weaker income effect.

Of course, the productivity of both working and consumption time increased secularly, and the true interpretation is somewhat between these extremes.

[21] It is possible that there are market components in nonmarket time and as such the statement in text requires qualification. This point is discussed later. However, in the specific context under discussion here (i. e., the allocation of previous working time to nonmarket activities), it is unlikely that these market components played any significant role.

[22] The alternative market wage for the 16th, 17th, etc. hours is probably significantly lower in general than the wage for the 1st, 2nd, . . ., 8th hours. But the 9th, . . ., 12th hours may have a substantial market alternative perhaps greater than the conventional eight hours—consider overtime pay. When one approaches the 24th hour in the day, the alternative wage may be negative because of inframarginal changes in the value of other hours: without sleep, the productivity of *all* the hours would decrease.

However, every attorney knows that there are instances in which even the 16th hour may have high market value. In this context, there are many who choose nonmarket employment of these times. How many prospective employees of the infamous "Wall Street" firms have chosen other employment because of an aversion to the "midnight oil" ?

[23] See, e. g., Cornelius J. Peck & William S. Hopkins, supra note 1; Norman Leonard, Future Economic Value in Wrongful Death Litigation, 30 Ohio State L.J. 502 (1969); Norman Leonard, Measurement of Damages: An Economist's View, 31 Ohio State L.J. 687 (1970); Leo M. O'Connor & Robert E. Miller, The Economist-Statistician: A Source of Expert Guidance in Determining Damages, 48 Notre Dame Lawyer 354 (1972). For a sophisticated discussion of the underlying economic analysis, see Herman P. Miller, Lifetime Income and Economic Growth, 55 Am.Econ.Rev. 834 (1965).

[24] Here as elsewhere in this discussion the extent to which the damage structure adjusts to any failures in articulation by *sub rosa* inclusion of the loss under some other category is unknown. In this context, the reader should question whether the diminution in perception just discussed in the text will be adjusted for by increases in the recovery under the *ad hoc* personal injury categories to be discussed subsequently. No hard evidence exists, but there is reason to doubt that categories not explicitly sensitive to units of time will fully adjust to this change in the allocation of time.

[25] There is another approach taken to wrongful death—punitive damages. Since this approach is not grounded in conceptions of compensation, it will be ignored here. It should be noted, however, that the distinction between compensatory and punitive damages is not meant to imply that the former may not be an attempt to affect the behavior of prospective defendants. The difference lies in the *means* of assessing damages, not the *purpose* of assessing damages.

The two wrongful-death approaches discussed in the text are not themselves unique and homogeneous. Each contains many variations and many jurisdictions have systems which are uneven fusions of parts of the two approaches. These permutations and combinations will be discussed more fully subsequently.

[26] The major source for the basic law in this area is McCormick which despite its age remains an excellent source. The relevant sections are §§ 91, 92, 94–96, 98–102. Changes in the law since he wrote and other sources will be noted where appropriate.

[27] The market role of the former has probably decreased over time while that of the latter has increased. The damage law seems to reflect the past state since any differences in treatment between these groups seem to view the child as more market oriented than the wife.

[28] See pp. 480–82, infra.

[29] Minor children have been unable to collect for loss of an injured parent's services. See, e. g., Jeune v. Del E. Webb Construction Co., 77 Ariz. 226, 269 P.2d 723 (1954) ; Hill v. Sibley Memorial Hospital, 108 F.Supp. 739 (D.C.D.C.1957); Halberg v. Young, 41 Hawaii 634 (1957); Feneff v. N. Y. C. & H. R. R. Co., 203 Mass. 278, 89 N.E. 436 (1909); Blair v. Sutner Dry Goods Co., 184 Mich. 304, 151 N.W. 724 (1915); Eschenbach v. Benjamin, 195 Minn. 378, 263 N.W. 154 (1935); Stout v. Kansas City Terminal Ry. Co., 172 Mo.App. 113, 157 S.W. 1019 (1913); Gibson v. Johnson, 144 N.E.2d 310 (Ohio App. 1956).

[30] In connection with this division between the wife's market and nonmarket time, the following comment again depicts the pervasiveness of the perception that real loss is confined to lost "market time" :

It is clear that if the husband can recover for loss of her future services and the wife can recover for loss of her future earning capacity, there is a real possibility of double counting.

Charles O. Gregory & Harry Kalven, Jr., Cases and Materials on Torts 428 (1959).

It is always possible that the consideration of both future earning capacity and future household productive capacity might lead to the inclusion of a future hour in both categories (i. e., double counting). However, given a normal eight-hour market-work-day, there exists sufficient *uncounted* time for household production that the recovery for lost household services would not appear to create any greater danger of double counting than exists in any damage system that has overlapping but primarily different categories of recovery.

[31] Cf. Florida Greyhound Lines, Inc. v. Jones, 60 So.2d 396 (Fla.1952), where an injured wife was allowed to recover for lost earning capacity despite the fact that there was no past history of market activity.

[32] Also included here is the value of the child's services in any family business operations.

[33] An older child on a farm or in a small family business might provide important market time inputs. In addition, there are rare examples of children who earn substantial market incomes. These notable exceptions usually involve the entertainment industry. A recent example of the potential "rich kid" is Rodney Allen Rippey, the five year old with the angelic face, who reportedly will earn at least $100,000 in market income this year and exceed that amount in each of the next few years. Parade Magazine, Nov. 18, 1973, at 22–23.

The greater pecuniary role of children in nineteenth century households is noted in Richard A. Posner, supra note 4, at 47.

[34] The choice to have children has received considerable recent consideration by economists in part as a concomitant of the development of the household production theory. See, e. g., the fifteen papers given at the Conference on New Economic Approaches to Fertility, 81 J.Pol.Econ., No. 2, pt. ii (March/April 1973).

[35] In the conventional home, a great part of the time allocated to the creation and rearing of the child comes from the mother. One measure of the value of the mother's time is its opportunity cost on the market, a concept discussed later in this article in connection with the loss of a housewife-mother's time.

The damage law reflects the importance of time inputs in child creation and rearing by recognizing the value of the services of mothers and even fathers as legitimate loss to surviving children. The recognition of the loss of father's services is especially remarkable since it is the only form of nonmarket time loss recognized in wrongful death actions of a husband-father.

Consider the extreme factual situation present in Hord v. National Homeopathic Hospital, 102 F.Supp. 792 (D.D.C.1952), where a newly born infant was killed due to negligence of the defendant's agent which occurred while the mother was still on the delivery table. The mother had already invested large amounts of her time, taken appreciable risks, and incurred considerable discomfort. While the court in that case rationalized its affirmance of the damage award on the basis of minority earning capacity and support for parents, it is more likely that the substantial recovery recognized the investment in the child rather than any lost potential pecuniary returns.

Note also that recent economic studies show that the per capita investment in the average child has risen over time despite the decrease in pecuniary earnings of the average child over the same period. See Dennis N. De Tray, Child Quality and the Demand for Children, 81 J.Pol.Econ. No. 2, pt. ii, 570 (March/April 1973).

[36] But see discussion at pp. 483–84, infra.

[37] See Harry Kalven, Jr., supra note 1, at 168–69.

Some courts have attempted to expand the conventional legal approach by resort to "loss of companionship." The Michigan courts were apparently on this track in Wycho and Currie (see Wycho v. Gnodtke, 361 Mich. 331, 105 N.W.2d 118 (1960); Currie v. Fiting, 375 Mich. 440, 134 N.W.2d 611 (1965)), but seem to have reversed this position in Breckon v. Franklin Fuel Co., 383 Mich. 251, 174 N.W.2d 836 (1970). See Note, 48 J.Urban Law 1014 (1971). Other recent cases include Wardkow v. City of Keokuk, 190 N.W.2d 439 (1971); Fussner v. Audert, 261 Minn. 347, 113 N.W.2d 355 (1961); Lockhart v. Besel, 71 Wash.2d 112, 426 P.2d 605 (1967); Hockstra v. Helgeland, 78 S.D. 82, 98 N.W.2d 669 (1959).

[38] See Leonard Decof, Damages in Actions for Wrongful Death of Children, 47 Notre Dame Lawyer 197, 202 (1971).

[39] At most recent count, thirteen American jurisdictions have allowed recovery either by statute or by "extensions" of common law principles. See Mo. Pac. Transp. Co. v. Miller, 227 Ark. 351, 299 S.W.2d 41 (1957); Bailey v. Wilson, 100 Ga.App. 405, 11 S.E. 2d 106 (2d Div.1959); Stenta v. Leblang, 55 Del. 181, 185 A.2d 759 (1962); Dini v. Naiditch, 20 Ill.2d 406, 170 N.E.2d 881 (1960); Acuff v. Schmit, 248 La. 272, 78 N.W.2d 480 (1957); Deems v. Western Md. Ry. Co., 274 Md. 95, 231 A.2d 514 (1967); Montgomery v. Stephan, 359 Mich. 33, 101 N.W.2d 227 (1960); Novak v. Kansas City Transit, Inc., 365 S.W.2d 539 (Mo.1963); Clem v. Brown, 32 Ohio Op.2d 477, 3 Ohio Misc. 167, 207 N.E.2d 398 (C. P. Paulding Co. 1965); Hockstra v. Helgeland, 78 S.D. 82, 98 N.W.2d 669 (1959); Moran v. Quality Aluminum Casting Co., 34 Wis.2d 542, 150 N.W.2d 137 (1967); Va.Code Ann. § 55–36 (1969); Ore.Rev.Stat. § 108–010 (1971).

[40] See, e. g., Allendorf v. Elgin, Joliet and Eastern Railway Co., 8 Ill.2d 164, 133 N.E. 2d 288 (1956); Miller v. Southern Pac. Co., 117 Cal.App.2d 492, 603 (1953).

[41] McCormick at 349.

[42] See discussion at pp. 477–80, infra.

[43] The hypothetical is not so different from the fact situation in McNulty v. Southern Pacific R. R. Co., 96 Cal.App.2d 841, 216 P.2d 534 (1950), an often discussed case (See

Harry Kalven, Jr., supra note 1, at 160, where he compares interpretations of the case by Melvin Belli and Professor Jaffe). In that case, a man 42 years of age previously employed as a bank teller lost both legs. He made a quick recovery, adjusted to artificial limbs, lost little time at work (his employer paid his salary during his absence), and appeared able to continue his employment. The jury awarded $100,000 and the appellate court affirmed the judgment. It mentioned the victim's outside or nonmarket activities briefly, but felt it necessary to rationalize its decision in terms of speculations about the victim's ability to advance in his chosen employment (banking).

44 See discussion at pp. 477–80, infra.

45 More accurately, the probability of damage recovery is better known. The circumstances of the incident are known and probabilities of defendant's liability assessable prior to decisions on convalescence production.

46 It is possible to imagine a situation in which only physical discomfort is present. In such a situation, the victim would perform in the market and in the household in precisely the same manner that he would have performed without the injury but with physical discomfort. The factual setting of the *McNulty* case, discussed supra at note 43, raises the possibility of such a situation at least in term of market time. The plaintiff there may have in reality performed his market duties in the same fashion, but not without physical discomfort.

47 This concept is referred to in economics as "productive consumption." See Becker at 503.

48 See, e. g., Springer v. George, 403 Pa. 563, 170 A.2d 367 (1961); Covell v. Colburn, 308 Mich. 240, 13 N.W.2d 275 (1944); Annotation, 15 A.L.R.2d 418 (1951); Stuart Speiser, Recovery for Wrongful Death 135–45 (1966).

49 See Norman Leonard (1969), supra note 26; Norman Leonard (1970), supra note 26; Leo M. O'Connor & Robert E. Miller, supra note 26.

50 Comment, The Unemployed Housewife-Mother: Fair Appraisal of Economic Loss in a Wrongful Death Action, 21 Buffalo L.Rev. 205 (1971); Comment, 33 Mo.L.Rev. 462 (1968); Cornelius J. Peck & William S. Hopkins, supra note 1, at 365–67.

51 For concise presentation of the basics of this approach in the case of an injured housewife, see Richard A. Posner, Economic Analysis of Law 80 (1972). The author also points out that if the market wage rate is employed as an opportunity cost figure it should be the market wage rate net of taxes since the return on nonmarket time is not taxable.

52 Reuben Gronau, The Intrafamily Allocation of Time: The Value of the Housewives' Time, 63 Am.Econ.Rev. 634 (1973). See also Gronau, The Effect of Children on the Housewife's Value of Time, 81 J.Pol.Econ. No. 2, pt. ii, S168 (March/April 1973); Yoram Ben-Porath, Labor Force Participation Rates and the Supply of Labor, 81 J.Pol. Econ. 697 (1973); Jacob Mincer, Labor Force Participation of Married Women: A Study of Labor Supply, in Aspects of Labor Economies 63–105 (Universities-Nat'l. Bur. Econ. Research Conference series 15, 1962); G. C. Cain, Married Women in the Labor Force: An Economic Analysis (1966).

53 Chong Soo Pyun, The Monetary Value of a Housewife: An Economic Analysis for Use in Litigation, 28 Am.J.Econ.Sociol. 271 (1969). See Harpen Truck Lines, Inc. v. Mills, 378 F.2d 705 (5th Cir. 1967).

54 Howard V. Hagglie & Kopp Michelotte, Multiple Jobholding in 1970 and 1971 (U. S. Dept. of Labor, Bur. of Labor Stat., Special Labor Force Report 139, 1972).

55 Also of interest is the close positive correlation between earnings in the first and second jobs. Such information combined with other variables could provide a useful projection of the value of the nonmarket time of a person who does not have a second job.

56 For an interesting discussion of the pattern of expenditure on children over time, see Theodore W. Schultz, The Value of Children: An Economic Perspective, 81 J.Pol. Econ. No. 2, pt. ii, at 2 (1973).

57 Wycho v. Gnodtke, 361 Mich. 331, 105 N.W.2d 118 (1960).

58 See Louis J. Dublin & Alfred J. Lotka, The Money Value of a Man 22–40 (1930).

59 See materials cited in note 34 supra.

60 Melvin M. Belli, The Use of Demonstrative Evidence in Achieving "The More Adequate Award" 32–35 (1951).

61 The cases are discussed along with the Belli argument in Harry Kalven, Jr. & Charles O. Gregory, supra note 33, at 459–62.

62 Consider the opinion of Diplock, L. J., in Wise v. Kay, [1962] 1 Q.B. 638, C.A. [1962] 2 W.L.R. 96, which contains a long discussion of the ability of a plaintiff to replace her actual loss or gain some measure of happiness from a pecuniary award.

*

PART 3

Public Goods, Collective Goods and Externalities

A Introduction

Probably no subjects have occasioned more heated controversy among interested economists in recent years than the related issues of public goods and externalities. Regardless of the terminology used, these subjects have provided the principal arena for those economists who find serious fault with free market allocational mechanisms, even when monopoly is not present.

The public goods problem arises because certain kinds of economic goods, once produced, can be enjoyed by individuals for whom they have positive value at zero marginal cost. If these goods are not given away free, less will be consumed than otherwise would be, though the additional consumption will be at no additional cost to anyone else. This violates the fundamental criterion of Pareto optimality that if anyone can be made better off without another person's being made worse off, that position is to be desired. This mode of criticism of *laissez-faire* economics is most commonly associated with the name of Paul Samuelson, whose highly technical work is discussed at length in the included readings.

The second argument popularly used today to defend greater government intervention into private arrangements is that there are various external costs generated by private behavior but not taken account of by the private actor. This causes over-investment in these activities because individual costs are less than the real social costs. This argument has in recent years achieved an intensity of interest rarely accorded technical economic doctrines. This is undoubtedly attributable to popular concern with various kinds of pollution problems.

It is anomalous nonetheless that most of the writings decrying the existence of uncontrolled externalities rarely, if ever, recognize that private arrangements also generate extraordinary external benefits for which no price is generally paid. The discussion of this topic has been extremely technical, and for that reason the two principle positions

appearing in the scholarly literature are not reprinted herein. They
are Paul A. Samuelson, "Contrast between Welfare Conditions for
Joint Supply and for Public Goods," 51 Rev.Econ. & Stat. 26 (1969);
and Harold Demsetz, "The Private Production of Public Goods," 13
Jnl.Law & Econ. 293 (1970). The most significant external benefit
provided by private arrangements is the utility enjoyed by almost everyone from the generally free availability of information about market
prices. The converse of this point, that government, policing, regulating,
or producing goods and services are costly, is the central theme of both
"The Exchange and Enforcement of Property Rights" by Demsetz and
"On the Distinction Between Public and Private Goods" by Davis and
Whinston.

The Section begins with the elegant, concise statement of the
underlying issue in R. Turvey's "On Divergences Between Social Cost
and Private Cost" (20). Turvey's article briefly reviews the basic literature critical of the Pigovian tradition in this field.

The Demsetz article included herein (21) points out the
weakness in using a definitional approach to what constitutes a public
good if that term is used to justify government action. The correct
approach, Demsetz suggests, is to determine which of the various private
and governmental methods available for dealing with these issues involves the lowest total cost, whether they be exchange costs, information costs, or policing costs. The recognition that there is
considerable efficiency value to policing private property rights, even
in connection with Samuelsonian public goods, leads Demsetz to conclude
that it may still be more efficient in the Pareto sense to exclude individuals from the free use of such goods.

Davis and Whinston (22) point out an apparent non sequitur in
Samuelson's work when he concludes that if the market is not working
"perfectly" to place all costs and benefits where they belong, the
appropriate solution is governmental action. Unfortunately, in his most
important early works, Samuelson made no attempt to examine what
we might term "government failures," or to compare the costs of less-
than-ideal market arrangements to the costs of less-than-ideal
government ones.

The article by Demsetz mentioned above but not appearing in
this collection, "The Private Production of Public Goods," argues
against the Samuelsonian position and defends the arguments for considering the public goods issue as simply a variant of the common joint
supply problem correctly analyzed by Alfred Marshall many years ago.
As Demsetz points out, the fact that benefits can be enjoyed by more
than one individual when television programs are broadcast is really
no different than recognizing that different individuals may benefit from

the hide and the meat when a cow is slaughtered.   And just as we do not
give the leather away free in the latter case, or turn immediately
to government ownership of slaughterhouses, so the same logic seems
to apply to the great range of items many economists today want the
government to supply.

Finally, a review article on the subject of externalities by E. Mishan
(23) is included, first to give the flavor of the modern debate from a
somewhat different perspective, but more importantly to include the
extensive bibliography attached to the article.   Nonetheless, it should be
noted that, for whatever reasons, Demsetz's writings then in existence are
not included in this bibliography.

Section C is designed to let the reader gain more concrete knowledge
of some specific cases in which either misallocation of resources or
failure of appropriate internalization of costs has been alleged to occur.
The 1954 work by Scott Gordon on fisheries (24) certainly is one of
the great classics of this literature, while S. Cheung's "The Structure
of a Contract and the Theory of a Non-Exclusive Resource" (25)
brings the analysis of the fishery problem right up to date with the application of the most recent advances in the theory of property rights.

The second article by Cheung, "The Fable of the Bees: An Economic
Investigation" (26) is likely in time to become a classic not merely
among economists and lawyers, but among apiarists as well.   It is
erudite, instructive, and, not least, charming.   And lawyers, skeptical
about economists but hopeful that economics may be useful, may take
satisfaction in Cheung's final two sentences: "My main criticism, rather,
concerns [economists'] approach to economic activity in failing to
investigate the real-world situation and in arriving at policy implications out of sheer imagination.   As a result, their work contributes
little to our understanding of the actual economic system."

The final article in this Section is R. Stroup and J. Baden's "Externality, Property Rights, and the Management of Our National Forests"
(27).   Here we are offered a close-up view of the points so tellingly
made by Demsetz, Davis and Whinston that there are costs attached
to any system of allocation of resources, be it market or governmental.
The discussion is really about the politics of the U. S. Forest Service
and the expenditures of resources made to control and influence that
agency.   The paper concludes with the economist's perennial cry for
more empirical research, but in its own way, like Cheung's "Fable,"
it tells us a great deal about the effects of economic misconceptions on
the actual selection of allocational policies.   It comprehends tellingly
the kind of information that lawyers need to know about the use of
economics and that economists need to know about the use of law.

*

B Public Goods and
Private Goods—
Theory

20: ON DIVERGENCES BETWEEN SOCIAL COST AND PRIVATE COST*

RALPH TURVEY

The notion that the resource-allocation effects of divergences between marginal social and private costs can be dealt with by imposing a tax or granting a subsidy equal to the difference now seems too simple a notion. Three recent articles have shown us this. First came Professor Coase's "The Problem of Social Cost", then Davis and Whinston's "Externalities, Welfare and the Theory of Games" appeared, and, finally, Buchanan and Stubblebine have published their paper "Externality".[1] These articles have an aggregate length of eighty pages and are by no means easy to read. The following attempt to synthesise and summarise the main ideas may therefore be useful. It is couched in terms of external diseconomies, i. e. an excess of social over private costs, and the reader is left to invert the analysis himself should he be interested in external economies.

The scope of the following argument can usefully be indicated by starting with a brief statement of its main conclusions. The first is that if the party imposing external diseconomies and the party suffering them are able and willing to negotiate to their mutual advantage, state intervention is unnecessary to secure optimum resource allocation. The second is that the imposition of a tax upon the party imposing external diseconomies can be a very complicated matter, even in principle, so that the *a priori* prescription of such a tax is unwise.

To develop these and other points, let us begin by calling *A* the person, firm or group (of persons or firms) which imposes a diseconomy,

Economica, Vol. 30, August 1963, p. 309.

and B the person, firm or group which suffers it. How much B suffers will in many cases depend not only upon the *scale* of A's diseconomy-creating activity, but also upon the precise *nature* of A's activity and upon B's *reaction* to it. If A emits smoke, for example, B's loss will depend not only upon the quantity emitted but also upon the height of A's chimney and upon the cost to B of installing air-conditioning, indoor clothes-dryers or other means of reducing the effect of the smoke. Thus to ascertain the optimum resource allocation will frequently require an investigation of the nature and costs both of alternative activities open to A and of the devices by which B can reduce the impact of each activity. The optimum involves that kind and scale of A's activity and that adjustment to it by B which maximises the algebraic sum of A's gain and B's loss as against the situation where A pursues no diseconomy-creating activity. Note that the optimum will frequently involve B suffering a loss, both in total and at the margin.[2]

If A and B are firms, gain and loss can be measured in money terms as profit differences. (In considering a social optimum, allowance has of course to be made for market imperfections.) Now assuming that they both seek to maximise profits, that they know about the available alternatives and adjustments and that they are able and willing to negotiate, they will achieve the optimum without any government interference. They will internalize the externality by merger[3], or they will make an agreement whereby B pays A to modify the nature or scale of its activity.[4] Alternatively,[5] if the law gives B rights against A, A will pay B to accept the optimal amount of loss imposed by A.

If A and B are people, their gain and loss must be measured as the amount of money they respectively would pay to indulge in and prevent A's activity. It could also be measured as the amount of money they respectively would require to refrain from and to endure A's activity, which will be different unless the marginal utility of income is constant. We shall assume that it is constant for both A and B, which is reasonable when the payments do not bulk large in relation to their incomes.[6] Under this assumption, it makes no difference whether B pays A or, if the law gives B rights against, A, A compensates B.

Whether A and B are persons or firms, to levy a tax on A which is *not* received as damages or compensation by B may prevent optimal resource allocation from being achieved—still assuming that they can and do negotiate.[7] The reason is that the resource allocation which maximises A's *gain less B's loss* may differ from that which maximises A's *gain less A's tax less B's loss*.

The points made so far can usefully be presented diagrammatically (Figure 1). We assume that A has only two alternative activities, I and II, and that their scales and B's losses are all continuously variable. Let us temporarily disregard the dotted curve in the right-hand part of the diagram. The area under A's curves then gives the total gain to A. The area under B's curves gives the total loss to B after he has made the best adjustment possible to A's activity. This is thus the direct loss as reduced by adjustment, plus the cost of making that adjustment.

If A and B could not negotiate and if A were unhampered by restrictions of any sort, A would choose activity I at a scale of OR. A scale of OS would obviously give a larger social product, but the optimum is clearly activity II at scale OJ, since area 2 is greater than area 1. Now B will be prepared to pay up to $(1a + 1b - 2a)$ to secure this result, while A will be prepared to accept down to $(1 + 1a - 2 - 2a)$ to assure it.

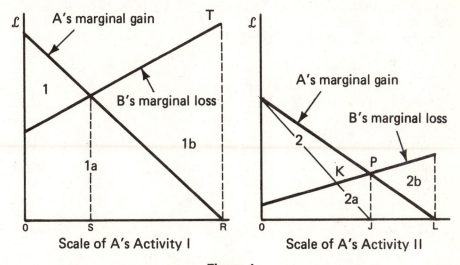

Figure 1

The difference is $(1b - 1 + 2)$, the maximum gain to be shared between them, and this is clearly positive.

If A is liable to compensate B for actual damages caused by either activity I or II, he will choose activity II at scale OJ (i. e. the optimum allocation), pay $2a$ to B and retain a net gain of 2. The result is the same as when there is no such liability, though the distribution of the gain is very different: B will pay A up to $(1a + 1b - 2a)$ to secure this result. Hence whether or not we should advocate the imposition of a liability on A for damages caused is a matter of fairness, not of resource allocation. Our judgment will presumably depend on such factors as who got their first, whether one of them is a non-conforming user (e. g. an establishment for the breeding of maggots on putrescible vegetable matter in a residential district), who is richer, and so on. Efficient resource allocation requires the imposition of a liability upon A only if we can show that inertia, obstinacy, etc. inhibit A and B from reaching a voluntary agreement.[8]

We can now make the point implicit in Buchanan-Stubblebine's argument, namely that there is a necessity for any impost levied on A to be paid to B when A and B are able to negotiate. Suppose that A is charged an amount equal to the loss he imposes on B; subtracting this from his marginal gain curve in the right-hand part of the diagram gives us the dotted line as his marginal net gain. If A moves to point J it will then pay B to induce him to move back to position K (which is sub-optimal) as it is this position which maximises the *joint* net gain to A and B together.

There is a final point to be made about the case where A and B can negotiate. This is that if the external diseconomies are reciprocal, so that each imposes a loss upon the other, the problem is still more complicated.[9]

We now turn to the case where A and B cannot negotiate, which in most cases will result from A and/or B being too large a group for the members to get together. Here there are certain benefits to be had from resource re-allocation which are not privately appropriable. Just as with collective goods,[10] therefore, there is thus a case for collective action to achieve optimum allocation. But all this means is that *if* the state can ascertain and enforce a move to the optimum position at a cost less than the gain to be had, and *if* it can do this in a way which does not have unfavourable effects upon income distribution, then it should take action.

These two "ifs" are very important. The second is obvious and requires no elaboration. The first, however, deserves a few words. In order to ascertain the optimum type and scale of A's activity, the authorities must estimate all of the curves in the diagrams. They must, in other words, list and evaluate all the alternatives open to A and examine their effects upon B and the adjustments B could make to reduce the loss suffered. When this is done, if it can be done, it is necessary to consider how to reach the optimum. Now, where the nature as well as the scale of A's activity is variable, it may be necessary to control both, and this may require two controls, not one. Suppose, for instance, that in the diagram, both activities are the emission of smoke: I from a low chimney and II from a tall chimney. To induce A to shift from emitting OR smoke from the low chimney to emitting OJ smoke from the tall chimney, it will not suffice to levy a tax of PJ per unit of smoke.[11] If this alone were done, A would continue to use a low chimney, emitting slightly less than OR smoke. It will also be necessary to regulate chimney heights. A tax would do the trick alone only if it were proportioned to losses imposed rather than to smoke emitted, and that would be very difficult.

These complications show that in many cases the cost of achieving optimum resource allocation may outweigh the gain. If this is the case, a second-best solution may be appropriate.   Thus a prohibition of all smoke emission would be better than OR smoke from a low chimney (since 1 is less than $1b$) and a requirement that all chimneys be tall would be better still (giving a net gain of 2 less $2b$).   Whether these requirements should be imposed on existing chimney-owners as well as on new ones then introduces further complications relating to the short run and the long run.

There is no need to carry the example any further.   It is now abundantly clear that any general prescription of a tax to deal with external diseconomies is useless.   Each case must be considered on its own and there is no *a priori* reason to suppose that the imposition of a tax is better than alternative measures or indeed, that any measures at all are desirable unless we assume that information and administration are both costless.[12]

To sum up, then: when negotiation is possible, the case for government intervention is one of justice not of economic efficiency; when it is not, the theorist should be silent and call in the applied economist.

FOOTNOTES

* I am indebted to Professor Buchanan, Professor Coase, Mr. Klappholz, Dr. Mishan and Mr. Peston for helpful comments on an earlier draft.

1 *Journal of Law and Economics*, Vol. III, October, 1960, *Journal of Political Economy*, June, 1962, and *Economica*, November, 1962, respectively.

2 Buchanan-Stubblebine, pp. 380–1.

3 Davis-Whinston, pp. 244, 252, 256; Coase, pp. 16–17.

4 Coase, p. 6; Buchanan-Stubblebine agree, p. 383.

5 See previous references.

6 Dr. Mishan has examined the welfare criterion for the case where the only variable is the scale of A's activity, but where neither A nor B has a constant marginal utility of income; Cf. his paper "Welfare Criteria for External Effects", *American Economic Review*, September, 1961.

7 Buchanan-Stubblebine, pp. 381–3.

8 Cf. the comparable argument on pp. 94–8 of my *The Economics of Real Property*, 1957, about the external economy to landlords of tenants' improvements.

9 Davis-Whinston devote several pages of game theory to this problem.

10 Buchanan-Stubblebine, p. 383.

11 Note how different PJ is from RT, the initial observable marginal external diseconomy.

12 Coase, pp. 18, 44.

B Continued

21: THE EXCHANGE AND ENFORCEMENT OF PROPERTY RIGHTS*

HAROLD DEMSETZ
University of Chicago

Our economic system, with its specialization of economic activities into separate ownership and decision units, requires both control over goods and exchange of goods if it is to cope with the diversity of wants of specialist producers. This paper is concerned with the fact that the exchange of goods and the maintenance of control over the use of goods impose costs on traders and owners. It is also concerned with the cost of government alternatives to the market place. We seek to establish both the importance and the wide role of these costs in economic life.

A large part of our argument will be illustrated by two important controversies in welfare economics in which we will show, on the one hand, that zero pricing of scarce goods need not result in inefficiency, and, on the other, that zero pricing of "public" goods may result in inefficiency. The standard criticisms of resource allocation by the market, which turn on the market's failure to price "external" effects and on its tendency to price "public" goods, are shown to be invalid. To do this we extend the well known axiom that there is no such thing as a free scarce good by including such goods as markets, government bureaus, and policing devices.

Throughout this paper, our attention is confined to the problem of efficiency within the framework of smoothly running markets and governments, in the sense that we assume that persons, whether in their capacity as civil servants or as private citizens, do not make arithmetic errors in calculating, or, at least, that they do not tend to make more errors in one

Journal of Law and Economics 11 (October 1964).

role than in another. We do not concern ourselves with problems of monopoly by either a firm or the government, but the problem of imperfect knowledge is treated.

Instead of "external effects" or "neighborhood effects" we will use the phrase "side effects" to identify those for which no account *seems* to be taken in the market place. This avoids the flavor of location and of being *necessarily* outside of the market place that seem to be associated with the more common names for these effects.

I. Exchange Cost

Recent Developments. R. H. Coase,[1] in an important article written recently for this *Journal*, demonstrates that there is, in general, nothing special about side effects that rules out the possibility of their being taken account of by the market. These effects can be taken into account by market transactions between the parties affected once the courts have established who has what right of action. Under competitive conditions and assuming zero exchange costs, these transactions will result in an efficient solution to the scarcity problem. Thus, if ranchers are given the right to allow their cattle to roam and the cattle stray accidentally onto unfenced farm land, it will be in the farmer's interest to bring the damage they cause to the rancher's attention by offering to pay the rancher to reduce the number of cattle foraging nearby. If the rancher disregards this offer, he sacrifices a potential receipt equal to the crop damage. Thus, the crop damage becomes a private cost to the rancher of raising additional cattle and will be taken account of in his calculations. Moreover, Coase points out the efficiency of the solution with respect to the number of cattle and the size of the crops in the absence of exchange costs is independent of whether the farmer or rancher is legally liable for the damage. The party not held liable, of course, acquires the right to act in ways which may have harmful side effects. The assignment of the liability for crop damage to the rancher would lead to a direct accounting for this cost in his operations and he would need to decide whether to reduce his herd or pay the farmer to reduce the crop he plants. Whether the farmer will find it worthwhile to pay enough to the rancher to reduce his herd or whether the rancher can pay enough to the farmer to reduce the area he cultivates depends on whether the value lost because of the crop reduction is greater or less than the value lost because the size of the herd is reduced. Whichever way the rights are initially assigned, the outcome of the subsequent bargaining will be that which maximizes the value of output.

Coase has advanced the analysis of the roles that can be played by the market and the government a step beyond its previous position. For now Coase has shown that if exchange costs are positive, it is necessary to ask whether government can take the harmful effects of an action into account at less cost than can the market or, indeed, if the resulting resource realignment is worth the cost of taking the side effects into account at all.

Misapplication of Optimality Theorems.   The question which asks whether or not realignment is worthwhile brings to light an improper usage to which we frequently have put our optimality theorems.   The cost of using the market relative to the cost of using a political mechanism has seldom been considered explicitly or in detail in the bulk of the theory of welfare economics.   This has led to an improper usage of those theorems. As a consequence of the conventional approach to these problems, it has not been recognized that the very conditions under which side effects are believed to lead to inefficiency are those conditions for which the welfare theorems used are inapplicable.

The usual analysis of market inefficiency in such cases attributes the difficulty to the absence of markets in which "appropriate" prices for measuring side effects can be revealed.[2]   But absence of a market or of a price can be consistent with efficiency when optimality theorems are appropriately interpreted.   *For produced goods*, the optimality theorems require equalities among various marginal rates of substitution.   These same optimality conditions, however, do not require such equalities for goods and services that are *not produced* in the final efficient equilibrium; for these we have corner solutions involving inequalities.   Thus, a basic premise in requiring equalities is that we are talking about goods which we require to be produced in positive quantities.

We then turn to the competitive model and observe that market prices will often bring about the equalities required for produced commodities and services.   But, we ask, what if some goods produce side effects which are not exchanged over a market?   We answer that the market fails to provide us with incentives which will guide behavior to take account of the side effects and that, therefore, the required equalities will be absent.   The allegation is that even perfectly competitive markets fail to achieve efficiency.   But, this reasoning generally fails to take account of the fact that the provision of a market (for the side effect) is itself a valuable and costly service.   Where a market, or the political action which would be its counterpart, does not exist, this service is not being produced.   If this service is not being produced some *in*equalities (instead of the equalities required for produced goods) among our marginal rates of substitution and marginal rates of transformation may be consistent with efficiency, as will be the case if the cost of taking account of side effects through either the market or the government exceeds the value of realigning resources. In such cases zero amounts of market pricing or the government equivalent will be efficient.   In asking the implications of the nonexistence of some markets, we seem to have forgotten the cost of providing market services or their government equivalent. The existence of prices to facilitate exchange between affected parties has been too much taken for granted. A price for every produced good or service is not a necessary condition for efficiency, so that the absence of a price does not imply that either market transactions or substitute government services are desirable. If we insist either that all actions (services or commodities) be priced in the market or that the government intervene, we are insisting that we do not economize on the cost of producing exchanges or government services. Thus, most welfare propositions concerned with side effects are based on an invalid use of the standard optimality theorems, i. e., they ignore the cost of some of the goods.

Some Examples. We shall consider two examples to illustrate our point. In the first rights of action are clearly defined; in the second they are not.

Our first example is zero-priced parking at shopping plazas in which unpaid-for benefits exist insofar as shoppers, in the prices they pay, confer benefits on nonshopping parkers. Most economists, regardless of their philosophical persuasion, would probably argue that the number of spaces is nonoptimal. But, when we say nonoptimal, we must have some idea of what is the optimal number of spaces. Assuming the absence of increasing returns, the less careful of us are apt to reply that the proper number of spaces is the number that would clear the market when a charge is levied to cover construction cost. A more careful reply would include exchange costs in the charge. *Neither* answer is necessarily correct.

It is true that the setting and collecting of appropriate shares of construction and exchange costs from each parker will reduce the number of parking spaces needed to allow ease of entry and exit. But while we have reduced the resources committed to constructing parking spaces, we have increased resources devoted to market exchange. We may end up by allocating more resources to the provision and control of parking than had we allowed free parking because of the resources needed to conduct transactions. By insisting that the commodity be priced, we may become less efficient than had we allowed persons to ration spaces on a first come, first serve basis. Similarly, rationing by government involves its own costs and may be no better. Those who purchase merchandise and indirectly pay for parking spaces may prefer to substitute the smaller total cost of constructing additional spaces to accommodate free-loaders rather than ration out the nonbuying parkers by paying the required exchange costs minus the savings of constructing fewer parking spaces. Since the cost of providing additional parking spaces depends largely on the price of land, it follows that we should expect to observe free parking allowed more frequently in suburbs than in the center of towns because of the differential prices of land. Given this differential, both methods of allocating parking may be efficient.

Is this example consistent with competition? Will not competing stores open nearby and charge lower prices because their customers use a free parking lot supplied by a competitor? Will they, thereby, force their competitor out of business? The desirability of providing parking spaces implies that we are dealing with a world of finite dimension in which all cars cannot be parked at zero cost on a dimensionless point. For this reason, differential land rent will be taken into account. Owners of land surrounding the free parking lot will enjoy windfall profits, a question of wealth redistribution, but potential competitors will have the advantages of the nearby lot capitalized and included in the rent they pay; they will enjoy no competitive advantage. The equilibrium is a stable competitive one although it gives rise to differential land rent. If the windfall is expected to be large enough to warrant the additional transactions required to purchase surrounding land, the (prospective) owners of the shopping plaza could take account of these gains in their calculations by purchasing the surrounding land before free parking is allowed. This option, which Coase refers to as extending the role of the firm, is alternative to both exchange and government action.[3]

In this particular example, the efficiency of producing this costly but zero-priced parking depends on the supplier being able to recoup the cost by other means, namely in the prices of his merchandise. This method of financing the parking lot becomes economically superior *only* if demand interrelations are such that a sale in combination arrangement reduces exchange costs sufficiently. Both the loose combination sale (not all parkers need to buy merchandise) as well as tighter tie-ins may, in fact, be methods which reduce the cost of allocating and which lead to optimal quantities of goods. We will have more to say on the relevance of this for the problems posed by public goods.

For contrast, our next example, one that has become a favorite, involves neither tie-in arrangements nor defined rights of action. It is the case in which market transactions do not take place in the the use of nectar by bees, so that prices do not arise which reflect the beneficial effects of apple blossoms on the productivity of bees. Clearly, as Coase would probably point out, it is possible for beekeepers and apple growers to strike a bargain over how many trees are to be planted, the bargain taking account of an apple tree's contribution to honey production and a bee's contribution to cross-fertilization of trees. Further, were there significant predictable benefits from the interaction, significant enough to offset any diseconomies of underspecialization, beekeeping and apple growing would be carried on by the same farmer. However, the benefits may be small relative to the costs of forsaking specialization. Merger will not then be the solution. Suppose, also, that estimates of benefits are small relative to estimates of the cost of developing the science of the apple-bee interaction and to either the costs of transacting in the market or providing substitute government services. Then efficiency requires that bees be allowed to "help themselves" on a first come, first serve basis, which is, after all, an alternative arrangement for settling scarcity problems.

Here no combination sales are directly involved. A valuable and costly good, nectar, is provided free of charge because it would be too costly to take account of the indirect benefits to beekeepers. In contrast to the parking and merchandising example, the separate marketing of the two products, apples and blossoms, is costly. Hence a zero-priced good may be efficient even though no combination sale is used. Since no low cost combination sale seems possible, the good (nectar) will be provided free if apples, *per se*, are worth producing. If apples are not worth producing, our recognition of the existence of a benefit to beekeepers will not make the production of apples desirable, for the cost of inducing the apple grower to take this benefit into account is too high to make it worthwhile.

II. Police Cost

Up to now we have largely limited our attention to situations in which direct bargaining between individuals requires an exchange cost that is larger than the benefits derived from the exchange. To take account of these side effects, the interested parties, therefore, resort to combination sales, to extensions of the firm, or they find it expedient not to modify these effects. All of these alternatives are consistent with efficiency and yet all fail to exhibit a market in the side effect. There are situations, however, which are somewhat different in that the cost of *policing* the effects of actions, rather than the cost of exchange, may be so high as to cause additional complications. The following discussion of these situations is designed to reveal the roles played by police cost and private property and to help clear up some public good problems.

Property Rights and the Valuation Problem. There are two tasks which must be handled well by any acceptable allocative mechanism. These are, firstly, that information must be generated about all the benefits of employing resources in alternative uses, and secondly, that persons be motivated to take account of this information. To the extent that both these tasks are solved by the allocative mechanism, the problem of attaining an efficient allocation of resources reduces to arithmetic. Setting aside the second problem, we turn to the first and, in particular to the necessity for protecting the right to use economically valuable resources if we are to obtain accurate information about benefits.

It is well known that prices can serve as guideposts to where resources are wanted most, and in addition, that exchangeability of goods at these prices can provide incentives for people to follow these guideposts. However, analytical concentration on the price mechanism has kept us from closely examining what it is that is being traded. The value of what is being traded depends crucially on the rights of action over the physical commodity and on how economically these rights are enforced. The enforcement of the accompanying property rights has an important impact on the ability of prices to measure benefits. An emphasis on this aspect or view of the problem, in conjunction with our emphasis on exchange cost, will allow us to unify our treatment of what is now largely a collection of special cases in which our measures of benefits diverge from actual benefits. The petroleum and fishery "pool" problems are good examples of problems created by treating economic goods as free goods. The general conclusion reached by the analysis of pool problems is that a resource, be it petroleum, fish, or game, is too rapidly worked. This conclusion is correct and if we think in terms of producible inventories, the absence of property right enforcement also can be shown to result in too little production of the good, or in too small an increment to the pool or inventory of the good. This is because the prices, which reflect private benefits, fail to measure the whole of the social benefit derived from the good. As a special case of this general proposition, if we assume that it costs nothing to police property rights, it follows that there exists a direct relationship between the degree to which private benefits approach social benefits and the degree to which the conveyed property rights are enforced. This relationship can be illustrated with two examples.

Given any definition of the rights that accompany ownership in an automobile, the price mechanism will ration the existing stock of automobiles. But the total private value of this stock will depend on the degree to which auto theft is reduced by our laws and police. If we pass a law *prohibiting* the arrest and prosecution of auto thieves, and also prohibiting the use of private protection devices, the bids that persons subsequently offer for the purchase of automobiles will fall below the social value of automobiles. The lower bids will result from the reduction in control that a purchaser can expect to exercise over the use of a purchased auto and, in addition, from his ability to "borrow" at no charge those autos which are purchased by others. The bids submitted after the passage of such a law will underestimate the social value of autos, for we can assume for our purposes that the usefulness of an auto remains the same whether it is used by the purchaser or by the legal thief. This is true even though the existing stock of autos is efficiently distributed among owners. The total value of autos will fall below social value and the subsequent increase in the stock of autos will be less than it should.

The lowering of bids that results from our law is similar to the lowering of bids that will take place when high police cost reduces the degree of private control that it is economical to guarantee owners. The provision of national defense provides us with a classic example of the impact of high police cost. Voluntarily submitted bids for defense will be lower than the social value of defense because the bidder can count on being able to enjoy (some of) the defense bought and also enjoyed by his fellow citizen. The effect on bidding is similar to that which takes place in our example of legalized auto theft except that the reason for lack of control is not merely the absence of an appropriate law but, rather, it is the high cost of defending a purchaser from a foreign aggressor while at the same time preventing his neighbors from enjoying protection. The cost of excluding those who have not contracted for benefits from the enjoyment of some of these benefits is so high that a general attitude of letting others bear the cost of defense can be expected. Consequently, voluntarily submitted bids will underestimate the social value of defense.

If a low cost method is available and is used to prevent those who do not contract for defense from benefiting from the defense bought by others, the market would reveal accurate information about the social value of defense. Such information would be extremely useful if the market or the planner is to allocate resources efficiently.

The institution of private property, which attempts to exclude nonpurchasers from the use of that which others have purchased, should, therefore, not be looked upon as either accidental or undesirable. On the contrary, its existence is probably due in part to its great practicality in revealing the social values upon which to base solutions to scarcity problems. This is precisely why we do not worry that bids for, say, candy will fail to reveal the social value of candy. The price of candy is accurate in its measure of social value because reflected in it is the ability of each purchaser to control the use of his purchase, whether that use be for resale or for charity, for his children, or for his own consumption. This valuation function is related to but distinct from the incentives to work provided by a property system, for even in a society where work is viewed as a pleasurable activity, and, hence, where incentives to work are not needed, it would still be necessary to properly value the varieties of alternative output that can be produced.

We have already observed that the value of what is being traded depends upon the allowed rights of action over the physical good and upon the degree to which these rights are enforced. This statement at once raises the question of which rights and which degrees of enforcement are efficient. If changing the mix of property rights that accompany ownership increases the value of property, such a change will be desirable from the viewpoint of wealth maximizing. For example, if the problem is whether to allow automobile owners to increase the speed at which they travel on side streets, one could assess whether there would result an increase in the total value of affected property. Would people be willing to pay higher prices for automobiles? It is by no means clear that they would, for some prospective owners may fear high speed more than they value it. And, if there would result an increase in the price of automobiles, would it be large enough to offset any increase in the cost of insuring life, limb, and home (i. e., the resulting decline in the value of other property)? If a net increase in the total value of property follows a change in the mix of rights, the change should be allowed if we seek to maximize wealth. Not to allow the change would be to refuse to generate a surplus of value sufficient to compensate those harmed by the change. The process of calculating the net change in value will, of course, involve the taking into account of side effects and this is a problem that we have already discussed. The enforcement of rights can be viewed in the same way. Indeed, we can insist that a proper definition of a right of action include the degree to which the owner or the community is allowed to enforce the right. Enforcement thus becomes the specification of additional rights and can be included in the above analytical framework. The conclusion we have reached depends, of course, upon the existence of competitive entry in the exercise of particular rights. It is therefore necessary to exclude rights which confer monopoly by restricting entry and to insist that all owners have the same rights of action. There are some difficult problems which we do not take up here. For example, since everyone has the right to take out a patent or a copyright on "newly created" goods or ideas, does the granting of this right involve the granting of monopoly power?

It is, of course, necessary to economize on police cost, so that we will not always want to guarantee full control to the purchaser; more will be said below about this aspect of the problem. But, this aspect aside, it is essential to note that the valuation power of the institution of property is most effective when it is most *private*. It is ironic, therefore, that one of the strongest intellectual arguments for expanding the role of government has been based on the alleged necessity for eliminating exclusivity and for allowing free access to the use of certain types of resources. These resources have been given the name "public goods" and they are characterized by their alleged ability to confer benefits on additional persons without thereby reducing the benefits conferred on others. The provision of national defense is a well known example.

The Public Goods Problem. The relevance of what we have been discussing for public goods is that if the cost of policing the benefits derived from the use of these goods is low, there is an excellent reason for excluding those who do not pay from using these goods. By such exclusion we, or the market, can estimate accurately the value of diverting resources from other uses to the production of the public good. Thus, even though extending the use of an existing bridge to additional persons adds nothing to the direct cost of operating the bridge, there is good reason for charging persons for the right to cross the bridge. Excluding those who do not pay for the use of the bridge allows us to know whether a new bridge is likely to generate more benefit than it is likely to cost.[4] Why should we desire information about a new bridge if the direct marginal cost of using the existing bridge is zero? Firstly, the bridge may depreciate with time rather than with traffic, so that the question of replacement remains relevant even though the marginal cost of use is zero. Secondly, there is a private marginal benefit to users of the bridge, at least in lessening their driving costs, and this benefit can be measured by pricing the use of the bridge. Such information would allow us to ascertain whether it is economic to have a new bridge closer to some persons than is the present bridge.

For some goods, air for example, the supply is so plentiful that diversion from some uses is not required to increase the intensity with which they are used elsewhere. Only where scarcity is absent is it *a priori* reasonable to charge a zero price. Superabundance is the only true *a priori* case for a zero-priced public good. All other goods are such that their provision forces us into resource allocation problems. To solve these problems efficiently, we need information which is obtained by excluding nonpurchasers, *provided that the additional information is worth more than the exchange and police costs necessitated.* In cases where the costs are greater, a zero price can be reconciled with efficiency requirements. If we must distinguish among goods, we had best do away with the "public goods" *vs.* private goods dichotomy and instead classify goods according to whether they are truly free or economic and classify economic goods according to whether marketing costs are too high relative to the benefits of using markets and to the costs of substitute nonmarket allocation devices.

Alternative Devices. The use of taxation for the provision of scarce goods must be defended on grounds other than the usual rationale of their being public goods. As we have seen, insofar as efficiency is concerned, the fact that side benefits can be derived by nonpurchasers from the acquisition by others of these goods is inconclusive. If the planner's or the market's calculation of benefits can be improved by a small expenditure to protect or to confer property rights, the use of price rationing to measure these benefits may be justified. The problem can be viewed as that of determining the degree to which it is desirable to purchase valuation information through the competitive pricing process. A purchase of valuation information reduces the utilization of a public good below the levels that seem to be warranted by the direct cost of extending utilization. If the direct cost of, say, increasing the volume of traffic carried by an existing bridge is zero, it may nonetheless be *un*desirable to charge a zero price because of the indirect costs implied by zero-pricing. These indirect costs are of two kinds.

Firstly, and obviously, valuation information about the bridge is sacrificed. (Is not valuation information one of the most important public goods?) Secondly, the alternative methods of financing the building of bridges may also lead to inefficiency, especially by degrading valuation information elsewhere. This is most easily seen by supposing that an excise tax is levied on other goods to finance bridges. Such a tax will lead to inefficiently small rates of production of these other goods (assuming competitive markets). Alternatively, the levying of an income tax will inefficiently reduce the quantities of income generating activities undertaken by those taxed. A tax on property values, even one on rent, would tend to discourage the seeking out of more valuable uses of property. A head tax would have the least effect because it is not concentrated on particular activities. Even a head tax, one could argue, would alter a person's choice of community, and moreover, a resident who refused to pay the tax might be excluded from use of the bridge. Taxes exclude just as do prices, so that on grounds of exclusion there is not much principle to guide us. Given these indirect costs of alternative methods of financing the provision of public goods, the desirability of zero-pricing is not at all clear, especially if the cost of policing is low.

For some goods, however, it must be recognized that police cost may seem too high to allow the market to generate accurate information on social benefits economically. In these cases taxation *may* be the most practical method of finance and zoning the most practical way of establishing rights, just as subsidies, excise taxes, and government nonprice rationing may be the most practical way of coping with high exchange costs. But it must be remembered that all these devices are "exclusionary" and have costs of their own. At best, they would be second best alternatives to a market in which police and exchange costs are small and in which there is no bias in arithmetic mistakes as between civil servants and others, for these devices are not as likely to turn up correct estimates of the social values of alternative goods.

In a world in which exchange and police cost and the cost of providing alternative political devices are all zero, reliance on the political mechanism of a smoothly run democracy will result in less efficiency than will reliance on the market. Aside from problems of monopoly in government or of errors in calculation, in a one-man, one-vote democracy, where votes are not for sale, the polling place will generate information that is based on majoritarian principles rather than on maximum benefit principles. Thus, suppose some citizens prefer a stronger national defense but that a majority prefer a weaker defense. Left to a vote, the weaker defense will be our chosen policy even though the minority is willing to pay more than the additional cost required to bring defense up to the level they desire (and so, if possible, they may hire private police services). An error in the opposite direction is also possible. The majority of voters may approve of a large space effort even though they would not be able to bid high enough to acquire these resources for space in the absence of forced tax contributions. (Here, however, the minority cannot privately adjust.)

Although taxation is sometimes the most practical way of dealing with the provision of high police costs goods, there are other methods which are likely to arise in the market and which will lower the required police cost. As we have seen, extending the firm and the practice of sale-in-combination may overcome many instances of high exchange cost. These devices can also be used to reduce high police cost.

In the famous railway example, sparks from passing trains destroy some crops. The damage caused was believed to be adequate grounds for the government to take action through one or more of the political devices we have already mentioned. Direct contracting between the farmers and the railroad might take account of this side effect were it not that a bargain struck between a farmer and the railway would automatically confer benefits on all surrounding farmers by reducing spark fall-out on their land. Police costs are too high to allow benefits to be conferred on the contracting farmer without at the same time conferring them on non-contracting farmers. Therefore, it is believed that each farmer will wait for someone else to buy a reduction in spark output. (This conclusion requires two preliminary assumptions. The exchange cost of farmers getting together to submit a joint bid must be high relative to the benefits they will receive so that it is blocked by the expense it entails, and the exchange cost of their getting together to submit a joint bid must be higher than the cost of their organizing politically to lobby for antispark legislation.)

However, once the spatial aspects of the problem are admitted, we must again consider the phenomenon of differential land rent. Presumably, land rents on property adjacent to railways have been suitably depressed to allow farmers to compete with those not affected by sparks. The landowners, who find it in their interest to reduce the railroad's output of sparks, also find themselves not willing to enter into contracts through which other landowners will benefit. To some extent each would wait for the other to transact with the railway for a reduction in spark output. However, the analysis is not yet finished. The railway may realize a profit by purchasng the surrounding land at its depressed price. The purchase of a parcel of land does not confer benefits on neighbors to the same degree as would a purchase of spark curtailment so that this action would not hamper the concluding of similar contracts with other landowners as much as would the sale of a reduction in sparks. After the railroad purchases title to enough land to make it worthwhile, it could take into account the effect of its output of sparks on land values and profitably bring about an adjustment of this output to the socially optimal amount—that which maximizes the joint value of railroading and land-owning. The land must, of course, be rented or resold with a contractual agreement requiring a continuance of reduced spark output. The low police cost associated with the purchase of land is substituted for the very high police cost that would be required to eliminate sparks on some land but not on other nearby land. The necessity for purchasing a reduction in spark output is obviated by substituting a purchase of land.

The extension of the firm together with the combination-sale devices that are associated with differential land rent are extremely important alternatives to government action. These devices can extend considerably the usefulness of markets for revealing and measuring the value of many side effects. The sale of land may entail much less exchange and policing cost than the direct exchange of whatever is producing the side effect. The smoke emitted from a nearby factory would, in principle, be subject to solution in the same manner. Now, of course, in many of these cases we do not observe such solutions taking place because exchange and police costs are not reduced sufficiently and because they may require too much underspecialization cost. Governmental devices, say, zoning laws, may help take account of such benefits, however inaccurately, at a lower cost (in which we should include those costs imposed by the rigidities of zoning laws). It may be, however, that both governmental and market solutions are too costly and that the most efficient alternative is not to attempt to take account of some side effects.[5]

There are other indirect devices for internalizing via combination sales. The activities of labeling, branding, and advertising allow for internalization of side effects by tying in the sale of information with other goods. Suppose persons would like their tuna boiled longer before canning. Each canner would find it in his interest to prepare the tuna more carefully except that, in a world without labels, all competitors would enjoy at no cost some of the benefits of the resulting increase in demand. Some, therefore, wait for competitors to act. Underinvestment in tuna boiling (or overinvestment in boiling tuna at home) takes place and government regulations governing canning procedures are instituted.

Suppose we allow each canner to state on the label both his name and the minimum boiling time. The name is required to establish responsibility and thereby to reduce policing cost, which is another way of saying that the cost of exercising the rights acquired by purchasers by reason of the purchase contract is reduced for the buyer. The sale of knowledge jointly with that of tuna allows the value of longer boiling to be taken into account by producers and buyers. Structural market imperfections of the monopolistic competition variety can be ruled out if both longer boiled and less boiled tuna have numerous producers. The demand for each producer's tuna will then be the going market price of the particular quality he produces.[6]

Still other institutional arrangements have been devised to combine extensions of the firm with the sale-in-combination device. Department stores and shopping plazas are organizational devices for overcoming high police cost. The owner of the department store or shopping plaza can provide a general environment that is conducive for shopping, such as pleasant plantings, escalators, and other customer services that merchants who owned their own land might hesitate to pay for, hoping instead that neighboring landowners would incur the necessary expenses from which all would benefit. The enclosing of the land into a single ownership entity which often undertakes to provide services usually provided by government from tax revenues, such as streets, sidewalks, refuse collection, and even police protection, allows the owner to exclude those who refuse to pay rentals which cover the cost of these services. The competition of various plazas and department stores will provide ample opportunity for merchants to select the services that they wish to buy without fearing or counting on free-loading. Apartment buildings can also be viewed in the same light, and especially the modern apartment building which combines office and recreational space with living space. The development of these institutional arrangements provides an interesting challenge to political institutions for the provision of many of the services generally presumed to be within the scope of the polling place.

The preceding discussion has taken as given the state of technical arts. The levels of exchange and police costs that are required for effective marketing and the costs of government substitute services depend on how well we master the technology of operating markets and governments. Attention is sometimes called to the fact that emerging technical developments will make the use of markets or governments more economic than they now are. There are surely many instances where this is true. However, our analysis suggests that technological developments can operate in the opposite direction. At the same time that technology is reducing the cost of using these alternative institutional arrangements for economizing, it is also reducing the cost of constructing parking spaces, of developing fire resistant corn, and of mass producing automobiles. Whether or not it pays to increase the extent to which we exchange via markets, protect private property rights, or use alternative government devices depends on how much we will thereby reduce production cost and crop damage. Markets or their government alternatives should come into greater prominence only if technical developments lower the costs of these institutional arrangements more than they reduce the costs of producing parking spaces and cars and the cost of crop damage.

Essentially, we have argued in this paper that there exist no qualitative differences between side effects and what we may call "primary" effects. The only differences are those that are implicitly based on quantitative differences in exchange and police cost. Suppose a factory invents a new more efficient furnace which can burn a cheaper grade of coal than can existing furnaces. The burning of cheap coal, we will assume, dirties homes in the neighborhood. We label this effect as side or neighborhood or external, but its real economic implication is to reduce the wealth of nearby homeowners. If this same factory, by virtue of its new furnace, successfully forces a nearby competing firm out of business, and if the resulting decline in demand for housing reduces the wealth of neighborhood homeowners, we do not become concerned. Why the difference in our attitudes toward these two situations which have the same effect on homeowners?

The decline in wealth which results from the fall in demand for housing is more than offset by an increase in wealth elsewhere. This increase accrues primarily to other homeowners and to persons purchasing the lower priced product produced by the factory. We accept the reallocation, I conjecture, because we feel that the existence of a smoothly operating market will insure that wealth is maximized. In the smoke case, exchange and police costs are high relative to the benefits of marketing smoke and, therefore, we do not have an existing market to rely on for the reallocation, although a potential one always stands ready. If the costs of exchanging and policing smoke contracts were zero (and if the cost of exchanging houses were zero) there would be no reason for distinguishing between the two cases insofar as "remedial" action is concerned. We have already argued that the most efficient arrangement may, in fact, require that nothing be done to prohibit smoke and we will not go into these matters again. Our present purpose is merely to emphasize that there is nothing special or qualitatively different about any of these effects, including the effects which stem from what we ineptly call public goods, and that any special treatment accorded to them cannot be justified merely by observing their presence.

FOOTNOTES

* The author wishes to thank Armen A. Alchian, Gary S. Becker, William H. Meckling, Peter Pashigian, and George J. Stigler for their comments.

1 Coase, The Problem of Social Cost, 3 J.Law & Econ. 1–44 (1960).

2 Cf. Arrow, Uncertainty and the Welfare Economics of Medical Care, 53 Am.Econ. Rev. 941, 944–45 (1963):
An individual who fails to be immunized not only risks his own health, a disutility which presumably he has weighed against the utility of avoiding the procedure, but also that of others. In an ideal price system, there would be a price which he would have to pay to anyone whose health is endangered, a price sufficiently high so that the others would feel compensated; or, alternatively, there would be a price which would be paid to him by others to induce him to undergo the immunization procedure. . . . It is, of

course, not hard to see that such price systems could not, in fact, be practical; to approximate an optimal state it would be necessary to have collective intervention in the form of subsidy or tax or compulsion.
and Bator, The Anatomy of Market Failure, 72 Q.J.Econ. 351, 353–54 (1958):
Pareto-efficient . . . points . . . are characterized by a complete set of marginal-rate-of-substitution . . . equalities (or limiting inequalities) which, in turn, yield a set of price-like constants.   Where no such constants exist, reference will be to *failure of existence* (of prices, and hence, of efficiency).   (Parenthetic phrase added.)

3 The existence of unique locations does not necessarily imply the inefficiency usually associated with monopolistic competition.   *Cf.* Demsetz, The Welfare and Empirical Implications of Monopolistic Competition, 74 Economic J. 623–41 (1964).   It should also be noted that if the landowners could know of the differential land rents that would result from the superior technology offered by free parking, they would be inclined to enter into an agreement sharing the differential rent accruing to land adjacent to the shopping plaza.   If they did not enter into such an agreement there would be an inclination to let the free parking facility be built on the other man's property.

4 See Coase, The Marginal Cost Controversy, 13 Economica 169–82 (1946), for an early application of this point in reference to the use of multipart pricing in natural monopoly situations.   See also Minasian, Television Pricing and the Theory of Public Goods, 7 J.Law & Econ. 71 (1964).

5 The ability of combination sales to take account of side benefits depends on how closely the value of the tied-in good reflects the value of the public good.   There is a direct and exact correspondence between the value of land and the (negative to farmers) value of spark output.   A less exact correspondence between the values of the tied goods, while not a perfect device, can nonetheless be useful for taking account of the value of public goods.

Even the stubborn classic case of providing for the national defense is amenable to some usable tie-in arrangements.   The provision of defense again presents us with a situation in which it is in the interest of a beneficiary to let others buy defense since he will benefit from their purchases.   Suppose, however, that instead of financing defense with taxes, the government resorts to the sale of insurance to citizens which covers their lives and property in the event of loss arising from war.   The tied goods, insurance and defense, are substitutes, but they do not fully correspond in value fluctuations.   For a stated premium per thousand dollars of insurance and a stated maximum, citizens would buy more insurance the more likely they thought war and the less able they thought our defense.   Those having more at stake would buy more insurance.   The premiums could then be used to finance the defense establishment.   The side effect is not fully captured, however, because your purchase of insurance, although it fully internalizes your losses in the event of war, also decreases the likelihood of war, and, hence, reduces the amount of insurance others would volunteer to buy.   This smaller remaining public aspect of the good could be accounted for by offering the insurance for premiums that are believed to be subsidized.

War, as well as other events, can topple governments, so that to make the insurance credible, the government might need to offer citizens the option of cancelling their insurance and receiving all or some of the premiums they have paid.   This cancellation option need be effective only up to the date before a war starts.   The insurance device is not without dangers.   By raising the maximum purchasable insurance (and lowering premiums), the government could induce a more aggressive attitude among the citizens than is warranted by actuarial fair insurance.

6 It is not really necessary for efficiency to obtain to require that producers take the product price as given and beyond their control.   See Demsetz, op. cit. supra note 3.

B Continued

22: ON THE DISTINCTION BETWEEN PUBLIC AND PRIVATE GOODS*

OTTO A. DAVIS
Carnegie Institute of Technology

ANDREW B. WHINSTON
Purdue University

I. Introduction

Some years ago, in a now classic series of articles [13] [14] [15], Professor Paul A. Samuelson made an admittedly polar distinction between public and private goods. Briefly, private consumption goods, like bread, must be parceled out among persons with one man getting a loaf more if another gets a loaf less. Thus, if x_{ij} represents the ith person's consumption of the jth private good and X_j represents the quantity available, then

$$\sum x_{ij} = X_j.$$

A public consumption good, on the other hand, differs in that one man's consumption does not diminish the quantity available for another. Thus, if Y_{ik} represents the ith person's consumption of the kth public good and Y_k represents the quantity available, $y_{ik} = Y_k$ for all men. Prime examples are supposed to be outdoor circuses, national defense, and, some may have thought, radio waves and TV signals.

Recently, responding to Minasian's argument [10] that market allocation (via subscription) of television might be a more desirable arrangement, Professor Samuelson [16] claimed that the possession by television of the characteristics of a public good did not constitute evidence either for or against a market arrangement via subscription. There is no doubt but that Samuelson's claim (or admission?) is correct. Aside from television and radio signals, there are many examples of goods which are allocated in the market

*Amer. Econ. Rev., Vol. 57, 1967, p. 360.

place and yet which exhibit various degrees of "Samuelsonian publicness." The products of the researcher's efforts, the outpouring of the jukebox and the record player, under-capacity indoor (why be restricted to the outdoors?) circuses and performances of movies and various forms of entertainment, the unhurried and uncrowded viewing of old masters which are owned by a private art collector, etc.—all exhibit aspects of publicness. Olsen [12] claims that the concept can be applied to all large organizations.[1]

When one is faced with such examples, it is only natural to wonder if it is possible to determine in any objective fashion whether a good should be governmentally or privately produced. Samuelson's classic articles seem to provide few clues to an answer. Yet, the problem appears to merit consideration.

II. Institutional Arrangements and Samuelson's Model

It is important to understand that, despite the title, Samuelson's model is not directly concerned with public expenditures. Rather, it is a model of market failure. What is shown is that in a system incorporating his "public" consumption goods, the market "fails" in the sense that the necessary conditions for the attainment of Pareto optimality are not automatically satisfied. One should observe two facts here. First, despite the name given to the public goods, the failure of the pricing mechanism to satisfy the necessary conditions for Pareto optimality does not constitute a prima facie case for public ownership, or even public regulation, of the relevant facilities for either production or distribution. Second, the institutional arrangements under which a good, even a public consumption good, is distributed in a market perform an important role in determining the characteristics of the performance of the pricing mechanism.

Recall the definition of Samuelson's public good. One of the implicit notions is that whatever is produced is available to all. Obviously, even if the appropriate maximization problem yields the necessary optimality conditions with the associated Lagrange multipliers, it is difficult to even imagine real prices performing the role indicated by the multipliers. Behaviorally, the problem appears to be much more complicated and rich than is indicated by the simple mathematics. At issue is the fact that paying the price does not give one control of the good. Instead, the act of paying the price is somehow separated from the act of consumption. Consider the following example in order to clarify the behavioral implications of this point.

Imagine that the government decided to alter the institutional arrangements or organization of the market for bread, which is certainly a private good. Suppose that the government decided to separate the act of paying from the act of obtaining the bread. Accordingly, imagine that payments for the desired quantity of bread were made by consumers to the government in the early morning at the "revenue center." Later in the day, bread could be obtained at the "distribution center." However, suppose that there is no communication between the revenue and distribution centers so that the acts of paying and obtaining are truly separated. The bread is distributed on a first come, first served basis. One might observe that this institutional arrangement would certainly affect the functioning of the market mechanism. Consumers could not be counted upon to reveal their preferences at the revenue center. Nor would the distribution center fare much better since consumers could simply take the bread they wanted, if it happened to be available, no matter what their payment at the revenue center. Price could not perform its traditional functions. The institutional arrangements cause market failure.

Observe that, at least under one interpretation, there are certain similarities between the above example and the Samuelsonian model of public consumption goods. By definition, a public good in Samuelson's model is available to all consumers no matter whether a consumer chooses to pay or not. From the standpoint of an individual consumer, a payment could not give one control over the public good in the sense of deciding the precise quantity to be consumed. The act of paying is separated from the act of consuming. It is not surprising that the market fails. For a consumer actually to make a payment would be nothing more or less than an act of pure charity.

III. Some Conditions Needed for the Operation of a Market

Since he was interested in the problem of attaining an efficient or Pareto optimal allocation, Samuelson did not discuss the possibility of making a market for public goods operate much as if it were allocating private goods. Nevertheless, such a possibility is often available as an alternative to the collective provision of the public good if the appropriate institutional arrangements can be accomplished. Accordingly, a brief and informal discussion of some of the conditions which seem to be needed if a market is to operate in a reasonable manner appears to be merited.

It is obvious that the first requirement is a provision for some type of ownership or property rights. Without ownership, at least in some form, there would seem to be no basis for exchange. Of course, there are complex issues involved in the definition of property rights. The very definition can affect the manner in which exchange takes place and the way in which a market operates.[2] The definition of property rights can sometimes determine whether externalities are allowed to exist in the market. Zoning ordinances, for example, can be interpreted as an effort to remove the influence of externalities in the urban property market.[3] It might be noted that in a sense a good may be characterized by the control an owner may exercise, so that the same piece of property is in effect a different good once the zoning ordinance is changed.

The second requirement, which is related to the issues of ownership and property rights, concerns "control" over the good or service. The act of buying or paying for the good or service must be related to the use or consumption of it. Even in the case of public good, purchase can sometimes be made to give some control and establish a connection between the act of paying and consumption as the example of television signals with scramblers illustrates.

The third requirement, which is related to both of the previous ones, concerns the possibility of exclusion. While perfect exclusion need not be required for markets to function reasonably well, as numerous examples of the presence of externalities amply illustrates, it is easily seen that exclusion does provide basic motivation for exchange.[4]

IV. The Market Allocation of Samuelsonian Public Goods

In part, the question of whether the above requirements can be satisfied for some particular good depends upon the technological characteristics of the good. In order to illustrate this point, consider the case of television. In the age of electronic scramblers, exclusion is possible. The signals can be "owned" and their services sold. Thus it is possible to establish a direct relationship between the consumption of the service and the payment for it. The above requirements for a market can be satisfied. Since the issue does not seem to have been considered fully, it appears appropriate to discuss briefly the operation of such a market on the basis of an excessively simple model.

Consider a society composed of people deciding upon viewing a pay television program. For simplicity, let the capital or fixed costs of producing the program be ignored. Assume that there is no advertising. Consider the following definitions:

$x_i = $ 0 if the ith person does not watch the program
$\qquad$ 1 if that person does watch the program

$y = $ 0 if the program is not produced
$\qquad$ 1 if the program is produced

$u_i(x_i)$: The value or "utility" to the ith person from watching the program.

$g(y)$: A function indicating the amount of some homogeneous (for simplicity) resource used to produce the program.

M: An arbitrarily large number.

K: The "minimal" amount of the homogeneous resource used to produce the program; i.e., $g(1) = K$.

Given these definitions, and assuming that the objective is to attain a Pareto optimum in television viewing, consider the following vector maximization problem:

$$\text{(1.1)} \quad \max \, [u_1(x_1), u_2(x_2), \cdots, u_n(x_n)] \tag{1}$$
$$\text{subject to}$$

$$\text{(1.2)} \quad \sum_i x_i - My \leq 0$$

$$\text{(1.3)} \quad g(y) \leq K$$

$$\text{(1.4)} \quad x_i = 0, 1; \; y = 0, 1 \quad i = 1, \cdots, n$$

It is convenient to replace the vector (1.1). Following the procedure introduced in [8], let α_i represent the reciprocal of the ith individual's marginal utility of income. Define $d_i = u_i(1)$ and $c_i = \alpha_i d_i$. Assuming for simplicity that the α_i are not affected by the decision to watch or not watch the program, one can replace the vector (1.1) by

$$\sum_i \alpha_i u_i(x_i) = \sum_i \alpha_i d_i x_i = \sum_i c_i x_i \tag{2}$$

and maximize (2) subject to the same constraints so that the problem is reduced to one of integer maximization. Note that the use of M in (1.2) means that once $y = 1$ the constraint is never binding. The program must be available if someone watches it.

Let p represent the price of the homogeneous resource and assume that p is given by a perfect market. Define $k = p \cdot g(1)$ so that $p \cdot g(y) = ky$. Problem (1) can now be replaced by the following equivalent problem:

$$\max \sum_i c_i x_i - ky \tag{3}$$

$$\text{subject to}$$

$$\sum_i x_i - My \leq 0$$

and the solution to (3) is obvious. If

$$\sum_i c_i \geq k \text{ for } c_i \geq 0,$$

then the program should be presented and all x_i corresponding to $c_i \geq 0$ should be set equal to one. If there is an i such that $c_i < 0$, then that $x_i = 0$. All persons who enjoy the program should be able to view it.

Consider whether the above solution could be achieved by a nondiscriminatory pricing device. Let λ denote the price of being able to view the program. Obviously, if no one who wishes to see the program is to be excluded, then the best that the television network can do is to set

$$\lambda = \min_i c_i \geq 0 \qquad (4)$$

so that the total revenue to the network is

$$\lambda \sum_i x_i$$

where the sum is over all i whose $c_i \geq 0$. Two issues are relevant here. First,

$$\lambda \sum x_i < k$$

is a likely outcome so that a subsidy may be required to pay for the costs of the program. The fact that total revenue is less than variable costs (recall that fixed costs are ignored here) does not necessarily indicate that the program is unwarranted. Second, there seems to be no feasible way for the network to determine the appropriate value of λ as indicated in (4). Obviously, the network cannot ask potential viewers to reveal the value of their c_i. One might think of starting with a zero price and raising it by successive increments until some viewer turned off his set; but surely viewers would catch on to this little game and bluff by turning off their set at any positive price so that it would be driven back down to zero. Therefore, it does not appear that pricing, with or without subsidization, can result in the achievement of the solution to (3).

Since the presence of market failure does not imply the existence of a superior nonmarket alternative, consider the "second-best" type of problem where the television program is priced, there is no subsidy and costs must be covered. It seems obvious in these circumstances that the "best of the second best" possibilities is one which allows costs to be covered exactly. In other words, values of both λ and the x_i must be determined such that

$$\lambda \sum_i x_i - k = 0 \qquad (5)$$

and the other conditions are also satisfied. It is not always true that such a solution exists or that it is unique. Assuming existence, presumably one could find such a solution by starting with an extremely low price and then raising it by increments until (5) was satisfied. Note that the existence of (5) removes the incentive for bluffing. In other words, in this second-best type of allocation by pricing, there is no problem of individuals emitting false signals or not revealing true preferences. Observe, however, that this second-best solution does impose costs of exclusion upon the society. This cost is given by

$$\sum c_i$$

where the sum is taken over those c_i satisfying the relation $0 \leq c_i \leq \lambda$ where here λ represents the particular value of λ which was selected to satisfy (5).

Note that no motivational premise, such as profit maximization, was introduced as the basis for the selection of the second-best constraint (5). However, it can be argued that in an expanded model where alternate networks compete for viewers of their programs, the very competition will cause the "no profit" condition (5) to be satisfied so that this analysis does provide a basis (at least as a first approximation) for the assessment of the costs of the private provision of television services by the pricing mechanism.

Observe again that the particular pricing arrangement analyzed above depended upon the technological feasibility of scrambling (and descrambling) devices. However, even if these devices were not available, market allocations are still possible if certain institutional actions are taken. Law might require that television sets be made in such a manner that a special device is required to tune into any given channel. The purchase of one of these special devices would give the owner of the set the right to view the specified channel as often as desired. Such an arrangement would not markedly differ from the practice of many private swimming clubs, for example, of selling a season pass instead of charging for each trip to the pool. Similarly, channels might be assigned to the networks who might "rent" the right to make sets capable of tuning into the specified channels to the various manufacturers. Obviously, various arrangements are possible. Each possibility has its own operating characteristics and corresponding social cost.

The point here is that technological considerations can determine partially which institutional arrangements are feasible. The feasibility of various institutional arrangements certainly has an influence in the determination of which particular one is to be selected as the most appropriate. Since technology changes over time, one can expect that institutions should be modified accordingly.

V. Institutional Choice for Samuelsonian Public Goods

The recent exchange between Minasian and Samuelson, which was concerned with the issue of subscription television, illustrates the fact that the optimality conditions are only of limited value in making an institutional choice.[5] Samuelson [16] emphasizes that there is no presumption that the particular arrangement which does satisfy the necessary conditions is one which produces a Pareto optimal allocation. Sufficient conditions must also be considered. Even more important, one must determine whether there are feasible institutional arrangements which could result in the satisfaction of both sets of conditions. It is obviously a fact that there is nothing inherent in the derivation of either necessary or sufficient conditions for a Pareto optimum which suggests that feasible arrangements for satisfying these conditions exist. It is interesting to note that Samuelson stressed this very point in the first of his series of papers on this topic.[6]

The consequence of a lack of feasible institutional arrangements for satisfying both necessary and sufficient conditions for Pareto optimality in systems which include public goods is the realization that institutional choice involves the comparison of alternative arrangements which are necessarily nonoptimal in the sense of Pareto. The problem is not to choose from the Pareto optimum positions that one considered ethically desirable. Rather, the problem is to choose from a feasible set of institutional arrangements that particular one which gives the most suitable or "best" allocation of the good under consideration.

It is obvious that in choosing between alternative institutional arrangements the actual operating characteristics of these various arrangements are factors of great importance. As Buchanan has argued so eloquently, it makes little sense to compare operating characteristics of unobtainably ideal arrangements in making an institutional choice.[7] Consequently, if one is choosing, for example, between the alternative institutional arrangements of subscription television, zero pricing and financing by advertising, or zero pricing without advertising with governmental provision of the service, it is not sufficient to argue that subscription television should be ruled out because a nonzero price violates the necessary condition for efficiency, that financing by advertising results in programs appealing to mass taste so that cultural and educational values are overlooked, and that these reasons indicate governmental provision. One cannot simply assume (and be correct) that governmental provision will be "ideal" simply because the other two arrangements are not. One must consider the actual operating characteri tics of all alternative arrangements. The problem of institutional choice often involves the comparison of alternative problems of second best which characterize the available possibilities.

For a Samuelsonian public good, there are certain costs associated with private provision and exclusion. When the requirements for a market are satisfied, at the expense of those costs imposed upon the system by exclusion and the operation of a pricing system, one obtains those advantages provided only by markets.[8] Information concerning desires is provided and can be incorporated into decisions concerning supply, quality of the good, etc. It is worthwhile noting that the relative intensity of desires can be at least partially revealed in even an imperfect market system while this kind of information is much more difficult to obtain under any other arrangement. Nevertheless, the costs of exclusion are not to be taken lightly.

Governmental provision of a public good at, say, a zero price, on the other hand, also has problems associated with it. How are the decisionmakers to decide, for example, the quantity which should be provided? One can give the easy answer to this question by saying that the political process makes the decision. However, such an answer only evades the issue. How does the politician get information which would lead to the proper decision? One must realize that politicians make decisions at least in part upon the basis of political costs which might be approximated in terms of votes. There does not appear to be any reason to suspect that votes are superior indicators of desires in a system where there are many issues and few elections, so that a vote may enjoy alternative interpretations.

There are obvious difficulties in analyzing those problems of second best where the institutional arrangement is governmental provision, or governmental regulation, of the good under consideration. One does not yet know the appropriate behavioral characteristics which should determine the form of the second-best constraints in the models. What are the behavioral rules which guide the decisions and the actions of governmental agencies? It appears that this question must be answered in a satisfactory and useful manner before there will be a very reasonable basis for analyses capable of adequately determining whether given "public" goods should be governmentally produced and distributed or left to the private sector, with or without regulation.

Finally, it should be noted that ethical considerations cannot completely be ignored in institutional choice. Strotz [17] emphasizes the fact that public goods have important distributional implications. Similarly, alternative institutional arrangements for the allocation of public goods have distributional implications.

VI. The Allocation of Non-Samuelsonian Public Goods

It has long been recognized that Samuelson's admittedly polar definition of public goods omits much of governmental activity. It can be argued that another class of goods which should be either governmentally provided or regulated is characterized by extreme decreasing costs. This class of goods involves a high, fixed, and negligible marginal cost coupled with the presence of a capacity constraint. Roads and bridges are prime examples. Leaving aside the question of whether these goods "should" be governmentally produced and distributed, and also leaving the question of how the government actually would do it, let us consider the problem of how such a good "should" be produced and its services allocated over time. One needs to have the benchmark of ideal performance in order to either access or influence actual performance.

Consider a good (say a bridge or a road) which must be constructed in an initial period and whose services must be allocated in that period and also T periods in the future. Supposedly this good becomes obsolete and disintegrates at the end of the Tth period. One incurs the high fixed cost in the initial period and only negligible costs thereafter. Two interrelated questions appear. One must choose the capacity (or decide "how much to consume") in the initial period and also determine an allocation over time.

In order to answer the above questions, let us consider a very simple model in which there are only two goods. One good (say bread) is produced and consumed during each period. It is an ordinary private good. The other good is the one discussed above. In our system it is often (but not necessarily always) a governmental good and for convenience will be termed such here. Consider the following definitions:

$x^i_1(t)$: The amount of the private good consumed by the ith person during period t.

$x^i_2(t)$: The amount of the governmental good consumed by the ith person during period t.

$y_1(t)$: The quantity of the private good produced and available for consumption during period t. For simplicity, assume no storage or carryover between periods.

$y_2(1)$: The quantity of the governmental good produced during the initial period and available for consumption during each of the T periods.

$g(y_1(t))$: An implicit "production possibility" function relating available resources (assumed to be one) to $y_1(t)$ during periods $t = 2, \cdots, T$.

$H(y_1(1), y_2(1))$: An implicit "production possibility" function relating available resources (assumed to be one) to the quantities $y_1(1)$, $y_2(1)$ of the two goods which are produced during the initial period.

U_t^i: The assumed concave utility function of the ith individual during period t.

It is convenient to simplify the problem by ignoring side issues and assuming that there are no externalities in the system. Consequently, it is assumed that in the initial period the productions of the two goods are not functionally interrelated so that H is separable and can be written in the form

$$H(y_1(1), y_2(1)) = h_1(y_1(1)) + h_2(y_2(1)) \qquad (6)$$

and that the decisions of the initial period do not affect the production possibilities of the following periods so that g can be given as indicated. It is also assumed that utility depends only upon consumption in the given period so that there are no functional interdependencies over time. In addition, it is convenient to assume that utility functions can be written in the separable form

$$U_t^i(x^i_1(t), x^i_2(t)) = u^i_{1t}(x^i_1(t)) + u^i_{2t}(x^i_2(t)) \qquad (7)$$

so that there is no interaction. The utility from bread does not influence the utility from crossing the bridge and vice versa.

Since interest here is centered upon deriving the conditions for Pareto optimality, it is obvious that the problem is one of vector maximization. It is convenient, however, to apply the Kuhn-Tucker equivalence theorem and follow the procedure outlined in [8] in order to state the criterion function in a more appropriate form. Accordingly, and as before, let α_i represent the (unspecified but assumed positive) reciprocal of the ith consumer's marginal utility of income. The maximization problem can be written as follows:

$$(8.1) \quad \max \sum_i \sum_t \alpha_i u_{1t}^i(x_1^i(t)) + \sum_i \sum_t \alpha_i u_{2t}^i(x_2^i(t))$$

subject to

$$(8.2) \quad \sum_i x_1^i(t) \leq y_1(t) \quad t = 1, \cdots, T \tag{8}$$

$$(8.3) \quad \sum_i x_2^i(t) \leq y_2(1) \quad t = 1, \cdots, T$$

$$(8.4) \quad h_1(y_1(1)) + h_2(y_2(1)) \leq 0$$
$$(8.5) \quad g(y_1(t)) \leq 0 \quad t = 2, \cdots, T$$
$$(8.6) \quad x_1^i(t) \geq 0, x_2^i(t) \geq 0, y_1(t) \geq 0, y_2(1) \geq 0 \quad \begin{matrix} t = 1, \cdots, T \\ i = 1, \cdots, n \end{matrix}$$

Note that (8.1) is the criterion (social welfare) function which is stated in a form useful for determining the conditions for Pareto optimality. Constraint (8.2) states that no more of the private good can be consumed than is available in any given period. Constraint (8.3) indicates that no more of the governmental good can be consumed in any period than is made available in the first period. Note that the quantity available of the governmental good is measured in terms of capacity. Constraints (8.4) and (8.5) indicate that no more of the goods can be produced than is allowed by the available resources. Finally, (8.5) indicates the nonnegativity conditions.

It is obvious from the very structure of problem (8) that the usual and familiar conditions apply for the private good. Accordingly, these Pareto conditions are not presented here. Competitive markets are fully capable of satisfying these conditions and performing the desirable allocation. Attention is centered on the conditions for the production and allocation of the governmental good. Let $\lambda(t)$ represent the multiplier associated with constraint (8.3). Recall that this multiplier can be interpreted as a shadow price. Then the conditions on the demand side are

$$\alpha_i \frac{\partial u_{2t}^i}{\partial x_2^i(t)} - \lambda(t) \left\{ \begin{matrix} \leq \\ = \end{matrix} \right\} 0 \text{ if } x_2^i(t) \left\{ \begin{matrix} = \\ > \end{matrix} \right\} 0, \quad \begin{matrix} i = 1, \cdots, n \\ t = 1, \cdots, T \end{matrix} \tag{9.1}$$

which are also the conventional and familiar Pareto conditions. If the governmental good is chosen, then an individual should consume that amount in each period which equates his weighted marginal utility to the price of the good during the period. Let β represent the multiplier associated with (8.4). Then on the supply side the condition is

$$\sum_t \lambda(t) - \beta \frac{\partial h_2}{\partial y_2(1)} \left\{ \begin{matrix} \leq \\ = \end{matrix} \right\} 0 \text{ if } y_2(1) \left\{ \begin{matrix} = \\ > \end{matrix} \right\} 0 \tag{9.2}$$

which has an interesting interpretation. Note that if one were to determine the quantity (or capacity) of the governmental good to be made available according to a profit maximization criterion with the prices taken as given, then one would consider the problem

$$\max_{y_2(1) \geq 0} \left\{ \sum_t \lambda(t)y_2(1) - \beta h_2(y_2(1)) \right\} \tag{10}$$

and the conditions for the solution to this problem are given by (9.2). Note that condition (9.2) can be interpreted as saying that if the governmental good is to be supplied, then that quantity (capacity) should be chosen in the initial period which will equate the sum of the prices to the marginal cost of supplying the selected quantity. The solution is that given by profit maximization.

Under the usual assumptions, the conditions derived from (8) are both necessary and sufficient for Pareto optimality. Observe that, in regard to the governmental good, one obtains as a solution to (8) a vector of consumption quantities

$$(x_2^i(1), \cdots, x_2^i(T))$$

for each i, a number $y_2(1)$ which is the quantity made available in each period (the capacity), and a vector of prices or charges

$$(\lambda(1), \cdots, \lambda(T)).$$

This solution is Pareto optimal. Note, however, that it cannot be decentralized period by period.

There are some interesting aspects to the solution to this problem which have important implications for the planning for the provision of the class of goods (such as bridges and roads) under consideration. Note that if demand is at all variable, it is likely that the charge $\lambda(t)$ which rations the available supply $y_2(1)$ is likely to be zero for some periods. From the point of view of planning, the zero charge does not imply no exclusion. It merely means that a person does not have to pay to obtain the right to use the bridge, but he must still obtain that right. Also note the implication of (9.2). The capacity (quantity supplied) should not be selected to be so large that the corresponding constraint (8.3) never becomes binding. The constraint must become binding during some periods so that the charge becomes positive. If demand is such that the charge can never become positive, the facility is not justified.[9] The implication for planning for this class of goods is that one should make a forecast of possible usage over the life of the facility. This forecast should be conditional upon the use of the appropriate charges during each period. Given that revenues can cover costs, one selects the appropriate capacity accordingly.[10] Once the facility is constructed, actual prices (as opposed to the forecasted ones) should be simply adjusted by the conventional rule to ration the available supply.

In terms of practical planning of bridges and roads, where it is usually assumed to be not feasible to use direct charges as a rationing device, the implications of the above analysis would seem to indicate that facilities should not be constructed so as to eliminate congestion during all periods. The constraint (8.3) must be binding during some periods in order to have a rational allocation of resources. Since congestion costs serve (imperfectly) as prices, the construction of facilities which never became congested during their useful life should serve as a clear indication of a misallocation of resources.[11] Rational action should not eliminate congestion but merely obtain a (here undefined) appropriate amount of it.

VII. Concluding Comments

This paper has not included a discussion of whether the so-called "governmental goods" should really be produced and distributed by the public sector. The issues here are much the same as those discussed for the so-called "public goods." All that is indicated in the previous section is a benchmark analysis against which the behaviors of private, regulated or public actors could be measured. It is true that analytic models of public actors are needed before institutional choices can be made on anything approaching a reasonable basis. Nevertheless, it does appear to be a shame that public goods are called "public."

FOOTNOTES

*This research was supported by grants from Resources for the Future and the National Science Foundation to the Graduate School of Industrial Administration, Carnegie Institute of Technology, and by a Ford Foundation Fellowship to one of the authors. The authors are greatly indebted to Professor James M. Buchanan, University of Virginia, who provided important support in the form of both stimulation and encouragement. We are also indebted to our colleagues G. Graves, M. Intriligator, and R. Wagner. Of course, only the authors bear responsibility for errors.

[1] But see Wagner's review [18] of Olsen's theme.

[2] This basic point seems to have been first pointed out by Coase [4] [5]. See also Buchanan and Stubblebine [3] and Davis and Whinston [7].

[3] See Davis [6].

[4] Musgrave [11] emphasizes the notion of exclusion.

[5] See Minasian [10] and Samuelson [16].

[6] See Samuelson [13], pp. 388-89.

[7] See Buchanan [1].

[8] The point that markets are costly to operate has been emphasized by Coase [5]. Demsetz [9] also makes this point but with a greater emphasis upon the costs associated with policing the property rights.

[9] Note, however, that supply is assumed to be infinitely divisible.

[10] Recall, however, the convenient assumption of no externalities. If there are externalities, then one has to make an adjustment in this rule to take them into account.

[11] One must make an exception here for the very real problem caused by indivisibility in rural areas. Recall the convenient assumption that the size of the facility was continuously divisible.

REFERENCES

James M. Buchanan, "Politics, Policy, and the Pigovian Margins," *Economica*, Feb., 1962, pp. 17–28.

———, "An Economic Theory of Clubs," *Economica*, Feb., 1965, pp. 1–14.

James M. Buchanan and W. Craig Stubblebine, "Externality," *Economica*, Nov., 1962, pp. 371–84.

Ronald H. Coase, "The Federal Communications Commission," *J. of Law and Econ.*, Oct., 1959, pp. 1–40.

———, "The Problem of Social Cost," *J. of Law and Econ.*, Oct., 1960, pp. 1–44.

Otto A. Davis, "Economic Elements in Municipal Zoning Decisions," *Land Econ.*, Nov., 1963, pp. 375–86.

Otto A. Davis and Andrew B. Whinston, "Some Notes on Equating Private and Social Cost," *S. Econ. J.*, Oct., 1965, pp. 113–26.

———, "Welfare-Economics and the Theory of Second Best," *Rev. of Econ. Studies*, Jan., 1965, pp. 1–14.

Harold Demsetz, "The Exchange and Enforcement of Property Rights," *J. of Law and Econ.*, Oct., 1964, pp. 11–26.

Jora R. Minasian, "Television Pricing and the Theory of Public Goods," *J. of Law and Econ.*, Oct., 1964, pp. 71–80.

Richard A. Musgrave, *The Theory of Public Finance* (McGraw-Hill, 1959).

Mancur Olson, *The Logic of Collective Action* (Harvard Univ. Press, 1965).

Paul A. Samuelson, "The Pure Theory of Public Expenditure," *Rev. of Econ. and Statis.*, Nov., 1954, pp. 387–89.

———, "Diagrammatic Exposition of a Theory of Public Expenditure," *Rev. of Econ. and Statis.*, Nov., 1955, pp. 350–56.

———, "Aspects of Public Expenditure Theories," *Rev. of Econ. and Statis.*, Nov., 1958, pp. 332–38.

———, "Public Goods and Subscription TV: Correction of the Record," *J. of Law and Econ.*, Oct., 1964, pp. 81–84.

Robert H. Strotz, "Two Propositions Related to Public Goods," *Rev. of Econ. and Statis.*, Nov., 1958, pp. 329–31.

Richard E. Wagner, "Pressure Groups and Political Entrepreneurs: A Review Article," G. Tullock, ed., *Papers on Non-Market Decision Making* (Charlottesville: Thomas Jefferson Center, Univ. of Virginia, 1966), pp. 161–70.

B Continued

23: THE POSTWAR LITERATURE ON EXTERNALITIES: AN INTERPRETATIVE ESSAY

E. J. MISHAN*
The London School of Economics
The American University

External effects on firms—or externalities, as they are now inelegantly referred to—make their appearance in Marshall's *Principles* as external economies; *i. e.,* economies external to the firm but internal to the industry. Little attention was given to this concept until Pigou's celebrated *Economics of welfare,* where, developed and extended, it appears as one of the chief causes of divergencies between "private net product" and "social net product." Expressed more generally, externalities today provide the standard exception to the equation of optimality with universal perfect competition. In addition to the increasingly overt recognition of this qualifying or limiting proviso, interest in the externality concept, as a phenomenon in the context of partial equilibrium analysis, has grown steadily and picked up momentum in the post-war period. Its current popularity warrants the demarcation of a new field of specialization within the broader terrain of welfare economics.

* * *

[Copy omitted (ed.).]

Journal of Economic Literature, no. 1 (1971), p. 1.

VII.   Solutions to the Externality Problem

Let us now turn our attention to several of the more familiar methods proposed for correcting outputs for external diseconomies.[26]

1.   Outright Prohibition.   The economist is prone to think of this solution as naive. It would be prohibitively expensive, if not impossible, it is argued, to eliminate entirely all trace of some of the pollutants that inflict losses on others.   Moreover, the argument continues, optimality does not require that external diseconomies be eliminated, simply that their amounts be consistent with the optimal amounts of the goods that create them.

This sort of argument is not conclusive for all pollutants. First of all, prohibition need not imply prohibition of every trace of a pollutant; it may be directed against producing "discernible" or "dangerous" amounts of the pollutant. Second, as we shall remark later, the cost of discovering and maintaining an optimal amount of the pollution may itself be prohibitive.   The community may then be faced with the choice of zero or unchecked pollution.

2.   The Tax/Subsidy Solution.   This is the classic solution, and the one until recently most favored by theorists.   The chief obstacle here is, of course, the costs of collecting the necessary information and the costs of supervision, costs which would be particularly heavy for industries in which demand and supply conditions are apt to vary frequently.[27]   It is alleged, moreover, that this solution, even if feasible, overlooks a particular contingency that can result in "overcorrection."

See Figure 1 where SS is the "private," or commercial marginal cost curve of the output of X, DD is the market demand curve, and the vertical distance between SS and the *social* marginal cost curve, $S'S'$, is the unit cost of spillovers generated in the production of X.[28]

Optimal output, OQ, can be achieved by an excise tax equal, at Q, to the vertical distance between SS and $S'S'$.   After the imposition of such a tax, however, the producers may regard $S'S'$ as the new marginal cost curve.

At the new tax equilibrium, OQ, the marginal damage of the spillover effect is equal to ab.   The victims of the spillover can then afford to pay producers as much as cb, equal to ab, to reduce output OQ by one unit, and so on for successive reductions.   From such reasoning we construct a curve $S''S''$ that is above $S'S'$ by the same vertical distance at all points as $S'S'$ is above SS.   Clearly there can now be mutual agreement between producers and victims to reduce output to Oq, below the optimal output OQ.[29]

However, this possibility cannot be taken very seriously. If producers and their spillover victims can indeed reach voluntary agreement, they have more incentive to reach it before the excise tax is levied than afterward. The government, in any case, can always take measures to ensure that no further arrangements of this sort take place in order to prevent output being reduced below optimum.[30]

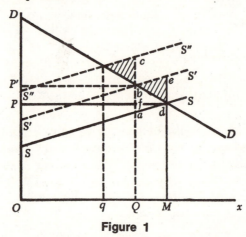

Figure 1

3.   **Regulation.**   Insofar as regulation of the production of goods that generate externalities is intended, much the same sort of information is required, and much the same sort of costs are incurred, as in the tax/subsidy solution.   If, however, regulation is to be applied to the extent, and manner, of the usage of spillover-generating products, there will be additional costs of enforcement—the more so if flexibility is sought, and regulations are devised, to vary according to time, area, and circumstances.

4.   **Voluntary Agreements.**   If transactions costs in the broadest sense (to be defined presently) are *nil*, the initiative by either the producer or the recipient of the spillover in negotiating a mutually satisfactory agreement will bring about an optimal output.   In Figure 1, for example, there will be an incentive to move from output OM to OQ since by so doing there will be a gain equal to the area of triangle *ebd* to be shared between the beneficiaries of X and the spillover victims.   The maximum sum the spillover victims will pay to reduce the market output by MQ is given by the parallelogram area *abed*, while the loss to producers and consumers from reducing output by MQ is equal to the area of the triangle *abd*.

Such agreements, however, unless they are between firms or industries (and supported by legal sanctions) are likely to be so expensive to negotiate and maintain as to be impractical.

5.   **Preventive Devices.**   For obvious reasons the professional economist is more likely to interest himself in optimal-output solutions than in the opportunities for installing preventive devices.   This latter form of remedy, however, cuts across those mentioned above inasmuch as either

government regulation or voluntary agreements can bring them into being. Whether there are opportunities for few or for many such devices, and whether they are less costly to the industry concerned than the alternative course of reducing the spillover-generating outputs, are, of course, empirical questions and ones to which economists are now turning.

VIII. The Abortive Consensus

Post-war developments seemed about to culminate in a broad consensus in the early 1960s when increased attention to environmental spillovers compelled economists to re-examine some of their basic simplifications as well as the conclusions based on them. The more crucial propositions of this emergent consensus are summarized below.

1. On the assumption that the most economic way of dealing with an externality involves an output adjustment, the optimal output is uniquely determined. In this connection, it was also believed [9, Coase, 1960, pp. 1–44] that Pigou had failed to make explicit the duality of the tax-subsidy remedy. Whether the government offers an excise subsidy to the manufacturer to induce him to reduce the output of a good generating external diseconomies, or whether it imposes an excise tax on such a good, was believed to be a matter of indifference so far as allocation is concerned. Similarly, in the absence of government intervention, and assuming transaction costs are low enough, it was believed to be a matter of indifference from the point of view of allocation whether a manufacturer is compelled to compensate the victims or whether the victims offer to bribe the manufacturer.

2. Nor can the question of liability for the spillover properly be settled by a consideration of the equity involved. To use an example from Coase's 1960 paper [9, pp. 3–5], if the machinery of a confectioner disturbs the practice of a physician on the floor above, so also does the installation of vibration-reducing devices lower the profits of the confectioner. The interests of the two parties are mutually antagonistic, and with respect to equity the case is symmetric.[31]

3. However the matter is actually resolved—whether an excise tax or an excise subsidy is used, or whether the one party or the other is compensated—optimality is not at issue, only the distribution of welfare. This statement does not, of course, imply approval of all measures that realize an optimum position, since in moving from a non-optimal to an optimum position only a *potential* Pareto improvement, at best, is assured (gains exceed losses), and not an *actual* Pareto improvement. Thus a movement to an optimal position is quite consistent with one that makes the poor yet poorer.

4. In the absence of government intervention, whatever the legal position, the unfavored party has a clear interest in trying to bribe the

other party to modify the "uncorrected" output. Successful mutual agreement between the parties, however, presupposes that the maximum possible amount of the shared gains, G, in moving to an optimal position, exceeds their combined transaction costs, T.   Since the transactions costs, T, are real enough, inasmuch as they are ultimately the valuation of scarce resources, successful mutual agreement produces a *net* Pareto improvement— $(G - T) > 0$.   Failure to reach mutual agreement, on the other hand, can be regarded as *prima facie* evidence that $(G - T) < 0$; that is, a *net* potential Pareto improvement is not possible.   Rationalizing the *status quo* in this way brings the economist perilously close to defending it.

Before subjecting the above propositions to scrutiny, it is as well to touch on an analytic difficulty of the partial analysis that seems to have been fudged.

The maximum social gain, G, from reducing the competitive output by MQ, in Figure 1, is generally calculated as follows: the gains to the spillover victims of reducing the output by MQ is equal to the area of the "parallelogram" *abed*.   From this gain, we subtract the loss from two other groups: consumers suffer a loss equal to the area of the "triangle" *fdb*, and producers suffer a loss equal to the area of the "triangle" *fda*.   The residual gain—*abed* less (*fdb* + *fda*)—is, of course, equal to the triangle, *dbe*.

However, if the supply curve is a long-period industry supply curve, one sloping upward in consequence of a relative price rise of the factor(s) used more intensively in this industry than in the economy as a whole, a zero Knightian profit is made by all firms in the industry in any long-period equilibrium.   The area above the supply curve cannot then be identified with any surplus to the producers.   Only if the upward slope of the long-period supply curve arises from the addition of increments of a constant-priced variable factor to the fixed amount of another factor— which may, however, include differences as between firms in the quality of the fixed factor—may the area between the supply curve and the price of the good be treated as a surplus.   Moreover, it is not a surplus that accrues to the firms, but to the owners of the fixed factor whether of uniform quality or not.[32]

However, even if we suppose this long-period supply curve to slope upward as a result only of a fixed amount of the scarce factor, we may note that the conclusion that mutual agreement between producers and spillover victims, if feasible, produces an optimal output, commonly ignores the consumer interest.   This neglect of the consumer interest is another consequence of the popular preference for the two-firm model, and of the occasional simplification of a horizontal sales curve facing each of the firms.

Ignoring transaction costs, the most favorable conditions for negotiation between producers and spillover victims would seem to exist when producers can be taken as a corporation, and the supply curve then treated as a long-period marginal cost curve (excluding rent). It will facilitate the analysis still further if we suppose the corporation to act as a discriminating monopolist, appropriating all the consumer surplus, thus equating its private marginal cost to the demand curve.

IX. Environmental Spillovers—Allocation (i)

The pertinent economic features of environmental spillovers, other than the observed fact that they appear to increase rapidly with economic growth, are 1) that their impact on the welfare of members of the public can be substantial, and 2) regarded as external diseconomies, they pose a problem not so much as between firms or industries, but as between, on the one hand, the producers and/or the users of spillover-creating goods and, on the other, the public at large. The implications of the latter feature are not diminished by the observation that, in important instances, the users of the spillover-creating goods and the affected public are all but indistinguishable—this being but a special case of external diseconomies internal to the activity in question.

A consequence of the first feature is that the so-called income-effects —or, more accurately, *welfare effects*, as we shall call them—can no longer be treated as negligible. A consequence flowing from the second feature is that the transaction costs are likely to be inordinately large. These two consequences assume particular relevance when we recognize that an alteration in the law, say from tolerating to the prohibiting of certain spillovers, or the reverse, has significant effects not only on the distribution of welfare, but on the outcome of the allocative criterion. In particular, the notion of a Pareto Optimum, or, more accurately, since we are to restrict ourselves to partial economic analysis, a potential Pareto improvement, is no longer uniquely determined. Nor, for that matter, is a *net* potential Pareto improvement, $(G - T) > 0$, uniquely determined.

These propositions will now be demonstrated in connection with each of these two features in turn.

(1) If we assume that the welfare effects are positive, or "normal," a man who is prepared to spend up to $60,000 for a particular house with a view will experience a rise in his welfare if, unexpectedly, he finds he can buy it, for, say, $40,000. In consequence of this "surplus" of $20,000, the minimum price he will sell it for, after buying it for $40,000, will be more than $60,000, say $65,000. Invoking familiar Hicksian terminology, the difference of $5,000 in this case is equal to the difference between his *compensating variation* of $20,000 (the maximum sum he would pay— thus restoring his welfare to its original level W_o—in order to be allowed to buy his house for a price of $40,000) and his *equivalent variation* of

$25,000 (the minimum sum he would accept to forego the opportunity of buying the house at $40,000, which sum raises his welfare to the level W_1 that he would have enjoyed had he indeed been permitted to buy the house at $40,000).

There is, however, another and possibly more potent factor in differentiating these magnitudes wherever the welfare involved is substantial. The maximum sum he will pay for something valuable is obviously related to, indeed limited by, a person's total resources, while the minimum sum he will accept for parting with it is subject to no such constraint. To take an extreme example, a man may be ready to sacrifice every penny he can spare in order to pay for an operation that will save his life. This may amount to a present value of $10,000 or $10,000,000, but it will be a finite sum. On the other hand, there may be no sum large enough to compensate him for going without the operation, and so parting from this life.

Let individual B, with disposable income of $12,000 per annum, be exposed to aircraft noise which can be escaped with certainty only by relocating hundreds of miles away in some deserted area. Given the choice, he would, if hypersensitive enough to aircraft noise, pay as much as $5,000 per annum to be entirely free of it. At the same time, if the law compelled the airlines concerned to compensate all injured parties, his true minimum claim could be, say, $15,000 per annum.

Now instead of regarding the maximum and minimum sums as compensating-variation and equivalent-variation measures of a change in welfare under the existing law, we can regard each respectively as the compensating variation corresponding to two opposing states of the law. Thus, if the existing law, L, is tolerant of environmental spillovers, in particular aircraft noise, the compensating variation of a contemplated change banning all aircraft noise is a payment by B of $5,000 this being the sum which, given up in exchange for the ban, maintains B's welfare at the level W_0 which prevails under the existing L law. If, on the other hand, the existing law is $\bar{L}$, one that effectively bans all aircraft noise, B's level of welfare is W_1, which is higher than the level W_0 that prevails under the L law. The compensating variation of a contemplated change introducing aircraft noise is then a receipt of $15,000 by B—this being the sum which, if the change occurs, will maintain his welfare at its original W_1 level.

Let A stand for the aircraft interests which extend, in this example, to all owning capital or employed in aircraft services as well as all the beneficiaries of air travel. The compensating variations of each of these persons will, in general, also vary according to which of the two kinds of law prevails. Let B stand for all those offended by aircraft noise. If the maximum sums that people are willing to pay to acquire a "good" (or to avoid a "bad") are prefixed by $+ve$ signs, while the minimum sums

they are prepared to accept to forego a good (or to put up with a "bad")
are prefixed by $-ve$ signs, the algebraic sum of all compensating variations indicates the social value of the change in question. In particular, if,
under the existing law, the algebraic sum of a contemplated change is
$+ve$, a potential Pareto improvement is possible. If, however, the algebraic sum is $-ve$, the existing unchanged situation is optimal; the change
in question would only result in a potential Pareto loss.

Imagine now that a costless and perfectly accurate method of obtaining all the relevant data has been invented. The end-product of much
research into the aircraft noise problem might then be summarized in
the figures of Table I.

Reading along the first row we interpret as follows: given the existing law L, that is permissive of aircraft noise, the A group must be paid
at least $55 million to secure agreement to change to $\bar{L}$ law, while the B

Table 1

Existing Law	A	B	Total
L	−$55m	+$40m	−$15m
L̄	+$45m	−$70m	−$25m

group will offer up to $40 million to have the L law changed to $\bar{L}$. Since
the changeover would incur a potential Pareto loss of $15 million, the
existing situation under L law is deemed Pareto Optimal. If, however,
the existing law is $\bar{L}$ to start with, the second row indicates that the A
group will pay up to $45 million to have the law changed to L. But this
sum falls short by $25 million of the minimum compensation required by
the B group to agree to the change. Again, therefore, the existing situation under the $\bar{L}$ law is Pareto Optimal.

We are to conclude, therefore, that irrespective of the existing distribution it is possible, if not likely, that for significant environmental spillovers, the arrangement that is optimal under one state of the law is not
optimal under the other state of law. In our example, if aircraft are
already allowed to fly unchecked (L law), then that situation appears
as optimal. If, on the other hand, aircraft were banned under $\bar{L}$ law,
that situation, too, would be optimal.[33] Under such conditions, how do
we decide how to act?

The above analysis, applicable to indivisible economic arrangements
as appear, say, in cost-benefit calculations, can easily be extended to
economic arrangements having perfectly divisible external effects. Suppose the number of aircraft permitted to fly over a residential area is to
be determined by reference only to optimality considerations—the exercise

being to locate the point at which the marginal benefit of the aircraft group A is equal to the marginal loss suffered by the residential group B. Prior to calculating the optimal number of flights, the existence of L law, which permits unchecked flying over the area, will result in a higher level of welfare for the A group than if, instead, the $\bar{L}$ law prevails and no planes are permitted to fly, the reverse being the case for the residents comprising the B group.

Suppose the L law to be in force; then, prior to any agreement between A and B, the number of planes flying over the area is given by OM in Figure 2. The minimum compensation acceptable to the A group for reducing successive flights is given by the marginal curve $M - A_L$, while the maximum sums that the B group will pay for successive flight reductions is given by $B_L - O$, the two curves intersecting at Q_L. If, however, $\bar{L}$ is in force to start with, then, prior to any mutual agreement between A and B, the number of flights over the area is zero, and the minimum sums acceptable to the B group for each successive flight are given by the marginal curve $O - B_{\bar{L}}$ while the maximum sums that the A group is willing to pay for each additional flight are given by the marginal curve $A_{\bar{L}} - A_{\bar{L}}'$. The intersection of these two $\bar{L}$ curves is $Q_{\bar{L}}$.

Now in reaching agreement, beginning from either initial position—OM flights with L law, or zero flights with $\bar{L}$ law—one, or both, groups

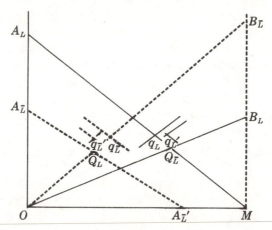

Figure 2

are made better off and, therefore (assuming normal welfare effects), one or both marginal valuation curves shift upwards, which implies that neither Q_L nor $Q_{\bar{L}}$ can be reached by bargaining alone. Nonetheless, if L law prevails, in which case flights are OM to begin with, and if we assume that in bargaining their way to an optimal position, all the gains go to the B group,[34] the increase in its welfare is still less than it would be, if instead $\bar{L}$ law initially prevailed and (without any payment from the B group) all flights were banned. Consequently the resulting maximum upward shift in B's marginal curve is still below the O–$B_{\bar{L}}$ curve, the optimal point being then q_{L}. However, if we suppose instead that A obtains some of the potential gains in the bargaining, B's marginal curve rises less and A's marginal curve rises somewhat, with the result that the revised optimal position, q_{L}' is to the right of q_{L}.

If, on the other hand, the $\bar{L}$ law prevails, and we assume first that all the gains in bargaining go to the A group, the increase in its welfare is less than it would be if the law were changed to L, and all flights were freely allowed. The resulting upward shift in A's original $A_{\text{L}} - A_{\text{L}}'$ curve is therefore below the $A_{\text{L}} - M$ curve, the optimal point being $q_{\bar{\text{L}}}$. However, according as the B group secures some of the gains in bargaining toward an optimal position, A's resulting marginal curve is somewhat lower while B's resulting marginal curve is above $O - B_{\text{L}}$. The revised optimal position $q_{\bar{\text{L}}}'$ being to the left of $q_{\bar{\text{L}}}$.[35]

We may conclude, then, that however the bargaining goes, the resulting optimum output under the L law entails more flights than an optimum output under the $\bar{L}$ law.[36]

X. Environmental Spillovers—Allocation (ii)

(2) Assuming that, whichever law prevails, the state does not oppose agreements tending to a Pareto improvement, any movement by any method toward such improvements involves a variety of costs, for which the term *transactions costs* is in common use. In general, the more favorable the law is in promoting mutual agreements of this sort, the lower will such transactions costs be. If, at first, we restrict ourselves to the method of voluntary agreement between two opposing groups in their attempt to reach a solution, either by curbing the activity of the offending industry, by installing preventive devices, or by moving the industry (or, alternatively, members of the B group) elsewhere—whichever method is the cheapest—the transactions costs, T, may be divided into three sub-categories: T_1, the initial costs leading to negotiations between the two groups; T_2, the costs of maintaining and, if necessary, revising, the agreement; and T_3, the capital expenditure, if any, required to implement the agreement.

The more important of these, the T_1 costs, can be broken down, for each group, into a number of phases: a) identifying the members of the group, b) persuading them to make, or to accept, a joint offer, c) reaching agreement within the group on all matters incidental to its negotiation with the other group, and d) negotiating with the other group.

It cannot be assumed, without investigation, that transactions costs would be any less under $\bar{L}$ law than they are under L law. What can be said, however, is that such costs, especially those subsumed under T_1, increase with the dispersion of the B group, and increase with the numbers involved, probably at an exponential rate. Whatever the magnitude of the T costs, however, relative to the maximum Pareto gains, G, three alternative cases exhaust the possibilities.

1.   A net potential Pareto improvement, $(G - T) > 0$ emerges for the industry under either type of law—though if $\bar{L}$ law prevails, the optimal output, both of goods and pollution, will be smaller.

2.   A net potential Pareto improvement for the industry emerges under neither type of law. By comparison with the (costless) potential optimum, therefore, we shall have "too much" pollution with the equilibrium output under the L law, and "too little" pollution under the zero output of the $\bar{L}$ law. Without further assumptions, however, it is not possible to say in general whether "too much" (under the L law) or "too little" (under the $\bar{L}$ law) is likely to be closer to the potential optimum, and, therefore, whether more is lost by adopting the L law rather than the $\bar{L}$ law.

3.   Where the potential optimum position is closer to the initial $\bar{L}$ position than to the initial L position, a net Pareto improvement may take place only if the L law prevails. If the reverse is true, a net Pareto improvement may take place only if the $\bar{L}$ law prevails.[37]   The former possibility is illustrated in Figure 3a; the latter in Figure 3b (welfare shifts being omitted so as not to encumber the diagrams).

Although it has been convenient to think of net potential Pareto improvements, through voluntary agreement between the A and B groups, in terms of output adjustments, if any, the above three possibilities are equally valid if other, and cheaper, methods of effecting net potential Pareto improvements are contemplated—such as moving factories, or processes (or members of the B group) to other areas, installing any of a variety of preventive devices (or, in general, modifying the technology as to reduce spillovers), or government regulation of output either directly or through excise taxes.

In the absence of evidence indicating a clear connection between the magnitude of transactions costs and the type of law, there appear to be no firm allocative implications—save, perhaps, the advisability of thinking more closely of technical and institutional innovations that are likely to reduce transactions costs. Thus, with respect to the costs of government regulation of output, directly or through excise taxes, economists may like to remind themselves that the pursuit of the ideal is the enemy of the better. A roughly calculated excise tax imposed on a pollutant is likely to effect a distinct improvement, even if it were as much as 20% or so higher, or lower, than the "ideal" excise tax. As an immediate response

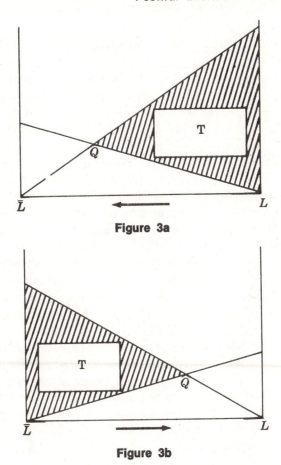

Figure 3a

Figure 3b

to clear cases of excessive pollution, a roughly calculated tax is likely to be superior to not imposing a tax at all—or to procrastinating indefinitely while engaged in research to refine data and methods in the attempt to produce an ideal tax.

There are, nevertheless, a couple of considerations which appear to favor L law rather than $\bar{L}$ law. First, although the magnitude of transactions costs have been assumed independent of the type of law, the likelihood of a member of one group taking the initiative in approaching the other group is not independent of the law. If L law is in force, the possibility of some limited benefit for the person(s) taking the initiative on behalf of a large and widely dispersed B group has to be set against the certain loss of time and effort, and also against a large risk of incurring substantial and irrecoverable expenses in the attempt to complete phases (a) and (b). Under $\bar{L}$ law in contrast, the necessary initiative comes from industry. No personal risk is undertaken by one or more of the executives acting on behalf of shareholders—though, in any case, such an initiative would hardly stand out from the routine activities involving decision-taking by the managers of industry.[38]   Indeed, under $\bar{L}$ law, firms are unlikely to invest in plant and machinery for the manufacture of pollution-prone products unless they are fairly confident that—after all economic "preventive technology" has been employed—they can afford to meet claims for residual damage.

Second, under an L law, there is little incentive for industry to switch resources from promoting sales, or from research into product innovations or from cost-reducing technology, in favor of pollution-reducing technology.   Assuming that firms allocate investable funds according to the equi-marginal principle, they will then, under the existing L law, misallocate resources because they tend to ignore all opportunities for social gains made by directing research funds into preventive technology.[39]   Under an L law, in contrast, full liability for pollution damage enters directly into production costs, along with expenditures on productive services, and the consequent incentive to engage in such research is inescapable.

Opportunities for private industry, under an $\bar{L}$ law, of reducing the social costs of pollution are not, however, restricted to curbing outputs and engaging in research on pollution-reducing technology.   There will be incentives for the polluting industries to investigate many other possible ways of reducing their liabilities for damage to the public.   They may find it cheaper to concentrate (parts of) their plant in remote areas, to re-design and re-route highways, to re-route air flights over less populous areas, in the pursuit of which they create conditions conducive to separate "amenity areas" for the public.[40]

XI.   Environmental Spillovers—Equity

On the issue of the relative merits of L law and $\bar{L}$ law, there remain a number of considerations which may be subsumed under equity.

1.   Distribution.   If it can be shown a) that goods which generate spillovers also earn incomes for, and are purchased by, groups having above-average incomes, and b) that the bulk of modern spillovers fall more heavily on families with below-average incomes, then it may be asserted that, compared with $\bar{L}$ law, L law is a force acting to increase the regressive distribution of welfare.   In the absence of any systematic research into the question, however, one can say only that it is not implausible to believe that the introduction of significant disamenities into a large area is likely to reduce the welfare of the more mobile rich less than that of the poor.[41]

2.   Malpractices.   If institutional innovations over time cause transactions costs to decline and initiative among the public to rise, there would be, under existing L law, a temptation for enterprising firms, and others in a position to do so, to produce unnecessary pollution in order to exact greater tribute from the public. This result can occur either prior to an initial agreement with the affected members of the public, or else subsequently—on the plea that market conditions have changed so radically that the existing agreement is irrelevant. Access to the detailed knowledge necessary to challenge businessmen's alleged expenditures on research and on consultations in attempting to meet public demands, or their subsequent allegations of changes in market conditions, is, if possible at all, likely to be costly and to lead to prolonged litigation.

3. **Culpability.** A part of the recent consensus was the belief that the conflict of interest entailed by an external diseconomy was symmetric in all relevant respects. The freedom of either group to pursue its interests or enjoyments necessarily interfered with the freedom of the other group. Thus, if the non-smokers' enjoyment is reduced by the smokers' freedom to smoke, so also, it is observed, is the smokers' enjoyment reduced by their abstaining for the greater comfort of the non-smokers. The question of who should compensate whom, it was occasionally stated, can be settled only arbitrarily or by reference to distributional implications.

But although they are indeed Pareto symmetric, such conflicts may not be ethically symmetric. In accordance with the classical liberal maxim, the freedom of a man to pursue his interests is qualified in so far as it tends to reduce the freedom, or the welfare, of others. It may then be argued that the freedom of the smoker to smoke in shared quarters is not on all fours with the freedom of the non-smoker to breathe fresh air, since the freedom to breathe fresh air does not, of itself, reduce the welfare of others. In contrast, the smokers' freedom to blow smoke into the air breathed by others does reduce their welfare. Similarly, it may be argued, the freedom to operate noisy vehicles, or pollutive plant, does incidentally damage the welfare of others, while the freedom desired by members of the public to live in clean and quiet surroundings does not, of itself, reduce the welfare of others. If such arguments can be sustained, there is a case in equity for the L law, and a case therefore for making polluters legally liable.[42]

4. **Amenity.** If, over time, transactions costs, and perhaps the costs of regulation also do not decline, the choice of L law or $\bar{L}$ law may imply that for a large class of spillovers the effective choice for society lies between "too much" spillover or "too little."[43] If the rate of growth of spillovers equals or exceeds[44] the growth of Gross National Product, and if one assumed diminishing marginal utility of man-made goods and increasing marginal disutility of man-made "bads," the prevalence of L law will be a factor accelerating the rate at which *per capita* growth of real income approaches zero, and beyond.

5. **Posterity.**   Indeed, for a range of spillovers, government regulation, intervention, or prohibition may be justified notwithstanding an apparent consensus among the groups immediately affected.   The possibility that the damage being wrought by particular spillover effects is virtually irreversible has to be taken seriously in the new vision of our tiny and unique planet.   In terms of man's life span, the continuing destruction of our limited resources of natural beauty, the poisoning of lakes and rivers, may be regarded as irrevocable.   Consequently the losses to be suffered by future generations [45] has to be added to those carried by existing populations.

6. **Information.**   If the pace of technological innovation extends the time lag between the immediate commercial exploitation of new products and processes, on the one hand, and, on the other, the knowledge of their long-term genetical and ecological effects, there is a presumption not only in favor of L law, but in favor also of direct prohibition of a number of hazardous polluting activities.   There is a case, too, for public control over the adoption of new processes, and the marketing of new products, in particular, chemical products.   The risks arising from insufficient knowledge of the long-term effects of any single innovation—or, indeed, the risks arising from insufficient knowledge of the long-term effects of any of a number of existing products and processes—may well be thought slight.   But even allowing for this more favorable contingency, as the number of such products spread over the globe—and today they tend to spread with incredible rapidity—the chance of some uncontrollable epidemic, or ecological catastrophe occurring becomes increasingly probable.

XII.   Epilogue

Many of the considerations brought forward in the last section do not, I recognize, lend themselves easily to analytic elegance.   But with respect to environmental spillover—the most urgent economic problem of our fragile civilization—they are more pertinent than those arising from traditional allocative analysis.   It is not, of course, hard to understand the somewhat exaggerated weight attached by economists to the allocative aspects of an economic problem as distinct, say, from those connected with equity.   For the former aspects lend themselves nicely to formal theorizing and, with patience and a little finesse, impressive measures of social losses and gains can be foisted on credulous civil servants and a gullible public.

Yet the priority given to allocative aspects in real economic problems cannot, I think, be justified; certainly not by recourse to welfare economics.   The more "affluent" a society becomes, the less important is allocative merit narrowly conceived.   And in any society in the throes of accelerating technological change (one in which, of necessity, pertinent knowledge of the human, social, and ecological consequences of what we are doing is generally slight and partly erroneous) complacency on the part of any economist, guided in his professional decisions by considerations alone of allocative merit or economic growth potential, is both to be envied and deplored.

REFERENCES

Ayres, R. V. and Kneese, A. V. "Production, Consumption, and Externalities," *Amer.Econ.Rev.*, June 1969, *59*(3), pp. 282–97.

Baumol, W. J. "External Economies and Second-Order Optimality Conditions," *Amer.Econ.Rev.*, June 1964, *54*(3), pp. 358–72.

Bohm, P. *External economies in production.* Stockholm: Almquist & Wiksells, 1964.

———, "Pollution, Purification and the Theory of External Effects," (Mimeograph, 1969). Also in French in *Annales de l'Insee*, 1970.

Buchanan, J. M. and Stubblebine, W. C. "Externality," *Economica*, Nov. 1962, *29*, pp. 371–84.

Buchanan, J. M. and Kafoglis, M. Z. "A Note on Public Goods Supply," *Amer. Econ.Rev.*, June 1963, *53*(3), pp. 403–14.

Buchanan, J. M. "An Economic Theory of Clubs," *Economica*, Feb. 1965, *32* (125), pp. 1–14.

Burrows, P. "On External Cost & the Visible Arm of the Law," *Oxford Econ. Pap.*, March 1970, *22*(1), pp. 1–17.

Coase, R. H. "The Problem of Social Costs," *J.Law Econ.*, Oct. 1960, *3*, pp. 1–44.

Davis, O. A. and Kamien, M. I. "Externalities, Information and Alternative Collective Action" in *The analysis of public expenditures: The PPB system.* Washington: Government Printing Office, 1969, pp. 67–86.

Davis, O. A. and Whinston, A. "Externalities, Welfare and the Theory of Games," *J.Polit.Econ.*, June 1962, *70*(3), pp. 241–62.

———, "On Externalities, Information and the Government-Assisted Invisible Hand," *Economica*, August 1966, *33*(131), pp. 303–18.

———, "Piecemeal Policy in the Theory of Second Best," *Rev.Econ.Stud.*, July 1967, *34*(3), pp. 323–31.

———, "On the Distinction between Public and Private Goods," *Amer.Econ. Rev.*, May 1967, *57*(2), pp. 360–73.

Dolbear, F. T., Jr. "On the Theory of Optimal Externality," *Amer.Econ.Rev.*, March 1967, *57*(1), pp. 90–103.

Duesenberry, J. *Income, saving and the theory of consumer behaviour.* Harvard: Harvard University Press, 1949.

Ellis, H. and Fellner, W. "External Economies and Diseconomies," *Amer. Econ.Rev.*, Sept. 1943, *23*(3), pp. 493–511. Reprinted in *Readings in price theory.* Chicago: Irwin, 1952.

Evans, A. W. "Private Goods, Externality, Public Good," *Scottish J.Polit. Econ.*, Feb. 1970, *17*(1), pp. 79–89.

Farrel, M. J. "In Defence of Public Utility Pricing," *Oxford Econ.Pap.*, Feb. 1958, *10*, pp. 109–23.

Graaff, J. de V. *Theoretical welfare economics*. Cambridge: University Press, 1957.

Green, H. A. J. "The Social Optimum in the Presence of Monopoly and Taxation," *Rev.Econ.Stud.*, 1962, *29*(1), pp. 66–78.

Hicks, J. R. "The Four Consumer's Surpluses," *Rev.Econ.Stud.*, 1943, *11*(1), pp. 31–41.

Kahn, R. F. "Some Notes on Ideal Output," *Econ.J.*, March 1935, *45*(177), pp. 1–35.

Kneese, A. V. *Approaches to regional water quality management*. Washington, D.C.: Resources for the Future, Inc., 1967.

Knight, F. H. "Some Fallacies in the Interpretation of Social Cost," *Quart. J.Econ.*, August 1924, *37*, pp. 582–606.

Lipsey, R. G. and Lancaster, K. "The General Theory of Second Best," *Rev. Econ.Stud.*, 1956–57, *24*(63), pp. 11–32.

Little, I. M. D. *A critique of welfare economics*. Oxford: University Press, 1957.

Margolis, J. "A Comment on the Pure Theory of Public Expenditure," *Rev. Econ.Statist.*, Nov. 1955, *37*, pp. 347–49.

Marshall, A. *Principles of economics* (8th ed.). London: Macmillan, 1925.

McGuire, M. C. and Aaron, H. "Efficiency and Equity in the Optimal Supply of a Public Good," *Rev.Econ.Statist.*, Feb. 1969, *51*(1), pp. 31–39.

Meade, J. "External Economies and Diseconomies in a Competitive Situation," *Econ.J.*, March 1952, *62*, pp. 54–67.

Mishan, E. J. "Welfare Criteria for External Effects," *Amer.Econ.Rev.*, Sept. 1961, *51*(4), pp. 594–613.

———, "Second Thoughts on Second Best," *Oxford Econ.Pap.*, Oct. 1962, *14*, pp. 205–17.

———, "Reflections on Recent Developments in the Concept of External Effects," *Can.J.Polit.Econ.*, Feb. 1965, *31*, pp. 3–34.

———, "Pareto Optimality and the Law," *Oxford Econ.Pap.*, Nov.1967, pp. 255–87.

——— "What is Producers' Surplus?" *Amer.Econ.Rev.*, Dec. 1968, *58*(5), pp. 1269–82.

———, "The Relationship between Joint Products, Collective Goods, and External Effects," *J.Polit.Econ.*, May 1969, *72*(3), pp. 329–48.

Musgrave, R. A. "Cost-Benefit Analysis and The Theory of Public Finance," *J.Econ.Lit.*, Sept. 1969, *7*(3), pp. 797–806.

Oakland, W. H. "Joint Goods," *Economica*, August 1969, *36*(143), pp. 253–68.

Olson, M. *The logic of collective action*. Harvard University Press, 1965.

Pauly, M. V. "Clubs, Commonality and the Core: An Integration of Game Theory and the Theory of Public Goods," *Economica*, August 1967, *34*(135), 314–24.

Pigou, A. C. *The economics of welfare* (4th ed.). London: Macmillan, 1946.

Plott, C. R. "Externalities and Corrective Taxes," *Economica*, Feb. 1966, *33* (129), pp. 84–87.

Ridker, R. G. *Economic costs of air pollution*. New York: Praeger, 1967.

Rosenstein-Rodan, P. W. "Problems of Industrialization of East and South East Europe," *Econ.J.*, June 1943, *53*, pp. 202–11.

Samuelson, P. A. "Contrast between Welfare Conditions for Joint Supply and for Public Goods," *Rev.Econ.Statist.*, Feb. 1969, *51*(1), pp. 26–30.

———, "The Pure Theory of Public Expenditure," *Rev.Econ.Statist.*, Nov. 1954, *36*, pp. 387–89.

———, "Aspects of Public Expenditure Theories," *Rev.Econ.Statist.*, Nov. 1958, *40*, pp. 332–38.

Schumacher, E. F. "Clean Air and Future Energy," *Des Voeux Memorial Lecture*, 1967.

Scitovsky, T. "Two Concepts of External Economies," *J.Polit.Econ.*, April 1954, *62*, pp. 70–82.

Turvey, R. "On Divergences between Social Cost and Private Cost," *Economica*, August 1963, *30*, pp. 309–13.

Vincent, P. E. "Reciprocal Externalities and Optimal Input and Output Levels," *Amer.Econ.Rev.*, Dec. 1969, *59*(5), pp. 976–84.

Viner, J. "Cost Curves and Supply Curves," *Zeit.Nationalokonomie*, Sept. 1931, *3*, pp. 23–46. Reprinted in *Readings in price theory*. New York: The Blakiston Co., 1953.

Williams, A. "The Optimal Provision of Public Goods in a System of Local Government," *J.Polit.Econ.*, Feb. 1966, *74*, pp. 18–33.

Wellisz, S. "On External Diseconomies and the Government-Assisted Invisible Hand," *Economica*, Nov. 1964, *31*, pp. 345–62.

Worcester, D. A. "Pecuniary and Technological Externality, Factor Rents, and Social Costs," *Amer.Econ.Rev.*, Dec. 1969, *59*(5), pp. 873–85.

FOOTNOTES

* *I wish to acknowledge with gratitude the helpful comments and suggestions of Abram Bergson, Otto Davis, Jack Ochs, and E. P. Seskin who read a first draft of this paper.*

[26] A comparable though not entirely similar commentary on the more commonly proposed solutions to the externality problem can be found in a recent paper by Davis and Kamien [10, 1969, pp. 78–86].

[27] It is, of course, possible that the industry producing the external diseconomy is a non-competitive industry. A monopoly firm equating marginal cost to marginal revenue will in any case produce an output smaller than the marginal (private) cost-price output, which may then be closer to the optimal output. In this connection, see D. A. Worcester [56, 1969].

[28] There is some slight geometric convenience in constructing $S'S'$ parallel to SS.

[29] See J. M. Buchanan and W. C. Stubblebine [5, 1962] and Turvey [51, 1963].

[30] A related objection to an effluent excise tax occurs in a paper by P. Bohm [4, 1970]. If the optimal excise tax increases with output, the firm (he argues) might become aware

of the relationship. Subtracting the schedule of optimal taxes from the demand price of the product would result in a downward-sloping net average revenue curve from which the firm could derive a marginal revenue curve. By equating marginal cost to this "marginal revenue" curve, the firm reduces its output below optimal.

However, the government is not obliged to impose a *uniform* effluent tax. It could as well make it clear that it would impose a *discriminating* tax, one equal at each unit of output to the marginal effluent and, therefore, at any output raising a total tax equal to the total loss inflicted by the effluent. Such a tax, already marginal, effectively precludes the industry from "exploiting" it by reducing its output. In addition, such a discriminating tax ensures that the total conditions are met. Thus, heavy effluent charges properly imposed on the initial units of the output could well prohibit production of the good.

* * *

31 This conclusion can be ascribed to the popularity in the literature of the two-firm or two-industry case.

32 The rents earned by lands of superior quality, or location, being one of the earlier examples in the history of economic thought.

33 The reader will observe that the above paradox (which depends on different compensating variations under different states of the law) has no affinity with that associated with the so-called "Kaldor-Hicks" and "Scitovsky" type welfare criteria. The latter paradox arises only from alterations in the set of relative prices (common to everyone) associated with the distributional changes whenever the community moves from producing one batch of goods to producing another.

34 That is, the B group pays for each successive flight reduction no more than the sums traced out by the $M-A_L$ curve.

35 Another incidental implication of this sort of analysis, one making explicit allowance for welfare effects, is that an excise tax alone can no longer be counted on to realize an optimal position. In this connection see F. T. Dolbear, Jr. [15, 1967].

36 The reverse being true for the improbable case of negative welfare effects.

37 It is of incidental interest to note, however, that in the first case society would be better off if the $\bar{L}$ law prevailed (notwithstanding that it would not pay to move from the resulting zero output), since it would save the T costs incurred in moving to Q under the L law. As for the second case, society would be better off if the L law prevailed.

38 We have ignored welfare effects in order to avoid minor distractions from the shifting of the marginal valuation curves.

Under the $\bar{L}$ envisaged, it is not necessary for a plaintiff to incur any expense in pursuing a claim against pollution in the courts of law, since pollution—in the absence of explicit permission to the contrary—is illegal. Punitive action which includes cessation of the pollution-creating activity is immediately taken by the public prosecutor unless the firm has a government permit issued periodically, which permit is never granted unless all claims to damages over the period in question are met. So severe a law will not prove costly to administer simply because businesses will almost certainly find it cheaper a) to move away from populous centers and/or b) to undertake further research into the technical changes necessary to reduce pollution as to be virtually undetectable.

39 Any hope that funds from the B group will be offered to industry to engage in research so as to reduce widespread pollutants can be ruled out both because of the heavy risks of initiative by individual victims and because of the costs of transactions referred to.

40 The conditions under which a separate areas' solution of group conflict is superior to the usual optimal solution that is constrained within a given area are discussed in Mishan [35, 1967].

41 The fact that in any given neighborhood the rich will respond to local forms of pollution by moving from the locality in larger proportion than the poor certainly bears on the question of whether disamenities tend to fall in the first instance more heavily on the neighborhoods of the poorer groups in the economy. But even if it were the case that disamenities were introduced into initially unpolluted neighborhoods, rich and poor, in an entirely random fashion—which is implausible—it does not follow that the growth in pollution does not have regressive welfare effects. Thus if a man earning $100,000 per annum is willing to give up a maximum sum of $30,000 per annum to be rid of some particularly noxious spillover, but discovers that he is able to move out of the polluted area for a loss of about $10,000 per annum, he becomes better off than he would be if he remained in the area (to the tune of $20,000 per annum). An equally sensitive man earning only $10,000 per annum may be willing to sacrifice a maximum of $1,500 per annum to be rid of the pollution. But if the movement out of the area would involve him in a loss (or in the risk of a loss) of more than $1,500 per annum, he has to stay put and bear the full loss in his welfare.

42 This argument, if coaxed a little, might be made to take a finer turn: thus, if a switch in my demand from x to y causes either the price of x or y to rise, it obviously affects the welfare of others also. Nevertheless, considerations of equity need not ignore differences of magnitude. If the world were indeed such that a simple increase in my demand for notepaper inflicted injury on innocent families, it is likely—though the question of equity was far from clear—that broad agreement could be secured on the need to develop countervailing government mechanisms. If, however, the effects of changing tastes on relative prices were slight and random, and the costs of continually tracing them back to those responsible were prohibitive, there would be an explicit agreement or tacit understanding to ignore them for the undeniable conveniences offered by a comprehensive price system.

43 As suggested, the adoption of $\bar{L}$ law will encourage the development of preventive technology more than will L law. The "too little" will not, then, be likely to last as long as the "too much."

44 Which is more likely, since familiar growth industries (automobiles, motor-boats, motorized garden implements, chemicals, nuclear power, tourism, etc.) also appear prolific of spillover.

45 Any discounting of the losses to be borne by *future* generations, moreover, cannot be justified on the usual arguments developed in the context of a single generation.

*

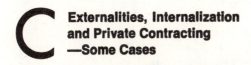

C **Externalities, Internalization
and Private Contracting
—Some Cases**

24: THE ECONOMIC THEORY OF A COMMON PROPERTY RESOURCE: THE FISHERY[1]

H. SCOTT GORDON
Carleton College, Ottawa, Ontario

I. Introduction

The chief aim of this paper is to examine the economic theory of natural resource utilization as it pertains to the fishing industry. It will appear, I hope, that most of the problems associated with the words "conservation" or "depletion" or "overexploitation" in the fishery are, in reality, manifestations of the fact that the natural resources of the sea yield no economic rent. Fishery resources are unusual in the fact of their common-property nature; but they are not unique, and similar problems are encountered in other cases of common-property resource industries, such as petroleum production, hunting and trapping, etc. Although the theory presented in the following pages is worked out in terms of the fishing industry, it is, I believe, applicable generally to all cases where natural resources are owned in common and exploited under conditions of individualistic competition.

II. Biological Factors and Theories

The great bulk of the research that has been done on the primary production phase of the fishing industry has so far been in the field of biology. Owing to the lack of theoretical economic research,[2] biologists have been

Journal of Political Economy (1954), p. 124.

forced to extend the scope of their own thought into the economic sphere
and in some cases have penetrated quite deeply, despite the lack of the
analytical tools of economic theory.[3]   Many others, who have paid no
specific attention to the economic aspects of the problem have nevertheless recognized that the ultimate question is not the ecology of life in the
sea as such, but man's use of these resources for his own (economic) purposes.   Dr. Martin D. Burkenroad, for example, began a recent article on
fishery management with a section on "Fishery Management as Political
Economy," saying that "the Management of fisheries is intended for the
benefit of man, not fish; therefore effect of management upon fishstocks
cannot be regarded as beneficial *per se.*"[4]   The great Russian marine
biology theorist, T. I. Baranoff, referred to his work as "bionomics" or
"bio-economics," although he made little explicit reference to economic
factors.[5]   In the same way, A. G. Huntsman, reporting in 1944 on the
work of the Fisheries Research Board of Canada, defined the problem of
fisheries depletion in economic terms: "Where the take in proportion to
the effort fails to yield a satisfactory living to the fisherman";[6] and
a later paper by the same author contains, as an incidental statement, the
essence of the economic optimum solution without, apparently, any recognition of its significance.[7]   Upon the occasion of its fiftieth anniversary
in 1952, the International Council for the Exploration of the Sea published
a *Rapport Jubilaire*, consisting of a series of papers summarizing progress
in various fields of fisheries research.   The paper by Michael Graham on
"Overfishing and Optimum Fishing," by its emphatic recognition of the
economic criterion, would lead one to think that the economic aspects of
the question had been extensively examined during the last half-century.
But such is not the case.   Virtually no specific research into the economics
of fishery resource utilization has been undertaken.   The present state
of knowledge is that a great deal is known about the biology of the various commercial species but little about the economic characteristics of the
fishing industry.

The most vivid thread that runs through the biological literature is the
effort to determine the effect of fishing on the stock of fish in the sea.
This discussion has had a very distinct practical orientation, being part of
the effort to design regulative policies of a "conservation" nature.   To the
layman the problem appears to be dominated by a few facts of overriding
importance.   The first of these is the prodigious reproductive potential of
most fish species.   The adult female cod, for example, lays millions of
eggs at each spawn.   The egg that hatches and ultimately reaches maturity
is the great exception rather than the rule.   The various herrings (Clu-
peidae) are the most plentiful of the commercial species, accounting for
close to half the world's total catch, as well as providing food for many
other sea species.   Yet herring are among the smallest spawners, laying a
mere hundred thousand eggs a season, which, themselves, are eaten in

large quantity by other species. Even in inclosed waters the survival and reproductive powers of fish appear to be very great. In 1939 the Fisheries Research Board of Canada deliberately tried to kill all the fish in one small lake by poisoning the water. Two years later more than ninety thousand fish were found in the lake, including only about six hundred old enough to have escaped the poisoning.

The picture one gets of life in the sea is one of constant predation of one species on another, each species living on a narrow margin of food supply. It reminds the economist of the Malthusian law of population; for, unlike man, the fish has no power to alter the conditions of his environment and consequently cannot progress. In fact, Malthus and his law are frequently mentioned in the biological literature. One's first reaction is to declare that environmental factors are so much more important than commercial fishing that man has no effect on the population of the sea at all. One of the continuing investigations made by fisheries biologists is the determination of the age distribution of catches. This is possible because fish continue to grow in size with age, and seasonal changes are reflected in certain hard parts of their bodies in much the same manner as one finds growth-rings in a tree. The study of these age distributions shows that commercial catches are heavily affected by good and bad brood years. A good brood year, one favorable to the hatching of eggs and the survival of fry, has its effect on future catches, and one can discern the dominating importance of that brood year in the commercial catches of succeeding years.[8] Large broods, however, do not appear to depend on large numbers of adult spawners, and this lends support to the belief that the fish population is entirely unaffected by the activity of man.

There is, however, important evidence to the contrary. World Wars I and II, during which fishing was sharply curtailed in European waters, were followed by indications of a significant growth in fish populations. Fish-marking experiments, of which there have been a great number, indicate that fishing is a major cause of fish mortality in developed fisheries. The introduction of restrictive laws has often been followed by an increase in fish populations, although the evidence on this point is capable of other interpretations which will be noted later.

General opinion among fisheries biologists appears to have had something of a cyclical pattern. During the latter part of the last century, the Scottish fisheries biologist, W. C. MacIntosh,[9] and the great Darwinian, T. H. Huxley, argued strongly against all restrictive measures on the basis of the inexhaustible nature of the fishery resources of the sea. As Huxley put it in 1883: "The cod fishery, the herring fishery, the pilchard fishery, the mackerel fishery, and probably all the great sea fisheries, are inexhaustible: that is to say that nothing we do seriously affects the number of fish. And any attempt to regulate these fisheries seems consequently, from the nature of the case, to be useless." [10] As a matter of fact, there was at this time relatively little restriction of fishing in European waters. Following the Royal Commission of 1866, England had repealed a host of restrictive laws. The development of steam-powered trawling in the 1880's, which enormously increased man's predatory capacity and the marked improvement of the trawl method in 1923 turned the pendulum, and throughout the interwar years discussion centered on the problem of "overfishing" and "depletion." This was accompanied by a considerable growth of restrictive regulations.[11] Only recently has the pendulum begun to reverse again, and there has lately been expressed in biological quarters a high degree of skepticism concerning the efficacy of restrictive measures, and the Huxleyian faith in the inexhaustibility of the sea has once again begun to find advocates. In 1951 Dr. Harden F. Taylor summarized the overall position of world fisheries in the following words:

> Such statistics of world fisheries as are available suggest that while particular species have fluctuated in abundance, the *yield of the sea fisheries as a whole or of any considerable region has not only been sustained, but has generally increased with increasing human populations*, and there is as yet no sign that they will not continue to do so. No single species so far as we know has ever become extinct, and no regional fishery in the world has ever been exhausted.[12]

In formulating governmental policy, biologists appear to have had a hard struggle (not always successful) to avoid oversimplification of the problem. One of the crudest arguments to have had some support is known as the "propagation theory," associated with the name of the English biologist, E. W. L. Holt.[13] Holt advanced the proposition that legal size limits should be established at a level that would permit every individual of the species in question to spawn at least once. This suggestion was effectively demolished by the age-distribution studies whose results have been noted above. Moreover, some fisheries, such as the "sardine" fishery of the Canadian Atlantic Coast, are specifically for *immature* fish. The history of this particular fishery shows no evidence whatever that the landings have been in any degree reduced by the practice of taking very large quantities of fish of prespawning age year after year.

The state of uncertainty in biological quarters around the turn of the century is perhaps indicated by the fact that Holt's propagation theory was advanced concurrently with its diametric opposite: "the thinning theory" of the Danish biologist, C. G. J. Petersen.[14] The latter argued that the fish may be too plentiful for the available food and that thinning out the young by fishing would enable the remainder to grow more rapidly. Petersen supported his theory with the results of transplanting experiments which showed that the fish transplanted to a new habitat frequently grew much more rapidly than before. But this is equivalent to arguing that the reason why rabbits multiplied so rapidly when introduced to Australia is because there were no rabbits already there with which they had to compete for food. Such an explanation would neglect all the other elements of importance in a natural ecology. In point of fact, in so far as food alone is concerned, thinning a cod population, say by half, would not double the food supply of the remaining individuals; for there are other species, perhaps not commercially valuable, that use the same food as the cod.

Dr. Burkenroad's comment, quoted earlier, that the purpose of practical policy is the benefit of man, not fish, was not gratuitous, for the argument has at times been advanced that commercial fishing should crop the resource in such a way as to leave the stocks of fish in the sea completely unchanged. Baranoff was largely responsible for destroying this approach, showing most elegantly that a commercial fishery cannot fail to diminish the fish stock. His general conclusion is worth quoting, for it states clearly not only his own position but the error of earlier thinking:

> As we see, a picture is obtained which diverges radically from the hypothesis which has been favoured almost down to the present time, namely that the natural reserve of fish is an inviolable capital, of which the fishing industry must use only the interest, not touching the capital at all. Our theory says, on the contrary, that a fishery and a natural reserve of fish are incompatible, and that the exploitable stock of fish is a changeable quantity, which depends on the intensity of the fishery. The more fish we take from a body of water, the smaller is the basic stock remaining in it; and the less fish we take, the greater is the basic stock, approximating to the natural stock when the fishery approaches zero. Such is the nature of the matter.[15]

The general conception of a fisheries ecology would appear to make such a conclusion inevitable. If a species were in ecological equilibrium before the commencement of commercial fishing, man's intrusion would have the same effect as any other predator; and that can only mean that the species population would reach a new equilibrium at a lower level of abundance, the divergence of the new equilibrium from the old depending on the degree of man's predatory effort and effectiveness.

The term "fisheries management" has been much in vogue in recent years, being taken to express a more subtle approach to the fisheries problem than the older terms "depletion" and "conservation." Briefly, it focuses attention on the quantity of fish caught, taking as the human objective of commercial fishing the derivation of the largest sustainable catch. This approach is often hailed in the biological literature as the "new theory" or the "modern formulation" of the fisheries problem.[16]

Its limitations, however, are very serious, and, indeed, the new approach comes very little closer to treating the fisheries problem as one of human utilization of natural resources than did the older, more primitive, theories. Focusing attention on the maximization of the catch neglects entirely the inputs of other factors of production which are used up in fishing and must be accounted for as costs. There are many references to such ultimate economic considerations in the biological literature but no analytical integration of the economic factors. In fact, the very conception of a *net economic yield* has scarcely made any appearance at all. On the whole, biologists tend to treat the fisherman as an exogenous element in their analytical model, and the behavior of fishermen is not made into an integrated element of a general and systematic "bionomic" theory. In the case of the fishing industry the large numbers of fishermen permit valid behavioristic generalization of their activities along the lines of the standard economic theory of production. The following section attempts to apply that theory to the fishing industry and to demonstrate that the "overfishing problem" has its roots in the economic organization of the industry.

III.   Economic Theory of the Fishery

In the analysis which follows, the theory of optimum utilization of fishery resources and the reasons for its frustration in practice are developed for a typical demersal fish. Demersal, or bottom-dwelling fishes, such as cod, haddock, and similar species and the various flat-fishes, are relatively nonmigratory in character. They live and feed on shallow continental shelves where the continual mixing of cold water maintains the availability of those nutrient salts which form the fundamental basis of marine-food chains. The various feeding grounds are separated by deep-water channels which constitute barriers to the movement of these species; and in some cases the fish of different banks can be differentiated morphologically, having varying numbers of vertebrae or some such distinguishing characteristic. The significance of this fact is that each fishing ground can be treated as unique, in the same sense as can a piece of land, possessing, at the very least, one characteristic not shared by any other piece: that is, location.

(Other species, such as herring, mackerel, and similar pelagic or surface dwellers, migrate over very large distances, and it is necessary to treat the resource of an entire geographic region as one. The conclusions arrived at below are applicable to such fisheries, but the method of analysis employed is not formally applicable. The same is true of species that migrate to and from fresh water and the lake fishes proper.)

We can define the optimum degree of utilization of any particular fishing ground as that which maximizes the net economic yield, the difference between total cost, on the one hand, and total receipts (or total value production), on the other.[17]   Total cost and total production can each be expressed as a function of the degree of fishing intensity or, as the biologists put it, "fishing effort," so that a simple maximization solution is possible.   Total cost will be a linear function of fishing effort, if we assume no fishing-induced effects on factor prices, which is reasonable for any particular regional fishery.

The production function—the relationship between fishing effort and total value produced—requires some special attention.   If we were to follow the usual presentation of economic theory, we should argue that this function would be positive but, after a point, would rise at a diminishing rate because of the law of diminishing returns.   This would not mean that the fish population has been reduced, for the law refers only to the *proportions* of factors to one another, and a fixed fish population, together· with an increasing intensity of effort, would be assumed to show the typical sigmoid pattern of yield.   However, in what follows it will be assumed that the law of diminishing returns in this pure sense is inoperative in the fishing industry.   (The reasons will be advanced at a later point in this paper.)   We shall assume that, as fishing effort expands, the catch of fish increases at a diminishing rate but that it does so because of the effect of catch upon the fish population.[18]   So far as the argument of the next few pages is concerned, all that is formally necessary is to assume that, as fishing intensity increases, catch will grow at a diminishing rate.   Whether this reflects the pure law of diminishing returns or the reduction of population by fishing, or both, is of no particular importance. The point at issue will, however, take on more significance in Section IV and will be examined there.

Our analysis can be simplified if we retain the ordinary production function instead of converting it to cost curves, as is usually done in the theory of the firm.   Let us further assume that the functional relationship between average production (production-per-unit-of-fishing-effort) and the quantity of fishing effort is uniformly linear.   This does not distort the results unduly, and it permits the analysis to be presented more simply and in graphic terms that are already quite familiar.

In Figure 1 the optimum intensity of utilization of a particular fishing ground is shown.   The curves *AP* and *MP* represent, respectively, the average productivity and marginal productivity of fishing effort.   The relationship between them is the same as that between average revenue and marginal revenue in imperfect competition theory, and *MP* bisects any horizontal between the ordinate and *AP*.   Since the costs of fishing supplies, etc., are assumed to be unaffected by the amount of fishing effort, marginal cost and average cost are identical and constant, as shown by the curve, *MC*, *AC*.[19]   These costs are assumed to include an opportunity in-

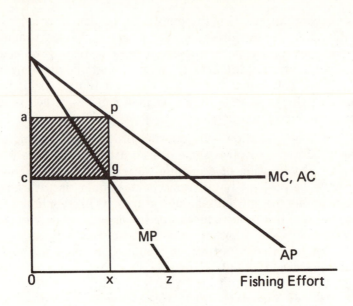

Figure 1

come for the fishermen, the income that could be earned in other comparable employments. Then Ox is the optimum intensity of effort on this fishing ground, and the resource will, at this level of exploitation, provide the maximum net economic yield indicated by the shaded area $apqc$. The maximum sustained physical yield that the biologists speak of will be attained when marginal productivity of fishing effort is zero, at Oz of fishing intensity in the chart shown. Thus, as one might expect, the optimum economic fishing intensity is less than that which would produce the maximum sustained physical yield.

The area $apqc$ in Figure 1 can be regarded as the rent yielded by the fishery resource. Under the given conditions, Ox is the best rate of exploitation for the fishing ground in question, and the rent reflects the productivity of that ground, not any artificial market limitation. The rent here corresponds to the extra productivity yielded in agriculture by soils of better quality or location than those on the margin of cultivation, which may produce an opportunity income but no more. In short, Figure 1 shows the determination of the intensive margin of utilization on an intramarginal fishing ground.

We now come to the point that is of greatest theoretical importance in understanding the primary production phase of the fishing industry and in distinguishing it from agriculture. In the sea fisheries the natural resource is not private property; hence the rent it may yield is not capable of being appropriated by anyone. The individual fisherman has no legal title to a section of ocean bottom. Each fisherman is more or less free to fish wherever he pleases. The result is a pattern of competition among fishermen which culminates in the dissipation of the rent of the intra-marginal grounds. This can be most clearly seen through an analysis of the relationship between the intensive margin and the extensive margin of resource exploitation in fisheries.

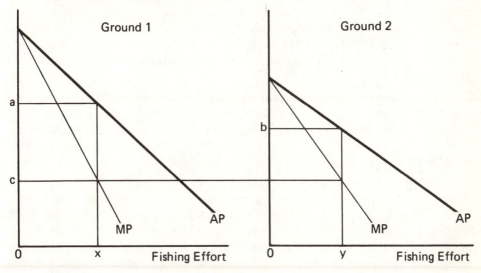

Figure 2

In Figure 2, two fishing grounds of different fertility (or location) are shown. Any given amount of fishing effort devoted to ground *2* will yield a smaller total (and therefore average) product than if devoted to *1*. The maximization problem is now a question of the allocation of fishing effort between grounds *1* and *2*. The optimum is, of course, where the marginal productivities are equal on both grounds. In Figure 2, fishing effort of *Ox* on *1* and *Oy* on *2* would maximize the total net yield of *Ox* + *Oy* effort if marginal cost were equal to *Oc*. But if under such circumstances the individual fishermen are free to fish on whichever ground they please, it is clear that this is not an equilibrium allocation of fishing effort in the sense of connoting stability. A fisherman starting from port and deciding whether to go to ground *1* or *2* does not care for *marginal* productivity but for *average* productivity, for it is the latter that indicates where the greater total yield may be obtained. If fishing effort were allocated in the optimum fashion, as shown in Figure 2, with *Ox* on *1*, and *Oy* on *2*, this would be a disequilibrium situation. Each fisherman could expect to get an average catch of *Oa* on *1* but only *Ob* on *2*. Therefore, fishermen would shift from *2* to *1*. Stable equilibrium would not be reached until the average productivity of both grounds was equal. If we now imagine a continuous gradation of fishing grounds, the extensive margin would be on that ground which yielded nothing more than outlaid costs plus opportunity income—in short, the one on which average productivity and average cost were equal. But, since average cost is the same for all grounds and the average productivity of all grounds is also brought to equality by the free and competitive nature of fishing, this means that the intramarginal grounds also yield no rent. It is entirely possible that some grounds would be exploited at a level of *negative* marginal productivity. What happens is that the rent which the intramarginal grounds are capable of yielding is dissipated through misallocation of fishing effort.

This is why fishermen are not wealthy, despite the fact that the fishery resources of the sea are the richest and most indestructible available to man. By and large, the only fisherman who becomes rich is one who makes a lucky catch or one who participates in a fishery that is put under a form of social control that turns the open resource into property rights.

Up to this point, the remuneration of fishermen has been accounted for as an opportunity-cost income comparable to earnings attainable in other industries. In point of fact, fishermen typically earn less than most others, even in much less hazardous occupations or in those requiring less skill. There is no effective reason why the competition among fishermen described above must stop at the point where opportunity incomes are yielded. It may be and is in many cases carried much further. Two factors prevent an equilibration of fishermen's incomes with those of other members of society. The first is the great immobility of fishermen. Living often in isolated communities, with little knowledge of conditions or opportunities elsewhere; educationally and often romantically tied to the sea; and lacking the savings necessary to provide a "stake," the fisherman is one of the least mobile of occupational groups. But, second, there is in the spirit of every fisherman the hope of the "lucky catch." As those who know fishermen well have often testified, they are gamblers and incurably optimistic. As a consequence, they will work for less than the going wage.[20]

The theory advanced above is substantiated by important developments in the fishing industry. For example, practically all control measures have, in the past, been designed by biologists, with sole attention paid to the production side of the problem and none to the cost side. The result has been a wide-open door for the frustration of the purposes of such measures. The Pacific halibut fishery, for example, is often hailed as a great achievement in modern fisheries management. Under international agreement between the United States and Canada, a fixed-catch limit was established during the early thirties. Since then, catch-per-unit-effort indexes, as usually interpreted, show a significant rise in the fish population. W. F. Thompson, the pioneer of the Pacific halibut management program, noted recently that "it has often been said that the halibut regulation presents the only definite case of sustained improvement of an overfished deep-sea fishery. This, I believe, is true and the fact should lend special importance to the principles which have been deliberately used to obtain this improvement." [21]   Actually, careful study of the statistics indicates that the estimated recovery of halibut stocks could not have been due principally to the control measures, for the average catch was, in fact, greater during the recovery years than during the years of decline. The total amount of fish taken was only a small fraction of the estimated population reduction for the years prior to regulation.[22]   Natural factors seem to be mainly responsible for the observed change in population, and the institution of control regulations almost a coincidence. Such coincidences are not uncommon in the history of fisheries policy, but they may be easily explained. If a long-term cyclical fluctuation is taking place in a commercially valuable species, controls will likely be instituted when fishing yields have fallen very low and the clamor of fishermen is great; but it is then, of course, that stocks are about due to recover in any case. The "success" of conservation measures may be due fully as much to the sociological foundations of public policy as to the policy's effect on the fish. Indeed, Burkenroad argues that biological statistics in general may be called into question on these grounds. Governments sponsor biological research when the catches are disappointing. If there are long-term cyclical fluctuations in fish populations, as some think, it is hardly to be wondered why biologists frequently discover that the sea is being depleted, only to change their collective opinion a decade or so later.

Quite aside from the *biological* argument on the Pacific halibut case, there is no clear-cut evidence that halibut fishermen were made relatively more prosperous by the control measures. Whether or not the recovery of the halibut stocks was due to natural factors or to the catch limit, the potential net yield this could have meant has been dissipated through a rise in fishing costs. Since the method of control was to halt fishing when the limit had been reached, this created a great incentive on the part of each fisherman to get the fish before his competitors. During the last twenty years, fishermen have invested in more, larger, and faster boats in a competitive race for fish. In 1933 the fishing season was more than six months long. In 1952 it took just twenty-six days to catch the legal limit in the area from Willapa Harbor to Cape Spencer, and sixty days in the Alaska region. What has been happening is a rise in the average cost of fishing effort, allowing no gap between average production and average cost to appear, and hence no rent.[23]

Essentially the same phenomenon is observable in the Canadian Atlantic Coast lobster-conservation program. The method of control here is by seasonal closure. The result has been a steady growth in the number of lobster traps set by each fisherman. Virtually all available lobsters are now caught each year within the season, but at much greater cost in gear and supplies. At a fairly conservative estimate, the same quantity of lobsters could be caught with half the present number of traps. In a few places the fishermen have banded together into a local monopoly, preventing entry and controlling their own operations. By this means, the amount of fishing gear has been greatly reduced and incomes considerably improved.

That the plight of fishermen and the inefficiency of fisheries production stems from the common-property nature of the resources of the sea is further corroborated by the fact that one finds similar patterns of exploitation and similar problems in other cases of open resources. Perhaps the most obvious is hunting and trapping. Unlike fishes, the biotic potential of land animals is low enough for the species to be destroyed. Uncontrolled hunting means that animals will be killed for any short-range human reason, great or small: for food or simply for fun. Thus the buffalo of the western plains was destroyed to satisfy the most trivial desires of the white man, against which the long-term food needs of the aboriginal population counted as nothing. Even in the most civilized communities, conservation authorities have discovered that a bag-limit *per man* is necessary if complete destruction is to be avoided.

The results of anthropological investigation of modes of land tenure among primitive peoples render some further support to this thesis. In accordance with an evolutionary concept of cultural comparison, the older anthropological study was prone to regard resource tenure in common, with unrestricted exploitation, as a "lower" stage of development comparative with private and group property rights. However, more complete annals of primitive cultures reveal common tenure to be quite rare, even in hunting and gathering societies. Property rights in some form predominate by far, and, most important, their existence may be easily explained in terms of the necessity for orderly exploitation and conservation of the resource. Environmental conditions make necessary some vehicle which will prevent the resources of the community at large from being destroyed by excessive exploitation. Private or group land tenure accomplishes this end in an easily understandable fashion.[24] Significantly, land tenure is found to be "common" only in those cases where the hunting resource is migratory over such large areas that it cannot be regarded as husbandable by the society. In cases of group tenure where the numbers of the group are large, there is still the necessity of co-ordinating the practices of exploitation, in agricultural, as well as in hunting or gathering, economies. Thus, for example, Malinowski reported that among the Trobriand Islanders one of the fundamental principles of land tenure is the co-ordination of the productive activities of the gardeners by the person possessing magical leadership in the group.[25] Speaking generally, we may say that stable primitive cultures appear to have discovered the dangers of common-property tenure and to have developed measures to protect their resources. Or, if a more Darwinian explanation be preferred, we may say that only those primitive cultures have survived which succeeded in developing such institutions.

Another case, from a very different industry, is that of petroleum production. Although the individual petroleum producer may acquire undisputed lease or ownership of the particular plot of land upon which his well is drilled, he shares, in most cases, a common pool of oil with other drillers. There is, consequently, set up the same kind of competitive race as is found in the fishing industry, with attending overexpansion of productive facilities and gross wastage of the resource. In the United States, efforts to regulate a chaotic situation in oil production began as early as 1915. Production practices, number of wells, and even output quotas were set by governmental authority; but it was not until the federal "Hot Oil" Act of 1935 and the development of interstate agreements that the final loophole (bootlegging) was closed through regulation of interstate commerce in oil.

Perhaps the most interesting similar case is the use of common pasture in the medieval manorial economy. Where the ownership of animals was private but the resource on which they fed was common (and limited), it was necessary to regulate the use of common pasture in order to prevent each man from competing and conflicting with his neighbors in an effort to utilize more of the pasture for his own animals. Thus the manor developed its elaborate rules regulating the use of the common pasture, or "stinting" the common: limitations on the number of animals, hours of pasturing, etc., designed to prevent the abuses of excessive individualistic competition.[26]

There appears, then, to be some truth in the conservative dictum that everybody's property is nobody's property. Wealth that is free for all is valued by none because he who is foolhardy enough to wait for its proper time of use will only find that it has been taken by another. The blade of grass that the manorial cowherd leaves behind is valueless to him, for tomorrow it may be eaten by another's animal; the oil left under the earth is valueless to the driller, for another may legally take it; the fish in the sea are valueless to the fisherman, because there is no assurance that they will be there for him tomorrow if they are left behind today. A factor of production that is valued at nothing in the business calculations of its users will yield nothing in income. Common-property natural resources are free goods for the individual and scarce goods for society. Under unregulated private exploitation, they can yield no rent; that can be accomplished only by methods which make them private property or public (government) property, in either case subject to a unified directing power.

426 Public Goods, Collective Goods and Externalities

IV. The Bionomic Equilibrium of the Fishing Industry

The work of biological theory in the fishing industry is, basically, an effort to delineate the ecological system in which a particular fish population is found. In the main, the species that have been extensively studied are those which are subject to commercial exploitation. This is due not only to the fact that funds are forthcoming for such research but also because the activity of commercial fishing vessels provides the largest body of data upon which the biologist may work. Despite this, however, the ecosystem of the fisheries biologist is typically one that excludes man. Or, rather, man is regarded as an exogenous factor, having influence on the biological ecosystem through his removal of fish from the sea, but the activities of man are themselves not regarded as behaviorized or determined by the other elements of a system of mutual interdependence. The large number of independent fishermen who exploit fish populations of commercial importance makes it possible to treat man as a behavior element in a larger, "bionomic," ecology, if we can find the rules which relate his behavior to the other elements of the system. Similarly, in their treatment of the principles of fisheries management, biologists have overlooked essential elements of the problem by setting maximum physical landings as the objective of management, thereby neglecting the economic factor of input cost.

An analysis of the bionomic equilibrium of the fishing industry may, then, be approached in terms of two problems. The first is to explain the nature of the equilibrium of the industry as it occurs in the state of uncontrolled or unmanaged exploitation of a common-property resource. The second is to indicate the nature of a socially optimum manner of exploitation, which is, presumably, what governmental management policy aims to achieve or promote. These two problems will be discussed in the remaining pages.

In the preceding section it was shown that the equilibrium condition of uncontrolled exploitation is such that the net yield (total value landings *minus* total cost) is zero. The "bionomic ecosystem" of the fishing industry, as we might call it, can then be expressed in terms of four variables and four equations. Let P represent the population of the particular fish species on the particular fishing bank in question; L the total quantity taken or "landed" by man, measured in value terms; E the intensity of fishing or the quantity of "fishing effort" expended; and C the total cost of making such effort. The system, then, is as follows:

$$P = P\ (L), \tag{1}$$
$$L = L\ (P, E), \tag{2}$$
$$C = C\ (E), \tag{3}$$
$$C = L. \tag{4}$$

Equation (4) is the equilibrium condition of an uncontrolled fishery.

The functional relations stated in equations (1), (2), and (3) may be graphically presented as shown in Figure 3. Segment *1* shows the fish population as a simple negative function of landings. In segment *2* a map of landings functions is drawn. Thus, for example, if population were P_3, effort of Oe would produce Ol of fish. For each given level of population, a larger fishing effort will result in larger landings. Each population contour is, then, a production function for a given population level. The linearity of these contours indicates that the law of diminishing returns is not operative, nor are any landings-induced price effects assumed to affect the value landings graphed on the vertical axis. These assumptions are made in order to produce the simplest determinate solution; yet each is reasonable in itself. The assumption of a fixed product price is reasonable, since our analysis deals with one fishing ground, not the fishery as a whole. The cost function represented in equation (3) and graphed in segment *3* of Figure 3 is not really necessary to the determination, but its inclusion makes the matter somewhat clearer. Fixed prices of input factors —"fishing effort"—is assumed, which is reasonable again on the assumption that a small part of the total fishery is being analyzed.

Starting with the first segment, we see that a postulated catch of Ol connotes an equilibrium population in the biological ecosystem of Op. Suppose this population to be represented by the contour P_3 of segment *2*. Then, given P_3, Oe is the effort required to catch the postulated landings Ol. This quantity of effort involves a total cost of Oc, as shown in segment *3* of the graph. In full bionomic equilibrium, $C = L$, and if the particular values Oc and Ol shown are not equal, other quantities of all four variables, L, P, E, and C, are required, involving movements of these variables through the functional system shown. The operative movement is, of course, in fishing effort, E. It is the equilibrating variable in the system.

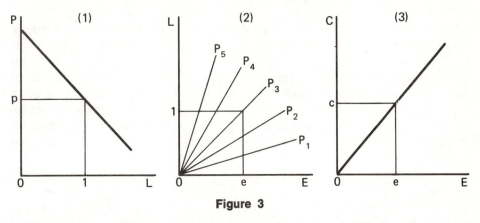

Figure 3

The equilibrium equality of landings (L) and cost (C), however, must be a position of stability, and $L = C$ is a necessary, though not in itself sufficient, condition for stability in the ecosystem.   This is shown by stable equilibrium could be found.   If the case were represented by C and Figure 4.   If effort-cost and effort-landings functions were both linear, no L_1, the fishery would contract to zero; if by C and L_2, it would undergo an infinite expansion.   Stable equilibrium requires that either the cost or the landings function be nonlinear.   This condition is fulfilled by the assumption that population is reduced by fishing (eq. [1] above).   The equilibrium is therefore as shown in Figure 5.   Now Oe represents a fully stable equilibrium intensity of fishing.

The analysis of the conditions of stable equilibrium raises some points of general theoretical interest.   In the foregoing we have assumed that stability results from the effect of fishing on the fish population.   In the standard analysis of economic theory, we should have employed the law of diminishing returns to produce a landings function of the necessary shape. Market factors might also have been so employed; a larger supply of fish, forthcoming from greater fishing effort, would reduce unit price and thereby produce a landings function with the necessary negative second derivative.   Similarly, greater fishing intensity might raise the unit costs of factors, producing a cost function with a positive second derivative. Any one of these three—population effects, law of diminishing returns, or market effects—is alone sufficient to produce stable equilibrium in the ecosystem.

As to the law of diminishing returns, it has not been accepted per se by fisheries biologists.   It is, in fact, a principle that becomes quite slippery when one applies it to the case of fisheries.   Indicative of this is the fact that Alfred Marshall, in whose *Principles* one can find extremely little formal error, misinterprets the application of the law of diminishing returns to the fishing industry, arguing, in effect, that the law exerts its influence through the reducing effect of fishing on the fish population.[27] There have been some interesting expressions of the law or, rather, its essential varying-proportions-of-factors aspect, in the biological literature. H. M. Kyle, a German biologist, included it in 1928 among a number of reasons why catch-per-unit-of-fishing-effort indexes are not adequate measures of population change.[28]   Interestingly, enough, his various criticisms of the indexes were generally accepted, with the significant exception of this one point.   More recently, A. G. Huntsman warned his colleagues in fisheries biology that "[there] may be a decrease in the take-per-unit-of-effort without any decrease in the total take or in the fish population. . . .   This may mean that there has been an increase in fishermen rather than a decrease in fish."[29]   While these statements run in terms of average rather than marginal yield, their underlying reasoning clearly appears to be that of the law of diminishing returns.   The point has had little influence in biological circles, however, and when, two years ago, I advanced it, as Kyle and Huntsman had done, in criticism of the standard biological method of estimating population change, it received pretty short shrift.

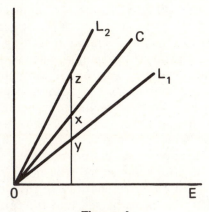

Figure 4

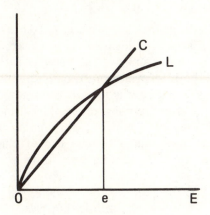

Figure 5

In point of fact, the law of diminishing returns is much more difficult to sustain in the case of fisheries than in agriculture or industry. The "proof" one finds in standard theory is not empirical, although the results of empirical experiments in agriculture are frequently adduced as subsidiary corroboration. The main weight of the law, however, rests on a *reductio ad absurdum*. One can easily demonstrate that, were it not for the law of diminishing returns, all the world's food could be grown on one acre of land. Reality is markedly different, and it is because the law serves to render this reality intelligible to the logical mind, or, as we might say, "explains" it, that it occupies such a firm place in the body of economic theory. In fisheries, however, the pattern of reality can easily be explained on other grounds. In the case at least of developed demersal fisheries, it cannot be denied that the fish population is reduced by fishing, and this relationship serves perfectly well to explain why an infinitely expansible production is not possible from a fixed fishing area. The other basis on which the law of diminishing returns is usually advanced in economic theory is the prima facie plausibility of the principle as such; but here, again, it is hard to grasp any similar reasoning in fisheries. In the typical agricultural illustration, for example, we may argue that the fourth harrowing or the fourth weeding, say, has a lower marginal productivity than the third. Such an assertion brings ready acceptance because it concerns a process with a zero productive limit. It is apparent that, ultimately, the land would be completely broken up or the weeds completely eliminated if harrowing or weeding were done in ever larger amounts. The law of diminishing returns signifies simply that such a zero limit is *gradually approached,* all of which appears to be quite acceptable on prima facie grounds. There is nothing comparable to this in fisheries at all, for there is no "cultivation" in the same sense of the term, except, of course, in such cases as oyster culture or pond rearing of fish, which are much more akin to farming than to typical sea fisheries.

In the biological literature the point has, I think, been well thought through, though the discussion does not revolve around the "law of diminishing returns" by that name. It is related rather to the fisheries biologist's problem of the interpretation of catch-per-unit-of-fishing-effort statistics. The essence of the law is usually eliminated by the assumption that there is no "competition" among units of fishing gear—that is, that the ratio of gear to fishing area and/or fish population is small. In some cases, corrections have been made by the use of the compound-interest formula where some competition among gear units is considered to exist.[30] Such corrections, however, appear to be based on the idea of an increasing catch-population ratio rather than an increasing effort-population ratio. The latter would be as the law of diminishing returns would have it; the idea lying behind the former is that the total population in existence represents the maximum that can be caught, and, since this maximum would be gradually approached, the ratio of catch to population has some bearing on the efficiency of fishing gear. It is, then, just an aspect of the population-reduction effect. Similarly, it has been pointed out that, since fish are recruited into the catchable stock in a seasonal fashion, one can expect the catch-per-unit-effort to fall as the fishing season progresses, at least in those fisheries where a substantial proportion of the stock is taken annually. Seasonal averaging is therefore necessary in using the catch-effort statistics as population indexes from year to year. This again is a population-reduction effect, not the law of diminishing returns. In general, there seems to be no reason for departing from the approach of the fisheries biologist on this point. The law of diminishing returns is not necessary to explain the conditions of stable equilibrium in a static model of the fishery, nor is there any prima facie ground for its acceptance.

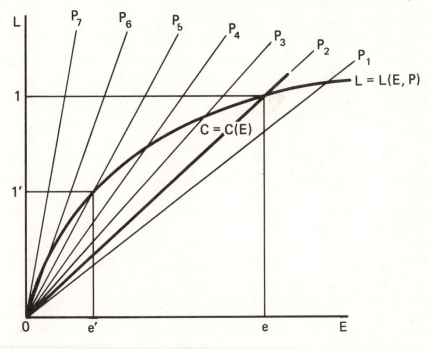

Figure 6

Let us now consider the exploitation of a fishing ground under uni-fied control, in which case the equilibrium condition is the maximization of net financial yield, $L - C$.

The map of population contours graphed in segment *2* of Figure 3 may be superimposed upon the total-landings and total-cost functions graphed in Figure 5. The result is as shown in Figure 6. In the system of interrelationships we have to consider, population changes affect, and are in turn affected by, the amount of fish landed. The map of popula-tion contours does not include this roundabout effect that a population change has upon itself. The curve labeled L, however, is a landings func-tion which accounts for the fact that larger landings reduce the population, and this is why it is shown to have a steadily diminishing slope. We may regard the landings function as moving progressively to lower population contours P_7, P_6, P_5, etc., as total landings increase in magnitude. As a con-sequence, while each population contour represents many hypothetical combinations of E, L, and P, only one such combination on each is actually compatible in this system of interrelationships. This combination is the point on any contour where that contour is met by the landings function L. Thus the curve labeled L may be regarded as tracing out a series of combinations of E, L, and P which are compatible with one another in the system.

The total-cost function may be drawn as shown, with total cost, C, measured in terms of landings, which the vertical axis represents.[31] This is a linear function of effort as shown. The optimum intensity of fishing effort is that which maximizes $L - C$. This is the monopoly solution; but, since we are considering only a single fishing ground, no price effects are introduced, and the social optimum coincides with maximum monopoly revenue. In this case we are maximizing the yield of a natural resource, not a privileged position, as in standard monopoly theory. The rent here is a social surplus yielded by the resource, not in any part due to artificial scarcity, as is monopoly profit or rent.

If the optimum fishing intensity is that which maximizes $L - C$, this is seen to be the position where the slope of the landings function equals the slope of the cost function in Figure 6. Thus the optimum fishing intensity is Oe' of fishing effort. This will yield Ol' of landings, and the species population will be in continuing stable equilibrium at a level indicated by P_5.

The equilibrium resulting from uncontrolled competitive fishing, where the rent is dissipated, can also be seen in Figure 6. This, being where $C = L$, is at Oe of effort and Ol of landings, and at a stable population level of P_2. As can be clearly seen, the uncontrolled equilibrium means a higher expenditure of effort, higher fish landings, and a lower continuing fish population than the optimum equilibrium.

Algebraically, the bionomic ecosystem may be set out in terms of the optimum solution as follows. The species population in equilibrium is a linear function of the amount of fish taken from the sea:

$$P = a - bL. \tag{1}$$

In this function, a may be described as the "natural population" of the species—the equilibrium level it would attain if not commercially fished. All natural factors, such as water temperatures, food supplies, natural predators, etc., which affect the population are, for the purposes of the system analyzed, locked up in a. The magnitude of a is the vertical intercept of the population function graphed in segment 1 of Figure 3. The slope of this function is b, which may be described as the "depletion coefficient," since it indicates the effect of catch on population. The landings function is such that no landings are forthcoming with either zero effort or zero population; therefore,

$$L = cEP. \tag{2}$$

The parameter c in this equation is the technical coefficient of production or, as we may call it simply, the "production coefficient." Total cost is a function of the amount of fishing effort.

$$C = qE.$$

The optimum condition is that the total net receipts must be maximized, that is,

$$L - C \text{ to be maximized.}$$

Since q has been assumed constant and equal to unity (i. e., effort is counted in "dollars-worth" units), we may write $L - E$ to be maximized. Let this be represented by R:

$$R = L - E, \tag{3}$$

$$\frac{dR}{dE} = 0. \tag{4}$$

The four numbered equations constitute the system when in optimality equilibrium. In order to find this optimum, the landings junction (2) may be rewritten, with the aid of equation (1), as:

$$L = cE \ (a - bL).$$

From this we have at once

$$L \ (1 + cEb) = cEa,$$

$$L = \frac{caE}{1 + cbE}.$$

To find the optimum intensity of effort, we have, from equation (3):

$$\frac{dR}{dE} = \frac{dL}{dE} - \frac{dE}{dE}$$

$$= \frac{(1 + cbE) \ (ca) - caE \ (cb)}{(1 + cbE)^2} - 1,$$

$$= \frac{ca}{(1 + cbE)^2} - 1;$$

for a maximum, this must be set equal to zero; hence,

$$ca = (1 + cbE)^2,$$
$$1 + cbE = \pm \sqrt{ca},$$
$$E = \frac{-1 \pm \sqrt{ca}}{cb}.$$

For positive E,

$$E = \frac{\sqrt{ca} - 1}{cb}.$$

This result indicates that the effect on optimum effort of a change in the production coefficient is uncertain, a rise in c calling for a rise in E in some cases and a fall in E in others, depending on the magnitude of the change in c. The effects of changes in the natural population and depletion coefficient are, however, clear, a rise (fall) in a calling for a rise (fall) in E, while a rise (fall) in b means a fall (rise) in E.

FOOTNOTES

[1] I want to express my indebtedness to the Canadian Department of Fisheries for assistance and co-operation in making this study; also to Professor M. C. Urquhart, of Queen's University, Kingston, Ontario, for mathematical assistance with the last section of the paper and to the Economists' Summer Study Group at Queen's for affording opportunity for research and discussion.

[2] The single exception that I know is G. M. Gerhardsen, "Production Economics in Fisheries," *Revista de economia* (Lisbon), March, 1952.

[3] Especially remarkable efforts in this sense are Robert A. Nesbit, "Fishery Management" ("U. S. Fish and Wildlife Service, Special Scientific Reports," No. 18 [Chicago, 1943]) (mimeographed), and Harden F. Taylor, *Survey of Marine Fisheries of North Carolina* (Chapel Hill, 1951); also R. J. H. Beverton, "Some Observations on the Principles of Fishery Regulation," *Journal du conseil permanent international pour l'exploration de la mer* (Copenhagen), Vol. XIX, No. 1 (May, 1953); and M. D. Burkenroad, "Some Principles of Marine Fishery Biology," *Publications of the Institute of Marine Science* (University of Texas), Vol. II, No. 1 (September, 1951).

[4] "Theory and Practice of Marine Fishery Management," *Journal du conseil permanent international pour l'exploration de la mer*, Vol. XVIII, No. 3 (January, 1953).

[5] Two of Baranoff's most important papers—"On the Question of the Biological Basis of Fisheries" (1918) and "On the Question of the Dynamics of the Fishing Industry" (1925)—have been translated by W. E. Ricker, now of the Fisheries Research Board of Canada (Nanaimo, B. C.), and issued in mimeographed form.

[6] "Fishery Depletion," *Science*, XCIX (1944), 534.

[7] "The highest take is not necessarily the best. The take should be increased only as long as the extra cost is offset by the added revenue from sales" (A. G. Huntsman, "Research on Use and Increase of Fish Stocks," *Proceedings of the United Nations Scientific Conference on the Conservation and Utilization of Resources* [Lake Success, 1949]).

[8] One example of a very general phenomenon: 1904 was such a successful brood year for Norwegian herrings that the 1904 year class continued to outweigh all others

in importance in the catch from 1907 through to 1919. The 1904 class was some thirty times as numerous as other year classes during the period (Johan Hjort, "Fluctuations in the Great Fisheries of Northern Europe," *Rapports et procèsverbaux, Conseil permanent international pour l'exploration de la mer*, Vol. XX [1914]; see also E. S. Russell, *The Overfishing Problem* [Cambridge, 1942], p. 57).

9 See his *Resources of the Sea* published in 1899.

10 Quoted in M. Graham, *The Fish Gate* (London, 1943), p. 111; see also T. H. Huxley, "The Herring," *Nature* (London), 1881.

11 See H. Scott Gordon, "The Trawler Question in the United Kingdom and Canada," *Dalhousie Review*, summer, 1951.

12 Taylor, op. cit., p. 314 (Dr. Taylor's italics).

13 See E. W. L. Holt, "An Examination of the Grimsby Trawl Fishery," *Journal of the Marine Biological Association* (Plymouth), 1895.

14 See C. G. J. Petersen, "What Is Overfishing?" *Journal of the Marine Biological Association* (Plymouth), 1900–1903.

15 T. I. Baranoff, "On the Question of the Dynamics of the Fishing Industry," p. 5 (mimeographed).

16 See, e. g., R. E. Foerster, "Prospects for Managing Our Fisheries," *Bulletin of the Bingham Oceanographic Collection* (New Haven), May, 1948; E. S. Russell, "Some Theoretical Considerations on the Overfishing Problem," *Journal du conseil permanent international pour l'exploration de la mer*, 1931, and *The Overfishing Problem*, Lecture IV.

17 Expressed in these terms, this appears to be the monopoly maximum, but it coincides with the social optimum under the conditions employed in the analysis, as will be indicated below.

18 Throughout this paper the conception of fish population that is employed is one of *weight* rather than *numbers*. A good deal of the biological theory has been an effort to combine growth factors and numbers factors into weight sums. The following analysis will neglect the fact that, for some species, fish of different sizes bring different unit prices.

19 Throughout this analysis, fixed costs are neglected. The general conclusions reached would not be appreciably altered, I think, by their inclusion, though the presentation would be greatly complicated. Moreover, in the fishing industry the most substantial portion of fixed cost—wharves, harbors, etc.—is borne by government and does not enter into the cost calculations of the operators.

20 "The gambling instinct of the men makes many of them work for less remuneration than they would accept as a weekly wage, because there is always the possibility of a good catch and a financial windfall" (Graham, op. cit., p. 86).

21 W. F. Thompson, "Condition of Stocks of Halibut in the Pacific," *Journal du conseil permanent international pour l'exploration de la mer*, Vol. XVIII, No. 2 (August, 1952).

22 See M. D. Burkenroad, "Fluctuations in Abundance of Pacific Halibut,". *Bulletin of the Bingham Oceanographic Collection*, May, 1948.

23 The economic significance of the reduction in season length which followed upon the catch limitation imposed in the Pacific halibut fishery has not been fully appreciated. E. g., Michael Graham said in summary of the program in 1943: "The result has been that it now takes only five months to catch the quantity of halibut that formerly needed nine. This, *of course*, has meant profit, where there was none before" (op. cit., p. 156; my italics). Yet, even when biologists have grasped the economic import of the halibut program and its results, they appear reluctant to declare against it. E. g.,

W. E. Ricker: "This method of regulation does not necessarily make for more profitable fishing and certainly puts no effective brake on waste of effort, since an unlimited number of boats is free to join the fleet and compete during the short period that fishing is open. However, the stock is protected, and yield approximates to a maximum if quotas are wisely set; as biologists, perhaps we are not required to think any further. Some claim that any mixing into the economics of the matter might prejudice the desirable biological consequences of regulation by quotas" ("Production and Utilization of Fish Population," in a Symposium on Dynamics of Production in Aquatic Populations, Ecological Society of America, *Ecological Monographs*, XVI [October, 1946], 385). What such "desirable biological consequences" might be, is hard to conceive. Since the regulatory policies are made by man, surely it is necessary they be evaluated in terms of human, not piscatorial, objectives.

[24] See Frank G. Speck, "Land Ownership among Hunting Peoples in Primitive America and the World's Marginal Areas," *Proceedings of the 22nd International Congress of Americanists* (Rome, 1926), II, 323–32.

[25] B. Malinowski, *Coral Gardens and Their Magic*, Vol. I, chaps. xi and xii. Malinowski sees this as further evidence of the importance of magic in the culture rather than as a means of co-ordinating productive activity; but his discussion of the practice makes it clear that the latter is, to use Malinowski's own concept, the "function" of the institution of magical leadership, at least in this connection.

[26] See P. Vinogradoff, *The Growth of the Manor* [London, 1905], chap. iv; E. Lipson, *The Economic History of England* [London, 1949], I, 72.

[27] See H. Scott Gordon, "On a Misinterpretation of the Law of Diminishing Returns in Alfred Marshall's *Principles*," *Canadian Journal of Economics and Political Science*, February, 1952.

[28] "Die Statistik der Seefischerei Nordeuropas," *Handbuch der Seefischerei Nordeuropas* (Stuttgart, 1928).

[29] A. G. Huntsman, "Fishing and Assessing Populations," *Bulletin of the Bingham Oceanographic Collection* (New Haven), May, 1948.

[30] See, e. g., W. F. Thompson and F. H. Bell, *Biological Statistics of the Pacific Halibut Fishery*, No. 2: *Effect of Changes in Intensity upon Total Yield and Yield per Unit of Gear: Report of the International Fisheries Commission* (Seattle, 1934).

[31] More correctly, perhaps, C and L are both measured in money terms.

C Continued

25: THE STRUCTURE OF A CONTRACT AND THE THEORY OF A NON-EXCLUSIVE RESOURCE *

STEVEN N. S. CHEUNG
University of Washington

The process of arriving at a useful concept of analysis is not only slow and painful, but also may go astray and attain nothing useful. Someone begins with one example or observation, followed by a theory which is intuitively plausible. A theoretical term associated with a vague concept is coined. Examples of a seemingly different type emerge, which call for another theory. The process goes on. As examples and theories continue to accumulate, the different categories under the same heading of analysis serve only to confuse, and each associated theory becomes *ad hoc*. Such has been the fate of the concept of "externality." [1]

A more useful approach, I think, is via contractual conditions. The example chosen for illustration is marine fisheries, where the fishing right is taken as non-exclusive, and where most economists agree that "externalities" exist in several directions.[2] In the absence of exclusive rights to the use of the fishing ground,[3] the right to contract so as to stipulate its use does not exist. This implies the absence of contractual stipulations governing resource use which would exist if the fishing ground were private property, thereby altering the constraint of competition and affecting resource allocation in a number of ways. The alleged "externalities" in fisheries are thus attributable to the absence of the right to contract.

Journal of Law and Econ., Vol. 3, 1970, p. 49.

I.   Property Rights and Contracting

Combining resources of several owners for production involves partial or outright transfers of property rights through a contract.[4]   A contract for the partial transfer of rights, such as leasing or hiring—embodies a *structure*.   The stipulations, or terms, which constitute the structure of the contract are, as a rule, designed to specify (a) the distribution of income among the participants, and (b) the conditions of resource use.   Under transferable rights, these stipulations are consistent with, or determined by, competition in the marketplace.   As shown elsewhere,[5] the choice of contracts is determined by transaction costs, natural (economic) risks, and legal (political) arrangements.   However, the familiar market prices are but one among many of the contractual terms (indeed, in share contracts, prices are not explicitly specified).

With private property rights governing the use of *all* resources, the postulate of wealth maximization implies that the contractual stipulations are designed to maximize the return to all resources subject to the constraint of competition.   Assume away the costs of transactions, the contractual stipulations for every resource use will be so designed that they are consistent with the equimarginal principle.   In general, the structure of the contract will be such that the marginal gain and cost are equal.   In specific details, however, the elements constituting gains and costs are multiple and the marginal equalities of a constrained maximization are several.   Since to satisfy one particular marginal equality, one or more contractual stipulations, implicitly or explicitly, are required, pages of stipulations in one contract can be found.

Two questions immediately arise.   First, given the contractual stipulations, do we know that the required marginal equalities are satisfied? And second, what bearing do these stipulations have on the actual outcome of income distribution and resource allocation?

The answer to the first is that we know at least whether the stipulations are *consistent* with the requisite marginal equalities.   The stipulations of a contract may be inconsistent with marginal equality of resource use (for example, a contract stipulating only a lump-sum charge without quantity stipulation); or the contract may not exist, implicitly or explicitly, as in the case of the use of a non-exclusive right.   A defective contract, or the absence of a contract, does not necessarily imply economic inefficiency, and can be traced either to the presence of transaction costs, the existing legal arrangements, or the lack of foresight and the costs of information.[6]   The second question—the relation between a set of stipulations and the actual outcome—is one of contractual enforcement.   While one may argue that non-enforceable stipulations will not be present in a contract, for our present purpose it suffices to point out that the absence of a contract will lead to different resource use than when an enforceable contract exists.

But the main point here is that a contract may encompass a large set of stipulations, governing a set of marginal equalities associated with various aspects of resource use. If outright transfers exist for all resources engaged in production, the owner alone is responsible for the decision aspects. If partial transfers exist, then the contracting parties mutually negotiate the terms. For any production process, multiple contracts may exist. Given the form of contract, the stipulations would be more complex the more complex the physical attributes of inputs and outputs.

It has become increasingly clear to me that the mushrooming of alleged "externalities" is attributable to either (1) the absence of the right to contract, (2) the presence of a contract but with incomplete stipulations, or (3) the presence of stipulations that are somehow inconsistent with some marginal equalities. Among these cases, however, differences are only a matter of degree. Since the conceivable number of different contractual stipulations is very large, the rapid growth rate in the literature in recognizing "new" externalities is natural.

As an example, let us examine marine fisheries, wherein the right to use the fishing ground is said to be non-exclusive and hence the right to contract is absent. The assumed condition of a lack of exclusive right to use the resource, free of institutional regulations, does not, of course, correspond to the real world where rules and regulations established by governments and unions are numerous.[7] The issue of regulation versus voluntary contractual arrangements in the marketplace will be discussed briefly in section IV.

Fish, like rice or any other growing (biological) asset, require "planting" as well as "harvesting." Different physical attributes of such resources, however, will lead to different degrees of emphasis on the alternative options of choice. In general, decisions will be made on the product to be produced, the method of production, the amount and type of investment over time, the financial maturity of the catch, and the intensity and method of harvesting. With private property rights, these decisions will result in stipulations mutually negotiated by the contracting parties (for example, the fishing-ground owner, the boat owner and the fisherman). Although the stipulations differ when the forms of contract differ, the implied resource use may not.

In the absence of exclusive rights governing the use of the fishing ground, not only will the intensity of its use be affected, but also the costs of policing (enforcing) the income generated by other private investment inputs will be higher. Higher policing costs will affect decisions pertaining to planting and financial maturity. For example: if the right to the use of land is non-exclusive, the cost of policing *private* fertilizers applied to land for the production of corn will be higher than if the land use is exclusive and is subject to contractual stipulation and enforcement. That is, if private landownership obtained, the owner could enter a contract with labor and fertilizer owners, and restrict non-participants from interfering in any undesirable way. The right to contract is also the *right to exclude*. The same applies to the non-exclusive fishing ground, despite the different physical attributes of fish and corn. Some implications are:

(1) The choice of product will be constrained by the higher costs of guarding private investment inputs, generated by the non-exclusive use of the resource. This implies that a product, the physical attributes of which entail relatively low costs of policing private investment inputs, will be preferred by the users of the non-exclusive resource. In Tripolitania, for example, potentially lucrative almond trees are reported to have been forsaken for cattle raising owing to the "common ownership" of land.[8] This can be explained by the fact that the cost of policing investment in a tree, perenially "attached" to the common land, is high, whereas cattle are driven home at night. The change in product as described results in a different composition of investment inputs; but the total value of investment may rise or fall. Furthermore, the collectable rent—a residual under non-exclusive landownership—will decline even before its dissipation under competition, owing to the choice of a product differing from that chosen to maximize rent under private property.

Does the lack of exclusivity in the fishing ground significantly affect the choice of product in marine fisheries? One impression is that it does not, since the fishing ground appears to be amenable to concurrent uses, or the existing types of marine product might be the most valuable choices. Still, there may be too many of some fish and too few of another, or the product choice in aquaculture may be affected.[9] The issue is an empirical one.

(2) Given the product, some types of investment input will predictably decline when a private fishing ground becomes non-exclusive. For example, privately owned paddy-field fisheries will receive more intensive feeding than if the same fish were placed in a common lake.[10] The phenomenon is again due to the higher cost of policing private feeding inputs, on account of the non-exclusive use of the common lake. In marine fisheries, the rate of return to this type of investment appears negligible, hence unimportant. But the same may not be true for all marine products.

(3) The physical attributes of marine fisheries, together with policing costs, also affect the value at maturity (size of catch) of the growing asset. Should the fishing ground be exclusively owned and its products costlessly enforced as private, the financial maturity of fisheries and the implied rate of rotation (that is, the mesh size) would be so chosen as to

maximize wealth.[11]   Similarly, the time shape of the income stream of harvesting will differ from that of maximizing wealth under non-exclusive rights.[12]   These factors, while significant in marine fisheries, do not appear so for cattle raising in common pastures, since the cost of policing cattle is lower.   That is, the cost of policing privately raised fish in a "common" ocean is higher than that of raising cattle in common pastures.

The several changes in decisions pertaining to planting and financial maturity discussed above are only some of the more prominent effects of the absence of exclusive rights in one of the factors of production.   While an exhaustive list is not attempted here, our discussion shows that since a contract embodies a structure, the absence of the right to contract, as with a non-exclusive resource, will affect resource allocation in a variety of ways.   And since production decisions are usually several, so are the marginal equalities affected: the marginal mesh size, marginal feeding inputs, marginal product choice, and so forth.   According to the current practice, these decision aspects affected by the absence of a contract are treated as different types of externalities.

While, in section III, I shall support the existing conclusion of the dissipation of rent under the non-exclusive use of a resource, I shall not endorse the traditionally accepted analysis through which this dissipation takes place.   This section has shown that the effects pertaining to planting and financial maturity, if they occur, will in themselves reduce the collectable rent.   And it is not difficult to conceive of a situation in which, by harvest time, there is nothing worthwhile to harvest.   But marine fisheries have better luck.

II.   Harvesting: Private Property Rights and the Margin of Damage

We now turn to analyze the intensity of fishery "harvesting" in two hypothetical worlds, one with private property in all resources and one with a non-exclusive fishing ground.   The harvesting issue is singled out here because the existing theoretical solution has been fundamental in recent economic analysis of marine fisheries and of the "common pool." Furthermore, externality is said to exist in its purest form: the catch of one fisherman depends not only on his own input, but also on the inputs of other competing fishermen.   In this section we discuss the private-property world, and the common pool in the next.   The simple manipulation of the law of diminishing returns serves to demonstrate further the function of contracting and the ambiguity of the concept of externality.

Consider two private factor inputs in fishery production: the fishing ground and fisherman labor (assume that fish grow by themselves and ignore biomass value, hence harvesting is the only consideration). The rent derivable from the fishing ground is thus the integral of the difference between the marginal product of labor and the wage rate. To maximize rent (income) under private ownership,[13] the rate of change of rent with respect to labor is required to be set at zero, implying that the marginal product of labor equals the wage rate.

The above equilibrium condition can be viewed in terms of the gain from adding labor to fishery harvesting and the damage the incremental labor inflicts on the productivity of the existing (intramarginal) labor input. Viewing the marginal gain per infinitesimal unit of labor added as it average product (its contribution) minus the wage rate (its alternative earning), we write

$$\Omega(L) = \frac{Q}{L} - W$$

On the other hand, "external" to the labor being added, the productivity of all existing (intramarginal) labor declines. Algebraically, we write

$$\Phi(L, L') = L \left[\frac{Q(L)}{L} - \frac{Q(L + L')}{L + L'} \right],$$

where the function Φ gives the value of damage caused by the increase in L', with L being the intramarginal labor. Taking the derivative of Φ with respect to L', we obtain

$$\frac{\partial \Phi}{\partial L'} = - \frac{\partial Q(L + L')}{\partial L'} \frac{L}{L + L'} + \frac{Q(L + L')L}{(L + L')^2}$$

The marginal damage $\Lambda(L)$, caused by an infinitesimal increase in labor is thus

$$\frac{\partial \Phi(L, O)}{\partial L'} = - \frac{\partial Q}{\partial L} + \frac{Q}{L} = \Lambda(L)$$

To maximize rent of the fishing ground, the marginal gain of adding labor must equal the associated marginal damage, that is, $\Omega(L) = \Lambda(L)$.

In the above simple model we see that the effects of an action are independent of the system of property rights. To prohibit damage entirely is, insofar as diminishing returns hold (as in our model), to prohibit output entirely. What counts is whether the incremental gain can more than offset the associated damage. And it is one main function of contracting to stipulate the margin of damage that is to be allowed. Private property in the fishing ground grants its owner the right to contract and stipulate. The absence of such a right, as in marine fisheries, will affect the margin of damage.

What, then, is an externality? Does it exist always? If so, why is it treated as a special problem? Does it exist only when the marginal gain from an action is not equal to the marginal damage it causes? If so, should we view an "externality" as becoming less "external" when the inequality diminishes? Does it exist only when the damage is so great that rental income (in our example) is reduced to zero? If so, what is the conceptual difference between a zero rent and a negligibly small rent? In the simple case presented, indeed it is impossible to draw a dividing line such that "externality" can be meaningfully identified. *Every economic action has effects.* Nor is it illuminating to view the damage as external or internal to a firm, for the firm is but a holder of contracts.[14] The same applies to all decisions on resource use. It follows that the classification of various kinds of "externalities," if at all useful, is *ad hoc* theorizing, a cumbersome way to treat a general problem. The problem is general because for every gain there is a cost.

Because the above conclusion appears abrupt, let me retreat for a moment to discuss, by way of illustration, several types of economic effects caused by actions of individual decision units. The first type includes actions which produce trivial effects *and* which are transacted (with contracts) "smoothly" in the market. The traditional term for this appears to be "perfect competition"—with perhaps "constant cost for the industry." Note, however, that the same trivial action may no longer be trivial without contracting (for example, to acquire an apple without payment).

The second type includes effects which are trivial and are not transacted with contracts. Examples for this are to say "sorry" for minor damages done among individuals, or be gentle to the neighbor's dog. Let me refer to this type of behavior as "customs." According to J. S. Mill, when an activity is a customary practice and "not of a varying convention, political economy has no laws of distribution to investigate."[15] While the persuasiveness of Mill may yield peace of mind, subsequent economists have frequently employed "custom" as an excuse to avoid analysis.[16] Even a practice that is truly customary may reflect the existence of costs in contracting. Furthermore, the effect of an action which resolves into a custom under one property right arrangement may be taken as a crime under another.

Third, there are actions which produce significant effects and which are transacted in the market place. Examples given have been cases of rising supply,[17] or of interactions among large and perhaps oligopolistic producers. Such actions have been termed "pecuniary external economies or diseconomies," [18] and do not necessarily entail specifiable economic waste.[19]

Fourth, there are actions which produce significant effects but contractual arrangements are absent—so significant, indeed, that "customs" simply will not bail them out. The classic example is a factory polluting the environment. This type of effect is traditionally termed "technological external economies or diseconomies." [20] Since these effects occur to consumption as well as production activities, in many cases it is difficult to see their "technological" attributes.[21]

Consider finally a fifth type of action, the effects of which may be trivial or significant, and which are governed by contracts. However, for some reasons certain marginal conditions required for the standard constrained maximization are not satisfied. Referring to our earlier exposition of fishery harvesting, such a case would arise if the marginal gain, $\Omega(L)$, from an increment of labor is either greater or smaller than the associated marginal damage, $\Lambda(L)$. The traditional term for this, I think, is "market imperfection."

In the above five paragraphs I have, as perceived in the light of contracting, sketched my impression of the literature relating to externalities. The arbitrariness of the division should be self-evident. What is trivial is at best a matter of degree, and the economic significance of the same actions varies under different circumstances. Similarly, "perfection" or "imperfection" is difficult if not impossible to define. And to call some effects of actions "externalities" and some—"internalities" (?)—is to me incomprehensible.

It would be ambiguous enough if "externalities" were confined to effects that are economically significant but with respect to which the rights of actions are not clearly delineated and thus not transacted in the market place. However, such a classification would have the merit of not doing much harm. But—perhaps prompted by the obvious non-existence of "internalities"—the concept of externality has been extended to virtually all economic activities,[22] with endless divisions of types.[23] And the many associated theories serve only to confuse.

The issue at stake is not merely a semantic one. And I do not propose to refine the concept of "externality." I propose to discard the concept entirely. The change in view through the analysis of contracting is not a redundant way of treating the same class of problems, for this change in view leads to different—and I believe more fruitful—questions. Why do market contracts not exist for certain effects of actions? Because of the absence of exclusive rights, or because transaction costs are prohibitive? Why do exclusive rights not exist for certain actions? Because of the legal institutions, or because policing costs are prohibitive? Why do some conceivably more efficient stipulations not exist in the structure of a contract? And what implications for resource allocation and income distribution can we deduce from all this?

III. Harvesting: The Dissipation of Rent

As we turn now to analyze the intensity of fishery harvesting—with the fishing ground as a non-exclusive resource—we should keep in mind that we refer to only one of several decision aspects affected by the absence of a contract. The puzzle at stake is, I believe, one of the sources of the stream of "externalities." My main concern in this section, however, is to correct an error in the existing solution. Thus the "externality" issue will be put aside until the next section.

Ever since F. H. Knight's exposition [24] of A. C. Pigou's example [25] of good and bad roads, which in a tilted mirror image is seen in H. Scott Gordon's analysis [26] of the common fishing ground, models of fishery harvesting have followed the conclusion that, in equilibrium, the *average* product of fishing effort (or labor) equals the wage rate (or the marginal factor cost).[27] Hence economic waste results, since the marginal product of labor in fishing is lower than of that employed elsewhere. The equalization of the average product of labor to the wage rate leads to the dissipation of rent for the fishing ground tautologically.

Obvious as it appears at first sight, two puzzles remain in the dissipation of rent. First, individual decisions are, by definition, made at the margin: how is it possible that the marginal product of fisherman labor be lower than the wage rate (in the social sense) if *no* fisherman (that is, a decision unit) will apply labor to fishing when its marginal product to *any fisherman* is less than the wage rate? Second, just what does a fisherman maximize if exclusive right to the fishing ground is absent? Failure to answer these questions satisfactorily renders the average-product argument, hence the dissipation of rent, an asserted and not a derived result.[28] In what follows I offer an analysis which answers these questions, and the associated solution yields some implications different from those of the existing analysis.

Before proceeding to the formal analysis, an introductory summary will help. Under private ownership of the fishing ground, the right to the rent (income) is exclusive, and a contractual arrangement will make rent a private cost of fishery production. With non-exclusive fishing rights and without collusion among fishermen, rent becomes a residual, with every decision-making unit—a fisherman or a fishing firm—maximizing the portion left behind by others. Behavior is thus consistent with wealth maximization subject to the wage constraint *and* the absence of contractual constraint on other people's use of the fishing ground. With independent maximization, the marginal product of each fisherman is equal to his wage rate.   In the absence of both legal and contractual restrictions on the use of the fishing ground, a fisherman will enter the industry so long as the residual (that is, earnings in excess of his alternative wage) for him is positive.   With each new entrant, however, the marginal product for all fishermen will fall, and, following the equimarginal rule, each of them will *curtail* their fishing effort (or labor input).   The process is thus analogous to Cournot's duopoly solution *with free entry*, with ocean rent replacing monopoly rent, average product of labor in place of demand for product, and a positive wage rate in place of the assumed zero cost of production.[29]   Assume that fisherman labor is homogeneous and supply to the industry perfectly elastic, the complete dissipation of rent in equilibrium implies that the *number* of individual fishermen (or firms) approaches infinity, with each committing a trifling amount of fishing effort.

*   *   *

[Pages omitted (ed.).]

From the social point of view, the equality of the would-be average product of labor under private exploitation of the fishing ground and the wage rate implies that rent is entirely dissipated, and the corresponding (would-be) marginal product of labor being lower than the wage rate (marginal social opportunity cost) implies economic waste—if all costs associated with defining and policing private property in the fishing ground are ignored.   Note that similar results can be obtained for share contracting between boat owner and fisherman, which is of some interest since we are informed that share contracts between boat owners and fishermen predominate in marine fisheries.[32]

Strange as the above results may seem to be, the analysis is consistent with maximization by the equimarginal rule, at the same time producing a condition that the social average product is equal to the wage rate.   The main feature in which this analysis differs from the traditional average-product argument is in the curtailment of fishing input by one decision unit when the number of competitors increases.   The implication is important: if the number of competing fishermen is reduced or restricted, each fisherman will capture part of the ocean rent even though none has an exclusive right to the fishing ground.

But in the real world the observed number of fishermen is finite.   To explain this we relax some of the hypothetical specifications which I have implicitly or explicitly employed in the analysis.   First, the fishermen are not identical and their supply to the industry is not infinitely elastic. Leaving aside the various meanings of a homogeneous factor, one may point out that not all fishermen are equally productive, and that their alternative earnings are not the same.   In other words, their comparative advantages in fishing are not equal.   Thus, not all decision units will commit the same trifling amounts of inputs. Second, the cost structure of fishery harvesting has been neglected. The costs of entry will reduce the number of fishermen. And the production function is not necessarily linear homogeneous. There is the possibility of economies of scale, in the minimum boat size, gear size, and distance of travel for operation. And third, institutional arrangements designed to restrict entry, such as fisherman and boat unions and legal regulations, will impose constraints on competition.

So finite they are. Still, the implications of the model remain. The following are worth noting. First, other things being equal, the total outlay per decision unit will be lower with non-exclusive rights over the fishing ground than if it were private property. This may be observed in boat sizes being voluntarily kept small, and the number of days per year engaged in fishing few. Conversely, an effective restriction on entry will result in an increase in outlay per decision unit.

Second, there exist incentives to fishermen to restrict the *number* of decision units who have access to the fishing right. That is, even if each decision unit is free to commit the amount of fishing effort, the "rent" captured by each will be larger the smaller the number of decision units. Could that explain the prevalence of boat and fisherman unions in marine fisheries? An interesting case for further study is the recent issuance of licenses to fishing boats in British Columbia. Implied by our model is that such a license, if transferable, will yield a market price representing the present value of the ocean rent to be captured.

A third implication is more complex. Consider three alternative arrangements. The first arrangement is a group of individuals forming a tribe, a clan or a union so as to exclude "outsiders" from competing for the use of a non-exclusive resource. In this arrangement each "insider" is free to use the resource as he pleases and derive income therefrom. According to our analysis, the fewer the insiders, the greater will be the "rent" captured by each. On the other hand, the cost of exclusion (for example, bloodshed) for each insider is a rising function of the number of outsiders excluded. In equilibrium, the number of insiders is determined when the gains and costs of excluding outsiders are equal at the margin.

The second arrangement involves not only the exclusion of outsiders, but, as in some cooperatives, there is central regulation of the amounts of work and income for the insiders. The third arrangement is private property rights governing all resources, where the property rights are exclusively delineated and enforced, and where resource use is guided by contracting in the marketplace.

All three arrangements are costly. While it appears that these costs are lowest for the first type and highest for the third, the gains from each arrangement are in a reverse order. Weighing these gains and costs, the choice of property right arrangements becomes predictable. Thus the analysis points to the possibility of a theory of property right formation. Such a theory, however, is not intended here.

IV.   The Nature of the Problem

In this concluding section, I discuss generally the nature of the problem in light of the suggested contractual approach. The economic problem of marine fisheries is not unique, although the physical attributes of the fish and the legal arrangements for that industry yield certain characteristic features.

If an idea must have an origin, then the growth of the concept of "externality" can be traced back to Pigou's analysis of the divergences between social and private net product,[33] although Pigou did not use either the term "externality" or a similar term. At a time when "economic efficiency" began to be understood in terms of the fulfillment of some marginal equalities, it was natural as well as important to think of situations under which certain marginal equalities may not hold. In imagination Pigou excelled. However, he had weaknesses.

One of Pigou's weaknesses, shown in his discussion of social and private net product, is that he took assertions of fact for granted, accepting claims of deficient contractual arrangements without demanding evidence.[34] The manifestation of this is that, years later, when someone came up with the example of an apple orchard and honey production, it was universally accepted as a clear case of resource misallocation requiring government intervention. No one, however, has ever investigated the actual contractual arrangements between the apple grower and the beekeeper, or even suggested that a contract might exist.[35]

Another weakness in Pigou's analysis is the lack of any thorough attempt to generalize the various kinds of possible "divergence." Pigou seems to say that each kind differs from the others, but with no convincing reason as to why they differ.[36] The ambiguity has since remained a tradition in the "externality" literature, and the nature of the problem remained obscure. Indeed, one wonders what the state of the art would be had Pigou taken advantage of Knight's exposition on "Some Fallacies in the Interpretation of Social Cost." [37] published in 1924, in the subsequent revisions of his book. Commenting on Pigou's example of good and bad roads, where "excessive" use of the good road is said to result in a lower marginal value for the users, Knight wrote:

> The [conclusion] does in fact indicate what would happen *if no one owned the superior* [road]. But under private appropriation and self-seeking exploitation of the [roads] the course of events is very different. It is in fact the social function of ownership to prevent this excessive [use of

the superior road]. Professor Pigou's logic in regard to the roads is, as logic, quite unexceptionable. Its weakness is one frequently met with in economic theorizing, namely, that the assumptions diverge in essential respects from the facts of real economic situations. . . . If the roads are assumed to be subject to private appropriation and exploitation, precisely the ideal situation which would be established by the imaginary tax will be brought about through the operation of ordinary economic motives.[38]

The associated analysis is not flawless,[39] but the argument is sound. There was an interval of several years in which Pigou could have revised his analysis on social and private product,[40] by incorporating Knight's "social function of ownership" to his various cases of "divergences." However, Pigou did not do so.

Some thirty years later,[41] R. H. Coase published "The Problem of Social Cost." [42] Although the contribution of this paper is justly well known, the reader may find the following statement of Coase's thesis unfamiliar. Commenting on Pigou, Coase wrote:

> Pigou seems to make a distinction between the case in which no contract is possible (the second class) and that in which the contract is unsatisfactory (the first class). . . . But the reason why some activities are not the subject of contracts is exactly the same as the reason why some contracts are commonly unsatisfactory—it would cost too much to put the matter right. Indeed, the two cases are really the same since the contracts are unsatisfactory because they do not cover certain activities.[43]

The *problem* of social cost, therefore, arises either in the absence of exclusive rights (hence the absence of the right to contract), or where the right to contract exists "but where contracts are peculiarly difficult to draw up and an attempt to describe what the parties have agreed to do or not to do . . . would necessitate a lengthy and highly involved document. . . ." [44] It is, therefore, strange that recent discussions of externality are almost invariably associated with Coase's work.[45]

Let us discuss the problem further. The transfer of property rights among individual owners through contracting in the marketplace requires that the rights be exclusive. An exclusive property right grants its owner a *limited* authority to make decision on resource use so as to derive income therefrom. To define this limit requires measurement and enforcement. Any property is multi-dimensional, and exclusivity is frequently a matter of degree. But without some enforced or policed exclusivity to a right of action, the right to contract so as to exchange is absent.

The absence of exclusivity in property may be due to the absence of recognition by legal institutions of that exclusivity, or to the costs of delineating and policing the limit of the right being prohibitively high. The general issue is thus whether contractual arrangements and exclusive rights exist so that gains and costs of actions are weighed in the market; if not, whether alternative legal arrangements or government regulations are economically desirable.

The costs associated with the formation of property and of the subsequent contracts may be viewed in two stages. At one stage, without exchange, there are costs of defining and policing exclusivity. These costs vary, among other things, according to the physical attributes of the resource in question. In our example of marine fisheries, the difficulty of assessing, quantifying, identifying and policing private fishing rights is evident. Even the branding of cattle is costly. At this stage also, these costs also depend on the size of holding: it may cost less per unit of holding if the entire fishing ground is owned by one individual, or a group of individuals through the issuance of stock; [46] it may cost more per unit of holding if all the land in the world is owned by one man. If the individual is left to make the decision, then the degree of exclusivity and the size of holding chosen, among other things, will be such that the marginal cost of enforcing exclusivity equals the associated marginal gain.

At a second stage, there are costs associated with negotiating and enforcing contracts for the exchange or transfer of property rights. At least two reasons may be offered for the difficulty of separating the costs of this second stage from the first. One reason is that the income derivable from an exclusive right, or the *gain* of enforcing it, depends on the existence of transferability in the marketplace, for without transfer the highest-valued option may not be realized. This implies that the lower the costs of contracting for transfer, the higher will be the gain of enforcing exclusivity. A second reason is that the *cost* of enforcing exclusivity also depends on the existence of transfer and its associated costs. The preferred size of resource holding so as to lower policing cost, for example, can be chosen insofar as the market exchange permits. For these reasons it is convenient, although somewhat arbitrary, to lump the costs at the two stages into one broad term, namely, transaction costs. As in the case of joint products, only *marginal* costs are relevant.

In modern societies, private property rights require the recognition and enforcement of law. There are reasons to believe that the existence of government lowers transaction costs. But history has repeatedly demonstrated that market response is much quicker than legal response to changing economic conditions.[47] What was not worthwhile to enforce as private yesterday may be so today: changes in supply and demand conditions, technological innovations and improved methods of organization may lower the transaction costs.[48]

In the case of marine fisheries, it is an empirical question whether the enforcement of private property is economically worthwhile. International conflicts of interest make the problem almost unmanageable. Still, economic theory predicts that since non-migratory marine products cost less to police, private property will be instituted earlier in these than in migratory products. Such has been the case with oyster beds, which in some states in America are recognized and enforced as private by law. Could the lag in government response alone account for the absence of property rights over the oyster beds in the remaining states, and similarly in other non-migratory and aquacultural products?

Finally, let us consider the issue of resource allocation channeled through the market versus government regulations. For any imaginary divergence between private and social costs, there exists an imaginary market contract through which the divergence will be eliminated. As emphasized in Section I, a contract entails a structure of stipulations. It follows that in many cases a single regulation, such as an imaginary tax, will not serve the same function as a contract.[49] To replace an imaginary contract, an imaginary *set* of regulations is required. Of course, some imaginary contracts—imaginable while ignoring transaction costs and information problems—are farflung and may have no resemblance in the real world.[50] But so are many "ideal" government regulations.

To evaluate economic efficiency by comparing imaginary contracts and regulations is futile, for in so doing any divergence between private and social costs is simply imagined away. Nor is it fruitful to compare the "imaginary" and the "actual," for Demsetz would rightly charge the "grass is greener" fallacy.[51] It is the "actual" compared with the "actual" that is relevant. The question is whether, given the same effects of an action, actual market contracts or realizable government regulations involve lower transaction costs so that a higher net gain or a lower net loss will result. And while facts and measurements are hard to come by, they still require theoretical interpretation.

The effectiveness of the market in weighing the gains and costs of some action is evident. The existence of a great variety of contracts in free markets suggests what an unmanageable situation it would be if all contractual stipulations were replaced by government regulations.[52] Elsewhere I wrote:

> For any resource, a number of individuals compete for ownership. Each potential buyer or user possesses some knowledge not only of alternative uses of the resource, but also of different transaction costs associated with different [contractual] arrangements by which the resource may enter into production. Assume away information problems that may exist in competitive trading in the marketplace; the resource will find that owner whose use of the resource yields the highest value. *Competition* for and *transferability* of the ownership right in the marketplace thus perform two main functions for contracting. First, competition conglomerates knowledge from all potential owners—the knowledge of alternative contractual arrangements and uses of the resource; and transfer-

ability of property rights ensures that the most valuable knowledge will be utilized.   Second, competition among potential contract participants and a resource owner's ability to transfer the right to use his resource reduce the cost of enforcing the stipulated terms in a contract.   This is because competing parties will stand by to offer or accept similar terms. In sum, competition *in the marketplace* reduces the costs of finding and pursuing the most valuable option in which a resource may be contracted for production.   While transaction cost determines, it is also determined.[53]

But the above quotation ignores the possibility that transaction costs may be so high as to result in the absence of exclusive rights and of contracting among individuals.   Gains and costs of an action are thus not weighed in the market.   Is it likely, then, that government action or regulation will actually be more efficient?   The question is difficult, and no answer to it will be attempted here.[54]

Let me conclude.   In light of the analysis of contracting, this section has discussed the problem of the divergence of private and social costs. Externality, on the other hand, seems to center on different cases of "divergence" and to ignore the economic problem involved.   The concept of "externality" is vague because every economic action has effects;   it is confusing because classifications and theories are varied, arbitrary, and *ad hoc*.   For these reasons, theories generated by the concept of "externality" are not likely to be useful.

FOOTNOTES

* This paper is an expanded version of my Contractual Arrangements and Resource Allocation in Marine Fisheries, which was prepared for the Proceedings of the H. R. MacMillan Symposium on the Economics of Fishing, held at the University of British Columbia, Vancouver, April, 1969.   The first two drafts were written at the University of Chicago.   Thanks for financial support are given to the Ford Foundation grant for International Studies at the University of Chicago, and to the Institute of Economic Research at the University of Washington.

The thesis of this paper was germinated by a set of equations which yield the traditionally accepted conclusions of the "common pool," but in which the constraint prescribed for the Langrangian expression has no economic content.   Turning to a more elementary analysis, I was surprised at my inability to define meaningfully "externality" for what I believed to be the simplest case.   A subsequent review of the literature left me deeper in doubt.

To raise a noticeable voice amidst a commotion requires the support of other voices of the same tone.   And I definitely would have given up shouting except for R. H. Coase's advice and encouragement at every turn.   I am also grateful to friends who either cheered for me from the side line, or commented on one draft or another.   They include David Anglin, Armen A. Alchian, Yoram Barzel, Zvi Griliches, D. Gale Johnson, Harry G. Johnson, Patricia Kuttner, John McGee, John McManus, Theodore W. Schultz, Anthony D. Scott, Vernon L. Smith, and George J. Stigler.   While ideas are not exclusive, errors are exclusively mine.

[1] For a fairly comprehensive count, see E. J. Mishan, Reflections on Recent Developments in the Concept of External Effects, 31 Can.J.Econ. & Pol.Sci. 3 (1965). Note, however, that the number of "externalities" has increased rapidly in the subsequent four years.

[2] See, for example, Ralph Turvey, Optimization and Suboptimization in Fishery Regulation, 54 Amer.Econ.Rev. No. 2., Pt. 1, at 64 (1964); and Vernon L. Smith, On Models of Commercial Fishing, 77 J.Pol.Econ. 181 (1969).

[3] What resource in marine fisheries is non-exclusive—the ocean bed, the water, or the fish? The answer is that any productive resource is multi-dimensional, and the term "fishing ground" is chosen to include all of them. This term is used synonymously with "fishery resource" or "fishing rights" in this paper.

[4] If only outright transfers exist for all resources, then only owner production will exist, and contractual stipulations on resource use will be absent. Partial transfers, such as leasing and hiring, are emphasized here because (1) they lead more directly to the problems involved and (2) they serve to illustrate more clearly the function of a contract.

[5] Steven N. S. Cheung, Transaction Costs, Risk Aversion, and the Choice of Contractual Arrangements, 12 J.Law & Econ. 23 (1969).

[6] See R. H. Coase, The Problem of Social Cost, 3 J.Law & Econ. 1 (1960); George J. Stigler, The Economics of Information, 69 J.Pol.Econ. 213 (1961); and Harold Demsetz, The Exchange and Enforcement of Property Rights, 7 J.Law & Econ. 11 (1964).

[7] The literature is immense. See, Francis T. Christy, Jr. & Anthony Scott, The Common Wealth in Ocean Fisheries (1965); James Crutchfield & Arnold Zellner, Economic Aspects of the Pacific Halibut Fishery, Fishery Industrial Research, no. 1 (April, 1962); Expert Meeting on the Economic Effects of Fishery Regulations, Ottawa, 1961, Economic Effects of Fishery Regulation (R. Hamliseh ed., 1962); Myres S. McDougal & William T. Burke, The Pubic Order of the Oceans (1962); Sol Sinclair, License Limitation-British Columbia: A Method of Economic Fisheries Management (Can. Dep't of Fisheries, 1960); and Int'l Technical Conf. on the Conservation of the Living Resources of the Sea, The Economics of Fisheries (Ralph Turvey & Jack Wiseman eds., 1956). Rules imposed by boat and fisherman unions can best be obtained from the unions themselves.

[8] See Anthony Bottomley, The Effect of Common Ownership of Land upon Resource Allocation in Tripolitania, 39 Land Econ. 91 (1963).

[9] See Anthony Scott, Economic Obstacles to Marine Development, (manuscript prepared for Conf. on Marine Aquaculture, Ore. St. Univ., May 1968).

[10] But investment of this type may not be reduced to zero. While no definitive solution for this is offered here, let me suggest an approach to the problem. Assume that the cost of policing private investment is so high as to be prohibitive. Let p be the marginal rate of return on investment and r be the rate of interest. If the return to investment is non-exclusive, then given n identical people, an individual will invest if $p/n \geqslant r$. It is, of course, possible that investment of this type be reduced to zero even if n is quite small. However, the number of individuals should be treated as a variable partly dependent on p.

[11] Although the "tree-cutting" problem is well known, I refer here to an early solution by Martin Faustmann (1849), which is resurrected in M. Mason Gaffney, Concepts of Financial Maturity of Timber and Other Assets (A. E. Information Series No. 62, mimeographed at N. Carolina St. Coll., 1960).

[12] The best exposition of "time shape" and wealth maximization is still found in Irving Fisher, The Theory of Interest, ch. 5 & 6 (1961).

13 Throughout this paper, the word "rent" is used synonymously with "income", the flow of returns to any private resource right. For constrained maximization, it is viewed as an annuity.

14 I believe this accords with R. H. Coase, The Nature of the Firm, 4 Economica 386 (n.s. 1937), reprinted in Readings in Price Theory (George J. Stigler & Kenneth Boulding, eds., 1952). Not every holder of contracts is a firm. The associated complexity is not yet relevant here.

15 John Stuart Mill, Principles of Political Economy 364 (4th ed., 1857). Mill was commenting on the terms of a share contract.

16 Some asserted "customs" are, in fact, market practices in which the contractual terms are not obvious. See, Steven N. S. Cheung, The Theory of Share Tenancy, ch. 3 & 4 (1969).

17 See Jacob Viner, Cost Curves and Supply Curves, in Zeitschrift fur Nationalokonomie (1931), reprinted in Readings in Price Theory, supra note 14; Joan Robinson, Rising Supply Price, 8 Economica 1 (1941), reprinted in id.; and Howard S. Ellis & William Fellner, External Economies and Diseconomies, 33 Amer.Econ.Rev. 493 (1943), reprinted in id.

18 See Jacob Viner, supra note 17; and Tibor Scitovsky, Two Concepts of External Economies, 62 J.Pol.Econ. 143 (1954).

19 The best exposition on this point appears to be Roland N. McKean, Efficiency in Government Through Systems Analysis 134–150 (1958).

20 See Jacob Viner, supra note 17; and Tibor Scitovsky, supra note 17.

21 Francis M. Bator has a somewhat different classification. See his The Anatomy of Market Failure, 72 Q.J.Econ. 351 (1958). Bator's classification would be incomplete if compared with the present count of externalities.

22 See, for example, James M. Buchanan & W. Craig Stubblebine, Externality, 29 Economica 371 (n.s. 1962). See also E. J. Mishan, supra note 1.

23 Vernon L. Smith, supra note 2, for example, has classified mesh externalities, stock externalities, and crowding externalities for fisheries alone. Classification according to physical attributes can be traced back to J. E. Meade's "creation of atmosphere." See J. E. Meade, External Economies and Diseconomies in a Competitive Situation, 62 Econ. J. 54 (1952). The frequency of new classifications in recent doctoral dissertations is striking. See, for example, Lawrence Schall, Technological Externalities and Resource Allocation, (unpublished doctoral thesis, University of Chicago, 1969).

24 Frank H. Knight, Some Fallacies in the Interpretation of Social Cost, Q.J.Econ. (1924), reprinted in Readings on Price Theory, supra note 14.

25 A. C. Pigou, The Economics of Welfare 194 (1920).

26 H. Scott Gordon, The Economic Theory of a Common Property Resource: The Fishery, 62 J.Pol.Econ. 124 (1954).

27 See, for example, Anthony Scott, The Fishery: The Objectives of Sole Ownership, 63 J.Pol.Econ. 116 (1955); Anthony Scott, Optimal Utilization and the Control of Fisheries, in The Economics of Fisheries, supra note 7; and James A. Crutchfield, Common Property Resources and Factor Allocation, 22 Can.J.Econ. & Pol.Sci. 292 (1956).

28 In Gordon's exposition, supra note 27, fishing grounds with different fertility are explicit. I find his analysis of the dissipation of rent unclear, particularly if only one homogeneous fishing ground exists.

29 Criticisms of Cournot's duopoly solution, however, are not applicable here because we are concerned with a large number of entrants, and, by the nature of a non-exclusive resource, collusion of any kind among firms does not exist. For two criticisms of Cournot's duopoly solution, see George J. Stigler, The Organization of Industry 36–37 (1968).

[32] See H. Zoeteweij, Fisherman's Remuneration, in The Economics of Fisheries, supra note 7.

[33] A. C. Pigou, The Economics of Welfare, Pt. 2, ch. 9 (4th ed., 1932).

[34] This charge is based on my checking of all the references cited in A. C. Pigou, supra note 33, at 174, 175, 178, 181 and 182, where deficient lease contracts in agriculture are said to be evident.

[35] However, Harold Demsetz, supra note 6, at 15, wrote: "Coase would probably point out, it is possible for beekeepers and apple growers to strike a bargain over how many trees are to be planted." Another alternative, of course, is that the apple growers keep the bees themselves, or purchase the beekeepers' resource ownerships outright. A similar neglect of contractual arrangements is found in the literature of economic development, where technological externalities are frequently said to exist for the training of workers in poor countries. "Undertraining" is alleged on ground that future returns are not capturable by the trainers. However, even casual conversation with teenage apprentices in Southeast Asia reveals the existence of complex training contracts.

[36] Although Pigou frequently referred to "kinds" or "classes" or divergences of social and private products, I have been unable to count them separately, or even to determine where one discussion begins and where it ends.

[37] Frank H. Knight, supra note 25.

[38] Frank H. Knight, supra note 25, at 163–64.

[39] See supra, sect. III. Also, Knight should be more specific on the kind of investment he has in mind when he speaks of "excessive investment in superior situations", supra note 25, at 163. A comment on the "imaginary tax" will come later.

[40] After 1924, The Economics of Welfare was revised in 1928 and in 1931. It is, of course, possible that Pigou never knew of Knight's article.

[41] The term "external economies or diseconomies" began, perhaps, with Marshall, and it was used frequently in the 1930's and early 1940's for the derivation of cost and supply curves. The works of both Marshall and Pigou were influential. (See Readings in Price Theory, supra note 14, at Pt. 2.) In the 1950's, however, "external" effects became popular in the literature of economic development. In fact, it was the main issue of the debate of balanced versus unbalanced growth and of investment criteria. The general theme is that, in order to achieve rapid economic growth, certain external effects should be maximized. The associated literature is immense. "Externalities" constitute a new trend in the 1960's.

[42] See supra note 6. Also important is Coase's earlier work, The Federal Communications Commission, 2 J.Law & Econ. 1 (1959).

[43] R. H. Coase, supra note 6, at 38–39.

[44] Id. at 16.

[45] See, for a few examples, James M. Buchanan, Politics, Policy and the Pigovian Margins, 29 Economica 17 (n.s. 1962); J. M. Buchanan & W. Craig Stubblebine, supra note 22; Stanislaw Wellisz, On External Diseconomies and the Government Assisted Invisible Hand, 31 Economica 345 (n.s. 1964); E. J. Mishan, supra note 1; Charles R. Plott, Externalities and Corrective Taxes, 33 Economica 84 (p.s. 1966).

[46] Note that monopoly in the fishery market is not necessarily implied. There may still exist a large number of fishing firms, potentially or actually, renting the fishing rights.

[47] The Japanese experience is notable. See Yasoburo Takekoshi, The Economic Aspects of the History of the Civilization of Japan (3 vol., 1967). Note, in particular, the duration of various land systems before and after the Taika reforms (chs. 4, 5 and 10), and that decades had passed before Meiji (1868) legally recognized some "grey" market activities existing in Tokugawa agriculture (chs. 81, 82 and 83).

48 See, as a case in point, Douglass North, Sources of Productivity Change in Ocean Shipping 1600–1850, 76 J.Pol.Econ. 953 (1968).

49 That an imaginary tax may not fully correct an imaginary divergence between private and social costs is seen in Charles R. Plott, supra note 45; and Otto A. Davis & Andrew Whinston, Externalities, Welfare, and the Theory of Games, 70 J.Pol.Econ. 241 (1962).

50 An imaginary contract for the "ideal" pricing of a "public" good—or a good amenable to concurrent consumption—would fall into this category. Needless to say, public goods have given rise to still another type of externality. See, for example, James M. Buchanan, Joint Supply, Externality and Optimality, 33 Economica 404 (1966).

51 See Harold Demsetz, Information and Efficiency: Another Viewpoint, 12 J.Law & Econ. 1 (1969).

52 A striking case is the experience of the People's Republic of China. On the one hand, the important role of contracts similar to those developed in the market was recognized; on the other hand, the property right constraints and regulations were at odds with market contracts. The result was the existence of a variety of contracts supervised by the government, involving great complexities and inconsistencies. See the informative Chung Hwa Jen Min Kung Ho Kuo Min Fa Chi Pen Wen Ti (A Textbook of Civil Law of the People's Republic of China, in Chinese, 1958). See also Richard M. Pfeffer, The Institution of Contracts in the Chinese People's Republic, 14, 15 China Q. 153, 115 (April-June, 1963; July-September, 1963); Contracts in China Revisited, With a Focus on Agriculture, 1949–63, 28 China Q. 106 (Oct.-Dec., 1966); and Gene T. Hsiao, The Role of Economic Contracts in Communist China, 56 Calif.L.Rev. (1965).

53 Steven N. S. Cheung, supra note 16, at 64.

54 But see R. H. Coase, supra note 6, at 19–28.

Continued

26: THE FABLE OF THE BEES: AN ECONOMIC INVESTIGATION*

STEVEN N. S. CHEUNG
University of Washington

Economists possess their full share of the common ability to invent and commit errors. . . . Perhaps their most common error is to believe other economists.

George J. Stigler

Ever since A. C. Pigou wrote his books on "welfare," [1] a divergence between private and social costs has provided the main argument for instituting government action to correct allegedly inefficient market activities. The analysis in such cases has been designed less to aid our understanding of how the economic system operates than to find flaws in it to justify policy recommendations. Both to illustrate the argument and to demonstrate the nature of the actual situation, the quest has been for real-world examples of such defects.

Surprisingly enough, aside from Pigou's polluting factory and Sidgwick's lighthouse, convincing examples were hard to come by.[2] It was not until 1952, more than thirty years after Pigou's initial analysis, that J. E. Meade proposed further examples and revitalized the argument for corrective government actions.[3] Meade's prime example, which soon became classic, concerned the case of the apple farmer and the beekeeper. In his own words:

Suppose that in a given region there is a certain amount of apple-growing and a certain amount of bee-keeping and that the bees feed on the apple blossom. If the apple-farmers apply 10% more labour, land and capital to apple-farming they will increase the output of apples by 10%; but they will also provide more food for the bees. On the other hand, the bee-keepers will not increase the output of honey by 10% by increasing the amount of

Journal of Law & Econ., Vol. 16, 1973, p. 11.

land, labour and capital to bee-keeping by 10% unless at the same time the
apple-farmers also increase their output and so the food of the bees by
10%. . . . We call this a case of an unpaid factor, because the
situation is due simply and solely to the fact that the apple-farmer cannot
charge the bee-keeper for the bees' food. . . .[4]

And Meade applied a similar argument to a reciprocal situation:

While the apples may provide the food of the bees, the bees may fertilize
the apples. . . . By a process similar to that adopted in the previous
case we can obtain formulae to show what subsidies and taxes must be
imposed. . . .[5]

In another well-known work, Francis M. Bator used Meade's example to
infer "market failure":

It is easy to show that if apple blossoms have a positive effect on honey
production . . . any Pareto-efficient solution . . . will associate
with apple blossoms a positive Lagrangean shadow-price. If, then, apple
producers are unable to protect their equity in apple-nectar and markets
do not impute to apple blossoms their correct shadow value, profit-maximizing decisions will fail correctly to allocate resources . . . at the
margin. There will be failure "by enforcement." This is what I would
call an *ownership* externality.[6]

It is easy to understand why the "apples and bees" example has enjoyed widespread popularity. It has freshness and charm: the pastoral
scene, with its elfin image of bees collecting nectar from apple blossoms,
has captured the imagination of economists and students alike. However,
the universal credence given to the lighthearted fable is surprising; for in
the United States, at least, contractual arrangements between farmers and
beekeepers have long been routine. This paper investigates the pricing
and contractual arrangements of the beekeeping industry in the state of
Washington, the location having been selected because the Pacific Northwest is one of the largest apple-growing areas in the world.

Contrary to what most of us have thought, apple blossoms yield little
or no honey.[7] But it is true that bees provide valuable pollination services
for apples and other plants, and that many other plants do yield lucrative
honey crops. In any event, it will be shown that the observed pricing and
contractual arrangements governing nectar and pollination services are
consistent with efficient allocation of resources.

I.   Some Relevant Facts of Beekeeping

Although various types of bees pollinate plants, beekeeping is confined
almost exclusively to honeybees.[8] The hive used by beekeepers in the state

of Washington is of the Langstroth design which consists of one or two brood chambers, a queen excluder, and from zero to six supers. A brood chamber is a wooden box large enough to contain eight or ten movable frames, each measuring $9\frac{1}{8}$ by $17\frac{5}{8}$ by $1\frac{3}{8}$ inches. Within each frame is a wax honeycomb built by the bees. In the hexagonal cells of this comb the queen lays her eggs and the young bees, or "brood," are raised. It is here also that the bees store the nectar and pollen which they use for food. Honey is not usually extracted from this chamber but from the frames of a shallower box, called a super, placed above the brood chamber. The queen excluder, placed between the super and the brood chamber, prevents the laying of eggs in the upper section.[9]

The bees, and consequently the beekeepers, work according to a yearly cycle. Around the beginning of March, a Washington beekeeper will decide whether he wants to prepare for the pollination season by ordering booster packages of bees from California to strengthen his colonies, depleted and weakened during the winter and early spring. Alternatively, he may decide to build up the colony by transporting the hives to farms or pastures in warmer areas, such as Oregon and California. The colony hatches continuously from spring to fall, and the growth rate is rapid. Reared on pollen, the infant bees remain in the brood stage for about three weeks before entering the productive life of the colony for five or six weeks. Active workers spend three weeks cleaning and repairing the brood cells and nursing the young, then live out the remainder of their short lives foraging for pollen and nectar.[10]

Because of the bees' quick growth, the working "strength" of a colony includes both brood and workers, and increases from about five frames in early spring to about twelve by late summer. Spring is the primary season for fruit pollination, and beekeepers usually market a standard colony strength of roughly four frames of bees and two to three frames of brood for pollination services. But since empty frames are needed to accommodate the expanding colony, two-story hives, with 16 or 20 frames, are used. The swarming period, beginning in mid-summer and lasting until early fall, is the peak honey season, and the yield per hive will vary positively with the colony strength. Because the maximization of honey yield requires that the colonies be of equal strength, they are usually reassorted in preparation for the major honey season, so that the number of colonies at the "peak" is generally larger than the number in spring.[11]

When pollen fails in late fall, the hives become broodless and the bee population begins to decline. During the idle winter months adult bees live considerably longer than in the active season, and they can survive the winter if about 60 pounds of nectar are left in the hive. But in the northern part of the state and in Canada, where cold weather makes the overwintering of bees more costly, the common practice is to eliminate the bees and extract the remaining honey. It should be noted here that bees can be captured, and that they can be easily eliminated by any of a large number of pesticide sprays.[12] The cost of enforcing property rights in nectar is therefore much lower than economists have been led to believe.

Few agricultural crops, to my knowledge, exhibit a higher year-to-year variance of yield than does the honey crop. Several natural factors contribute. Cold weather and rain discourage the bees from working, and winds alter their direction of flight. Also, the nectar flows of plants are susceptible to shocks of heat and cold.[13] The plants yielding most honey are mint, fireweed, and the legumes, such as alfalfa and the clovers. Fruit trees usually have low nectar flows, although orange blossoms (in California) are excellent. Indeed, the pollination of fruits, especially the cherry in early spring, may actually detract from the yield of honey: less honey may be in the hive after pollination than was there initially, owing to the bees' own consumption. Another reason for the low honey yield from fruit trees is the relatively short time that the hives are left in the orchards.

Cross-pollination is accidentally effected as the bees forage for nectar and pollen. Pollination services were not marketed before World War I, primarily because small firms had enough flowering plants and trees to attract wild insects. It was not until 1910 and the advent of modern orcharding, with its large acreage and orderly planting, that markets for pollination services began to grow rapidly.[14] Today, the services are demanded not only for production of fruits but also for the setting (fertilizing) of seeds for legumes and vegetables. Evidence is incontrovertible that the setting of fruits and seeds increases with the number of hives per acre, that the pollination productivity of bees is subject to diminishing returns, and, despite some beekeepers' claims to the contrary, beyond some point the marginal productivity may even be negative.[15] There is also strong evidence that pollination yield will improve if the hives are placed strategically throughout the farm rather than set in one spot.[16] The closer a particular area is to a hive, the more effective will be the pollination within that area. Although each individual bee will forage only a few square yards, the bees from one hive will collectively pollinate a large circular area,[17] and this gives rise to a problem: given a high cost to control fully the foraging behavior of bees, if similar orchards are located close to one another, one who hires bees to pollinate his own orchard will in some degree benefit his neighbors. This complication will be further discussed in the next section.

In the state of Washington, about 60 beekeepers each own 100 colonies or more; at the peak season the state's grand total of colonies is about 90,000. My investigation, conducted in the spring of 1972, covered a sample of nine beekeepers and a total of approximately 10,000 spring colonies. (One of these beekeepers specialized in cut-comb honey and he will be treated separately in a footnote.) Table 1 lists the bee-related plants covered by my investigation. As seen from Columns (3) and (4), some plants (such as cherry trees) require pollination services for fruit setting but yield no honey; some (such as mint) yield honey while requiring no pollination service; and some (such as alfalfa) are of a reciprocal nature. Note that when alfalfa and the clovers are grown only for hay, pollination services are not required, although these plants yield honey.

The practice of relocating hives from farm to farm, by truck, enables the beekeeper to obtain multiple crops a year, either in rendering pollination service or in extracting honey. However, while the maximum observed number of crops per hive per year is four and the minimum is two, my estimate is that a hive averages only 2.2 crops a year. More frequent rotation not only involves greater costs of moving and of standardizing hives, but abbreviates the honey yield per crop. In the southern part of the state, where the relatively warm climate permits an early working season, beekeepers usually begin by pollinating either cherry or almond (in California) in early spring. The hives may or may not then be moved northward in late spring, when apple and soft fruits (and some late cherry) begin to bloom.[18]

The lease period for effective pollination during spring bloom is no more than a week. But then, for a month or two between the end of fruit pollination and the beginning of summer nectar flow, the hives have little alternative usage. Since this period is substantially longer than the time needed for the beekeeper to check and standardize his hives for the honey crops, he will generally be in no hurry to move them and will prefer to leave them in the orchards with no extra charge, unless the farmer is planning to spray with insecticide. The appropriate seasons for the various plants listed in Column (5) of Table 1, may not, therefore, match the lengths of hive leases. Lease periods are generally longer for honey crops, for the collection of nectar takes more time.

The sixth column in Table 1 indicates the various hive-densities employed. The number of hives per acre depends upon the size of the area to be serviced, the density of planting, and, in the case of fruit pollination, the age of the orchards. For the pollination of fruits, the hives are scattered throughout the farm, usually with higher densities employed in older orchards because the trees are not strategically placed to facilitate the crossing of pollen. The most popular choices are one hive per acre and one hive per two acres. It is interesting, and easily understood, that farmers demand significantly fewer hives for pollination than the number

Table 1 Bee-Related Plants Investigated (State of Washington, 1971)

(1) Plants	(2) Number of Beekeepers	(3) Pollination Services Rendered	(4) Surplus Honey Expected	(5) Approximate Season	(6) Number of Hives Per Acre (range)
Fruits & Nuts					
Apple & Soft Fruits [a]	7	Yes	No	Mid-April—Mid-May	0.4 to 2
Blueberry (with maple)	1	Yes	Yes	May	2
Cherry (early)	1	Yes	No	March—Early April	0.5 to 2
Cherry	2	Yes	No	April	0.5 to 2
Cranberry	2	Yes	Negligible	June	1.5
Almond (Calif.)	2	Yes	No	February—March	2
Legumes					
Alfalfa	5	Yes and No [c]	Yes	June—September	0.3 to 3
Red Clover	4	Yes and No	Yes	June—September	0.5 to 5
Sweet Clover [b]	1	No [d]	Yes	June—September	0.5 to 1
Pasture [b]	4	No	Yes	Late May—September	0.3 to 1
Other Plants					
Cabbage	1	Yes	Yes	Early April—May	1
Fireweed	2	No	Yes	July—September	n.a.
Mint	3	No	Yes	July—September	0.4 to 1

a Soft fruits include pears, apricots, and peaches.
b Pasture includes a mixture of plants, notably the legumes and other wild flowers such as dandelions.
c Pollination services are rendered for alfalfa and the clovers if their seeds are intended to be harvested; when they are grown only for hay, hives will still be employed for nectar extraction.
d Sweet clover may also require pollination services, but such a case is not covered by this investigation.

recommended by entomologists: [19] both are interested in the maximization of yield, but for the farmer such maximization is subject to the constraint of hive rentals.   When bees are employed to produce honey only, the hives are placed together in one location, called an apiary, for greater ease of handling.[20]   The relatively large variation in hive densities required if legumes are, or are not, to be pollinated is discussed in the next section.

Before we turn to an analysis of the pricing and contractual behavior of beekeepers and farmers, I must point out that the two government programs which support the beekeeping industry did not constitute relevant constraints for the period under investigation.   The honey price-support program, initiated in 1949, involves purchase of honey at supported prices by the Commodity Credit Corporation.[21]   For the period under investigation, however, the supported price was about 20 per cent lower than the market price.[22]   Section 804 of the Agricultural Act of 1970, effectuated in 1971 and designed to reimburse beekeepers for any loss due to pesticide sprays, has been largely ignored by beekeepers because of the difficulty of filing effective claims with the federal government.[23]

II.   The Observed Pricing and Contractual Behavior

It is easy to find conclusive evidence showing that both nectar and pollination services are transacted in the marketplace: in some cities one need look no further than the yellow pages of the Telephone Directory.   But the existence of prices does not in itself imply an efficient allocation of resources.   It is, therefore, necessary to demonstrate the effectiveness of the market in dictating the use even of those resources—bees, nectar, and pollen—which, admittedly, are elusive in character and relatively insignificant in value.   In doing so, I shall not attempt to estimate the standard sets of marginal values which an efficient market is said to equate: the burden of such a task must rest upon those who believe the government can costlessly and accurately make these estimates for the imposition of the "ideal" tax-subsidy schemes.   Rather, I offer below an analysis based on the equimarginal principle.   To the extent that the observed pricing and contractual behavior fails to falsify the implications derived from this analysis we conclude that (1) the observed behavior is explained, and (2) the observations are consistent with efficient allocation of resources.

A.   The Analysis

The reciprocal situation in which a beekeeper is able to extract honey from the same farm to which he renders pollination services poses an interesting theoretic riddle.   The traditional analysis of such a condition relies on some interdependent production functions, and is, I think, unnecessarily complex.[24]   The method employed here simply treats pollination services and honey yield as components of a joint product generated by the hive. That is, the rental price per hive received by a beekeeper for placing his hives on a farm may be paid in terms of honey, of a money fee, or of a combination of both.   The money fee or the honey yield may be either positive or negative, but their total measures the rental value of the hive.

*   *   *

[Pages omitted (ed.)]

C.   Characteristics of the Contractual Arrangements

Contracts between beekeepers and farmers may be oral or written.   I have at hand two types of written contracts.   One is formally printed by an association of beekeepers; another is designed for specific beekeepers, with a few printed headings and space for stipulations to be filled in by hand.[36]   Aside from situations where a third party demands documented proof of the contract (as when a beekeeper seeks a business loan), written contracts are used primarily for the initial arrangement between parties; otherwise oral agreements are made.   Although a written contract is more easily enforceable in a court of law, extra-legal constraints are present: information travels quickly through the closely knit society of beekeepers and farmers,[37] and the market will penalize any party who does not honor his contracts.   Oral contracts are rarely broken.

Pollination contracts usually include stipulations regarding the number and strength of the colonies, the rental fee per hive, the time of delivery and removal of hives, the protection of bees from pesticide sprays, and the strategic placing of hives.   Apiary lease contracts differ from pollination contracts in two essential aspects.   One is, predictably, that the amount of apiary rent seldom depends on the number of colonies, since the farmer is interested only in obtaining the rent per apiary offered by the highest bidder.   Second, the amount of apiary rent is not necessarily fixed.   Paid mostly in honey, it may vary according to either the current honey yield or the honey yield of the preceding year.[38]

In general, contractual arrangements between beekeepers and farmers do not materially differ from other lease contracts.   However, some peculiar arrangements resulting from certain complications are worth noting.   First, because of the foraging behavior of the bees a farmer who hires bees may benefit his neighbors.   Second, the use of pesticide sprays by one farmer may cause damage to the bees on an adjacent farm. And third, fireweed, which yields good honey, grows wild in forests. Let us discuss each in turn.

The Custom of the Orchards.   As noted earlier, if a number of similar orchards are located close to one another, one who hires bees to pollinate his own orchard will in some degree benefit his neighbors. Of course, the strategic placing of the hives will reduce the spillover of bees. But in the absence of any social constraint on behavior, each farmer will tend to take advantage of what spillover does occur and to employ fewer hives himself. Of course, contractual arrangements could be made among all farmers in an area to determine collectively the number of hives to be employed by each but no such effort is observed.

Acknowledging the complication, beekeepers and farmers are quick to point out that a social rule, or custom of the orchards, takes the place of explicit contracting: during the pollination period the owner of an orchard either keeps bees himself or hires as many hives per area as are employed in neighboring orchards of the same type. One failing to comply would be rated as a "bad neighbor," it is said, and could expect a number of inconveniences imposed on him by other orchard owners.[39] This customary matching of hive densities involves the exchange of gifts of the same kind, which apparently entails lower transaction costs than would be incurred under explicit contracting, where farmers would have to negotiate and make money payments to one another for the bee spill-over.[40]

The Case of Pesticide Sprays. At the outset, we must remember that to minimize the loss of bees from insecticide usage is not necessarily consistent with efficient allocation of resources. The relevant consideration is whether the gain from using the pesticide is greater than the associated loss of bees, in total and at the margin. Provided that the cost of forming contracts permits, beekeepers and farmers will seek cooperative arrangements such that the expected marginal gain from using the pesticide is equal to the value of the expected marginal bee loss. In the absence of the arrangements, however, the total gain from using the pesticide may still be greater than the associated loss; the greater the expected damage done to bees, the greater will be the gain from the cooperative arrangements.[41]

When a pollination contract is formed, the farmer usually agrees to inform the beekeeper before spraying his crop, but this assurance will not protect the bees from pesticide used on neighboring farms. In areas dominated by orchards which require pollination at roughly the same time, such as the apple-growing districts, this agreement will suffice, for no farmer will apply the spray during the pollination period. But in regions where adjacent farms require bee pollination at different times, or do not require it at all, a farmer with no present obligation to any beekeeper may spray his fields and inflict damages to the bees rented by other farms. In this situation, only cooperation over a large geographic area can avoid bee loss, and we find just such arrangements in the pollination of cranberries but not of red clover.

Cranberry farms near Seattle are usually found in clusters, and spraying is conducted shortly after the bloom, which may vary by as much as a week or two among neighboring farms. Although each cranberry grower agrees not to spray until the contracted beekeeper removes the bees from his farm, this does not protect bees which may still remain on adjacent farms. Therefore the beekeepers make a further arrangement among themselves to remove all hives on the same date, thus insuring that all the bees are protected.

Red clover presents a different situation. Since the plant is often grown in areas where neighboring farms require no bee pollination, the pesticide danger is reportedly high and beekeepers demand an additional $1.00 to $2.00 per hive to assume the risk. But just as the beekeepers cooperate with one another during cranberry pollination, a clover farmer could make arrangements with his neighbors. Given that neighboring farmers have the legal right to use pesticide, the clover farmer would be willing to pay them an amount not exceeding the beekeeper's risk premium if they would refrain from spraying during the pollination period. Although no such arrangements are observed, it would seem that the costs of reaching an agreement would be no higher than those encountered in the case of the cranberries, and we must infer, pending empirical confirmation, that the gain from using the sprays is greater than the associated loss. This would particularly apply when a single farm requiring pollination is located amidst a large number of farms which require spraying during that same period.

The Case of Fireweed. I have at hand two types of apiary contract pertaining to fireweed, a honey plant which grows wild in the forest. The first is between a beekeeper and the Weyerhaeuser Company, owner of private timber land; the second is between a beekeeper and the Water Department of the City of Seattle. Two distinctions between them are worth noting. First, while both contracts stipulate 25 cents per hive, Weyerhaeuser asks a minimum charge of $100, and the Water Department a minimum of $25. In the apiary for fireweed honey, the number of hives used by a beekeeper is more than 100 but less than 400. Thus it happens that in the case of Weyerhaeuser, the apiary rent is independent of the number of hives, whereas with the Water Department it is dependent. The "underpriced" rent levied by the Water Department would have implied some sort of queuing except that a second unique feature is incorporated in its apiary contracts: no beekeeper is granted the exclusive right to the fireweed nectar in a particular area. The implication is that competition among beekeepers will reduce the honey yield per hive until its apiary rent is no more than 25 cents; while no beekeeper attempts to exclude entrants, the parties do seek a mutual division of the total area to avoid chaotic hive placement. Finally, fireweed also grows wild in the national forests and for this case I have no contract at hand. My information is that apiary rent is measured by the hive, is subject to competitive bidding among beekeepers, and has a reported range of 25 to 63 cents with the winner being granted exclusive right to a particular area.

III.   Conclusions

Whether or not Keynes was correct in his claim that policy makers are "distilling their frenzy" from economists, it appears evident that some economists have been distilling their policy implications from fables. In a desire to promote government intervention, they have been prone to advance, without the support of careful investigation, the notion of "market failure." Some have dismissed in cavalier fashion the possibility of market operations in matters of environmental degradation, as witnesses the assertion of E. J. Mishan:

> With respect to bodies of land and water, extension of property rights may effectively internalize what would otherwise remain externalities. But the possibilities of protecting the citizen against such common environmental blights as filth, fume, stench, noise, visual distractions, etc. by a market in property rights are too remote to be taken seriously.[42]

Similarly, it has been assumed that private property rights cannot be enforced in the case of fisheries, wildlife, and whatever other resources economists have chosen to call "natural."   Land tenure contracts are routinely taken as inefficient, and to some the market will fail in the areas of education, medical care, and the like.

Then, of course, there is the fable of the bees.

In each case, it is true that costs involved in enforcement of property rights and in the formation of contracts will cause the market to function differently than it would without such costs.   And few will deny that government does afford economic advantages.   But it is equally true that any government action can be justified on efficiency grounds by the simple expedient of hypothesizing high enough transaction costs in the marketplace and low enough costs for government control.   Thus to assume the state of the world to be as one sees fit is not even to compare the ideal with the actual but, rather, to compare the ideal with a fable.

I have no grounds for criticizing Meade and other economists who follow the Pigovian tradition for their use of the bee example to illustrate a theoretical point: certainly, resource allocation would in general differ from what is observed if the factors were "unpaid."   My main criticism, rather, concerns their approach to economic inquiry in failing to investigate the real-world situation and in arriving at policy implications out of sheer imagination.   As a result, their work contributes little to our understanding of the actual economic system.

FOOTNOTES

* Facts, like jade, are not only costly to obtain but also difficult to authenticate. I am therefore most grateful to the following beekeepers and farmers: Leonard Almquist, Nat Giacomini, Ancel Goolsbey, L. W. Groves, Rex Haueter, Harold Lange, Lavar Peterson, Elwood Sires, Clarence Smith, Ken Smith, John Steg, P. F. Thurber, and Mrs. Gerald Weddle. All of them provided me with valuable information; some of them made available to me their accounting records and contracts. R. H. Coase inspired the investigation, Yoram Barzel saw that it was conducted thoroughly, and Mrs. Lina Tong rendered her assistance. The investigation is part of a proposed research in the general area of contracts, financially supported by the National Science Foundation.

[1] A. C. Pigou, Wealth and Welfare (1912); and The Economics of Welfare (1920).

[2] Pigou had offered other examples. The example of two roads was deleted from later editions of The Economics of Welfare, presumably in an attempt to avoid the criticism by F. H. Knight in Some Fallacies in the Interpretation of Social Cost, 38 Q.J.Econ. 582 (1924). The railroad example has not enjoyed popularity. Most of Pigou's examples, however, were drawn from land tenure arrangements in agriculture, but an exhaustive check of his source references has revealed no hard evidence at all to support his claim of inefficient tenure arrangements.

[3] See J. E. Meade, External Economies and Diseconomies in a Competitive Situation, 52 Econ.J. 54 (1952).

[4] Id. at 56–57.

[5] Id. at 58.

[6] Francis M. Bator, The Anatomy of Market Failure, 72 Q.J.Econ. 351, 364 (1958).

[7] The presence of apple honey in the market is therefore somewhat mysterious. While occasionally apple orchards in the Northwest do yield negligible amounts of nectar, beekeepers are frank to point out that the dandelion and other wild plants in the orchard are often the sources of "apple" honey, so called. Elsewhere, as in New York, it was reported that apple orchards yielded slightly more nectar. See, for example, A. I. & E. R. Root, The ABC and XYZ of Bee Culture 386 (1923). The explanation for this divergence of facts, to my mind, lies in the different lengths of time in which the hives are placed in the apple orchards: in Root's day the hives were probably left in the orchards for longer periods than today.

[8] See George E. Bohart, Management of Wild Bees, in U. S. Dep't of Agriculture, Beekeeping in the United States 109 (Ag. Handbook No. 335, 1971). [Hereinafter cited as Beekeeping . . .]. Leafcutters, for example, have recently been introduced for the pollination of alfalfa and clover seeds. But these bees yield no honey crop and are seldom kept.

[9] For further details see Spencer M. Riedel, Jr., Development of American Beehive, in Beekeeping . . . 8–9; A. I. & E. R. Root, supra note 7, at 440–58; Carl Johansen, Beekeeping (PNW Bulletin No. 79, rev. ed. March 1970).

[10] For further details see Carl Johansen, supra note 9; F. E. Moeller, Managing Colonies for High Honey Yields, in Beekeeping . . . 23; E. Oertel, Nectar and Pollen Plants, in Beekeeping . . . 10.

[11] According to a survey conducted by Robert K. Lesser in 1968, based on a sample of 30 out of 60 commercial beekeepers in the state of Washington, the total number of peak colonies is 14.6% higher than that of spring colonies. See Robert K. Lesser, An Investigation of the Elements of Income from Beekeeping in the State of Washington 74 (unpublished thesis, Sch. of Bus. Admin., Gonzaga Univ., 1969).

12 See, for example, A. I. & E. R. Root, supra note 9, at 97–103; Eugene Keyarts, Bee Hunting, Gleanings in Bee Culture 329–33 (June 1960); U. S. Dep't of Agriculture, Protecting Honey Bees from Pesticides (Leaflet 544, 1972); Carl A. Johansen, How to Reduce Poisoning of Bees from Pesticides (Pamphlet EM 3473, Wash. St. Univ., College of Ag., May 1971); Philip F. Torchio, Pesticides, in Beekeeping . . . 97.

13 See E. Oertel, supra note 10; C. R. Ribbands, The Behaviour and Social Life of Honeybees 69–75 (1953); Roger A. Morse, Placing Bees in Apple Orchards, Gleanings in Bee Culture 230–33 (April 1960). Owing to its weather, Washington is not one of the better honey yielding states in the Union. Data made available to me by the U. S. Dep't of Agriculture indicates that over the years (1955–1971) Washington ranks 24th among 48 states in yield per colony and 20th in the total number of colonies. The U. S. Dep't of Agriculture data, like those obtained by Lesser, provide no information on the different honey yields and pollination requirements of various plants and are therefore of little use for our present purpose. It should be noted that the U. S. Dep't of Agriculture overall yield data are significantly lower than those obtained by Lesser and by me. See Robert K. Lesser, supra note 11.

14 See M. D. Levin, Pollination, in Beekeeping . . . 77.

15 Id.; 9th Pollination Conference, Report, The Indispensable Pollinators (Ag. Extension Serv., Hot Springs, Ark., October 12–15, 1970); G. E. Bohart, Insect Pollination of Forage Legumes, 41 Bee World 57–64, 85–97 (1960); J. B. Free, Pollination of Fruit Trees, 41 Bee World 141–51, 169–86 (1960); U. S. Dep't of Agriculture, Using Honey Bees to Pollinate Crops (Leaflet 549, 1968); Get More Fruit with Honey Bee Pollinators (Pamphlet EM 2922, Wash. St. Univ., March 1968); Protect Berry Pollinating Bees (Pamphlet EM 3341, Wash. St. Univ., February 1970); Increase Clover Seed Yields with Adequate Pollination (Pamphlet EM 3444, Wash. St. Univ., April 1971); Honey Bees Increase Cranberry Production (Pamphlet EM 3468, Wash. St. Univ., April 1971).

16 See, for example, Douglas Oldershaw, The Pollination of High Bush Blueberries, in The Indispensable Pollinators, supra note 15, at 171–76; Roger A. Morse, supra note 13.

17 There is, however, little agreement as to how far a bee could fly: estimated range is from one to three miles. For general foraging behavior, see M. D. Levin, supra note 14, at 79; O. W. Park, Activities of Honeybees, in The Hive and the Honeybee 125, 149–206 (Roy A. Grout ed., 1946); C. R. Ribbands, supra note 13.

18 Following the practice of local beekeepers, we use the term "soft fruit" to refer to peaches, pears, and apricots, generally grown in the same area, and often in the same orchard, as apples. (By standard usage, the term refers only to the various berry plants.)

19 See note 15 supra.

20 See, for example, W. P. Nye, Beekeeping Regions in the United States, in Beekeeping . . . 17.

21 See Harry A. Sullivan, Honey Price Support Program, in Beekeeping . . . 136.

22 From 1970 to 1972 the supported prices were near 11.5 cents per pound, whereas the market wholesale price was above 14 cents per pound. Between 1950 and 1965 were seven years in which the CCC purchased no honey, and two years of negligible amounts. See Harry A. Sullivan, supra note 21, at 137.

23 See 7 U.S.C. § 135 b, note (1970); Pub.L. No. 91–524 § 804. My judgment is based both on the behavior of beekeepers (see next section) after the initiation of the Act and on the complexity of relevant claim forms which I have at hand. In April 1972 beekeepers associations were still lobbying for easier claiming conditions.

24 In J. E. Meade, supra note 3, at 58, this problem is set up in terms of the interdependent functions $x_1 = H_1 (l_1, c_1, x_2)$ and $x_2 = H_2 (l_2, c_2, x_1)$. I find Meade's analysis difficult to follow. Elsewhere, Otto A. Davis and Andrew Whinston employ the functions

$C_1 = C_1 (q_1, q_2)$ and $C_2 = C_2 (q_1, q_2)$ in their treatment of certain "externalities." It is not clear, however, that the authors had the bee example in mind. See Otto A. Davis & Andrew Whinston, Externalities, Welfare, and the Theory of Games, 70 J.Pol.Econ. 241 (1962).

* * *

[36] Some beekeepers use just postal cards. The general contractual details reported below are similar to those briefly mentioned in Grant D. Morse, How About Pollination, Gleanings in Bee Culture 73–78 (February 1970).

[37] During my conversations with beekeepers, I was impressed by their personal knowledge of one another, including details such as the number of hives owned, the kinds of farms served, and the rents received.

[38] While we may attribute this behavior to the aversion of risks, the apiary contracts are not the same as share contracts. Rather, they resemble fixed-rent contracts with what I have called "escape clauses." For discussion of the "escape clause" and the stipulations of the share contract, see Steven N. S. Cheung, The Theory of Share Tenancy, ch. 2 & 4 (1969). One impression I obtain is that apiary rents generally involve such low values in Washington that elaborate formations and enforcements of apiary contracts are not worthwhile. In further investigations of these contracts, states with higher honey yields are recommended.

[39] The distinction between an oral or an implicit contract and a custom is not always clear. A common practice in some areas is that each farmer lets his neighbors know how many hives he employs. Perhaps the absence of a court of law to enforce what could in fact be a highly informal agreement is the reason why farmers deny the existence of any contract among them governing the employment of hives.

[40] Since with a sufficiently high reward the notoriety of being a "bad neighbor" will be tolerated, the likelihood of explicit contracting rises with increasing rental values of hives. Alternatively and concurrently, with a high enough rental price of hives the average size of orchards may increase through outright purchases, or the shapes of the orchards may be so tailored as to match the foraging behavior of the bees. By definition, given the gains the least costly arrangement will be chosen.

Some beekeepers reported that there are peculiar situations where the foraging behavior of the bees forces a one-way gift, but these situations are not covered by the present investigation. Even under these rare situations, the absence of both contractual and customary restraints may not result in a different allocation of resources. See Steven N. S. Cheung, The Theory of Inter-individual Effects and The Demand for Contracts (Univ. of Washington, Inst. of Econ. Res.).

[41] For a fuller discussion, see Steven N. S. Cheung, supra note 40.

[42] E. J. Mishan: A Reply to Professor Worcester, 10 J.Econ.Lit. 59, 62 (1972). As immediate refutation of Professor Mishan's claim, I refer the reader to a factual example: Professor John McGee has just purchased a house, separated from that of his neighbor by a vacant lot. That the space would remain vacant had been assured by the previous owner who (upon learning that a third party was planning to buy the lot and construct a house there) had negotiated with the neighbor to make a joint purchase of the ground, thus protecting their two households from the "filth, fumes, stench, noise, visual distractions, etc." which would be generated by a new neighbor.

C Continued

27: EXTERNALITY, PROPERTY RIGHTS, AND THE MANAGEMENT OF OUR NATIONAL FORESTS*

RICHARD STROUP
Montana State University

JOHN BADEN
Utah State University

During the past few years the Sierra Club and its allies have come to agree with those in the forest products industry. Nearly all parties agree that the National Forests are not being "properly" managed. In brief, this means that none of the various competing interests feel that the National Forests are managed for *them*. From this we can infer that the Forest Service has not been "captured" by any single group. Thus, given that the Forest Service has responsibility for substantial and highly valued resources and that it has great managerial discretion, we may be confident that the various interested parties will continue efforts to impose their policy preferences upon the decisions of the Forest Service.

New policy decisions shift costs and benefits. In effect, property rights in forest resources are granted and revoked without normal negotiation and without full compensation. Thus, the policy making process is inherently the result of a conflict. As applied to the National Forests, new policies can be fostered in two broad ways. The first, we might call "intramural." In this case the fundamental congressional acts are accepted. Within these constraints the various interest groups as well as

Baden and Stroup, "Externality, Property Rights, and the Management of Our National Forests," 16 J.Law & Econ. (1973), from page 303 to page 312.

interested individuals attempt to influence the Forest Service in its exercise of discretion.   For example, the forest supervisor might be encouraged to restrict snowmobiles from a winter feeding area or to refrain from road building on a watershed feeding a prime trout area.   In localized cases of this type, at issue is the *emphasis* placed upon the various uses and values that are produced within the forest.   A similar "intramural" process might occur at the regional or national level where representatives from the various interested groups might prevail upon the Forest Service to give greater weight to their concerns.   Under these circumstances one factor that might reasonably come into play is the threat of changing the congressional mandate or "rules of the game" under which the various parties, including the Forest Service, operate.

This second possibility may be viewed as an attempt to change the range of discretion available to the Forest Service, or, as in the case of the Multiple-Use Sustained Yield Act of 1960, to codify and hence to defend and secure the amount of discretion available to the Forest Service.[1] The so-called National Timber Supply Act of 1969 was an effort to channel policy making within the Forest Service in a particular direction, in this case toward greater emphasis on timber production.[2]   In addition to increasing annual harvests in the short run, the reliable and adequate source of funds provided by these additional sales would have funded the Forest Service at a higher level, for the stated purpose of allowing more intensive management efforts to increase long-run yields.   In contrast with this aborted effort is S.1592, the McGee Clearcut Moritorium Bill.   The impact of this bill would also be to limit the discretion of the Forest Service, by prohibiting the practice of clearcutting on the National Forest for a limited time.[3]   The proponents of this bill argue that the Forest Service gives far too much weight to the interests of the forest products industry and hence that those of the more general public must be protected by a statutory enactment.   In each of these cases we note that groups with particular interests invoke the political process in efforts to foster policy decisions which advance their claims to rights in the public forests.

In general, all policy making in the American political context follows a similar pattern.   Demands for rights to public assets are made by individuals or groups upon the political system at some level.   The component of the political system responds by ignoring the demands, by converting the demands into public policy, or by taking steps to strengthen the existing policy.   If the interested group is not successful, it can make the demand at what it considers to be a more vulnerable place within the political system.   This brief sketch of political mechanics is included to emphasize one point—that current management of the National Forests is substantially dependent upon the effective strength of the various demands placed upon its managers.

Conflict regarding the management of the National Forest arises from a simple fact.   One cannot maximize its use for one purpose without sacrificing to some degree some other uses.   Beyond certain limits domestic cattle and sheep are competitors for browse with wild animals; logging demands compete with fishing for the maintenance of a given level of water quality.   In brief, while some uses are reinforcing, (for example, logging tends to encourage high deer population) tradeoffs among competing values are an inherent aspect of the management of a public (or private) resource.   Within this context it is unreasonable to expect "politics" to be absent from the management of the National Forests.

Proposed solutions to existing management problems range from small changes in criteria or practices to rather drastic changes in the form and function of management itself.   In the latter category is a proposal, voiced by Milton Friedman and others,[4] that government agencies should not manage these forests at all.   Instead management would be left to private managers and the present value of *wealth* captured for public use by auctioning off rights (title) to the lands in question.   It is our purpose in this paper to discuss the issues involved in evaluating the potential costs and benefits of such a solution, to predict changes which might occur due to adoption of such a policy, and to comment on the probability of its occurrence.

The effectiveness of management, however measured, depends on the combination of information and incentives facing the decision maker, who has a given level of resources and technology available.   Thus the organizational context influences the choices actually made by management by affecting the incentive structure and information constraints within which they operate.   Important in defining the organizational context, as well as in determining effective results, are the terms of "ownership" of property rights to assets, and thus the appropriability of rewards to efficient management.

In a market system with private ownership of rights to assets, incentives and much of the information flow are handled through prices.   Not only do bid and asked prices convey condensed information on the relative values of alternative uses of resources, but the same prices also give resource owners and managers a powerful incentive to use their resources in the manner most helpful to others.   We need not count on good will, morality, or principle: greed will suffice.   Within a market context people are of course free to ignore the wishes of others—expressed through bid and asked prices—but when prices are not distorted, resource users and owners sacrifice wealth exactly to the extent that they ignore those wishes.   It is largely the efficiency of prices in transmitting information, and their effectiveness in providing incentive without coercion, which make the market system attractive.

The advantages claimed for this sort of resource management system include diversity, individual freedom, adaptiveness, the production of information, and a certain equity.   Diversity is fostered because there is no single, centralized decision maker but many asset owners and entrepreneurs each of whom can exercise his own vision.   Those who correctly anticipate people's desires are most rewarded.   Individual freedom is preserved as those who wish to participate in and support each activity may do so on the basis of willing consent.   Adaptiveness is encouraged in both management and consumptive activities, since prices provide immediate information and incentive for action as soon as changes are seen.   If only a *few* see scarcities or opportunities ahead, they can buy, sell,—or just provide expertise as a small group of consultants—and thus direct resource use *without* convincing 51 per cent of the voters (or their bureaucracy) of the advantages of their preferences.   In this case profits will reward foresight and quick action, while losses discipline those who divert resources foolishly.

Production of *information* in a market situation is slowly being recognized for its importance.[5]   Activities *not* marketed are proving very difficult to manage rationally for there is little or no concrete evidence of how people *really* evaluate nonmarketed activities relative to other resource-using activities.[6]   We know, for example, how much people are willing to sacrifice for a thousand board feet of lumber of a given species and grade, but how much *would* they pay for a day's access to a wilderness area?   In the latter case we have only rough estimates.

Even the most conscientious and competent manager cannot make good management decisions on resource inputs without knowledge of the absolute and relative values of his various outputs.

Finally, there is a measure of equity in having those people who *use* a resource, or wish to reserve it for use, pay for it by sacrificing some of their wealth.   The proceeds from the sale of public assets could be distributed, or invested and perpetually distributed to the poor or whomever.   Those using the forests would be required to pay, whether it be for recreation, timber harvest, or even research in a unique area.

Unfortunately, the orderly picture above does not fully describe all real-world market situations.   The prime villain in disturbing the beauty of the picture is what economists and political scientists call "externalities." [7]   Broadly, this means that asset owners or managers may not be in a position to capture all the benefits or pay for costs of their various actions.[8]   It is clear that in a market situation there is normally little incentive to provide goods or services that offer no return.   If, for example, a forest owner could not (at low cost) exclude those recreationists who did not pay for access, receipts would understate recreational valuation, and he would have a diminished incentive to preserve or provide recreational opportunity—assuming the benefits of *alternatives* uses, such as timber harvests, are fully captured by the owner. We are confident that among potential externalities (aspects difficult to contract for) are some of the effects of flood control, watershed provision, weather modification, animal habitat, biotic diversity, and environmental buffering. These effects might be partially internalized by placing restrictions on the title transfer, constraining the buyers to avoid certain socially costly decisions. But to the extent this happens, the benefits of market organization and individually expressed preferences are eschewed. In practice we have generally gone much further, leaving management directly in the hands of managers who have relatively little incentive to listen to or be guided by individual preferences as expressed in relative prices. To summarize briefly, the existence of externality is recognized by many economists and political scientists as a necessary—but not sufficient—condition for government interference with markets to possibly improve efficient resource management.[9] A significant point to remember here is that an important form of externality is pervasive also in all governmental forms of organization. At best, decision makers are held "accountable" by the threat of replacement if their decisions are not desirable to their superiors or to politically influential clientele. They do not, however, receive directly the gains from better management (or declines in resource values from poor management) as private resource owners generally do. This follows, as do market externalities, from the fact that property rights are attenuated.[10]

Many resource managers find the above anti-market argument based upon externalities—both positive and negative—sufficient to justify departures from market determined resource utilization. Another tack, however, is taken by some of those who criticize market results. If people gnerally do not know what is best for themselves, then they make bad decisions in a market. In contrast, if bureaucrats are making the decisions while working under political representatives, the people may be "saved from themselves." It is quite clear to some that from this perspective the average man demonstrates bad taste in preferring developed recreational areas to pristine wilderness. The fact that many people will pay much more for a cabin near the former than near the latter is clear evidence to them that "common" people should not be trusted to manage their own affairs. The fear that fewer wilderness areas might exist if the relatively few users had to pay for the resources withheld from other uses, understandably disturbs wilderness buffs. An assumption implicit in this position is that people who make unwise decisions in the market place make wise decisions at the ballot box.

Another group of people opposing the sale of forests to private operators recognizes the desirable and undesirable aspects of private management, but objects precisely on equity grounds. Many of us in the West who use National Forests extensively are greatly subsidized. We realize that we would have to pay for what we now get free, or at reduced cost. Such subsidies are much more likely to be provided (especially to the relatively wealthy recipients) when they are hidden by the lack of cash transactions that characterize many of the uses of the public forests. A private manager's desire to allocate resources where they are most valued and to extract the maximum rent might be inconsistent with our continued subsidy.[11]

In summary, there are three major arguments against market management. The first is that market externalities may be great enough to overcome the advantages of using prices to transmit information efficiently and to provide noncoercive incentives for effective management. Problems of externality (attentuated property rights) in governmental operation typically are ignored by people accepting this argument. The second argument, essentially elitist, is that people's preferences as expressed in the market are simply wrong. Thus, good managers and policies must be selected through governmental action. In this manner we may expect to improve upon the results of market choices. A third factor, not often stated publicly, is that the current subsidy given to many users of natural resources (such as National Forests) would be made explicit and hence might be reduced if a market system of resource management were introduced.

What effects then could we predict if our National Forests were sold and if forests were operated by governmental units only when those units paid for forests as they pay for other resources? The first and most obvious impact would be a large revenue windfall to the government. Some of this presumably would be reserved for continued public provision of forest access and improvement. The costs of these services would, however, be explicit rather than hidden as currently is the case. The (presumed) reduction in *public* provision of forest services at low or zero cost to users would mean a transfer of real wealth from forest resource users to the beneficiaries of the programs subsequently increased. Thus, forest users would more often pay for the rights to resources they withdraw from alternative uses.

A second impact would be an increase of forest use of the types people are willing to pay for. Simultaneously, information would be produced on just how each competing forest use *is* valued by people. Some forest areas would no doubt be subject to very intense development for use by masses of people with preference for easy access and comfort. Also, however, some wilderness areas could be expected to be more strongly protected than now, as some entrepreneurs catered to those willing and able to pay for access to pristine wilderness. Just as we have restaurants of all kinds, in about the proportions people want and will pay for, we could expect an immense diversity in forest use and perhaps even the development of use patterns not yet attempted, as private owners tried to increase the usefulness (value) of their land.

A change *not* to be expected is a shift to strictly short-sighted goals, such as immediate exploitation of logging potential to the expected detriment of long-run productivity in the land. The owner of a forest may be 50 years old and expect to live only to 70; but, even if he wants to leave his heirs nothing, he will maximize his own returns by managing the forest in such a way as to maximize *long-run expected value*. He would thus sell out when he wants cash and would receive expected market value. Of course, if timber prices are expected to rise *less* rapidly than other prices, due perhaps to expected development of wood substitutes, *then* immediate harvest may make sense both privately and socially, depending on timber growth rates, and the effects of timber harvest on alternative forest land uses. Only in those cases when the private owner *cannot capture* increased values of better management, as in the case where recreationists cannot be charged for their use of land, will private owners be "short sighted" or "lacking vision."

In the absence of constraints upon private owners, a new set of externalities would likely become important. While government operations stifle creative activity, adaptiveness, and response to important efficiency questions by making the benefits of these attributes and actions inaccessible to the decision maker, private operation reduces responsiveness to *politically* expressed desires. Thus the costs of poor watershed or recreation management will not fully accrue to the private operator unless property rights are enforceable at reasonable costs. That is, if the benefits of better watershed management or enhanced recreation opportunities do not redound directly to the private forest owner to reduce law suits or reduce cash receipts, the private forest will most likely be mismanaged.

In summary, three kinds of effects are expected. First, one kind of externality is exchanged for another. Both benefits *and* costs (except extra work) of nearly *all* improvements in management are external to governmental managers. Diversity and adaptiveness, if they mean more work or risk, are probably more likely with private than with public management. Secondly, income is redistributed from those who *now* use forests without paying full costs to the beneficiaries of newly expanded government programs or tax cuts. The third kind of change is the production of valuable information, as users compete in the bidding for resources formerly allocated by decree or other nonmarket methods.

The net desirability of selling our national forests, then, depends on judgements as to (1) which set of externalities is most acceptable, (2) whether the *general* public, rather than the forest users as such, deserve the value produced by public forest lands, and (3) how valuable the extra information produced by market operation, on relative values of competing forest land uses, actually is. Further research hopefully will shed light on questions (1) and (3), but (2) is basically a value judgement, so that research could at most indicate the size and distribution of changes in wealth.

As we noted in our introduction, however, the management of our public lands is inherently political. It is compellingly obvious that the mere consideration of a change in the form of management as drastic as that discussed will generate political heat. Thus we might reasonably expect powerful and possibly diffuse resistance to this alternative. It seems clear that many classes of forest users are so highly subsidized by the general public that they might be made worse off by this change. Examples of such groups would include cattlemen who receive grazing rights far below market rates, and certain logging firms, who have reportedly [12] exercised oligopsony power in obtaining stumpage at less than what would be the prevailing rates. Several such groups have recurrently demonstrated political skill in affecting policy. While often in opposition, in the case at hand they would have strong incentive to work in concert. The political strength of these groups is formidable. Finally, we must consider the position of the Forest Service (as well as the Bureau of Land Management) and other governmental agencies. Given the propensities of bureaucracies for survival and growth, and the political dexterity repeatedly evidenced by the Forest Service, it seems certain that they would offer formidable opposition to the sale of the National Forests. In view of the bias inherent in their position and their natural advantage of access to data, it seems quite possible that even without the direct aid of their clientele interest groups, the Forest Service could block legislation aimed at the sale of the National Forest.

On the other side of the ledger, those who would strongly support this kind of proposal are less easily identifiable. Certainly those entrepreneurs who saw the greatest potential return from given types of forest services (and who thus could out-bid others for the resources without giving up all the expected value of the resource) could be expected to support such a proposal. If revenues from a sale of forest were ear-marked for specific projects, then the beneficiaries of those projects also could be expected to support the change. Among consumers of the forest services however, the extent of support would depend heavily on the results of study into projected patterns of actual use and the prices expected to accompany those patterns. For example, Sierra Club members might even be expected to support private ownership if it became apparent that the really pristine wilderness experience in America, like bird hunting in Britain, is best preserved in a private setting. If back packers in general became convinced that the development of high density recreational areas, which reduced the pressure on wilderness areas, would proceed much more rapidly with private development, then they too might endorse the notion of private management of large blocks of forest.

Concluding Remarks

The authors are convinced that: (a) current management institutions leave serious problems of efficiency and equity unsolved, (b) misconceptions abound concerning the nature of a market solution to this problem, (c) a simple market solution, unbounded by continuing government intervention of some sort, would involve serious externality problems, and (d) the empirical information needed to predict and compare the results of increased use of the market mechanism is largely unavailable now, so that much empirical research is called for.   We hope that this paper has illuminated the issue and raised the sorts of questions that might stimulate research in this important area.

FOOTNOTES

* The authors wish to thank R. Bish, R. d'Arge, D. Gardner, V. Ostrum, and G. Tullock for their helpful comments, while retaining responsibility for any remaining errors.

1 Act of June 12, 1960, Pub.L. 86–517, 74 Stat. 215.

2 The original legislation was rewritten by the House Agriculture Committee ". . . to provide for more-efficient development and improved management of national commercial forest land in order to increase the annual timber harvest and to establish a high timber yield fund." Timber Supply, 27 Cong.Q.Wkly.Rep. 2491 (Dec. 5, 1969). The rewritten bill was called the National Forest Timber Conservation and Management Act of 1969 (H.R. 12025, 91st Cong., 1st Sess.), and was reported out of the Agriculture Committee on November 18, 1969 (H.R.Rep. 91–655). Despite being granted a rule by the House Rules Committee, the bill was never brought to debate because the House rejected, by a 228–150 roll call vote, the rule under which the bill was to be considered. The vote reflected the lobbying of such "conservation interests" as the National Rifle Association, the United Auto Workers, the Izaak Walton League, the National Audubon Society and the Sierra Club. Interests supporting the bill were the National Association of Home Builders, the National Forest Products Association, the United Brotherhood of Carpenters and Joiners, and others. Thus the so-called National Timber Supply Act of 1969 was killed in the House on a procedural vote. Timber Sales, 28 Cong.Q.Wkly.Rep. 679 (March 6, 1970) ; Conservationists Kill Increased Federal Timber Cuts, id. at 695–697.

3 A Bill to Establish a Commission to Investigate and Study the Practice of Clearcutting of Timber Resources of the United States on Federal Lands, S.1592, § 6, at 5, 92nd Cong., 1st Sess. (1971). For more information on clearcutting and its regulation by Congress (including McGee bill), see Clearcutting: Pressures on Congress for Decision, 30 Cong. Q.Wkly.Rep. 492–96 (March 4, 1972).

4 Milton Friedman, Capitalism and Freedom 31 (1962). See also Edwin D. Dolan, TANSTAAFL, the Economic Strategy for Environment Crisis, ch. 7 (Preserving the Wilder-

ness: Public Interest or Special Interest?); esp. at 92 (1971). On April 6, 1971, Representative Wayne Aspinall (D.Colo.) submitted a bill, H.R. 7211, which would have allowed the sale, under certain conditions, of some public lands including National Forest Land. The bill was reported out of the Committee on Interior and Insular Affairs on August 7, 1972 (H.R.Rep. 92–1306). Digest of Public General Bills and Resolutions, 92d Cong., 2d Sess., pt. 1, at 399–401 (Library of Congress, Cong., Res.Serv., 1972).

[5] For importance of price system in providing information in our American market system, see Robert L. Bish, The Public Economy of Metropolitan Areas 9–10 (1971).

[6] For an explanation of this problem, see Richard A. Musgrave, The Theory of Public Finance: A Study of Public Economy 10 (1959).

[7] Discussion of externalities, public goods, and monopolies (see note 8 for the introduction of public goods and monopolies) abound in the literature of political economics. William J. Baumol, Welfare Economics and the Theory of the State 24–36 (1965) is a summary of literature "on the theory of externalities." Robert L. Bish, supra note 5, at 18–25 discusses "externalities" ; and his discussion of "public goods," id. at 25–30, cites several other good discussions of public goods. See Richard Musgrave, supra note 6 at 7, for external economies or diseconomies; and Francis M. Bator, Government and the Sovereign Consumer, in Private Wants and Public Needs 118, 123–31 (Edmund S. Phelps ed., 1965) for the role of monopolies in the market system. Elinor Ostrom, in a mimeographed paper entitled On the Variety of Potential Public Goods (Indiana Univ., undated), also discusses these issues, with frequent citations to past work.

[8] Note that this definition is broad enough to include technical externalities, pecuniary externalities, public goods, and even ordinary monopoly where sellers cannot fully capture the benefits of increased production but must pass on some of those benefits to the customers in the form of lower prices. Steven N. S. Cheung, The Structure of a Contract and the Theory of a Non-exclusive Resource, 13 J.Law & Econ. 49 (1970) suggests that the term "externality" is so broad as to be useless, and that we should focus on the inability of users and potential users of the resource to contract among themselves in such a way as to maximize efficiency by properly adjusting marginal productivity conditions. We believe this to be a cogent and productive perspective.

[9] William J. Baumol, supra note 7, discusses this point at 19–22 ; and his entire book is a discussion of the proper role of the state. See also Paul W. Barkley & David W. Seckler, Economic Growth and Environmental Decay: The Solution Becomes the Problem, chs. 8 (Market Failure Externalities) and 9 (Market Failure Collective Goods); and Elinor Ostrom, supra note 7.

[10] For an excellent discussion of attenuated rights in this context see, Roland N. McKean, Property Rights Within Government, and Devices to Increase Governmental Efficiency, 39 So.Econ.J. 177 (1972).

[11] Note, however, that even here it is not clear that the consumers now being subsidized would be made worse off. The new pattern of goods and services provided with forest resources might be worth enough more that even at higher prices, the consumer would be better off. Services or experiences now unavailable might be marketed by imaginative resource owners eager to maximize the value of rents.

[12] Walter J. Mead, in Competition and Oligopsony in the Douglas Fir Lumber Industry (1966), documents this statement as applied to stumpage.

PART **4**

Property Rights in Associational Relationships

*

A Introduction

It seems obvious at this juncture that as the newer economics of property rights has developed in sophistication and complexity, certain older economic problems would yield to new solutions. Two of the more puzzling questions in the earlier literature have been why individuals should ever organize into firms if markets and market specialization were working efficiently (28); and second, how large, unwieldy entities like modern corporations could be fit into any systematic theory of markets and property rights (29 and 30).

The first of these puzzles, that about the firm, began to give way in Ronald Coase's early article, "The Nature of the Firm" (4 *Economica* 386 (1937)), belatedly recognized for the classic that it is. Coase was, as he seems usually to be, well ahead of his time in utilizing the puzzle-solving qualities of information and transactions costs to clarify our understanding of market events. Coase's foundation has been further built upon by Alchian's and Demsetz's important concept of "monitoring" to explain much of the behavior we observe in connection with firms both large and small (32). This concept, like the related notions of information and transactions costs, gives promise of significant new insights into such areas as the behavior of union officials, agency relationships, not-for-profit enterprises, and various other fiduciary arrangements.

The second great issue now being effectively addressed by the newer economics was popularly posed by Berle and Means in their highly influential *The Modern Corporation and Private Property* (1932). Berle (for this was uniquely his contribution) thought that normal market forces could not appropriately constrain the managers of large corporations with diffused share ownership. This led to the famous "separation of ownership and control" epigram and all that has logically followed from it.

But now it is clear that the Berle thesis must be significantly revised. Concepts like a market for corporate control, property rights in votes (31), the monitoring function of residual claimants (32), and internalized market competition (29) have all helped in this regard. Other recent discoveries have influenced the newer theory of large corporations as well, but they have been omitted as inappropriate to this set of readings. They concern the so-called Random Walk hypothesis and the Efficient Market theory. These notions help us understand how capital markets can supply the information necessary for the effective functioning of the other restraints mentioned above.

The relationship of capital market theory to corporate behavior is touched upon in H. Manne's "Our Two Corporation Systems: Law and Economics" (30). However, for a later and much fuller elaboration of the significance of these new findings see H. Manne, "Economic Aspects of Required Disclosure under Federal Securities Laws," in H. Manne and E. Solomon, *Wall Street in Transition* (New York Univ. Press, 1974), pp. 21–109.

Ironically, the very writers who have perhaps been most critical of Berle's view of the large private corporation find that his thesis has considerable merit when applied to profit-limited businesses or non-profit institutions. Alchian and Kessel (33) give an overview of this analysis, and subsequent readings examine the functioning of the modern university system in detail (34 and 35). There is a comparable literature, omitted here, relating to hospitals and public utilities.

Here again we see a major analytical breakthrough resulting from the tremendous insights afforded by the newer economic theory. Berle was correct in suggesting that there would have to be compensating benefits (or controls) to overcome the lessened power of monitorization resulting from diffused ownership. But he did not see that a private market solution to that problem was impossible only in those cases in which private ownership rights are attenuated by law, as with rate-regulated public utilities; or where transferability is limited, as in the case of not-for-profit institutions.

The significance of transferability finds unexpected application in the article by D. Martin on property rights in jobs (36). Although as yet we have no literature analyzing union organizations and the behavior of trade union leaders and members comparable to that developed for corporations and not-for-profit organizations, this article does give some important insights into several aspects of trade unionism. It is safe to predict that this important area will be carefully investigated before long.

As mentioned earlier, that old devil scarcity required foregoing inclusion of the important and fascinating literature on bureaucracies being developed by such writers as W. Niskanen, R. Posner, G. Tullock, R. Noll, A. Downs and G. Stigler.   The interested reader is referred in the first instance to Niskanen's pathbreaking book, *Bureaucracy and Representative Government* (1971).   Nonetheless, as a small sop thrown in this "political" direction, and hopefully for a chuckle along with an insight, I have included H. Manne's "Parable of the Parking Lots" (37).   It is short, but it does tell something about the interrelation- ship—or perhaps I should say identity—of market forces and politics.

*

28: THE BASIS OF SOME RECENT ADVANCES IN THE THEORY OF MANAGEMENT OF THE FIRM

ARMEN A. ALCHIAN

Attacks on the theory of the firm—or more accurately on the theory of behavior of individuals in the firm—have called attention to logical inconsistencies in the profit maximizing criterion and to empirical evidence refuting its implications in a wide class of firms. The empirical evidence seemed overwhelming that individuals working within a firm as managers or employees (and even as employers), pursued policies directed at, for example, increasing sales, gross assets, employees, expenditures for various equipment and facilities beyond those that yield a profit maximum.

Attempts to defend the profit maximizing theory by rigorously treating profits as capital value increments, rather than as current transitory rates of net earnings—so as to avoid the short- and long-run pitfall—removed some conflicting evidence. Similarly a defense asserting that the aberrations are temporary deviations in a search process does eliminate some more of the embarrassing evidence. However, the defense is not adequate; a vast class of behavior conflicting with wealth maximizing remains to be explained.

The observations of behavior that refute the profit or wealth maximizing theory are the 'facts' that some managers incur expenditures apparently in excess of those that would maximize wealth or profits of the owners of the firm. Managers of corporations are observed to emphasize growth of total assets of the firm and of its sales as objectives of mana-

Reprinted from *Journal of Industrial Economics* (November 1965), pp. 30–41.

gerial actions. Also managers of firms undertake cost reducing, efficiency increasing campaigns when demand falls; under wealth maximization they would already have been doing this. Managerial actions not conducive to the greatest wealth to the stockholders are taken to be well-established facts—and with which there appears to be no quarrel. Baumol emphasizes the managerial objective of sales increases, even to the extent of postulating that sales maximization is an objective. Penrose emphasizes the growth of the asset size of the firms. None of these can be made consistent with stockholder wealth maximization. If one postulates asset growth or sales maximization he will explain some cases but reject a lot of others in which that simply does not hold. Similarly, attempts to posit asset or sales maximization subject to a minimum wealth or profit constraint also runs into the objection that it implies the firm will not make *any* sacrifice in sales no matter how large an increment in wealth would thereby be achievable. Observed behavior simply does not support that attempted revision of the theory. Thus the Baumol type of attempt to modify the theory flounders—which in no way diminishes the importance of the insistence on recognizing inadequacies in the then existing state of theory.

Attacking any theory is easy enough, since none is perfect. But the wide class of empirical observation that *is* explained by economic theory should caution one against sweeping that theory aside and setting up new *ad hoc* theories to explain *only* or *primarily* those events the standard theory will not explain. What is wanted is a generalization of economic theory to obtain an expanded scope of validity without eliminating any (or 'too much') of the class of events for which it already is valid. Too many new theories happen to be *ad hoc* theories, valid only for a smaller class of cases. And among recent attempts to increase the power of the theory of the firm one can find some sparkling examples. Though there is no point in our giving attention to those failures, credit is due them as reminders of the areas in which economic theory awaits valid generalization.

Deserving our attention here are those in which scientific progress toward a more generalized and valid theory is realized. Two recent works serve as good examples. Especially distinguished is the contribution in Oliver E. Williamson's *The Economics of Discretionary Behavior: Managerial Objective in a Theory of the Firm*, a doctoral thesis (which won a Ford Foundation award) [11]. The other is Robin Marris, *The Economic Theory of Managerial Capitalism* [7]. Now that we have some advances we can look back and determine what prior works served as foundations for the advance. Especially noticeable as pathbreaker was Gary Becker's *Economics of Discrimination* [4], also a doctoral dissertation completed almost ten years ago. From Becker to Marris and Williamson there is worth noting here, the works of Downie [6], Baumol [3], Penrose [9], Simon [10], Averch and Johnson [2], Cyert and March [5].

Perhaps the nature of the advance can be characterized by asserting that the old schizophrenia between consumption and production behavior has been replaced by a consistent, more powerful criterion of utility maximizing.   In a sense the utility theory underlying individual behavior in the consumption sphere has swallowed up producer or management theory —with, if we judge the recent literature aright, significant improvements in economic theory.   Rather than concentrate on a detailed statement of who said what (and why he should or should not have said it), this paper is an attempt to indicate the nature of that advance—as a sort of survey review of the recent literature.

A means of advance was made explicit by Becker, who insisted that non-pecuniary sources of utility be included in the utility function of an income earner.   An owner, manager or employee is prepared to sacrifice some pecuniary income as a source of utility if he is offered enough non-pecuniary goods, which also contribute to utility.   Becker concentrated on race, religion and congeniality of colleagues or employees as a source of non-pecuniary utility.   He emphasized the production trade-offs or transformation rates between money income and working conditions (including color of colleagues and other non-pecuniary goods) and he pointed out that changes in the trade-off rates would affect the extent to which a person chose non-pecuniary sources (goods) of utility relative to pecuniary income.

There is, of course, nothing novel in this proposition.   One can find it in Adam Smith.[1]   But with the growth of formalism and rigor of mathematical modes of analysis it seems to have dropped out of the theory. Becker's dissertation stimulated applications of the principle to see if different kinds of institutions implied different trade-off rates between pecuniary and non-pecuniary incomes to managers and employees.   Thus, a paper by the present author and R. Kessel [1] applied the analysis to profit limited and regulated businesses—public utilities, for example, and derived the implication that discrimination against racial and religious groups is greater in profit controlled firms.   Any firm already earning the maximum *allowable* profit found it almost costless (of profits) to 'buy' that kind of discrimination.   Evidence was also presented to corroborate the analysis.   Averch and Johnson applied the principle to investment activities of owners of public utilities and derived an implication about the extent to which investment in cost *increasing* activities would be induced.

Marris says the managers will be induced to sacrifice some increment of owner's profits for the sake of the increment of size of firm (and consequent increment of managerial salary).   Manager's salaries are larger in larger firms.   Therefore they will have an incentive to enlarge the firm beyond the owner's wealth, or profit, maximizing size. Marris makes explicit that stockholders are not blind to this; the costs of their detecting this effect and exerting controls are large enough to make it more economical for stockholders to tolerate the reduced wealth than to incur the costs required to keep the managers more strictly in line with the stockholder's wealth maximizing criterion.

Unfortunately Marris's analysis appears to be slightly marred by a logical confusion between rates of profit *per unit of investment* and absolute growth of wealth (profit)—in view of the fact that the investment is a discretionary *variable.*[2] If I am correct in my understanding, the implication derived by Marris, wherein the manager will seek a growth rate of assets beyond that which maximizes the above mentioned ratio, is completely consistent with simple wealth maximization *to the owners.* Diminishing marginal rate of return on *additional* investment calls for setting that marginal rate of return equal to the rate of interest—maximizing neither the marginal nor the average rate of return per dollar of (variable) investment. However, it would be a simple task to set the analysis aright by formalizing into the manager's opportunity set of choices among wealth to stockholders versus wealth to managers the costs to stockholders of enforcing a stockholders' wealth maximizing criterion on the managers.

Marris says he uses a utility maximizing approach wherein the person has his utility increased not only by higher salaries but also by greater security in his continued incumbency. In a strict sense, this is a wealth maximizing rather than a utility maximizing, approach for the manager. It is that because a greater security is an increase in wealth. If risk of loss of future receipts is reduced, the present value is increased. Hence Marris uses a wealth function in which two components of greater wealth are made explicit—the projected future receipts and the probability of their being realized.

Competing with the utility maximizing approach is a wealth or growth of wealth maximizing criterion. Marris devotes most of his book to an exposition of a model in which the growth of the firm is constrained by internal saving out of its business generated income. As it turns out, a wealth growth maximizing criterion is a wealth maximizing criterion. Although Marris offers interesting observations it is his utility maximizing proposition that makes his approach most fruitful—in this reviewer's judgment.

As of the present moment, the best formulation of a theory that seems to be both more general and more valid than the wealth maximizing theory is the utility maximizing approach more fully presented by Williamson. He postulates that the manager can direct the firm's resources to increase his own utility in at least three ways. First, he can get a higher salary by obtaining greater profits for the owners, as in the older profit maximizing model. Second, he can direct the firm's resources so as to increase his salary at the expense of a decrease in profits. In particular, if the manager believes that a large firm is correlated with higher salaries (holding profits constant as a *ceteris paribus*), he will strive more to enlarge the gross asset size of the firm.

Third, the manager can sacrifice some increments to stockholder profits in order to increase expenditures for his own non-pecuniary emoluments within the firm. The extent to which these three avenues are used depends on the costs to the stockholders of detecting and policing the manager's behavior and effectiveness, *i. e.* on the costs, of enforcing contracts. In the modern, large corporation these costs are higher than in the single owner enterprise (and are absent in the owner-operated enterprise).

The third of the avenues listed above is formally admissible if one uses a utility maximizing theory rather than a pecuniary wealth maximizing postulate. By doing so, the manager's behavior is interpreted as choosing among opportunities to obtain increments of non-pecuniary goods in his utility function (*e. g.*, pretty secretaries, thick rugs, friendly colleagues, leisurely work load, executive washrooms, larger work staff, relaxed personnel policies involving job security, time off for statesmanlike community activities, gifts of company funds to colleges, out of town hotel suites, racial and religious discrimination in personnel policy, etc.). The utility maximizing theory is applicable and useful if, and only if, (1) we can identify some of its components (beside direct pecuniary wealth) *and* if (2) we can identify circumstances that involve differences in the costs of each of the various types of managerial non-pecuniary 'goods'. By satisfying these two conditions, we can deduce the relative extent of such activities in each of those circumstances.

One circumstance is the type of ownership of the firm, *e. g.*, corporate ownership, non-profit firm, public utility (with a restricted profit rate), and governmentally owned organizations. In this context, the contributions of the recent literature lie in the clues about the differences in relative costs among various types of organizations.

In conformity with the familiar fundamental theorem of demand, the lower the cost of a good or activity (whether it be a traditional type of economic good or one of a more general class of goods, like pleasant surroundings and those mentioned above) the more it will be demanded. This is all merely standard economic theory applied in a broader nexus of utility affecting components and is in no way an abandonment of the traditional basic theorems.

Williamson and Marris provide advances along the second and third avenues, indicate how to test the theory, and provide examples of tests. Williamson considers emoluments and staff preference as two ways of spending beyond the profit maximizing rate. The preference for larger staffs exists because salaries to a manager are correlated with a larger staff under a manager—a phenomenon best explained, to my knowledge, by Mayer [8].[3]

The approach used by Williamson is expressible as a maximization of the manager's utility, which is a function of several specified variables (*e. g.*, size of staff and profits of the firm). The utility is subject to constraints on the choices he can make about staff and profit. Williamson postulates that profits are affected by the size of the staff (at first profits and staff size are positively related for increasing staff up to level and thereafter negatively related for larger staffs—given the demand environment of the firm). The owners of the firm, by detecting and policing their employees' actions, seek to induce them to select the maximum profit combination, which maximizes owners' utility. Unfortunately for the owners, there are costs of detecting and policing his actions so as to make sure he does select that point. Once these costs are recognized, it is obviously better to avoid some of these costs if the profits saved are less than the costs. Cash registers, sales books and accounting systems are in part devices to enable more efficient detecting and policing of employees' deviations from profit maximization. The greater the costs of this detection and policing, the greater will managers sacrifice profits for the sake of staff size and other means of increasing management utility.

Perhaps Williamson's analysis can be most easily illustrated without doing it too much violence, by his graphic technique. In Figure 1, the vertical axis measures profit to the owner-stockholders. The horizontal axis measures staff (or emoluments) to the manager. Curve *AA* is the feasibility curve portraying the opportunity set of combinations of profits and 'staff' open to the manager. The initial positively sloped portion indicates joint increases in staff and profits; the negative portion indicates staff can be larger than the profit maximizing level indicated at the point *K*. One typically shaped utility curve is drawn *UU*. Profits to stockholders enter the manager's utility function in so far as larger profits imply larger salaries to the manager. Similarly, staff enters as an argument in the manager's utility or wealth function in that this too is correlated with salary as well as with emoluments. The familiar conflict of interest between stockholders and manager or between owner and employee, or between taxpayer and government employee is portrayed by the utility curves of the employee-manager's utility function which contains the firm's staff or emolument component whereas only the profit or net value of the firm enters the stockholder's utility function. Point *L* is chosen by the manager. That point *K* is not chosen reflects the costs that must be borne by stockholders if he tried to detect and prevent *all* deviations from point *K*. The opportunity set bounded by *AA* would be vertically bounded

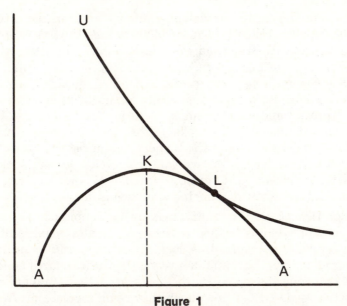

Figure 1

**Stockholder Profits and Staff Size as Sources of Utility or Pecuniary Income
to Manager Shift Equilibrium beyond Maximum Profit Size**

on the right by the dotted line straight down from K if, and only if, detection of profit maximizing actions and the policing were costless.

Any events, circumstances or factors that affect the feasibility curve (taxes, changes in business conditions) can shift the optimum tangency point. (Similarly, anything that shifts the shapes of the utility map will shift the equilibrium position.) Williamson derives the implied effects of corporate tax changes on the position and shape of the opportunity set bounded by AA. He also analyses the effects of a decline in business conditions on the curve AA. Williamson shows that the decrease in demand (and profitability) implies an increased effort to achieve greater *efficiency* in staff size—such as presumably would already have been achieved if the managers were maximizing profits of the stockholder owners. Thus the results differ from those of profit maximization, and they are more like those that seem to be observed in reality.

The significant point is that the equilibrium or solution values involve staff size, corporate expenditures and emoluments beyond the maximum profit combination of profits and staff or emoluments. Thus the owner's profit maximizing hypothesis is apparently replaced with a more general utility maximizing postulate for the manager with the indicated resultant implications. A fixed total tax shifts the AA downward vertically; this leads to a solution with smaller gross size of firm, emoluments and staff. Williamson points out that a firm with several subdivisions could in effect impose a fixed tax on each subdivision—calling it an overhead cost—thereby inducing the subdivision managers to shift their actions more toward profits and less toward staff and gross asset size. The lower the profit to the subdivision the greater the marginal rate of substitution in consumption for managers between profit and other 'goods'. The tax does not change the feasible or opportunity rate of substitution between salary from larger profits and gains from the size and staff, because the slope of the AA curve is unchanged as it is shifted vertically downward. This leads to the leftward revision of the tangency point between the curve AA and the utility line. Marris, as we said, came close to the same result; in fact his book presents a diagram much like Williamson but the axes are different and no utility maximizing approach is involved.

The significance of the utility maximizing approach for the sales maximization approach is rather interesting. Sales maximization, advanced conjecturally by Baumol, is constrained by a 'minimum requisite' profit. Unfortunately, this minimum requisite profit squares neither with the rest of economic theory nor with the facts of life. Managers do not maximize sales regardless of how much they could increase profits if they sacrificed some increment of sales. While sales maximization subject to the postulated constraint gives *some* implications that agree with observed events, it also implies many other things that are refuted by all available evidence. The hypothesis cannot be held out as a serious proposition. Instead, Williamson's model seems to explain the facts that Baumol was seeing and emphasizing. He saw some firm's managers with their eyes on sales—even to the point of increasing sales beyond what everyone would have agreed was the profit maximizing level. Williamson makes this sensible, in that the incentive to increase sales is not treated as a single criterion for maximization, but rather as *a* means of the manager increasing his salary—in much the same fashion as a larger staff under the manager has the same effect. Substitution between these various components (salaries correlated with firm's profits, sales, assets, employees, etc.) affecting the manager's income or utility is the crucial factor, and Williamson emphasizes the factors making the substitution rate non-zero.

Without tarnishing the brilliance of Williamson's work, we can point out a bit of ambiguity. The derivation or basis of his profit-staff feasibility curve AA is not clear. In particular, he does not indicate exactly what is being held constant as a constraint defining the opportunity set. Furthermore, pecuniary and non-pecuniary benefits are mixed together on his emolument and staff division, thus making the utility isoquant an ambiguous concept. However, this can be easily corrected, formally, by adding a new dimension by which he can separate the pecuniary from the non-pecuniary goods to the manager. This would require at least a three dimensional graph and a more detailed mathematical formulation.

One could then include business expenditures designed to increase, not the manager's pecuniary salary, but rather the *non-pecuniary* benefits available within the firm, like those mentioned above in the 'third avenue'. If quantities of these non-pecuniary benefits were explicitly included in the utility function and also indicated along one of the axes of the graph, we could draw iso-utility curves, showing combinations of pecuniary and non-pecuniary goods that yield a constant *utility* to the manager. Then the tangencies of the utility function with the feasibility function (production function of wealth and non-pecuniary benefits) would yield the solution values of profits and types of non-pecuniary managerial benefits for the managers.

If one formulates his analyses in this way, the changes in taxes and especially of changes in ownership structures (which affect the costs for owners to detect and punish non-profit maximizing behavior by their employees) will be reflected in the feasibility set or production function on which the managers can operate. For example, the incentive to achieve maximum feasible profits for any given level of emoluments depends upon the costs of the owners detecting that full realizability and appropriately rewarding or punishing the manager. If a large corporation with many stockholders involves higher detection and policing costs, the inducement for managers to depart from the objective of their employers is increased. In effect the profit-emolument curve is lowered and made flatter, pushing the manager toward greater emolument and less profit to stockholders.

This model can, and has been, applied to profit-limited public utilities and to non-profit corporations. A lesson to be drawn from these applications is that we can readily improve our analysis of managerial behavior if we first categorize firms according to whether the firm is a public utility (with constraints on the retainable profits) or is a non-profit organization (rather than according to size or simply to corporate versus non-corporate firms). Much loose talk and erroneous blanket generalizations about managerial behavior would be avoided if the differences among *types* of corporate ownership were recognized. Drawing inferences from the behavior of managers of *large* (public utility firms) and applying those inferences to managers of non-public utility firms is not generally justified. What is more viable in one firm is not so viable in another. A further temptation to compare the small manager's behavior with that of a large non-profit or public utility is to confound size with different forms of ownership. Improvements in this direction await merely the application of some routine intellectual toil.

This model certainly can be applied to government ownership, where it may serve to shock some people who think that more government ownership or regulation will solve the problem of making managers conform more to the criteria they are 'told' to seek.

The approach in the literature reviewed here is in stark contrast to that which attempts to use new types of utility functions, such as lexicographic or discrete utility functions. Lexicographic functions rank goods by some criterion and assert that those of a lower rank provide no utility until those of a higher rank achieve some critical amount. For example, there may be no utility of non-pecuniary goods (via prestige, leisure, emoluments, pretty secretaries, etc.) until profits or income achieve some minimum level. Furthermore, increments of the higher ranking goods beyond the critical level have zero utility, so that in effect, substitution among goods is denied. The analyses covered in this review retain the classic utility function but revise the types of constraints on the opportunity set of choices open to the utility maximizer (instead of revising the utility function). It is difficult for this reviewer to place much hope in this lexicographic type of utility function—in view of the clear cut refutation of its implications. The refutation of some of the implications derived with the classic utility functions seem (now that one examines these new analyses) to the result of the postulated constraint system. By revising the constraints, rather than the utility function, new implications are being derived. Instead of postulating classic constraints of private property with zero costs of detecting and policing employee behavior, a more general theory can be derived from more general or varied types of property constraints. Perhaps unwittingly the literature of managerial behavior is enlarging the realm of formal economic theory to be applicable to more than conventional, individual private property systems.

Another apparent 'casualty' of the utility maximizing approach under the revised constraints is the 'satisficing' or 'aspiration' approaches. The discussion by Marris [10: pp. 266–77] is especially effective in bankrupting 'satisficing', perhaps even more than Marris intended. As he points out, in one sense it amounts to a statement of a constraint, rather than an objective. That is, certain conditions must be satisfied (*i. e.*, losses not incurred). In another sense it indicates a 'maximum'—given the costs of getting more information about the possibility and location of still superior positions. As Marris suggests, the subject faced with a problem involving effort in finding the solution, sets up a tentative solution or target as an aspiration or satisficing level. If he happily succeeds in exceeding that level, he raises his 'aspiration', target or 'satisficing' level. And conversely. In this sense the word is simply a name of the search process for maximizing some criterion—not a replacement or substitute.

There is no sense in trying to summarize a review. Instead a couple of personal impressions are offered. First, and least important, it is embarrassing that some economists feel compelled to preface or defend their work by an attack on the irrelevancy of existing economic theory. Even more embarassing is their subsequent erroneous use of that theory.

Second, it is a genuine puzzle to me why economics has no 'field' or section (analogous to the 'fields' of money and banking, international trade, public finance, labor, etc.) devoted to 'property rights'. The closest thing to it is the field known as comparative economic systems; yet even there the fundamental role of the particular set of property right, as a specification of the opportunity set of choices about uses of resources, seems inadequately recognized. Especially puzzling is this in view of the fact that Adam Smith's *Wealth of Nations* is heavily concerned with exactly such questions. Perhaps the answer is that the whole of economics is the analysis of property rights in non-free goods. But if that is so, it is puzzling why it has taken so long to bring rigorous analytical techniques to bear on the implications about behavior under different forms of property rights. In any event, a substantial start has now been made—even if it has not been explicitly recognized. Hence one of the major points of this paper has been to try to make explicit and emphasize this basis which, I think, underlies the advances of analyses here reviewed.

REFERENCES

Armen A. Alchian and Reuben A. Kessel, 'Competition, Monopoly and the Pursuit of Pecuniary Gain', *Aspects of Labor Economics*, Princeton: National Bureau of Economic Research 1962.

H. Averch and L. L. Johnson, 'Behavior of the Firm Under Regulatory Constraint'. *American Economic Review*, December 1962, 52, 1052–69.

William J. Baumol, *Business Behavior, Value and Growth*, Macmillan Co., New York, 1959.

Gary Becker, *The Economics of Discrimination*, University of Chicago Press, Chicago, 1957.

Richard M. Cyert and James G. March, editors, *A Behavioral Theory of the Firm*, Prentice-Hall, Englewood Cliffs, 1963.

Jack Downie, *The Competitive Process*, Gerald Duckworth & Co., London, 1958.

Robin Marris, *The Economic Theory of 'Managerial' Capitalism*, Free Press of Glencoe, 1964.

Thomas Mayer, 'The Distribution of Ability and Earnings', *The Review of Economics and Statistics*, May 1960, pp. 189–95.

Edith T. Penrose, *The Theory of the Growth of the Firm*, John Wiley and Sons, New York, 1959.

J. G. March and H. A. Simon, *Organizations*, John Wiley and Sons, New York, 1958.

Oliver E. Williamson, *The Economics of Discretionary Behavior: Managerial Objectives in a Theory of the Firm*, Prentice-Hall, Englewood Cliffs, 1964.

FOOTNOTES

[1] Book V, Chapter 1, Article 2 and 3 of his *Wealth of Nations*.

[2] Pp. 254–60.

[3] Mayer's explanation, in terms of the dependence of marginal product of managers upon the size of assets affected by the managers' decisions, avoids many of the superficial, misleading or downright erroneous explanations relying on convention, prestige, privilege of rank, etc.

B Continued

29: CORPORATE MANAGEMENT AND PROPERTY RIGHTS

ARMEN A. ALCHIAN

Though we know securities regulation is what securities regulators do, we may not know "why." Why should exchange of corporate property rights be permitted only under restricted conditions, whereas exchanges of non-corporate rights—such as rights in nonprofit corporations, or to proprietorships in houses and lands—are not equally regulated? What is there about corporate rights that calls for distinctive treatment?

Varied answers can be offered by economists. For example, securities in a corporation are homogeneous and purchased by many people; each potential stockholder in a corporation would bear a cost of independently discovering essentially the same information about the firm—a cost repeated for each potential buyer in some degree. If this information is required from each firm and made public, information search costs are reduced. For houses or privately-owned, noncorporate enterprises the turnover of identical rights is sufficiently small that potential costs savings are insufficient to justify the costs of compulsory revelation of "all" material and relevant data.

But one may still wonder why we insist that all public, corporate firms reveal information. Why not let those that choose to do so file "full-disclosure" reports; potential buyers could then ignore those which do not. Stockholders could then decide whether the change in stock values consequent to reduced information costs about the corporation is worth the cost of general disclosure. This would permit buyers to act on less information if they wish. It is hard to see how one can argue against

Economic Policy and the Regulation of Corporate Securities (H. Manne, ed.), Washington, D. C., 1969, p. 337.

such optional behavior unless he takes a paternalistic attitude—a position not without its advocates.

Another argument for compulsory disclosure is the reduction in fluctuation in security prices (as distinct from later or earlier fluctuation), but strong theory or evidence to support that proposition—or indeed even to deny it—is lacking.

Probably the most popular basis for regulation of the conditions under which corporate securities may be sold rests in the ingenious phrase "separation of ownership and control." Writers who have tried to put content into that phrase have elaborated by saying "no group of stockholders would be able under ordinary circumstances to muster enough votes to challenge the rule of management."[1] Or "barring blatant incompetence, management can count on remaining in office. . . . [S]o long as management possesses the confidence of the board [of directors], that body will usually not actively intervene to dictate specific policies."[2] "Control lies in the individual or group who have the actual power to select the board of directors" and these presumably are some group other than the stockholders.[3]

Competition is said to be so restricted by the market power of large corporations as to change the role of competition; behavior by managers and employers is so insulated from the wealth-increasing interests of the owners that the conventional view of managers operating to increase owners' wealth is no longer germane.[4]

Though these pronouncements lack empirically refutable content, their emotional impact rivals that of a national anthem.

The empirical evidence for the "separation" theme, if we judge by the data brought to bear, is the dispersion of stockholdings in our largest corporations, combined with management advantages in a proxy fight. Recent data suggest the dispersion of stockholdings over holders with small proportional amounts has increased.[5] Yet surely the music about separation of ownership and control requires more lyrics than that stockholding is dispersed among many stockholders with no holders having, say, 10 or more percent of the holdings. If that were all there were to the theme, it would mean merely that the expression "separation of ownership from control" had replaced the expression "dispersion of stockholdings." I would have thought that anyone propounding or testing a phenomenon to be called the separation of ownership from control would identify it with more than a measure of degree of stock ownership dispersion.

The expression probably suggests some behavioral implications. What are they? Is it that more dispersed holdings give less certainty to any one holder that his preferred use of the corporate resources will be the actual one? Or that the agent he prefers as the manager is not the one who is? Or that the probability that a *private* proprietor of $10,000 of goods can determine the use of those resources is higher than the probability that the preferred decision of an individual with a $10,000 interest in a million dollar enterprise will be the one executed.   (But note that through his power of decision making on $10,000 is reduced, it is increased over the remaining $990,000.)   Any of these might denote the behavioral phenomenon implicit in the expression "separation of ownership from control."   But I suspect it is not what is meant.

For clues to the meaning, we can note that a necessary attribute of ownership is the bearing of the value consequences of resources.   We can interpret control to mean the authority to control decisions that will affect the value of resources.   What must be meant by those who speak of separation of control from ownership is a reduced ability of the owners to revoke and reassign delegations of decision-making authority that will affect value.

In other words, it is assumed that the probability that any majority can be formed to reassign authority is lower the greater the dispersion of stock ownership.   This may rest on two factors: (1) Knowledge of negligence or inefficiency by an agent will be more expensive to disperse over a majority.   (2) The knowledge of harmful managerial decisions will be less influential on each stockholder, as the proportionate interest of the largest stockholders is smaller and the number of stockholders is greater.   In this sense, a manager's deviations from stockholders' interests are less likely to be "policed."   This is one empirically meaningful interpretation of the expression, "greater separation of control from ownership." [6]

But some features of group ownership cut against this argument. A greater number of owners implies a greater variety of owners, some with more knowledge of the particular business.   We can not assume legitimately that when there is one stockholder, he is the person most able to detect deviant behavior.   Specialization of knowledge is not to be ignored; the corporate form enables a greater utilization of specialization of expert business knowledge.   Despite the difficulty in reconciling several points of view, the variety of talents and the special knowledge may more than compensate.   Committees are not entirely vehicles for blocking action.

Corporate voting mechanisms are frequently alluded to as both a principal cause and as "evidence" of a separation of stockholders from "control."   Management, with its accessibility to proxies at corporate expense, is alleged to dominate the voting.[7]   No minority group can be formed to fight the management.   The picture is completed with an etching of a monolithic management group with common interests, no interpersonal conflicts of interest, and capable of perpetuating itself in office. (One is reminded of the naive cartel theory in which a group of erstwhile competitors agree to share a market, apparently with no conflicts of interests to be resolved or suppressed.)

But in fact, if a management group is exploiting stockholders by operating an enterprise in a diversionary manner, opportunities will arise within the group for some to gain personally by eliminating that "inefficient" behavior. Management cannot be adequately analyzed if it is regarded as a single person; there is competition within management; managers can move to new jobs; and they compete for jobs by superior performance on present jobs. For example, few of us at the University of California strive to produce superior products in research and teaching because the taxpayers of California are uppermost in our interests. It is the appeal we offer to other potential employers that induces us to act as if we were trying to satisfy our present employer's interests. Only if my future were irrevocably tied, like a slave, to my present employer would my behavior match that of the folklore indolent manager.

While we can leap from a monolithic view of management to the idea of effective separation of management from stockholder interest and control, we can not do so if we recognize other significant management constraints. If that leap were valid, then I conjecture the tenure of office of managers in "management controlled" corporations, as they are called, should be greater than in other corporations. Is the management more able to stay in office at unaffected salaries? Are stockholder profits in such corporations smaller? Is management compensation greater? Is the transition probability matrix of larger dispersed corporations different from others? I know of no empirical tests of these possible implications. Is what I have called the superficial analysis of the "separation" thesis incorrect, or is the alternative which does not dismiss so readily the competitive forces valid? Absent any empirical evidence in favor of the former, I shall not reject the latter.

In sum, demonstration of greater dispersion of stockholdings, along with our proxy system, does not establish that bearing-of-value consequences have been separated from the effective control of the decision maker, nor that the wealth of the stockholder is less well guarded.

There seems to have been an embarrassing delay or unwillingness to formulate the thesis in such a way as to make it refutable or testable. One would have expected the advocates to have presented evidence. But in 30 years, we remain with almost no empirical evidence. *So, presumed implications still remain to be validated by empirical study,* and I know of none. There is one test, the survival test, but that is given almost no attention.

Since we observe an increased dispersion in corporate ownership, we should wonder why stockholders whose interests are less heeded by the top management would purchase stock in such corporations. Perhaps other advantages of the corporate form more than offset losses to stockholders imposed by the increased divergence of managers from stockholders' interests. This *could* be correct, and the fact that the dispersed ownership has increased certainly does not lend *support* to the implications of the general thesis that managerial activity in these situations will be less consistent with the shareholders' interests. Absence of a theory does not prove the phenomena are absent, but the concomitance of unspecified implications, little evidence and inadequate logic is certainly not conducive to confidence.

Weaknesses in Theory of New Corporate Economy

Some analytical and conceptual mistakes have been committed in attempts to deduce a "distortion" in managerial behavior. It has been said that profits accrue to those who bear risks and make innovative decisions. Indeed, you can find economists who have referred to profits as rewards for innovative activity, with the value effects serving to induce such innovation by rewarding the risk takers. But it is something else to say that managers who select the innovative uses are those who bear or should bear consequent value effects. Whether or not they do depends upon prearranged contractual relationships with respect to property rights.

The economic concept of "profits" refers to a particular value phenomenon—unpredicted value changes. Whoever has the title to goods is the person who bears the profits and losses. "Owner" is the name given to that person. It does not advance rigorous analysis to talk about profits as the "reward" to both the owners *and* to managers who exercise delegated decision authority in determining uses of resources. This careless conjunction, common in the lay literature, leads to sentences like "if the courts, following the traditional logic of property seek to insure that all profits reach or be held for the security owners, they prevent profits from reaching the very group of men (managers) whose action is most important to the efficient conduct of enterprise. Only as profits are diverted into the pockets of control do they, in a measure, perform their second function" (i. e., inducing innovation).[8]

To believe that employed managers, with delegated authority to determine uses of someone else's resources, are the bearers of resultant profit or loss is to lose sight of the essential attributes of the ownership-agency relation. Managers do *not* bear those realized profit gains or losses. Owners do. The manager does not acquire those realized profits any more than does the designer or builder of a profitable apartment house acquire or share in the realized profits—all of which go to the apartment owner. Profits (or losses) from the construction of an apartment house are borne by the owner, not the architect or builder. The profits they initiated are not theirs and are not distributed to them unless they initially had a contract to share in them—i. e., unless they initially had become co-owners in the assets. Yet, although that is true, it does not follow that the wealth or income of the architect or builder is unaffected or that he is left unrewarded. A profitable apartment brings more demand for its architect or builder. Increased demand leads to higher incomes for the architects and builders—or managers.

It is one thing for agents with delegated authority to be rewarded for creating profits for owners; it is a far different thing for delegated agents to share *in those* profits. Profit receivers do not give up any of their accrued profits when their agents are subsequently paid higher incomes for future services. The *past, realized* profits are not redirected to or redivided among the managers in the form of new subsequent contractual terms. Rather, the initial realized profits of the resource owners were smaller because people anticipated that the wages of the superior manager would be bid up in efforts to obtain his services. No *prior* contractual provision explicitly arranged between the parties is necessary for the superior manager to realize a gain for superior services. His revealed superiority is reflected in his higher market value.

I conjecture that confusion has arisen from the impression that a person gets what he produces—a manifestly false, if not empty, proposition. Instead he may get, via a contract, in the context of competition for his services, an amount commensurate with the most optimistic employer's belief of what he is *expected* to produce. If he prefers a different kind of contractual reward, viz., one in which his reward is contingent upon realized results, then he can become a co-owner of the resources whose values are to be affected and part of which value is to be his.

In sum, the fact that delegated agents are paid to produce value changes in goods by the way they use them, does not in any sense imply that the agents deserve or will obtain part of *that* value change. This stands even though their subsequent contracts reflect their earlier performance in successfully producing past profits.

Belief that earlier realized profits must be shared among the owners and the so-called responsible superior managers or innovators results from a failure to recognize anticipatory capitalization in the market's valuation of resources. If the manager had to be rewarded by a payment out of the initial profits realized by the initial employer, then those who worry about separation of ownership and management functions would indeed have pointed out a problem.[9] But that is not the way a market values resources.

Neither is that the logic of economic theory nor the logic of conventional profit theory, despite some assertions to the contrary.[10] The conventional and still valid wisdom presumes competitive market capitalization of foreseeable future events and assumes that once a manager displays evidence of a superior activity, the market (i. e., other people) will not ignore the implications about the future demand and costs for his services. Ignoring or denying the forces of open competitive market capitalization is, in my opinion, a fundamental error in the writing about ownership and control and about the modern corporate economy. Neither the role of competition in the markets for capital goods and services, nor its logic, is upset by the presence of large corporations with dispersed ownership.

Not only is market valuation ignored in the misinterpretation of the role of profits, but it is ignored also in the contention that the modern stockholder's wealth is less well protected in the dispersed than in the concentrated ownership corporation. We have only to ask if anyone would pay as much for a share of stock in a corporation with dispersed ownership if he knows his wealth would be given less diligent interest by corporate managers. He would pay less in the knowledge he was to get less. The lower bid prices for stock would protect investor-owners from the foreseeable losses anticipated from less diligent concern for their wealth. Yet, corporations have thrived, and they would not have if the dispersed ownership corporation suffered from this value discounting.

Resolution of these two conflicting interpretations lies in the possibility that either (1) the alleged greater diversionary activity is a myth, or (2) the dispersed large corporation is so advantageous in other respects that the diversionary tactics of the managers are financed out of those advantages while the stockholders get as much as they would in less dispersed corporations. If the former were true, the whole issue would collapse. If the latter were true, it would imply only that the *forms* (but not value) of managerial behavior and of rewards in the dispersed ownership corporation are different and more costly (inefficient), but the managers would reap no extra gain. The consumer of products of those corporations would be paying a higher price than he otherwise would (but still, a price lower than if there were *no* dispersed ownership corporations). But could it not still be argued that the stockholders could have received a larger return? It would seem not, for if they could have, the number of dispersed corporations would have increased, thus lowering returns to the equivalent of what is being obtained in less dispersed ownership corporations. Let me elaborate on these points.

Managers do not reap some special or additional gain or economic rent from their ability to engage in diversionary tactics. Awareness of greater diversionary capability by managers or employees results in lower pecuniary salaries as managers and employees compete for the jobs permitting diversionary tactics.[11] Competition among managers and employers in seeking attractive, easy, or secure jobs implies a lower pecuniary reward in those jobs. A job with more leisure yields a lower wage; one with greater security yields a lower wage; one with more leisure and a given wage will have its security competed down. Substitution among the various facets of jobs occurs so that, on *net* of all considerations, the advantage of one job over another is competed away. All the various facets constitute "forms" of payment to the employee, whether the facets be leisure, wages, types of colleagues, working hours, vacation provisions, extent of surveillance by the employer, or what have you. Pecuniary salary will be lower for the same reasons that salaries of people working in factories or shops in more pleasant surroundings will be lower than they would have been with less attractive working conditions. Stockholders need not be activists in bringing this about.

This argues that the dispersed ownership corporation implies a difference in the vector or form of payments to managers and employees. But not all forms of "compensation" to employees are equally costly. The form of compensation in a dispersed corporation may indeed represent a higher cost vector to the corporation, but if the corporation can earn enough because of its advantages, it can in equilibrium bear this higher cost vector of a managerial "salary." This does not mean the employees or managers are getting a more valuable or preferable return than in less dispersed corporations. Instead they are being paid with a different, higher cost (i. e., less efficient), vector of rewards—one that costs more to provide but is no more preferable on net that those used in other corporations or businesses. It is different simply because the costs of controlling the various facets of the vector and changing it to a different one (say one with higher wages and less leisure) is greater than the saving. The higher costs of such vectors (of given attractiveness to employees) can be financed out of the advantages of this type of corporation. If the costs of these forms of rewards to managers had not been higher, one might think there would have been larger earnings for the owners. But this would not be an entirely correct conclusion, for the number and scope of such corporations would have been greater, with consequent lower prices to consumers. The higher cost salary vectors, if indeed they are more costly, simply mean a sacrificed output potential for consumers—evidenced by higher prices than would have been paid for the larger output if the dispersed ownership corporation could police and control its managers' and employees' behavior as efficiently as is alleged for a smaller, less dispersed, corporation.

To repeat, all this argues that the dispersed corporation changes the *forms* (and efficiency) of payment to employees and managers. It does *not* imply lower wealth for the stockholders, nor higher earnings for employees and managers, than in less dispersed corporations. If employees tend to be thieves, and if employers or employees are aware of this tendency, contractual money salaries will be adjusted so that part of the total salary is taken as legitimatized "theft." The employers do not necessarily lose. The higher policing costs are borne by (i. e., discounted by lower wage offers to) the employees whose past conduct determines their present reputation and beliefs about future behavior. Similarly, if dispersed corporate ownership permits managers greater scope for anti-stockholder activity and if the stockholders or the employees are aware of this tendency, the terms of employment compensation will be adjusted.

The resultant implication is that in large, dispersed-ownership, for-profit corporations, we should expect different types of managerial and employee behavior and rewards than in small and closely held corporations. The large corporate pattern should reflect the greater costs of policing and revising delegated authority, but *without* necessarily resulting in lower wealth for the stockholder than in less dispersed corporations. These effects, insofar as they are foreseen or predictable, on the average will be reflected in anticipatory behavior, and therefore in the valuation of initial capital investments or in stock prices on subsequent stock transfers. The stockholders are not any the poorer or their wealth less well secured.

How valid is this competitive market equalization process in reality? We do not know. But that does not mean that we can gratuitously assume it is absent or weak as does most of the writing on the "ownership and control separation" theme. Nor can we cavalierly assume the opposite.

Do dispersed ownership firms have historically lower rates of growth of stockholders' wealth (allowing for dividends and capital value growth) than less dispersed ownership firms? I have yet to see a test of this, though this appears to be a feasible evaluation. With attention to the "regression phenomenon" and with controls for types of industry, this should make a fine project for several doctoral dissertations—several, because of the value of replication and competitive testing of results.

Let us consider the presumed monolithic structure of management in the business firm. In reality, the firm is a surrogate of the marketplace, but differs in that longer-term general service contracts exist without continuous renegotiations at every change of type of service. To analyze the firm as a single-operator institution within which it is assumed there is not the competition that exists in markets is to miss a significant portion of the competitive processes. Though a firm may continue with unchanged name, and possibly even the same stockholders, the internal shifting of personnel within, as well as among, firms is market competition. The many people within a firm competing with each other and with people in other firms should suggest that the unit of analysis for competitive activity is the individual rather than an institution, which serves as an internalized market. Top management of a firm engages in screening employees, techniques, and proposals for new products which, if performed externally by separate firms, would be clearly evident as market functions. But when these functions are performed within the firm, the competitive market forces are hidden from obvious view and mistakenly ignored by careless analysts.

More significant than the rise and fall of firms, for purposes of behavioral analysis, is the rise and fall of individuals within firms. For many purposes (though not all) we can think of a firm (call it General Electric) as a marketplace, as if it were a city, within which individuals engage in atomistic competition. Competition among cities takes the form of individuals moving among cities and exporting ideas that have passed the test of profitability. While it is not correct to carry this analogy too far—and just how far "too far" is, I do not yet know—the analogy is very good in some resepcts. The long survival of some firm or of a few firms cannot be interpreted as evidence of a lack of market competition either within or between firms.

If it be argued that corporations with dispersed ownership or with so-called management control have separated the interests of stockholders from those of managers, we should expect differences in the rates of transition of individual employees within and between firms. We should perhaps expect a lower turnover of management in the dispersed corporation. Do we have any evidence of it? I have been unable to find it. However, I shall cite some evidence later for implying different types of behavior. For example, to continue to speak of a mythical firm called General Electric, the directors and president are quick to fire or demote a division chief whose profit record shows inferiority to some other potential division head. Replacement of an inefficient division head *may* be quicker within General Electric than if the division manager owned the division. The internal capital and personnel market may be more efficient than the external open market. I could go on and assert that there is greater mobility of managers and technical personnel within General Electric than among firms in an atomistic market economy, that new ideas are internally evaluated more quickly, cheaply, accurately, and on a broader scale than in a society made up of several firms aggregating the same size. I could assert that the labor market within General Electric is superior to the atomistic, so-called, pure competitive market and is superior because there are specialists within General Electric who are rewarded more fully for collecting and evaluating information about people. Thus the usual outside employment agencies that specialize in providing personnel information would be less efficient than the personnel employment agencies operating within General Electric. But what the truth is, I do not know.

Further, the investment funds (capital) market *within* General Electric is fiercely competitive and operates with greater speed to clear the market and to make information more available to both lenders and borrowers than in the external "normal" markets. In fact I conjecture that the wealth growth of General Electric derives precisely from the superiority of its internal markets for exchange and reallocation of resources—a superiority arising from the greater (cheaper) information about people and proposals. Many "knowledge effects" that would be externalistic in an ordinary market are converted into beneficial internalities within the firm as incentives and rewards to those producing them.

The foregoing is intended to suggest that the traditional theory of profits, of private property, markets, and competition is not obsolete, and also that the "separation of ownership from control" theme still lacks validly deduced and established implications about exploitation of stockowners' wealth. Long prior to the wide dispersal of stockholdings in a corporation, potential conflicts of interest among stockholders were recognized. Political theory if not legal history tells us much about the probability of subgroups exploiting the remainder by the group decision process. Furthermore, the conflict of interest between principals and their agents has long been recognized, though I presume that it is not that idea which the "separation of ownership and control" is supposed to designate.

If I appear to be defending the old theory as adequate, let me beg off. Inadequacies in the old theory exist, but they derive from its use of a wealth instead of a utility maximizing postulate. The wealth maximizing postulate is usually appropriate (or less inappropriate) when applied to the "firm" as a unit of analysis. But in seeking to explain individual behavior *within* the firm, utility maximizing criteria are more general and powerful than wealth maximizing criteria. And I believe this would be equally true for the old-fashioned small firm.

Instead of a change in the modern society, it is the change in the objectives of economic theory that points up inadequacies in the old theory. We want now to interpret individual behavior, not merely firm survival as an entity. Although I say this is a change in objectives, I should be the first to assert that good old Adam Smith did exactly that in his *Wealth of Nations*. The adherents of the theme of a new modern corporate economy are saying what Smith said about corporations. Yet they are denying that the old competition theory is applicable; a somewhat strange twist, indeed.

There have been changes in our economy. But I do not believe that the idea of a replacement of a competitive era by an era of "market-power" large firms will enrich our theory or understanding of behavior.

My own impression is that moves toward an economy with less open-market competition reflect a diversion of competition to the political processes, as resort is made to greater governmental control over economic access to markets and terms of exchange.   Much of what passes for the new corporate economy should more accurately be called the new mercantilist, or the new "political" or politically regulated, economy, since it involves more political competition and the greater use of political rewards and penalties.   And this move to political influence has occurred in both small and large firm industries.   The "solution" offered (if such a "political" economy is a problem) usually is more political controls and political competition.   This is beneficial to those most adept at political competition, for they would benefit from increased demand for their services as political competition displaces market competition in controlling economic activity.   And this is what the "obsolete" economic theory implies.

*   *   *

[Balance of Article omitted (ed.).]

FOOTNOTES

1 R. J. Larner, "The 200 Largest Nonfinancial Corporations," *American Economic Review*, September, 1966, p. 779.

2 P. A. Samuelson, *Economics*, 7th ed. (New York: McGraw-Hill, 1966), pp. 89–90.

3 A. Berle and G. Means, *The Modern Corporation and Private Property* (New York: Macmillan, 1933), p. 69.

4 C. Kaysen, "Another View of Corporate Capitalism," *Quarterly Journal of Economics* (1965), p. 43.

5 Larner, op. cit.

6 Notice that one of the premises underlying this was *not* that in a group decision process one subgroup can exploit another, such as occurs in political voting for say a tariff or licensing restriction on entry to a profession.

7 Berle and Means, op. cit., p. 139.

8 Ibid., p. 350.

9 Note that I refer to a separation of *functions*, not a separation of interests or a loss of control.

10 Berle and Means, op. cit., pp. 341–51.

11 Unless you believe, with Kaysen, that executive compensation is not within control of the stockholders, op. cit.   If I knew what that really meant, I might test it.   If it means what I suspect it was intended to mean, I think it is wrong.   But then, ask yourself, "Does an owner have 'control' of the wages he pays in any kind of firm? "

30: OUR TWO CORPORATION SYSTEMS: LAW AND ECONOMICS

HENRY G. MANNE*

In the past thirty-five years a large literature has developed criticising what is sometimes termed the traditional theory of corporations.[1] Unfortunately, there is no such theory,[2] and, as a result, much of this criticism has simply tilted at windmills. To make matters even worse for the critics of nonexistent theory, it is not one but two theories that are missing, one for large, publicly traded companies[3] and one for small, closely held ones. By and large the legal-historical developments and the economic functions of these two systems are quite different, and meaningful legal or economic analysis must begin by recognizing this fact. This Article represents an effort to outline a dual theory of corporations. It may serve as a basis for criticizing our traditional corporate system or simply for understanding it better.

The history of the large corporation in America begins essentially in the 1830's with the first wide public promotions of railroads. There is little in the history of corporation law before that which contributes significantly to later developments. The older law did provide some of the forms, vocabulary and legal formulas used by lawyers in the transition to a different kind of institution. Indeed 14th and 15th century English common law dealing with corporations sole and aggregate (towns, the church and the king) also served this purpose. But these formal aspects should not be confused with the fundamental business pressures which generated mid-19th century corporate legal norms. Undoubtedly this inheritance of form and language was important—especially from the law-

Virginia Law Review, Volume 53, March 1967, Number 2, p. 259.

yer's point of view. But its functional significance was very small. New forms of vocabulary could have been easily invented, as indeed many were. Where we find older forms employed by modern corporations, it seems safe to conclude that they are used because they function satisfactorily, not because no alternative system can be devised. To attribute the success of the modern corporation specifically to law and lawyers is a professional conceit which will not bear scrutiny.[4]

The Publicly Traded Corporation—Economics

The fundamental fact about the development of American corporations in the 19th century is that they came into existence because entrepreneurs, or promoters, needed some device to raise capital from a relatively large number of investors.[5] The implications of this simple fact are almost astounding in their reach. It is possible to predict or describe much of the legal structure of the large corporation system from the logical implications of this one notion.

The first important legal norm which can be derived from the central concept of the corporation as a capital-raising device is that of centralized management, which has been virtually sanctified in the classical words of every state's corporation statute: "The business of a corporation shall be managed by its board of directors." A moment's thought will show how the concept of centralized management is directly related to the idea of the large corporation as a capital-raising device. At the stage of selling securities, promoters have already performed the entrepreneurial function. Traditionally, this includes not only conceiving an idea, but also engaging in those steps necessary to bring the idea to successful fruition.[6] As generally understood, this means that promoters, in forming a corporation and marketing its shares, perform an entrepreneurial function. But it also implies that the selection of the managerial group is a function of the entrepreneur, and not of the capitalist investors.

Thus if the principal economic function of the corporate form was to amass the funds of investors, *qua* investors, we should not anticipate their demanding or wanting a direct role in the management of the company. Management, and the selection of particular managers, is not, in theory at least, a function of capital investors. Management is a discrete economic service or function, and the selection of individuals to perform that function, whether undertaken at the outset or during the later life of a company, is a part of the entrepreneurial job.[7] Centralizing management serves simply to specialize these various economic functions, and to allow the system to operate more efficiently.

It is sometimes assumed that centralized management is merely a practical outgrowth of the early law's concern with large corporations.

Thus it is argued that direct democracy would not be feasible with a large number of shareholders and that representative governance is the only feasible alternative.[8]   But this approach can never explain why the law was mandatory on this subject.   The matter could have been left to the interested parties to decide for themselves if size and practicality were the only issues.[9]

It is perhaps less obvious that the concept of limited liability also flows logically from the concept of the corporation as a capital-raising mechanism.   One of the great advantages of the large corporate system is that it allows individuals to use small fractions of their savings for various purposes, without risking a disastrous loss if any corporation in which they have invested becomes insolvent.   In any given promotion there may be substantial investors and small investors, and clearly each of them cannot be made equally liable for all the debts of the business operation, as in a partnership.   If this were the case, small investments in corporations would tend to come only from individuals who were nearly insolvent already.   Wealthy individuals would never make small investments in a corporation.

An alternative would be to make every shareholder liable on a pro-rata basis for that portion of the corporation's debts represented by his interest.   Here again, substantial difficulties would plague the rule (as demonstrated by those cases imposing liability upon shareholders of defectively formed corporations).   Some individuals will have received substantial shares for promotional activities or other non-cash consideration, thus indicating unwillingness or inability to shoulder a financial burden. A rule of pro-rata liability could prove highly arbitrary in its actual effect and would not necessarily give creditors any real protection.   There are practical difficulties as well, since the costs involved in assessing and collecting fractional liabilities from large numbers of small investors might frequently be greater than the anticipated recovery.   Limited liability, of course, obviates all these questions, and directly shifts an easily recognizable risk to the corporation's creditors.

There is still another explanation of limited liability for corporate shareholders.   It is one thing for a corporate investor to assume the risk of losing a specified part of his assets.   But the possibility of liability arising at an unforeseen time and in an unpredictable amount would probably be too great a risk for large numbers of small investors to shoulder. Limited liability is probably an essential aspect of a large corporate system with widespread public participation.

This matter can also be analyzed by comparing the costs of alternative methods of allocating the risk of corporate insolvency.   The costs of placing this burden on investors might be prohibitive, but the real economic cost of locating this burden on those dealing with corporations is probably relatively low. First of all, many creditors of corporations will also be corporations, and thus the shock of one corporate debtor's bankruptcy may be cushioned through a series of corporations. Perhaps more important, at least in the case of voluntary creditors—which certainly includes most business creditors—the risk of insolvency is regularly understood and, where significant, treated as any other cost. This explains why business associations with limited liability are required to record information about financial limitations in some public place.

This last explanation of limited liability does not account for the problem of the involuntary creditor, or others who might in some sense be considered noncommercial creditors. One group overwhelmingly affected in this way is the labor force. As the principal victims of industrial accidents, they formerly constituted the most numerous group of involuntary creditors. The modern counterpart of this group is composed, of course, of the victims of the corporation's automobile or truck accident. And laborers are today the noncommercial participants most dependent on corporate solvency for their income. If the problem presented by these groups had not been resolved in other ways, it is possible that tort victims or employees would have been regularly excluded from the concept of limited liability. In fact, shareholders in New York and several other states to this day may be held liable for wage claims.[10] Bankruptcy law was early adjusted to avoid any heavy impact on employees,[11] and unemployment compensation may also have removed some of the sting from limited liability as it might affect employees. The solution to the industrial accident problem was simply shifted out of the corporate arena, and its modern counterpart, the auto accident, seems to place no special pressure on the limited liability concept.

A prime requisite for the functioning of the corporation system as a capital-raising device is liquidity for investment. Even with limited liability an investor must still consider the possibility of a change in his own or in corporate circumstances which may affect his investment interest. While the concept of limited liability looks to the danger of corporate insolvency, liquidity or marketability of securities is perhaps most important when the corporation is not threatened with bankruptcy. An individual may decide at a particular time that his needs are best served by a high-risk investment. But it is a far different matter to suggest that this decision must be made on a near-permanent basis. Any rational investor will recognize that his investment needs or interests will change as he grows older, as his family circumstances change, as the size or nature of his estate changes, or as alternative opportunities for utilization of funds present themselves. And death must ultimately bring in a new owner with different needs and circumstances.

Furthermore, even if the position of the investor remains constant, circumstances within the corporation may change so that the investment no longer serves its initial function for him. For instance, the corporation may change its dividend policy, or embark on more or less speculative activities, or change its mode of operation in such a way as to have unhappy tax consequences for a shareholder. Any of these may dictate the desirability of some alternative use of the funds and the liquidation of present holdings. Thus, in most instances, a functioning stock market will be of more interest to a potential corporate investor than will the limitation of his liability in the event the corporation is not successful. The latter interest will, of course, vary with the degree of speculation involved in the investment.

Another aspect of market liquidity relates not to changes in investment needs but to the investor's freedom to dissociate himself from a particular corporation if for any reason he becomes dissatisfied with its management. There is only one alternative to market liquidity as a way out for corporate investors. That alternative is dissolution of the corporation and the sale of its assets, with subsequent distribution to the shareholders of the proceeds. But the market allows discrete decisions to be made by individual investors, whereas the dissolution alternative requires some level of general agreement among the shareholders before it can be utilized. A system in which a minority shareholder is given the power to force dissolution of a large corporation because of his own dissatisfaction or a change in his own investment needs would not be workable. At the time an investor makes a decision to purchase a security he must assume that his investment opportunity will continue in substantially its present form and that there will be no arbitrary dissolutions.

But the market cannot be made the exclusive way out. Legal provisions relating to dissolutions are necessary in any system of business associations since it may be in the financial interests of all the investors to redistribute these particular assets rather than to wait for an inevitable bankruptcy. But market liquidity provides such an efficient alternative for investors that dissolution can safely be made relatively difficult to obtain, thus giving greater protection to those shareholders who wish to remain with the venture, without injuring those who prefer leaving. Not surprisingly, therefore, voluntary dissolution and other so-called organic changes in a corporation require more than a simple majority of shareholder votes.[12]

So far we have examined two discrete markets which have influenced the development of legal norms in the large corporation. One of these was the market for investment capital, primarily illustrated by the promotors' search for new funds. The other market is that for the buying and selling of existing securities, mainly exemplified by the organized securities exchanges. Now we will examine briefly a third market, one which has been referred to as the market for corporate control.

The market for corporate control can function only because shares carrying votes can be bought and sold. Thus, given the concept of majority determination of corporate control, it is possible to buy control of the corporation directly by buying fifty-one per cent of the voting shares. In corporations with widely diffused ownership,[13] the figure may be considerably less than fifty-one per cent, and control may be secured through methods other than direct purchase, such as merger and proxy fights.

The market for corporate control serves an extraordinarily important purpose in the functioning of the corporate system. Unless a publicly traded company is efficiently managed, the price of its shares on the open market will decline, thus lowering the price at which an outsider can take over control of the corporation.[14] The constant pressure provided by the threat of a takeover probably plays a larger role in the successful functioning of our corporate system than has been generally recognized. It conditions managers to a specific point of view perfectly consistent with the shareholders' interest, to wit, keeping the price of the company's shares as high as possible. Even this, of course, is no guarantee that an outsider will not feel that he can do better; but if the management group performs relatively efficiently, the dangers of losing control are not great.

It is necessary to examine two minor points relating to markets to understand fully the economic framework of the large corporate system. The discussion of a market for corporate control assumes that the price of the company's securities will in general accurately reflect the relative efficiency of a company's management. Is there then any basis for assuming the necessary inputs of knowledge to guarantee that market prices will accurately reflect the management's efficiency? One need make only one assumption to answer in the affirmative. That assumption is that insiders, or any others who have accurate and reliable information about the corporation's activities and prospects, actively trade in its shares. If an individual has information indicating that the price of a particular share will eventually increase, it would be in his interest to buy the shares, thus causing the price to rise, even though the information is not yet disseminated to the public. If he knows depressing news, he will sell. Thus, insiders, by engaging in profitable transactions, tend constantly to move the price of shares in the correct direction.[15] Their interest in maintaining control, however, may introduce some upward bias, though this is probably insignificant in corporations with widely diffused ownership. The role just described for the stock market assumes that so-called insider trading will not have injurious effects.[16] And in fact the long-term investor in a publicly traded corporation can almost never be injured by this practice. In the first place, the less frequently he trades, the less likely he is ever to encounter an inside trader. More important, the true investor will tend to buy or sell for reasons relating to his own financial circumstances or to various factors having a personal impact on him. He would tend to sell at the same time whether or not a rule allowing insider trading existed. The impact of insider trading on long-term investors will be almost insignificant. The short-term trader, however, is in a very different position. His motivation is likely to be that of a gambler,[17] and he is trying to insinuate himself into the position of someone with reliable, undisclosed information. Since most of his information will in fact not be reliable, he will be trading frequently against other short-term traders and against insiders. It is the latter group who will tend to make the process an unprofitable one for the short-term trader.

We have seen that insider trading serves the important function of constantly moving share prices in the correct direction. This practice serves still another important competitive function, perhaps going to the very heart of the corporate system. If an individual makes an important invention, our legal system allows him a temporary monopoly called a patent. He may then sell the patent or license its use as he sees fit. But many innovations in the business world are not patentable under present laws. How then can such an inventor or innovator gain the value of his development? Generally classical economists assumed that the normal process of exploitation of an idea involved the establishment of a new business through which the innovator would exploit his idea. His return on the idea would generally be mixed with the return for his capital contribution and his performance of the managerial function. It is not evident, however, that this mixed mode of entrepreneurial compensation can be made available to innovators in existing, publicly held companies. On the other hand, the corporation with publicly traded shares is in a position to make discrete purchases of entrepreneurial services, no matter who performs them. Such services may be purchased from employees of the corporation or from outsiders such as lawyers or investment bankers. Basically this is done through the practice of insider trading. Where an individual is responsible for a development which will have an impact on the price of the corporation's stock, the most appropriate method of paying him is to let him exploit the value of his information in the stock market. The argument has been spelled out at length elsewhere [18] but the important point is that, if a competitive market for entrepreneurial services exists, insider trading allows large corporations to compete effectively with small, privately owned or newly founded businesses for these services.

The Publicly Traded Corporation—Legal Norms

If the implications of the economic forces discussed above are carefully interpolated, it is possible to develop the major outlines and many details of the typical general corporation act up to about 1930. These statutes, for reasons which are still unclear, were adopted with the publicly held

corporation almost exclusively in mind.   Although there are a few exceptions, it is not until the late 1930's that we begin to find numerous amendments designed for corporations with the shares closely held and rarely
sold on an open market.

Since one of the aims of general incorporation acts was to avoid the
administrative problems inherent in special chartering, these acts had to
provide the detailed mechanics for incorporation.   For instance, one of the
requirements of early general corporation acts was that there be a minimum of three directors, each of whom should be a shareholder of the
corporation.   Because of the use of dummy directors, this provision soon
ceased to have any importance, but like many traditional statutory provisions, it did reflect the notion of some multiplicity of investors.[19]   Statutes required various financial provisions to appear in the articles of incorporation which were to be registered and made a matter of public
notice.   In this way, creditors were to be notified of the risk they assumed by dealing with a limited-liability enterprise, though again the
practice did not conform to the expectations.   Similarly, the articles
were required to give the name and address of a registered agent to accept service of process, thus aiding creditors in reaching corporate assets.

Many other provisions required to appear in the articles of incorporation were designed to inform shareholders of the nature and identity of
their investment.   For instance, the name of the company, its period of
existence, its principal business activity, limitations on powers, the names
of incorporators, and certain financial information performed this function.   Special provisions relating to voting, preemptive rights and preferences in dividends or liquidation also served to inform shareholders.

The statutes determined the moment at which the corporation came
into legal existence and generally required public filing of the articles
in the county of the principal place of business as an additional protection to creditors.   The function of the government official, usually the
secretary of state, in issuing the certificate of incorporation was purely
a ministerial one.   His job was solely to determine whether or not the
provisions of the statute had been complied with, and not to question the
desirability of the provisions made by the incorporators.   These acts,
true to their special-charter ancestry, were largely permissive and flexible.   By and large this philosophy of corporation statutes has continued
until today.[20]   The changes in the system have taken place outside the
framework of these statutes, largely through the development of blue sky
and federal securities laws.[21]

Perhaps the provision most characteristic of American corporate
philosophy was that the business of the corporation should be managed
by the board of directors.   The reasons for this provision have been examined above and require no further elaboration here.   As we should

anticipate, the statutes provided for election of the board of directors by majority vote, though classes of nonvoting shares were generally allowed. The idea of free transferability of voting shares was well understood, though it was not explicitly provided for in the statutes, and many early cases attest to the strictness with which courts treated any attempt to restrict alienability. Whether this was an unconscious recognition of the importance of a market for corporate control or the direct application of common-law precedents, as it appeared to be superficially, is not clear. But given the amazing aptitude of common-law courts sometimes to come up with appropriate solutions to complex economic issues, the former explanation does not seem far-fetched.

The idea of corporations functioning within a competitive, free-enterprise system, coupled with the 19th century's suspicion of or unfamiliarity with government regulation, leads to one of the most important doctrines of corporation law. This is the so-called "business judgment rule," probably one of the least understood concepts in the entire corporate field. It is still widely believed that this rule was designed to encourage individuals to take positions on boards of directors by protecting them from liability for mistakes of business judgment, even though the same action would constitute negligence under ordinary standards. But that encouragement could as well have taken the form of compensation for service as a director, as it did in England. More recent discussions of directors' liability have centered on the problems of indemnification provisions, suggesting still another alternative to the business judgment rule as a device to protect directors. However, the liability aspect of the rule may well have been incidental to its principal function. The rule is more likely to have survived because it functioned as a quasi-jurisdictional barrier to prevent courts (as the only available governmental agency) from exercising regulatory powers over the activities of corporate managers.[22]

To avoid undesirable judicial intervention, two alternatives were available. Courts could simply restate the verbal formula for liability (usually by compromising on standard of care) and apply it very gingerly. This approach, however, has reflected all the difficulties inherent in trying to describe by a literary generalization a way to measure the "quantity" of negligence. The business judgment rule, while not entirely obviating that problem, provides a brilliant partial solution. In effect, the court applying the rule must first examine the facts to see if this is the kind of case which it should hear. The test for this is more objective and straightforward than that for negligence. It will preclude the courts from any consideration of honest if inept business decisions, and that seems to be the purpose of the rule.

The requirements for invoking the rule have a logic of their own, which dictates most of the standards with which we are familiar in business judgment cases.   First, the decision in question must have been one actually contemplated by the directors.   Consequently the business judgment rule cannot be used as a defense to a charge that a director neglected to attend meetings and to guard the corporation's interests, or that he attempted to delegate his responsibility to a third person.   Since the corporate system is premised on some coincidence of interest between managers and shareholders, the decision-making process must be one which on its face can be presumed to be in the interest of the shareholders.   Therefore, if a colorable allegation of conflict of interest or fraud is made, the business judgment rule should not apply.   Manifestly, this would be the case where directors were voting on their own salary or on contracts with other companies in which they held an interest.   The assumed identity of interest between particular managers and the shareholders may not exist when matters of corporate control are in question. Consequently the rule is properly applicable only to so-called "ordinary" business decisions and not to mergers, liquidations and other changes upon which we do not want simple majorities to pass.

If a court finds after a preliminary investigation that some necessary prerequisite to allowing full managerial discretion is missing, it should proceed to the merits of the case with no further consideration of the business judgment rule.   If, on the other hand, it finds that all these elements do reasonably appear, or that the allegation is really one of negligence, it should refuse to investigate the matter further, without regard to the amount of loss the directors may have caused the corporation. The idea of gross negligence, while not without difficulties, probably has to be maintained and dealt with in the familiar manner of gross negligence cases in other areas.

But corporation law must still provide some device for recovering damages from dishonest, disloyal or grossly negligent managers.   The technique established for this purpose, the shareholders' derivative suit, is an independent American legal invention, though it borrowed its form from very early English equity practice.[23]   There are basically two problems in allowing shareholders to sue corporate managers.   The device must not require or even allow every shareholder of a corporation to sue for his aliquot share of the total recovery.   This would be an extremely inefficient scheme, since the share of the damages of many shareholders in a company with widely diffused ownership would be too small to warrant their bringing a suit.   It might also require the courts to litigate the same issue over and over again.   Furthermore, as a technical legal matter, individual suits in which the corporation was not joined as a party would not be binding on the corporation, and consequently, in many instances, the courts would not be able to design an effective remedy since they would have no jurisdiction over a crucial party.

The second problem is that recovery by individual shareholders would be tantamount to a court decision that this money could or should be paid out to the shareholders as a dividend. Without the wrongdoing, the corporation would have had greater assets available to satisfy creditors' claims. However, to protect the corporate creditors, the corporation statutes contained detailed provisions regulating the payment of dividends, and the declaration of dividends is explicitly made the responsibility of the board of directors. Without very special circumstances the courts should not use the occasion of a claim of mismanagement to authorize a pay-out to individual shareholders which the courts would not have ordered directly.

Thus the two major problems inherent in allowing shareholders to police management activities through lawsuits are the danger of a multiplicity of suits and the matter of creditor protection. To meet both of these problems the derivative suit was devised. In this action the shareholder sues on behalf of the corporation and any recovery is awarded directly to the corporation and not to the individual. This could be taken as the one great contribution of the legal order to the functioning of the modern corporate system. Unfortunately the cases couched the standards for such suits in terms of a dichotomy between harm to the corporation and harm to the individual shareholders. By failing to recognize the underlying purpose of the requirement of a derivative suit in certain cases, the courts obscured and needlessly complicated the whole area.

Many legal writers have tended to view the derivative suit as the exclusive mode of shareholder protection. In fact, it is a relatively unimportant one which can be used only to police the more blatant forms of wrongdoing. It can never be effective as a device for the policing of mere inefficiency in management. Given the jurisdictional impact of the business judgment rule and the extreme complexity of derivative suit procedures, it is quite clear that if this were the only protective device, the corporate system could not function as well as it does. Manifestly, the various market forces discussed above both goad and constrain managers in a far more significant fashion than does the derivative suit, though the latter definitely answers a special need.

Another important rule of traditional corporation law is that directors (and a fortiori officers) owe no special fiduciary duty to individual shareholders. This rule too is explainable in terms of the economics of the large corporate system. We have seen that the position of the shareholder is assumed to be that of the capitalist investor of traditional economic theory. His economic function is to put out money at risk for use by entrepreneurs and managers. Apart then from having the shareholders' funds used in the corporation's interest and his contracted-for return paid to the investor, economics suggests no other relationship between investors and managers. The shareholder might retain his investment, receiving his return in the form of dividends; or he might use the market way out, realizing his return in the form of capital gains on the sale.

We have already noted the importance of allowing the most knowledgeable insiders to trade in a company's stock in order constantly to correct the share price. When these insiders buy shares they must buy from existing corporate shareholders. Since we posit that the insiders do—indeed must—have special knowledge which is unavailable to the selling shareholder, the question naturally arises whether a general duty to disclose is owed the noninsider. Traditional corporation law, built on the various market foundations already discussed, unequivocally said no. So long as fraud or deceit was neither proved nor intimated by surrounding circumstances, insiders were not required to disclose information about the company to outside buyers or sellers. But this too was a rule which made sense mainly for companies whose shares were actively traded. In the last section of this Article we shall see how the logic of the close corporation system required a modification of this rule.

Two minor limitations in traditional corporation law should be noted here. Each of them is logically connected to the concept of shareholders investing risk capital in the corporation. The first of these is the concept of equality among holders of the same class of shares. Thus the directors may not declare a dividend to some holders of a class of shares but not to others holding shares of the same class. Nor may particular shares in a class be accorded different voting rights from other shares in the same class. In the large publicly traded corporation, this limitation has not proved significant, though, as we shall see, it suggests an important distinction in the closely held company. The same may be true of another limitation, the so-called pre-emptive rights of shareholders. Here the idea is to protect existing shareholders against dilution of their financial or voting interest by the sale of new securities at less than market price. This protection is afforded by giving them a first option on new issues of stock. In practice this idea has proved both unworkable and unnecessary in large corporations, since directors have no incentive to issue shares at bargain prices to anyone other than themselves, and normal shareholder suits are available to handle that problem.

We have already noted that certain decisions about corporate affairs are not left exclusively to the discretion of the directors. These include mergers and consolidations, dissolutions, liquidations and sales of substantially all the assets. It is sometimes suggested that these activities are simply too important to leave to the directors and that a fundamental interest of the shareholders is involved requiring their approval. But these matters involve business decisions which could easily be delegated to directors. Certainly the shareholders are not better equipped to make these decisions than the directors. That conclusion leaves the somewhat nagging question why, in addition to the vote by the board of directors, even the earliest statutes required higher-than-majority votes by the shareholders to approve an organic change. The answer seems to relate to the concept of majority rule in the corporate sphere. The board of directors is simply the living representation of the controlling block of shares. That is, the concept of centralized management is fundamentally the same notion as majority rule.

In connection with the organic changes under discussion, the unanimity principle would really seem to be more appropriate. This is because each shareholder has in a sense entered into a complex contractual arrangement with all the other shareholders, and such an arrangement could simply not function if one party, even a large majority shareholder, had the power to dissolve it at any time. The unanimity rule, based on constitutional notions of vested property rights, was actually the common-law rule in the absence of a statutory provision lowering the required vote. Under a unanimity rule, every shareholder who wished to remain would receive the maximum security possible. But the difficulty with any rule of unanimity is the problem of the "holdout," or the high costs necessary to secure agreement. Some shareholders, particularly the very small ones, will find it in their interest to vote against a proposed dissolution so that they may be "bought off" by major shareholders.[24] The statutes therefore effected a compromise between a simple majority standard, normally dictated by the need to prevent control by minority shareholders, and the concept of unanimity. Traditionally the statutes selected either two-thirds or three-fourths as the compromise figure. Clearly without cumulative or class voting there is no way to deal with this problem solely through the board of directors, since each director represents the interests of fifty-one per cent of the shareholders, or even less.

But if there are dangers of a fifty-one-per-cent control group abusing minority contractual interests, the same danger exists if the control group happens to own two-thirds of the stock when the statute requires that fraction to vote for a merger or liquidation. Consequently, it is not surprising that the courts have shown some willingness to investigate the fairness of these organic changes even though the statute is strictly complied with.[25] This is actually one of the rare instances in which a problem quite common to small corporations exists for publicly held ones as well.

It was also true that there were no important restraints on the right to sell shares carrying votes. The courts probably made an error of sorts in the early cases holding that a sale of votes separate from the underlying share interest was illegal. This proposition makes some sense if the separation of the vote from the underlying share is made permanent or made to extend over a long period of time, since that would prevent the market for corporate control from functioning effectively. But the legalization of sales of discrete votes for one election would probably represent a marginal improvement in corporation law. The practical difference between allowing a sale of a vote and allowing a sale of the vote-share package is not great. The only difference in cost would be the interest paid (or foregone) on the additional cost necessary to buy the shares outright and hold them for a relatively short period of time.

The Close Corporation—Law and Economics

We have now seen the general outline of both the law and economics applicable to large corporations. It is quite clear that these forces were at work in the development of mid-19th century corporation law, although the exact mechanics of the relationship between market forces and legal developments have never been adequately explored. Probably the experience gained by businessmen and lawyers during the pragmatic period of special chartering in the early part of the 19th century played the most significant role. It is also clear that in the great period of adoption of general corporation acts, from about 1850 to 1875, no radical innovations in corporation law appeared, with the obvious exception of automatic, ministerial incorporation. The general laws simply codified what were understood to be the requirements for a system of publicly held corporations.[26]

These general incorporation acts, while perhaps not necessarily adopted in order to allow close corporations to exist, had that effect, since incorporations without public promotion were facilitated and made less expensive.[27] It seems likely that the adoption of general corporation laws made the use of the corporate form for small enterprises quite attractive. Undoubtedly limited liability, permanent life, easily transferable shares and organizational efficiencies contributed to the large number of small incorporations in the last half of the nineteenth century. But just as the underlying economic principles of the existing corporate system were not understood, their inapplicability to small corporations was overlooked. With hindsight, we can see that the problems that began to develop for small corporations were logically predictable.

Actually, the greatest rate of increase in the number of incorporations by small business seems to have come in the 1940's with the advent of high personal income tax rates.[28] The corporate income tax meant that money earned by the corporation and distributed to the shareholders as dividends was in fact taxed twice. But it was relatively easy to avoid this consequence by making payments from the corporation in the form of salary, interest or rent, which was tax-deductible by the corporation. The rest of the corporate earnings could simply be reinvested in the business. This caused an increase in the value of the shares, and if the shares were held until death, there would be no tax on this gain. They could also be exchanged for easily marketable shares in a merger which visited no tax consequences. And if the shares were sold, the entire increment would represent capital gains rather than ordinary income. For these and other more specialized tax reasons (particularly those relating to executive compensation), many sole proprietorships and partnerships incorporated, with no intention of "going public." The process became so mechanical that today the partnership form is relatively unusual in all but the smallest, most temporary or most informal kind of business arrangements.

As we begin to examine the differences between publicly traded corporations and close corporations, it becomes apparent that the two are extremely dissimilar. First of all, it cannot be said that the guiding need for the organization of a close corporation is to amass capital. It is quite possible that one or even several of the participants in a close corporation, as might be true in a partnership, have been invited solely to contribute capital, and they anticipate no active role in the affairs of the company. But unlike the large corporation, this is not the general rule.

Generally, in small businesses, a few individuals, perhaps each with some specialized function to perform, associate in order to exploit an idea. Their contribution may be capital; it may be an invention; it may be a long-term employment contract; it may be organizational ability; or it may be some other form of property, such as land, machinery, or raw materials. There is simply no way to catalog the various reasons why individuals may contract to associate in a business enterprise.

Since the close corporation is not peculiarly a capital-raising device, we should anticipate much less acceptance of a passive role by shareholders in connection with the management of the business. This is not to say that in many instances such a passive role will not be assumed, but we should simply not expect it to be the almost unvarying norm as in the case of the large corporation. It is quite clear that many of the problems of the small corporation result because of the insistence by the various participants on some role in managing or on some control of management policies.

A connection can readily be seen between the fact that participants in a small corporation are not generally passive investors and the question of the transferability of shares. We saw with the large corporation that a functioning stock market was almost a necessary precondition for the existence of such organizations, primarily in terms of liquidity but also in terms of the market for corporate control. Generally in the small corporation these characteristics will not be desired. Shareholders in a close corporation may frequently provide for direct participation in management. Thus the concept of free transferability of shares could have a quite different impact from the one it has in large companies where only one's status as a passive participant is traded in a stock transaction. Participants in a small business have a very real interest in knowing and controlling the identity of other participants. Thus it is not surprising to find that restrictions on share transferability are very common with small corporations.[29]

By and large the courts have been relatively liberal in allowing share transfer restrictions, even though these are clearly at odds with the norms underlying traditional corporation law. The courts simply borrowed from other common-law areas and concluded that the restraint was valid if it was "reasonable." There is a substantial body of law on the question of what is a reasonable restraint. The most popular device today is the so-called right of first refusal in which the shareholders or perhaps the corporation are given a right to buy shares before they may be sold to outsiders. This device has given rise to a tremendous number of complications. There are the problems of knowing to whom and in what proportion the option will run; whether the outside offer is a good faith offer; how the price of the shares will be determined; and many others. Accounting and legal problems abound, though it would serve no purpose to catalog them here. Suffice it to say that these problems arise in only one small aspect of planning for a close corporation. On the other hand, these complexities simply do not arise in the corporation with publicly traded shares. The market provides a very effective substitute for detailed and complex business planning.

The absence of a ready market for controlling shares, and the existence of various constraints relating to management policies and to the appointment and removal of directors and officers, combine to prevent any smooth functioning of a market for corporate control. Of course, the controlling group may decide to sell out, and this may benefit minority shareholders. But mere inefficiency in management will never be sufficient to signal potential raiders that a profitable opportunity exists, for there is no active trading of shares from which this information can be gleaned, and even if it were known, the individuals responsible for the bad management may be personally "locked in" to their position by very high compensation. That is, the premium which must be paid for control becomes higher as the control block of shares is more securely held [30]—a phenomenon quite typical of close corporations.

The absence of an effective market for corporate control has far-reaching implications for the law of small corporations. With the large corporation, the business judgment rule can be used to prevent the courts from second-guessing corporate managers. Their review is not necessary because other more effective schemes regularly protect the shareholders. But with the close corporation the same thing is not true. For instance, in a large corporation, the failure to pay dividends sufficient to satisfy the shareholders will reflect itself in a lowered stock price and the danger of a proxy fight or a takeover. Thus there is no incentive for management to follow such a policy, and it is quite logical to remove substantially all discretion from the courts on the matter of forcing dividends from large corporations.

In the small corporation, on the other hand, the dividend policy will most frequently reflect the personal and perhaps peculiar financial needs of the controlling shareholders. There will be no market to reflect dissatisfaction with this policy. Furthermore, a failure to pay dividends may be used by the controlling group in small corporations to force minority shareholders to sell their shares at a bargain price. Here it can be seen that it makes considerably less sense to adopt a judicial hands-off attitude. In fact, it would not be too extreme to put the burden of proving the propriety of its dividend policy on the controlling shareholders. The cases may be moving in that direction, but by and large the courts have applied large-corporation norms to these problems.

The dividend example is merely one illustration of how controlling shareholders in close corporations can bring pressure on or abuse minority interests. A full catalog of these methods would require a small book,[31] and yet most of them look on the surface simply like any business decision. Unless minority shareholders in small corporations have made adequate advance preparation, they will not receive adequate protection from either the market or the legal system.

We saw earlier that at common law a corporate director could deal at arm's length with any shareholder. Barring fraud, he had no duty to disclose important information, and indeed his trading on such information seemed both to compensate the entrepreneur and to keep the market price of shares at the correct level. In the small corporation, however, all this is turned on its head. There is no market price to correct; there tends to be an identity between investors and entrepreneurs; transactions will be face-to-face rather than across an exchange; and the relationship of the parties involved will often be close, personal and obscure to outsiders. The last point is important because it explains why fraud or subtle coercion may be so very difficult to prove in many cases.

The net effect of all this was that the practice known as insider trading was not so completely condoned in the small corporation as in the large. The courts did not adopt the partnership standard requiring full disclosure, though this could be contracted for by the parties. Instead the courts developed the "special facts" rule, which is usually called into play when the dangers of abuse seem greatest and the possibility of proving fraud is very small.[32] This ad hoc approach to the problem has worked reasonably well, though it has never been extended to a transaction in listed shares.[33]

By and large the partnership form comprehends the kinds of protection participants in small businesses would want. Interests are not transferable without the permission of the remaining partners. Unless there is a specific provision to the contrary, each partner has a veto power over partnership activities, although the usual rules of apparent authority protect third persons. And (subject to the possibility of contract damages) any partner may dissolve the partnership whenever he wishes. There is also a strong fiduciary duty owed one partner by another. These are essentially the elements desired or needed for close corporations, but none of them is a part of traditional corporation law.

If we examine some of the standard planning provisions for close corporations, it will be apparent how inappropriate traditional corporate norms were for the purposes at hand. First, shareholders in a small corporation might want a greater voice in management than was provided by the number of voting shares held. Identical shares cannot be given disparate numbers of votes, though different classes of shares could be used with each class given the right to elect a certain number of directors. In most cases, the shareholders simply entered into an agreement providing that X would be elected as a director of the corporation. Interestingly enough, this was one of the few small corporation provisions which did not experience substantial difficulties in the courts. The reason is paradoxical, since the courts, borrowing from the logic of the large corporation, repeated the familiar doctrine that a shareholder may vote as he pleases and in his own interest and that, unlike a director, he owes no duty actively to use his business judgment. Thus he did not owe a duty to all shareholders which would be violated by a contractual obligation to vote in a certain way. When these agreements did not require a formal separation of the vote from the underlying shares, the courts upheld them.

Manifestly, however, simply being guaranteed a seat on the board of directors does not in and of itself establish all the authority that an individual may want. He can still be outvoted by a majority of the directors. Participants then tried to specify certain corporate arrangements, such as the identity, salary, powers or tenure of officers or key employees. This time, however, the courts generally refused to allow the agreement to prevail. The statutes provided that the directors should elect officers, and that it was exclusively the directors' duty to determine officers' salaries, etc. The courts almost mechanically repeated that the business of the corporation should be managed by the board of directors. And true to large corporate norms, individual directors were not free to contract among themselves for arrangements respecting any of these provisions.

Many shareholders' agreements took a different approach to the problem. Instead of trying to spell out precise positions, powers and restrictions, they settled for a veto arrangement which ordinarily would provide all the bargaining power necessary. It will be recalled, however, that the corporate norm dictated majority voting by shareholders. The statutes also required majority voting by the board of directors. Thus, when shareholders entered into agreements requiring higher-than-majority votes for shareholder or director action, the courts found that this was in violation of the statutes and regularly struck down these provisions.[34]

When these arrangements were finally approved, mainly by legislation, a new problem arose. By virtue of a greater-than-majority requirement or a unanimity rule, it became an easy matter for a small shareholder to deadlock a meeting of the shareholders or of the board and prevent any action from being taken. In the partnership this does not present insuperable problems, because the nondeadlocking partners have the power to force a dissolution of the partnership. But in the corporation, as we have seen, the large corporate norm dictated rather strict standards for dissolution. It was assumed that the dissatisfied shareholder would remove himself from the association by selling his shares. In the small corporation this frequently is not feasible. As a result, shareholders were forced to complicate their agreements even further by providing such solutions as arbitration, provisional directors, or forced purchase of shares under these circumstances. Again, each of these solutions raised problems, since provisional directors were not provided for in the statute; arbitration was frequently hampered by judicial hostility; and the sale of shares to the other party raised various financial problems.

Legislative approval of small corporate norms developed long before the courts began to reflect a more sympathetic approach. As early as 1901, for instance, state legislatures approved voting trusts which had earlier been declared illegal by courts because of the separation of the vote from the underlying share interests.[35] Later legislatures began to adopt provisions expressly approving various exceptions to the formal parliamentary requirements appropriate only to large companies. Thus waivers of notice were allowed after a meeting, and attendance could substitute for notice. More important, in a great variety of instances statutes were amended by the simple addition at the beginning of a section of the words, "unless otherwise provided in the articles of incorporation" (or frequently, in the alternative, in the bylaws).

Today these "unless otherwise provided" provisions or their equivalent have become so common that there are few truly mandatory provisions left in the typical general corporation act. This reflects an interesting demonstration of the fact that large corporations function in a largely permissive framework and that market forces rather than legal ones have dictated their organization and structure. There is no indication that, since the advent of "unless otherwise provided" provisions, public corporations have taken advantage of this liberalization to establish provisions contrary to those contemplated by the earlier, less permissively worded statutes. One is almost tempted to suggest that the large corporation system could and would function substantially as it does if there were almost no state corporation statutes beyond provisions for incorporation. This may not be so far-fetched, for the effect of most modern amendment programs dealing with basic provisions of the corporation acts has been to modify them in the interest of the close corporation. Our general corporation laws seem to be in the process of becoming general close corporation laws with only incidental relevance to large companies.

FOOTNOTES

* Professor of Law, George Washington University Law School. B.A., 1950, Vanderbilt University; J.D., 1952, University of Chicago; LL.M., 1953, S.J.D., 1966, Yale University. This Article is a revised version of a paper presented at the Annual Meeting of the Southern Economics Association in November 1966.

[1] The seminal work is Berle & Means, The Modern Corporation and Private Property (1932). And see Berle, *Modern Functions of the Corporate System*, 62 Colum.L.Rev. 433 (1962).

[2] There are, to be sure, bits and pieces of theory but no general overview of the entire system putting these pieces into a coherent whole.

[3] On occasion I will refer to "large" and "small" corporations but, unless the context clearly indicates the contrary, the reference is actually to corporations with or without regularly traded shares.

[4] It might be added that those few rules of corporation law which are the most inappropriate economically seem to stem from legal analogies wrongly applied to the newer business form. For instance, the absurdly strict applications of the ultra vires doctrine clearly derived from earlier legal attitudes. The strict interpretation of powers granted a corporation made sense in the period when corporations were granted monopoly privileges as a matter of course, but it was not a workable doctrine for a complex competitive capitalist system governed by general corporation laws. Compare the later development of the business judgment rule, discussed infra, pp. 271–72. Furthermore, the failure to develop suitable rules regarding the separation of votes from underlying share interests seems to have resulted from false analogies to older laws regarding voting in political bodies. See Manne, *Some Theoretical Aspects of Share Voting*, 64 Colum.L.Rev. 1427 (1964).

[5] This is not to say that this was the exclusive reason for the formation of corporations. Clearly that is not true in the case of nonprofit enterprises. Furthermore, there is another dimension to the problem, since many corporations were established for quasi-political purposes. That is, they were established to perform functions which today we commonly think of as governmental, but which the government was unable to perform directly during much of the 19th century. But capital raising does remain a necessary hallmark of every public business promotion, and, as will be seen, its impact on the development of corporation law is probably more pervasive than is that of alternative explanations.

[6] See generally Schumpeter, The Theory of Economic Development (1934).

[7] The fact that management selection remains an entrepreneurial function throughout the life of the firm has considerable significance for the modern debate about corporate democracy. There is no reason to believe a priori that this critical entrepreneurial function can be easily or effectively performed at any stage of a corporation's

life through majority voting by shareholders. The advocates of corporate democracy have probably been widely misled by political analogies. See Manne, *The "Higher Criticism" of the Modern Corporation*, 62 Colum.L.Rev. 399, 407–13 (1962).

8 Ballantine, Corporations § 1, at 4 (1946).

9 In the discussion of the market for corporate control, infra pp. 265–66, we will again see the importance of centralized management as related to the difference between the capitalist's and the entrepreneur's function. There, however, it will be the outsider trying to take over control of a corporation (i. e., selecting himself or another as the manager) rather than the corporate promoter who performs as an entrepreneur. The need for centralized management is the same in either case, however.

10 N.Y.Bus.Corp.Law § 630.

11 In fact, the second highest priority given creditors under the Federal Bankruptcy Law is for wages. 11 U.S.C. § 104(a)(2) (1964). Prior to 1926, federal taxes enjoyed a higher status. See Federal Bankruptcy Act § 64, 30 Stat. 563 (1898). The first priority has always been for the fees of the administrator of the bankrupt estate. See 11 U.S.C. § 104(a)(1) (1964).

12 See, e. g., Del.Code Ann. tit. 8, § 275(c) (1953); N.Y.Bus.Corp.Law § 1001.

13 The reference is generally to ownership of voting shares, though in some special situations where class voting is required, even nonvoting shares may have to be considered.

14 For further elaboration of the thesis, see Manne, *Mergers and the Market for Corporate Control*, 73 J.Pol.Econ. 110 (1965).

15 It is somewhat doubtful that outsiders can ever perform this function as effectively as insiders. Even the mass of data required to be disclosed under the Securities Act of 1933, 15 U.S.C. §§ 77a–77aa (1964), and the continuing disclosure provisions of the Securities Exchange Act of 1934, 15 U.S.C. §§ 78a–78jj (1964), will not guarantee the necessary information. There are two primary reasons why this is so. First, this disclosure can never really explain many aspects of corporate management. The true story of interpersonal relationships, subtle personal contributions and the relative importance of specific individuals often cannot even be articulated, much less made the subject of a specific disclosure requirement. More important, however, the backbone of most disclosure requirements is financial data. But without tremendous sophistication about a company, its industry, its modes of accounting and other factors which are generally available only to a few people, no individual can really evaluate this data. Accounting may or may not be an art form, but it certainly is not a science. Insiders, however, will have (perhaps unconsciously) a key to the meaning of all developments, and they are in an immeasurably better position to "value" their company's stock than are any outsiders.

16 For detailed treatment of this subject see Manne, Insider Trading and the Stock Market (1966).

17 Implicit in this assumption is an acceptance of the so-called "random walk" hypothesis of the stock market. Briefly, this suggests that there is no discernible interdependence between successive price changes in a particular stock, and so-called "technical" factors are thus considered insignificant. The short-term trader is assumed to rely more on "technical" factors than on "fundamental" factors. Thus, his transactions are apt to contain more of the characteristics of gambling than are those of the long-term investor. For detailed consideration of the random walk theory, see The Random Character of Stock Market Prices (Cootner ed. 1964).

18 See Manne, op. cit. supra note 16, at 138–41.

19 There is an amazing case which recognizes this proposition. It is amazing because it was decided in 1956 and seems to be the only holding of its kind in American

corporation law. In Park Terrace, Inc. v. Phoenix Indem. Co., 243 N.C. 595, 91 S.E.2d 584 (1956), the North Carolina Supreme Court held that a corporation, all of whose shares had been transferred to a single individual, ceased thereby to exist, since a one-man corporation was not contemplated by the statute. The case was promptly overruled by the North Carolina legislature. A leading corporation authority said that

> no previous judicial decisions of the Court would have led one to anticipate this rationale. One ventures that nowhere in American decisions of the 20th century has a court for the first time cast so dark a cloud on a form of business organization so commonly accepted, so entrenched in the business mores of the business world, as the one-man and two-man corporation and the wholly owned subsidiary of a parent corporation. Literally thousands of such corporations exist in this state, as well as in other states.

Latty, *A Conceptualistic Tangle and the One- or Two-Man Corporation*, 34 N.C.L.Rev. 470, 476 (1956). Professor Latty was undoubtedly correct. The case appears simply to have been decided one hundred years too late. It might have exercised a very healthy influence on our legal system had it been decided in 1856.

[20] See Katz, *The Philosophy of Mid-century Corporation Statutes*, 23 Law & Contemp.Prob. 177 (1958). This permissiveness in state general corporation statutes is probably a function of our federalist system. Because promoters are free to incorporate in any state and to do business in that or any other state, "shopping" for the most desirable incorporation statute developed quite early. Since the states found various advantages to flow from encouraging more incorporations, a competition, sometimes termed "charter mongering," developed for new incorporations. The "currency" with which the states competed were the provisions of the general corporation laws. The necessary effect of this process was to guarantee that most states would generate highly permissive laws and that ultimately there would be few significant differences among the several states. Although this process has generally been criticized in the literature, it has probably saved our corporate system from a substantial dose of undesirable state regulation. It has had a secondary and unnoticed advantage of making the corporation law of every state generally familiar to lawyers over the entire country.

[21] See, e. g., Fleischer, *"Federal Corporation Law" : An Assessment*, 78 Harv.L.Rev. 1146 (1965); cf. Ruder, *Pitfalls in the Development of a Federal Law of Corporations by Implication Through Rule 10b-5*, 59 Nw.U.L.Rev. 185 (1964).

[22] See Pound, The Formative Era of American Law (1938). See also Hurst, Law and the Conditions of Freedom in the Nineteenth-Century United States (1956). The development of the business judgment rule in the last half of the 19th century contrasts sharply with the seemingly inconsistent ultra vires doctrine, which clearly was an anachronism from the 18th and early 19th centuries.

[23] See Foss v. Harbottle, 2 Hare 461, 67 Eng.Rep. 189 (Ch.1843); Prunty, *The Shareholders' Derivative Suit: Notes on Its Derivation*, 32 N.Y.U.L.Rev. 980 (1957).

[24] For a detailed elaboration of the theory of voting majorities, see Buchanan & Tullock, The Caculus of Consent (1962).

[25] An attempt to deal with this problem by statute was made in the so-called shareholder appraisal statutes, allowing dissenting shareholders to receive an amount for their shares fixed by a court. These statutes are at least implicitly premised on the notion that the market is too imperfect to be relied upon by dissatisfied shareholders. But all indications are that these statutes have been unnecessary and even harmful as applied to companies with publicly traded shares. See Manning, *The Shareholder's Appraisal Remedy: An Essay for Frank Coker*, 72 Yale L.J. 223 (1962).

[26] Probably the greatest single mystery in corporation law history is why, with a significant number of small corporations in existence, the statutes which developed in

the 19th century dealt so exclusively with the problems of the large company. One tentative hypothesis is that the political influence of individuals concerned with larger companies was far greater than that of small business associates. Another conceivable thesis is that these statutes were (erroneously, to be sure) conceived as regulatory provisions rather than enabling acts. Consequently, there would have been less concern with legislation for the close corporation. At any rate, to the author's knowledge this question has never been investigated.

27 Available histories indicate that this may have been exactly what the forces pushing for general incorporation laws had in mind. See, e. g., Cadman, The Corporation in New Jersey: Business and politics, 1791–1875, at 124–26 (1949). But if this is so, it involved the very naive assumption that a law appropriate for publicly held companies could be transferred wholesale to small ventures. There is some empirical evidence that the number of incorporations swelled considerably after the adoption of general incorporation laws. See Evans, Business Incorporation in the U. S., 1800–1943, at 75 (1948).

It should be remarked that the "going public" of a previously closely held corporation entails the same economic considerations as the initial promotion of a publicly held company. Only the identity of the individuals performing the entreprenurial function will be different.

28 The total number of corporations in the United States rose from approximately 450,000 in 1944 to well over a million ten years later. U. S. Bureau of the Census, Historical Statistics of U. S., Colonial Times to 1957, at 572 (1960).

29 This statement, and others where the context makes it clear, must be explained. Most incorporations of small businesses probably use a "boiler-plate" set of articles of incorporation and bylaws. Little use seems to be made in articles and bylaws of the optional provisions allowed by the statutes. See the important study by Dykstra, *Molding the Utah Corporation: Survey and Commentary*, 7 Utah L.Rev. 1 (1960). If a shareholders' agreement or a pre-incorporation agreement among participants exists, in most instances it will be informal and limited to a small number of issues. This probably reflects the fact that small businesses cannot afford the expense required to convert large corporate norms into more fitting arrangements. Dykstra implies that the lawyers may be at fault as well. And legislators may be to blame for not having established a simple boiler-plate close corporation form. Regardless of the reason, it does signify that many small corporations are operating under an inappropriate system. Thus when we say that share transfer restrictions are very common, it means that they are very common only in those cases where the parties do some close corporation planning and not that such restrictions are common in terms of the absolute number of close corporations. There are no data available on the latter point at this time.

30 See Manne, supra note 4.

31 For such a catalog, see O'Neal & Derwin, Expulsion or Oppression of Business Associates: "Squeeze-Outs" in Small Enterprises (1961).

32 See Strong v. Repide, 213 U.S. 419 (1909); Manne, op. cit. supra note 16, at 21–24.

33 Basically the SEC, in cases involving its rule 10b–5, seems to be asking the courts to extend the common-law rule to listed companies and relax some of the common-law strictures on recovery for failure to disclose. See SEC v. Texas Gulf Sulphur Co., 258 F.Supp. 262 (S.D.N.Y.1966); Fleischer, *Securities Trading and Corporate Information Practices: The Implications of the Texas Gulf Sulphur Proceeding*, 51 Va.L.Rev. 1271 (1965).

34 See Annot., 159 A.L.R. 290 (1945).

35 See Delaware General Corporation Act of 1901, ch. 167, § 18, 22 Del.Laws 293 (amending Delaware General Corporation Act of 1899, ch. 273, § 23, 21 Del.Laws 451).

31: SOME THEORETICAL ASPECTS OF SHARE VOTING

An Essay in Honor of Adolf A. Berle

HENRY G. MANNE*

If we were building the American economic system anew, we might wonder whether the present system of stockholders' votes was the best way, or even a good way, of choosing managers or of locating power.

Adolf A. Berle [1]

A developing literature on the theory of political voting holds great promise for its applicability to corporate voting. While questioning our usually oversimplified approach to majoritarian democracy, these works have offered a theoretical foundation for careful scientific analysis of political phenomena. Although the two principal studies [2]—Downs, *An Economic Theory of Democracy*, and Buchanan and Tullock, *The Calculus of Consent*—emphasize different aspects of the subject, they demonstrate the manner in which voting tends to generate optimal solutions to political problems and the likelihood that, with certain limitations peculiar to political voting, more desirable solutions may be reached when some exchange or trading of votes is allowed.

The theoretical proof of this last proposition is both simple and important. Different individuals have different intensities of feeling regarding the subjects or candidates on which they vote. Consequently, assuming that every individual acts in his own self-interest as he sees it, simple majoritarianism can give awkward and undesirable results. If fifty-one percent of the voters favor a project or candidate only very

Columbia Law Review, Vol. 64, (1964) p. 1427.

slightly, they would generally defeat a forty-nine percent minority whose dislike is extremely intense. But if the forty-nine percent are allowed to make some transfer payment to the fifty-one percent, and the transfer payment is sufficient to shift the votes of the majority, total individual welfare would thereby be increased.[3]

This result stems from the application of a fundamental proposition upon which most of economic theory is built: free individuals engaged in exchange because it benefits each of the participants. If I own a book which I value at two dollars and another individual values the same book at three dollars, each of us will gain from a sale at any price from $2.01 to $2.99. This, in its simplest form, is the mechanism by which the free market tends to optimize individual welfare and allocate resources efficiently.

This same advantage from exchange can be had even though the item exchanged is a vote. It is not so obvious as ordinarily assumed why we do not allow the direct buying and selling of political votes. Downs argues that the forty-nine percent do not have to make a transfer payment to the entire fifty-one percent but rather to only two percent in order to win the election; he concludes that vote buying would generally allow no protection for the interests of substantial minorities.[4] Asserting a variant of Downs' view, Buchanan and Tullock claim that imperfections in the vote market would probably allow the creation of a permanently disadvantaged group of voters.[5] These imperfections are analogized to monopoly and perhaps other imperfections in more traditional economic markets, but the point is not elaborated at length. Objections based on these imperfections are heightened by the fact that a redistribution of wealth may result from political voting. The issue on which A, B, and C are voting may cause a transfer of wealth from A to B and C, and so forth. This is one of the reasons why we do not allow all issues to be decided on a purely majority vote basis and why constitutional amendments have high voting requirements. It is possible that political vote selling could result in a redistribution from the less wealthy to the more wealthy, though it is not clear that this would necessarily occur.

There are at least two possible approaches to the analysis of vote selling. Downs sees the actual casting of a vote for a candidate as tantamount to a "sale of the vote" insofar as the voter exchanges a vote for the actions promised him by the candidate. His theory places considerable emphasis on the need for voters to be personally informed in order to know whether voting is worth their effort at all, and, if so, for whom they should vote. Indeed, the cost of informing themselves dictates the not irrational conclusion for many voters that abstention is their best policy.[6] Those voters who feel most intensely about the issues or candidates will be less interested in acquiring new information that may change their views, but they will find it more important to vote according to their preference. In Downs' scheme, therefore, intenseness of feeling will correct to some extent the mal-allocation of resources that might otherwise result from majority voting.

The approach of Buchanan and Tullock to the problem of optimizing individual welfare by political means is more detailed and perhaps more attuned to the American scene.[7] They shift their attention from the mass electorate of a party "government" along the lines of the British system, which is Downs' chief interest, to the activities of individual, elected legislators. Although recognizing the necessity for avoiding the results of simple majoritarianism, the authors present a carefully drawn argument against the legalization of vote selling. They conclude that political logrolling in the legislatures gives most of the advantages to be derived from vote trading while allowing none of the disruptive forces that might result from legalization of direct vote selling.

Corporate voting procedures exhibit similarities and differences when compared with political voting procedures. The high voting device of the latter, for example, is employed in corporate voting to protect investors' fundamental expectations against change through simple majority votes; a two-thirds or other high vote is required for mergers and other organic changes. Contrary to the ban on the sale of political votes, however, corporate vote selling is permitted so long as the vote is sold in combination with the investment portion of the share. Limitations on the power to sell voting or nonvoting shares are indeed treated very strictly by our courts.[8] They generally hold that the discrete sale of a vote is illegal, some solemnly declaring that corporate vote buying is sinful and tantamount to bribery.[9] Nonetheless, the buying and selling of *shares carrying votes* is the standard and not the exception. Indeed, today the marketing of share votes is deemed so important that the New York Stock Exchange, probably for different reasons than those to be offered in this paper, will no longer list shares of a corporation which also has an issue of nonvoting stock.[10] Since the tying together of shares and votes does not fundamentally alter the fact that vote selling is regularly occurring, the corporate "political" system provides a laboratory for the observation and analysis of the dynamics of vote selling.

I. The Market for Corporate Control[11]

An individual voting share of stock is a package composed of two parts—an underlying investment interest and a vote. The two bear a complex relationship to each other, and to understand this relationship it is necessary first to know why corporate control is a valuable asset. There are four distinct reasons why corporate control is sought. The first of these, of perennial concern in the antitrust field, is the monopoly power one firm may achieve by the elimination or control of a competing firm. Next there is the legitimate advantage that may be derived from cost-saving technological efficiencies or other economies of scale which are unavailable to the single firm. The third reason is the simple desire for salaries and the other perquisites normally associated with control of a corporation. Finally, and most important from the point of view of this paper, there is the substantial gain that may be realized in the price of shares when the company receives improved management.

With the first three reasons, the price of the vote segment of the share package would tend to rise with the price of the investment portion of the share and for the same underlying reason.[12] However, this relationship is completely reversed in the case of increased capital gains through improved management. As the price of a voting share declines because of any recognizable inefficiency in the management of the company, the possibility of capital gains from improved management increases accordingly. Control will be worth more, and the vote portion of the share package will appreciate at the same time that the price of the share package is declining. The vote therefore becomes valuable largely as a result of the potential for appreciation of the underlying share interest; when the potential gain in shares is lowest, the value of the vote will tend towards zero. This may explain why takeovers motivated by a desire for large capital gains [13] are quite rare in regulated industries. The possibility of great improvements in the earnings of a rate-regulated monopoly are extremely small; thus little incentive is provided outsiders to compete for control of these companies. In this way, regulation of rates, with its concomitant legalization of monopoly, may have the undesirable side effect of locking-in the incumbent management. By virtue of this "protection" for managers of public utilities, regulation tends to create a true Berle and Means separation of ownership and control.[14]

In a well-managed company, the value of the vote attributable to potential capital gain approaches zero, and the market price of the package will tend to be identical with that of the investment portion. But the value of the vote portion of the package will also tend to be zero if for any reason a change in control cannot be implemented. Too strict rules against mergers have this effect if alternative take-over techniques are not available. Any move along a continuum away from a completely free market for control tends to cause a decline in the market value of the vote. The various proposals for abolishing share voting and for curtailing a free market for control blocks of shares clearly have that effect.[15]

Outsiders, those who create the market demand for control, must be able to recognize when control has achieved a high potential for gain. Typically, though not necessarily, this will occur when a poor showing by the present managers is reflected in the stock market.[16] This in turn generally results from the shareholders' dissatisfaction with their investment in the company. Consequently, at the base of the entire analysis in this paper lies the necessity of a free stock market—ultimately, the single great protective device for shareholders.

Only as an active market for control develops (in one of the several ways to be discussed below) will the value of the vote tend to be realized. But this does not mean that there will necessarily be a simple proportional distribution of the value of control to each share of stock. The exact manner of distribution and amount of this value as well as the determination of who will receive it relates to many factors still to be analyzed.

Depending on his own financial circumstances, his motivation in the acquisition, and the distribution and price of shares, an outsider seeking control of a corporation may select one or more of several different devices for taking over control of another corporation. The three principal devices are direct purchase of shares, mergers, and the proxy fight. Each of these devices still requires that some premium for control be paid, though the form and size of the premium and its recipients may differ under each of the techniques. Some brief description of the strategy considerations of the outsider is necessary in order to understand the choices posed for the shareholders.

The most obvious and direct method of acquiring control of a corporation is the outright purchase of the necessary number of shares.[17] This may be done through private negotiations with large individual shareholders, purchases on the open market, or by the use of tender bids. This last form of direct purchase is most appropriate when the shareholdings are widely diffused and there is a chance of a fast increase in market price if the news spreads that there is a heavy buyer in the market for the company's shares.

If there is a controlling shareholder, the payment of a premium for control will ordinarily be made directly to that person.[18] If the outsider seeks simple but absolute control, and one person owns fifty-one percent of the shares of the company, nothing will be paid for the votes attached to the other shares. The less securely that control is held in one block, however, the more likely a noncontrolling shareholder will participate in the premium, and the less will an outsider be willing to pay one shareholder for his control. As we move along a continuum towards complete diffusion of ownership, so that no one shareholder or small group has control, it is clear that small shareholders will tend to receive a larger price per share than would be true if a control block existed. Both proxy fights and multiple competitive tender bids are more likely to occur under these conditions.

The most popular method of taking over control of a corporation is the merger. Not included in this category, however, are those mergers following an acceptance by existing shareholders of an exchange of stock in another company; in effect, the control change in these transactions has already occurred through a mechanism that is frequently a variant of the tender bid, and the subsequent merger only formalizes the control change. The merger arrangement under discussion is more like a proxy fight, since the shareholders are simply asked to vote for or against the merger, that is, for or against a new management. But there are also critical differences: the required shareholder vote is typically two-thirds rather than a simple majority, and, most important, the existing management must give its approval to the merger before the shareholders can vote.[19]

If we assume that corporate control has a market value, those actually controlling the corporation will not vote for a merger in which control is given up and nothing is gained by them in return. The only general exception to this occurs when the control is worth less to the present holder than the potential gain in his shares from more efficient management of the corporation.[20] Nonetheless, it is quite likely that in most mergers motivated by the goal of realizing capital gains through more efficient management of the company, some form of side-payment to the incumbents occurs. This may on occasion take the form of a direct payment of some sort, but it generally involves a position with the new corporation, a consulting contract, or access to valuable information.

The formula for determining the price to be paid for control in a merger is difficult to state. Unlike the holders of control in the tender bid situation, directors in a merger situation cannot guarantee delivery. Both the high vote requirement for shareholder approval and the possibility of a competing offer by another outsider prevent this. Therefore the side-payment to directors will not equal the full value of control. That is, in a merger situation some part of the value of control will be captured either by existing shareholders or by the outsiders trying to take over. But the outcome of this bargaining situation is indeterminate.

The most dramatic but least used of the take-over devices is the proxy fight. In a pure proxy fight, one in which the parties do not combine the solicitation of proxies with a direct purchase of shares, nothing will be paid directly for control; rather, the only expenditures will be the cost involved in influencing shareholders to give proxies. Shareholders voting for the insurgent in a proxy fight perform a function which the outsiders could otherwise accomplish only by expenditures for the acquisition of shares. Presumably the outsider has chosen this method of seeking control after comparing the cost of acquiring votes through expenditures on persuasion and the cost of direct acquisition of share votes. The matter is not simple, however. If the outsider is motivated by a desire for increased capital gains, he would normally prefer to buy share packages, getting the shares on which he anticipates a gain along with the vote he needs for control. For the outsider to get votes without shares means that others participate in his better management without his necessary expenditures of funds. But, from the shareholders' point of view, as we shall see, holding the shares and voting rather than selling does represent an alternative benefit foregone and thus a cost.

II. The Strategy of Shareholders

A. Tender Bids

We have now set the stage for an analysis of how shareholders may react to an attempted take-over of the corporation. Generally, the simplest set of alternatives is presented to the shareholder by a direct attempt to purchase control, as with a tender bid, though even here the analysis entails some degree of complexity. If the bid is for one hundred percent of the shares of the corporation, many shareholders would see this as an opportunity to attach some part of the control value to their own shares. That is, any individual shareholder who assumed everyone else would sell at the announced price and that the bidder was intent on securing one hundred percent of the shares might reasonably view himself as holding a controlling block of shares for which he would try to receive a premium. Consequently, tender bids rarely are made to acquire all of the shares. Indeed, a figure like ninety-five percent is better designed to acquire all the shares than is one hundred percent, though even with that figure some shareholders may still try to be holdouts.[21]

Following through on the same continuum, the larger the individual shareholding, the more likely it is to command a premium for some part of control. At the end of this continuum is found the situation in which control is actually held in one block of shares. The entire premium for control will be commanded by that one block, and nothing will be paid for the vote of other shares.[22] Short of this extreme point, however, some amount will likely be offered to induce each shareholder to forego his potential holdout position. The price to be paid, as indicated above, will vary with the percentage of shares desired for control and the distribution of shareholdings.

Even if the noncontrolling shareholder recognizes that the holdout alternative is not practicable for him, he is still faced with an important question. He must decide whether to accept the price offered for his shares or to continue as a shareholder under the new control group.[23] He may offer his shares under the tender bid, or he may take his chances on the new management, hoping to participate in a substantial appreciation of his stock.

Ordinarily the outsider seeking control has some reason to believe that he can manage the corporation more efficiently than the incumbents. Sophisticated shareholders will typically recognize this inducement. Consequently, if they could remain in the corporation as shareholders and participate in the better management *at no cost to themselves,* most would prefer to do so. But the difference between the offering price and the market price also measures the cost to shareholders who do not accept the offer. This difference represents the alternative foregone. The price offered for shares must therefore be sufficient to cover the gain the shareholders otherwise see themselves losing, discounted by the probability of the bid's being unsuccessful if the deciding shareholder does not participate. This provides another reason why tender bids are invariably made at a price considerably above the current market price of the company's shares.[24]

Many shareholders will not offer their shares under the tender bid because they value the potential appreciation in the underlying investment interest more highly than the price offered for that investment and the vote. Many might prefer, however, to sell the vote alone. The outsider would prefer to buy both parts of the package, as he must have control in order to realize any capital gains. But, since his funds may be limited, he may conclude at some point that he must forego some of the potential capital gain in order to guarantee the acquisition of control. That is, he may decide that he can only afford to buy votes without the rest of the share package. And some shareholders—those most interested in capital appreciation and sanguine about the outsider's potential —also would be willing to sell votes without the rest of the package. But we do not allow the separate and discrete buying and selling of votes; the entire share package must be traded. However, the control purchaser is free, after he has achieved control, to sell these same shares to others who want to participate in the better managed company. Thus the rule against vote selling merely causes an additional transaction. So long as individuals are free to borrow money to purchase share packages that can be sold immediately after they are voted, the rule against vote selling merely adds two cost items for the outsider: a brokerage fee and the amount of interest on that part of a short-term loan which would be necessary to finance the purchase of the investment portion of the share package.[25]

The rule requiring package selling may result in an unnecessary transaction for shareholders as well. Many shareholders will find it to their advantage to offer their shares under the tender bid in order to realize the market value of the vote. Subsequently, they may buy back the shares. What they actually purchase, however, is primarily the investment portion of the package, since the vote will normally have only minimal value immediately after the successful take-over. The price will nonetheless reflect any market expectations of improved management. Undoubtedly a number of individuals would have preferred in the first instance merely to sell their vote, hold their shares, and participate in the better management.

There would seem to be no strong policy reason why the New York Stock Exchange should not be allowed to list corporate votes for trading whenever a tender bid or a proxy fight is announced.[26] To permit this practice the New York statutory provisions against vote buying [27] might have to be repealed. These votes should probably be valid only until the next stockholders' meeting. Ultimately, the proper working of the corporate system requires that proportionate share interests, in a sense, "generate" their own vote. But the vote on each separate control issue can be viewed as discrete: the vote in a fight one year has nothing to do with the vote in a fight some years later. For each discrete contest, however, it is important that shareholders be allowed complete freedom to use their vote *for that contest* as they see fit. There well may be long periods in which the vote will be valueless and ignored, but protection of the interests of shareholders through the functioning of a corporate control market demands that votes represent proportionate investment interests in the corporation at the time they become valuable.

B. Mergers

In the ordinary merger situation, the shareholder must make a simple decision between continuation of the *status quo* and a change of control through merger. By and large, he will be furnished with sufficient free information to make an intelligent decision, since typically the merger plan will call for an exchange of the acquired company's securities for a marketable security of known value. He need only determine the value to himself of his present holdings and make the relevant comparison in order to determine how to vote. The usual requirement of a two-thirds vote for a merger approval by shareholders provides little opportunity for any small shareholder to become a holdout. As a result, he can participate in better management only by retaining his shares and voting for the merger. Although this sounds quite similar to the tender bid discussed above, it is really similar only to tender bids for all shares when there exists a strong control block of shares. It will be recalled that in this situation very little would be offered the noncontrolling shareholders.

It is not hard to find why little will be offered to shareholders in exchange for their votes in favor of a merger. Under almost all state statutes the board of directors of a corporation must approve a merger before it is submitted to shareholders for a vote.[28] This means that ordinarily there is no way for an outsider to reach the shareholders directly as they can with tender bids or proxy fights.[29]   Therefore, the existing managers of a corporation are in a position to claim for themselves the full value of control discounted only by the probability of not getting a two-thirds vote of shareholders.   Moreover, the probability of not getting the requisite shareholder vote is very small.   Typically merger negotiations are very well kept secrets, as it is in the interest of both negotiating parties to prevent the development of a competitive offer.   The value per share that the shareholders will receive if the plan is approved will generally be higher than the preannouncement market price of the shares.   A competitive offer may be an extremely complex matter, frequently impossible to develop without the assistance of the company's managers in time to head off the prior offer.[30]   As a result, the shareholders have little bargaining power for their vote in most merger situations.

It would seem to follow that the value of shares offered in a merger plan on which shareholders are asked to vote would be less than the price offered in the tender bid when there is no control block of shares, or even less than the price that shares of a corporation would reach during the course of a proxy fight.[31]   Both the tender bid and the proxy fight normally allow the shareholder to gain some of the value of control by a sale of his vote.   But in the merger situation, as in tender bids for non-controlling shares when there is a control block, the value of control will not be distributed in proportion to shareholdings.   This is not to say, however, that the cost to the outsider will be substantially less.   The control group will still try to get the full value of control.   Since the outsider can generally threaten a proxy fight or even disclosure of the negotiations, the cost to him for control will often be less in the case of mergers than with any other device, though there is no way of predicting the precise results of this bargaining situation.   The popularity of the merger as a take-over device would seem to bear out the general conclusion.[32]

An exception to this analysis occurs when active opposition to a merger offer develops and proxies are solicited in opposition to the management's decision.   In this case, the shareholders will receive additional gain for their vote even though they may not be conscious that this is occurring.   Solicitation materials in opposition to a merger ordinarily take the form of a more attractive merger offer.[33]   The difference in what will be offered to the shareholders in the two plans will result from an attempt in the later plan to shift part of the premium for control from the management to the shareholders.[34]   If the second bidder offers the shareholders the full value of control, then, under the assumption that the actual value of the investment interest is the same to each of the bidders, there is nothing left for the existing management.   Consequently, no matter how bad the prior offer, the interest of management would lie in approving the subsequent one.   It is very doubtful, however, that an actual deadlock situation would ever develop because the shareholders ultimately have the upper hand if two-thirds wish to accept one or the other of the merger offers. They must first depose the existing directors, but that too can be done in the unlikely case that the directors do not accede to their wishes in advance.

The directors, even in this situation, have some indeterminate amount of bargaining power, and it is quite likely that in order to settle the matter quickly a second bidder would prefer making a side-payment to them, albeit smaller than that of the first bidder. But it is the possibility of the shareholders ultimately gaining some of the value of their own votes that probably dictates much of the strategy—and much of the secrecy—in merger arrangements. A change in state statutes to require several months notice to shareholders of a proposed merger might be highly desirable. The difficulty for outsiders trying to receive information from hostile directors would remain, but the possibility of competitive offers would be greatly increased.

C. Proxy Fights

The most complex take-over technique is undoubtedly the proxy fight. Here the number of options open to the shareholder is the greatest. He may simply do nothing, neither voting, selling nor giving a proxy; he may vote the shares himself for one side or the other; he may give a proxy to one side or the other; or he may sell the shares. Basically, the critical element in making this decision involves the cost and reliability of information that he can obtain about the respective positions of the parties in the contest. There is one bit of information—readily available to and easily understandable by the shareholder—that he may confidently rely upon to the exclusion of almost everything else. This is the price at which the shares are selling relative to the price of other investments the shareholder might have made at the time he bought these shares.[35] If he learns that the shares of other companies are doing much better than his own, either in terms of capital gains or dividends, it may be quite rational to vote for any group willing to incur the expense of a fight for control. The mere fact of a proxy fight indicates some probability that an outsider believes that the lower price has resulted from poor management and that he can make improvements.

The shareholder may, of course, be wrong, but at some point it is perfectly rational to vote or give a proxy on this basis alone. Additional expenditures on information might have too low a probable return to warrant their being made. This suggests why in many proxy fights—especially those motivated by an outsider's attempt to realize large capital gains by giving more efficient management—many shareholders do vote their own shares or make an independent decision about their proxy. If, however, the proxy fight seems motivated by other factors, such as an attempt by a dissident insider group to distribute management compensation differently, or if the share price is not relatively low but the outsider promises a much higher price, shareholders will be less likely to trust their own information, and therefore less apt to vote their own shares.[36]

There are three kinds of informational costs involved for shareholders in a proxy fight. The first is the cost involved in actually securing specific bits of information in the form of reliable statements about relevant aspects of the business and the contestants. The second kind of information cost is basically that incurred to gain financial sophistication or education, that is, the ability to read and understand the information available. The third kind of cost results from the time and effort necessary to absorb the available information and reach the appropriate decision.

The only one of these costs in any way alleviated by the Securities Exchange Act of 1934 [37] is the first. There are at least three reasons why the mere availability of reliable data about contestants does not necessarily provide sufficient incentive for all shareholders to vote. Many shareholders will not find it possible to comprehend the true impact of proxy solicitation materials; [38] nor will small shareholders find it economical to hire individual experts to assist them. The resulting higher uncertainty will lessen the incentive to vote, since the uninformed shareholder cannot know that his vote will do more good than harm.

Even for the shareholder who is sophisticated enough to deal intelligently with proxy solicitation materials, the effort will not necessarily be undertaken. He must decide, in advance of making the comparison of the contending propositions, whether the projected gain to be made from making a correct decision on the matter is greater than the value of the effort he will have to expend. The very making of this decision, beset as it is by obvious uncertainties, entails some cost, as will the delegation of the decision to an agent. Moreover, as the size of the holdings becomes smaller, the likelihood that the preliminary cost will be incurred decreases because the effort required to reach a "correct" conclusion remains constant over a fairly wide range of sizes of shareholdings. Thus there are definite returns to scale in this endeavor.

An additional basis upon which small shareholders—and perhaps some larger ones—may rationally abstain from corporate voting goes to a crucial difference between political and corporate elections. With very rare exceptions, there are no conflicts in the corporate interests of voting shareholders.[39] Unlike many governmental decisions, corporate decisions almost never have a direct wealth redistribution effect among the shareholders, that is, one changing relative participations of the shareholders. In those areas where this is not the case, such as reorganization proceedings or those involving discretionary dividends on preferred shares, the courts are more likely to have a say in the ultimate decision. But these are special situations which cannot be treated in this paper.

A conflict between shareholders interested in high dividend payments and those interested in capital gains would seem likely. This issue, however, is largely settled in the market place. If the dividend policy of a corporation is known and felt to be consistent, the shareholders will tend to be those who are favored by that policy. Nor should we expect to find a random distribution of types of shareholders in any corporation. Thus, shareholders in a public utility corporation that pays out a high percentage of earnings will include a much higher percentage of older, retired individuals than we would find in a "growth" electronics corporation. Few fights for control of a corporation, therefore, are likely to involve any fundamental difference of opinion among shareholders on ultimate goals; they are much more likely to represent differences about how the company can best assure the maximization of a common interest.

This identity of interests among the shareholders of corporations sharply differentiates the politics of the corporation from the politics of government. Many shareholders may simply feel that since their interests are the same as those of the other shareholders, the others will inform themselves and, in effect, vote in the interest of all. This strategy is indeed quite rational for small shareholders, especially if there are some substantial holdings of stock in the company. But a large shareholder must measure the cost saving of disinterest against the possibility that too few shareholders will vote or that those voting will be in error. Manifestly this strategy of nonparticipation is more sensible the smaller the individual holding and the less widely diffused all other holdings.

In the absence of party loyalty, moral suasion or high "entertainment" value, small shareholders have little incentive to incur any costs to aid in the election of corporate management.[40] If they vote, it is likely to be on the basis of whether the *status quo* seems tolerable or intolerable. But the information problem in the typical proxy fight presents a classic opportunity for small shareholders to utilize economies of scale. If a large number of shareholders with the identical financial interest can find a third party with no inconsistent interests to do the job for them, it would be to their benefit to turn over both the information-absorbing function and the decision-making function.[41] The group most appropriate for this job would be those individuals who regularly sold or recommended shares—the brokers. It is in the brokers' interest to have their customers get a maximum return in the market, and it would therefore be in their interest to advise their customers as correctly as possible about how to vote in a proxy fight.

The broker must have a large number of customers with a position in the corporation's shares. Otherwise it will not be worth his cost to inform himself about the dispute.   It is generally true, however, that brokers specialize in the stocks of a few companies, and their customers' holdings tend to be concentrated in shares of those companies.   Therefore, those brokers or investment advisers whose customers in total may have a large position in the corporation's shares are likely nominees for collective delegation of proxy powers.

One difficulty with leaving the matter entirely to broker-proxies is that these are the same brokers who may on occasion have an overriding interest in the present management.   If this fact is known to the shareholders, a decision to leave a proxy with these brokers is tantamount to a *vote* for the incumbents.   Full disclosure of any relationship between the brokerage firm and the corporate management would certainly be in order.

None of this is intended to suggest that the much heralded proxy solicitation rules have been without effect.   On the contrary they have undoubtedly lowered the cost of securing information and thereby opened the voting option to some shareholders who would otherwise have taken a different course.   Also the costs of securing information have been lowered for brokers and investment advisers, thus making collective action for a large number of shareholders more feasible than might otherwise have been the case.   At the same time, the proxy regulations have undoubtedly raised the cost of proxy fights to the contestants, those who must furnish the information and deal with the administrative hurdles erected under the 1934 act.   On balance, the degree of shareholder participation has probably increased, but the actual competition for control of corporations has probably declined.   It is doubtful, however, that the advantages of the former have offset the disadvantages of the latter.[42]

The saving grace of the difficult quest for information about groups contending for control is the fact that the shareholder is still allowed to sell his share, including his vote.   If the contestants are actively in the market buying shares as well as merely soliciting proxies, the price of the shares will tend to rise.   There is no way of gauging in advance the quantitative impact of this buying, although generally the price rise should be less than that required for a successful tender bid.

This will not be the only factor affecting share prices during the course of a proxy fight.   Even if the contestants themselves are not in the market for shares, the price of the shares should still appreciate.   Some individuals—whether large shareholders or outsiders—will undoubtedly have found it to their advantage to inform themselves fully as to the relative merits of the opposing parties.   If they conclude that the outside group offers the prospect of better management of the corporation than the incumbents are presently providing, it will be in their interest to purchase shares, causing the price to rise to the point where it accurately reflects the value of their information.

The market for votes, therefore, serves two critical functions. It gives the advantage of someone else's information-gathering to all the shareholders willing to sell. It also causes votes to move into the hands of those shareholders to whom the vote itself is most valuable, that is, those who know how to use it most profitably. The value of the vote, as opposed to the value of voting the shares one way rather than another, rests with those who have the most reliable information. Without the market, many small shareholders could not have any idea of what the vote itself was actually worth to them. Thus, the corporate system of allowing the sale of votes guarantees an electorate that is both relatively well-informed and more intensely interested in the outcome of the election than would be the case if votes were not transferable. And it does this with no harm to the interests of anyone associated with or affected by the corporation.

Conclusion

Although the analysis in this paper has drawn heavily on theories developed for political voting, it is clear that fundamental differences between the corporate and political spheres prevent any simple transfer of theory from one area to the other. The conclusion which is unmistakably implied by the foregoing analysis is that vote selling plays an invaluable role in the operation of the American corporate system and negatives many of the criticisms often leveled at the modern corporation.[43]

While recognizing the advantages of direct vote selling, the newer theorists of political voting have concluded that it should not be permitted because of the possible existence of monopoly-type imperfections in the market for votes. They have not, however, subjected this view to exhaustive research and analysis. It is important, nonetheless, that in the corporate area we know what imperfections might be interfering with the share vote market. As suggested in the body of this paper, some of the government regulations designed to aid shareholders may have the opposite effect. In addition, many of the conclusions about costs and other subjects reached in the body of this paper must be qualified by a variety of tax considerations.

Modern political voting theorists have demonstrated that where some form of trading or exchange is inevitable, intenseness of feeling will often compensate, at least over a period of time, for a lack of numerical strength. In corporate power struggles, however, intensity of feeling is seldom relevant. In the first place there is rarely an issue about which the voters will have emotional feelings; on the contrary, wealth maximization usually calls for cool heads rather than high tempers, and programs for the redistribution of wealth among shareholders are not ordinarily condoned. In fact if a corporation is in a competitive industry, there is rarely any real choice about what ultimate policies it may pursue.[44]

Even more important is the fact that in the corporate system votes are bought and sold. The corporate shareholders who might be considered analogous to political voters holding very strong views, are those who have reliable information about the contestants and the company. The share votes will tend to move into the hands of those who know best how to maximize their use value. Any inclination toward disagreements among shareholders about how the company should be managed tends to be halted automatically, as one side will simply buy out the other. Indeed, much of this is occurring so constantly and so automatically in the stock market that dramatic events do not often emerge; the uninspiring reports in the daily financial press of personnel changes, mergers and stock prices are the significant data that indicate the functioning of our corporate system.

Nothing comparable is possible in the political arena even if we allowed blatant vote buying and selling. We should still be faced with the problem of adjusting to differences about ultimate goals and the possibility of redistribution of wealth. The simple mobility of funds provided by the stock market has no direct counterpart in politics. Voters would have to move physically from one jurisdiction to another to gain the analogous advantage; and, while politically motivated moves do occur, the cost is generally too high, relative to the gain for this device to become an important institutionalized pattern. In a comparison of the corporation with the political system, the basic problems are, of course, far simpler in the corporation. The issues are not as profound, and a market mechanism for appropriate determination of the corporate constituency is readily available. The corporation is probably a far more democratic mechanism from the viewpoint of shareholders than is government from the point of view of voters.

FOOTNOTES

* This article represents both a descriptive and a normative model of the functioning of certain aspects of the American corporate system. The intermingling of the two may create some confusion, though care has been taken to make it clear when the reference is intended to be a description of reality and when it is intended to state an ideal that may or may not be reached in actual practice. A pure ideal theory of the corporation would probably not be very helpful. It would be too far removed from the familiar technical realities of corporation law and regulation to be meaningful. On the other hand a pure description, if that is a meaningful concept at all, would not offer any standards by which to judge and improve the present arrangement. The confusion between the descriptive and the normative is further aggravated at many points in this article by the unavailability of relevant empirical data. The reader is advised that some factual assertions are made with no reference to sources. These statements are, unless indicated to the contrary, believed by the author to be correct statements of fact. But if the reader feels any doubts about the veracity of such assertions, he

should take them only as statements of supposition or belief by the author, necessary for the development of a helpful normative model.

The dearth of relevant empirical data is perhaps not too hard to explain. One does not simply gather facts; a framework, a working hypothesis, is necessary. However, we simply have not had a coherent, integrated theory about corporations. An attempt has been made in this rather brief and abstract introduction to the theory of corporate voting to point out the areas where empirical research would be most helpful. But the effort calls for considerabe cooperation between lawyers and economists. A dialogue on the order of that long familiar in the antitrust field seems necessary. And it seems highly appropriate to dedicate this article to Adolf A. Berle.

1 Power Without Property 107 (1959).

2 Buchanan & Tullock, The Calculus of Consent (1962) [hereinafter referred to as Buchanan & Tullock]; Downs, An Economic Theory of Democracy (1957) [hereinafter referred to as Downs].

3 Buchanan & Tullock 125–30; Downs 64–69.

4 Downs 192. Downs also favors, however, the ban on vote selling on subjective, ethical grounds, especially since there is no agitation for the legalization of vote selling today. See Id. at 192 n. 17.

5 Buchanan & Tullock 272–76.

6 Downs 260–76.

7 Buchanan & Tullock 265–81.

8 See cases cited in Baker & Cary, Cases on Corporations 314–57 (3d ed. 1959).

9 See Sneed, *The Stockholder May Vote as He Pleases: Theory and Fact*, 22 U.Pitt. L.Rev. 23, 45–47 (1960) and authorities cited. But cf. Lilienthal, *Corporate Voting and Public Policy*, 10 Harv.L.Rev. 428, 438 (1897).

10 N.Y. Stock Exch., Company Manual at A280.

11 This section constitutes a brief summary of an analysis of the market for corporate control. A more detailed discussion of this market by the author entitled "Mergers and the Market for Corporate Control" will appear in a forthcoming issue of *The Journal of Political Economy*. That article and this section analyze the "demand" side of the control market, comparing the advantages and disadvantages for an outsider of various techniques for gaining control of a corporation. The major part of this article may be viewed as a companion piece analyzing the same phenomena principally from the point of view of the corporate shareholders.

12 Each of these first three situations involves a high positive correlation between the benefits to the company and to the holder of control. The salary point is included on the assumption that higher compensation is more likely if the company is efficiently operated. This point is, however, subject to considerable question. See Marris, The Economic Theory of Managerial Capitalism 89–99 (1964); Roberts, Executive Compensation 62–78 (1959). The technological advantages included here are only those available as a result of integration of two or more firms, with the advantages running to both firms. If the economies are available to the single firm at no extra cost but are not being put into effect, this would be characterized, for our purposes, as inefficient management.

Managerial efficiency in this analysis is measured by one criterion only. That is the effect on the market price of the company's shares of any managerial activity. Any failure to take feasible action which would have the effect of increasing the price is an indication of managerial inefficiency. The concept then is very broad, certainly covering more than is usually connoted by the word "management," but only this definition is helpful in the present analysis.

It should be noted that no theoretical distinction between acquisitions by firms and acquisitions by individuals is being made in the present context.

13 The phrase "capital gain" in this context is not intended to have any necessary relationship to the Internal Revenue Code concept. Here we simply use it to mean an accretion in the market price of shares.

14 Berle & Means, The Modern Corporation and Private Property (1932). Perhaps, in part, the legal monopoly position of utilities is a *quid pro quo* for this disadvantage to shareholders. There are important implications in this notion for the management of nonprofit organizations as well as for legal monopolies. Indeed, the Berle and Means thesis fits foundations, universities, and other nonprofit organizations far better than it does the large corporation for which it was designed. See Alchian & Kessel, *Competition, Monopoly and the Pursuit of Money*, in Aspects of Labor Economics 157 (Nat'l Bureau of Economic Research, 1962).

15 See Drucker, The New Society 340 (1950); Chayes, *The Modern Corporation and the Rule of Law*, in The Corporation in Modern Society 25, 40–41 (Mason ed. 1959); cf. Berle, Power Without Property 98–110 (1959). Manning does not propose vote abolition, although he does consider it hypothetically. Book Review, 67 Yale L.J. 1477, 1490–93 (1958), reviewing Livingston, The American Stockholder (1958). For proposed restrictions on sales of control, see Berle, *"Control" in Corporate Law*, 58 Colum.L.Rev. 1212 (1958); Jennings, *Trading in Corporate Control*, 44 Calif.L.Rev. 1 (1956). But see Hill, *The Sale of Controlling Shares*, 70 Harv.L.Rev. 986 (1957); Katz, *The Sale of Corporate Control*, 38 Chicago B. Record 376 (1957).

16 Much of the theory set forth in this article is based on the premise that the stock market, over some period of time, accurately reflects the best possible estimate of the present worth of the company. Some evidence for this proposition is offered in the author's article referred to in note 10 supra.

17 This figure may of course vary with the purpose for which control is wanted. Simple control of a corporation with widely diffused share ownership may be guaranteed by a relatively small percentage of the shares. See Essex Universal Corp. v. Yates, 305 F.2d 572 (2d Cir. 1962). If absolute assurance of a merger is wanted, usually two-thirds of the shares must be acquired. See Del.Code Ann. tit. 8, § 251(c) (1953). Unless the contrary is clearly indicated, references in this paper will be to simple, absolute control acquisitions, that is, the acquisition of 51% of the shares. For the most part, however, the necessary extrapolations for other situations will be obvious.

18 *Compare* Jennings, supra note 14, at 18 n. 68, *with* Hill, supra note 14, at 1038–39 n. 150.

19 ABA Model Bus.Corp.Act Ann. § 65, ¶ 2.02(3)(d) (1960 ed., Supp.1964).

20 This case also suggests the possibility of a conflict between a controlling shareholder and his nominees on the board who hold managerial positions with the corporation. For an account of a fight of this type, see Berle & Means, op. cit. supra note 13, at 82–83.

21 Presumably there will always be some shareholders who will assume that no matter how small the percentage of shares requested, the bidder ultimately wants 100%. This is another factor determining the offering price.

22 This does not mean, however, that the control holder must sell his entire block. He may sell only enough to defeat his control, or he may retain all his shares and transfer the voting power, for example, by use of a voting trust. Or, if satisfactory compensation arrangements can be made, he may merely "hire" new management as an alternative to selling control.

23 No consideration will be given here to such typically small costs as those involved in computing the probability of success of the tender bid. Small shareholders undoubtedly ignore such costs, but for a large shareholder such considerations may occasionally become important.

24 It should be noted then that there are several factors determining that price. The first is the simple holdout problem referred to previously in the text. The second is the cost-for-participation matter just described. The third aspect may be said to be a simple function of the supply schedule for the corporation's shares. That is, a higher price than the existing market price will be necessary to call forward more shares than are currently being offered. To some extent, the supply schedule may be determined by the first two factors. But it also seems clear that, even if no public announcement of a take-over is made and no one suspects that one is in the offing, the price of the shares would still increase as other expectational factors became operative. This is not, however, a decision by the shareholders as to the price for which they will sell votes.

25 Another inhibition on this practice is Regulation U of the Federal Reserve Board prohibiting commercial banks from lending money for share purchases. 12 C.F.R. § 221.1 (1963). Swiss banks, however, do perform this function for active participants in the market for corporate control. Consideration should be given to an exemption from Regulation U for participants in control fights.

26 The vote might be considered a "security" under the Securities Act of 1933, § 2(1), 48 Stat. 74, as amended, 15 U.S.C. § 77b(1) (1959), but no reason appears why an additional registration should be required of shareholders who do not have "control" within the meaning of the Securities Act of 1933, § 2(11), 48 Stat. 75, as amended, 15 U.S.C. § 77(b)(11) (1959). "Controlling" shareholders would probably not use this mechanism, as they would negotiate directly with the vote buyers. The direct buying of votes would not seem to be a solicitation of proxies within the meaning of the Securities Exchange Act of 1934, § 14, 48 Stat. 895, 15 U.S.C. § 78n (1959), as amended, Securities Acts Amendments of 1964, § 5, 78 Stat. 569.

The actual mechanics of any such program would present difficulties not considered in this essentially theoretical approach. For instance, because of uncertainties as to which shareholders would be entitled to vote, proxies rather than actual votes might have to be listed. These and other considerations, however, should remain secondary to consideration of the substance of the proposal.

27 N.Y.Bus.Corp.Law § 609(e); N.Y.Pen.Law § 668(1). Only the latter would seem to apply to foreign as well as domestic corporations, though the matter is certainly not clear.

28 A.B.A. Model Bus.Corp.Act Ann. § 65, ¶ 2.02(3)(d) (1960 ed., Supp.1964).

29 There is an interesting possibility, never judicially explored, of requiring a shareholder's vote on a merger question in the absence of a vote by the board or in spite of a negative vote. If the right of merger is viewed as one belonging fundamentally to the shareholders (and consistent with that approach, the statutory requirement of a vote by the board of directors would have to be viewed as a purely administrative or ministerial device preliminary to a shareholder vote), it is possible that the SEC's "shareholder proposal" rule might be available for this purpose. See SEC Rule 14A–8, 17 C.F.R. § 240.14a–8 (1964). Compare SEC v. Transamerica Corp., 163 F.2d 511 (3d Cir. 1947), cert. denied, 332 U.S. 847 (1948). Currently the SEC seems to take the position that this is a proper subject for shareholder action, but it is advisory only in its effect and not mandatory. 2 Loss, Securities Regulation 908 (2d ed. 1961).

30 The statutory minimum time periods of notice to shareholders ranges from five to thirty days. ABA Model Bus.Corp.Act.Ann. § 67, ¶ 2.02(3)(b) (1960). The directors may, of course, set a higher figure. See MacCrone v. American Capital Corp., 51 F.Supp. 462 (D.Del.1943) (dictum). This suggests that the real drawback to shareholder appraisal

statutes may lie with evaluation difficulties rather than with the idea that shareholders need no help. See Manning, *The Shareholder's Appraisal Remedy: An Essay for Frank Coker*, 72 Yale L.J. 223, 231–33, 261 (1962).

[31] See Manne, *The "Higher Criticism" of the Modern Corporation*, 62 Colum.L.Rev. 399, 412 (1962).

[32] There are, of course, other economic reasons for the popularity of mergers as well. See the author's article cited in note 10 supra.

[33] The best known of these occurred in the recent fight for control of the Rock Island Railroad with the original offer of merger coming from the Union Pacific and opposition proxies being solicited by the Chicago and North Western. Union Pac. R. R. v. Chicago & N. W. Ry., 226 F.Supp. 400 (N.D.Ill.1964). Presumably the Chicago & North Western had been familiar with the Rock Island properties for some time before the Union Pacific's offer. Sometimes the competition develops before the directors have voted on the merger or at least before it has been presented to the shareholders. In that case the competitive offers may be presented first to the board of directors. The recent spate of offers for the shares of Pure Oil Co., illustrates this point, although this may be a situation in which management actually solicited offers. See Wall St. J., Oct. 1, 1964, p. 7, col. 2.

[34] This assumes that all parties are fully informed and that neither of the offering companies has any unique quality which will allow it to offer more for control than the other company. But the mere presence of such unique quality would still not necessarily prevent the operation of the mechanism described in the text.

[35] If the shareholder is more interested in dividend policy than capital gains, he would make the appropriate comparison of announced dividends.

[36] The same should be true for fights motivated by technological reasons, as may have occurred in some recent situations involving railroads.

[37] § 14(a), 48 Stat. 895, 15 U.S.C. § 78n(a) (1959), as amended, Securities Acts Amendments of 1964, § 5, 78 Stat. 569. It should be clear that we are speaking only of giving a proxy in the context of a fight for control. Many of the discussions in this area do not clearly distinguish that situation from the solicitations which historically were for the principal purpose of getting a quorum at the shareholders' meeting. See, e. g., S.Rep. No. 1455, 73d Cong., 2d Sess. 387–88 (1934) (testimony of Mr. Thomas Lamont). Apparently the great bugbear in these early hearings was shareholder ratification of fraudulent or self-dealing activity by management. But little attention ever seems to have been given to common-law rules regarding ratification which would normally have made such a purpose futile if anyone questioned the underlying act in court. See Restatement (Second), Agency, §§ 91, 101(a) (1958). The principal focus today seems to be on proxy solicitations as a device for keeping shareholders generally informed rather than for aiding them when there is a fight for control. See 2 Loss, op. cit. supra note 28, at 1027. Thus, the New York Stock Exchange has for some time required annual solicitation of proxies whether there is a fight for control or not. N.Y. Stock Exch., op. cit. supra note 9, at A134. The 1964 amendments to the Securities Exchange Act of 1934 make mandatory the annual disclosure of information comparable to that required for proxy solicitations whether proxies are solicited or not. Securities Acts Amendments of 1964, § 5(c), 78 Stat. 569, amending 15 U.S.C. § 78a (1959). The "contested meeting" seems now to be merely one of the detailed parts of the over-all regulation of proxy solicitations. See, e. g., von Mehren & McCarroll, *The Proxy Rules: A Case Study in the Administrative Process*, 29 Law & Contemp.Prob. 728, 730–32 (1964).

Ironically the rules of the New York Stock Exchange, approved by the SEC, have the effect of making it most costly for brokers to aid shareholders in just those situations in which private collectivization of decision-making is most desirable, that is, when

there is a proxy fight, a merger vote, or other complex matters.   They do this principally by requiring brokers who seek to give proxies on shares held in street names to
obtain specific permission from beneficial owners.   In non-contested elections, specific
permission is not required.   See N.Y. Stock Exch., op. cit. supra note 9, at A143–45.   See
also id. at A147–48 (discouraging initiation of various actions by brokers).

38 See Williams, *Thinking Ahead*, Harv.Bus.Rev., July-Aug. 1955, p. 21.

39 The principal exceptions occur when there are different classes of shares with
differing dividend or liquidation rights.

40 Compare Downs 244–47.   The directors have considerable incentive to have a quorum
at shareholders' meetings.   Consequently costly effort will be exerted by the corporation,
usually on brokers holding shares in street names, to get a sufficient number of proxies.

41 Compare id. at 230–34.   It should be noted that the share vote delegator has no problem with standards of evaluation as his political counterpart might.

42 Empirical data on this point would be extremely helpful in evaluating the desirability of the present scheme.   Unfortunately the *Special Study of Securities Markets* by
the Securities and Exchange Commission merely assumed the desirability and urged extension of the system to over-the-counter stock issuers.   H.R.Doc. No. 95, 88th Cong., 1st
Sess., pt. 3, at 12–14 (1963);   see Stigler, *Public Regulation of the Securities Markets*, 19
Bus.Law. 721 (1964).   Congress promptly obliged.   Securities Acts Amendments of 1964,
§ 5, 78 Stat. 565, amending 15 U.S.C. § 78n (1959).

43 See Manne, *Current Views on the "Modern Corporation,"* 38 U.Det.L.J. 559 (1961),
Corporate Practice Commentator, Aug. 1962, p. 1.

44 Mahoney, *What Happened at Endicott Johnson After the Band Stopped Playing*,
Fortune, Sept. 1962, p. 127.

32: PRODUCTION, INFORMATION COSTS, AND ECONOMIC ORGANIZATION

ARMEN A. ALCHIAN
HAROLD DEMSETZ*

The mark of a capitalistic society is that resources are owned and allocated by such nongovernmental organizations as firms, households, and markets. Resource owners increase productivity through cooperative specialization and this leads to the demand for economic organizations which facilitate cooperation. When a lumber mill employs a cabinetmaker, cooperation between specialists is achieved within a firm, and when a cabinetmaker purchases wood from a lumberman, the cooperation takes place across markets (or between firms). Two important problems face a theory of economic organization—to explain the conditions that determine whether the gains from specialization and cooperative production can better be obtained within an organization like the firm, or across markets, and to explain the structure of the organization.

It is common to see the firm characterized by the power to settle issues by fiat, by authority, or by disciplinary action superior to that available in the conventional market. This is delusion. The firm does not own all its inputs. It has no power of fiat, no authority, no disciplinary action any different in the slightest degree from ordinary market contracting between any two people. I can "punish" you only by withholding future business or by seeking redress in the courts for any failure to honor our exchange agreement. That is exactly all that any employer can do. He

Alchian and Demsetz, "Production, Information Costs, and Economic Organization," 62 American Economic Review (December 1972), from page 777 to page 795.

can fire or sue, just as I can fire my grocer by stopping purchases from him or sue him for delivering faulty products. What then is the content of the presumed power to manage and assign workers to various tasks? Exactly the same as one little consumer's power to manage and assign his grocer to various tasks. The single consumer can assign his grocer to the task of obtaining whatever the customer can induce the grocer to provide at a price acceptable to both parties. That is precisely all that an employer can do to an employee. To speak of managing, directing, or assigning workers to various tasks is a deceptive way of noting that the employer continually is involved in renegotiation of contracts on terms that must be acceptable to both parties. Telling an employee to type this letter rather than to file that document is like my telling a grocer to sell me this brand of tuna rather than that brand of bread. I have no contract to continue to purchase from the grocer and neither the employer nor the employee is bound by any contractual obligations to continue their relationship. Long-term contracts between employer and employee are not the essence of the organization we call a firm. My grocer can count on my returning day after day and purchasing his services and goods even with the prices not always marked on the goods—because I know what they are—and he adapts his activity to conform to my directions to him as to what I want each day . . . he is not my employee.

Wherein then is the relationship between a grocer and his employee different from that between a grocer and his customers? It is in a *team* use of inputs and a centralized position of some party in the contractual arrangements of *all* other inputs. It is the *centralized contractual agent in a team productive process*—not some superior authoritarian directive or disciplinary power. Exactly what is a team process and why does it induce the contractual form, called the firm? These problems motivate the inquiry of this paper.

I. The Metering Problem

The economic organization through which input owners cooperate will make better use of their comparative advantages to the extent that it facilitates the payment of rewards in accord with productivity. If rewards were random, and without regard to productive effort, no incentive to productive effort would be provided by the organization; and if rewards were negatively correlated with productivity the organization would be subject to sabotage. Two key demands are placed on an economic organization—metering input productivity and metering rewards.[1]

Metering problems sometimes can be resolved well through the exchange of products across competitive markets, because in many situations markets yield a high correlation between rewards and productivity. If a farmer increases his output of wheat by 10 percent at the prevailing market price, his receipts also increase by 10 percent. This method of organizing economic activity meters the *output directly*, reveals the marginal product and apportions the *rewards* to resource owners in accord with that direct measurement of their outputs. The success of this decentralized, market exchange in promoting productive specialization requires that changes in market rewards fall on those responsible for changes in *output*.[2]

The classic relationship in economics that runs from marginal productivity to the distribution of income implicitly *assumes* the existence of an organization, be it the market or the firm, that allocates rewards to resources in accord with their productivity. The problem of economic organization, the economical means of metering productivity and rewards, is not confronted directly in the classical analysis of production and distribution. Instead, that analysis tends to assume sufficiently economic— or zero cost—means, as if productivity automatically created its reward. We conjecture the direction of causation is the reverse—the specific system of rewarding which is relied upon stimulates a particular productivity response. If the economic organization meters poorly, with rewards and productivity only loosely correlated, then productivity will be smaller; but if the economic organization meters well productivity will be greater. What makes metering difficult and hence induces means of economizing on metering costs?

II. Team Production

Two men jointly lift heavy cargo into trucks. Solely by observing the total weight loaded per day, it is impossible to determine each person's marginal productivity. With team production it is difficult, solely by observing total output, to either define or determine *each* individual's contribution to this output of the cooperating inputs. The output is yielded by a team, by definition, and it is not a *sum* of separable outputs of each of its members. Team production of Z involves at least two inputs, X_i and X_j, with $\partial^2 Z/\partial X_i \partial X_j \neq 0$.[3] The production function is *not* separable into two functions each involving only inputs X_i or only inputs X_j. Consequently there is no *sum* of Z of two separable functions to treat as the Z of the team production function. (An example of a *separable* case is $Z = aX_i^2 + bX_j^2$ which is separable into $Z_i = aX_i^2$ and $Z_j = bX_j^2$, and $Z = Z_i + Z_j$. This is not team production.) There exist production techniques in which the Z obtained is greater than if X_i and X_j had produced separable Z. Team production will be used if it yields an output enough larger than the sum of separable production of Z to cover the costs of organizing and disciplining team members—the topics of this paper.[4]

Usual explanations of the gains from cooperative behavior rely on exchange and production in accord with the comparative advantage specialization principle with separable additive production. However, as suggested above there is a source of gain from cooperative activity involving working as a *team*, wherein individual cooperating inputs do not yield identifiable, separate products which can be *summed* to measure the total output. For this cooperative productive activity, here called "team" production, measuring *marginal* productivity and making payments in accord therewith is more expensive by an order of magnitude than for separable production functions.

Team production, to repeat, is production in which 1) several types of resources are used and 2) the product is not a sum of separable outputs of each cooperating resource. An additional factor creates a team organization problem—3) not all resources used in team production belong to one person.

We do not inquire into why all the jointly used resources are not owned by one person, but instead into the types of organization, contracts, and informational and payment procedures used among owners of teamed inputs. With respect to the one-owner case, perhaps it is sufficient merely to note that (a) slavery is prohibited, (b) one might assume risk aversion as a reason for one person's not borrowing enough to purchase all the assets or sources of services rather than renting them, and (c) the purchase-resale spread may be so large that costs of short-term ownership exceed rental costs. Our problem is viewed basically as one of organization among different people, not of the physical goods or services, however much there must be selection and choice of combination of the latter.

How can the members of a team be rewarded and induced to work efficiently? In team production, marginal products of cooperative team members are not so directly and separably (i. e., cheaply) observable. What a team offers to the market can be taken as the marginal product of the team but not of the team members. The costs of metering or ascertaining the marginal products of the team's members is what calls forth new organizations and procedures. Clues to each input's productivity can be secured by observing *behavior* of individual inputs. When lifting cargo into the truck, how rapidly does a man move to the next piece to be loaded, how many cigarette breaks does he take, does the item being lifted tilt downward toward his side?

If detecting such behavior were costless, neither party would have an incentive to shirk, because neither could impose the cost of his shirking on the other (if their cooperation was agreed to voluntarily). But since costs must be incurred to monitor each other, each input owner will have more incentive to shirk when he works as part of a team, than if his performance could be monitored easily or if he did not work as a team. If there is a net increase in productivity available by team production, net of the metering cost associated with disciplining the team, then team production will be relied upon rather than a multitude of bilateral exchange of separable individual outputs.

Both leisure and higher income enter a person's utility function.[5] Hence, each person should adjust his work and realized reward so as to equate the marginal rate of substitution betwen leisure and production of real output to his marginal rate of substitution in consumption. That is, he would adjust his rate of work to bring his demand prices of leisure and output to equality with their true costs. However, with detection, policing, monitoring, measuring or metering costs, each person will be induced to take more leisure, because the effect of relaxing on *his realized* (reward) rate of substitution between output and leisure will be less than the effect on the *true* rate of substitution. His realized cost of leisure will fall more than the true cost of leisure, so he "buys" more leisure (i. e., more nonpecuniary reward).

If his relaxation cannot be detected perfectly at zero cost, part of its effects will be borne by others in the team, thus making *his* realized cost of relaxation less than the true total cost to the team. The difficulty of detecting such actions permits the private costs of his actions to be less than their full costs. Since each person responds to his private realizable rate of substitution (in production) rather than the true total (i. e., social) rate, and so long as there are costs for other people to detect his shift toward relaxation, it will not pay (them) to force him to readjust completely by making him realize the true cost. Only enough efforts will be made to equate the marginal gains of detection activity with the marginal costs of detection; and that implies a lower rate of productive effort and more shirking than in a costless monitoring, or measuring, world.

In a university, the faculty use office telephones, paper, and mail for personal uses beyond strict university productivity. The university administrators could stop such practices by identifying *the* responsible person in each case, but they can do so only at higher costs than administrators are willing to incur. The extra costs of identifying each party (rather than merely identifying the presence of such activity) would exceed the savings from diminished faculty "turpitudinal peccadilloes." So the faculty is allowed some degree of "privileges, perquisites, or fringe benefits." And the total of the pecuniary wages paid is lower because of this irreducible (at acceptable costs) degree of amenity-seizing activity. Pay is lower in pecuniary terms and higher in leisure, conveniences, and ease of work. But still every person would prefer to see detection made more effective (if it were somehow possible to monitor costlessly) so that he, as part of the now more effectively producing team, could thereby realize a higher pecuniary pay and less leisure. If everyone could, at zero cost, have his reward-realized rate brought to the true production possibility real rate, all could achieve a more preferred position. But detection of the responsible parties is costly; that cost acts like a tax on work rewards.[6] Viable shirking is the result.

What forms of organizing team production will lower the cost of detecting "performance" (i. e., marginal productivity) and bring personally realized rates of substitution closer to true rates of substitution? Market competition, in principle, could monitor some team production. (It already *organizes* teams.) Input owners who are not team members can offer, in return for a smaller share of the team's rewards, to replace excessively (i. e., overpaid) shirking members. Market competition among potential team members would determine team membership and individual rewards. There would be no team leader, manager, organizer, owner, or employer. For such decentralized organizational control to work, outsiders, possibly after observing each team's total output, can speculate about their capabilities as team members and, by a market competitive process, revised teams with greater productive ability will be formed and sustained. Incumbent members will be constrained by threats of replacement by outsiders offering services for lower reward shares or offering greater rewards to the other members of the team. Any team member who shirked in the expectation that the reduced output effect would not be attributed to him will be displaced if his activity is detected. Teams of productive inputs, like business units, would evolve in apparent spontaneity in the market—without any central organizing agent, team manager, or boss.

But completely effective control cannot be expected from individualized market competition for two reasons. First, for this competition to be completely effective, new challengers for team membership must know where, and to what extent, shirking is a serious problem, i. e., know they can increase net output as compared with the inputs they replace. To the extent that this is true it is probably possible for existing fellow team members to recognize the shirking. But, by definition, the detection of shirking by observing team output is costly for team production. Secondly, assume the presence of detection costs, and assume that in order to secure a place on the team a new input owner must accept a smaller share of rewards (or a promise to produce more). Then his incentive to shirk would still be at least as great as the incentives of the inputs replaced, because he still bears less than the entire reduction in team output for which he is responsible.

III. The Classical Firm

One method of reducing shirking is for someone to specialize as a monitor to check the input performance of team members.[7] But who will monitor the monitor? One constraint on the monitor is the aforesaid market competition offered by other monitors, but for reasons already given, that is not perfectly effective. Another constraint can be imposed on the monitor: give him title to the net earnings of the team, net of payments to other inputs. If owners of cooperating inputs agree with the monitor that he is to receive any residual product above prescribed amounts (hopefully, the marginal value products of the other inputs), the monitor will have an added incentive not to shirk as a monitor. Specialization in monitoring plus reliance on a residual claimant status will reduce shirking; but additional links are needed to forge the firm of classical economic theory. How will the residual claimant monitor the other inputs?

We use the term monitor to connote several activities in addition to its disciplinary connotation. It connotes measuring output performance, apportioning rewards, observing the input behavior of inputs as means of detecting or estimating their marginal productivity and giving assignments or instructions in what to do and how to do it. (It also includes, as we shall show later, authority to terminate or revise contracts.) Perhaps the contrast between a football coach and team captain is helpful. The coach selects strategies and tactics and sends in instructions about what plays to utilize. The captain is essentially an observer and reporter of the performance at close hand of the members. The latter is an inspector-steward and the former a supervisor manager. For the present all these activities are included in the rubric "monitoring." All these tasks are, in principle, negotiable across markets, but we are presuming that such market measurement of marginal productivities and job reassignments are not so cheaply performed for team production. And in particular our analysis suggests that it is not so much the costs of spontaneously negotiating contracts in the markets among groups for team production as it is the detection of the performance of individual members of the team that calls for the organization noted here.

The specialist *who receives the residual rewards* will be the monitor of the members of the team (i. e., will manage the use of cooperative inputs). The monitor earns his residual through the reduction in shirking that he brings about, not only by the prices that he agrees to pay the owners of the inputs, but also by observing and directing the actions or uses of these inputs. *Managing or examining the ways to which inputs are used in team production is a method of metering the marginal productivity of individual inputs to the team's output.*

To discipline team members and reduce shirking, the residual claimant must have power to revise the contract terms and incentives of *individual* members without having to terminate or alter every other input's contract. Hence, team members who seek to increase their productivity will assign to the monitor not only the residual claimant right but also the right to alter individual membership and performance on the team. Each team member, of course, can terminate his own membership (i. e., quit the team), but only the monitor may unilaterally terminate the membership of any of the other members without necessarily terminating the team itself or his association with the team; and he alone can expand or reduce membership, alter the mix of membership, or sell the right to be the residual claimant-monitor of the team. It is this entire bundle of rights: 1) to be a residual claimant; 2) to observe input behavior; 3) to be the central party common to all contracts with inputs; 4) to alter the membership of the team; and 5) to sell these rights, that defines the *ownership* (or the employer) of the *classical* (capitalist, free-enterprise) firm. The coalescing of these rights has arisen, our analysis asserts, because it resolves the shirking-information problem of team production better than does the noncentralized contractual arrangement.

The relationship of each team member to the *owner* of the firm (i. e., the party common to all input contracts *and* the residual claimant) is simply a "quid pro quo" contract. Each makes a purchase and sale. The employee "orders" the owner of the team to pay him money in the same sense that the employer directs the team member to perform certain acts. The employee can terminate the contract as readily as can the employer, and long-term contracts, therefore, are not an essential attribute of the firm. Nor are "authoritarian," "dictational," or "fiat" attributes relevant to the conception of the firm or its efficiency.

In summary, two necessary conditions exist for the emergence of the firm on the prior assumption that more than pecuniary wealth enter utility functions: 1) It is possible to increase productivity through team-oriented production, a production technique for which it is costly to directly measure the marginal outputs of the cooperating inputs. This makes it more difficult to restrict shirking through simple market exchange between cooperating inputs. 2) It is economical to estimate marginal productivity by observing or specifying input behavior. The simultaneous occurrence of both these preconditions leads to the contractual organization of inputs, known as the *classical capitalist firms* with (a) joint input production, (b) several input owners, (c) one party who is common to all the contracts of the joint inputs, (d) who has rights to renegotiate any input's contract independently of contracts with other input owners, (e) who holds the residual claim, and (f) who has the right to sell his central contractual residual status.[8]

Other Theories of the Firm

At this juncture, as an aside, we briefly place this theory of the firm in the contexts of those offered by Ronald Coase and Frank Knight.[9] Our view of the firm is not necessarily inconsistent with Coase's; we attempt to go further and identify refutable implications. Coase's penetrating insight is to make more of the fact that markets do not operate costlessly, and he relies on the cost of using markets to *form* contracts as his basic explanation for the existence of firms. We do not disagree with the proposition that, *ceteris paribus*, the higher is the cost of transacting across markets the greater will be the comparative advantage of organizing resources within the firm; it is a difficult proposition to disagree with or to refute. We could with equal ease subscribe to a theory of the firm based on the cost of managing, for surely it is true that, *ceteris paribus*, the lower is the cost of managing the greater will be the comparative advantage of organizing resources within the firm. To move the theory forward, it is necessary to know what is meant by a firm and to explain the circumstances under which the cost of "managing" resources is low relative to the cost of allocating resources through market transaction. The conception of and rationale for the classical firm that we propose takes a step down the path pointed out by Coase toward that goal. Consideration of team production, team organization, difficulty in metering outputs, and the problem of shirking are important to our explanation but, so far as we can ascertain, not in Coase's. Coase's analysis insofar as it had heretofore been developed would suggest open-ended contracts but does not appear to imply anything more—neither the residual claimant status nor the distinction between employee and subcontractor status (nor any of the implications indicated below). And it is not true that employees are generally employed on the basis of long-term contractual arrangements any more than on a series of short-term or indefinite length contracts.

The importance of our proposed additional elements is revealed, for example, by the explanation of why the person to whom the control monitor is responsible receives the residual, and also by our later discussion of the implications about the corporation, partnerships, and profit sharing. These alternative forms for organization of the firm are difficult to resolve on the basis of market transaction costs only. Our exposition also suggests a definition of the classical firm—something crucial that was heretofore absent.

In addition, sometimes a technological development will lower the cost of market transactions while, at the same time, it expands the role of the firm. When the "putting out" system was used for weaving, inputs were organized largely through market negotiations. With the development of efficient central sources of power, it became economical to perform weaving in proximity to the power source and to engage in team production. The bringing in of weavers surely must have resulted in a reduction in the cost of negotiating (forming) contracts. Yet, what we observe is the beginning of the factory system in which inputs are organized within a firm. Why? The weavers did not simply move to a common source of power that they could tap like an electric line, purchasing power while they used their own equipment. Now team production in the joint use of equipment became more important. The measurement of marginal productivity, which now involved interactions between workers, especially through their joint use of machines, became more difficult though contract negotiating cost was reduced, while managing the behavior of inputs became easier because of the increased centralization of activity. The firm as an organization expanded even though the cost of transactions was reduced by the advent of centralized power. The same could be said for modern assembly lines. Hence the emergence of central power sources expanded the scope of productive activity in which the firm enjoyed a comparative advantage as an organizational form.

Some economists, following Knight, have identified the bearing of risks of wealth changes with the director or central employer without explaining why that is a viable arrangement. Presumably, the more risk-averse inputs become employees rather than owners of the classical firm. Risk averseness and uncertainty *with regard to the firm's fortunes* have little, if anything, to do with our explanation although it helps to explain why all resources in a team are not owned by one person. That is, the role of risk taken in the sense of absorbing the windfalls that buffet the firm because of unforeseen competition, technological change, or fluctuations in demand are not central to our theory, although it is true that imperfect knowledge and, therefore, risk, in *this* sense of risk, underlie the problem of monitoring team behavior. We deduce the system of paying the manager with a residual claim (the equity) from the desire to have efficient means to reduce shirking so as to make team production economical and not from the smaller aversion to the risks of enterprise in a dynamic economy. We conjecture that "distribution-of-risk" is not a valid rationale for the *existence* and organization of the *classical* firm.

Although we have emphasized team production as creating a costly metering task and have treated team production as an essential (necessary?) condition for the firm, would not other obstacles to cheap metering also call forth the same kind of contractual arrangement here denoted as a firm? For example, suppose a farmer produces wheat in an easily ascertained quantity but with subtle and difficult to detect quality variations determined by how the farmer grew the wheat. A vertical integration could allow a purchaser to control the farmer's behavior in order to more economically estimate productivity. But this is not a case of joint or team production, unless "information" can be considered part of the product. (While a good case could be made for that broader conception of production, we shall ignore it here.) Instead of forming a firm, a buyer can contract to have his inspector on the site of production, just as home builders contract with architects to supervise building contracts; that arrangement is not a firm. Still, a firm might be organized in the production of many products wherein no team production or jointness of use of separately owned resources is involved.

This possibility rather clearly indicates a broader, or complementary, approach to that which we have chosen. 1) As we do in this paper, it can be argued that the firm is the particular policing device utilized when joint team production is present. If other sources of high policing costs arise, as in the wheat case just indicated, some other form of contractual arrangement will be used. Thus to each source of informational cost there may be a different type of policing and contractual arrangement. 2) On the other hand, one can say that where policing is difficult across markets, various forms of contractual arrangements are devised, but there is no reason for that known as the firm to be uniquely related or even highly correlated with team production, as defined here. It might be used equally probably and viably for other sources of high policing cost. We have not intensively analyzed other sources, and we can only note that our current and readily revisable conjecture is that 1) is valid, and has motivated us in our current endeavor. In any event, the test of the theory advanced here is to see whether the conditions we have identified are necessary for firms to have long-run viability rather than merely births with high infant mortality. Conglomerate firms or collections of separate production agencies into one owning organization can be interpreted as an investment trust or investment diversification device—probably along the lines that motivated Knight's interpretation. A holding company can be called a firm, because of the common association of the word firm with any ownership unit that owns income sources. The term firm as commonly used is so turgid of meaning that we can not hope to explain every entity to which the name is attached in common or even technical literature. Instead, we seek to identify and explain a particular contractual arrangement induced by the cost of information factors analyzed in this paper.

IV. Types of Firms

A. Profit-Sharing Firms

Explicit in our explanation of the capitalist firm is the assumption that the cost of *managing* the team's inputs by a central monitor, who disciplines himself because he is a residual claimant, is low relative to the cost of metering the marginal outputs of team members.

If we look within a firm to see who monitors—hires, fires, changes, promotes, and renegotiates—we should find him being a residual claimant or, at least, one whose pay or reward is more than any others correlated with fluctuations in the residual value of the firm. They more likely will have options or rights or bonuses than will inputs with other tasks.

An implicit "auxiliary" assumption of our explanation of the firm is that the cost of team production is increased if the residual claim is not held entirely by the central monitor. That is, we assume that if profit sharing had to be relied upon for *all* team members, losses from the resulting increase in central monitor shirking would exceed the output gains from the increased incentives of other team members not to shirk. If the optional team size is only two owners of inputs, then an equal division of profits and losses between them will leave each with stronger incentives to reduce shirking than if the optimal team size is large, for in the latter case only a smaller percentage of the losses occasioned by the shirker will be borne by him. Incentives to shirk are positively related to the optimal size of the team under an equal profit-sharing scheme.[10]

The preceding does not imply that profit sharing is never viable. Profit sharing to encourage self-policing is more appropriate for small teams. And, indeed, where input owners are free to make whatever contractual arrangements suit them, as generally is true in capitalist economies, profit sharing seems largely limited to partnerships with a relatively small number of *active*[11] partners. Another advantage of such arrangements for smaller teams is that it permits more effective reciprocal monitoring among inputs. Monitoring need not be entirely specialized.

Profit sharing is more viable if small team size is associated with situations where the cost of specialized management of inputs is large relative to the increased productivity potential in team effort. We conjecture that the cost of managing team inputs increases if the productivity of a team member is difficult to correlate with his behavior. In "artistic" or "professional" work, watching a man's activities is not a good clue to what he is actually thinking or doing with his mind. While it is relatively easy to manage or direct the loading of trucks by a team of dock workers where input activity is so highly related in an obvious way to output, it is more difficult to manage and direct a lawyer in the preparation and presentation of a case. Dock workers can be directed in detail without the monitor himself loading the truck, and assembly line workers can be monitored by varying the speed of the assembly line, but detailed direction in the preparation of a law case would require in much greater degree that the monitor prepare the case himself. As a result, artistic or professional inputs, such as lawyers, advertising specialists, and doctors, will be given relatively freer reign with regard to individual behavior. If the management of inputs is relatively costly, or ineffective, as it would seem to be in these cases, but, nonetheless if team effort is more productive than separable production with exchange across markets, then there will develop a tendency to use profit-sharing schemes to provide incentives to avoid shirking.[12]

B.   Socialist Firms

We have analyzed the classical proprietorship and the profit-sharing firms in the context of free association and choice of economic organization. Such organizations need not be the most viable when political constraints limit the forms of organization that can be chosen.   It is one thing to have profit sharing when professional or artistic talents are used by small teams.   But if political or tax or subsidy considerations induce profit-sharing techniques when these are not otherwise economically justified, then additional management techniques will be developed to help reduce the degree of shirking.

For example, most, if not all, firms in Jugoslavia are owned by the employees in the restricted sense that all share in the residual.   This is true for large firms and for firms which employ nonartistic, or nonprofessional, workers as well.   With a decay of political constraints, most of these firms could be expected to rely on paid wages rather than shares in the residual.   This rests on our auxiliary assumption that general sharing in the residual results in losses from enhanced shirking by the monitor that exceed the gains from reduced shirking by residual-sharing employees. If this were not so, profit sharing with employees should have occurred more frequently in Western societies where such organizations are neither banned nor preferred politically.   Where residual sharing by employees is politically imposed, as in Jugoslavia, we are led to expect that some management technique will arise to reduce the shirking by the central monitor, a technique that will not be found frequently in Western societies since the monitor retains all (or much) of the residual in the West and profit sharing is largely confined to small, professional-artistic team production situations.   We do find in the larger scale residual-sharing firms in Jugoslavia that there are employee committees that can recommend (to the state) the termination of a manager's contract (veto his continuance) with the enterprise.   We conjecture that the workers' committee is given the right to recommend the termination of the manager's contract precisely because the general sharing of the residual increases "excessively" the manager's incentive to shirk.[13]

C.   The Corporation

All firms must initially acquire command over some resources.   The corporation does so primarily by selling promises of future returns to those who (as creditors or owners) provide financial capital.   In some situations resources can be acquired in advance from consumers by promises of future delivery (for example, advance sale of a proposed book).   Or where the firm is a few artistic or professional persons, each can "chip in" with time and talent until the sale of services brings in revenues.   For the most part, capital can be acquired more cheaply if many (risk-averse) investors contribute small portions to a large investment. The economies of raising large sums of equity capital in this way suggest that modifications in the relationship among corporate inputs are required to cope with the shirking problem that arises with profit sharing among large numbers of corporate stockholders. One modification is limited liability, especially for firms that are large relative to a stockholder's wealth. It serves to protect stockholders from large losses no matter how they are caused.

If every stock owner participated in each decision in a corporation, not only would large bureaucratic costs be incurred, but many would shirk the task of becoming well informed on the issue to be decided, since the losses associated with unexpectedly bad decisions will be borne in large part by the many other corporate shareholders. More effective control of corporate activity is achieved for most purposes by transferring decision authority to a smaller group, whose main function is to negotiate with and manage (renegotiate with) the other inputs of the team. The corporate stockholders retain the authority to revise the membership of the management group and over major decisions that affect the structure of the corporation or its dissolution.

As a result a new modification of partnerships is induced—the right to sale of corporate shares without approval of any other stockholders. Any shareholder can remove his wealth from control by those with whom he has differences of opinion. Rather than try to control the decisions of the management, which is harder to do with many stockholders than with only a few, unrestricted salability provides a more acceptable escape to each stockholder from continued policies with which he disagrees.

Indeed, the policing of managerial shirking relies on across-market competition from new groups of would-be managers as well as competition from members within the firm who seek to displace existing management. In addition to competition from outside and inside managers, control is facilitated by the temporary congealing of share votes into voting blocs owned by one or a few contenders. Proxy battles or stock-purchases concentrate the votes required to displace the existing management or modify managerial policies. But it is more than a change in policy that is sought by the newly formed financial interests, whether of new stockholders or not. It is the capitalization of expected future benefits into stock prices that concentrates on the innovators the wealth gains of their actions if they own large numbers of shares. Without capitalization of future benefits, there would be less incentive to incur the costs required to exert informed decisive influence on the corporation's policies and managing personnel. Temporarily, the structure of ownership is reformed, moving away from diffused ownership into decisive power blocs, and this is a transient resurgence of the classical firm with power again concentrated in those who have title to the residual.

In assessing the significance of stockholders' power it is not the usual diffusion of voting power that is significant but instead the frequency with which voting congeals into decisive changes.   Even a one-man owned company may have a long term with just one manager—continuously being approved by the owner.   Similarly a dispersed voting power corporation may be also characterized by a long-lived management.   The question is the probability of replacement of the management if it behaves in ways not acceptable to a majority of the stockholders.   The unrestricted salability of stock and the transfer of proxies enhances the probability of decisive action in the event current stockholders or any outsider believes that management is not doing a good job with the corporation.   We are not comparing the corporate responsiveness to that of a single proprietorship; instead, we are indicating features of the corporate structure that are induced by the problem of delegated authority to manager-monitors.[14]

D.   Mutual and Non-profit Firms

The benefits obtained by the new management are greater if the stock can be purchased and sold, because this enables *capitalization* of anticipated future improvements into present *wealth* of new managers who bought stock and created a larger capital by their management changes.   But in nonprofit corporations, colleges, churches, country clubs, mutual savings banks, mutual insurance companies, and "coops," the future consequences of improved management are not capitalized into present wealth of stockholders.   (As if to make more difficult that competition by new would-be monitors, multiple shares of ownership in those enterprises cannot be bought by one person.)   One should, therefore, find greater shirking in nonprofit, mutually owned enterprises.   (This suggests that nonprofit enterprises are especially appropriate in realms of endeavor where more shirking is desired and where redirected uses of the enterprise in response to market-revealed values is less desired.)

E.   Partnerships

Team production in artistic or professional intellectual skills will more likely be by partnerships than other types of team production.   This amounts to market-organized team activity and to a non-employer status. Self-monitoring partnerships, therefore, will be used rather than employer-employee contracts, and these organizations will be small to prevent an excessive dilution of efforts through shirking.   Also, partnerships are more likely to occur among relatives or long-standing acquaintances, not necessarily because they share a common utility function, but also because each knows better the other's work characteristics and tendencies to shirk.

F.   Employee Unions

Employee unions, whatever else they do, perform as monitors for employees. Employers monitor employees and similarly employees monitor an employer's performance. Are correct wages paid on time and in good currency? Usually, this is extremely easy to check. But some forms of employer performance are less easy to meter and are more subject to employer shirking. Fringe benefits often are in nonpecuniary, contingent form; medical, hospital, and accident insurance, and retirement pensions are contingent payments or performances partly in *kind* by employers to employees. Each employee cannot judge the character of such payments as easily as money wages. Insurance is a contingent payment—what the employee will get upon the contingent event may come as a disappointment. If he could easily determine what other employees had gotten upon such contingent events he could judge more accurately the performance by the employer. He could "trust" the employer not to shirk in such fringe contingent payments, but he would prefer an effective and economic monitor of those payments. We see a specialist monitor—the union employees' agent—hired by them and monitoring those aspects of employer payment most difficult for the employees to monitor. Employees should be willing to employ a specialist monitor to administer such hard-to-detect employer performance, even though their monitor has incentives to use pension and retirement funds not entirely for the benefit of employees.

V.   Team Spirit and Loyalty

Every team member would prefer a team in which no one, not even himself, shirked. Then the true marginal costs and values could be equated to achieve more preferred positions. If one could enhance a common interest in nonshirking in the guise of a team loyalty or team spirit, the team would be more efficient. In those sports where team activity is most clearly exemplified, the sense of loyalty and team spirit is most strongly urged. Obviously the team is better, with team spirit and loyalty, because of the reduced shirking—not because of some other feature inherent in loyalty or spirit as such.[15]

Corporations and business firms try to instill a spirit of loyalty. This should not be viewed simply as a device to increase profits by *over*working or misleading the employees, nor as an adolescent urge for belonging. It promotes a closer approximation to the employees' potentially available true rates of substitution between production and leisure and enables each team member to achieve a more preferred situation. The difficulty, of course, is to create economically that team spirit and loyalty. It can be preached with an aura of moral code of conduct—a morality with literally the same basis as the ten commandments—to restrict our conduct toward what we would choose if we bore our full costs.

VI. Kinds of Inputs Owned by the Firm

To this point the discussion has examined why firms, as we have defined them, exist? That is, why is there an owner-employer who is the common party to contracts with other owners of inputs in team activity? The answer to that question should also indicate the kind of the jointly used resources likely to be owned by the central-owner-monitor and the kind likely to be hired from people who are not team-owners. Can we identify characteristics or features of various inputs that lead to their being hired or to their being owned by the firm?

How can residual-claimant, central-employer-owner demonstrate ability to pay the other hired inputs the promised amount in the event of a loss? He can pay in advance or he can commit wealth sufficient to cover negative residuals. The latter will take the form of machines, land, buildings, or raw materials committed to the firm. Commitments of labor-wealth (i. e., human wealth) given the property rights in people, is less feasible. These considerations suggest that residual claimants—owners of the firm—will be investors of resalable capital equipment in the firm. The goods or inputs more likely to be invested, than rented, by the owners of the enterprise, will have higher resale values relative to the initial cost and will have longer expected use in a firm relative to the economic life of the good.

But beyond these factors are those developed above to explain the existence of the institution known as the firm—the costs of detecting output performance. When a durable resource is used it will have a marginal product and a depreciation. Its use requires payment to cover at least use-induced depreciation; unless that user cost is specifically detectable, payment for it will be demanded in accord with *expected* depreciation. And we can ascertain circumstances for each. An indestructible hammer with a readily detectable marginal product has zero user cost. But suppose the hammer were destructible and that careless (which is easier than careful) use is more abusive and causes greater depreciation of the hammer. Suppose in addition the abuse is easier to detect by observing the way it is used than by observing only the hammer after its use, or by measuring the output scored from the hammer by a laborer. If the hammer were rented and used in the absence of the owner, the depreciation would be greater than if the use were observed by the owner and the user charged in accord with the imposed depreciation. (Careless use is more likely than careful use—if one does not pay for the greater depreciation.) An absentee owner would therefore ask for a higher rental price because of the higher *expected* user cost than if the item were used by the owner. The expectation is higher because of the greater difficulty of observing specific user cost, by inspection of the hammer after use. Renting is therefore in this case more costly than owner use. This is the valid content of the misleading expressions about ownership being more economical than renting—ignoring all other factors that may work in the opposite direction, like tax provision, short-term occupancy and capital risk avoidance.

Better examples are tools of the trade. Watch repairers, engineers, and carpenters tend to own their own tools especially if they are portable. Trucks are more likely to be employee owned rather than other equally expensive team inputs because it is relatively cheap for the driver to police the care taken in using a truck. Policing the use of trucks by a nondriver owner is more likely to occur for trucks that are not specialized to one driver, like public transit busses.

The factor with which we are concerned here is one related to the costs of monitoring not only the gross product performance of an input but also the abuse or depreciation inflicted on the input in the course of its use. If depreciation or user cost is more cheaply detected when the owner can see its use than by only seeing the input before and after, there is a force toward owner use rather than renting. Resources whose user cost is harder to detect when used by someone else, tend on this count to be owner-used. Absentee ownership, in the lay language, will be less likely. Assume momentarily that labor service cannot be performed in the absence of its owner. The labor owner can more cheaply monitor any abuse of himself than if somehow labor-services could be provided without the labor owner observing its mode of use or knowing what was happening. Also his incentive to abuse himself is increased if he does not own himself.[16]

The similarity between the preceding analysis and the question of absentee landlordism and of sharecropping arrangements is no accident. The same factors which explain the contractual arrangements known as a firm help to explain the incidence of tenancy, labor hiring or sharecropping.[17]

VII. Firms as a Specialized Market Institution for Collecting, Collating, and Selling Input Information

The firm serves as a highly specialized surrogate market. Any person contemplating a joint-input activity must search and detect the qualities of available joint inputs. He could contact an employment agency, but that agency in a small town would have little advantage over a large firm with many inputs.   The employer, by virtue of monitoring many inputs, acquires special superior information about their productive talents.   This aids his *directive* (i. e., market hiring) efficiency.   He "sells" his information to employee-inputs as he aids them in ascertaining good input combinations for team activity.   Those who work as employees or who rent services to him are using him to discern superior combinations of inputs.   Not only does the director-employer "decide" what each input will produce, he also estimates which heterogeneous inputs will work together jointly more efficiently, and he does this in the context of a privately owned market for forming teams.   The department store is a firm and is a superior private market.   People who shop and work in one town can as well shop and work in a privately owned firm.

This marketing function is obscured in the theoretical literature by the assumption of homogeneous factors.   Or it is tacitly left for individuals to do themselves via personal market search, much as if a person had to search without benefit of specialist retailers.   Whether or not the firm arose because of this efficient information service, it gives the director-employer more knowledge about the productive talents of the team's inputs, and a basis for superior decisions about efficient or profitable combinations of those heterogeneous resources.

In other words, opportunities for profitable team production by inputs already within the firm may be ascertained more economically and accurately than for resources outside the firm.   Superior combinations of inputs can be more economically identified and formed from resources already used in the organization than by obtaining new resources (and knowledge of them) from the outside.   Promotion and revision of employee assignments (contracts) will be preferred by a firm to the hiring of new inputs.   To the extent that this occurs there is reason to expect the firm to be able to operate as a conglomerate rather than persist in producing a single product.   Efficient production with heterogeneous resources is a result not of having *better* resources but in *knowing more accurately* the relative productive performances of those resources.   Poorer resources can be paid less in accord with their inferiority;   greater accuracy of knowledge of the potential and actual productive actions of inputs rather than having high productivity resources makes a firm (or an assignment of inputs) profitable.[18]

VIII.   Summary

While ordinary contracts facilitiate efficient specialization according to comparative advantage, a special class of contracts among a group of joint inputs to a team production process is commonly used for team production.   Instead of multilateral contracts among all the joint inputs' owners, a central common party to a set of bilateral contracts facilitates efficient organization of the joint inputs in team production. The terms of the contracts form the basis of the entity called the firm—especially appropriate for organizing team production processes.

Team productive activity is that in which a union, or joint use, of inputs yields a larger output than the sum of the products of the separately used inputs. This team production requires—like all other production processes—an assessment of marginal productivities if efficient production is to be achieved. Nonseparability of the products of several differently owned joint inputs raises the cost of assessing the marginal productivities of those resources or services of each input owner. Monitoring or metering the productivities to match marginal productivities to costs of inputs and thereby to reduce shirking can be achieved more economically (than by across market bilateral negotiations among inputs) in a firm.

The essence of the classical firm is identified here as a contractual structure with: 1) joint input production; 2) several input owners; 3) one party who is common to all the contracts of the joint inputs; 4) who has rights to renegotiate any input's contract independently of contracts with other input owners; 5) who holds the residual claim; and 6) who has the right to sell his central contractual residual status. The central agent is called the firm's owner and the employer. No authoritarian control is involved; the arrangement is simply a contractual structure subject to continuous renegotiation with the central agent. The contractual structure arises as a means of enhancing efficient organization of team production. In particular, the ability to detect shirking among owners of jointly used inputs in team production is enhanced (detection costs are reduced) by this arrangement and the discipline (by revision of contracts) of input owners is made more economic.

Testable implications are suggested by the analysis of different types of organizations—nonprofit, proprietary for profit, unions, cooperatives, partnerships, and by the kinds of inputs that tend to be owned by the firm in contrast to those employed by the firm.

We conclude with a highly conjectural but possibly significant interpretation. As a consequence of the flow of information to the central party (employer), the firm takes on the characteristic of an efficient market in that information about the productive characteristics of a large set of specific inputs is now more cheaply available. Better recombinations or new uses of resources can be more efficiently ascertained than by the conventional search through the general market. In this sense inputs compete with each other within and via a firm rather than solely across markets as conventionally conceived. Emphasis on interfirm competition obscures intrafirm competition among inputs. Conceiving competition as the *revelation and exchange* of knowledge or information about qualities, potential uses of different inputs in different potential applications indicates that the firm is a device for enhancing competition among sets of input resources as well as a device for more efficiently rewarding the inputs. In contrast to markets and cities which can be viewed as publicly or nonowned market places, the firm can be considered a privately owned market; if so, we could consider the firm and the ordinary market as competing types of markets, competition between private proprietary markets and public or communal markets. Could it be that the market suffers from the defects of communal property rights in organizing and influencing uses of valuable resources?

REFERENCES

M. Canes, "A Model of a Sports League," unpublished doctoral dissertation, UCLA 1970.

S. N. Cheung, *The Theory of Share Tenancy*, Chicago 1969.

R. H. Coase, "The Nature of the Firm," *Economica*, Nov. 1937, *4*, 386–405; reprinted in G. J. Stigler and K. Boulding, eds., *Readings in Price Theory*, Homewood 1952, 331–51.

E. Furobotn and S. Pejovich, "Property Rights and the Behavior of the Firm in a Socialist State," *Zeitschrift für Nationalökonomie*, 1970, *30*, 431–454.

F. H. Knight, *Risk, Uncertainty and Profit*, New York 1965.

S. Macaulay, "Non-Contractual Relations in Business: A Preliminary Study," *Amer.Sociological Rev.*, 1968, *28*, 55–69.

H. B. Malmgren, "Information, Expectations and the Theory of the Firm," *Quart J.Econ.*, Aug. 1961, *75*, 399–421.

H. Manne, "Our Two Corporation Systems: Law and Economics," *Virginia Law Rev.*, Mar. 1967, *53*, No. 2, 259–84.

S. Pejovich, "The Firm, Monetary Policy and Property Rights in a Planned Economy," *Western Econ.J.*, Sept. 1969, *7*, 192–200.

M. Silver and R. Auster, "Entrepreneurship, Profit, and the Limits on Firm Size," *J.Bus.Univ. Chicago*, Apr. 1969, *42*, 277–81.

E. A. Thompson, "Nonpecuniary Rewards and the Aggregate Production Function," *Rev.Econ.Statist.*, Nov. 1970, *52*, 395–404.

FOOTNOTES

* Professors of economics at the University of California, Los Angeles. Acknowledgment is made for financial aid from the E. Lilly Endowment, Inc. grant to UCLA for research in the behavioral effects of property rights.

1 Meter means to measure and also to apportion. One can meter (measure) output and one can also meter (control) the output. We use the word to denote both; the context should indicate which.

2 A producer's wealth would be reduced by the present capitalized value of the future income lost by loss of reputation. Reputation, i. e., credibility, is an asset, which is an-

other way of saying that reliable information about expected performance is both a costly and a valuable good. For acts of God that interfere with contract performance, both parties have incentives to reach a settlement akin to that which would have been reached if such events had been covered by specific contingency clauses. The reason, again, is that a reputation for "honest" dealings—i. e., for actions similar to those that would probably have been reached had the contract provided this contingency—is wealth.

Almost every contract is open-ended in that many contingencies are uncovered. For example, if a fire delays production of a promised product by A to B, and if B contends that A has not fulfilled the contract, how is the dispute settled and what recompense, if any, does A grant to B? A person uninitiated in such questions may be surprised by the extent to which contracts permit either party to escape performance or to nullify the contract. In fact, it is hard to imagine any contract, which, when taken solely in terms of its stipulations, could not be evaded by one of the parties. Yet that is the ruling, viable type of contract. Why? Undoubtedly the best discussion that we have seen on this question is by Stewart Macaulay.

There are means not only of detecting or preventing cheating, but also for deciding how to allocate the losses or gains of unpredictable events or quality of items exchanged. Sales contracts contain warranties, guarantees, collateral, return privileges and penalty clauses for specific nonperformance. These are means of assignment of *risks* of losses of cheating. A lower price without warranty—an "as is" purchase—places more of the risk on the buyer while the seller buys insurance against losses of his "cheating." On the other hand, a warranty or return privilege or service contract places more risk on the seller with insurance being bought by the buyer.

3 The function is separable into additive functions if the cross partial derivative is zero, i. e., if $\partial^2 Z/\partial X_i \partial X_j = 0$.

4 With sufficient generality of notation and conception this team production function could be formulated as a case of the generalized production function interpretation given by our colleague, E. A. Thompson.

5 More precisely: "if anything other than pecuniary income enters his utility function." Leisure stands for all nonpecuniary income for simplicity of exposition.

6 Do not assume that the sole result of the cost of detecting shirking is one form of payment (more leisure and less take home money). With several members of the team, each has an incentive to cheat against each other by engaging in more than the average amount of such leisure if the employer can not tell at zero cost which employee is taking more than average. As a result the total productivity of the team is lowered. Shirking detection costs thus change the form of payment and also result in lower total rewards. Because the cross partial derivatives are positive, shirking reduces other people's marginal products.

7 What is meant by performance? Input energy, initiative, work attitude, perspiration, rate of exhaustion? Or output? It is the latter that is sought—the *effect* or output. But performance is nicely ambiguous because it suggests both input and output. It is *nicely* ambiguous because as we shall see, sometimes by inspecting a team member's input activity we can better judge his output effect, perhaps not with complete accuracy but better than by watching the output of the *team*. It is not always the case that watching input activity is the only or best means of detecting, measuring or monitoring output effects of each team member, but in some cases it is a useful way. For the moment the word performance glosses over these aspects and facilitates concentration on other issues.

8 Removal of (b) converts a capitalist proprietary firm to a socialist firm.

9 Recognition must also be made to the seminal inquiries by Morris Silver and Richard Auster, and by H. B. Malmgren.

10 While the degree to which residual claims are centralized will affect the size of the team, this will be only one of many factors that determine team size, so as an approximation, we can treat team size as exogenously determined. Under certain assumptions about

the shape of the "typical" utility function, the incentive to avoid shirking with unequal profit-sharing can be measured by the Herfindahl index.

11 The use of the word active will be clarified in our discussion of the corporation, which follows below.

12 Some sharing contracts, like crop sharing, or rental payments based on gross sales in retail stores, come close to profit sharing. However, it is gross output sharing rather than profit sharing. We are unable to specify the implications of the difference. We refer the reader to S. N. Cheung.

13 Incidentally, investment activity will be changed. The inability to capitalize the investment value as "take-home" private property *wealth* of the members of the firm means that the benefits of the investment must be taken as annual income by those who are employed at the time of the income. Investment will be confined more to those with shorter life and with higher rates or pay-offs if the alternative of investing is paying out the firm's income to its employees to take home and use as private property. For a development of this proposition, see the papers by Eirik Furobotn and Svetozar Pejovich, and by Pejovich.

14 Instead of thinking of shareholders as joint *owners*, we can think of them as investors, like bondholders, except that the stockholders are more optimistic than bondholders about the enterprise prospects. Instead of buying bonds in the corporation, thus enjoying smaller risks, shareholders prefer to invest funds with a greater realizable return if the firm prospers as expected, but with smaller (possibly negative) returns if the firm performs in a manner closer to that expected by the more pessimistic investors. The pessimistic investors, in turn, regard only the bonds as likely to pay off.

If the entrepreneur-organizer is to raise capital on the best terms to him, it is to his advantage, as well as that of prospective investors, to recognize these differences in expectations. The residual claim on earnings enjoyed by shareholders does not serve the function of enhancing their efficiency as monitors in the general situation. The stockholders are "merely" the less risk-averse or the more optimistic member of the group that finances the firm. Being more optimistic than the average and seeing a higher mean value future return, they are willing to pay more for a certificate that allows them to realize gain on their expectations. One method of doing so is to buy claims to the distribution of returns that "they see" while bondholders, who are more pessimistic, purchase a claim to the distribution that they see as more likely to emerge. Stockholders are then comparable to warrant holders. They care not about the voting rights (usually not attached to warrants); they are in the same position in so far as voting rights are concerned as are bondholders. The only difference is in the probability distribution of rewards and the terms on which they can place their bets.

If we treat bondholders, preferred and convertible preferred stockholders, and common stockholders and warrant holders as simply different classes of investors—differing not only in their risk averseness but in their beliefs about the probability distribution of the firm's future earnings, why should stockholders be regarded as "owners" in any sense distinct from the other financial investors? The entrepreneur-organizer, who let us assume is the chief operating officer and sole repository of control of the corporation, does not find his authority residing in common stockholders (except in the case of a take over). Does this type of control make any difference in the way the firm is conducted? Would it make any difference in the kinds of behavior that would be tolerated by competing managers and investors (and we here deliberately refrain from thinking of them as owner-stockholders in the traditional sense)?

Investment old timers recall a significant incidence of nonvoting common stock, now prohibited in corporations whose stock is traded on listed exchanges. (Why prohibited?) The entrepreneur in those days could hold voting shares while investors held nonvoting shares, which in every other respect were identical. Nonvoting share-holders were simply investors devoid of ownership connotations. The control and behavior of inside owners in such corporations has never, so far as we have ascertained, been carefully studied. For example, at the simplest level of interest, does the evidence indicate that nonvoting shareholders fared any worse because of not having voting rights? Did owners permit the nonvoting holders the normal return available to voting share-holders? Though evidence is prohibitively expensive to obtain, it is remarkable that voting and nonvoting shares sold for essentially identical prices, even during some proxy battles. However, our casual evidence deserves no more than interest-initiating weight.

One more point. The facade is deceptive. Instead of nonvoting shares, today we have warrants, convertible preferred stocks all of which are solely or partly "equity" claims without voting rights, though they could be converted into voting shares.

In sum, is it the case that the stockholder-investor relationship is one emanating from the *division* of *ownership* among several people, or is it that the collection of investment funds from people of varying anticipations is the underlying factor? If the latter, why should any of them be thought of as the owners in whom voting rights, whatever they may signify or however exercisable, should reside in order to enhance efficiency? Why voting rights in any of the outside, participating investors?

Our initial perception of this possibly significant difference in interpretation was precipitated by Henry Manne. A reading of his paper makes it clear that it is hard to understand why an investor who wishes to back and "share" in the consequences of some new business should necessarily have to acquire voting power (i. e., power to change the manager-operator) in order to invest in the venture. In fact, we invest in some ventures in the hope that no other stockholders will be so "foolish" as to try to toss out the incumbent management. We want him to have the power to stay in office, and for the prospect of sharing in his fortunes we buy nonvoting common stock. Our willingness to invest is enhanced by the knowledge that we can act legally via fraud, embezzlement and other laws to help assure that we outside investors will not be "milked" beyond our initial discounted anticipations.

15 *Sports Leagues:* Professional sports contests among teams is typically conducted by a *league* of teams. We assume that sports consumers are interested not only in absolute sporting skill but also in skills *relative* to other teams. Being slightly better than opposing teams enables one to claim a major portion of the receipts; the inferior team does not release resources and reduce costs, since they were expected in the play of contest. Hence, absolute skill is developed beyond the equality of marginal investment in sporting skill with its true social marginal value product. It follows there will be a tendency to overinvest in training athletes and developing teams. "Reverse shirking" arises, as budding players are induced to overpractice hyperactively relative to the social marginal value of their enhanced skills. To prevent overinvestment, the teams seek an agreement with each other to restrict practice, size of teams, and even pay of the team members (which reduces incentives of young people to overinvest in developing skills). Ideally, if all the contestant teams were owned by one owner, overinvestment in sports would be avoided, much as ownership of common fisheries or underground oil or water reserve would prevent overinvestment. This hyperactivity (to suggest the opposite of shirking) is controlled by the league of teams, wherein the league adopts a common set of constraints on each team's behavior. In effect, the teams are no longer really owned by the team owners but are supervised by them, much as the franchisers of some product. They are not full-fledged owners of their business, including the brand name, and can not "do what they wish" as franchises. Comparable to the franchiser, is the league commissioner or conference president, who seeks to restrain hyperactivity, as individual team supervisors compete with each other and cause external diseconomies. Such restraints are usually regarded as anticompetitive, antisocial, collusive-cartel devices to restrain free open competition, and reduce players' salaries. However, the interpretation presented here is premised on an attempt to avoid hyperinvestment in team sports production. Of course, the team operators hav an incentive, once

the league is formed and restraints are placed on hyperinvestment activity, to go further and obtain the private benefits of monopoly restriction. To what extent overinvestment is replaced by monopoly restriction is not yet determinable; nor have we seen an empirical test of these two competing, but mutually consistent interpretations. (This interpretation of league sports activity was proposed by Earl Thompson and formulated by Michael Canes.) Again, athletic teams clearly exemplify the specialization of monitoring with captains and coaches; a captain detects shirkers while the coach trains and selects strategies and tactics. Both functions may be centralized in one person.

16 Professional athletes in baseball, football, and basketball, where athletes having sold their source of service to the team owners upon entering into sports activity, are owned by team owners. Here the team owners must monitor the athletes' physical condition and behavior to protect the team owners' wealth. The athlete has *less* (not, *no*) incentive to protect or enhance his athletic prowess since capital value changes have less impact on his own wealth and more on the team owners. Thus, some athletes sign up for big initial bonuses (representing present capital value of future services). Future salaries are lower by the annuity value of the prepaid "bonus" and hence the athlete has *less* to lose by subsequent abuse of his athletic prowess. Any decline in his subsequent service value would in part be borne by the team owner who owns the players' future service. This does not say these losses of future salaries have no effect on preservation of athletic talent (we are not making a "sunk cost" error). Instead, we assert that the preservation is reduced, not eliminated, because the amount of loss of wealth suffered is smaller. The athlete will spend less to maintain or enhance his prowess thereafter. The effect of this revised incentive system is evidenced in comparisons of the kinds of attention and care imposed on the athletes at the "expense of the team owner" in the case where athletes' future services are owned by the team owner with that where future labor service values are owned by the athlete himself. Why athletes' future athletic services are owned by the team owners rather than being hired is a question we should be able to answer. One presumption is cartelization and monopsony gains to team owners. Another is exactly the theory being expounded in this paper—costs of monitoring production of athletes; we know not on which to rely.

17 The analysis used by Cheung in explaining the prevalence of sharecropping and land tenancy arrangements is built squarely on the same factors—the costs of detecting output performance of jointly used inputs in team production and the costs of detecting user costs imposed on the various inputs if owner used or if rented.

18 According to our interpretation, the firm is a specialized surrogate for a market for team use of inputs; it provides superior (i. e., cheaper) collection and collation of knowledge about heterogeneous resources. The greater the set of inputs about which knowledge of performance is being collated within a firm the greater are the present costs of the collation activity. Then, the larger the firm (market) the greater the attenuation of monitor control. To counter this force, the firm will be divisionalized in ways that economize on those costs—just as will the market be specialized. So far as we can ascertain, other theories of the reasons for firms have no such implications.

In Japan, employees by custom work nearly their entire lives with one firm, and the firm agrees to that expectation. Firms will tend to be large and conglomerate to enable a broader scope of input revision. Each firm is, in effect, a small economy engaging in "intranational and international" trade. Analogously, Americans expect to spend their whole lives in the United States, and the bigger the country, in terms of variety of resources, the easier it is to adjust to changing tastes and circumstances. Japan, with its lifetime employees, should be characterized more by large, conglomerate firms. Presumably, at some size of the firm, specialized knowledge about inputs becomes as expensive to transmit across divisions of the firms as it does across markets to other firms.

*

Non-Profit and Other Private Associational Activities

33: COMPETITION, MONOPOLY, AND THE PURSUIT OF MONEY

ARMEN A. ALCHIAN

REUBEN A. KESSEL
University of California at
Los Angeles and
University of Chicago*

The Problem

Generally speaking, the observations of economists on the subject of monopoly fall into two classes. One set of observations, which flows directly from monopoly theory, is that resources in the competitive sector of the economy would be underutilized if used by monopolists. The other, which does not arise as an implication of either monopoly or competitive theory, consists of a series of observations of empirical phenomena: that monopolistic enterprises, by comparison with competitive enterprises, are characterized by rigid prices, stodgy managements, and relaxed, easygoing working conditions. Alternatively, it is alleged that employees of competitive enterprises work harder, managements are more aggressive and flexible, and pricing is more responsive to profit opportunities.[1]

To regard this second class of observations as not an implication of either monopoly or competitive theory is only partly correct. More correctly, these observations are inconsistent with the implications of the standard profit or wealth maximization postulate. For analyzing the behavior described by Hicks, the pecuniary wealth maximization postulate is clearly inappropriate and should be replaced by a utility maximization postulate.

Aspects of Labor Economics, National Bureau of Economic Research, 1962, p. 152.

Utility Maximization, Not Wealth Maximization

That a person seeks to maximize his utility says little more than that he makes consistent choices.   In order to employ this postulate as an engine of analysis, one must also specify what things are regarded as desirable.   This is the class that includes all those things of which a person prefers more rather than less: money, wealth, love, esteem, friends, ease, health, beauty, meat, gasoline, etc.[2] Then, assuming that a person is willing to substitute among these variables, that is, he will give up wealth in return for more peace and quiet, or better looking secretaries, or more cordial employees, or better weather, the behavior described by Hicks can be analyzed.

Economics cannot stipulate the exchange value that these things have for any particular person, but it can and does say that, whatever his preference patterns may be, the less he must pay for an increase in one of them, the more it will be utilized.   This principle, of course, is merely the fundamental demand theorem of economics—that the demand for any good is a negative function of its price.   And price here means not only the pecuniary price but the cost of whatever has to be sacrificed.

For predicting the choice of productive inputs by business firms, where only the pecuniary aspects of the factors are of concern, the narrower special-case postulate of pecuniary wealth is usually satisfactory.   But this special-case postulate fails when a wider class of business activities is examined.   Therefore we propose to use the general case consistently, even though in some special cases simpler hypotheses, contained within this more general hypothesis, would be satisfactory.[3]

An example of the power of the generalized utility maximizing postulate is provided by Becker.[4]   He shows that under the more general postulate a person, deliberately and even in full knowledge of the consequences for business profits or personal pecuniary wealth, will choose to accept a lower salary or smaller rate of return on invested capital in exchange for nonpecuniary income in the form of, say, working with pretty secretaries, nonforeigners, or whites.   The difference in money return between what an entrepreneur could earn and what he does earn when he chooses to discriminate is an equalizing difference that will not be eliminated by market pressures.   If these persisting, equalizing differences exist, their size, and consequently the extent of discrimination, will differ when institutional arrangements lead to differences in the relative costs of income in pecuniary form relative to income in nonpecuniary form.   Thus, if one can determine the direction in which relative costs are affected by activities or variables that enhance a person's utility, then it should be possible to observe corresponding differences in behavior.

Monopolistic versus Competitive Behavior

The wealth-maximizing postulate seems to imply that both competitive and monopolistic enterprises pursue profits with equal vigor and effectiveness, that their managements are equally alert and aggressive, and that prices are just as flexible in competitive as in monopolized markets. Both the competitive and monopoly model imply that the assets of an enterprise, be it a monopolist or competitive firm, will be utilized by those for·whom these assets have the greatest economic value. One might object to this implication of similarity between competition and monopoly by arguing that, when a monopolistic enterprise is not making the most of its pecuniary economic opportunities, it runs less risk of being driven out of business than a similarly mismanaged competitive enterprise. The answer to this is that despite the absence of competition in product markets, those who can most profitably utilize monopoly powers will acquire control over them: competition in the capital markets will allocate monopoly rights to those who can use them most profitably. Therefore, so long as free capital markets are available, the absence of competition in product markets does not imply a different quality of management in monopolistic as compared with competitive enterprises. Only in the case of nontransferable assets (human monopoly rights and powers like those commanded by Bing Crosby) does classical theory, given free capital market arrangements, admit a difference between competition and monopoly with respect to the effectiveness with which these enterprises pursue profits.[5]

The preceding argument implies that there is no difference in the proportion of inefficiently operated firms among monopolistic as compared with competitive enterprises. (Inefficiency here means that a situation is capable of being changed so that a firm could earn more pecuniary income with no loss in nonpecuniary income or else can obtain more nonpecuniary income with no loss in pecuniary income.) As Becker has shown, discrimination against Negroes in employment is not necessarily a matter of business inefficiency. It can be viewed as an expression of a taste, and one's a priori expectation is that discrimination is characterized by a negatively sloped demand curve. From this viewpoint, discrimination against Negroes by business enterprises, whether competitors or monopolists, would not lessen even if managements were convinced that discrimination reduced their pecuniary income. Presumably, the known sacrifice of pecuniary income is more than compensated for by the gain in nonpecuniary income. But if discrimination does not constitute business inefficiency, then the frequency of discrimination against Negroes ought to be just as great in competitive as in monopolistic enterprises, since both are presumed to be equally efficient. This implication is apparently inconsistent with existing evidence. Becker's data indicate that Negroes are discriminated against more frequently by monopolistic enterprises.[6] But why do monopolistic enterprises discriminate against Negroes more than do competitive enterprises? One would expect that those who have a taste for discrimination against Negroes would naturally gravitate to those economic activities that, for purely pecuniary reasons, do not employ Negroes. Free choice of economic activities implies a distribution of resources that would minimize the costs of satisfying tastes for discrimination. Consequently the managements of competitive enterprises ought to discriminate against Negroes neither more nor less than those of monopolistic enterprises.

If there is greater discrimination by monopolists than by competitive enterprises, and if it cannot be explained by arguing either that people with tastes for discrimination also have special talents related to monopolistic enterprises or that monopolists are in some sense less efficient businessmen, what, then, explains Becker's data and similar observations? More generally, what is the explanation for the contentions that monopolists pursue pecuniary wealth less vigorously, do not work as hard, have more lavish business establishments, etc.? It is to this problem that this paper is addressed.

Monopoly and Profit Control

Stigler and others have pointed out that monopolies, both labor and product, are creatures of the state in a sense which is not true of competitive enterprises.[7] Monopolies typically are protected against the hazards of competition, not simply by their ability to compete, but by the state's policy of not permitting competitors to enter monopolized markets. Laws are enacted that encourage and lead to the creation of monopolies in particular markets. Monopolies so created are beholden to the state for their existence—the state giveth, the state taketh away. Accordingly, they constrain their business policies by satisfying the requirements that they shall do what is necessary to maintain their monopoly status.

Public utilities are an example. Under this head one should include not only gas, electric, and water companies, but all franchised and licensed industries. Railroads, busses, airlines, and taxis fall in this category of business for which permission of a public authority is required, and for which rate and profit regulation exists. For many other businesses, entry regulation exists: commercial and savings banks, savings and loan associations, insurance companies, and the medical profession. All these are formally regulated monopolies, since they are licensed and operated with the approval of the state. Their cardinal sin is to be too profitable.[8] This constraint upon monopolists does not exist for firms operating in competitive markets. This difference in constraints implies differences between the business policies of competitive firms and those of monopolies. The remainder of this paper is devoted to indicating specifically the character of the constraints that are postulated and exploring the observable implications of this postulate.

Even a firm that has successfully withstood the test of open competition without government protection may manifest the behavior of a protected monopoly. Thus a firm like General Motors may become very large and outstanding and acquire a large share of a market just as a protected monopoly does. If, in addition, its profits are large, it will fear that public policy or state action may be directed against it, just as against a state-created monopoly. Such a firm constrains its behavior much in the style of a monopoly whose profit position is protected but also watched by the state. This suggests that the distinction between publicly regulated monopolies and nonregulated monopolies is a false distinction for this problem. As the possibility of state action increases, a firm will adapt its behavior to that which the state deems appropriate. In effect, state regulation is implicitly present.

The cardinal sin of a monopolist, to repeat, is to be too profitable. Public regulation of monopolies is oriented about fixing final prices in order to enable monopolists to earn something like the going rate of return enjoyed by competitive firms. If monopolists are too profitable, pressures are exerted to reduce profits through lowering prices. Only if monopolists can demonstrate to regulatory authorities that they are not profitable enough are they permitted to raise prices.

Implications

If regulated monopolists are able to earn more than the permissible pecuniary rate of return, then "inefficiency" is a free good, because the alternative to inefficiency is the same pecuniary income and no "inefficiency." Therefore this profit constraint leads to a divergence between private and economic costs. However, it is easy to be naive about this inefficiency. More properly, it is not inefficiency at all but efficient utility maximizing through nonpecuniary gains. Clearly one class of nonpecuniary income is the indulgence of one's tastes in the kind of people with whom one prefers to associate. Specifically, this may take the form of pretty secretaries, of pleasant, well-dressed, congenial people who never say anything annoying, of lavish offices, of large expense accounts, of shorter working hours, of costly administrative procedures that reduce the wear and tear on executives rather than increasing the pecuniary wealth of the enterprise, of having secretaries available on a moment's notice by having them sitting around not doing anything, and of many others. It is important to recognize that to take income in nonpecuniary form is consistent with maximizing utility. What is important is not a matter of differences in tastes between monopolists and competitive firms, but differences in the terms of trade of pecuniary for nonpecuniary income. And given this difference in the relevant price or exchange ratios, the difference in the mix purchased should not be surprising.[9]

If wealth cannot be taken out of an organization in salaries or in other forms of personal pecuniary property, the terms of trade between pecuniary wealth and nonpecuniary business-associated forms of satisfaction turn against the former. More of the organization's funds will now be reinvested (which need not result in increased wealth) in ways that enhance the manager's prestige or status in the community. Or more money can be spent for goods and services that enhance the manager's and employees' utility. There can be more luxurious offices, more special services, and so forth, than would ordinarily result if their costs were coming out of personal wealth.

For the total amount of resources used, these constrained expenditure patterns necessarily yield less utility than the unconstrained. The man who spends a dollar with restrictions will need less than a dollar to get an equivalent satisfaction if he can spend it without the restriction. This constrained optimum provides the answer to the question: If a person does spend the wealth of a business as business-connected expenditures for thick rugs and beautiful secretaries, can they not be treated simply as a substitute for household consumption, since he can be regarded as voluntarily choosing to spend his wealth in the business rather than in the home? The answer is that business spending is a more constrained, even if voluntary, choice. This whole analysis is merely an illustration of the effects of restricting the operation of the law of comparative advantage by reducing the size of the market (or range of alternatives).

Employment policies will also reflect the maximization of utility. Assume that an employer prefers clean-cut, friendly, sociable employees. If two available employees are equally productive, but only one is white, native born, Christian, and attractive, the other will not get the job. And if the other employee's wages are reduced to offset this, it will take a greater cut or equilibrating difference to offset this in a monopoly. Why? Because the increase in take-home profits provided by the cost reduction is smaller (if it is increased at all) in the monopoly or state-sheltered firm. Thus one would expect to find a lower fraction of "other" employees in "monopolies" and other areas of sheltered competition.

What this means is that the wages paid must be high enough to attract the "right" kind of employees. At these wages the supply of the "other" kind will be plentiful. A rationing problem exists, so that the buyer, when he offers a higher price than would clear the market with respect to pecuniary productive aspects clears the market by imposing other tests, like congeniality, looks, and so on. For the right kind of employee the price is not above the market clearing price. In a competitive situation this price differential would not persist because its elimination would all redound to the benefit of the owners, whereas in monopoly it will persist because the reduction in costs cannot be transformed into equally large take-home pecuniary wealth for the owners.

The question may be raised: Even if all this is true of a regulated monopoly like a public utility, what about unregulated, competitively superior monopolies? Why should they act this way? The answer is, as pointed out earlier, that the distinction between regulated and unregulated monopolies is a false one. All monopolies are subject to regulation or the threat of destruction through antitrust action. And one of the criteria that the courts seem to consider in evaluating whether or not a firm is a "good" monopoly is its profitability.[10] It behooves an unregulated monopoly, if it wants to remain one, not to appear to be too profitable.

The owners of a monopoly, regulated or "not," therefore have their property rights attenuated because they do not have unrestricted access to or personal use of their company's wealth. This suggests that the whole analysis can be formulated, not in terms of monopoly and competition, as we have chosen to for present purposes, but in terms of private property rights. There is basically no analytic difference between the two since an analysis made in terms of monopoly and competition identifies and emphasizes circumstances that affect property rights. The same analysis can be applied to nonprofit organizations, governments, unions, state-owned, and other "non-owned" institutions, with almost identical results.

One word of clarification—the contrast here is between monopoly and competition, not between corporate and noncorporate firms. We are analyzing differences in implications for behavior that arise from factors other than the corporate structure of the firm. Although there may be differences between corporate, diffused ownership firms and single proprietorships that may affect the many kinds of behavior discussed in this paper, we have been unable to derive them from the corporate aspect. Nor are those features derived from considerations of size per se—however much this may affect behavior.[11]

The preceding propositions stated that more of some forms of behavior would be observed among monopolies. But more than what and of what? More than would be observed in competitive industries. It is not asserted that every monopolist will prefer more than every competitor; instead, it is said that, whatever the relative tastes of various individuals, all those in a monopolistic situation pay less for their actions than they would in a competitive context. And the way to test this is not to cite a favorable comparison based on one monopolist and one competitor. Rather the variations in individual preferences must be allowed to average out by random sampling from each class.

Tests of the Analysis

What observable populations can be compared in testing these implications? One pair of populations are the public utilities and private competitive corporations. Public utilities are monopolies in that entry by competitors is prohibited. Yet, as indicated earlier, the utility is not allowed to exercise its full monopoly powers either in acquiring or distributing pecuniary wealth as dividends to its owners. The owners therefore have relatively weak incentives to try to increase their profits through more efficient management or operation beyond (usually) 6 per cent. But they do have relatively strong incentives to use the resources of the public utility for their own personal interests, but in ways that will count as company costs. Nor does the public utility regulatory body readily detect such activities, because its incentives to do so are even weaker than those of the stockholders. The regulatory body's survival function is the elimination of publicly detectable inefficiencies. Furthermore, the utility regulatory board has a poor criterion of efficiency because it lacks competitive standards.

Public utility managements, whether or not they are also stockholders, will engage in activities that raise costs even if they eat up profits. Management will be rational (i. e., utility maximizing and efficient) if it uses company funds to hire pleasant and congenial employees and to buy its supplies from salesmen who have these same virtues. They cost more, of course, but how does the regulatory commission decide that these are unjustifiable expenditures—even though stockholders would prefer larger profits (which they aren't allowed to have) and customers would prefer lower product prices? Office furniture and equipment will be of higher quality than otherwise. Fringe benefits will be greater and working conditions more pleasant. The managers will be able to devote a greater part of their business time to community and civic programs. They will reap the prestige rewards given to the "statesman-businessman" class of employers. Vacations will be longer and more expensive. Time off for sick leave and for civic duties will be greater. Buildings and equipment will be more beautiful. Public utility advertising will be found more often in magazines and papers appealing to the intellectual or the culturally elite, because this is a low "cost" way of enhancing the social status of the managers and owners. Larger contributions out of company resources to education, science, and charity will be forthcoming—not because private competitors are less appreciative of these things, but because they cost monopolists less.[12]

Job security, whether in the form of seniority or tenure, is a form of increased wealth for employees. Since it makes for more pleasant employer-employee relations, it is a source of utility for employers. The incentive or willingness of owners to grant this type of wealth to employees and thereby increase their own utility is relatively strong because profits are not the opportunity costs of this choice. The owners of a competitive firm, on the other hand, would have to pay the full price either in profits or in competitive disadvantage. Therefore the viability of such activities is lower in that type of firm. The relative frequency or extent of job security should be higher in monopolies and employee turnover rates lower. Also, the incidence of tenure in private educational institutions will be less than in nonprofit or state-operated educational institutions—if the foregoing analysis is correct.[13]

The relative incidence of employee cooperatives will also provide a test. Some employee cooperatives are subsidized by employers. This subsidy often takes the form of free use of company facilities and of employees for operating the cooperative. For any given set of attitudes of employers towards employee cooperatives, costs are lower for monopolists with "excess" profits. Consequently their frequency will be greater among these enterprises.

Inability to keep excess profits in pecuniary form implies that monopolists are more willing than competitive enterprises to forego them in exchange for other forms of utility-enhancing activities within the firm. Fringe benefits, cooperatives, and special privileges for certain employees will be more common. Employees whose consumption preferences do not induce them to use the cooperatives or fringe benefits are not necessarily stupid if they complain of this diversion of resources. But their complaints do reflect their differences in tastes and their ignorance of the incentives and reward patterns that impinge upon owners and administrators. Instead of complaining, they might better seek benefits of special interest to themselves. But since this involves a power play within the firm, the senior people are likely to be the ones who win most often. Hence one would expect to find such benefits more closely tailored to the preferences of the higher administrative officials than would be observed in a competitive business.

Wage policies will also differ in monopoly and nonmonopoly enterprises. If business should fall off, the incentive to resort to fringe or wage reductions (unpleasant under any circumstances), will be weaker for a public utility because the potential savings in profits, if profits are not below the maximum permissible level, cannot be as readily captured by the management or stockholders. One would expect to find wages falling less in hard times, and one would also expect a smaller turnover and unemployment of personnel. The fact that these same implications might be derived from the nature of the demand for the utility's product does not in itself upset the validity of these propositions. But it does make the empirical test more difficult.

Seniority, tenure, employee cooperatives, and many other fringe benefits—instead of increased money salaries or payments—can be composed of mixtures of pecuniary and nonpecuniary benefits, though the inducement to adopt them despite their inefficiency is enhanced by the relatively smaller sacrifice imposed on the owners of organizations in monopolistic situations, as defined here. The relative cost of take-home wealth for the owners is higher; hence they are more willing to utilize other consumption channels.[14]

Constraints on the opportunity to keep profits that are above the allowable limit reduce the incentive to spend money for profitable expansion of services. An upper limit on profits, with strong protection from competition but no assurance of protection from losses of over-expansion, will bias the possible rewards downward in comparison with those of competitive business. An implication of this is "shortages" of public utility services. Despite the fact that prices are above the cost of providing some services, the latter will not necessarily be available. It is better to wait until the demand is already existent and expansion is demanded by the authorities. The possible extra profits are an attenuated inducement.

But these implications hold only if the public utility is earning its allowable limit of profits on investment. If it is losing money—and there is no guarantee against it—stockholders' take-home pay will be curtailed by inefficiency. Until profits reach the take-home limit, profitable and efficient operations will be desirable. If the state regulatory commission is slow to grant price increases in response to cost increases, the utilities should find their profits reduced below the allowable limit during a period of inflation. As a result there should be a tightening up or elimination, or both, of some of the effects predicted in the preceding discussion.[15] One would expect the opposite to occur during periods of deflation.

The present analysis also suggests that there may be an economic rationale for the "shock theory" of wage adjustments. This theory asserts that the profit-reducing wage increases imposed by labor will shock management into greater efficiencies. Suppose that monopolies are induced to trade pecuniary wealth (because they are not allowed to keep it) for nonpecuniary forms of income financed out of business expenditures. This means that, under the impact of higher wage costs and lower profits, the monopolies can now proceed to restore profit rates. Since some of their profit possibilities had been diverted into so-called nonpecuniary forms of income, higher labor costs will make realized profits, broadly interpreted, at least a little smaller. In part, at least, the increased pecuniary wages will come at the expense of nonpecuniary benefits, which will be reduced in order to restore profit levels.   Actually, the shock effect does not produce increases in efficiency.   Instead, it revises the pattern of distribution of benefits.   Left unchanged is the rate of pecuniary profits—if these were formerly at their allowable, but not economic, limit.

Evidence relevant for testing the hypothesis presented here has been produced by the American Jewish Congress, which surveyed the occupations of Jewish and non-Jewish Harvard Business School graduates.   The data consist of a random sample of 224 non-Jewish and a sample of 128 Jewish MBA's.[16]   The 352 Harvard graduates were classified by ten industry categories: (1) agriculture, forestry, and fisheries, (2) mining, (3) construction, (4) transportation, communication, and other public utilities, (5) manufacturing, (6) wholesale and retail trade, (7) finance, insurance, and real estate, (8) business services, (9) amusement, recreation, and related services, and (10) professional and related services.

Categories (4) and (7) must be regarded as relatively monopolized. Therefore, if the hypothesis presented here is correct, the relative frequency of Jews in these two fields is lower than it is for all fields combined.[17]   The relative frequency of Jews in all fields taken together, in the entire sample, is 36 per cent.   These data show that the frequency of Jews —74 MBA's—in the two monopolized fields is less than 18 per cent.   If a sample of 352, of whom 36 per cent are Jews, is assigned so that 74 are in monopolized and 278 in nonmonopolized fields, the probability that an assignment random with respect to religion will result in as few as 18 per cent Jews in monopolized fields (and over 41 per cent in nonmonopolized fields) is less than 0.0005.   This evidence, therefore, is consistent with the hypothesis presented.

One might object to classifying all finance, insurance, and real estate as monopolized fields.   This classification includes the subcategories of banking, credit agencies, investment companies, security and commodity brokers, dealers and exchanges, other finance services, insurance, and real estate.   Of these, only insurance and banking are regulated monopolies.   If only these two subcategories are used, then there are 6 Jews among a group of 39 or a frequency of less than 15 per cent.   If a sample of 352, of whom 36 per cent are Jews, is assigned so that 39 are in monopolized and 313 in nonmonopolized fields, the probability that an assignment that is random with respect to religion will result in as few as 15 per cent Jews in the monopolized fields (and over 39 per cent in the nonmonopolized fields) is less than 0.005.   This evidence is also consistent with the hypothesis presented.

Applications to Labor Unions

This application of monopoly analysis need not be restricted to public utilities. Any regulated activity or one that regulates entry into work should show the same characteristics. Labor unions, because of their control over entry or because of exclusive union representation in bargaining, have monopoly potential. Insofar as a union is able to use that potential to raise wages above the competitive level, unless the jobs are auctioned off, the rationing problem is a nonprice one. A "thoroughly unscrupulous" agent could, in principle, pocket the difference between the payment by the employer and the receipts to the employee, where this difference reflects the difference between the monopolistic and the competitive wage. The moral pressures and the state regulation of union monopoly operate against the existence of thoroughly unscrupulous union officers. But so long as the fruits of such monopoly are handed on to the employed members of the union, the state seems tolerant of monopoly unions. Because of the absence of free entry into the "union agent business," competitive bidding by prospective union agents will not pass on the potential monopoly gains fully to the laborers who do get the jobs.

The necessity of rationing jobs arises because the union agents or managers do not keep for themselves the entire difference between the monopoly wage and the lower competitive wage that would provide just the number of workers wanted. If they did keep it, there would be equilibrium without nonprice rationing. If any part of that difference is captured by the laborers, the quantity available will be excessive relative to the quantity demanded at the monopolized wage rate. The unwillingness of society to tolerate capture of all that difference by the union agents means that either it must be passed on to the workers, thus creating a rationing problem, or it must be indirectly captured by the union agents— not as pecuniary take-home pay, but indirectly as a utility derived from the expenditure of that difference in connection with union business.

To the extent that the monopoly gains are passed on, the preceding rationing problem and its implications exist. But to the extent that they are not, the union agents or persons in control of the monopoly organization will divert the monopoly gains to their own benefit, not through outright sale of the jobs to the highest bidder, but through such indirect devices as high initiation fees and membership dues. This ties the monopoly sale price to the conventional dues arrangement. Creation of large pension funds and special service benefits controlled by the unions redounds to the benefit of the union agents and officers in ways that are too well publicized as a result of recent hearings on union activities to need mention here.[18]

The membership of monopoly unions will tolerate such abuses to the point where the abuses offset the value of monopoly gains accruing to the employed members.   We emphasize that these effects are induced by *both* the monopoly rationing problem and by the desire to convert the monopoly gains into nonpecuniary take-home pay for the union officers or dominant group.   We conjecture that both elements are present; part of the monopoly gain is passed on to the workers, and part is captured as a nonpecuniary source of utility.   When the former occurs the rationing problem exists, and the agents or those in the union will exclude the less desirable type of job applicants—less desirable not in pecuniary productivity to the employer but as fellow employees and fellow members of the union. Admission will be easier for people whose cultural and personal characteristics conform to the interests of the existing members.[19]   And admission will be especially difficult for those regarded as potential price cutters in hard times or not to be counted on as faithful members with a strong sense of loyalty to the union.   Minority groups and those who find they must accept lower wages because of some personal or cultural attribute, even though they are just as productive in a pecuniary sense to the employer, will be more willing to accept lower wages if threatened with the loss of their jobs.   But these are the very types who will weaken the union's monopoly power.   All of this suggests that young people, Negroes, Jews, and other minority or unorthodox groups will be underrepresented in monopolistic unions.[20]

There exists a symmetry in effects between nonprice rationing of admission to monopolistic trade unions and the allocation of rights to operate TV channels, airlines, radio stations, banks, savings and loan associations, public utilities, and the like.   In the absence of the sale of these rights by the commission or government agency charged with their allocation, nonprice rationing comes into play.   This implies that Negroes, Jews, and disliked minority groups of all kinds will be underrepresented among the recipients of these rights.   The symmetry between admission to monopolistic trade unions and the allocation of monopoly rights over the sale of some good or service by a government agency is not complete.   The rights allocated by the government, but not by trade unions, often become private property and can be resold.   Therefore this analysis implies that entrance into these economic activities is more frequently achieved by minority groups, as compared with the population as a whole, through the purchase of outstanding rights.

The chief problem in verifying these implications is that of identifying relative degrees of monopoly power.   If the classification is correct, there is a possibility of testing the analysis.   A comparison of the logic of craft unions with industry-wide unions suggests that the former have greater monopoly powers.   Therefore if this classification is valid, the preceding analysis would be validated if the predicted results were observed.

For classic economic reasons, we conjecture that the craft unions are more likely to have monopolistic powers than industry-wide unions. Therefore we would expect to observe more such discrimination in the first type of union than in the second. And included in the category of craft unions are such organizations as the American Medical Association, and any profession in which admission involves the approval of a governing board.[21]

Conclusions and Conjectures

This analysis suggests that strong nonrestrained profit incentives serve the interests of the relatively unpopular, unorthodox, and individualistic members of society, who have relatively more to gain from the absence of restrictions. Communists are perhaps the strongest case in point. They are strongly disliked in our society and, as a matter of ideology, believe that profit incentives and private property are undesirable. Yet if this analysis is correct, one should find communists overrepresented in highly competitive enterprises. Similar conclusions hold for ex-convicts, disbarred lawyers, defrocked priests, doctors who have lost their licenses to practice medicine, and so forth.

The analysis also suggests an inconsistency in the views of those who argue that profit incentives bring out the worst in people and at the same time believe that discrimination in terms of race, creed, or color is socially undesirable. Similarly, those concerned about the pressures toward conformity in our society, i. e., fears for a society composed of organization men, ought to have some interest in the competitiveness of our markets. It is fairly obvious that the pressures to conform are weaker for a speculator on a grain or stock exchange than they are for a junior executive of A. T. and T. or a university professor with or without tenure.

FOOTNOTES

[1] Hicks concludes: "The best of all monopoly profits is a quiet life." This conclusion appears in a theoretical paper on monopoly; yet it does not flow from the theory presented.

Preceding the foregoing quotation is: "Now, as Professor Bowley and others have pointed out, the variation in monopoly profit for some way on either side of the highest profit output may often be small (in the general case it will depend on the difference between the slopes of the marginal revenue and marginal cost curves); and if this is so, the subjective costs involved in securing a close adaption to the most profitable output may well outweigh the meagre gains offered. It seems not at all unlikely that people in monopolistic positions will often be people with sharply rising subjective costs; if this is so, they are likely to exploit their advantage much more by not bothering to get very near the position of maximum profit, than by straining themselves to get very close to it. The best of all monopoly profits is a quiet life. John R. Hicks, "Annual Survey of Economic Theory: The Theory of Monopoly." *Econometrica*, January 1935, page 8.

2 The following impression is not uncommon. "To say that the individual maximizes his satisfaction is a perfectly general statement. It says nothing about the individual's psychology of behavior, is, therefore, devoid of empirical content." T. Scitovsky, "A Note on Profit Maximization and Its Implications," *Review of Economic Studies*, 1943, pp. 57–60. But this is also true of profit or wealth maximization—unless one says what variables affect profit or wealth and in what way. And so in utility maximization, one must similarly add a postulate stating what variables affect satisfaction or utility. This leads to meaningful implications refutable, in principle, by observable events. For example, an individual will increase his use of those variables that become cheaper. Utility maximization, like wealth maximization, is not a mere sterile truism.

3 Failure to give adequate heed to the special-case properties of wealth maximization may have been responsible for some complaints about the inadequacy of economic theory and may even have led to the curious belief that people themselves change according to which postulate is used. For example, Scitovsky says (ibid.):

"The puritan psychology of valuing money for its own sake, and not for the enjoyments and comforts it might yield, is that of the ideal entrepreneur as he was conceived in the early days of capitalism. The combination of frugality and industry, the entrepreneurial virtues, is calculated to insure the independence of the entrepreneur's willingness to work from the level of his income. The classical economists, therefore, were justified in assuming that the entrepreneur aims at maximizing his profits. They were concerned with a type of business man whose psychology happened to be such that for him maximizing profits was identical with maximizing satisfaction.

"The entrepreneur today may have lost some of the frugality and industry of his forefathers; nevertheless, the assumption that he aims at maximizing his profits is still quite likely to apply to him—at least as a first approximation. For this assumption is patently untrue only about people who regard work as plain drudgery; a necessary evil, with which they have to put up in order to earn their living and the comforts of life. The person who derives satisfaction from his work—other than that yielded by the income he receives for it—will to a large extent be governed by ambition, spirit of emulation and rivalry, pride in his work, and similar considerations, when he plans the activity. We believe that the entrepreneur usually belongs in this last category."

Aside from the dubious validity of (1) alleged differences between the entrepreneurs of the "early days" of capitalism and those of today, and (2) the allegation that the early entrepreneur was one whose utility function had only a single variable—wealth—in it, the more general analysis obviates the urge to set up two different and inconsistent behavior postulates, as if people were schizophrenic types—utility maximizers when consumers and wealth maximizers when businessmen.

The special-case property of the wealth maximizing postulate has been noted by M. W. Reder ("A Reconsideration of the Marginal Productivity Theory," *Journal of Political Economy*, October 1947, pp. 450–458). But in suggesting alternatives he did not postulate the more general one, which includes the valid applications of the special-case postulate as well as many more, without leading to the invalid implications of the special-case postulate.

4 Gary S. Becker, *The Economics of Discrimination*, University of Chicago Press, 1957.

5 For a statement of this position, see Becker, *The Economics of Discrimination*, p. 38. Becker argues that, insofar as monopoy rights are randomnly distributed and cannot be transferred, there are no forces operating to distribute these resources to those for whom they are most valuable. Consequently monopolists, when rights are nontransferable, would be less efficient, on the average, than competitive firms.

6 Ibid., p. 40, Table II.

7 George J. Stigler, "The Extent and Bases of Monopoly," *American Economic Review*, June 1942, Supplement Part 2, p. 1; H. Gregg Lewis, "The Labor Monopoly Problem: A Positive Program," *Journal of Political Economy*, Aug. 1951, p. 277; C. E. Lindbloom, *Unions and Capitalism*, Yale University Press, 1949, p. 214; and Milton Friedman, "Some Comments on the Significance of Labor Unions for Economic Policy," in *The Impact of the Union*, David M. Wright, ed., Harcourt Brace, 1951, p. 214.

8 The notorious suggestion of the medical profession that doctors not drive around town in expensive Cadillacs when visiting patients is an example of the point being made.

9 Usually in economics consumers are presumed to maximize utility subject to fixed income or wealth. What is the wealth or income constraint here? In one sense it is not merely wealth or income that is the pertinent limitation. Many people have access to the use and allocation of resources even though they don't own them. An administrator can assign offices and jobs; he can affect the way company or business resources are used. In all of these decisions, he will be influenced by the effects on his own situation. Therefore to gauge his behavior by the usual wealth or income limitation is to eliminate from consideration a wider range of activities that do not fall within the usual "wealth" or ownership limitation. By straining it is possible to incorporate even this kind of activity with the wealth constraint but we find it more convenient for exposition not to do so. In this paper, in a sense, we are discussing the institutional arrangements which determine to what extent constraints are of one type rather than another.

10 See Aaron Director and Edward H. Levi, "Trade Regulation," *Northwestern Law Review*, 1956, p. 286 and ff.

11 We were originally tempted to believe that the same theory being applied here could be applied to corporate versus noncorporate institutions, where the corporate form happens to involve many owners. Similarly the size factor could also be analyzed via the effects on the costs and rewards of various choice opportunities. Subsequent analysis suggests that many of the appealing differences between corporate, dispersed ownership and individual proprietorship proved to be superficial.

12 We could compare a random sample of secretaries working for public utilities with a random sample of secretaries working for competitive businesses. The former will be prettier—no matter whom we select as our judges (who must not know what hypothesis we are testing when they render their decision). The test, however, really should be made by sampling among the secretaries who are working for equal salaried executives in an attempt to eliminate the income effect on demand. Another implication is that the ratio of a secretary's salary to her supervisor's salary will be higher for a public utility—on the grounds that beauty commands a price. Other nonpecuniary, desirable attributes of secretaries also will be found to a greater extent in public utilities (as well as in nonprofit enterprises) than in private competitive firms. In a similar way, all of the preceding suggested implications about race, religion, and sex could be tested.

Another comparison can be made. Consider the sets of events in the business and in the home of the public utility employee or owner having a given salary or wealth. The ratio of the thickness of the rug in the office to that of the rug at home will be greater for the public utility than for the private competitive firm employee or owner. The ratio of the value of the available company car to the family car's value will be higher for the public utility than for the private competitive firm. And similarly for the ratios of secretary's beauty to wife's beauty, decorations in the office, travel expenses, etc.

13 See Armen A. Alchian, "Private Property and the Relative Cost of Tenure," *The Public Stake in Union Power*, P. Bradley, ed., University of Virginia Press, 1958, pp. 350–371.

14 The other commonly advanced reasons for such benefits or "inefficiencies" are the income tax on pecuniary wealth and the influence of unions. The former force is obvious;

the latter is the effect of desires by union officials to strengthen their position by emphasizing the employee members' benefits to the union administration, as is done in many fringe benefits. But whether or not these latter factors are present, the one advanced here is an independent factor implying differences between monopoly and competition.

15 This analysis suggests that, with the decline in profitability of railroads, the principle of seniority advancement in railroad management has become relatively less viable. Similar arguments are applicable for other fringe benefits. With respect to negotiation with unions, it implies that railroad managements will more vigorously resist giving the unions extravagantly large concessions because these costs are being borne by owners.

The analysis also implies that unions do better in dealing with monopolistic as contrasted with competitive industries.

16 The existence of these data became known to the authors as a result of an article that appeared in the New York Times on the first day of the conference at which this paper was presented. Subsequently the American Jewish Congress released a paper, "Analysis of Jobs Held by Jewish and by Non-Jewish Graduates of the Harvard Graduate School of Business Administration," which contains the data reported here.

17 Similarly, one would expect Jews and Negroes to be underrepresented among enterprises supplying goods and services to monopolists for the same reason that they are underrepresented as employees.

18 Relevant for the analysis of monopoly power is the character of the protection afforded by the state. For utilities the state actively and directly uses its police powers to eliminate competition. For other monopolies—and this is especially relevant for union monopoly—the state permits these monopolies to use private police power to eliminate competition. The powers of the state passively and indirectly support these monopolies by refusing to act against the exercise of private police power. This suggests that there ought to exist a link between those who have a comparative advantage in the exercise of private police powers (gangsters), and monopolies that eliminate competition through "strong arm" techniques.

19 If the employer is the nonprice rationer, i. e., if the employer does the hiring and not the union, as is true for airplane pilots, he too will display a greater amount of discrimination in nonpecuniary attributes than with a competitive wage rate. If the wage rate has been raised so that he has to retain a smaller number of employees, he will retain those with the greater nonpecuniary productivity. If the wage rate would have fallen in response to increased supplies of labor but instead is kept up by wage controls, then the supply from which he could choose is larger, and again he will select those with the greater nonpecuniary attributes—assuming we are dealing with units of labor or equal pecuniary productivity.

20 See Reuben A. Kessel, "Price Discrimination in Medicine," *Journal of Law and Economics*, 1958, p. 46 and ff.

21 For evidence of the existence of discrimination, see H. R. Northrup, *Organized Labor and the Negro*, Chap. 1, New York, Harpers, 1944; and Kessel, *Price Discrimination in Medicine*, p. 47 and ff.

C Continued

34: THE ECONOMIC AND SOCIAL IMPACT OF FREE TUITION

ARMEN A. ALCHIAN*

Rarely do educational issues provoke as much passion as the proposal to raise tuition fees in California colleges. Unfortunately, the passion has not been matched by reason—it is hard to find a clear statement of the consequences of or reasons for a zero tuition or a high tuition fee. It is hard to determine from the public comments whether the antagonists differ about what the consequences of alternative tuition arrangements would be or have different preferences with respect to well perceived consequences. Some defenders of zero tuition have asserted that zero tuition is necessary for aid to poorer students, for the maintenance of our great system of higher education, for the preservation of free and prosperous society, for achievement of great social benefits, for educational opportunity for all, is a hallowed century-old tradition, and that tuition is a tax on education. Some proponents of tuition fees have argued, for example, that the university and colleges are haboring delinquents who would not be there with full tuition, the poor are aiding the rich, students should pay tuition in order to appreciate their education, taxes are excessive, and low tuition requires exploitation of an underpaid faculty, to cite a few. Most of these arguments are so patently fallacious or nonsensical or irrelevant that they do disservice to the more intelligent arguments. But there are some propositions that merit closer examination. To evaluate them it is first necessary to identify at some length the issues that are involved in analyzing and thereby choosing among

New Individualist Review, Winter 1968, p. 42.

the alternatives—and in the process make clear my own preferences. If I overlook significant objectives or consequences, perhaps others will be stimulated to fill the gaps.

The issues represent a classic topic for applied economics—the effects of different means of allocating scarce resources among competing claimants. A rational analysis of the consequences of tuition systems requires separation of two questions: (1) Who should bear the costs of education? (2) If someone other than the student should pay for his education, in what form should the aid be given?

Unless the distinction between these two issues is grasped, confusion is inevitable. The case for zero tuition is *not* established by demonstrating that aid to students is desirable. Full tuition may still be desirable, with the desired aid taking the form of explicit grants-in-aid or scholarships from which the student pays the tuition fee of his chosen school.

The issue of the most desirable form of aid should be separated from still another closely related question: What is the desired method of financing and controlling *colleges*—as distinct from financing *students*? For example, aid to students in the form of zero tuition means also that the state finances the colleges' activities directly by legislative appropriations with the students and their parents having less influence on financing and controlling the activities of colleges. Where student aid is in the form of grants-in-aid or scholarships, students and parents paying full tuition to their chosen colleges have a greater role in determining which colleges shall be financed and rewarded for superior performances. Recognition of these differences in effect explains why some people have asserted the administrators and members of state universities and colleges, which are currently financed by direct legislative appropriation, have sought from self-interest, rather than educational interest, to maintain the impression that zero tuition is the only feasible or sensible means of aid to students—in order to repress student influence and control over the colleges while retaining the influence of politicians.

Advocates of subsidization of college students (regardless of the method) assume that if each student bore the full cost there would be too little college education as well as a decrease of educational opportunity. What makes it desirable to have more education than if students pay full costs? Several arguments are advanced. Let us discuss these in ascending order of sophistication.

(1) "Although the costs of education are less than the gains to the students themselves, some are unable to finance their education now. A subsidy would provide educational opportunity to the poor." (2) "Cultural education, though not profitable in market earnings, and hence not capable of being paid for out of enhanced earnings, is nevertheless

desirable." (3) "Even if every student acquires as much education as is worthwhile to him, he would take too little, because the individual ignores the beneficial social gains indirectly conferred on other members of society —giving what some people call 'external social effects.' Therefore, society at large should induce students to take more education than indicated by their private interests."

The argument that the poor can not afford to pay for a profitable college education is deceptive. What is meant by a "poor" person? Is he a college calibre student? All college calibre students are rich in both a monetary and non-monetary sense. Their inherited superior mental talent—human capital—*is* great wealth. For example, the college calibre student is worth on the average about $200,000, and on the average, approximately $20,000—$50,000 of that has been estimated as the enhanced value derived from college training, depending upon his major field and profession.

Failure to perceive this inherent wealth of college calibre students reflects ignorance of two economic facts. One is the enormous human wealth in our society. Every good educator recognizes that inanimate capital goods are not the only forms of wealth. The second fact is the difference between current earnings and wealth. For example, a man with a million dollars worth of growing trees, or untapped oil is a rich man—though he is not *now* marketing any of his wealth or services. So it is with the college calibre student. Though his *current* market earnings are small, his wealth—the present wealth value of his future earnings—is larger than for the average person. This is true no matter what the current earnings or wealth of his parents. It is *wealth*, not current earnings nor parent's wealth, that is the measure of a student's richness. College calibre students with low current earnings are not poor. Subsidized higher education, whether by zero tuition, scholarships, or zero interest loans, grants the college student a second windfall— a subsidy to exploit his initial windfall inheritance of talent. This is equivalent to subsidizing drilling costs for owners of oil-bearing lands in Texas.

There remains an even more seriously deceptive ambiguity—that between the subsidization of college education and provision of educational *opportunity*. Educational *opportunity* is provided if any person who can benefit from attending college is enabled to do so despite smallness of *current* earnings. Nothing in the provision of full educational *opportunity* implies that students who are financed during college should not later repay out of their enhanced earnings those who financed that education. Not to ask for repayment is to grant students a gift of wealth at the expense of those who do not attend college or who attend tuition colleges and pay for themselves. This is true because, for one reason our tax bills do not distinguish between those directly benefitted by having obtained a zero tuition educational subsidy and those not so benefitted. Alumni with higher incomes pay more taxes, but they do not pay more than people with equal incomes who financed their own education or never went to college.

Many discussions about educational opportunity refer to proportions of students from poorer and richer families at tuition free colleges. However strong the emotional appeal, the proportion of rich and poor family students is relevant only to the separate issue of wealth redistribution, per se, consequent to state operated zero tuition education. It has nothing to do with the extent of educational opportunity. Though data for California colleges and taxes suggest that lower income groups provide a smaller proportion of students than of taxes to support education, such comparisons are irrelevant, so far as provision of educational *opportunity* is concerned. These data tell how much wealth redistribution there is among the less educated, the poor, the educated, and the rich. That wealth redistribution is good or bad depending upon whether one believes the educational system should be used as a device to redistribute wealth as well as to enhance wealth, knowledge, and educational opportunity. No matter how zero tuition in tax supported schools may redistribute wealth, the provision of full educational opportunity does *not* require redistributions of wealth. Yet, it seems to me, many people confuse these two entirely separate issues or think the latter is necessary for the former. To think that college calibre students should be given zero tuition is to think that smart people should be given wealth at the expense of the less smart.

When some zero tuition university alumni say that without zero tuition they could not have attended college, they should have a modest concern for the implications of that statement. One poor, "uneducated" resident of Watts, upon hearing Ralph Bunche say that he could not have had a college education unless tuition were free, opined, "Perhaps it's time he repay out of his higher income for that privilege granted him by taxes on us Negroes who never went to college." That reply spots the difference between educational opportunity and a redistribution of wealth.

Full educational *opportunity* would be provided if college calibre students could borrow against their future enhanced earnings. Students could repay out of their enhanced future earnings. Although, currently, loans are available from private lenders and also from publicly supported loans, a subsidy could provide a state guarantee of repayment of educational loans exactly as housing loans are guaranteed for veterans. Students could select among optional repayment methods. Some could contract to repay in full with interest; others could opt for a sort of insurance system, whereby the amount repaid was related to their income, with upper and lower limits to amounts repaid being specified. A host of possibilities are available. In fact today with income taxes, the college alumni are repaying part of the educational costs via taxes (but so are others who did not attend college).

Some people are impressed by the size of the debt that a college graduate would have to repay, but they should be impressed with the fact that the debt is *less* than the enhanced earnings he has thereby obtained and is an indication of the wealth bonanza given the student who is subsidized by society.

There remains one more facet of the educational opportunity argument. Even if a college education may be a very profitable investment for some person, he may, because of inexperience or lack of confidence, not appreciate his situation or be willing to borrow at available rates of interest. This presumably is an argument for subsidizing those students who lack confidence or understanding of their possibilities, and it may be a meaningful argument on its own ground, but it is not an argument for subsidizing "poor" students.

Pleas are made for subsidizing *cultural* education which, though it may add nothing to the student's future market earnings, will enhance his general welfare. But a person's welfare is increased if he gets more food, housing, recreation, beer drinking, and fancier cars. It would seem therefore that the relevant argument for helping students is one of helping them regardless of whether they wish their welfare increased via cultural education or better food. A grant of money to be spent as the recipient deems appropriate is an efficient form of aid—as judged by the recipient. Subsidized cultural education rather than money gifts could be justified if the giver knows better than the recipient what is good for the recipient. I cannot make that leap of faith for the collegiate student, although other people do it easily and confidently.

A case can be made for subsidizing the poor *and* the rich to take more education—more than a person would take when motivated by his own interests alone. It is often said there are privately unheeded, net social benefits, so each person will under-invest in education from the social point of view, regardless of whether he is rich or poor; but we must separate the illusory from the real external available gains.

Education makes a person more productive, as a doctor, lawyer, merchant, or engineer. Other people benefit from his greater productivity, because more engineers enable lower costs of engineering services for the rest of society. Engineers, looking only to their private gain would, it is said, undervalue the total benefit of having more engineers; too few people would seek sufficient engineering education. If this sounds persuasive, economics can teach you something. The increased supply of engineers reduces the prices of engineering services—even if by only a trivial amount

—and thereby reduces the income of *other* engineers. Their income loss is the gain to the rest of society. This is a *transfer* of income from existing engineers to non-engineers; it is *not* a net social gain. The benefitted parties gain at the expense of existing members of the engineering profession, who lose some of their scarcity value as more educated people are created. This is a transfer from the more educated to the less educated. A striking awareness of this effect is evident in the advocacy by labor groups of immigration restriction. Restricting the inflow of laborers of particular skills prevents reductions in wages of incumbent workers with similar skills and prevents a transfer of wealth from them to the rest of American society. An immigrant or a more educated person would have provided an increased product and he would have obtained that value by the sale of his services, but the lower wages to that *type* of services would have transferred some of the incomes of similar workers to the rest of society. This external *transfer* effect is not a net contribution to social output. It is not a reason for subsidizing education.

For external effects to serve as a valid basis for more education two conditions must be satisfied: (1) There must be a net social *gain* (not transfer) unheeded by the student. The ability to read reduces dangers and inconvenience to other people; ability to be sanitary enhances health of other people, or economic education may—but probably will not—prevent passage of socially detrimental, special interest legislation. These are examples of education with external social gains, which we shall assume are not heeded by the student in his private actions because they do not affect the marketable value of his services. Professional education of doctors, engineers, lawyers, economists, mathematicians, etc., has not been shown to fit in that category. Perhaps education at the undergraduate collegiate level in the elements of law, psychology, political science, mathematics, economics may make for better *nonmarket* decisions or actions.

I confess to a strong suspicion that such education is most significant at the grade school level, diminishes at higher levels, and disappears for professional or cultural, artistic, personal satisfaction courses, and is possibly *reversed* at graduate levels (by overtraining and insistence on excessively high standards of training for granting of licenses to practice in some professions—though this is a point the validity of which is not crucial to the main issue here).

(2) The second condition is that there must be *further* external gains unheeded by students at the college level. The fact of having *achieved* net external gains is not sufficient to warrant subsidization. The crucial condition is the failure to achieve still further available *incremental* net social gain from *further* education. Before concluding that they exist because of a tendency for people to ignore them, we should

note that people attend college for reasons other than financial marketable gain.   College attendance for personal reasons includes cultural,
artistic education, and attendance to find mates.   All these tend to extend
education beyond maximizing one's market wealth and possibly even beyond that yielding unheeded social gains.   But the facts are not conclusive
in *either* direction.

Incidentally, an especially common but erroneous contention, presumably relying on the external effect, is that the growth, prosperity, and
unusual position of California depend upon the free tuition, higher education system.   What does this mean?   If this means that free tuition has
contributed to higher wealth for the educated then this is no argument
for either free tuition or more education.   If it means the prosperity and
growth of aircraft, electronics, motion picture, or agricultural industries
in California are dependent upon free tuition, the contention remains
unsupported by any analytic or factual evidence, and in fact can be falsified by comparisons with other states.   Even if it could be demonstrated that *subsidized* higher education was responsible, the issue of *free*
tuition would still not be touched.   If this means that free tuition did attract some people to seek their education in California, they proceeded
to reap the gain in their own higher income.   If they provided a real
net social benefit, it should have exceeded the extent of their subsidization to be justifiable.   The same proposition holds for residents of California.   If this argument is accepted, it is difficult to justify charging
newcomers a full tuition while permitting existing residents a "free tuition."   Yet, we have seen no proponent of zero tuition advocate zero tuition for all newcomers from all other states.   If this means that the higher
incomes for more people increase tax receipts, then the relevance of that
completely escapes me.   If this means California has a larger population,
then this means higher land prices.   But in so far as benefits to "California" have any relevance, I believe they should be viewed as benefits to
people in California rather than as benefits to owners of a geographically
identified piece of land, unless by "California" one means "land owners or
politicians," who indeed do prefer larger populations as a source of political power and higher land values.

To induce students to take more education than is privately worth
their while—in order to obtain the otherwise unheeded external gains—
does call for payments to students.   If a student were paid for doing what
he would have done anyway, or if his education were subsidized to increase
his wealth, he would be receiving a gift.   But a payment (whether as
zero tuition or a money payment) to the student to *extend* his education,
for the sake of achieving *real*, external benefits that he otherwise would
have not produced, is a payment for services, much as if he were to build
houses, for the benefit of the rest of society.   Such payments may well be
independent of the income or future income of the students as well as of his

parents. Though there is nothing that says the rich would provide less real external effects from more education, my conjecture is that the rich would in any event take more education than the poor for cultural reasons and would therefore require a smaller inducement to take the "optimal" extra amount of education for external social benefits. This can form a basis for advocating more educational inducements to the poor than to the rich, but not necessarily by a zero tuition inducement to rich and poor alike.

It should be noted however that there is already subsidization of higher education by private philanthropy on a scale that staggers the imagination. The endowment funds of colleges and philanthropic foundations aiding education runs into the scores of billions. Even if only half that were used to subsidize education (and the rest for research), the amount can not be regarded as minor, on any standard.

No matter what your beliefs about the validity or relevance of the preceding consideration, let us accept them, for the sake of analysis of alternative *means* of providing aid, for full educational opportunity, cultural aid, or extra inducements to education. (Of course, those who think the preceding arguments are too weak to warrant taxpayers' giving aid to college students can ignore all that follows, for to them there is no case for any state action, nor of zero tuition). The rest will want to ask, "What is the best form of aid or inducement?"

We can enable or induce students to take more education with the following offer: "On the condition that you take certain kinds of education, we shall bear enough of the costs to induce you to do so." The costs he would have borne are the income foresaken and the tuition costs. (Food and living costs can be ignored for he would be incurring them no matter what he did). Which of the following is the preferred way of extending that aid to potential students? (1) We pay directly the costs of extra education by operating the school to provide the extra education; this is the zero tuition system. (2) We pay him an equal amount on the condition he take the additional, specified type of education, but he decides which school to attend and he pays the tuition to the school. This is an educational voucher or G.I. type educational bill-of-rights (used after World War II for veterans).

The first requires *also* that the state directly finance and operate the school providing the education; the second permits the student to choose from competing schools and direct payment to the school he chooses. These two alternatives are sufficient to illustrate the major implications of zero versus high tuition modes of subsidy. The wealth effect for the student is superficially the same in either case, and the financial cost to the subscriber can be the same in each case, once it is decided how much education to subsidize for whom. The costs to the subscriber may be the same, but the results are not.

In the California state system of higher education, the tuition fee is zero for *all* state schools and for *all* kinds of training, regardless of whether it contributes to a net social gain or not, and regardless of how rich the student is.

Zero tuition implies that the appropriate aid or subsidy for every student of a state school is exactly equal to the tuition cost no matter what subject he takes. No basis for zero tuitions as being the proper amount has ever been presented; maybe the aid should be even larger, to compensate for foresaken earnings.

Because low or zero tuition schools are believed to have a larger proportion of less wealthy students than high tuition colleges, zero tuition schools are believed to do a better job of providing educational opportunity for less wealthy students. But this entails the earlier confusion between provision of *opportunity* and provision of a wealth *bonanza*; zero tuition schools give bigger wealth gifts to the mentally able students than do the high tuition schools.

Of course, higher tuition will, *other things left unchanged,* reduce the number of financially insecure students attending tuition colleges. The case for raising tuition is not that aid should be denied but instead that "zero tuition" is a less desirable means of providing aid to students; it entails undesirable controls and political interference with education and lowers the quality of education. Yet there is another method of providing full educational opportunity *and* at the same time improving the quality and quantity of education and reducing political controls. That alternative is a system of full tuition supplemented by grants-in-aid to those who qualify as financially insecure and deserving students.

It is important to note that the financing of *colleges* to provide education is different from subsidizing *students.* The zero tuition is a subsidy to the *college* as well as to the student. Subsidies to *students* alone can be provided with a full tuition system; in fact they are now being so provided by many private schools that do charge full tuition.

The alternative to the zero tuition method of providing educational opportunity or giving aid is tuition, *with* loans or with grants of money. The critical difference, in my opinion, between no tuition and tuition, under these circumstances is that the former lets the state politician and college administrator and faculty directly exert more control over education whereas the latter enables the student to exercise more power by his choice of college.

Subsidies to whatever extent desired could be provided by a system of grants-in-aid via scholarships. That would appear to be more expensive *administratively* (but only administratively) than zero tuition, precisely because an effort is made to eliminate the haphazard bonanzas in the zero tuition system. The presumption is that the cost of selecting the students to be subsidized is less than the savings from the avoidance of subsidies to all students.

Tuition with grants-in-aid to students is not visionary. It is proven, practical, economical and currently used. New York State already has a large system of Regents scholarships. California has a smaller scale system with about 2,000 scholarships. After World War II, the Federal government granted millions of veterans educational vouchers for tuition, books and incidental expenses under an enormously successful act known as the G. I. Bill. All these granted aid regardless of the student's current financial status. In California the university and state colleges now receive about $500 million annually directly from the legislature. That would finance 250,000 scholarships of $2000 each. The university's budget would finance 125,000 students, more than the number now attending.

At present many arrangements exist whereby private colleges take into account the financial status of students in deciding how much tuition to charge each student. Even more efficient would be a system of loans with interest to be repaid after graduation out of the student's enhanced earnings. Under a loan system, the problem of filtering rich students from the financially distressed would be reduced to trivial dimensions, since the rich would have little, if anything, to gain by borrowing. This would provide full educational opportunity with little need for a means test.

Full tuition does not in any way restrict the achievability of full education opportunity. That can be achieved explicitly and openly by the scope of grants and subsidized loans. Just as social security and welfare payments are made in money with the recipient choosing his purchases from competing producers, so a full tuition system with grants-in-aid or loans would enable separation of the issue of the amount, if any, of the subsidy from that of the best means of providing and controlling education.

Under a system of full tuition fees, with whatever loans and scholarship voucher grants are deemed desirable, students could choose their education from the whole world. Any accredited college or educational institution whether it be for barbers, television technicians, beauty operators, mechanics, butchers, doctors, lawyers, or historians could serve. Ours would then really be the best educational system in the world; no longer would Californians be confined to California state operated schools. Whatever one's beliefs about the desirable degree of subsidy for more education, and whatever his beliefs about who should get it, the full tuition voucher coupled with scholarships and loans would magically open a new, larger world of choice.

An alternative form of aid to students is a tax-credit allowance whereby parents, or students, could later receive a tax offset to their payments for tuition. This would put private college students on a more equal basis with a low tuition public colleges. In my opinion, this would be equality at the wrong level of equality. Rather than give tax credits as a means of maintaining zero tuition, I would prefer placing a tax *liability* on students attending public colleges with low or zero tuition. Whereas the tax credit provides subsidies and aid to all students at the expense of non-students, the tax-liability assessment places the costs of providing the education more squarely on those who benefit from the education. A tax credit gives *equal* treatment to private and public college students—at the expense of non-students. A tax-liability gives equality to private and public college students and to college and non-college people, with each bearing only the costs of service provided for their benefit. If tax-liability assessments are out of the question politically, the tax credit would be the next best; but it would not achieve one of the major purposes of a full tuition system.

With full cost tuition, competition among California colleges, and even among academic departments would change. Instead of competition for funds being negotiated among university committees, deans, regents, state college boards, and legislators, competition would rely more on classroom behavior of instructors who would be more dependent on student attendance *vis-a-vis* other departments and other colleges. This would enormously enhance the power of the student in the former zero tuition colleges. Giving students more attention and influence in the university would indeed occur, exactly as the customer exercises more power at the grocery—by his purchases and choice among competing products and stores, but not by leaping over the counter and insisting on power to run the store, as occurs with current protest. Currently at the grade school level many parents are turning to private schools precisely because the parents can choose more fully the kind of education given their children —via the power of the purse. The poorer people do not have that option —but they would with a tuition-grant system.

Since the producer usually knows more about what he is producing than does the consumer, the producer illogically tends to conclude that he is a better judge about the appropriate quality and quantity for the consumer. This tendency is especially rewarding if the producer can thereby obtain a sheltered competitive position in the production of the good. He would tend to produce a quality and quantity in a style related more to that which enhances his welfare and less to what students and parents prefer.

It is easy to see that with zero tuition the university faculty benefits from research and graduate activity that builds an impressive publication record and research status, with the currently less rewarding teaching of undergraduates being relegated to the less "distinguished," lower-ranking faculty or graduate students. The "publish or perish" rule would be less powerful under full tuition, because teaching would become a more important source of student directed funds. Survival of the better teachers who are weak in publication would be enhanced. It is interesting and amusing to note, incidentally, that students at the University of California are now attempting to protect some members of the faculty from being dropped because of inadequate research and publication. The protection comes by the students "donating" funds to hire the man to give classes; this *is* a voluntary, spontaneous full tuition system. If allowed to expand, students would determine who was on the staff and who got the bigger incomes, just as they now decide which restaurants shall survive and prosper.

This is a simple application of the old, powerful, fundamental principle of behavior. The lower the price at which goods are distributed, relative to the market value, the greater the degree of discrimination and arbitrary criteria that the "seller" will display. Its corollary is that the lower the seller's right to the monetary proceeds, the greater his gain from underpricing the goods. The gains to the university administration and faculty from low tuition are classic examples, first expounded in Adam Smith's *The Wealth of Nations*. The greater the portion of a college's funds coming from tuition fees, the greater the power of the students and the greater the role teaching will play in the survival and prosperity of the members of the faculty. The less will the faculty choose which students shall attend, how they shall behave, etc. The lower is the ratio of tuition payments, the greater the power of the faculty over the students because the students are less able to exert significant effects on the financing of schools or departments as a reward for "good" performance—as they can with restaurants. The faculty says "education is different" and students are poor judges of good education; students are swayed by popular, theatrical teachers and do not appreciate the more valuable scholarly teachers. One wonders how students happen to go to the better and possibly tougher schools in the first place. The faculty of any college prefers lower tuition—until the budget expenditures can not be met from non-tuition sources. And even then there is conflict of interest within the college between those who are threatened by the budget cut and those with tenure who are not. If the cut, or loss of income, would mean merely fewer undergraduates and fewer *new* teachers, clearly the least difficult resolution from the current faculty's interest is the reduction in new students, rather than an increase in tuition.

With zero tuition the state schools have expanded relative to higher tuition private colleges, and the state university with its higher salaried teachers and more expensive education is more attractive to students than the state colleges and junior colleges. The ex-president and the administrators of zero tuition institutions correctly insist that *zero* tuition is the great principle underlying the *growth* of the university; but it is not a source of better education for California students. We should not confuse the *amount* of money with the *way* the money is obtained. More and better education, as judged by students, could be obtained at the same, or less, cost with the full tuition control of colleges coupled to loans and whatever grants-in-aid are desirable.

With full cost tuition, the less expensive junior colleges would attract students and income from the university and colleges. Predictably, the few administrative voices heard in favor of higher tuition seem, from my observation, to come from junior college administrators—who believe they would out-perform the university if put on a quality-cost basis of competition for students.

A counter argument to the preceding propositions is that junior college education is "inferior" to university education. Although the quality of the university as a research institution is high, not as much can be established for its quality as a teaching institution to educate college students. The move to junior colleges with full tuition would occur if the more expensive university education were not matched by the higher quality as judged by students and parents. The university would have to improve its teaching to hold students at its higher costs. If it could not, the results would constitute evidence that the high cost and high quality combination was not a superior combination of quality, cost, and quantity. A Rolls-Royce gives higher quality transportation than a Ford, but it does not follow that more Rolls should be produced than Fords. *Education* must be judged by the quality, quantity, and costs rather than in terms of only those who are educated at the highest, most expensive levels.

Yet, despite this patent fact of life, when faced with a budget cut the administrators of the state university plump four square for "quality at all costs"—for maintenance of quality education for a selected few regardless of how many must be turned away and given instead an "inferior" education. On what criterion is it established that it is better to maintain the level of quality of education for fewer students at the cost of sacrificing education for others? Would one argue that in the event of a social security reduction, we should reduce the *number* of recipients in order to maintain the quality of those lucky enough to keep getting social security payments? But analogies aside, the elite, authoritarian arguments by university administrators and faculty for a given level of quality, regardless of the sacrifices imposed on excluded students or on tax payers is sobering evidence of the seductiveness of self-interest pleading.

The faculty and administration of higher education in California has evolved in the zero tuition environment, with appropriately adapted behavioral traits. They have learned to use that political structure; they have learned how to appeal to the political processes and to legislators and governors for more financing.   They have been almost exclusively reliant on the political process.   They praise politicians for statesmanlike, responsible behavior when the university budget is increased; but if it is decreased, they cry of political interference.   Having accepted almost exclusive dependence on financing directly from the political and legislative processes, they should not complain of "political interference" when that same political process examines more intently the budget and the operations of the university.   Are they really surprised that the venerable law "He who pays, controls" still is effective?

Legislators generally tend to favor direct state legislative financing of education coupled with no tuition, rather than full tuition with grants-in-aid.   The closer the tuition approaches full cost, the less the power of the legislators over the educational institutions.   It is not entirely accidental that Congress used a grant-in-aid system for veterans; there was no Federal college system.

We must constantly remember the difference between paternalism and independence.   Independence from the competition of political processes and politicians' interests can be enhanced by full tuition, but it will bring greater dependence on competition among educators in satisfying students' whims and interest.   Either the students pay and control, or the political processes and politicians do.   Yet some of the faculty seem to think they can avoid both.   For educators there is no free lunch nor "free" tuition.

The situation reminds one of the Russian plight.   Dissatisfaction with the quality of goods produced by Russian firms is sparking attempts to restore market prices as reflections of consumers' interests.   While the Russian economists and consumers advocate more control via the market, producers and politicians show far less interest in weakening their power by moving away from Socialism.

There remains a subtle, but effective means whereby full tuition would lead to *more* education than if directly provided by government at zero tuition.   As matters stand now, an education at a tuition school may be worth $2000, or say, $500 *more* than the education at zero tuition state schools.   For that superior education worth $500 *more*, the student would have to pay the full tuition cost of $2000.   He gets no relief for not using state schools.   If education were on a full tuition basis, this obstacle to more and higher quality education would be removed.   We should not assume that spending more by government for *direct* provision of education necessarily yields more education.   This phenomenon, I conjecture, is powerful at all levels of education.

A preference for full tuition implies nothing whatsoever about the desirable extent of aid or subsidy to students.   Unfortunately much of the debate has erroneously assumed that zero tuition is a necessary or a preferred method of aid while full tuition is a device to avoid aid to students. No matter how much aid, if any, should be given to students, the case for full tuition does not rest on a denial of aid. It rests on the premise that, whether or not aid is given to students, the financing of schools should be controlled more directly by students and their parents because the kind of education thereby made available is deemed to be better—by those who advocate full tuition.

Full tuition, plus grants-in-aid to whatever extent one believes is justified, directs educational activities more to the interest of students and less to that of the university staff. And after all, is it not the students whose interests are fundamental rather than the university's, as an instituition? Is it the students' interests as reckoned by students and parents rather than the convenience to the educators that is a better guide? My choice of answers is obvious. I suspect that these are the crucial issues on which advocates of zero tuition will differ with me.

My opposition to zero tuition arises because I do not like the way it redistributes wealth, nor do I like the totality of the effects of the kinds of competition it induces relative to that which would prevail under full tuition, supplemented by grants and loans. The latter yields more variety of educational opportunities and just as much educational opportunity and presumptively, greater detectability and survival of superior education. It reduces the producers' control over the products that the customers can have. The influence of selecting their colleges and controlling payments is a trait with high survival in the world outside of academia and which should be cultivated. The decreased role of the state and political activity in administering education is also a consequence I find congenial. Higher tuition would improve the quality of education rather than reduce it. The quantity would be affected not by either a zero or high tuition, but by how much is spent for education. Zero tuition does not mean more is spent for education, nor that more poor people can attend. To believe it does is to think zero tuition is the only or best way to subsidize or aid students— and that contention begs the fundamental question of what is the best way.

All these consequences seem to work against my interests as a member of a zero tuition college. If I thought this one exposition of economic analysis and one man's preferences really were capable of converting our system of educational subsidies from the zero tuition to a full tuition system with scholarships, loans, and vouchers, I might be less willing to expose it, for the price may be high enough to make me join with those who, whatever may be their reason, prefer the Holy Zero, (excuse me, the *free*) tuition system.

FOOTNOTE

* Armen A. Alchian is Professor of Economics at the University of California, Los Angeles. He is co-author of the textbook *University Economics* and author of a number of important articles on costs and property rights. Acknowledgement is made to the Lilly Endowment, Inc. for a research grant to U.C.L.A. during which the present article was written. The opinions expressed here in no way reflect any conditions of that research grant.

C Continued

35: THE POLITICAL ECONOMY OF MODERN UNIVERSITIES

HENRY G. MANNE

An attempt will be made in this paper to examine the modern private university from an organization theory approach. The organizational arrangements of the modern university will be analyzed in an effort to explain the behavior of various individuals connected with these institutions. The list of characters includes trustees, administrators, faculty, graduate students, and undergraduates. The approach of this paper is somewhat different than that of related works by such authors as Ben Rogge, Armen Alchian, and James Buchanan. These authors have focused on the economic effects of less-than-full-cost tuition, and, while many of their points will be touched upon in this paper, the principal focus here is somewhat broader.

The theme of this paper is that the nonprofit organization of universities is probably the principal determinant of less-than-full-cost tuition, with all its implications, and also of many other aspects of university life. Hopefully, this broader approach will explain a wider range of issues and behavior patterns that can be related exclusively to the less-than-full-cost tuition circumstance.

No effort will be made to examine in detail the full behavioral implications of state-owned and state-operated universities, though the development of state universities, it will be argued, played an important role in establishing some aspects of the modern private university. Obviously, there are a number of similarities between the two, but these extrapolations will be left to the reader.

Education in a Free Society, Anne Husted Burleigh (ed.), Liberty Fund, Inc. (1973).

This paper is offered in some respects as a complex hypothesis about universities rather than as an absolute proof of the propositions offered. To this end some historical developments in the American university scene will be sketched, but only to serve certain analytical purposes. No historical research has been done on the development of American universities, and, for the most part, conjecture about that development is offered here rather than hard data. Nonetheless, the broad outlines of that development are well enough known that any errors in this regard should not affect the analysis significantly.

Origins of Modern Organization Form

Until near the end of the nineteenth century there were basically two traditions in American universities, all of which, for practical purposes, were private, nonprofit institutions. The first, and unquestionably more important, of these traditions was that of the church-related college. These were schools founded either to promote religion and inculcate certain values or to train students for the ministry. And, of course, some schools did both. In one fashion or another the great bulk of private universities in America, ranging all the way from the very early schools like Harvard and Dartmouth to the later group of small midwestern colleges like Antioch or the primeval University of Chicago, had strong denominational influence.

The fact that many of these schools were founded in order to give religious training had a direct effect on the behavior of everyone concerned with these schools. Unlike the modern university, with many and diverse goals, these schools had a specific objective. The trustees, administrators, and faculty, as well as students, all understood that the school was basically a means to achieve doctrinal conviction. It could be said that the donors of funds were purchasing primarily religious training and only incidentally other kinds of education.

The founders of these schools, in effect, "purchased" their own utility in the form of religious training for their and others' children. Presumably their satisfaction came from the knowledge of the religious values held by the students. Had the market provided purveyors of college religious training, the founders of these schools might as well have taken advantage of market specialization and allowed others to produce what they purchased. As it was, they had to produce this commodity for their own use. Their situation was analogous to that of mid-nineteenth-century farmers who mortgaged their lands in order to help finance railroads. The farmers did not do this to become investors in the railroad industry. Their motivation was rather to purchase transportation in order to get their commodities to market. Their concern, as illustrated by numerous nineteenth-century law cases on the subject of *ultra vires,* was with access to freight cars rather than with profitability from the operation of the railroad.

Under this approach, discretion in the allocation of the college's resources was very limited. The responsibility of all individuals to maximize the religious training purchased with the given funds was well understood. Thus, the behavior of trustees and administrators was not unlike that of any businessman interested in producing at a specific and definite cost the largest amount of a specific commodity possible; and the trust form of organization was eminently suited to this outlook. It allowed the donors of funds or the friends of the organization to manage the operation without any interference from market competitors; that is, they did not want the flexibility and potential for change inherent in a business firm competing in a marketplace. That form of organization would only have been appropriate for entrepreneurs planning to profit from the sale of education to consumers of it.

Another special aspect of academic denominationalism played a role in the development of modern universities. Probably because of constitutional doubts on the issue, these schools were regularly extended exemptions from local taxation. Most nonprofit institutions that received this privilege in late eighteenth- and early nineteenth-century America were church-related, and the First Amendment's interdiction of laws "respecting a religious establishment" was thus easily converted into an indirect form of government subsidy to denominational colleges. Again the legal history of this phenomenon is not altogether clear, and there were nondenominational charitable institutions in America as well. But the fact remains, nonetheless; that quite early this form of government subsidy was well established for private schools. Clearly, it influenced any school's founders to adopt the nonprofit form of organization.

The second great tradition in American private education, while not inconsistent with the other, is distinguishable enough to be addressed separately. This was the notion of elitist, liberal education. In this tradition, education was viewed as a kind of luxury "consumption good," designed to train an affluent class of aristocrats or dilettantes in the humane arts. Undoubtedly, a number of the private colleges originally founded as denominational schools moved into this second category. At the present a great many of these have ceased to acknowledge any denominational interests whatever.

Strangely, however, the political economy of this kind of school was not fundamentally different from that of the denominational school. These institutions were, in the truest sense of the word, "class" establishments, and the class was unmistakably upper. It would have been very difficult in nineteenth-century America to find many people who could afford the luxury of three or four years of humane studies. This would be true even though tuition was free and other costs were subsidized, since few students would have the necessary educational background, a vast number would simply have no interest, and an even larger number would not be able to afford the sacrifice of four years without gainful employment.

But be that as it may, these institutions were in large measure consciously managed so as to preserve them as intellectual and social sanctuaries for America's version of an aristocracy. Again, the trustees of such schools had a clear purpose by which to test their every action. So long as administrators and faculty understood the purpose, there could be no question about the location of authority.

Manifestly, the ultimate locus of control rested with those individuals who financed the institutions. It is probably the case that individuals giving large sums to quasi-denominational or nondenominational private schools did so with the idea of benefiting their own social class and perhaps occasionally the "deserving poor." This class, of course, was not a European-type aristocracy. However, that made no difference, since the goals were fundamentally the same; i. e., to insulate their children from other social classes, to educate them in a rather luxurious fashion, and, finally, to inculcate in them the values of the system in which their families had prospered.

There were certain characteristics of these schools, of which Princeton, Northwestern, Vanderbilt, and Stanford could serve as prototypes, that followed from their purpose and mode of organization. The individuals who gave large sums of money to these schools either became the trustees of the schools or selected the trustees or had fairly close relations with them. That is, these individuals, like the churches and religious donors to denominational schools, were still primarily interested in producing a certain kind of education for a select group of individuals. They did not intend to be establishing anything like a business firm selling to the public but incidentally operated on a not-for-profit basis. Since the money was really used to "purchase" a commodity, trustees kept a close watch on who were admitted as students, who taught courses, and indeed what was taught.

Certainly, no one in most of these schools would have thought of admitting blacks, or even whites who could not readily afford some financial drain, albeit subsidized. When members of minority religious groups were admitted, it was inevitably on a strict quota basis. Brilliance and scholarship were not the virtues most highly regarded for either students or teachers. Loyalty to the cultural or religious ideals of the institution must have been far more important than grades, publications, or inventions. This is not to say that trustees were necessarily opposed to the other qualities in teachers but, rather, that there was no reason to focus exclusively on intellectuality.

Further, there must have existed something approaching an implicit oath of loyalty to the ideals and attitudes the institution was established to preserve. Certainly the notion of academic freedom as a protection for teachers in their search for truth would not have been advanced in most nineteenth-century universities. This is not to say that scientists would not have been concerned to protect their objectivity and integrity, but science was not the kingpin of universities then.

Clearly, if universities were to function efficiently as the means by which donors "produced" attitudes for a certain set of students, it was necessary to avoid a competitive market situation. This could only be guaranteed if the education was offered at a "bargain" price; that is, below full cost. If schools began to cover all costs by tuition, students or their parents would have been converted into "consumers" and would have exercised normal market controls over competing sellers. Only by maintaining the form of a nonprofit institution subsidizing, as it were, the students who could take advantage of the program could the donors continue to control the substance of what was taught, who taught it, and to whom it was taught. Thus, there were no "consumers" who could be sovereign, since no school was established to "sell" its product on a competitive, businesslike basis.

This pattern, which probably predominated in the late nineteenth century, generated much of the popular image of universities. The college graduate had not only an education but a certain social status that others aspired to. But it was not a potential for high income resulting from education that gave him this status; on the contrary, this status was proof that he had "already arrived," socially and financially.

In passing, we might note what this pattern would probably dictate for the behavior of college administrators. Presidents would be selected by the trustees to carry out their bidding on all aspects of educational policy. There would be no other constituency to which college administrators would even think of answering. Disapproval by the faculty or students of administrative actions could only influence the administrator if the actions were also disapproved of by the trustees.

All in all, then, there was a fairly neat package, in which university donors caused the kind of education they wanted for certain students to be produced and the entire institution was managed to that end. While there was no consumer sovereignty on the part of students or their parents, at least in the usual sense, there were likewise none of the problems we find in the modern university. The reason for problems today, as we shall see, is not that the organizational form adopted by founders of colleges was not appropriate then. It is, rather, that it is no longer appropriate to the changed attitudes about education.

New Influences

Probably the pattern just described could have gone on almost indefinitely. As vocational training became more desirable, and as larger numbers of people recognized that education was a good investment, proprietary schools of various sorts developed. At one time these probably predominated in the United States in such areas as medicine, law, dentistry, accounting, engineering, and other vocational areas. The story of the disappearance of those schools is an interesting chapter in itself, but not directly germane to the present paper. Typically, these schools declined because of governmentally imposed "standards," which, in fact, were political devices to curtail competition for existing professionals. But the big change in American higher education patterns came with the expansion of state university systems, particularly after the Morrill Acts of 1862 and 1890.

State universities probably illustrate nicely the thesis of Allen Wallis that government welfare programs are generally adopted only when the need alleged is already being adequately served in the private sphere. The economic point of this is that only those already purchasing the particular service receive 100% of the value of the government's contribution. Anyone who was not already purchasing the service must value it at less than its market price; thus, he benefits less by the government's largess than the actual market consumer. The chances are pretty good that research would show political pressure for state universities to have come from the economic class that already realized the value of higher education for its children. Like all welfare programs, this one, too, was undoubtedly alleged to be for the welfare of the poor; that is, for those who could not "afford" college education for their children. In fact, as is true even today, the allocation of public funds to students in the form of university education usually represents a reallocation of wealth from the relatively poor to the relatively more affluent.

There were significant educational effects that flowed directly from the introduction on a large scale of political forces into the world of higher education. Though the children of wealthier parents gained the advantage of this subsidized education, it was also true that there ceased to be any guiding purpose for these institutions. Especially with the constitutional inhibitions on religious training, the goal of state-operated universities became a matter of considerable uncertainty. We know, of course, that the tradition of liberal arts education survived in considerable measure. More important, as schools came to be thought of as places where one learned a vocation, political pressures pushed schools toward the more "practical" programs, ones designed to help students earn a living. Even today, the tradition of humane letters and liberal arts is felt more strongly in the private universities than the public ones. No longer does the provider of funds, now the taxpayer, have much opportunity to exercise control over the educational program offered. So long as state universities do not interfere with the interests of the politicians responsible for channeling public funds into these ventures, things go smoothly. But if politically unpopular activities become too prevalent, the government must respond.

With the advent of the public university, a great deal of the support that had formerly gone for private universities disappeared. Competition for students became much more keen, as few parents could afford to forgo the implicit subsidy of the low-tuition state university. And very important for the analysis to follow, the demand for teachers became much greater. Since the state universities could not politically or legally hold to a particular religious or cultural standard, instructors began to be selected from religious and socioeconomic groups which were not regularly considered previously. These individuals, of course, could not necessarily be expected to feel a loyalty to a different culture. Thus, the attitudes prevalent on campuses began to undergo a radical shift, if for no other reason than that they became neutral or positivist, rather than religiously oriented or culturally directed.

Other important influences on the modern university are strictly twentieth-century developments. First among these would be high personal income tax rates, with contributions to nonprofit universities or foundations deductible from gross income. This had the effect of lowering the "price" of charity, thus increasing the amount of utility "purchased" through charitable contributions. This increase in contributions might have generated more of the kind of control traditional donors exercised over universities, but, by and large, it was too late. No longer could a donor "purchase" anything but the satisfactions afforded by his contributions to education as directed by others. Only in rare instances and for very large sums could he impose his will on the object of his charity. This might not be true of the modern foundation, which, on occasion, may make very large contributions. By and large, however, the foundations have avoided giving any positive direction to universities, while they have certainly done almost nothing to counteract economic and political biases of most of them. In effect, then, both individual and foundation donations have probably tended merely to strengthen the pattern which has developed in universities for other reasons.

Recent years have also seen a tremendous increase in the amount of government-sponsored research, as well as government contributions to private universities for buildings, salaries, and tuition. And, finally, the advent of large-scale private consulting, particularly by the science faculties, has probably had a significant influence on the behavior of academics.

The effect of most of these new influences has tended in the same direction. Trustees and other individual sources of funds who might have tried to direct the policies or values of universities are simply not as important to administrators and faculties as they originally were. As competition has driven the real income of faculties higher, the faculties have also discovered that a nonprofit institution allows them to take part of their gain in various nontaxable forms, like more leisure or time for research on a personally preferred topic. Furthermore, as government and foundations increased in financial importance relative to individual donors —at least for many of the specific things that individual faculty members wanted—it became more and more difficult for trustees to influence faculties at all. And as outside consulting and research became readily available for academics, this, too, tended to loosen the financial hold of donors and trustees.

There is no longer any way for trustees to keep faculty members "in line." There is not even a "line" for trustees, as such, at all. Their interest in serving has become only the quite weak reed of community status or prestige. Instead of being directed by trustees, the modern private university has become "democratized," with an almost total loss of trustee control over student admissions, faculty hiring, and curriculum.

Behavior of University Functionaries

The Trustees

The most significant characteristic of the modern university trustee is his almost total lack of real interest in exercising any authority. He could hardly feel a real personal responsibility for the "values of western civilization" or whatever amorphous goal he might talk about at annual dinners. He does not have any feeling, certainly, for the question of who, generally, should be admitted to receive the school's subsidy in the form of lower-than-full-cost tuition. This right was given up long ago, as American society culturally forbade the older, restrictive standards and as the faculty, the only group with a real interest in selecting the students, took over the task.

Somewhat similarly, the trustees have no power whatever to determine what views will be taught in universities. There are still denominational schools where this is not completely true, but, save these, the modern notion of "academic freedom" has given the faculty effective power over subject matter in the university and its curriculum. Particularly in very technical fields, this was said to have represented merely the trustees' deferring to the expertise of the faculty. But what that indicates is that the trustees had nothing significant to gain by exercising this power; therefore, it was no great loss to give it up to teachers who did have something to gain by it, as we shall see.

While it might be possible for one very wealthy individual to organize a university along certain lines, it would be extremely difficult for anyone to influence an existing institution by the use of donations. First of all, professional associations of teachers and accrediting agencies have removed some of the power to deal with that group. Secondly, laws now exist that forbid certain types of discrimination in the selection of students and faculty. Finally, even a very large donation to an existing institution does not give the donor any legal power of disposition over preexisting funds.

There is always a board of trustees that operates as a self-perpetuating oligarchy. Even though an individual may "buy" his way onto such a board, he will still only be one among many. This is not to say that in some instances wealthy individuals have not exercised considerable influence over an entire board of trustees, which in turn actually gave some direction to the university. Normally, however, this would require a rather unusual set of circumstances, including a top administrator committed to the goals of this individual.

Any prestige left to the position of university trustee no longer comes from the power the position carries. No longer are these favors that can be allocated to one's friends. Such prestige as there is today comes only from the traditional prestige of the office and certainly not from fighting for any particular ideology or standard. Although the trustees are still expected to assist in fund-raising for the university, it is largely on the same basis as they would assist in fund-raising for the local art gallery, orchestra, or museum. It is just that the university is usually larger and still carries greater prestige than other community activities. But it is doubtful whether, in years to come, the relative status position of universities' trustees will be much higher than that of any other comparable-sized eleemosynary institutions' trustees.

The last sporadic fights for the vestiges of control left in the hands of trustees are now being waged. These fights may frequently result in great losses of time, in embarrassment, or in unfavorable publicity for members of boards of trustees. These have become new "costs" of being a trustee. Consequently, we should anticipate that, in future years, there will be some lessened willingness on the part of prominent individuals to assume the risk of serving on a university board. Thus, trustees' power will shrink even more.

This is a rather bleak forecast for the future of boards of trustees of universities; in fact, that group seems well on its way to complete impotence. Since universities and faculties have developed independent sources of funds, there is not the compulsion that used to exist to appoint affluent trustees. In fact, the composition of these boards is already changing, as we find students, teachers, and even employees serving on the boards. It must be acknowledged, however, that for most schools there is still some concern with the flow of funds from trustees and their friends. Where that factor is still important, the college board tends to exercise more control of university policy. Probably this degree of control will never completely disappear.

The legal form of trustee "ownership" of the university is a fairly efficient one, and it has the added advantage of familiarity. Like the English monarchy, it would probably change only if the trustees actually tried again really to control academic policy. And that does not seem very likely, since there is really very little for them to gain by the exercise of such power. All indications are that the sterilization of boards of trustees will continue, with occasional signs of life here and there, usually based on an unusually strong individual personality. But these will be like comets that flash brilliantly for awhile and then disappear.

The Administration

When we refer to the administration, we generally mean the top administrative executive, here called the president. Not surprisingly, the general style and character of a university president will reflect the real power interests within the institution. That is, he will be selected on the basis of characteristics that please those individuals actually exercising the selection power.

It should be possible, therefore, to make some accurate deductions about the characteristics that will be demanded under different selection-power arrangements. Thus, in the goal-directed, traditional universities, presidents were probably subservient to an active and powerful Board of Trustees. We would not expect such individuals to be selected for, or show, qualities of imagination, competitiveness, and innovation. Only as trustees delegated part of their managerial power to the president do we find imposing figures like William Murray Butler at Columbia or William Rainey Harper at Chicago. Unquestionably, such appointments reflected a true dedication on the part of trustees to creating an institution of very high academic standing.

But the much more significant change in preferred characteristics of college presidents came as the real decision-making power shifted from the trustees to the faculty. Whereas, in an earlier era, the trustees may have wanted simply a supply-and-personnel manager, the interest of faculties was in a different kind of president. Perhaps first and foremost they were interested in a fund-raiser. He was not supposed to bring his personal influence to bear on issues of educational policy. He was simply supposed to keep the money flowing in from outside sources.

Thus, as the main source of funds began to shift from individuals to large foundations and government, the interest of presidential selection committees shifted to individuals with political know-how or good contacts in the government and foundation worlds. Recently, as money matters have seemed to take a back seat to the explosive issue of campus violence, the search has been for men best suited for resolving disputes and mediating between contending factions. Thus, it is no accident that Duke, Case Western, and Harvard have in the past year tapped the deans of their law schools as top university administrators. But this is probably only temporary. As the violence dies down, faculties will again recognize that the president is the key man for raising funds, and probably the earlier presidential recruiting pattern will reappear.

None of this is to suggest that in some simpleminded fashion the committee of trustees that used to select presidents is now a committee of tenured professors. As we shall see, the traditional form in universities has been maintained, while the real power has shifted. In the case of presidential selection, it is largely a matter of the trustees having no interests that they feel need to be protected or furthered by the selection of an individual dedicated to those interests. The faculty, on the other hand, address themselves to amorphous but generally accepted standards like "a man of high academic reputation" or "someone prominent in the university world" to guarantee that the man selected is, in fact, dedicated to the kind of university that faculties want.

University presidents today have almost no authorized discretionary power over academic matters like faculty selection and course content. They can, however, still wield some influence by tactical use of their power over budget matters. A strong president, with trustee support, can use the budget as a lever to gain some academic policy ends. But actually, in crucial areas like personnel selection and course content, few presidents really have any preferences contrary to those of the faculties.

A skilled president can still make matters uncomfortable for professors who are personally obnoxious to him, but even that power must be used sparingly, since faculties today understand the techniques necessary to force a president to resign. If enough trustees are made uncomfortable or embarrassed by complaints rightly or wrongly aired by the faculty about the president, most trustees will probably take the easy way out. Since trustees usually have no great interest in the doctrinal aspects of the dispute between the president and the faculty, their best strategy is generally to capitulate in a face-saving way to the faculty. In the last few years we have seen numerous examples of precisely this process. Cornell is probably the most notable.

All of this is not to say that a university president is a eunuch simply there to do the faculty's bidding. The principal point is that it requires a very different personality to serve a goal-directed board of trustees than it does to serve an amorphous, ill-directed power group like a university faculty. But it is the latter that most presidents must serve today in order to survive.

The publicity given to university disruptions in recent years generally suggested that there was a power struggle going on, with the faculty and students on one side arrayed against the administration on the other. The trustees were normally depicted as sitting on the sidelines or else grudgingly intervening only when the situation had become hopeless. But that is not what the real struggle was. What we have been witnessing is simply one of the last battles in the conflict between faculties and trustees for control of universities. The ultimate conclusion to this struggle is already foregone, and these are mainly mopping-up operations by the faculties. The students' interest, apart from the fact that they were largely manipulated by the faculties, seems to have been mainly in having a good time.

In this struggle the administration frequently served as a scapegoat, though just as often it operated as a shield or a battering ram for the faculty in dealing with the trustees. Only in the few unusual cases of presidents with strong views and a strong personality was the president a significant force in this power struggle. Not unexpectedly, then, he felt an obligation to protect the power position of the trustees and, indeed, to protect the integrity of the trustees themselves. But, unless the board itself is highly unusual, the faculty need only bide its time until it can select a president who will behave as they wish.

The Faculty

So much has been said about the economics of faculty behavior that very little that is new can be added here. Professors Rogge and Alchian have both pointed out many of the circumstances that flow from less-than-full-cost tuition, and James Buchanan has shown how the university provides insulation between the economic force of the buyers (students) and the producers (faculty) so that no normal market response to demand is likely. It is, indeed, a topsy-turvy world in which grown men actually receive great powers with no responsibility for how they are wielded and large rewards without having to produce anything in return.

As we saw earlier, the development of American universities can be viewed as a transition from an arrangement in which trustees or donors, in effect, purchased an economic good to one in which we think of students as purchasers of a different economic good. The trustees established certain arrangements for the allocation of the educational goods it was in their power to distribute. The thing that has now changed so radically is the trustees' ability to secure any personal satisfaction or gain from the power to allocate this good. Since they could no longer guarantee that the kind of education they were offering certain students would be accepted by the students, they had less incentive to "buy" this right. But the power to make this allocation did not disappear as a result of the trustees' loss of interest in allocating in a particular way. Faculties developed real interests in exercising this power, and it was a simple matter for the faculty to move into the power vacuum created by the trustees' loss of interest, since no one else offered any objective standards for selection of students.

It was, of course, very much in the interest of faculties to select the most intelligent and intellectual students they could for admission to the university. There were many reasons for this. In the first place, these students were simply more enjoyable to teach. Related to this is the fact that outside sources of funds are always more available to a school that has a "good reputation." Since academic reputation came to be based on the quality of students, a strong incentive was built into the system to secure as good students as possible, since this, in turn, meant a greater claim on public or private funds.

In a slightly different vein, the faculty preferred intellectual students to make their own work easier. Frequently, this simply meant that inexpensive or free research assistance was readily available to the teacher. Related, but probably more important, was the fact that better students frequently became teachers; they could thus carry their own professors' fame with them. This last point, of course, is more relevant for graduate students than undergraduates, but it was all part of the intellectualization of universities.

There is another reason, too, why this demand for intelligent students developed. As faculties ceased to be selected on the basis of commitment to either religious or cultural ideals, some other objective standards for discriminating between those to be hired and those who were not to be hired was necessary. Camaraderie, similarity of outlook, friendships all play a role in this, but they cannot be the announced and avowed criteria for selection. Only one possible criterion suggests itself, that of intelligence and scholarly accomplishment. The race for senior professorships became, in effect, a race to produce the most highly regarded scholarly works. This, in turn, created a value system permeating the entire university. As Professor Tonsor has pointed out, this may have very little to do with the search for objective truth in most areas of scholarship, but it did tend to put a premium on certain intellectual characteristics, not the least of which were high IQ, verbal facility, and an ability to copy and regurgitate the works of others in the profession without seeming to plagiarize them. Quite clearly, if professors were to act as if they honestly believed in the standard of intellectualism, they must extend this to the selection of students as well. One wonders at times, however, how many would not have preferred to select only pretty girls if other constraints were not present.

In recent years we have witnessed a somewhat strange phenomenon. Faculties have insisted on the selection of black students for admission to college exclusively on the basis of color and regardless of their lack of the usual intellectual achievements. Part of the reason for this departure from direct self-interest may have been the money available from government and other sources for black-student programs. For the most part, however, the professors were simply following their own inclinations, since there seemed to be no cost to them in doing so. But it is interesting to notice what is now happening. The expansion of outside funds has stopped, and there have actually been cutbacks. Those individuals who wished to establish desirable positions for themselves have already done so, and the rest find that they receive little satisfaction any longer from the issue. Furthermore, the black students who are ill-equipped for the work they confront demand a great deal more time and effort than the faculties originally contemplated. Interest is clearly beginning to wane in special programs for black students, and the next few years will probably witness, under various rationalizations, a return to the standard of scholastic ability as the near-exclusive criterion for admission, other than payment of tuition. The cost of this episode will be a small generation of very peculiarly educated black students convinced of the hypocrisy of a white university world that did not live up to its promises.

There is one other odd aspect to the policy decision that has been made to allocate the available educational subsidy to the more intelligent. Since local and federal taxes underwrite the cost of education to a significant degree, the universities are involved in a peculiar reallocation of wealth, in this case from the relatively less intelligent to the relatively more intelligent. That this is probably undesirable public policy goes without saying, but the rationalizations and dogma of intellectualism run very deep.

Although the change in desired characteristics for students has been one of the most significant results of the shift in authority from trustees to faculty, other aspects of the shift have been written about more frequently. Probably no other has received quite the attention given to the professors' single-minded interest in not teaching. The light teaching load has become almost the stock joke among university faculties today. And, of course, the principal device for attracting a "star" has long been the promise of little or no teaching. Undoubtedly, this reflects to a considerable extent the greater payoff to professors from research and consulting, but the significant thing is that there is no meaningful way of rewarding a professor for more or better teaching, and thus competing for the time he spends on other pursuits. This, of course, was not the case when trustees took responsibility for running universities; it is, rather, one of the direct results of the shift to faculty power. Only if someone has a direct interest, financial or otherwise, in transmitting knowledge to students will there be any increase in the incentive to teach. At this time, the incentives are very small, if not actually negative.

The same idea runs throughout other administrative policies in faculty-run institutions. The faculties argue that these matters are not really their responsibility, since they do not exercise universitywide authority. That is true. But it is also true that the aspects of university life that most affect students educationally come through the academic departments, and here the faculties reign supreme. We find, for instance, that the list of courses offered in a department will strongly reflect the individual, and often very peculiar, interests of the faculty and not, in any degree, the interests of the students. Graduate students will naturally be preferred to undergraduates, and gradually budgets and programs will be shaped to that end. The policy of the department and the university must be very liberal with regard to leaves of absence and consulting. And, of course, the faculty must not be asked to spend much time out of class with undergraduates. Signs on faculty doors like "Office hours —Wednesday, 2–3 P. M." are not uncommon. They are outdone only by signs reading "Office hours—by appointment only."

Another more serious consequence of faculty control of universities develops in the area of faculty hiring. Again we can draw on some of the economic behavioral theories of Armen Alchian to set the general framework for this discussion. Basically, faculty members making decisions about hiring colleagues ar esubject to almost no competitive market constraints. Like the public utility manager who cannot take home all the earnings he might be able to produce for the company, the faculty, too, tries to maximize its self-interest at the office. As a result, tenure faculty will inevitably look for young professors who (a) will not disrupt the department and (b) have views that seem reasonable to the senior people. Given the proclivity for personality fights sometimes to follow doctrinal lines, these two may not even be very different, but, in any event for present purposes, the second is the more interesting.

The problem for tenure professors considering a new man is to find out what his real views are. By and large, fairly safe guesses can be made. Actually, little attention is paid to other than the appearance, the personality, and perhaps the level of intellect of a candidate for a teaching position. Much more important is the recommendation given him by a senior professor under whom he has done his doctoral research. Since the views of that individual will almost certainly be widely known, it can be safely assumed that any graduate student he strongly recommends will have substantially the same point of view. Graduate students who understand this process ingratiate themselves with their senior professors by never advancing views fundamentally contrary to those of the older man.

This process almost guarantees a kind of monolithic uniformity of viewpoints, at least in those academic areas where complete objectivity is not possible (and perhaps even in the hard sciences where this objectivity is claimed). An open market for varying points of view would mean that varying views would be publicized and schools selected by students on the basis of their preference. At any given moment, the professors already in teaching have little incentive to create this kind of competition. It would, of course, almost automatically result if schools were generally profit-oriented, competitive firms. It should be noted that there are some exceptions to the generalization about monolithic viewpoints. An economics department like that of the University of Chicago or the political science department at the University of Rochester does attract students because of the publicized point of view of these departments, but such "sports" are rare.

Since a professor competes for a higher salary from universities rather than for a higher payment from students, faculty members tend to write for the former audience and to hold views that will not cause them to lose professional status. This further reinforces the pressures for a single point of view to be popular at any given moment in all departments in all universities within a given discipline. Change in this general viewpoint can come only very slowly, much in the style of changes in taste in the arts. Thus, if even a radical point of view becomes popular in a field, then, regardless of its merits and its lack of popularity in the world at large, it becomes nearly impossible to root it out or even to challenge it from within the university. Almost every area of the social sciences and humanities reflects the process just described.

The Students

The role of graduate students has been sufficiently explored in connection with the question of faculty appointments. But the position of undergraduates still deserves some additional consideration. Though the more vocal of these students may talk about the "reactionary" trustees and the "fascist" administration, the real truth is that among the various participants in the university community, the only real and significant conflict of interest exists between the faculty and the undergraduate students. Each of these groups wants more of exactly the same thing, and that is the faculty's time. Students want smaller classes, more courses, more liberal faculty office hours, and more individual conferences. The faculties avoid these things as much as they can and "jokingly" say how nice the university would be if there were no students.

As has been well described, particularly by James Buchanan, there is really no way that students can make their demands felt in this nonprofit environment. Those who make decisions in universities cannot profit personally by operating the university in the educational interests of students. The result, therefore, is from the students' point of view an appalling disregard of their wishes. A lot of what passes as modern permissiveness at the university level would more accurately be characterized as utter disinterest. Today this is being reflected in such matters as parietal rules, grading policy, so-called bulletin board courses, no attendance requirements, pass-fail grading, and many other devices passed off as innovations.

There are two principal factors that have prevented students from more effectively revolting against this monolithic system. One, obviously, was the draft, but the repeal of the college students' exemption removed that circumstance. The other is much more complicated. In many occupations, there is simply no way to secure the necessary government licensing without showing compliance with certain educational prerequisites. This is true of such popular fields as medicine, law, teaching, architecture, and many others. Obviously, many students do not realize why they are in a lockstep from high school to college to a professional school, and they probably see this simply as an initiation rite that our culture requires of its young. That they do not particularly care for it is clear from the variety of suggestions students make for varying their educational fare. Unfortunately, the one appropriate suggestion, forcing universities to compete for the students' favor, is unthinkable to them, since they have been so carefully taught through high school and college that that form of competition is evil and immoral.

* * *

[Balance of article omitted (ed.)].

C Continued

36: JOB PROPERTY RIGHTS AND JOB DEFECTIONS *

DONALD L. MARTIN
University of Virginia

Recent interest in the ownership arrangements or types of property rights that exist throughout the world has led economists to theorems which apply to wide classes of behavior. Writers have focussed on the comparative discretionary behavior of managers of resources in government, private not-for-profit institutions, and private for-profit firms,[1] with differences in behavior being explained by testable, utility-maximization models. The specification of rights to direct resources and bear the consequences, and the costs of enforcing rights are determinants of the constraints that are faced. That is, different kinds of property rights affect the marginal rates of transformation that confront individuals in trading off alternative sources of utility.[2]

This has yielded testable implications that appear to be borne out by observed differences in the behavior of *"firms."* Two obvious extensions of this analysis would be to (1) the behavior of labor unions (and their leaders) and (2) the behavior of employees where employer discretion in allocating labor resources is narrowed (by law or collective contract).

With respect to the latter extension, economists and students of industrial relations have long been interested in many of the legislated and contractual constraints attendant to employment relationships. These constraints are of two kinds: (a) those that limit the uses to which employees may be put (for example, the number and type of complementary resources with which they may be combined, the geographical boundaries within which they may be allocated, and the maximum rate at which they

Journal of Law and Economics, Vol. 15, no. 2, 1972, p. 385.

may produce output [3]) ; and (b) those that weaken an employer's discretion in selecting among alternative employees or would-be employees (for the purposes of initial employment, job assignment, promotion, layoff, recall, and discharge).   For example, an employer is compelled by law to select among alternative employees according to criteria other than sex, race, religion, national origin, or union membership.   Similarly, he has often been required by collective contract, explicitly or implicitly, (and sometimes by legislation or administrative decree) to use selection criteria based on seniority, union status, or work rotation.

Because the latter constraints are *exclusionary* in nature and can be identified with individuals, they convey enforceable rights to job access that are related to certain classes of property rights.   Rights to job access, in this article, will be called *job property rights* and will be considered as determinants of the cost-reward systems that affect employee behavior.   The analysis of job property rights, like the analysis of property rights in general, offers a useful means of explaining and predicting certain classes of behavior.   This article attempts to derive and test specific hypotheses about the behavioral consequences of job property rights such as seniority and union preference rules.   Because of the availability of data, I have confined this investigation to observations in the American longshore industry.

Employment Arrangements

Longshoring may be broadly defined as those services primarily concerned with the movement of cargo to and from awaiting ships at dockside and the securing of that cargo on departing vessels.   Longshoremen are individuals performing many of these services including the operation of cargo moving gear, the handling of cargo, baggage, and ships stores, and the covering and uncovering of hatches.[4]   The demand for longshoring services is a function of the uncertain comings and goings of ships and the physical disposition of their cargoes.   The demand for longshoremen is volatile and relatively hard to predict; it is not uncommon for the quantity of labor employed, at a given wage rate, to change by 50 per cent within a twenty four hour period.   With longshoremen's labor constituting a relatively large fraction of longshoring costs,[5] the volatile demands for their services have encouraged employers to seek employment relationships that are coterminous with the specific task to be performed.   This has commonly resulted in the hiring of workers at different specified times in a given day, (that is, daily multiple hiring calls).   In fact almost all deep water ports in this country use daily multiple hiring calls.   The number of hiring calls per day is generally a function of the average value of cargo and its variance, the structure of wage rates, the cost of information about ship arrivals and departures, the topography of the given port's facilities, and the provisions of the collective bargaining agreement (if any).

Job Defections and Job Rejections

In 1964 the U. S. Department of Labor (U.S.D.L. or Department) published a study of hiring practices and manpower problems existing in the American longshore industry.[6] In it the U.S.D.L. calls attention to certain employee practices, found in some ports, that we will call *job defections* and *job rejections*. For example, in one port the Department finds:

> .   .   .   evidence that the present [hiring] system has certain serious deficiencies. Frequently it fails to provide adequate manpower to meet the needs of the port. [Work] Gangs report short because men refuse [reject] certain jobs; men accept jobs but they quit before the work is completed.[7] This is particularly likely to occur if a better job opportunity becomes available [that is, men defect from one job to another] . . . .[8]

In another port the U.S.D.L. observes:

> Apparently [men in] gangs occasionally ignore orders to return [to the ship they had been working on] and will shape [that is, offer their services] instead for work on a ship that promises more work. In order to search for more lucrative employment men will leave their ship at 11:00 a.m. and shape at 11:45 a.m. for another job.[9]

The behavior was not found in all ports studied. However, where job defections and job rejections are detected the U.S.D.L. asserts that the productivity of work gangs is slowed, that workers are polarized into gangs of skilled and unskilled longshoremen, and that the period of time goods and ships lie idle in port is unduly prolonged. What accounts for the very different behavior of longshoremen among the various ports?

* * *

[Pages omitted (ed.).]

Job Property Rights

The hiring criteria in American longshore labor markets are not uniform.[17] For example, in the port of New York the hiring system is administered and enforced by the Waterfront Commission of New York Harbor. Longshoremen, in each of the port's seventeen official employment sections, are organized into work gangs and assigned to specific piers. Gangs, on their respective piers, have exclusive rights to the available work there. However, employment opportunities at the various piers differ from day to day. Longshoremen in unemployed work gangs may seek work opportunities as individuals, on other piers and in other sections, during two daily hiring periods conducted at the Commission's employment centers. Almost all longshoremen have been assigned seniority classifications that define hiring priorities, during these daily employment periods, directly proportional to the level of seniority held. Holders of seniority classifications within a given employment section have exclusive rights to all available work opportunities in this section *vis-à-vis* longshoremen from other sections. An employer must respect the seniority hiring rights of the longshoremen he selects or risk revocation of his license (issued by the Commission) to do business in the harbor.[18]

Conversely, the hiring of longshoremen in Charleston, South Carolina, and Jacksonville, Florida, is not constrained by a regulatory commission or by selection criteria that acknowledges a hierarchy of *claims to work opportunities* among longshoremen. At both ports the daily selection of longshoremen is at the discretion of the respective employers.

In Houston, as in New York, longshore hiring is governed exclusively by the respective seniority claims of would-be employees. However, the administration and enforcement of this system is the sole responsibility of the port's union locals.[19] Each day longshoremen are allocated to employers from two hiring halls. Employers place orders with the halls for the *number* of work gangs they desire; they may not specify particular gangs or particular individuals. In New Orleans, where there is a large and frequent turnover of longshore personnel and where a collective contract specifies a union shop, workers have no seniority hiring rights. Moreover, employers may ignore the union membership status of any would-be worker within the first thirty days of initial employment. Thereafter, a would-be worker must be a union member. By comparison, the hiring criterion at the port of Boston is considerably more restrictive. It is an unwritten but strictly enforced rule that all union card holders have preference to available work opportunities in the port. Membership in the union is effectively closed and union cards are bequeathable to immediate family members.

Each of the above ports has some peculiarity in its hiring system that differentiates it from the others. However, it is obvious that hiring practices in the ports of New York, Boston, and Houston have a common characteristic not present in the ports of Charleston, Jacksonville, and New Orleans. The employment criterion in each of the former ports narrows employer discretion, in selecting among would-be workers, by assigning to some longshoremen preferential rights to job access. These rights are defined for individual workers, they are exclusionary in purpose and effect, and they are either legally enforceable within the limits of collective contracts and labor legislation or enforced *extra*-legally (as in the case of Boston).[20] For analytical purposes it would be both accurate and useful to identify them as a class or kind of property right. In this context preferential rights to job access will be termed *job property rights*.[21] This is not to suggest that job property rights are private or alienable *de jure*. In this respect they are on all fours with other non-transferable (but enforceable) rights to use resources. For example, "managers" of government agencies are assigned legal authority (that is, enforceable rights) to take actions and use public resources in pursuit of the "public interest" and in accordance with some prescription.[22]

For their holders, job property rights increase the probability of securing and maintaining employment relative to all other would-be workers. Other things the same, this greater probability increases the expected income, and hence wealth, of any given "claim-holder". This implies an increase in the "level" of his budget constraint for decisions concerning the individual's supply of labor services and his consumption choices. Less obviously, perhaps, the greater probability associated with a job right also affects the slope of the budget constraint, or the exchange rates, between some *utility-affecting options*.[23] If a given longshoreman is not indifferent to the timing, duration, pecuniary rewards, and arduousness of alternative employment opportunities, any given hiring call will present the following options to him:

(a) he may accept the first assignment offered to him and work it to its completion.

(b) he may search among currently available assignments seeking his best offer and work it to its completion.

(c) he may reject all current offers and wait for an expected alternative at a later hiring call and work it to its completion.

(d) he may accept a current work assignment, but desert it later when a more desirable alternative presents itself.

Each option could be a utility maximizing one depending upon the expected cost and benefits of securing any assignment at will. For example, suppose a current opportunity (option a or b)[24] promises hourly earnings of $2.50 for a guaranteed minimum of four hours and an expected maximum of eight hours. The probability associated with the additional four hours is .5. The expected value of this opportunity is $10 + $10(.5) = $15. Alternatively, (option c) a known, and mutually exclusive, future opportunity promises hourly earnings of $3.00 for a guaranteed minimum of four hours and an expected maximum of eight hours. The probability associated with the additional four hours is .5. Since the opportunity has not yet been offered, the chance of securing it is less than unity and depends upon the number of positions open and the number of competitors. Let us assume that the probability of securing this later alternative is .5. The expected value of this opportunity is then [$12 + 12(.5)] .5 = $9, and the current work assignment will presumably be accepted. However, a probability of securing work above .83 (at .85 the expected value of the future assignment is $15.30) would encourage rejection of the current offer for the later alternative.   That is, option c would be chosen over options a or b; unless of course option d is more profitable.   If we assume that within the given structure of hourly earnings longshoremen wish to work eight hours, then in the current example option d is actually more profitable.   By accepting the current offer (with expected value $15) and then leaving after four hours for the later assignment (with expected value $15.30) the longshoreman can earn $10 + ($12).85 = $20.20.[25] This analysis also applies to employment opportunities with different non-pecuniary characteristics.

Since job property rights raise the probability of securing employment, the expected value (pecuniary or non-pecuniary) of any given assignment should be relatively higher where these rights are held.   Moreover, the opportunity costs of forsaking other assignments (through rejections and defections) are more likely to be limited to immediate foregone earnings than where employees do not hold these rights.   That is, with relatively less discretion in selecting among would-be workers, employers cannot readily foreclose future employment opportunities to those defecting from or rejecting current assignments.   Therefore, if we assume that all "desirable" assignments are not concentrated in the initial hiring call, job rejections and defections will be more prevalent where employees hold job property rights.   The above analysis is summarized in the following way.[26]

> Hypothesis B: Job property rights lower the expected costs and raise the expected gains from (1) rejecting some assignments for others and (2) defecting from some assignments to others.   Thus job property rights encourage job rejections and job defections.

Given the auxiliary assumption that longshoremen maximize utility, subject to constraints that are affected by job property rights, two implications derive directly from Hypothesis B.

> Implication B(1):   Relatively more job rejections will occur at ports where employees hold job property rights than at ports where they do not.
> Implication B(2):   Relatively more job defections will occur at ports where employees hold job property rights than at ports where they do not.

Implications B(1) and B(2) would be falsified (*ceteris paribus*) if the incidence of rejections and defections at some ports with job property rights was found to be similar (or lower than) the incidence of rejections and defections at ports without these rights.   Since ports differ in labor force size and in the volume of shipping they service, tests of B(1) and B(2) would require a comparison of rejections and defections per worker or per work opportunity.[27]   As was the case in testing hypothesis A, quan-

titative data on rejections and defections are extremely scarce.[28]   There
is, however, some qualitative evidence that provides support for hypothesis
B and its two implications.   New York, Boston, and Houston have been
identified as ports where employees hold job property rights.   The available evidence suggests that rejections and defections are relatively more
conspicuous at these ports.

In its reports on manpower utilization and job security in New York,
the Department does not explicitly cite job rejections or job defections but
it does call attention to the high degree of absenteeism that occurs there.
Workers are judged absent where they fail to appear for jobs to which
they have been assigned and where they fail to return to work they have
accepted.   This does not necessarily imply that absenteeism is tantamount
to job rejections and job defections.   Absenting oneself from work may
simply mean going home.   Rejections and defections, however, lie within
the set of possible actions open to absentees and thus the absentee rate is
a crude measure of that behavior.   In a survey of absenteeism during June
and July of 1963 the Department finds that:

> . . . approximately 350,000 gang men were ordered for work on the
> various piers.   Approximately 37,800 or 10.8 percent did not appear [and
> return] for work as ordered. . . .   The percent of absentees ranges
> from as low as none on one little used pier, to as high as 41.9 percent on
> another. . . .   Absenteeism of less than six percent was reported by
> eight piers.[29]

Consistent with these findings an independent researcher at the port of
New York, Vernon Jensen, notes that:

> A negative kind of mobility is observable in some sections when men
> defect from their gangs in order to take more attractive assignments
> elsewhere.   The work to be done by the gang may involve cargo whose
> handling is distasteful to some of the men and they prefer not to work
> it.   They might simply absent themselves of course [that is, go home] but
> they might know that acceptable work is available elsewhere and go to
> it.[30]

Before each hiring call, at the Commission's employment centers, longshoremen are checked to determine if they have already been given orders
at their home pier.   Jensen points out, however:

> If he has been given orders, a [computer] message is printed in red
> letting the [hiring] agent know where he should be and making him in-
> eligible, technically, for hiring at . . . the hiring center.   Neverthe-
> less some hiring agents will hire such men in spite of prior orders for
> . . . another pier . . .[31]

According to the Waterfront Commission's Director of Employment Centers, "red slip" violations are a continuing problem and can run as high as

200 men per day.[32]   With respect to job rejections, Jensen observes that
there are " .   .   . always a good number of high seniority men from the
section available   .   .   . They may not be willing to accept any employment whatsoever and may pass [it] up if it is not to their liking." [33]

We have already seen some evidence that job rejections and job defections occur in Boston [34] and Houston.[35]   Since the U.S.D.L. did not compute
data on absenteeism for any of the other ports it studied, quantitative comparisons with New York are not possible.   To obtain some estimate of the
relative importance of rejections and defections among the various ports a
questionnaire was sent to members of the respective employer associations at each port under study.   Only the New York Shipping Association
(N.Y.S.A.) membership failed to provide any respondents.   Along with
other questions,[36] employers were asked if job rejections and defections occur on their docks; or if men decline work or desert work for different or
unknown reasons; and if rejections and defections occur in less than 0.5
per cent or between 0.5 per cent and 15.0 per cent or over 15.0 per cent
of all work assignments.   Table 1 shows that employers in ports where
workers do *not* hold job property rights consistently estimate rejection and
defection rates lower than do employers in Boston and Houston.   This
qualitative evidence is consistent with B(1) and B(2) and complements the
Department's failure to report rejection or defection behavior in its
Charleston, Jacksonville, and New Orleans studies.[37]

Finally, the relative importance of job defections in Houston, compared with other ports, is suggested by a perusal of its *Daily Labor Reports* (DLR).   The DLR, among other things, provides for the daily reporting of job defectors, the cargoes on which they were employed, and
the time of their defections.[38]   The reporting system enables the Houston
Maritime Association (H.M.A.) to measure the magnitude of defections
and to identify defectors.   Its institution reflects the marked concern
registered by the H.M.A. with the U.S.D.L. during the latter's 1964 research study of Houston.   During the first seven months of the reporting
system, 1,234 defections were recorded.   Total employment of longshoremen in that period has been estimated to be 5,312.[39]   Thus between December of 1966 and July of 1967, Houston longshoremen had an aggregate
defection rate of 23.1 per cent.   This figure is not inconsistent with the
crude measures of rejections and defections for Boston and New York as
compared with the measures of rejections and defections for Charleston,
Jacksonville, and New Orleans.   The weight of all the qualitative and
quantitative evidence presented above suggests support for hypothesis B
and its implications B(1) and B(2).

Employee Behavior within Hiring Systems

Since job property rights raise the expected gains and lower the expected costs of rejections and defections for any given claim-holder, hypothesis B should also explain the *relative* behavior of longshoremen *within* a given hiring system. In both New York and Houston holders of higher-ranking seniority cards or badges must be hired before holders of lower-ranking seniority cards or badges may be employed. In Boston, the hierarchy of job rights is limited to union card holders and all others. At first this might suggest the following implication:

> B(3) Within a given hiring system, job rejections and job defections vary positively with the ranking of job property rights.

It is conceivable, however, that rejections and defections could be *inversely* related to the ranking of job rights (*ceteris paribus*). That is, without some qualification, B(3) is not logically implied by hypothesis B. The following example [40] will demonstrate this point and provide the auxiliary assumption necessary for B(3) to be implied by hypothesis B.

Let S_i be the monotonic ranking of a job right or claim to work opportunity in the hiring process.[41] Let R be the announced earnings for a prospective work opportunity (the product of wage rate and hours). For a holder of an ith ranked job right, let H_i be the expectation of being hired, at a given hiring call, (H_i varying positively with the ranking of job rights) and let C_i be the opportunity cost of leaving a current assignment before its completion. The *net expected value* from defecting, V, is then equal to:

$$V_i = R \cdot H_i - C_i$$

Let pD_i, the probability of defection by holders of an ith ranked job right, be some function g of V_i; and let $\triangle g(V_i) > 0$. The probability of defection varies positively with the *net expected value* from defecting. The absolute number of defections by holders of ith ranked job right is written as D_i, and it is a positive function of pD_i and N_i; N_i is the number of holders of an ith ranked job right. If $N_i = n(S_i)$, let $\triangle n(S_i), < 0$; the higher the rank (class) of the job right the fewer its holders (members). Because the representation of claim-holders in the hierarchy of job rights is unequal, a comparison of defections by job right class should be in terms of defections per class member. The defection rate, r_i is then equal to D_i/N_i.

The behavior of defections and the defection rate, with respect to the hierarchy of job rights, is therefore determined by the behavior of V_i with respect to the hierarchy of job rights. The latter variable may vary in-

versely with claims to work opportunity if the proportionate change in $R \cdot H_i$ (the *gross expected value* from defecting) is smaller than the proportionate change in C_i as S_i moves from higher to lower priorities in the hiring process. For example, assume a distribution of diverse R's associated with prospective future work assignments: $R_a = \$4.80$; $R_b = \$4.50$; $R_c = \$4.25$; $R_d = \$4.00$ and a distribution of hiring expectations; $H_1 = .9$; $H_2 = .8$; $H_3 = .7$; and $H_4 = .6$ associated with the ranking of job rights. The higher the expectation of securing employment the higher the prospective R associated with it.[42] Given that the opportunity costs of defecting are distributed among the hierarchy of job rights as $C_1 = \$4.25$; $C_2 = \$3.50$; $C_3 = \$2.75$; $C_4 = \$2.00$, the *net expected value* from defecting will vary inversely with the ranking of job rights or S_i. Since the probability of defection pD_i and consequently the number of defections D_i always vary positively with $V_i D_i$ will be *inversely* related to job rights; contrary to B(3). The defection rate D_i/N_i however, is indeterminate in this example because both numerator and denominator move in the same direction.

We may conveniently express the *gross expected value* from defecting, $R \cdot H_i$, as some positive function z of the hierarchy of job rights; $R \cdot H_i = z(S_i)$. The proportionate changes in $R \cdot H_i$ and C_i *with respect to changes in the ranking of job rights* can then be written as $\triangle z(S_i) \cdot 1/z_i$ and $\triangle C(S_i) \cdot 1/C_i$ respectively. If implication B(3) is to be logically inferred from hypothesis B it is necessary and sufficient (*ceteris paribus*) that

$$|\triangle z(S_i) \cdot 1/z_i| > |\triangle C(S_i) \cdot 1/C_i|;$$

where there is a distribution of diverse R's and C's. This condition permits the *net expected value* from defecting to vary *positively* with the ranking of job rights and thus the number of defections D_i and the defection rate D_i/N_i to behave likewise. We may rewrite B(3) as:

B(3′) Within a given hiring system, job rejections and job defections vary positively with the ranking of job rights if the *net expected values* from rejections and defections vary positively with the ranking of job rights.

As discussed above, the Department's ten port study provides no quantitative data on the numbers and rates of defections and rejections, *per se*. In New York and Boston, however, the U.S.D.L. and independent researchers do provide qualitative evidence that bears favorably on B(3′). Observations of New York seniority hiring practices, made by Jensen, suggest that it is the holders of higher seniority cards that are most associated with defections and rejections.

> There are . . . always a good number of *high seniority* men . . .
> available, particularly when they anticipate a good employment oppor-

tunity. They may not be willing to accept any employment whatsoever and may pass up employment [that is, reject work opportunities] if it is not to their liking.[43]

In discussing the absentee behavior of some longshoremen, when ordered by their home-pier-employer for a work assignment at a distance from that pier, Jensen observes:

> This reluctance to "travel," as it is called, is one of the most pervasive attitudes found among the *older* and reasonably well established [i. e. class A or class B card holding] longshoremen.[44]

Nowhere does Jensen discuss or cite lower seniority card holders as significant job rejectors.

As a proxy for the distribution of rejections and defections by seniority class, a comparison of absenteeism and seniority concentration by employment center suggests further support for B(3').[45] In mid-1963, the three hiring centers with the largest concentrations of class A card-holders (36 per cent of all class A men) were responsible for approximately 42 per cent of the absenteeism recorded in the port of New York. These centers *did not*, at the same time, have the largest concentrations of lower seniority classes. Moreover, the center with *the* greatest number of class A workers registered the greatest rate of absenteeism among all hiring centers.[46] The three hiring centers with the largest concentrations of *lower* seniority-card-holders were responsible for less than 30 per cent of the recorded absenteeism. The center with the greatest number of lower ranked seniority men registered a relatively low rate of absenteeism.[47] Consistent with these observations the U.S.D.L. relates that:

> In its 1962 negotiations, the New York Shipping Association proposed [unsuccessfully] . . . certain disciplinary actions and loss of seniority for excessive and unexcused absenteeism.[48]

Clearly, if seniority were not an important determinant of absenteeism, to which rejections and defections contribute, the proposed punishment would present a poor deterrent to longshoremen.

In the port of Boston, employer responses to questionnaires[49] together with the descriptions of hiring practices reported by another independent researcher suggest that defection behavior, as in New York, is positively related to the ranking of job property rights. Those responding members of the Boston Shipping Association who confirmed that some longshoremen leave work assignments before completion, to attend the next "pick-up" or hiring call,[50] were then asked to identify which group(s) *if any* does (do) so more often as a fraction of their respective employed membership. The respondents chose from the following answers: (a) union men in "extra" gangs,[51] (b) non-union men in "extra" gangs, (c)

union men in a foreman's "regular" gang, (d) non-union men in a foreman's "regular" gang, (e) no clear difference between groups. All selected (a), union men in "extra" gangs.

There remains the question: Why should defections be so prominent among union-card-holders in "extra" gangs relative to "regular" gangs? The answer is presumably that members of "regular" gangs have relatively higher expected opportunity costs of leaving assignments. The additional cost is the prospect of forsaking the relatively steadier earnings stream, at the contract wage, that is associated with regular gang membership. Defections by "regular" gang members can result in their being passed over by the hiring foreman of that gang at future hiring calls. "Extra" gang members have no expected attachment to such future income prospects.[52]

Another piece of qualitative evidence, is revealed in an employer's letter of complaint to the B.S.A., cited in a 1950 collective bargaining report.

> . . . Condition[s] [are] further aggravated by the port practice of the *union* men leaving the operation before completion, seeking employment on newly arrived vessels. They are usually replaced by non-card, inexperienced men, if available. This condition disrupts the operation considerably and in many instances affects the contemplated dispatch of vessels after owners and operators may have incurred expenditures for overtime.[53]

* * *

[Pages omitted (ed.).]

Exchanges for Job Rights

An alternate route to an explanation of the Houston data (consistent with hypothesis B) would be to accept the initial auxiliary assumption necessary to B(3′) [63] and instead attack the *ceteris paribus* conditions necessary to B(3′). More specifically, if we relax the assumption that job property rights are *not* transferable among workers [64] it can be shown that defection behavior (with respect to the hierarchy of job rights) would always be characterized by the data at Houston, irrespective of the relationship between $|\triangle z(S_i)\cdot 1/z_i|$ and $|\triangle C(S_i)\cdot 1/C_i|$. In neither New York nor Houston are seniority badges the private alienable property of their holders, *de jure*. That is, the sale, rental, or bequeathal of such claims are not legally enforceable. Except for the bequeathal of a union card, (to a son, stepson, father, or brother) [65] the transfer of cards among Boston longshoremen is also not enforceable.[66] But the incentive to transfer or enter into exchanges for job rights is present. To the extent that a job right entitles (within contractual limits) its holder to a protected share of the available work it can create for him a monopoly rent, and as such it is an economic

good. So long as the marginal rates of substitution between job rights and other economic goods differ among longshoremen, and so long as transaction costs are not prohibitive, economic theory implies that exchanges for *claims to work opportunity* will be mutually profitable, albeit *sub rosa*. That is, economic theory suggests that holders of job rights will behave as if those rights or claims were, to some degree, private and alienable, *de facto*.

In the longshore industry exchanges for claims can be consummated by the physical transfer of a seniority badge or a union card and sometimes by the *prearrangement* of a replacement on the job of one man for another. To the extent that holders of lower ranking claims replace higher ranking claim holders (by prearrangement), at assignments promising premium wages or promising longer periods of employment, an *implicit* sale or rental of job rights is suggested. The replacement, himself, may be a new arrival to the hiring hall or a person who has rejected other offers or defected from another assignment. Whether by explicit or implicit transfers, holders of lower ranked job rights would get to earn relatively higher incomes than they might otherwise expect. The lower the values of their own job rights the lower the probability of independently securing more remunerative employment, and the higher their voluntary payment would be to get it. That payment would be some portion of their expected differential income.

This suggests that higher ranking claim holders will seek to replace themselves with holders of the lowest ranked job rights when defections to other assignments appear profitable.[67] Moreover, holders of lower valued hiring rights will tend to engage in rejections and defections as do their senior coworkers. This follows if the former are to replace the latter on "premium jobs", since they could accept current assignment offers and prearrange to *defect* from them, to the premium job, later. Or, on the other hand, they can *reject* current offers and prearrange to replace senior men at later jobs. With an *explicit* transfer of job rights the new users will also find it relatively less costly to reject some assignment offers or defect to others since the probability of securing employment at any hiring call has increased for them. However, there will be some class of claimholders whose associated probability of securing work assignments is high enough so that the return from the explicit or implicit use of an even higher valued claim will be less than the cost of securing it. The cost of securing the higher ranking job right is equal to the bid price of the lowest ranking claim-holders. Holders of these "middle" hiring priorities will have the lowest defection and rejection rates, for they will make relatively fewer purchases of other people's job rights. Therefore defection rates should be relatively greater at the extremes of the job right hierarchy.

It might be argued, however, that, if the *net expected value* from defecting does *not* vary positively with the ranking of job rights, holders of higher valued claims would not find it as profitable to defect as would holders of the lowest ranking claims. If this were the case, it would appear that the evidence at Houston could not be explained by simply permitting exchanges for job rights because there would be less incentive for high seniority men to defect. But this argument rests solely on the premise that holders of higher ranking job rights will defect only to assignments with expected earnings *greater* than forsaken earnings. If implicit exchanges for job rights are possible, however, the above premise must be invalid. By prearranging replacements, high ranking claim-holders may even find it profitable to move to *ostensibly* less lucrative employment. For example, in securing a substitute for a premium wage rate job, the most senior men will find holders of the lowest ranked claims willing to pay an absolutely larger portion of the pecuniary differential between the senior men's current expected earnings and those of the junior men than would holders of the next highest ranked claims. This portion together with earnings from a prospective alternative employment at a later hiring call, paying slightly *lower* earnings and equally attractive otherwise, may sum to more than the senior men could earn at their initial "premium" assignment; thus the incentive to defect even to *lower valued jobs*. Implicit exchanges for job rights therefore render irrelevant the behavior of the *net expected value* from defection with respect to the hierarchy of job rights. The following implication is therefore inferred from hypothesis B:

> B(4) Where exchanges for job rights occur, rejection and defection rates should vary positively with higher valued job rights and negatively with lower valued job rights.

Both B(3′) and B(4) are logically implied by hypothesis B and empirically valid if it can be established that exchanges for job rights occur in Houston but not in New York or Boston. The available evidence supports both propositions. In its study of the port of Houston, the Department of Labor reports that:

> The seniority plan went into effect in January of 1961 and almost immediately ran into several administrative snags. High seniority men . . . engaged in a lively trade in seniority buttons. To put a stop to this, a worker's picture was inserted in his badge but this only resulted in picture switching.[68]

Also, Local 1273, acknowledges exchanges for claims in its *By-Laws and Hiring Hall Procedure.*

> (d) No member shall . . . use another person's or allow another person to use his classification button to secure a referral [a work assignment].[69]

It is interesting to observe that while this local imposes substantial financial penalties on its members for "drinking, intoxication, fighting, unnecessary noise and abusive, profane or vulgar language, in membership meetings and at all times in the union hall   .   .   . " [70], it imposes no penalty for the *sub rosa* transfer of job rights. *Implicit* exchanges for claims, as we have seen, broaden the set of possible defection opportunities to higher-ranking claim-holders, thus reenforcing the tendency for defection rates to be higher at the extremes of the hierarchy of job rights. The institutions at Houston are very conducive to such exchanges.

> A gang member who wishes to leave a work assignment before being relieved by his employer, is *expected* [by employer and union] to arrange with a longshoreman registered with the hiring hall to replace him. His decision is based strictly on who is available.[71]

On the other hand, the Department's published and unpublished reports on Boston reveal no evidence of exchanges for job rights. Similarly McLaughlin's research [72] and the experience of the Boston Shipping Association [73] provide no evidence of these exchanges. Finally, employer respondents to my questionnaire answered *no* to the question, "Do you know of any instances where union men have traded or exchanged their union cards, or the use thereof, with non-union men so that the latter may be eligible for more favorable work assignments?" [74] In the port of New York, the Department's published and unpublished reports make no mention of seniority card transfers, as they did for the port of Houston. Moreover, the Secretary to the Commission of the Waterfront Commission of New York Harbor [75] and the Research Director of the New York Shipping Association [76] stated that exchanges for or transfer of seniority cards *since* the Commission began policing and enforcing seniority hiring rights (March 1963) have not been in evidence. These statements fit in with Jensen's observations that, prior to the Commission taking over the hiring process, seniority cards were traded among longshoremen and card counterfeiting was practiced.[77] The apparent absence of transactions in seniority rights after March of 1963 does not conflict with the observed behavior of absentee rates during the June and July survey of 1963.[78]

While the Commission's administration of the hiring process has evidently made transactions in seniority rights more costly, the common obstacle to such exchanges in Boston and New York is the absence of a *replacement rule*. The absence of a replacement rule comparable to that in Houston makes the costs of selling and renting job rights at the other two ports relatively higher (perhaps prohibitively higher). *Prearranged* replacement or substitution on the job permits implicit transactions for job property rights and therefore defections by holders of higher and lower ranking job rights simultaneously. Without such a rule, transactions are made more costly because they are limited to the explicit or physical transfer of seniority cards and union cards among longshoremen. If holders of higher valued claims must physically transfer them to consummate exchanges, they cannot simultaneously use these claims to secure other assignments *via* defection. This suggests that the higher the transactions cost, the less likely defection rates will be greater at *both* extremes of the hierarchy of job rights.

Conclusion

The analysis of job property rights presented in this article, is analogous to the approach taken in the literature on property rights in general. Alchian, Coase, Demsetz, Williamson, and others [79] have argued that social arrangements defining "ownership" and the costs of enforcing and transferring that "ownership" are determinants of the cost-reward systems that constrain individuals in maximizing utility. Differences in the specification of, and costs of enforcing, property rights (*ceteris paribus*) imply predictable differences in behavior. This central hypothesis has been tested in longshore labor markets and has not been falsified by the evidence. Holders of job property rights find it relatively less costly to pursue sources of utility that conflict with employer goals. Consequently, job rejections, job defections, and the sub-rosa transfer of job rights are observable. There is no reason for this analysis of job rights to be applicable only to longshore labor markets.[80] Moreover, it may be useful in explaining differences in certain aspects of labor market behavior among nations.[81]

FOOTNOTES

* I am indebted to R. H. Coase, Kenneth G. Elzinga, Bennett T. McCallum, Roland N. McKean, and John H. Moore for their suggestions and criticisms on drafts of this article. Financial support was provided by the National Science Foundation Institutional Grant to the University of Virginia and, for earlier work, by the Lilly Endowment Inc. grant to U.C.L.A.

1 See Armen A. Alchian, Private Property and the Relative Cost of Tenure, in The Public Stake in Union Power 350 (Philip D. Bradley ed., 1959); Armen A. Alchian & Reuben A. Kessel, Competition, Monopoly and the Pursuit of Money [Pecuniary Gain], in Aspects of Labor Economics ([Universities]—Nat'l Bur. of Econ.Res. Special conf. ser. no. 14, 1962); R. H. Coase, The Problem of Social Cost, 3 J.Law & Econ. 1 (1960); Louis De Alessi, Implications of Property Rights for Government Investment Choices, 59 Amer.Econ.Rev. 13 (1969); Harold Demsetz, The Exchange and Enforcement of Property Rights, 7 J.Law & Econ. 11 (1964); G. Warren Nutter, Markets Without Property: A Grand Illusion, in Money, The Market, and the State 137 (N. Beadles & A. Drewry eds., 1968); Oliver E. Williamson, The Economics of Discretionary Behavior: Managerial Objectives, in A Theory of the Firm (1964).

2 See Armen A. Alchian, The Basis of Some Recent Advances in the Theory of Management of the Firm, 14 J.Indus.Econ. 30 (1965).

3 See for example, Robert D. Leiter, Featherbedding and Job Security (1964).

4 These services are to be distinguished from tasks performed by other longshore workers such as clerks, checkers, coopers, sack sewers and warehousemen. See Charles P. Larrowe, Shape-up and Hiring Hall 84–85 (1955); Edward E. Swanstron, The Waterfront Labor Problem: A Study in Decasualization and Unemployment Insurance 16–20 (1938).

5 See Arthur D. Little, Inc., North Atlantic Port Survey; Report to Boston Shipping Association 50–56 (1966).

6 Most of the evidence that will be presented in this analysis is the product of the Department's ten port study. See U.S., Dep't of Labor, Manpower Utilization-Job Security in the Longshore Industry (1964). The study has been issued in separate reports for the ports of New York, Boston, Philadelphia, Baltimore, New Orleans, and Mobile. Joint reports were issued for Jacksonville, Florida, Charleston, South Carolina, and Houston-Galveston, Texas. It should be noted that every East coast and Gulf coast port has a collective contract with the Int'l Longshoremen's Ass'n (I.L.A.).

7 U.S., Dep't of Labor, Houston, supra note 6, at 41.

8 Id. at 47.

9 U.S., Dep't of Labor, Boston, supra note 6, at 34.

17 Six of the ten ports studied by the Department (Boston, New York, Houston, New Orleans, Charleston, South Carolina, and Jacksonville, Florida) have been selected for analysis because their hiring regimes clearly reflect differences in the configuration of job property rights (defined below). However, since 1968 two of these ports (Boston and New Orleans) have altered their respective hiring systems so that the above descriptions cannot be considered valid beyond that date. I have not discussed the implication of these events because data and other information are not yet available.

18 For a detailed description of the hiring institutions at the port of New York and of the origins and powers of the Waterfront Commission of New York Harbor see Vernon H. Jensen, Computer Hiring of Dock Workers in the Port of New York, 20 Ind. & Lab.Rel. Rev. 414–18 (1967).

19 Of course, violations of seniority rights by employer or union are subject to the provisions of our national labor legislation. See note 20, infra.

20 See for example, Hargrove v. Bhd. of Locomotive Eng'rs, 116 F.Supp. 3 (D.D.C.1953); NLRB v. Local 1367, Int'l Longshoremen's Ass'n, 368 F.2d 1010 (5th Cir. 1966).

21 The concept of job property rights is not a new one. To a certain degree it may be traced to Selig Perlman, who wrote: "When a guild or a trade union applies . . . rules for the occupancy and tenure of opportunity which abolish and check competition for jobs . . . it creates a solid bargaining front against [the] employer and tends to bring about a distribution of opportunity fair to all." See Selig Perlman, Theory of the Labor Movement 243 (1928). Labor writers used the concept in a less normative sense. For example, Walton Hamilton suggested that: "The card of the union is a property, for it confers upon its holder the right to search for work where the person without it is excluded. . . . The right conveyed is not in an estate but in an opportunity." See Walton Hamilton, Property Rights in the Market, 1 J.Legal & Pol.Sci. no. 3–4, 10, 15 (1943); also, Frederic Meyers, The Analytic Meaning of Seniority, 18 Indus.Rel.Res.Ass'n Proceedings 1 (1965). The economics of job property rights, however, has not advanced beyond this conceptualization. To my knowledge, few writers have sought to derive and test implications, from economic theory, about the behavior of workers with job property rights. See Armen A. Alchian, supra note 1; also Simon Rottenberg, Property in Work, 15 Indus. & Lab.Rel.Rev. 402 (1962).

22 See Armen A. Alchian, Some Economics of Property (Rand Corp., 1961); also Louis De Alessi, supra note 1.

23 Armen A. Alchian, supra note 22, at 9–12.

24 The conditions in which one of these options would be substituted for the other will not be discussed here.

25 Given the probabilities of securing work and of work materializing, in our example, the chances that option c will be chosen over option d will be greater the greater is the wage rate of the future assignment relative to the current offer. If the current offer has hourly earnings equal to $1.25 and the future alternative has hourly earnings equal to $3.00, option c would be chosen over option d.

26 For the purposes of this analysis it is assumed that employers must hire strictly according to the hierarchy of job rights; that employers may not arbitrarily reassign job rights among employees; that employers may not make *individual* transactions with unionized employees for job rights or any other contractual right. It is also assumed that an employee may not independently or privately transfer his job right, to other employees or to his employer, as private property. The exception to this assumption occurs in Boston where union cards are bequeathable to immediate family members.

27 These measures are comparable, to some degree, since the size of the work force is a function of the number of work opportunities made available by the employer. Differential "work rules" or "mimimum size work gangs" will modify this relationship.

28 Houston is the only port that collects defection data (per se).

29 U.S., Dep't of Labor, Charts on the Port of New York 114 (unpublished, 1964). These data are filed with the Labor Management Services Ad. The New York Shipping Ass'n (N.Y.S.A.) has computed absentee rates by employment center from June through November of 1963. Its data also show high absentee rates among work gangs. The N.Y.S.A. data will be provided by this writer upon request. See also, U.S., Dep't of Labor, New York, supra note 6, at 40–42.

30 See Vernon H. Jensen, supra note 18, at 430.

31 Id. at 427.

32 I am indebted to Charles E. McGee, Secretary to the Commission, Waterfront Comm'n of N.Y. Harbor, for this information.

33 Vernon H. Jensen, supra note 18, at 426.

34 Evidence of job rejections at this port is suggested when the Department reports that "Shortages of . . . [certain] men show up on strong demand days when some of them take jobs as talley clerks [a preferred position apart from the basic work gang]." See U.S. Dep't of Labor, Boston, supra note 6, at 35.

35 Supra notes 7 & 8.

36 Copies of questionnaires for all six ports are presented in Donald L. Martin, Claims to Work Opportunity: An Economic Analysis of Alternative Configurations of Hiring Rights (unpublished Ph.D. dissertation, U.C.L.A., 1969).

37 The most explicit questionnaire response was volunteered by the Asst. Director of Labor Relations of the New Orleans Steamship Ass'n, "I am familiar with the problem that exists in Houston with regard to longshoremen leaving one job early to go to another job that may be more to their liking. There is no comparison between New Orleans and Houston in this respect. In fact, this problem is nonexistent in New Orleans."

38 For a sample Daily Labor Report see Donald L. Martin, supra note 36, at 182. Data from the Reports were kindly provided by the Houston Maritime Ass'n.

39 Employment data courtesy of Local 1273 and Local 872, Int'l Longshoremen's Ass'n, Houston, Texas.

40 I am indebted to William W. Brown for his assistance in the discussion that follows. For the purposes of exposition I have limited the discussion to job defections. The analysis, however, is directly applicable to job rejections as well.

41 Holders of S_i have a higher priority in the hiring process than holders of S_{i+1}.

42 $R_a'H_1 = \$4.32$; $R_b'H_2 = \$3.60$; $R_c'H_3 = \$2.97$; and $R_d'H_4 = \$2.40$.

43 Vernon H. Jensen, supra note 18, at 426. Italics supplied.

44 Id. at 430. Italics supplied. Neither Jensen nor the U.S. Dep't of Labor provide an age distribution of longshoremen by seniority class. The Dep't, however, has computed an age distribution and a seniority distribution of longshoremen by employment centers. A study of these distributions reveals that the highest concentration of men 65 years and older and the highest concentration of class A card holders occurs at the same employment center (center #2). Data are from U.S., Dep't of Labor, Charts on the Port of New York, supra note 29, at Chart 34, at 93, and Chart 37A, at 109–111. Copies of the latter charts will be provided by this writer upon request.

45 U.S., Dep't of Labor, supra note 29, at Charts 33, 34 and 39A, at 90–93 and 118b.

46 The absentee rate is the ratio of men absent to number of men ordered. Employment center #2 had a rate of 17% for "regular" gangs and 27.4% for "extra" gangs during June and July of 1963. While the absentee rates were highest at center #2 its total number of absences ranked second to center #9 which had the second highest number of class A men. See note 51 infra.

47 8.9% as compared with 9.1% for the employment centers with the second and third largest numbers of low security card-holders.

48 U.S., Dep't of Labor, Port of New York Manpower Utilization: Absenteeism 3 (unpublished on file at Labor-Management Services Ad.). Italics supplied.

49 See supra note 36, at 176, 180. A similar questionnaire generated no response from members of the New York Shipping Ass'n.

50 Four out of a possible six B.S.A. employers responded to the questionnaire. All answered "yes" to this question.

51 "Extra" gangs are those not regularly hired by the gang foreman.

52 It is also consistent with economic theory to argue that holders of job rights in "extra gangs" have different risk preferences from regular gang members.

53 Cited in Francis M. McLaughlin, Industrial Relations in the Boston Longshoremen Industry chap. V, at 181 (unpublished Ph.D. dissertation, M.I.T., 1969). Italics supplied.

63 That is, $\left|\triangle z(S_i) \cdot 1/z_i\right| > \left|\triangle C(S_i) \cdot 1/C_i\right|$.

64 Supra note 26.

65 I am indebted to Professor Francis M. McLaughlin, of the Alfred P. Sloan School of Management, at M.I.T. for this information.

66 As an interesting exception, a Seattle longshore union, at the turn of the century, issued negotiable stock certificates to its members. Each certificate represented a claim to work opportunity over non-certificated longshoremen. Any claim owner could sell his share(s?) to the highest bidder; it was his private alienable property. See Charles P. Larrowe, supra note 4, at 88.

67 A similar argument is put forth by Paul A. Weinstein, Racketeering and Labor: An Economic Analysis, 19 Indus. & Lab.Rel.Rev. 402 (1966). He argues that would-be longshoremen with the lowest opportunity costs will offer the largest "kick backs" to union agents who monopolize the allocation of jobs on the waterfront. It is in the interest of hiring agents to seek out these longshoremen for the purposes of selling work assignments to them.

68 U.S., Dep't of Labor, Hiring and Seniority Practices in the Port of Houston, Tentative Working Draft 11–12 (unpublished, on file at the Labor Management Services Ad., 1964).

[69] Int'l Longshoremen's Ass'n, Local 1273, By-Laws and Hiring Hall Procedure (1964). No pagination.

[70] Id.

[71] Personal correspondence with William F. Arnett, Director of Labor Relations and Vice-President, Houston Maritime Ass'n, March 28, 1969.   Italics supplied.

[72] Personal correspondence with Francis M. McLaughlin, March 5, 1968.

[73] Personal interview with John S. Dennehy, Manager, Boston Shipping Ass'n, Boston, Mass., July 20, 1967.

[74] See note 36, at 176.   Responding Houston employers (to an equivalent question) answered in the affirmative.

[75] Personal interview with Charles McGee, Secretary to the Comm'n, Waterfront Comm'n of N.Y. Harbor, July 3, 1967.

[76] Personal interview with Edward P. Tastrom, Research Director, N.Y. Shipping Ass'n, July 2, 1967.

[77] See Vernon H. Jensen, Hiring of Dockworkers and Employment Practices in the Ports of N.Y., Liverpool, London, Rotterdam and Marseilles 115 (1964).

[78] Supra at 400 and supra note 46.

[79] Supra note 1.

[80] For an earlier attempt at an analysis of job rights in the printing trades, see Arthur R. Porter, Job Property Rights: A Study of the Job Controls of the Int'l Typographical Union (1954).

[81] See J. P. Windmuller, Legal Restrictions on Employment Termination in the Netherlands, 18 Lab.L.J. 39 (1967).

37: THE PARABLE OF THE PARKING LOTS

HENRY G. MANNE

In a city not far away there was a large football stadium. It was used from time to time for various events, but the principal use was for football games played Saturday afternoons by the local college team. The games were tremendously popular and people drove hundreds of miles to watch them. Parking was done in the usual way. People who arrived early were able to park free on the streets, and latecomers had to pay to park in regular and improvised lots.

There were, at distances ranging from 5 to 12 blocks from the stadium, approximately 25 commercial parking lots all of which received some business from Saturday afternoon football games. The lots closer to the stadium naturally received more football business than those further away, and some of the very close lots actually raised their price on Saturday afternoons. But they did not raise the price much, and most did not change prices at all. The reason was not hard to find.

For something else happened on football afternoons. A lot of people who during the week were students, lawyers, school teachers, plumbers, factory workers, and even stock brokers went into the parking lot business. It was not a difficult thing to do. Typically a young boy would put up a crude, homemade sign saying "Parking $3." He would direct a couple of cars into his parents' driveway, tell the driver to take the key, and collect the three dollars. If the driveway was larger or there was yard space to park in, an older brother, an uncle, or the head of the

Manne, "The Parable of the Parking Lots," 23 The Public Interest (Spring 1971), from page 10 to page 15.

household would direct the operation, sometimes asking drivers to leave their keys so that shifts could be made if necessary.

Some part-time parking lot operators who lived very close to the stadium charged as much as $5.00 to park in their driveways. But as the residences-turned-parking-lots were located further from the stadium (and incidentally closer to the commercial parking lots), the price charged at game time declined. In fact houses at some distance from the stadium charged less than the adjacent commercial lots. The whole system seemed to work fairly smoothly, and though traffic just after a big game was terrible, there were no significant delays parking cars or retrieving parked cars.

But one day the owner of a chain of parking lots called a meeting of all the commercial parking lot owners in the general vicinity of the stadium. They formed an organization known as the Association of Professional Parking Lot Employers, or APPLE. And they were very concerned about the Saturday parking business. One man who owned four parking lots pointed out that honest parking lot owners had heavy capital investments in their businesses, that they paid taxes, and that they employed individuals who supported families. There was no reason, he alleged, why these lots should not handle all the cars coming into the area for special events like football games. "It is unethical," he said, "to engage in cutthroat competition with irresponsible fender benders. After all, parking cars is a profession, not a business." This last remark drew loud applause.

Thus emboldened he continued, stating that commercial parking lot owners recognize their responsibility to serve the public's needs. Ethical car parkers, he said, understand their obligations not to dent fenders, to employ only trustworthy car parkers, to pay decent wages, and generally to care for their customers' automobiles as they would the corpus of a trust. His statement was hailed by others attending the meeting as being very statesmanlike.

Others at the meeting related various tales of horror about non-professional car parkers. One homeowner, it was said, actually allowed his fifteen-year-old son to move other peoples' cars around. Another said that he had seen an $8,000 Cadillac parked on a dirt lawn where it would have become mired in mud had it rained that day. Still another pointed out that a great deal of the problem came on the side of the stadium with the lower-priced houses, where there were more driveways per block than on the wealthier side of the stadium. He pointed out that these poor people would rarely be able to afford to pay for damage to other peoples' automobiles or to pay insurance premiums to cover such losses. He felt that a professional group such as APPLE had a duty to protect the public from their folly in using those parking spaces.

Finally another speaker reminded the audience that these "marginal, fly-by-night" parking lot operators generally parked a string of cars in ther driveways so that a driver had to wait until all cars behind his had been removed before he could get his out. This, he pointed out, was quite unlike the situation in commercial lots where, during a normal business day, people had to be assured of ready access to their automobiles at any time. The commercial parking lots either had to hire more attendants to shift cars around, or they had to park them so that any car was always accessible, even though this meant that fewer cars could park than the total space would actually hold. "Clearly," he said, "driveway parking constitutes unfair competition."

Emotions ran high at this meeting, and every member of APPLE pledged $1 per parking space for something mysteriously called a "slush fund." It was never made clear exactly whose slush would be bought with these funds, but several months later a resolution was adopted by the city council requiring licensing for anyone in the parking lot business.

The preamble to the new ordinance read like the speeches at the earlier meeting. It said that this measure was designed to protect the public against unscrupulous, unprofessional and under-capitalized parking lot operators. It required, *inter alia*, that anyone parking cars for a fee must have a minimum capital devoted to the parking lot business of $25,000, liability insurance in an amount not less than $500,000, bonding for each car parker, and a special driving test for these parkers (which incidentally would be designed and administered by APPLE). The ordinance also required, again in the public's interest, that every lot charge a single posted price for parking and that any change in the posted price be approved in advance by the city council. Incidentally, most members were able to raise their fees by about 20 per cent before the first posting.

Then a funny thing happened to drivers on their way to the stadium for the next big game. They discovered city police in unusually large numbers informing them that it was illegal to pay a non-licensed parking lot operator for the right to park a car. These policemen also reminded parents that if their children were found in violation of this ordinance it could result in a misdemeanor charge being brought against the parents and possible juvenile court proceedings for the children. There were no driveway parking lots that day.

Back at the commercial parking lots, another funny thing occurred. Proceeding from the entrance of each of these parking lots within twelve blocks of the stadium were long lines of cars waiting to park. The line got larger as the lot was closer to the stadium. Many drivers had to wait so long or walk so far that they missed the entire first quarter of the big game.

At the end of the game it was even worse. The confusion was massive. The lot attendants could not cope with the jam up, and some cars were actually not retrieved until the next day. It was even rumored about town that some automobiles had been lost forever and that considerable liabilities might result for some operators. Industry spokesmen denied this, however.

Naturally there was a lot of grumbling, but there was no agreement on what had caused the difficulty. At first everyone said there were merely some "bugs" in the new system that would have to be ironed out. But the only "bug" ironed out was a Volkswagen which was flattened by a careless lot attendant in a Cadillac Eldorado.

The situation did not improve at subsequent games. The members of APPLE did not hire additional employees to park cars, and operators near the stadium were not careful to follow their previous practice of parking cars in such a way as to have them immediately accessible. Employees seemed to become more surly, and the number of dented-fender claims mounted rapidly.

Little by little, too, cars began appearing in residential driveways again. For instance, one enterprising youth regularly went into the car wash business on football afternoons, promising that his wash job would take at least two hours. He charged five dollars, and got it—even on rainy days—in fact, especially on rainy days. Another homeowner offered to take cars on consignment for three hours to sell them at prices fixed by the owner. He charged $4.00 for this "service," but his subterfuge was quickly squelched by the authorities. The parking situation remained "critical."

Political pressures on the city council began to mount to "do something" about the inordinate delays in parking and retrieving cars on football afternoons. The city council sent a stern note of warning to APPLE, and APPLE appointed a special study group recruited from the local university's computer science department to look into the matter. This group reported that the managerial and administrative machinery in the parking lot business was archaic. What was needed, the study group said, was less goose quills and stand-up desks and more computers and conveyor belts. It was also suggested that all members of APPLE be hooked into one computer so that cars could really be shifted to the most accessible spaces.

Spokesmen for the industry took up the cry of administrative modernization. Subtle warnings appeared in the local papers suggesting that if the industry did not get its own house in order, heavy-handed regulation could be anticipated. The city council asked for reports on failures to deliver cars and decreed that this would include any failure to put a driver in his car within five minutes of demand without a new dent.

Some of the professional operators actually installed computer equipment to handle their ticketing and parking logistics problems. And some added second stories to their parking lots. Others bought up additional space, thereby raising the value of vacant lots in the area. But many simply added a few additional car parkers and hoped that the problem would go away without a substantial investment of capital.

The commercial operators also began arguing that they needed higher parking fees because of their higher operating costs. Everyone agreed that costs for operating a parking lot were certainly higher than before the licensing ordinance. So the city council granted a request for an across-the-board ten per cent hike in fees. The local newspaper editorially hoped that this would ease the problem without still higher fees being necessary. In a way, it did. A lot of people stopped driving. They began using city buses, or they chartered private buses for the game. Some stayed home and watched the game on TV. A new study group on fees was appointed.

Just about then several other blows fell on the parking lot business. Bus transportation to the area near the stadium was improved with a federal subsidy to the municipal bus company. And several new suburban shopping centers caused a loss of automobile traffic in the older areas of town. But most dramatic of all, the local university, under severe pressure from its students and faculty, dropped intercollegiate football altogether and converted the stadium into a park for underprivileged children.

The impact of these events on the commercial parking lots was swift. Income declined drastically. The companies that had borrowed money to finance the expansion everyone wanted earlier were hardest hit. Two declared bankruptcy, and many had to be absorbed by financially stronger companies. Layoffs among car parkers were enormous, and APPLE actually petitioned the city council to guarantee the premiums on their liability insurance policies so that people would not be afraid to park commercially. This idea was suggested to APPLE by recent Congressional legislation creating an insurance program for stock brokers.

A spokesman for APPLE made the following public statement: "New organizations or arrangements may be necessary to straighten out this problem. There has been a failure in both the structure of the industry and the regulatory scheme. New and better regulation is clearly demanded. A sound parking lot business is necessary for a healthy urban economy." The statement was hailed by the industry as being very statesmanlike, though everyone speculated about what he really meant.

Others in the industry demanded that the city bus service be curtailed during the emergency. The city council granted every rate increase the lots requested. There were no requests for rate decreases, but the weaker lots began offering prizes and other subtle or covert rebates to private bus companies who would park with them. In fact, this problem became so serious and uncontrollable that one owner of a large chain proclaimed that old-fashioned price competition for this business would be desirable. This again was hailed as statesmanlike, but everyone assumed that he really meant something else. No one proposed repeal of the licensing ordinance.

One other thing happened. Under pressure from APPLE, the city council decreed that henceforth no parking would be allowed on any streets in the downtown area of town. The local merchants were extremely unhappy with this, however, and the council rescinded the ordinance at the next meeting, citing a computer error as the basis for the earlier restriction.

The ultimate resolution of the "new" parking problem is not in sight. The parking lot industry in this town not very far from here is now said to be a depressed business, even a sick one. Everyone looks to the city council for a solution, but things will probably limp along as they are for quite a while, picking up with an occasional professional football game and dropping low with bad weather.

Moral: If you risk your lot under an apple tree, you may get hit in the head.

INDEX